Praise for
CHOSEN LAND

"Fast-paced and lucidly written, *Chosen Land* should be required reading for anyone who wants to understand American religion, and for anyone who wants to understand America."

—Kristin Kobes Du Mez, *New York Times*–bestselling author of *Jesus and John Wayne*

"Matthew Sutton has written a sweeping, riveting history of how Christianity and America have been perilously entwined. *Chosen Land* shows us how faith has been both a balm and a weapon, a force of unity and division, and how it remains at the very heart of the American story."

—Kate Bowler, *New York Times*–bestselling author of *Everything Happens for a Reason*

"With a sweeping narrative and soaring prose, Matthew Sutton makes a powerful argument that the history of American Christianity is inextricable from the history of America itself. *Chosen Land* is a must read for anyone concerned about the past, present, and future of the Christian faith in the United States."

—Kevin M. Kruse, author of *One Nation Under God*

"Matthew Sutton's *Chosen Land* is an insightful, compelling, and deftly written new interpretation of the history of Christianity in America. Sutton's redefinition of America as a Holy Land is a powerful tool to understand America's history, and its future."

—Anthea Butler, author of *White Evangelical Racism*

"The scope of *Chosen Land* is breathtaking, spanning the nation's story from the late 15th century to yesterday, from the political far left to far right, from elite to popular culture, and from outside to inside the worldview of a plethora of distinct Christian traditions. With a pitch-perfect ear for the cadences of ordinary speech, Sutton successfully works within the sonic world of the home as well as the factory, library, and pulpit. Sutton's main argument—that all of US history can be profitably viewed through the lens of Christianity—is carefully framed and boldly presented. Readers may find some parts more persuasive than others, but that forthrightness adds to the book's appeal. *Chosen Land* is sure to rank as one of the premier overviews of the entire history of American Christianity."

—Grant Wacker, author of *America's Pastor*

"No book has ever told us as much as *Chosen Land* does about the role of religion in the most enduringly Protestant nation in the industrialized world. Not since Martin Marty's *Righteous Empire* of more than a half-century ago has a single scholar addressed this topic with the analytic acumen Matthew Sutton brings to the task. Building upon the recent generation's excellent body of scholarship but speaking always in his own voice, Sutton has given us a comprehensive narrative that promises to define professional and popular discussions of religion and politics in American life for a very long time."

—David A. Hollinger, author of *Christianity's American Fate*

CHOSEN LAND

ALSO BY MATTHEW AVERY SUTTON

Double Crossed: The Missionaries Who Spied for the United States During the Second World War

Faith in the New Millennium: The Future of Religion and American Politics (coeditor)

American Apocalypse: A History of Modern Evangelicalism

Jerry Falwell and the Rise of the Religious Right: A Brief History with Documents

Aimee Semple McPherson and the Resurrection of Christian America

CHOSEN LAND

How Christianity Made America and Americans Remade Christianity

MATTHEW AVERY SUTTON

BASIC BOOKS
New York

Copyright © 2026 by Matthew Avery Sutton

Cover design by Ann Kirchner
Cover image © YangYin via Getty Images
Cover copyright © 2026 by Hachette Book Group, Inc.

Hachette Book Group supports the right to free expression and the value of copyright. The purpose of copyright is to encourage writers and artists to produce the creative works that enrich our culture.

The scanning, uploading, and distribution of this book without permission is a theft of the author's intellectual property. If you would like permission to use material from the book (other than for review purposes), please contact permissions@hbgusa.com. Thank you for your support of the author's rights.

Basic Books
Hachette Book Group
1290 Avenue of the Americas, New York, NY 10104
www.basicbooks.com

Printed in Canada

First Edition: March 2026

Published by Basic Books, an imprint of Hachette Book Group, Inc. The Basic Books name and logo is a registered trademark of the Hachette Book Group.

The Hachette Speakers Bureau provides a wide range of authors for speaking events. To find out more, go to www.hachettespeakersbureau.com or email HachetteSpeakers@hbgusa.com.

Basic books may be purchased in bulk for business, educational, or promotional use. For more information, please contact your local bookseller or the Hachette Book Group Special Markets Department at special.markets@hbgusa.com.

The publisher is not responsible for websites (or their content) that are not owned by the publisher.

Print book interior design by Bart Dawson.

Library of Congress Cataloging-in-Publication Data

Names: Sutton, Matthew Avery, 1975- author
Title: Chosen land : how Christianity made America and Americans remade Christianity / Matthew Avery Sutton.
Description: First edition. | New York : Basic Books, 2026. | Includes bibliographical references and index.
Identifiers: LCCN 2025037467 | ISBN 9781541646339 hardback | ISBN 9781541646346 ebook
Subjects: LCSH: Christianity—United States—History | Church and state—United States—History | United States—Church history
Classification: LCC BR515 .S775 2026 | DDC 277.3—dc23/eng/20251119
LC record available at https://lccn.loc.gov/2025037467

ISBNs: 9781541646339 (hardcover), 9781541646346 (ebook)

MRQ-T

10 9 8 7 6 5 4 3 2 1

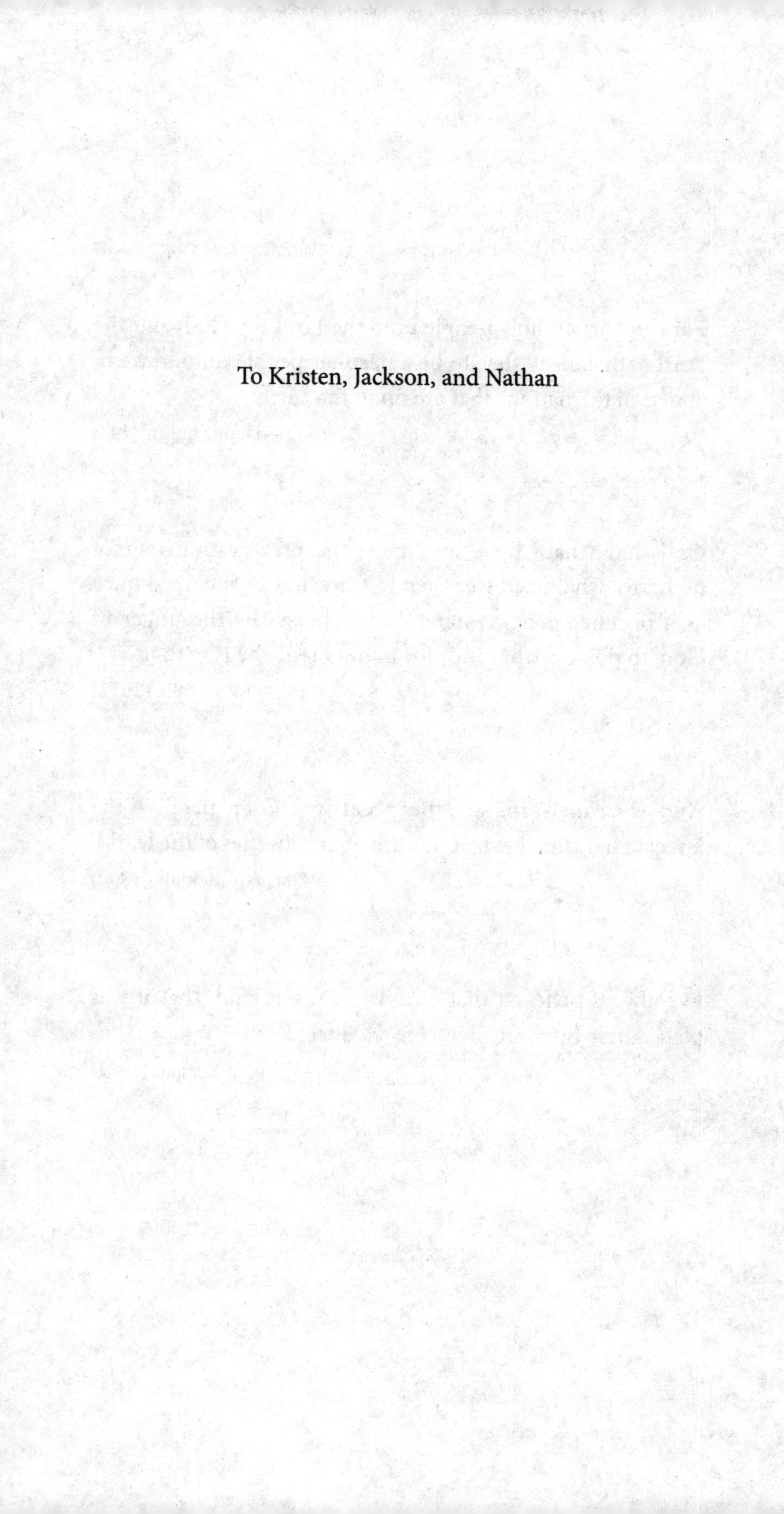

To Kristen, Jackson, and Nathan

For thou art an holy people unto the Lord thy God, and the Lord hath chosen thee to be a peculiar people unto himself, above all the nations that are upon the earth.

—Deuteronomy 14:2

Gods hand hath bene mighty in the preservation thereof hetherto; what need wee then to feare, but to goe up at once as a peculier people, marked and chosen by the finger of God, to possess [the land] for undoubtedly he is with us.

—John Rolfe (1617)

And we Americans are the peculiar, chosen people—the Israel of our time; we bear the ark of the liberties of the world.

—Herman Melville (1850)

I've always believed that ours is a chosen land, that it was placed here by some divine providence.

—Ronald Reagan (1984)

CONTENTS

Introduction 1

PART I
ORIGINS

1 The Christian Invasion Begins 19
2 The City on the Hill 32
3 Varieties of Christian Liberty 48
4 The Birth of Revivalist Christianity 61
5 Revolution 77
6 Sanctifying the West 93

PART II
BUILDING A CHRISTIAN EMPIRE

7 Disestablishing Christianity 109
8 Reviving the New Republic 124
9 Liberated Christianity 142
10 Creating American Originals 155
11 Building the Moral Establishment 172

PART III
A NATION IN CRISIS

12 Going into All the World 191
13 Setting Captives Free 205
14 An Almost Chosen People 223
15 Reconstructing the Nation 241

PART IV
THE CHALLENGES OF THE MODERN WORLD

16 Immigrating Faith 263
17 Saving and Purifying Bodies 279

18 Christianity, Capitalism, and the Signs of the Times 295
19 New Christianities for the New Century 316

PART V
SHAPING THE AMERICAN CENTURY

20 Making the World Safe for Democracy 333
21 The Rise of Fundamentalism 354
22 Relaunching Culture Wars 370
23 The Populist Revolt 390
24 Wars of Faith 411

PART VI
UNRAVELING THE RELIGIOUS ESTABLISHMENT

25 One Nation Under God 433
26 Still Seeking Liberation 456
27 Apocalypse Now 473
28 The Terminus of the Mainline 491

PART VII
REMAKING AMERICAN CHRISTIANITY

29 The Religious Right 509
30 Living at the Close of the Millennium 529
31 The End of Christian America or a New Beginning? 543

Conclusion 565

Acknowledgments 569
Notes 571
Index 618

INTRODUCTION

In 1846, a quirky, self-taught lawyer with a flair for tall tales burst onto the national political scene. He hoped to represent the State of Illinois in Congress. But his unconventional religious views and lack of traditional Christian commitments nearly derailed his blossoming political career. His name? Abraham Lincoln.

Lincoln's opponent for the House seat, Methodist minister Peter Cartwright, worked relentlessly to make religion the central issue of the campaign. Lincoln complained that Cartwright "slyly" insinuated that the hardscrabble lawyer's unorthodox religious views made him unworthy of political office. In Lincoln's view, keeping voters fixated on religion "was the chief object" of Cartwright's crusade.[1]

As a youth, Lincoln had rejected his family's traditional Christian faith and probably flirted with skepticism and atheism. He may have even written a book in his twenties on "infidelity" that his friends destroyed to save his reputation. At the time atheism and agnosticism almost always disqualified people from securing positions in public life. As Lincoln matured, his beliefs evolved. He came to trust in God's overriding providence. He studied the scriptures, read religious books, and asked insightful questions about faith. But doubt always plagued him. Over time Lincoln became a man who very much believed in God. Except when he didn't.

Cartwright's faith, in contrast, never wavered, and it drove his political zeal. He was a religious reformer who aimed to remake the culture, to Christianize the United States. He spent decades building revivalist Methodism in the West, becoming one of the nation's most effective and colorful ministers and leaders. He personified the quintessential itinerant, a manly man galloping on horseback from community to community armed with a rifle in one hand and the good book in the other. He believed that the success of Christianity and the success of the United States required not just righteous ministers, but godly laws and faithful public servants. Cartwright saw the fulfillment of America's divine destiny as contingent upon the election of virtuous individuals to political office and their support of Christian policies. Cartwright believed that Lincoln was no such individual. He saw sabotaging Lincoln's career as his divine duty.

During the 1846 campaign, Lincoln supposedly attended one of Cartwright's revival meetings, seeking to assess his political rival. In true Methodist fashion, Cartwright concluded the service by asking all who wanted to spend eternity in heaven to rise from their seats. Then, trying to catch the rest of the crowd, he asked those who hoped to avoid hell to stand as well. At that point only Lincoln had not budged. "Many responded to the first invitation," Cartwright told the audience, "to give their hearts to God and go to heaven. And I further observe that all of you save one indicated that you did not desire to go to hell. The sole exception is Mr. Lincoln, who did not respond to either invitation." The minister then pivoted toward his political opponent. "May I inquire of you, where you are going?"

"Brother Cartwright asks me directly where I am going," Lincoln replied as he turned and addressed the assembly. "I desire to reply with equal directness: I am going to Congress."[2]

To get there, Lincoln knew that he had to address the religion issue—he had to convince the public that he supported mainstream Christianity. As the election neared, he published a handbill laying out his views. Cartwright's charge "that I am an open scoffer at Christianity," Lincoln began, was a lie. "That I am not a member of any Christian Church, is true; but I have never denied the truth of the Scriptures;

and I have never spoken with intentional disrespect of religion in general, or of any denomination of Christians in particular." He wrote that he believed in God's sovereignty over human events. He would never "support a man for office, whom I knew to be an open enemy of, and scoffer at, religion," and he fully supported the prominent role of churches in American society.[3]

Lincoln's defense of his religious views satisfied voters, who rewarded him with a victory on Election Day. As Lincoln prepared to go to Congress, no one could have imagined that just a decade and a half later he would lead the nation through a ferocious, blood-drenched conflict saturated with religious fervor, or that Lincoln, perhaps more effectively than any other leader in American history, would fuse faith with national identity.

The Lincoln–Cartwright political contest exemplified themes fundamental to the American story. It epitomized the intricate interplay in the United States between religion and politics, faith and social reform, geographic expansion and religious freedom. It also illustrated the power of the people. Cartwright calibrated his ministry to match the changing needs and the demands of the public. Lincoln, in turn, had to make his religious convictions palatable to secure election.

In a country where the Constitution seemingly separated church from state, Christian activists such as Cartwright worked to infuse all aspects of American life with religious faith. They largely succeeded. They drove even those like Lincoln, whose spiritual beliefs did not align with the majority, to comply. They believed—as many Americans still do today—that God had made them a peculiar people, and that their nation was God's chosen land.

In the United States, people love God and they love his son, Jesus Christ. Nearly two-thirds of Americans currently identify as Christian. They are Catholics and Baptists and Methodists and Lutherans. They are pentecostals and Mormons and Quakers. They are your friends and they are your neighbors. They might even be you.[4]

The gospel preached by a humble carpenter from Nazareth two millennia ago has left an indelible mark on nearly every aspect of American life. It inhabits the lives of its peoples, haunts their dreams, and inspires their actions. It has motivated Christians to seek influence everywhere from politics to culture to business to foreign policy.

Chosen Land is the first book to chronicle Christians' epic five-hundred-year mission to turn North America into a holy land, a prelude to God's millennial kingdom. This mission is all the more remarkable since the nation's founders wrote a deliberately godless Constitution and never meant to establish an explicitly Christian nation. Yet Christianity, this book argues, became the dominant engine of American political and cultural life, shaping law, policy, popular entertainment, and ideals of gender, race, and nationhood. To ignore its power is to misunderstand American history—and America itself.

This argument is significant in at least three ways. First, it challenges the traditional narrative of the United States as a secular republic by emphasizing how the country developed one of the most Christian cultures in the modern world—ironically through the very mechanisms that were supposed to ensure religious neutrality. It demonstrates that "separation of church and state" was not a barrier to religious influence, but stimulated religious innovation, expansion, and integration into every part of American life.

Second, the book redefines how American culture was forged. It emphasizes the central role of grassroots religious actors—preachers, entrepreneurs, and movement leaders—who thrived in the free-market religious environment created by the First Amendment. These figures operated both inside and outside the halls of power, constantly reinventing Christianity to meet changing political, social, and economic realities. In doing so, Christians took an ancient religion and reconstructed it over and over again, tuning it to their times and places and to the demands of the public—even as they claimed to be doing nothing more than upholding the "traditional" faith. They fashioned a version of Christianity that was thoroughly American—and made America, in turn, profoundly Christian.

Finally, *Chosen Land* places Christianity at the center of American national identity. It links Christianity to key facets of national development, suggesting that to understand American distinctiveness fully, we must account for how Christianity shaped and was shaped by every major historical development from education to war. Americans' success at weaving Christianity into all aspects of their culture is what made the United States so unique. Understanding this makes *Chosen Land* essential for understanding the ideological foundations of both domestic and international policy.

Religion, however, never functions alone. Recent books have placed race and racism at the core of US history, others Indigenous peoples, and others still technology and economic class. My book draws on this excellent work while I focus my story on the centrality of Christian activism to the American story. This, perhaps more than anything else, is what distinguishes the United States from its peer nations. The work of Christian activists affected (and affects) the lives of all Americans, which makes understanding this history essential.[5]

Unlike in many European and Latin American countries, where the state finances churches and mandates religious training in public schools, in the United States the government does not keep houses of worship in business. With no state funding for religion, we might expect the United States to have a more secular identity than nations with established churches, and American Christians to have less power and influence. Some founders, such as Thomas Jefferson, wanted it this way. But the reality is just the opposite.

The religion clauses of the First Amendment empowered religious activists as they sought to erect the kingdom of God in the United States. The clauses read: "Congress shall make no law respecting an establishment of religion, or prohibiting the free exercise thereof." The "disestablishment" clause guaranteed that no single denomination would secure a monopoly on state funding. But rather than hindering Christian faith in the United States, it propelled competition and forced religious leaders to make religion broadly attractive, to study and meet the needs of the people.

Disestablishment did not, however, create an even playing field on which all religions competed equally. The men who drafted the Constitution and the nation's laws essentially rigged the game. Most sought to ensure that mainstream protestants would maintain the upper hand in the United States. Although the founders refused to establish a single, national denomination, they limited opportunities and constrained choices. They wanted religious leaders who upheld traditional hierarchies, deferred to political authorities, and championed market capitalism. While separation blocked the creation of an official state church, it simultaneously facilitated the rise of a decentralized, evolving, dominant protestant power structure, an independent, unofficial, quasi-establishment.

The protestant leaders directing the unofficial establishment often collaborated with ruling authorities. They worked with policymakers to shape Americans' views of topics ranging from clothing styles to birth control to same-sex relationships to popular culture. They crafted laws regulating abortion, blasphemy, commerce, cussing, dancing, gambling, marriage, media, the Sabbath, sodomy, and almost every other part of American life. They taught wide swaths of the American public how to understand race relations, mass media, pop culture, gender, sex, sexuality, economics, politics, and domestic policy. Nothing fell outside their sphere of influence.

Protestant leaders persuaded politicians and the courts to interpret the second clause in the First Amendment, the free exercise clause, in ways that usually benefited them. They encouraged a broad range of Christians to practice their faith unhampered, but they established outer limits. Protestants delineated the "orthodox" faith. They decided which groups might ostensibly strengthen the nation and which ones should be ostracized as "cults." They sought to eliminate competition from alternative religions at home and abroad. Some Christian groups faced substantial persecution, sometimes from mobs and sometimes from government officials. Meanwhile, those outside of Christianity had fewer rights and liberties than what the Constitution seemed to promise. The founders created a world in which Christian activists could impose their versions of the faith on the rest of the nation.

Yet the power of Christian leaders always depended on popular support. With church severed from state, ministers could not rely on institutional backing. They had no pope or bishop or king to legitimate them. They needed the people. If they lost their appeal, others stepped in to take their place. This democratization forced religious leaders to craft messages that resonated broadly, making faith relevant, accessible, and responsive to lay concerns.

In this competitive, free-market religious landscape, pastors and activists became entrepreneurs of faith. They vied for followers not only against each other but also against secular alternatives. Success demanded innovation, charisma, and the savvy use of emerging technologies. Those who excelled gained national influence, recasting Christianity. Their popularity allowed them to claim a mandate to speak for American Christianity as a whole, contributing to the nation's sense of religious and cultural exceptionalism. They produced one of the most dynamic, creative, enduring, and powerful Christian cultures in the world, and inspired a faith that can be oppressive, racist, sexist, exclusionary, and homophobic. They spun Christianity into the United States' most popular and enduring product, something packaged, advertised, and sold to Americans and exported to people around the world.

The Christian faith has permeated almost every aspect of American life. Yet it is so common and pervasive in the United States, we often don't notice its effects. It has compelled action and validated choices. It has stimulated righteousness and provided cover for evil. It has provided common language that gives meaning to the momentous and the mundane. It has defined individuals' relationships, conditioned their analyses of politics, colored their views of the economy, informed their voting priorities and patterns, determined their perspectives on social issues, influenced the curriculum they want their children to study, and helped structure how they understand natural disasters, geopolitical changes, and war. It has influenced Americans' priorities in ways both pedestrian and profound. It has filled in blanks, rationalized choices, and connected dots. Christianity has provided Americans with frameworks through which to interpret their lives, their communities, and the future. Whether Christian or not, Americans live their lives in cultural and political paradigms defined by Christian ideas.

Chosen Land focuses on the intersection between religion and culture. Rather than attempt to provide an exhaustive account of every notable Christian movement and activist in American history, in this book I highlight those groups and individuals who have substantially influenced the trajectory of the nation, those who have guided everything from colonization to war to civil rights. Because I emphasize social, political, and cultural power, this is a predominately White protestant story. But it is also the story of non-White religious activists who challenged White supremacy and sought to expand civil and religious freedoms. Their critiques of the nation's religious power structure sharpen our grasp of the First Amendment's promise—revealing both its expansive reach and its enduring limitations.

American religious life is remarkably diverse, encompassing a multitude of traditions and paths, yet competing groups of protestants have exercised enough power to give it a distinctive hue. White protestant leaders have subtly—and oftentimes not so subtly—drawn others into the orbit of their tradition. Under the canopy of their cultural authority, protestants set the terms for legitimacy, public presence, and institutional forms. Those who rejected protestantism—and even Christianity in general—had to use its terms, language, and idioms. In the United States, protestant Christianity is inescapable. So, while it may seem like in America there is wide-open religious freedom, it's actually structured by a deep, organizing logic—both diverse and centrally harmonized.

Beneath the broad protestant canopy lies a varied and evolving array of religions. Catholics had their own goals and priorities and spent generations working to integrate those into mainstream American life. They built their own faith-infused power structures that became especially influential in education, media, and law. Other

Christian groups on the fringes of American life often had to fight for equal rights. And non-Christian communities—Jews, Muslims, Buddhists, Hindus, and others—all lived and practiced their beliefs in the shadow of White protestant dominance.

In telling this story, I address a few dominant misconceptions about the American past. I demonstrate that the concept of "Christian nationalism," which journalists, sociologists, and pollsters have found especially useful in recent years, is not new. Although it takes many forms that change over time, Christian nationalism has influenced activists across the political and religious spectrum, Black and White, left and right, for centuries. Americans have never really separated church from state, nor have they truly championed the free exercise of religion. Christian activists from Frederick Douglass to Jerry Falwell used the Bible to try to impose their values and beliefs on the nation.

I also challenge the vague and often misleading use of the term "evangelical" by recent generations of scholars. Most historians treat modern evangelicals as the carriers of a long and rich historic tradition that ran through American history from the 1740s until today. But this is not accurate. Much as Cold War–era conservatives established the concept of the "traditional family" and then treated it as an eternal force that existed outside of time and place, so too was the creation of "evangelicalism" as we know it today an invented, post–World War II tradition.

In 1942 a group of Christian fundamentalists resurrected the old and by that time mostly discarded term "evangelical"—which dated back to the Protestant Reformation—to rebrand themselves. They hoped to distance themselves from the negative connotations that had developed around the term "fundamentalism," which they had been using for their movement. The postwar evangelicalism that they promoted was not the continuation of an older tradition but the start of a new American religious movement, a reinvigorated fundamentalism. There is no singular evangelical throughline dating from the colonial period to today. Those scholars who use the term to describe eighteenth- and nineteenth-century Christians inevitably bolster the move made by both contemporary evangelicals and their academic allies to position their movement at the center of American history in order to shape contemporary politics and the nation's path forward.[6]

Finally, in recent decades, polling data revealed that religious affiliation—or the lack thereof—has become one of the most reliable predictors of voting behavior. The more religious a person is, the more likely he or she is to vote Republican. I offer a new explanation for how this alignment took shape. Throughout the twentieth century, leaders of liberal protestant denominations often challenged American power, criticizing foreign interventions and denouncing imperialism. They also advocated for progressive social reforms such as civil rights, feminism, and LGBTQ+ equality. Over time these stances, often rooted in moral reckoning, alienated many of their White congregants, who were less inclined to embrace such changes. As the gap between clergy and laity widened, mainline churches began to hemorrhage members. Meanwhile, evangelical churches—offering a more culturally conservative message—grew rapidly.

Sensing an opportunity, partisan right-wing political operatives forged alliances with evangelical leaders eager to mobilize their flocks. These partnerships proved mutually beneficial: Politicians gained a loyal voting bloc, while evangelical leaders amplified their influence through politics. Together, they transformed the Republican Party into a vehicle for White Christian nationalism, persuading millions that the GOP alone stood for God and traditional American values. Meanwhile, they depicted the Democratic Party as one of secularism and hostility to religion. Rather than push back, many leading Democrats ceded the religious ground to Republicans, a move that some party leaders, including Barack Obama, have long regretted.

Chosen Land begins with Christopher Columbus's voyages to the Caribbean and his conviction that his actions fulfilled an end-of-days divine plan. Over the next two centuries, European colonizers followed in Columbus's wake, importing dozens of competing versions of Christianity to North America. Their diversity laid the foundations for the revolutionary generation to embrace a sense of divine mission while rejecting a state church. They defended religious liberty, not out of principle, but out of pragmatism.

Following the American Revolution, coalitions of mainstream protestants joined together to launch a multicentury campaign to build a religious utopia by infusing law, politics, education, and policy with protestant ideals. In the nineteenth century, they had tremendous success, exercising near absolute power. But in the last decades of the 1800s, the arrival of millions of Catholics and Jews produced a more diverse population, and intellectual trends driven especially by new scientific theories created opportunities for some Americans to challenge traditional ideas and beliefs. During the early twentieth century, the dominant protestant consensus began to unravel. Some protestants responded by heralding ecumenism, pluralism, and eventually secularism as the best path forward for the nation, while others launched a multigenerational quest to reclaim power, to reestablish the United States on Christian foundations.

I end the book with the ongoing struggle to define the place of religion in public life. In recent decades, some protestants, joined by groups of Catholics and Latter-day Saints, have resurrected a form of Christian nationalism and seek Christian supremacy. They are working through partisan politics—with the benefit of a sympathetic Supreme Court—to create a new Christian establishment to reign over an ever more diverse and pluralistic nation. Others seek to limit such activists' influence and power and to drive religion out of the public sphere. They argue that the First Amendment erected a "high wall" between church and state. The struggle among different religious groups and those with no religion at all continues to play out everywhere from school board meetings to presidential politics.

In seeking to build the kingdom of God on earth, American protestants have drawn from many versions of Christianity to serve their own purposes. In the colonial period, settlers tapped into the wide and forceful river of European Christianity, channeling its waters to nourish their fledgling communities with many imported styles and forms of Christian faith. As the nation matured, Christians divided that river into four distinctive American streams: what I am calling the conservative, revivalist, liberal, and liberationist streams. Each carved its own path through the American religious terrain, sometimes converging, often diverging, and continuously reshaping the religious landscape.

Those who drew from the conservative stream emphasized tradition, historic creeds, and the importance and centrality of the church and the church community. Nineteenth-century Lutherans and most Catholics, for example, sought to conserve the historic Christian faith as they understood it. They were skeptical of new knowledge and new insights, but they nevertheless generally changed with the times—albeit slowly and cautiously. For many conservatives, faith was something one was born into and that helped create an identity. The conservative stream included both elites who labored to maintain the status quo and those who worshipped in immigrant, ethnic congregations organized around a shared culture and language. The constant influx of immigrants to North America gave conservatives new life generation after generation. Of the four major types of Christians, conservatives tended to be the most isolated. They focused on strengthening their own communities and didn't often obsess over what other Americans were doing. Why, they asked, should they expect non-Christians to behave like Christians? They knew the world was a fallen place and hoped that their example would attract others to Christianity.

Those who drew from the revivalist stream developed a different approach to the Christian faith. They emphasized the autonomy of individuals, the preeminence of emotions and feelings, the importance of having a relationship with God, and the need for individual salvation and transformation. Although often called "conservatives," they were not. They pioneered new ways of thinking and believing. From Jonathan Edwards to Peter Cartwright to Billy Graham, they rejected both the churchly crowd's conservatism and liberals' embrace of secular knowledge (although both influenced them). More than any other group, they made Christianity a commodity, a choice, something one could purchase or return like a pair of shoes based on the whims of the day. They shifted the act of conversion from being the means of entry for non-Christians into an end unto itself—a sacrament required of everyone to authenticate one's faith.

Revivalists believed that just as God wanted to immediately transform the individual, so too did he want to transform the nation. They acted aggressively and unapologetically to try to impose their values on the United States. They had few doubts about their mission and rarely sought compromise. God, they felt sure, had absolute standards, and for them to make the United States God's promised land, they must execute his will—or at least their understanding of it—on everyone else.

The third stream consisted of liberals. They ranged from late eighteenth-century Congregationalists to nineteenth-century Deists to the twentieth-century leaders of many mainline denominations. They emphasized rationality and seeking truth, which they often saw as independent of community or experience. As learning and science changed, they assumed faith should change too, which kept it in constant flux. They embraced new ideas and worked relentlessly to keep religion up to date with the latest intellectual trends. They accommodated faith to outside ideas and values. They sought to apply Christian morals and ethics to social issues. They aspired to synchronize faith with science, new knowledge, and sometimes other religions. They rejected parochialism and tried to think and act globally, but in so doing, they often defended their privileged positions. Their substantial faith in individual freedom and autonomy helped further commodify faith in the United States. Of all the major Christian groups, they had the most patience and willingness to compromise, and they were uniquely confident that good would come through incremental steps. As they worked on making the United States a holy land, they forged alliances with others, including those outside their particular faith.

Those who sought to disrupt the status quo often drew from a fourth stream, the liberationist stream. This stream included everyone from Indigenous preachers speaking against removal policies to gay rights activists seeking equality within protestant churches. Liberationists emphasized the Old Testament God of Exodus who freed the Hebrew captives, and they trumpeted Jesus as a liberator who battled for the oppressed. They saw in the gospel a call to action—faith without deeds, they asserted, was dead. They fought to free people from stifling gender norms, economic inequalities, and racism. This stream was frequently the smallest and had the least power, but it served to remind other Christians that too often more popular versions of Christianity revealed more about race and class and geographic location than about any kind of eternal religious ideas or practices. They emphasized justice and emphatically reminded other Christian groups that they often embedded sexism and racism into their visions of the kingdom of God. They aspired to build a truly peaceable kingdom free of racism and discrimination, where all were equal.

Liberationists made explicit what was always implicit. Issues of race, ethnicity, and gender guided all four streams—the entire river—of North American Christianity. While Whites debated how to make North America the city on the hill for the rest of the world to emulate, Black, Latine, and Indigenous people; immigrants; and other groups had to fight to ensure that it was not hell on earth. White American Christians in practice almost always treated race as more important than theology or worship styles, often refusing to ally with those from minority groups even if they held the same or similar religious beliefs. Meanwhile, Black, Latine, Asian, and other Christians worshipped on their own and worked when possible to influence the White mainstream.

Furthermore, the history of American Christianity is the history of women. Women have filled the majority of church pews in just about every denomination and movement in North American Christianity. This was true among protestants and Catholics, White, Black, and Latine, in the North and the South and the West. They have also exercised religious leadership more often than many of us realize. While men have held disproportionate power in American Christianity, much of that power derived from the support of women.[7]

The four streams sometimes flowed together as a single river, sometimes flowed in different directions, and sometimes mingled and merged. But none of the streams remained static. As American Christians made them their own, Christians channeled the currents in new directions. At times some streams swelled, flooding the nation. Others stagnated and temporarily dried up. Some split, sending the faithful off in new directions. Nevertheless, categorizing the different kinds of Christianities in this way helps us make sense of the tactics, approaches, goals, similarities, and differences among competing types of Christians.

For centuries the river of American Christianity surged with overwhelming force. Separation of church from state, the commodification of faith, and the empowering of ordinary people to remake religion kept the waters churning. Competing Christian visions shaped our politics, our culture, and our very identity. But in recent decades, the river has slowed. Fewer Americans have claimed Christianity as their own. When asked to state their religious preference, growing numbers simply replied, "None of the above." Yet the decline now appears to be leveling off.

Americans are at a crossroads. Will the nation's Christian population begin to shrink again, leaving churches empty and politics secularized? Will our religious profile soon resemble that of Western Europe or Canada?

Or is another revival just over the horizon?

Whatever the future holds, we cannot understand the United States without understanding the faith that built it. The past that Christians constructed defines the present for both believers and unbelievers alike. American Christianity and American history are not two parallel stories—they are the same story. The history of the United States is the history of American Christianity, and the history of American Christianity is the history of the United States.

PART I

ORIGINS

1

THE CHRISTIAN INVASION BEGINS

Fifteenth-century North America was a vibrant and diverse place. Hundreds of tribes spanned the continent, with complex and distinctive cultures, practices, and politics. Most did not separate the sacred from the secular, or the natural from the supernatural. In subsequent centuries Europeans, and, later, scholars, divided "religion" from culture, but such distinctions would have made little sense to Indigenous peoples.

The North American population in the 1400s probably numbered between five million and seven million people. The largest city in what became the United States, Cahokia, developed on the Mississippi River near present-day St. Louis, although its residents had largely abandoned it by the late 1400s. It had served as a kind of crossroads, a trading center for people around the region. Most people, however, lived in smaller groups. Their lifestyles and cultural practices reflected the environments around them. Those near major waterways fished. Those on the plains hunted. Some built permanent residences. Others lived nomadically, following the game and the seasons. Extensive trade networks linked tribes to one another across the continent.

Then the Christian invasion began.

The man leading the first major expedition from Europe to the Americas, Christopher Columbus, believed that God had chosen him for this work. An avid and ambitious explorer, he viewed his conquests as the fulfillment of the Bible's ancient prophecies about the last days. Blending faith and violence, he aimed to grow the Catholic Church and European power by transforming and subjugating tribal cultures. He claimed that God had prescribed his mission, that it represented part of God's end-times plan for the world.

Columbus, with his religious justifications, disregard for the fundamental humanity of non-Europeans, and blend of missionary ambition with plunder, established precedents that would characterize European work in North America for the next couple of centuries. A long line of Spanish colonizers followed in his wake, seeking treasure, territory, and to impose European versions of the Christian faith on the land. They established footholds in what would become Florida, Mexico City, and the US Southwest. For the peoples of North America, however, the encounter with Christian explorers marked a different kind of discovery—they realized that rather than offering mutually beneficial partnerships, the Christian invasion brought with it death and destruction. Yet rather than succumb to the devil, they used the devil's tools to fight back.

Born in Genoa, Italy, in 1451, Columbus grew up on the sea. As he matured, he sailed the Mediterranean and North Atlantic. He studied the latest scientific discoveries and used the best technology to navigate from port to port. European leaders and merchants coveted the valuable commodities available in India and China. Rather than rely on long, arduous existing overland roads, they hoped to find a new ocean route to facilitate more economical trade. Although many Europeans thought that finding a westward course to India was impossible, Columbus convinced King Ferdinand and Queen Isabella of

Spain to invest in his project. By sailing west, he contended, he could find a faster route to the East. Columbus expected to locate treasure and spices, and to win new converts to Christianity. He recorded in his journal that the mission would benefit the "Catholic Christians and Princes who love the holy Christian faith" and ensure the "propagation" of their faith.[1]

For Columbus to frame his expedition in Christian terms made good sense. Life was precarious, and venturing to sea was risky. Columbus had to contend with storms, accidents, disease, and mutiny. Trusting in a sovereign god gave Europeans a way to see and understand the world. If the Old Testament God protected the Hebrew people and led them to the promised land, wouldn't he do the same for his church in the modern era? If Columbus aspired to expand Christianity's reach, how could the almighty let anything stop him? Columbus's beliefs inspired more than self-serving rationales for profit and plunder. They made risk more manageable and threats less ominous. Faith, for Columbus and for the many who followed in his path, made bold action possible.

Expanding Christendom, however, meant vanquishing competing belief systems. At home, Spanish leaders worked in concert with the Catholic Church to identify and persecute alleged heretics, including Jews and Muslims. Spain had just completed its Reconquista, driving African Muslims (called "Moors") from the Iberian Peninsula. Columbus praised the actions taken by the Spanish crown against "the sect of Mahoma and to all idolatries and heresies." In 1492, Ferdinand and Isabella required that all remaining non-Christians still living in their lands convert to Christianity and join the Catholic Church. They eventually expelled those who did not.[2]

On August 3, 1492, Columbus and about ninety men set sail from Spain aboard three ships, the *Niña*, the *Pinta*, and the *Santa María*. After just over a month at sea, the crews reached an island in the Bahamas. Columbus named the island San Salvador. From the very start of their expeditions, explorers began a process of imposing Christian names, ideas, and language on locations in the Western Hemisphere.

Astute planning and adoption of the latest insights from science and astronomy made the voyages a success. Even though Columbus never got anywhere near Asia and didn't quite understand where in the world he had actually disembarked, the Italian believed that God had directed the ships. "For the voyage to the Indies," he concluded, "neither intelligence nor mathematics nor world maps were of any use to me; it was the fulfillment of Isaiah's prophecy." The admiral understood the trip as about much more than securing a route to India; he expected the profits generated by the new route to serve Christendom and God's plan for the world.[3]

From the start, European and Indigenous men and women traded goods and communicated as best they could. The locals "should be good servants and intelligent," Columbus recorded in his journal, "for I observed that they quickly took in what was said to them." He made converting the people he encountered a top priority. He thought "they would easily be made Christians" since "they had no religion." Europeans typically assumed that peoples in the Americas had no religion. Most Indigenous peoples practiced complicated and holistic religions, but because their practices did not look to Europeans like Christianity, Judaism, or Islam, they assumed they had no religion at all. They were mistaken.[4]

Columbus had hoped to find large supplies of gold. When he failed to find riches, he drafted plans for how best to enslave Indigenous people and use their labor for profit. Here too he set a precedent. For the next few centuries, European Christians in the Americas sought both to convert those they encountered to their faith and to enslave them—and they rarely saw any contradiction between these actions. For some, conversion and enslavement reinforced each other. Making slaves increased opportunities for exposing non-Christian peoples to Christianity, which seemingly justified human theft. Although Columbus promised to show God's love to the Natives, love is the opposite of what he and his men practiced, a point made by some Europeans. Spanish priest Bartolomé de las Casas, for example, penned a scathing book criticizing Columbus and his allies for the pain they inflicted on local peoples.

Christopher Columbus believed that God had called him to launch an end-times mission to spread Christianity. He and his men brought both cross and sword to the Caribbean. (credit: New York Public Library)

Columbus hoped that the wealth he extracted, whether commodities or slave labor, would help Spain fund its crusade against Muslims in the Middle East. He expected "that all the profits of this my enterprise may be spent in the conquest of Jerusalem." In this way, his work linked Indigenous tribes in the Americas, Spanish plans for religious conquest and empire, and the long-running Christian–Muslim conflict over the Holy Land. Indigenous people inadvertently became bit players in an enduring religious war waged on the other side of the globe.[5]

In the last years of his life, Columbus compiled his *Book of Prophecies* seeking to explain how current events, including his voyages and the quest for the Holy Land, fulfilled biblical predictions about the end-times. "Holy Scripture," Columbus explained, indicated that "this world will end" in the year 1655, which meant time was running out. But before Jesus returned, Christians had to spread the gospel to all peoples. The opening up of the Americas to the Catholic faith, for Columbus, represented the partial fulfillment of this prophecy. "Much that has been prophesied remains to be fulfilled," he noted, "and I say that a sign of this is the acceleration of Our Lord's activities in this world. I know this from the recent preaching of the gospel in so many lands." In sharing his faith with the Indigenous peoples he met, he helped speed the world to its climax.[6]

While the Spanish battled for territory in the Americas, a religious hurricane bore down on the Catholic Church. A high priest based in Rome, the pope, led the church. Bishops and priests scattered around Europe served under him. They taught that salvation came only through the church and its clergy, who offered penitents seven holy sacraments: baptism, communion, confirmation, confession, holy orders, anointing the sick, and marriage.

One of those priests, a German Augustinian monk named Martin Luther, went through a personal religious crisis. Was he truly saved? How could he know? Over time, he found that clinging to two core Christian principles brought him peace: *sola gratia*, grace alone, and *sola fide*, faith alone. Sin and corruption so tainted humans, he believed, that nothing they did could earn their salvation—no actions could possibly atone for their sins. Instead, they had to rely solely on God's grace received through faith. Luther claimed that the Bible provided the basis for his views, which led him to a third principle, *sola scriptura*, the Bible alone. He believed that the holy text provided the only true account of human history, humans' relationship to God, and the means of salvation.

The church still mattered to Luther, but it no longer constituted a necessary vehicle for salvation. The monk's own encounters with church leaders had led him to question religious authorities. They seemed more Jezebel than Jesus. When a Dominican priest arrived in Germany in 1517 selling "indulgences" to help fund the construction of St. Peter's Basilica in Rome, Luther decided to act. "Indulgences" served as currency that a person could use to buy reduced punishments for sins, or for the sins of members of their departed family. More indulgences meant less time spent in purgatory waiting to join Jesus in heaven. So if a person wanted to escape God's punishment, he need only contribute to Rome.

Luther outlined his opposition to the sale of indulgences and other forms of corruption in a series of ninety-five theses, or brief arguments. On October 31, 1517, he posted the theses on the door of the local church in his hometown of Wittenberg.

Angered by Luther's actions, church authorities put the cleric on trial. While they had silenced or burned at the stake others who had ideas like Luther's, the German monk had powerful allies, including local princes who resisted the church's interference in their realms. A friend put Luther in protective custody and allowed him to continue his work. Luther spent the next few years applying his theological principles to religious practice. He developed a German translation of the Bible that laypeople could read for themselves, wrote vernacular hymns for Christians to sing, and restructured the format of church services. He aimed to help churchgoers understand the purposes behind religious rituals and encouraged individual participation. Rather than promote the seven holy sacraments championed by medieval Catholicism, he emphasized the two that he believed the Bible most clearly identified: communion and baptism.

As Luther worked through the implications of his theology, he celebrated the priesthood of all believers, arguing that Christians needed no intermediators between themselves and God, and he encouraged individuals to approach the almighty directly. He believed that God called all people to serve him. From God's perspective, a monk, a priest, a teacher, a farmer, and a prince were all the same.

Luther's work, and the actions of those who supported it, led to a schism in Western Christianity. The Catholic Church remained powerful and maintained the loyalty of much of Europe, but Luther sparked the rise of a major alternative called protestantism (from the Latin "to protest"). The religious divides that the Reformation inspired produced new geopolitical divides as well.

As Luther's ideas spread in Germany, Spain looked to expand its empire in North America. In 1519, Hernán Cortés invaded Mexico with five hundred men. By the time Cortés appeared in the heart of the Mexica (or Aztec) empire in Tenochtitlan (later Mexico City), its leader, Moctezuma II, seemed eager for peace and an alliance. But the Spaniards wanted power and riches, not negotiation. Cortés took Moctezuma prisoner, sparking two years of fighting. Moctezuma's death and a brutal epidemic eventually gave the Spaniards the upper hand.

Within a few decades of Columbus's explorations, Spanish leaders had laid the foundations for a powerful new extension of their empire centered in Mexico City. They hoped that the Americas would provide them with new wealth and power, and an opportunity to grow the Catholic Church.

With their base secure, Spanish soldiers spread out from Mexico City in search of gold. Francisco Vázquez de Coronado led one expedition into the region the Spaniards called "New Mexico" in 1540, in what is now the American Southwest. A few decades later, Franciscan friars followed the trails blazed by soldiers into New Mexico, seeking to share the Christian gospel with the Pueblo peoples. One Spaniard testified that he expected conversions to be relatively easy since "they are a submissive people." The Spanish tended to view and treat those they met as innocent, naive, childlike creatures. They did not realize that the Pueblo calibrated their actions toward Christians with the goal of building beneficial alliances. The locals were savvy, not submissive.[7]

The local Pueblo peoples had sacred origins myths that explained who they were, where they came from, and how the world was structured. They envisioned a universe in which the natural and supernatural blended, and actions in one realm influenced the other. Their sacred cosmology helped explain natural occurrences like droughts and floods, and periods of famine or bounty. It also helped them interpret conflict, war, and the Christian incursion.

Europeans in North America routinely failed to understand the beliefs of Indigenous peoples. The Spanish especially failed to realize how Pueblos integrated the supernatural into all aspects of life. One explorer reported that the Pueblo "have medicine men who talk to the devil," and he observed religious spaces called kivas, but nevertheless asserted that "they have no churches." They "worship some small idols made of stone or wood," he added, "but they do not have much attachment for them and do not mind abandoning them."[8]

The Franciscans' early reports on their New Mexican work impressed King Felipe II. Buoyed by the potential of establishing a Spanish-led colony in the region, Felipe's representative, the viceroy, dispatched Juan de Oñate from Mexico City to claim the land and govern the region for Spain. Born in Mexico, Oñate had a Spanish father and a mother who descended from Moctezuma. "Your main purpose," the viceroy instructed him, "shall be the service of God Our Lord, the spreading of His holy Catholic faith, and the reduction and pacification of the natives of the said provinces." Oñate would fail on every count.[9]

In 1598, Oñate led an expedition into New Mexico. The Pueblo peoples he encountered in the Rio Grande region represented at least six different language groups. But they had much in common. They lived in permanent apartments made of stone or adobe organized into towns ("pueblos"), and they cultivated farms. Their permanent location made them easier to missionize compared with more nomadic groups such as the nearby Apache and Navajo.

Rather than convince the Pueblo of the glories of Spanish rule or of the Christian faith, Oñate brought terror to the region. When the Spanish tried to take more supplies from the locals in the town of Ácoma than they were willing to give, the Natives resisted. Seeking to punish the Pueblo and maximize their suffering, the Spanish snatched the town's children and turned them over to the Franciscans. The fathers, complicit in this action, likely sold some children into slavery. They justified their actions by claiming to have made Christians of the captives. This was not the first time, and it would not be the last time, that colonizers used Christianity as a rationale for subjugating non-Christian peoples.

Oñate punished all the remaining men in the village over age twenty-five by chopping off one of their feet and assigning them to twenty years of servitude. He spared the limbs of all men between twelve and twenty-five, and all women over twelve, but sentenced them to twenty years of servitude. The Spanish cut one hand off each of two Natives who happened to be visiting Ácoma from other pueblos at the time, to warn others of the consequences of defying them. Jesus had once told his disciples, "And if thy right hand offend thee, cut it off, and cast it from thee: for it is profitable for thee that one of thy members should perish, and not that thy whole body should be cast into hell." Oñate seems to have missed the point as he cut the hands off those who offended him and tried to consign them to a Spanish-made hell. He later forced the surviving locals to construct a mission church, a symbol of the Spanish seizure of the territory.

Executing the crown's orders to pacify the local tribes and expand the Catholic faith proved more challenging than the Spanish had expected. People facing attack and subjugation often reject the religious sentiments of their oppressors. The Franciscan friars sometimes understood this, and they occasionally objected to some of Oñate's more brutal tactics, setting up a clash between church and government authorities. One Franciscan friar complained that the actions of the soldiers, including beating and killing local men and raping women, "brought great discredit on our teaching." "If we who are Christians," the friars reflected, "caused so much harm and violence, why should they become Christians?"[10]

Indeed, why? This question perfectly summed up the challenge of the entire European colonial enterprise in North America.

Despite the setbacks, representatives of the king remained optimistic about the region. The Franciscans reported that they had seven thousand "converts" in need of continuing spiritual leadership, and one soldier concluded that although the mission probably would not make much money, the friars could do a lot of good with minimal financial support. Convinced of the value of the church fathers' work, the king decided to maintain the Spanish presence in New Mexico.

Franciscan records show a steady increase in the number of acolytes. In 1620, the Catholic missionaries claimed seventeen thousand followers in New Mexican missions. In 1632, they counted sixty thousand converts. But what these numbers mean is difficult to discern. The notion of "conversion" is a Western concept. Did the people the fathers counted as "converts" understand what it meant to join the Catholic faith and to renounce their old ways? Most probably did not. Furthermore, the blending of Christian and Indigenous rituals revealed that many probably believed they did not have to choose between Christianity and their own traditions.

Christianity often worked more as an addition to traditional beliefs than a complete replacement. Converts wove Christianity into their existing way of life rather than embarking on an entirely new path. This kind of blending—where different faiths mix and create something new—happened again and again throughout Christian history. Because of ongoing contact, combination, and exchange, Christianity kept evolving over time, always adapting from one generation to the next.

Over the next few decades, tensions between Indigenous populations and colonizers continued to grow. The friars routinely punished local people for perceived sins, and sometimes the tribes punished religious leaders. Dozens of Franciscans suffered what their fellow brothers considered martyrdom at the hands of locals.

The situation in New Mexico began to unravel even further in the late 1660s. Famine and pestilence wreaked havoc on the region. By 1670, the local population had dropped to less than half of what it had been in 1640. Nearby Apaches and Navajos, suffering from drought and pestilence, increased their attacks on Pueblo peoples. Frustrated and angry, growing numbers of Pueblo turned their backs on the Christians and revitalized their old traditions. They believed that perhaps they had dishonored their gods, and by rejecting Christianity, peace and prosperity might return. In 1672, one group of Pueblo burned a local church; captured the friar; and stripped, tortured, and then killed him. They tied his lifeless, naked body to a cross. A few years later, Indigenous people killed seven more Franciscans, which the latter blamed on witchcraft.

Rather than reassess their own actions, the Christians tried to force the locals into submission. But they were frequently outnumbered. They could not push Natives too far without facing retribution. In 1675, a new governor, Juan Francisco Treviño, arrived in Santa Fe, the Spanish base of operations in New Mexico. He demanded that the Pueblo cease their "idolatry." He hung some "sorcerers" and arrested, flogged, and sold into slavery forty-seven medicine men. The Spanish seized or destroyed kivas and altars, forbade traditional dances, and destroyed masks and prayer sticks. A local group of Pueblo, the Tewa, intervened and demanded the release of those held captive. Treviño relented and released the men.

One of Treviño's captives, a charismatic leader and medicine man named Popé, plotted his revenge. After regaining his freedom, Popé moved to Taos, away from the watchful eyes of the Spanish. He believed that the time had come to drive out the Spanish. He brought together war chiefs, dissidents, and exiles from among the Tiwa, Tewa, Towa, Zuni, and Hopi. He called on them to work together to overthrow the Christians and their god, promising that if they did, an era of prosperity and good fortune would descend on them. Like the Franciscans, he had visions of a coming apocalyptic battle between good and evil. But the future he saw looked very different from that of the friars.

Popé launched an attack on August 10, 1680. The Pueblo captured horses first, which allowed them to fight and retreat more effectively. Although the Spanish had better weapons, Popé's men considerably outnumbered them. They split the region in half by cutting off roads and shutting down supply and communications routes. One by one, the revolutionaries advanced on settler towns, killed colonizers, and seized their weapons. Those Spanish who could retreat to Santa Fe did. On August 13, Popé's warriors surrounded the city. The governor refused to surrender, and a siege began. After nine days, the governor and his men counterattacked the insurgents, scattering the warriors. The Pueblo allowed some of the Hispanics to escape south and then took the capital.

Popé had secured victory, and he counseled the Pueblo to restore their old ways and return to the traditions and practices that predated the Christian invasion. This meant destroying all things Christian, from crosses to churches to altars to Bibles. According to the first full government report on the uprising, the Natives "set fire to the temples, seizing the images of the saints and profaning the holy vessels with such shocking desecrations and insolences that it is indecent to mention them." Rebel leaders instructed the people to "burn all the images and temples, rosaries and crosses, and that all the people should discard the names given them in holy baptism and call themselves whatever they liked." They warned them "not to mention in any manner the name of God, of the most holy Virgin, or of the Saints, on pain of severe punishment." Popé and the other leaders banned use of the Castilian dialect and replaced Spanish crops with traditional maize and beans, the "crops of their ancestors." Many converts returned to the river to wash off the Christian faith in a kind of reverse baptism.[11]

The conflict revealed the centrality of religion and religious freedom to both sides. Natives expressed outrage at Christians' desecration of their traditions, beliefs, and rituals. The Christians felt the same way once the tables had turned. Both sides defiled what the other deemed holy, both believed that spiritual forces guided worldly events, and both claimed their own interests matched those of the divine. In assessing what had happened, one of the Franciscans captured Indigenous sentiments more accurately than he probably realized. The local peoples were "so pleased with liberty of conscience and so attached to the belief in the worship of Satan that up to the present not a sign has been visible of their ever having been Christians." In the North American Southwest, liberty of conscience represented a principle the Pueblo, not the Christian invaders, went to war to defend.[12]

The Pueblo revolt sparked a major crisis among Spanish religious leaders. Columbus had sailed into the Western hemisphere believing God accompanied him. The Franciscans moved into the Southwest believing the same. Generation after generation of Christian conquerors acted in what they viewed as righteous and holy ways, confident that tribes would find salvation through them. They could not understand how they could have been so wrong, how their efforts could have inspired such a violent reckoning. Spanish colonizers, rather than herald the coming of the prince of peace, brought with them the sword. The first forms of Christianity to appear in North America came drenched in blood. But the Spanish were not the only Europeans looking to build Christian empires in North America. Others soon followed, equally confident that through them God was starting a new work, offering a new means of global salvation.

2

THE CITY ON THE HILL

Two thousand miles away from the Catholic enclaves in Santa Fe, the first major protestant utopian experiment in colonial North America seemed to be unraveling. New England minister Samuel Danforth wondered aloud "whether we have not in a great measure forgotten our Errand into the Wilderness." The founding generation of "Puritan" migrants—reformers set on purifying the Church of England from afar—had made great sacrifices to worship how they believe God wanted. Yet things had seemingly changed. Danforth fretted that "a careless, remiss, flat, dry, cold, dead frame of spirit" had invaded the community. "Pride," he harangued, "Contention, Worldliness, Covetousness, Luxury, Drunkenness and Uncleanness break in like a flood upon us, and good men grow cold in their love to God and to one another."[1]

Others felt similarly. Minister Increase Mather warned that the "day of trouble is near." He sensed "manifold transgressions, and mighty sins amongst us." Like Danforth, Mather believed that the Puritans had lost their way. "We can now see little difference between Church-members and other men, as to their discourses, or their spirits, or their walking, or their garb." Those who professed Christianity "fashion themselves according to the world."[2]

In the last few decades of the seventeenth century, a handful of events seemed to verify Puritan leaders' fears that their mission had failed. Danforth and Mather catalogued their community's many evils, any of which might provoke God's judgment. Bestiality ranked near the top of their lists. In 1674, Danforth preached a jeremiad to mark the execution of a young man named Benjamin Goad and his steed. That Goad enjoyed mare-buggering did not surprise Danforth. Goad had "lived in Disobedience to his Parents; in Lying, Stealing, Sabbath-breaking, and was wont to flee away from Catechism." Prior sexual sins, Puritans believed, often led to greater ones, and Goad's included "self-pollution, and other Sodomitical wickedness." The minister warned his audiences that without proper discipline they too might end up with an animal for a lover. Executing Goad (and his four-legged companion) served as "the onely way to turn away the wrath of God from us." Yet the man's death did not mark the end of the colony's problems or a return to better days. The Puritan utopia remained in crisis.[3]

Americans have subjected the New England Puritans to more analysis than any other group of immigrants to North America. Nineteenth-century French tourist Alexis de Tocqueville believed that we could find in the Puritans the entire "destiny" of the United States. He was correct, but what that destiny entailed varied from person to person. The Puritans became the American Rorschach test; people saw in them what they wanted. Some credited the Puritans with establishing democracy and freedom. Others saw them as killjoys who squashed individual liberty. Some saw them as the Founding Fathers' founding fathers. Others viewed them as genocidal murderers. Some saw them as the architects of the separation of church and state. Others saw them as religious tyrants who established a theocracy. However we assess them, the Puritans established a pattern that Americans repeated over and over again. They set out to build a new, pure, godly, utopian community. They made their Christian convictions central to every part of their lives. They believed that God had made them his peculiar people, destined to build a new chosen land. And they failed.[4]

The Puritans who first arrived in North America fled England to avoid persecution. Their journey was born out of the ongoing upheaval of the Protestant Reformation. In the 1530s, King Henry VIII broke with the pope and persuaded Parliament to declare him "Supreme Head" of the English church. His actions reverberated in countless unintended ways. A religious leader, the pope, no longer ruled the English church, but instead a political leader, the king, now had supremacy over religious affairs.

Over the next few decades, some protestant activists pushed for further change. They criticized the church's hierarchical structure and believed that Jesus, not a pope or a human sovereign, should rule the church. Critics dubbed the reformers "Puritans" for their zealous efforts to "purify" the church. The reformers preferred to call themselves the brethren, or the saints, or the godly. Eventually, however, the term "Puritan" stuck, although the boundaries between Puritans and other protestant reformers remained fuzzy.

A handful of core convictions animated the Puritans. They took the principle of *sola scriptura* to its logical end, convinced that the Bible and only the Bible, rather than reason and tradition, should provide the basis for religious belief and action. Puritans stressed the importance of the church as essential to God's plan to support salvation within the community. Preaching occupied the center of worship services, and they viewed its purpose as to illuminate the scriptures. Church music, Puritans believed, should consist of singing the Psalms, the actual words of scripture. They generally held a broad view of the second commandment: "Thou shalt not make unto thee any graven image." They believed that having images or representations of the divine violated this commandment, so they stripped their places of worship of statues, images in stained glass, paintings, and even altars.

Yet Puritans lacked consensus on many issues. The Bible is ambiguous and readers interpret it in many ways. One of the most significant debates centered on how far to extend the power of local congregations. Puritans believed that church leaders' authority came from the Holy Spirit and the people and not from bishops or the king. But if authority did not reside in established authorities, did every congregation have total autonomy? If so, how could religious leaders ensure that congregations did not fall into heresy, and if they did, how might church leaders correct them? Some Puritans advocated for the autonomy of the local church, but others believed that designated authorities should maintain some oversight through presbyteries, or bodies of elders, that oversaw local congregations.

In the early 1600s, James VI of Scotland (James I of England) concluded that Puritans' reform efforts had gone too far. One source of their mistaken ideas, he surmised, was the English-language Geneva Bible, which seemed to encourage radicalism. He established a committee to produce a new English version of the sacred text. Drawing on the latest scholarship and written in beautiful prose, the "Authorized" or "King James" Bible, published in 1611, became one of the most important publications in human history.

One group of Puritans during James's reign navigated an especially perilous route. They refused to acknowledge the authority of the Church of England at all but called instead for true believers to separate totally from the state church. Based on their reading of the New Testament, they concluded that church authority resided only in the local congregation. Some of these reformers established their own secret churches in England. Others, longing for the freedom to worship openly as they pleased, left for Holland.

The emigrants did not plan to be permanent exiles but expected the English to see the value of their ways and the truth of their convictions, and to welcome them back to remake the church. When that did not happen, some decided to change tactics. They concocted a genius plan—maintain their English citizenship but move to North America, one of England's most remote outposts where they could build a new community and worship in peace.

William Bradford, a member of the group and its chronicler, observed that in leaving the Netherlands, "they knew they were pilgrimes." In calling the group "pilgrims," Bradford casually used a common biblical metaphor drawn from the book of Hebrews. The verse reads, "They were strangers and pilgrims on the earth." Christians had always considered themselves "strangers and pilgrims," but later generations of historians and chroniclers dubbed this particular group the "Pilgrims" to distinguish it from other kinds of Puritans.[5]

The first group of English Puritans to settle in North America arrived in 1620. They came onboard the *Mayflower* at about the same time that the Franciscans were expanding their work in New Mexico. Although some came as servants and others in search of work, most of the men and women on the *Mayflower* were religious extremists in an era of religious extremists. Before the group disembarked, the men on the ship drafted a statement that put into words the explicit purpose behind their mission. They said they had "undertaken for the Glory of God, and Advancement of the Christian Faith, and the Honour of our King and Country, a Voyage to plant the first Colony in the northern Parts of Virginia." They affirmed their intention to "covenant and combine ourselves together into a civil Body Politick." Their statement aimed to unite the group as they began their work together.[6]

These Pilgrims, or separatist Puritans, secured a charter to settle in North America through the Virginia Company, one of England's colonial enterprises. They planned to join a recently established colony in Jamestown, but ocean currents drove them off course. They landed in Cape Cod in early November and then sailed down to an area they named Plymouth. Rather than continue further down the coast to the Jamestown settlement, they opted to stay. God, they believed, wanted them there. They did not encounter many people but found evidence of past human activity in the area, including human skulls and bones. Many of the region's Pokanoket people (a branch of the Wampanoag tribe) had suffered through a recent plague, and most survivors had moved away.

Bradford described the region as "vast & unpeopled" and "devoyd of all civill inhabitants." He and his fellow travelers encountered "only savage & brutish men" little different from "wild beasts of the same." His language revealed the racial and religious hierarchy that shaped the worldviews of most Englishmen and women. They viewed Indigenous groups as perhaps not fully human, and if they were human, as inferior. They treated tribal lands as "uninhabited."[7]

Over half the Pilgrim colony died during the first winter. That anyone survived was due in part to the help of a local man named Tisquantum (or Squanto). He shared supplies on behalf of Massasoit, the local Wampanoag leader. The Pilgrims believed that the Natives' generosity represented God's grace and support. Massasoit, in contrast, saw helping the Pilgrims as a shrewd political move. He and the Wampanoag people were at war with the powerful Narragansett people. Massasoit likely believed that an alliance with the English might tip the odds in his favor against his old enemy.

With the help of local Wampanoag, the colonists learned the best fishing spots and how to grow crops in the region. In the fall of 1621, they had a harvest celebration with their Indigenous allies. Two and a half centuries later this festival inspired the myth of the "first Thanksgiving," but the Pilgrims certainly did not intend this. They would have been horrified to know that their descendants established a holiday in their honor that had no precedent in the Bible, and that Americans reduced their life-and-death struggle to presidential pardons of turkeys, pecan pies, and salt and pepper shakers in the form of miniature Pilgrims.

In the late 1620s, a group of London merchants sympathetic to Puritan ideas formed a new company with the goal of establishing another settlement on North America's Atlantic coast. King Charles I supported their efforts and approved a charter for the Massachusetts Bay Company, granting investors land not far from the Pilgrims' Plymouth settlement. Company leaders recruited ministers and families willing to migrate. They elected John Winthrop governor, who for the next two decades helped lead the colony.

Unlike the separatist Pilgrims, this group aimed to reform and purify the Church of England. The Puritans hoped that their actions might help spark a religious and national revolution. Winthrop laid out the stakes in a sermon that he likely delivered either just as they were leaving or onboard their ship the *Arbella*. The sermon does not seem to have made a big impression on the group, but in retrospect we can see how it identified many of what became the central themes of the Puritan experiment. It eventually took on a life of its own, becoming a key document in the collective American memory. "For wee must consider," Winthrop admonished the group, "that wee shall be as a citty upon a hill. The eies of all people are uppon us." Winthrop and his fellow colonists, like the Pilgrims, had an extraordinarily inflated view of the importance of themselves and their endeavor. Their project meant little for the rest of the world, but their sense of mission elevated—exaggerated—the stakes for those involved.[8]

The Massachusetts Bay Colony Puritans believed that they had entered a covenant with God similar to God's Old Testament covenant with Abraham. If Abraham and his descendants abided by God's commands, God had promised to make them a great people. If the Puritans fulfilled the terms of their covenant, God would do the same for them. But if they broke the covenant, Winthrop warned, God would "withdrawe his present help from us."[9]

In organizing the Massachusetts Bay community, the Puritans drew on ideas associated with the French-born theologian John Calvin. A cleric and a lawyer in the mid-sixteenth century, Calvin became one of the most influential theologians of the Reformation. He emphasized God's absolute sovereignty over human affairs. God, Calvin taught, initially created humans with free will, but Adam and Eve's decision in the Garden of Eden to eat the forbidden fruit permanently imbued them and their descendants with a sin nature. The sin nature made it impossible for people to recognize God and his goodness and permanently estranged them from him. Only through Jesus's atoning sacrifice and the shedding of his pure, sinless blood on the cross could humans reconcile to God. Nevertheless, because of their sin, humans could not understand and accept the good work that Jesus had done unless and until God revealed himself to them by choosing them for salvation. In Calvin's view, people were careening toward a raging hellfire, but a merciful God would rescue a lucky few before they reached the inferno.

Puritans grew obsessed with determining whether God had chosen them for salvation. Anxiety about their eternal fate inspired them to vigorously analyze their own lives, seeking to identify and fix even trivial blemishes. If God had not predestined everyone for salvation, how could one know that he or she was among the elect? Only by living a life that reflected God's glory. This meant that Puritans constantly looked for sins—theirs and others'—to see if they could discern the true state of their souls.

Not all reformers placed as much emphasis as Calvin on God's sovereignty. Dutch theologian Jacobus Arminius believed that God offered humans some choice in the matter of their salvation. Arminius taught that God knew who would accept salvation, and therefore he offered it to all who would accept. While Calvinism won the day among the early settlers in North America, over the next few centuries Arminianism's influence grew, eventually becoming the dominant theology of salvation among American protestants.

Puritans in New England aimed to build a Christian commonwealth as Calvin had done in Geneva. The Puritan colonists saw themselves as the new Israel, which had both a spiritual and a political meaning. They believed that when God's original chosen people, the Hebrews, rejected Jesus as their messiah, the almighty opened up his grace to gentiles. At that point God's people became in part a spiritual community rather than an ethnic tribe, the universal Christian church rather than the Jewish people. However, many Puritans continued to believe that the Old Testament's depiction of God's people as a political community still had enduring relevance. The Puritans thought that they represented the new chosen people for the modern era. As God had revealed himself to the world through the ancient Hebrews, he was now revealing himself through the Puritans. Hence, they might really embody that city on the hill for all the world to emulate.

In establishing a form of government for the new colony, Puritans generally aimed to separate religious power and political power. God had established both church and state, they believed, to play essential roles, but their obligations and responsibilities differed. Yet since to the Puritans the stakes seemed so high, they did not harbor dissent. They expected magistrates to reward righteousness and to punish heresy and idolatry.

Puritan leaders built their community around hierarchies of class and gender. As Winthrop noted, they believed that "GOD ALMIGHTY in his most holy and wise providence" had destined some to be rich and some to be poor (lucky for Winthrop he ranked among the rich). Class disparities would demonstrate "the variety and difference of the creatures, and the glory of his power in ordering all these differences for the preservation and good of the whole." God, they believed, would restrain the "riche and mighty" so they would not "eate upp the poore" and the poor would not "rise upp against and shake off theire yoake."[10]

Puritans viewed material prosperity as a sign of God's blessing. They linked economic success with religious success and economic failure with religious failure. These precepts led later sociologists to conclude that Puritans laid the foundations for the rise of free market capitalism in the United States. Had they aimed to establish a New Testament–type communist community, things might have turned out differently. But for these faithful, God ordained the pursuit of wealth rather than equality.

The Puritan defense of divinely ordained class distinctions naturalized the community's embrace of certain forms of slavery. The Bible, as Puritans read it, forbade "man stealing." They could not enslave people themselves, but they could purchase those who others had enslaved. By the mid-seventeenth century, New England was home to a small number of enslaved Africans. For the most part, however, Puritans facilitated the Atlantic slave trade through their role as merchants and sailors rather than by direct enslavement.

Puritans believed that the family served as a model for society. God had established a clear hierarchy to maintain order. Although all people were equal before God, they had different roles to play in the world. Magistrates ruled over civil societies, elders over churches, husbands over wives, parents over children, and masters over servants (and those they enslaved). Anything that challenged or upset the hierarchy might provoke God's wrath. Like a successful sports team, the group flourished when everyone understood their assigned position.

The Puritans established Harvard College in 1636 to train new ministers. The college also served as a symbol of the community's commitment to education. Believing that producing godly children ensured the expansion of the kingdom, Puritans placed strong emphasis on the spiritual formation of their offspring. To ensure that young adults could read and understand the Bible, Puritans invested in schools. By the end of the seventeenth century, New England had one of the highest literacy rates in the world.

Most Puritans saw themselves as part of the Church of England—the purest part. But over time they grew more independent. Those who settled in New England, far from bishops and church hierarchies, adopted a congregational polity. They located power in the body of believers who covenanted together to form a local congregation. Eventually the Puritans came to be called Congregationalists based on their form of church government.

From the start, building a godly utopia proved difficult. In assigning power to the local congregation, elevating the individual, and encouraging Christians to read the Bible for themselves, the Puritans inadvertently opened the door for conflict and rebellion. It did not take long for some colonists to view local leaders as nearly as flawed if not as flawed as those they had escaped back in England.

One of the first challenges to the unified godly commonwealth that Winthrop and others hoped to establish in New England came from a Puritan minister. Roger Williams arrived in the Massachusetts Bay Colony in 1631. A separatist at heart, he believed that the Puritans had by their actions abandoned the Church of England; they should not pretend to be doing anything less. They had forsaken bishops, the official liturgy, and the *Book of Common Prayer*—the core text leaders used for organizing church life—so they might as well admit they had left the church altogether.

Even more controversially, Williams criticized the foundation of the Puritan mission. The Puritans had left England hoping to secure the freedom to worship according to the dictates of their conscience. But they would not allow others to do the same. They had erected a coercive political establishment whose members believed they could judge the souls of others and could interpret scripture more accurately than any who might disagree with them. They rejected the religious coercion of the bishops because it differed from their brand of coercion, but they did not reject religious coercion in principle. Williams advocated instead for a firmer separation of church and state than that promoted by most other Puritans.

Many of Williams's ideas threatened the New England Puritan project. All citizens, he wrote, should be allowed to worship freely, including the "Paganish, Jewish, Turkish, or anti-christian." Civil leaders are "not judges, governors, or defenders of the spiritual" and they should not pretend otherwise. If they did, Williams predicted, "sooner or later" they would incite a "civil war." Entwining church and state encouraged violations of conscience, persecution of Christians, and "destruction of millions of souls." The best defense against false religion was not civil authority but the Bible, "the sword of God's Spirit, the word of God."[11]

Williams also expressed a practical concern with the New England project. No one had sought or received the permission of the local tribes to settle on their land. While the king had granted the Puritans' claim, what made it his to grant? This theft guaranteed, in Williams's eyes, the inevitable collapse of the mission. How could God reward a land grab? To pretend that God had made "empty" land available to the colonists, he asserted, poisoned the endeavor from the start.

Williams's ideas revealed a fatal flaw in the Puritan mission. How do you build a community around shared beliefs when one of those beliefs is that the individual has the right and ability to interpret scripture and define belief for himself?

In 1635, a New England court expelled Williams from the colony. He moved near the headwaters of the Narragansett Bay to a spot he called "Providence," believing God in his providence had led him there. He set out to build a new colony as "a shelter for persons distressed of conscience." Rather than just resettle the land, he purchased it from Narragansett leaders. He separated civil government from religious authority, keeping state independent from church and church separate from the Church of England. The king eventually granted a royal charter to the Colony of Rhode Island and Providence Plantations. It promised "full liberty in religious concernments," making it one of the most liberal charters in the world at the time.[12]

The Puritan community faced another crisis in the mid-1630s, one that challenged church—and male—leadership in the colony. Puritan laypeople often organized weekly meetings to discuss recent sermons and some of the fine points of theology. Such meetings revealed the communal nature of the church. The congregation did not passively receive theology from their ministers but worked through it together.

Anne Hutchinson led one of the most popular meetings in the Massachusetts Bay Colony. Since the Hutchinsons lived just across the street from Governor Winthrop, Hutchinson's growing influence drew the attention of colonial authorities. Her minister had been preaching on the nature of grace and its relationship to works. He taught that humans could do nothing to merit God's favor. Hutchinson and her friends debated the implications of these teachings. She determined that since humans were incapable of living by the law of God, they should stop worrying about it. Instead, they should focus on God's grace. If a person did not live up to a minister's, or a magistrate's, or the community's moral code, who were others to judge? All had sinned and had fallen short of God's standards. Hutchinson asserted that ministers who emphasized right behavior rather than grace taught a false faith, a salvation by works. Although Hutchinson's position made solid theological sense, it posed a serious problem for the Puritan mission. How could the Puritans build a holy commonwealth if everyone was free to live by the grace of God alone? If they decided that righteous behavior didn't matter?

Colonial leaders regarded Hutchinson's ideas and popularity as jeopardizing their authority. Hoping to silence the woman leader, they charged her with sedition and put her on trial for meetings that were "not tolerable nor comely in the sight of God nor fitting" for her "sex." Hutchinson refused to relent, which turned the hearing into a lively debate that pit the popular midwife against some of the colony's leading authorities. Hutchinson based most of her arguments on the Bible and she repeated well known, commonly accepted theological principles. When pressed near the end of the trial to explain how she knew which directives took priority, she replied that the truth came to her by "immediate revelation. . . . By the voice of his own spirit to my soul."[13]

This was a step too far. To claim immediate revelation was to make every member of the community, every Christian, answerable only to God—not to their ministers, their churches, or their magistrates. Winthrop concluded that the "troublesomeness of her spirit and the danger of her course amongst us" was "not to be suffered." Hutchinson was "unfit for our society." The court agreed and banished Hutchinson from the colony. Governing authorities additionally expelled a minister and punished dozens of others as they sought to quell this "antinomian" ("against the law") controversy.[14]

In 1638 Hutchinson left Boston for Rhode Island. A few years later, while she was on Long Island, a group of Siwanoy warriors killed her and her family. For the Puritans in Massachusetts, God's vengeance had finally come. They saw Hutchinson's death as vindication of their judgment.

The Puritans, like all invading colonists, forged complicated relationships with local tribes. The seal of the Massachusetts Bay Colony, drawn in 1629, depicts an Indigenous man surrounded by a banner that reads, "Come Over and Help Us," an allusion to the Macedonian Call in Acts 16:9. But the locals did not want help, nor is help what the Puritans delivered.

Most Puritans, like the Pilgrims before them, believed that their faith and their charter entitled them to North American land. Indigenous land use, from the perspective of the Europeans, seemed like no use at all, which Christians used to justify conquest. "This savage people," Winthrop claimed, "ruleth over many lands without title or property."[15]

Indigenous people not only presented a real, physical obstacle to the Puritans' plans, they also presented an ideological challenge. Puritans asked themselves, Were Natives fully human? If so, what explained their "savagery" (in the eyes of the Puritans) compared to Europeans? Had the North American wilderness done this to them? Did this mean that the American environment might also transform Puritans? Whenever challenges arose in the colony, Puritans worried that perhaps they were becoming more like those they aimed to dispossess.

Unlike the Spanish in New Mexico, most Puritans made little effort to convert Natives. Minister John Eliot, however, believed that God had called him to evangelize local tribes. For decades he ministered to local people and studied the Massachusett language. In 1663, with the help of Indigenous aides, Eliot published a full Bible in the local language—the first Bible printed in North America. Eliot sought to make the faith accessible to his neighbors, and he and his allies established areas for Christian Indians to live together called "praying towns." Yet despite years of effort by Eliot and others, few Natives opted for baptism.

Occasional hostilities arose as the English encroached on ever more territory. The first serious conflict occurred in 1636 and 1637, when the Puritans, joined by allies from among the Narragansett and Mohegan, went to war against the Pequot. Then in 1675, Puritans waged another bloody war against their Indigenous neighbors at nearly the same time that the Pueblo revolted against the Spanish on the other side of the continent. The Puritan controversy began when Plymouth leaders executed three Wampanoag men after finding them guilty of murdering a Wampanoag Christian who had worked closely with the colonists.

The Wampanoag leader Metacom (also called Philip) rallied various local groups together against the colonists. The ensuing war proved extraordinarily brutal and violent. It took the lives of about a quarter of the people in the region (about three Indigenous lives for every English). The colonists captured thousands of Natives and sold them into slavery, mostly to the West Indies. The war proved particularly vicious for converts to Christianity. Colonists feared that "praying Indians" might be disloyal or might be spies, and so they turned against them. For the next few years, violence plagued those living on the edges of English colonization.

In 1692, the New England colonies faced yet another test. Witches and witchcraft seemed to overtake the town of Salem. The crisis began when two young women claimed that they felt "afflicted." Medical examiners could not find the source of their pain. Some adults concluded that dark forces must be at work, and to save the girls, they aimed to root out the source of their affliction. Over the next year, colonial authorities put almost one hundred fifty people on trial for witchcraft, and more than fifty confessed. Local leaders jailed many of them and executed at least twenty colonists. But almost as quickly as the controversy exploded, it died out. In late 1692 the courts stopped the trials, and in early 1693 freed the remaining prisoners.

The witchcraft controversy revealed the deep influence of magic and the supernatural in Puritan life. While colonists worked to build a godly society, they believed unseen forces influenced their efforts. Despite their professed reliance on the holy scriptures, a mix of conscious beliefs and unconscious assumptions molded their worldview. They viewed natural events—storms, sudden deaths, or women's afflictions—as signs of deeper spiritual realities. Puritans consulted almanacs filled with astrology, visited fortune tellers, and used metaphysical means to ward off curses. They reported ghostly visions, strange sounds, and supernatural occurrences. Drawing on classical meteorology and astrology, they interpreted comets, rainbows, and celestial patterns as messages from God. For them, nature was not random but a divine text filled with meaning to be read alongside the Bible.

In many ways, jeremiads, witch trials, and the heresy hunts have come to define the Puritans. While it is easy to disparage them for their many mistakes, Puritans left Americans with a deep and complicated record of an imperfect people trying to build a political community, trying to care for one another, trying to grow as one. And they show us how difficult that can be. They also remind us how oftentimes those claiming to do God's work overlook how their actions negatively affect those around them. Many Indigenous people died as Puritans tried to establish their holy community on seized land, expecting God to bless them for their actions.

The Puritans helped justify and establish the foundation for many Americans' sense of exceptionalism. That the Puritan project failed did little to quell Americans' enthusiasm for the Massachusetts Bay Colony experiment. Generations of writers, ministers, politicians, and activists drew a straight line from ancient Israel to Puritan New England to the modern United States, seeing the latter as God's chosen vehicle for implementing his plans and bringing his truth to the world. They believed that the Puritan covenant made Americans an exceptional people, chosen by God for a special work, and their nation the city on the hill, a light for all the world to see and to emulate. But this required that Americans pick up where the Puritans had left off. They needed to build a righteous nation to receive God's blessings; if they did not, as Winthrop predicted, they would provoke his wrath. The future was in their hands.

As the Puritans sought to expand their community, other Christian groups challenged their vision for North America. From Quakers to Catholics, they had their own ideas of what it meant to build the kingdom of God on earth.

3

VARIETIES OF CHRISTIAN LIBERTY

During the 1650s, missionaries from the Society of Friends, called "Quakers" by their enemies, targeted Boston Puritans for conversion. But every time the pesky enthusiasts entered the city, colonial leaders arrested them. They inspected their bodies for witches' marks and burned the books they carried with them. They even boarded up the town's jail cell windows to keep the Quakers from evangelizing those lingering nearby. Their fear that the Quakers might make converts revealed the precarious nature of the Puritan mission. To be the city on the hill required the violent suppression of dissent—including dissent from competing groups of Christians.

Englishman George Fox organized the Society of Friends in the 1640s. His followers aimed to recapture the mystery and aura of first-century Christianity and to return the faith to its essentials, to its original forms. Quakers believed that the Holy Spirit resided within each human in the form of an "inner light." During Quaker worship, which happened in large, plain rooms with men on one side and women on the other, participants sat in silence until someone felt the inner light inspiring them to speak or testify. As the power of the Holy Spirit pulsed through their bodies, participants occasionally shook, trembled, or "quaked." This behavior earned Friends their derogatory nickname.

Convinced they had discovered God's truth, Quakers eagerly shared their faith. Some bolted for the North American colonies, hoping to evangelize colonists. A small number moved to New England, mostly split between the unincorporated town of Plymouth and the somewhat more religiously tolerant Rhode Island. Others moved to the new colony of West Jersey (which later merged with East Jersey to form New Jersey), and some went to English colonies in the Caribbean.

Despite Puritan efforts to block them, Quakers aggressively sought converts in Boston and used provocations to garner attention. Sometimes they appeared nude in public to symbolize humanity's nakedness before God, provoking colonial authorities. One critic claimed that Quakers greeted local residents with the phrase, "Thou Serpent, thou Liar, thou deceiver, thou childe of the devil, thou cursed hypocrite, thou dumb dogge." Seeking to drive away the rabble-rousers permanently, Boston authorities began slicing off parts of their ears before expelling them, making it more difficult for them to return unnoticed.[1]

As the confrontations escalated, the Massachusetts general court passed a law mandating that the colony hang any Quakers who returned after being banished. Colonial leaders worried that Quakers might destroy everything they had worked so hard to build. Three previously banished Quakers, two men and one woman, returned in 1659, claiming that God had sent them. The Puritans captured and hung the two men but spared the life of the woman. Disappointed not to die as a martyr, eight months later she returned. This time Puritans executed her.

Quakers were one of dozens of religious groups from all over Europe who believed that perhaps in North America they might have the chance to worship freely. As more and more groups found refuge in the colonies, the Atlantic Seaboard became a haven for a broad range of competing European Christianities as well as home to a few other small religious groups. Anglicans dominated Virginia and the Carolinas, Quakers moved into Pennsylvania, and English and French Catholics carved out space in Maryland and on the edges of other colonies. Presbyterians filled the middle colonies and Baptists built small communities from north to south. Some French immigrants called Huguenots introduced another version of reformed protestantism to the continent. Jews settled in small communities, and Africans carried with them native religions, Islam, and Christianity. Indigenous peoples had made North America a diverse place; the arrival of Europeans and Africans made it even more so.

Many immigrant groups hoped to escape religious persecution and to grow their movements in the British colonies. Some thrived while others encountered violent opposition. The hodgepodge of competing religious communities set the colonies on an imperfect path toward increasing religious freedom by default. Although most individual colonies had established churches, no individual sect of protestants had the size or power to dominate the Atlantic Seaboard. By the time colonial leaders moved to form an independent nation, they championed religious liberty not only out of principle but also out of pragmatism.

In the first years of the seventeenth century, a group of London investors formed the Virginia Company. They expected to find in North America a land rich in resources and valuable metals. They also planned to establish new trade routes to further English power and prestige. The first colonists the company sent arrived in 1607 on three small ships in a region the local Algonkian people called Tsenacomoco. They settled on a swampy peninsula, christened the land Virginia, and established the Jamestown Colony.

The colony's first years proved difficult. The land was indeed rich, but not in the way colonists expected. They found no cities of gold to conquer, no treasures to snatch. The English suffered from disease, famine, and occasional troubles with the local tribes. During the first winter more than half the original settlers died. Those who survived had to work the land, which they had not anticipated.

Although the Jamestown pioneers did not place as much emphasis on religion as their Massachusetts Bay counterparts, Christianity still mattered to the colonial founders. The Virginia charter claimed that colonists would spread the Christian faith to those living "in Darkness and miserable Ignorance of the true Knowledge and Worship of God." They expected to "bring the Infidels and Savages, living in those parts, to human Civility." English leaders hoped that establishing protestant colonies in North America and converting tribes would challenge Catholic Spain's influence in the Western Hemisphere. Just as in Massachusetts, the English in Virginia came with a sense of total superiority that matched their total lack of curiosity about their new neighbors.[2]

As soon as the English disembarked, they held a communion service. John Rolfe, one of the early leaders, noted that he and his fellow colonists were "a peculiar people marked and chosen by the finger of God" to "possess" the land. "Undoubtedly," they claimed, "He is with us." Like the Franciscans to the west, they believed that God had specific plans to use the North American colonies to spread the faith. They quickly formed a parish and built a small chapel. Colonial leaders required everyone to attend Sabbath services, and their laws reflected the strict moral codes of the era. They established the Church of England in the colony and prohibited preaching by any ministers who did not have the blessing of church bishops back home. The colonies of North Carolina, South Carolina, and Georgia later joined Virginia in making the Church of England the official establishment church. Catholics and some closeted atheists also settled in Virginia.[3]

Virginia's colonists initially dispersed along the rivers feeding into the Chesapeake rather than forming towns. As the colony expanded, its leaders built churches on these waterways. Unlike Puritan New England, churches in Virginia did not serve as the central focus of colonial life.

The colony struggled to attract and retain competent ministers. Some who made their way to Virginia weren't answering a spiritual call but were escaping personal disgrace, including scandals, drunkenness, or unhappy marriages. Throughout much of the colony's first century, a shortage of clergy meant that ministers had to serve vast territories, often traveling long distances to reach scattered congregations.

The most powerful leader in the region, the Algonquin Wahunsonacock (the English called him Powhatan), oversaw a confederacy of multiple villages. He sought to expand his power and viewed the English as potential allies. At almost every stage of colonization, Indigenous leaders worked to benefit from the arrival of the English. Wahunsonacock secured knives and guns from the English and offered corn and other food in return.

In 1607 Wahunsonacock took Virginia leader John Smith captive. Unable to talk his way out of the predicament, Smith thought the Algonquins intended to execute him. "Two great stones were brought before Powhatan," Smith wrote in his journals in the third person as if observing rather than participating in this ritual. They readied to "beate out his braines" with clubs. But at the last minute Wahunsonacock's gutsy young daughter Matoaka, whom the English called Pocahontas, intervened, physically shielding the colonist. "Pocahontas the Kings dearest daughter," Smith explained, "got his head in her armes, and laid her owne vpon his to saue him from death." Smith may have made up the story, or his rescue by Matoaka might have represented some kind of scripted performance set up by Wahunsonacock to signify the dependence of the English on him and his people. Either way, Matoaka served as an important link between the Algonquins and the English.[4]

A few years later, members of the colony kidnapped Matoaka, hoping to secure a ransom from Wahunsonacock. John Rolfe fell in love with the captive. He agonized over his yearnings and studied the Bible to determine whether to pursue marriage with someone of a different culture. He knew that God had punished the Israelites "for marrienge of straunge wyves." But he remained nevertheless "in love wth one" whom he saw as far below him. Her "education hath byn rude," he continued, "her manners barbarous, her generacon Cursed, and soe discrepant in all nutriture from my selfe."

This was not exactly a Shakespearean love story. Or maybe it was. Rolfe could not stop thinking about Matoaka, which he blamed on the devil. "Surely theise are wicked instigations hatched by him whoe seeketh and delighteth in mans distruction." Rolfe eventually embraced his feelings and developed a thorough defense of the mixed-race marriage. Wahunsonacock supported the union, believing it would establish a solid alliance between the Algonquins and the English and that any children the couple produced would further cement relations between the groups.[5]

For colonial leaders to accept the marriage, Matoaka needed to convert to Christianity. Apparently she did, as far as the English were concerned. They baptized her and gave her a new name, Rebecca, after the Old Testament mother of two peoples. We do not know what Matoaka really thought of Rolfe, Christianity, or her marriage. Perhaps she fell in love, or perhaps her father orchestrated the partnership. In 1616 Matoaka traveled with Rolfe to London, where she came down with a fever. She died there at the age of twenty.

In the first decade of English settlement in Virginia, colonists failed to find the immediate riches that had inspired their venture. But they nevertheless learned how to make money by cultivating tobacco, a crop that became the colony's salvation. Growing tobacco, however, quickly drained soil of its nutrients, which required the colony to expand. Year by year, immigrant by immigrant, the English encroached further into Algonquin territory, inciting conflict.

The growth of the tobacco trade in the Chesapeake required that the colony expand its labor pool. In 1619, a group of enslaved Africans arrived in Jamestown. They had come onboard the *White Lion*, a ship under the command of English privateers. The sailors had seized the men and women from the Portuguese galleon the *São João Bautista*, which had left Angola with about three hundred captives. While en route to Vera Cruz, Mexico, the *White Lion* and another ship overtook the *São João Bautista* and stole its cargo. The captain of the *White Lion* then sailed to Virginia, where he sold more than twenty of the Africans to the English in exchange for food and supplies.

To the Virginia colonists, acquiring enslaved men and women was nothing remarkable. Slavery in various forms had been occurring in and around Europe and Africa for centuries. It had also been happening in North America. The Spanish had brought enslaved Africans to Florida decades earlier, and Indigenous tribes sometimes enslaved their vanquished enemies. Over the coming decades, the number of Africans in the Virginia colony grew as its leaders became ever more dependent on forced labor to build their economy.

The presence of enslaved people in the colonies forced political and religious leaders to address the relationship between human bondage and Christianity. Initially, White Chesapeake colonists made little effort to convert those they enslaved. Their economic interests outweighed any concern they might have felt for lost souls, and they feared that they might have to free baptized slaves. By the early eighteenth century, many colonies passed legislation that clarified the continuing legal obligation of enslaved people after conversion.

Enslavers had additional reasons for worrying about those they enslaved becoming Christians. Many believed that people with darker skin lacked the mental and spiritual capacities essential to joining the faith. Drawing from a racist anthropology, enslavers did not think it necessary to convert the enslaved—African peoples lacked the "soul" for Christianity. They feared Christianity's egalitarian nature as well. Enslavers could not envision a world in which their laborers could also be their brother or sister in the faith. Finally, enslavers worried that the Christian faith might make the enslaved feel empowered to rebel. They knew outcasts might find in the Christian gospel a story of liberation.

Most of the enslaved men and women in the colonies had little curiosity about the faith of their oppressors. They cherished their free time and seldom chose to spend it with Whites. Most worked every day but Sunday and used the Sabbath for cultivating their own gardens or meeting together. Not until the nineteenth century did Black North Americans convert to Christianity in large numbers.

Unlike those forcibly brought to North America, English Catholics came voluntarily, seeking freedom. In the wake of the English Reformation, Catholics in England struggled perhaps more than any other mainstream religious group. Protestant authorities had persecuted Catholic leaders and seized much of their property, and their right to worship ebbed and flowed depending on the monarch. English Catholics yearned to worship freely, and some looked abroad, hoping to discover a land where they could live in peace. One group thought they had found what they wanted in the North American colonies.

In 1632, King Charles granted a charter to Catholic nobleman Cecil Calvert for Maryland, a territory around the Chesapeake just north of the Virginia settlements. Calvert launched this mission to North America, he explained, for three reasons. First, to convert "the savages to Christianity." Second, to bring the new territory "under the subjection of his Crowne." And third, to help his fellow Catholics as they sought freedom and fortune.[6]

Calvert recruited both Catholics and protestants for his colony. He believed that by granting religious freedom to all Christians, he could secure and protect the rights of his fellow Catholics. Nevertheless, he asked Catholic emigrants to avoid inciting religious controversies. He told them on the voyage to Maryland to perform "all Acts of Romane Catholique Religion" as "privately as may be," and to "be silent upon all occasions of discourse concerning matters of Religion." He also called on the colonial leaders to "treate the Protestants with as much mildness and favor as Justice will permitt. And this to be observed at Land as well as at Sea."[7]

The first of Calvert's ships arrived in Maryland in 1634, with both Catholic and protestant passengers. Right away Catholic priest Andrew White offered mass. He and his allies then went to work, seeking to grow the church.

In the mid-seventeenth century, tensions between Catholics and protestants in England increased, which leaders in Maryland worried might affect the colony. In 1649, the colonial assembly passed an act of "toleration" that reiterated the founders' goal of making the colony a safe space for both religious groups. Anyone "professing to beleive in

Jesus Christ," the act declared, should not be in "any waies troubled, Molested or discountenanced for or in respect of his or her religion." Authorities granted all Christians—whether protestant or Catholic—"the free exercise" of their faith.

But the act also included several prohibitions. Colonists could not blaspheme or "curse" God, deny "our Saviour Jesus Christ to bee the sonne of God," or reject the Trinity. The punishment for such insolence was "death and confiscation or forfeiture of all his or her lands and goods." The assembly forbade residents from using a list of religious slurs against their fellow countrymen. They included: "heritick, Scismatick, Idolator, puritan, Independant, Prespiterian popish prest, Jesuite, Jesuited papist, Lutheran, Calvenist, Anabaptist, Brownist, Antinomian, Barrowist, Roundhead, Separatist" or anything else "in a reproachfull manner relating to matter of Religion." Leaders also forbade colonists from compelling residents toward "the beleife or exercise of any other Religion against his or her consent." The Toleration Act did not tolerate everything.[8]

Over the next few decades religious tensions in the Chesapeake region waxed and waned. As the number of protestants grew, the power and freedom of Catholics declined. Protestants occasionally attacked their rivals and vandalized their churches. By the latter part of the seventeenth century, protestants had forced most Catholics to practice their faith covertly, outside of worship houses, and without priests. In 1692 the Maryland legislature made the Church of England the established church of the colony. Nevertheless, Baltimore remained an important city for North American Catholics. Calvert had laid important foundations in Maryland upon which other Catholics later built.

While the leaders of the southern colonies made the Church of England the establishment church, the leaders of New Amsterdam, Rhode Island, and Pennsylvania cultivated more diversity. The Dutch West India Company founded New Amsterdam on the island of Manhattan shortly after the Pilgrims arrived in Plymouth in the 1620s. The colony's founders ignored English claims to the region and bought rights from the local Lenape people to use the land. They hoped that the colony would contribute to their growing fur trade. Although leaders officially supported the Dutch Reformed Church, profits and not God drove the colony's development. It attracted a diverse group of tradesmen and merchants representing many nationalities who practiced many versions of the Christian faith.

New Amsterdam proved welcoming to Jews as well. Jews had likely sailed with Columbus, and others had immigrated in small numbers to the colonies, but they mostly avoided attention. In 1564 a new group arrived in New Amsterdam. They had been living in a Dutch settlement in Brazil, but when the Portuguese captured the colony, they fled north. Local colonial leaders in New Amsterdam initially wanted to block the immigrants from settling, but some Jewish shareholders in the Dutch West India Company insisted that local leaders let the refugees stay. The immigrants formed the first Jewish congregation on land that later became part of the United States. In 1664, the Dutch ceded control of New Amsterdam to the English, who renamed it New York.

The most religiously diverse English colony in North America was Roger Williams's Rhode Island. As the colony's reputation grew, it became a haven for dissidents. In 1638, a group of reformers left England and established the first Baptist church in North America in Providence. Baptists, like Puritans and Presbyterians, aspired to purify the Church of England. But their commitment to "believer's baptism" distinguished them. They did not think that parents should baptize children but insisted that only those old enough to choose baptism for themselves should undergo the rite. Baptists placed considerable emphasis on the autonomy of local church congregations, and they believed that civil rulers should have no jurisdiction over churches. As a dissident, minority sect, they had a lot to gain in separating church from state, and much to lose in communities with existing, established churches.

As the Society of Friends faced persecution in England, more members of the faith looked abroad. One ambitious convert, William Penn, believed that North America could be a Quaker paradise. The English government owed Penn's father a substantial amount of money. Penn convinced King Charles II to settle the debt in 1681 by granting him a charter to create a colony called Pennsylvania ("Penn's

Woods") on a large swath of land on the mid-Atlantic. Penn named the capital of the colony "Philadelphia," or City of Brotherly Love.

While most Christian groups viewed social hierarchies as reflections of the authentic faith, members of the Society of Friends turned such beliefs upside down. Quakers believed that the inner light resided in everyone—God had not predestined some and damned others, but all could be saved and achieve perfection. Such beliefs led Friends to reject traditional social roles. They treated women as just as capable as men of following the Holy Spirit's lead in giving public testimony. Class distinctions, they insisted, simply hid or covered humans' true identities as children of God. They refused to recognize social hierarchies or to defer to their supposed betters. Friends embraced pacifism, convinced that God called them to turn the other cheek and love their enemies.

Like some of the other religious dissenters who had left England for North America, Penn hoped to establish a vibrant community that the rest of the world might emulate. He drafted a "frame of government" that made religious diversity a hallmark of the colony. "All persons living in this province," the document read, "who confess and acknowledge the one Almighty and eternal God" and agree to "live peaceably and justly in civil society, shall, in no ways, be molested or prejudiced for their religious persuasion, or practice, in matters of faith and worship." Nor would colonial authorities compel colonists "to frequent or maintain any religious worship, place or ministry whatever." However, colonial leaders drew the line at atheists; they could not live openly in the colony.[9]

While Penn tolerated a diversity of beliefs, he did not tolerate a diversity of actions. He expected everyone to abide by a strict moral code since "a careless and corrupt administration of justice draws the wrath of God upon magistrates," and "the wildness and looseness of the people provoke the indignation of God against a country." Like the Puritans, Quakers believed that God intervened in human affairs, doling out blessings and punishments. Therefore, Penn admonished, the colony would not endure "offences against God." They included "swearing, cursing, lying, prophane talking, drunkenness, drinking of healths, obscene words, incest, sodomy, rapes, whoredom, fornication, and other uncleanness (not to be repeated), all treasons, misprisions, murders, duels, felony, seditions, maims, forcible entries, and other violences, to the persons and estates of the inhabitants within this province." Penn also forbade "all prizes, stage-plays, cards, dice, May-games, gamesters, masques, revels, bull-battings, cock-fightings, bear-baitings, and the like, which excite the people to rudeness, cruelty, looseness, and irreligion." Those committing such sins, Penn asserted, would be "severely punished."[10]

Pennsylvania contained rich, abundant land for farming, and the city of Philadelphia, laid out on a grid pattern, proved a model of efficiency. As the colony grew, it attracted not just Quakers but also Presbyterians and immigrants from around much of Europe, including many German-speaking families, making it one of the most ethnically diverse colonies on the Atlantic Seaboard. Philadelphia soon rivaled Boston as one of North America's most prosperous trade centers.

Quakers tended to have better relations with local and regional tribes compared with those living in many of the other colonies. Penn learned the local Delaware language and tried to treat his neighbors relatively fairly. As problems arose between settlers and tribes in other regions, some Natives even migrated to Pennsylvania.

By the late seventeenth century, Puritans and Anglicans led a majority of the colonies' churches. Quakers had footholds in Pennsylvania and parts of New England. Catholics had some influence in parts of Maryland and led Christian communities in the Southwest, Florida, and on the borders of the Northern English colonies. Baptist and Presbyterian numbers were also growing. English colonists came to North America for the freedom to practice their faith as they wished, but usually not to extend such freedoms to their Christian competitors. Yet with so many different versions of Christianity represented in North America, no single group could dominate the colonial project or create a monopoly with its version of Christianity. In Europe, religious differences historically led to war. Colonists hoped to avoid that fate. But to keep the peace meant they had to blaze a new trail, to find a new way to balance the competing demands of church and state. They knew it would not be easy.

Then, beginning in the 1730s, a new revival of Christian excitement and devotion burst forth. It promised to complicate an already complicated set of relationships among Christian groups and to upend the status quo.

4

THE BIRTH OF REVIVALIST CHRISTIANITY

James Davenport, the scion of an elite Connecticut Puritan family, did exactly what his father expected. He went to Yale College to train for ministry and, after graduation, planned to find an established pulpit where he could contribute to the Puritan mission of building a godly commonwealth. But what happened next was not what he or his family anticipated. His ministry nearly cost him his pants.

After graduating in 1732, Davenport accepted a call to minister at a Long Island Congregational church. The Puritan-founded Congregationalists remained the dominant religious authorities in the region, but they faced ever-increasing competition from other Christian sects as well as more secular amusements. Davenport hoped to keep his church vibrant and growing.

A couple of years into his work, Davenport attended a New York revival meeting led by a traveling British minister named George Whitefield. The evangelist pitched salvation as a highly individualized experience rather than something that one pursued in a church community and across a lifetime. Whitefield offered faith as a commodity one could accept immediately as a guaranteed means of avoiding hell and damnation.

Davenport compared the steadfast but uninspiring faith he saw practiced in local congregations with the excitement in Whitefield's meetings. What, he wondered, made Whitefield different from other ministers? Perhaps, he concluded, church leaders had not themselves been truly saved. What else could account for the seeming declension of faith in the century since the Puritans had arrived in New England?

Davenport translated thought into action and started warning people against following "unconverted" ministers. The more he railed against his fellow clergymen, the more successful his own revivals became. He discovered that publicly calling out local clergy drew large audiences, and large audiences bred energy, and energy bred conversions.

In 1741, Davenport left his church to work full time as a traveling revivalist. He held raucous services where people fell under the influence of the Holy Spirit, laughing and shaking and convulsing. While Davenport thrilled the crowds who came to see him, his tactics and jeremiads against ministers offended local leaders. When ministers cut off his access to their pulpits, Davenport simply relocated his services to fields, greens, and barns. He preached at all hours, and sometimes meetings stretched late into the night. Critics complained that he drove his followers to madness.

Davenport's career stoked more controversy in New England than almost anything since the witch trials. During a meeting in New London, Davenport invited his audience to cleanse themselves of their sins. Medical doctor Alexander Hamilton was traveling though the region at the time and heard about Davenport from a friend. He wrote about the minister in his diary, calling him "a fanatick preacher" who "told his flock in one of his enthusiastic rhapsodies that in order to be saved they ought to burn all their idols." The audience seemed eager to participate. They began with a book burning, sacrificing many

Puritan classics, "and sung psalms and hymns over the pile" while it smoldered.

After destroying their intellectual idols, the revival mob turned to their material stumbling blocks. "The women made up a lofty pile of hoop petticoats, silk gowns, short cloaks, cambrick caps, red heeld shoes, fans, necklaces, gloves and other such aparrell." Then Davenport joined in. "And what was merry enough," Hamilton continued, "Davenport's own idol with which he topped the pile, was a pair of old, wore out, plush breeches." The pants, however, along with the rest of the pile, survived the ordeal. One observer "more moderate than the rest" found "means to perswade them that making such a sacrifice was not necessary for their salvation, and so every one carried off their idols again." This was lucky for Davenport, Hamilton concluded, "who, had fire been put to the pile, would have been obliged to strutt about bare-arsed."[1]

Davenport and others like him went to war against the imperial forms of Christianity that Europeans had carried to the colonies. By the mid-eighteenth century many Congregationalists and Anglicans had grown conservative. Critics saw them as staid, boring, and overly intellectual. Seeking to channel the faith in a new direction, Davenport and others drew a "revivalist" stream from the headwaters of North American Christianity. They formed it into an emotional, spiritually democratic, and highly individualized form of Christianity that eventually redesigned political life in North America. Their version of faith reinforced colonists' independence and their suspicion of established authority. It also offered entertainment and appealed to the masses. Although revivalist leaders later claimed to have restored traditional protestantism, in reality they created something attuned to the time and place. Launched in the 1730s, revivalist Christianity has vied for dominance in North America in every generation since, transforming individual lives and with them the culture and politics of the nation.

Revivalist ministers and theologians recycled and reconfigured ideas and practices from seventeenth-century Pietism, a religion of the heart. European Pietists emphasized individuals' relationship to God and personal morality, and they believed that faith required transformation for both the individual Christian and the broader community. Although many Pietists drew on Calvinist theology, they lived, acted, and talked as if God made salvation available to all. To those who wondered how they might know that God had saved them, Pietists offered an answer. A true Christian felt his or her salvation. Pietists had little patience for intellectualism, rationality, and rote, formal practices.

Pietist ideas helped Christian leaders adjust to the perceived declension of religious life by offering an easier path to salvation. The old way of viewing conversion—as a lifetime journey through the wildness of this world—gave way among some to a sharper focus on conversion as something that one felt in a single moment. Like falling in love, a person may not recognize their conversion the instant it happened, but in retrospect they could look back and identify the exact moment God had transformed them.

A small number of New England Congregationalists integrated pietistic ideas into their work. Solomon Stoddard, the pastor of a Northampton church about one hundred miles west of Boston, oversaw occasional pietistic revivals. When Stoddard retired, his grandson, Jonathan Edwards, took over the ministry. Perhaps colonial America's most important theologian, Edwards read widely and deeply and engaged with the ideas of not only prominent theologians but also Enlightenment philosophers such as John Locke and Isaac Newton. Edwards wrote many books focused on issues of religion, philosophy, and the nature of conversion. A frugal person, he drafted his ideas on random scraps of paper, filling every inch with nearly indecipherable chicken scratch that scholars have spent decades decoding. Like his grandfather, he made revivals central to his work.

In the summer of 1741, the Northampton divine preached a sermon titled "Sinners in the Hands of an Angry God." Like other revivalists, he hoped to provoke an emotional response and to lead his audience to a conversion experience. "Your Wickedness," he told those in the pews, "makes you as it were heavy as Lead, and to tend downwards with great Weight and Pressure towards Hell; and if God should

let you go, you would immediately sink and swiftly descend & plunge into the bottomless Gulf." And there was nothing they could do about it. "Your healthy Constitution," he continued, "and all your Righteousness, would have no more Influence to uphold you and keep you out of Hell, than a Spider's Web would have to stop a falling Rock." They had incensed God, he reminded them. "The Bow of God's Wrath is bent, and the Arrow made ready on the String, and Justice bends the Arrow at your Heart, and strains the Bow, and it is nothing but the mere Pleasure of God, and that of an angry God, without any Promise or Obligation at all, that keeps the Arrow one Moment from being made drunk with your Blood." As he read the sermon in a dry monotone, his audience wept and screamed.[2]

A few years later, Edwards picked up his pen to justify revivalist Christianity. In *A Treatise Concerning Religious Affections,* he tried to capture the euphoria of a conversion. He used as his primary exhibit the experience of an acquaintance—his wife Sarah (although he did not name her or identify her gender). Sarah's experience of revival, he observed, left her "in a kind of heavenly Elysium" and she felt like she was swimming "in the rays of Christ's love." Her "heart was swallowed up in a kind of glow of Christ's love, coming down from Christ's heart in heaven," which produced "a constant flowing and reflowing" of love "from heart to heart." This led her to a near out-of-body experience. "The soul," Edwards explained, "seemed almost to leave the body; dwelling in a pure delight." She felt "omnipotent joy, as to cause the person (wholly unavoidably) to leap with all the might, with joy and mighty exultation." Probably no one before or after Edwards better expressed the emotions and feelings of a revivalist conversion experience. In describing it, Edwards, like other revivalists, emphasized the emotional feelings of conversion, as well as the sense of conviction—or deep awareness—of sin that they inspired. People lacking such an experience, revivalists concluded, may not be saved.[3]

Edwards's defense of his own actions proved less successful than his defense of the revivals. Despite all he had done for the Northampton church, his congregation eventually turned on him. He caused a major row when he repudiated his grandfather's practice of offering communion to all who wanted it rather than just church members. He also angered congregants when he disciplined some of the teenage boys in the church for passing around a midwife's manual—the closest thing to pornography most boys in that era could find. He eventually left New England in 1758 for the presidency of the College of New Jersey but died shortly thereafter. A man of science, he had voluntarily taken a smallpox inoculation. It killed him.

While revival fires occasionally ignited in Northampton, a young Anglican was defying convention in England. George Whitefield had hoped to have a career on the stage, but as he grew in the Christian faith, he came to see acting as immoral. He went to Oxford to train for the ministry. Nevertheless, he never lost faith in the power of drama to change how people viewed the world. He and other students, including John and Charles Wesley, established a small pietistic fellowship that detractors called the "Holy Club." Group members dedicated themselves to holy living and caring for their fellow humans.

After graduating from Oxford in 1736, Whitefield preached around the region. To compete for audiences, he stripped his sermons to their essence. He delivered his messages extemporaneously, or without notes. He acted out biblical stories, playing characters and changing his voice to mimic past religious heroes, both men and women. He cried somewhat regularly when delivering sermons, conveying his passion for the gospel and his heartfelt piety. Whitefield's physical appearance may have added to his appeal. He had crossed eyes, which likely came from battling measles as a child. His eighteenth-century audiences seemed to interpret this unique characteristic as a sign of special or supernatural gifts and talents; they believed that perhaps he had a touch of the divine.

The preacher also made good use of the press. He fed stories to journalists to benefit his work. As his reputation grew, newspaper coverage of Whitefield snowballed. The more the papers talked about the minister, the more eager people were to see him, and as his crowds grew, so did newspaper coverage.

Whitefield's many tactics all directed audiences toward the same goal—individual salvation. The evangelist hoped to affect his listeners.

He wanted to generate in them an emotional and physical response, a transformation. He aimed to convince audiences of the importance of the "new birth," an instantaneous conversion experience.

In 1738, Whitefield visited North America, making the first of seven trips to the colonies. He pioneered a new form of ministry, working as a traveling or itinerant evangelist, a preacher without a permanent pulpit. Others had served as traveling ministers in sparsely populated areas, but Whitefield aspired to preach in places with established churches and ministers. His ambitious itinerary helped him create an Atlantic revival network that linked England, Scotland, Ireland, and North America.

Whitefield embraced another innovation—outdoor preaching. Holding services in open areas freed him of the constraints of local leaders, allowed him to minister to larger crowds, and provided less limiting physical structures for his dramatic performances. Outdoor services also demolished social hierarches. In many churches people often sat in family pews that corresponded to their class status; in a field the rich and the poor, the saved and the unregenerate all mingled together freely. Revivalist Christianity, sometimes intentionally and sometimes inadvertently, made faith more democratic. In vying for public attention, Whitefield competed against stage plays, horse races, merchant stands, music, and various other entertainments. He offered a product to the masses, and he needed to sell it as well as an actor sells a performance, or his show would close as quickly as it opened.

Needing a permanent institutional base in North America from which to launch colonial revival tours, Whitefield founded an orphanage in Georgia called "Bethesda." The orphanage, like many Southern institutions, relied on the labor of enslaved men and women. As Whitefield's work expanded, he became an advocate of the slave system, lobbied for its expansion, purchased his own slaves, and used coerced labor to help run his Georgia work. In this way American revivalism and racism became mutually supportive.

In the fall of 1739, Whitefield returned to North America for a second preaching tour. He stopped first in Philadelphia, where he delivered his first sermons inside church buildings, but local ministers'

Controversial revivalist George Whitefield often spoke extemporaneously, outdoors rather than in churches, and used drama to great effect. This cartoon depicts Whitefield as having his head filled by the devil with a liquid used for enemas while his revivals are characterized by chaos, sexual immorality, and financial corruption. (credit: Library of Congress)

opposition to his tactics along with surging crowds forced him to move outside. His approach made little sense to the regular clergy, and they sensed relatively quickly that he represented a new kind of competition from within Christendom rather than outside of it.

The evangelist's ability to hold a crowd and project his voice outdoors impressed Benjamin Franklin. "I had the Curiosity to learn how far he could be heard," Franklin recalled. So he did some calculations. He walked backward from where Whitefield was preaching until he could no longer hear the evangelist clearly. "Imagining then a Semi-Circle," Franklin continued, "of which my Distance should be the Radius, and that it were fill'd with Auditors, to each of whom I allow'd two square feet, I computed that he might well be heard by more than Thirty-Thousand." This verified for Franklin the newspaper accounts "of his having preach'd to 25000 People in the Fields, and to the antient Histories of Generals haranguing whole Armies, of which," he admitted, "I had sometimes doubted."[4]

Whitefield hoped to raise money in Philadelphia for his orphanage. Franklin initially "refus'd to contribute." But the printer had underestimated Whitefield's ability to cast a spell on those in his audience. "I silently resolved he should get nothing from me," Franklin vowed. "I had in my Pocket a Handful of Copper Money, three or four silver Dollars, and five Pistoles in Gold. As he proceeded I began to soften, and concluded to give the Coppers." But Whitefield had not ended the call. "Another Stroke of his Oratory made me asham'd of that, and determin'd me to give the Silver; and he finish'd so admirably, that I empty'd my Pocket wholly into the Collector's Dish, Gold and all." A master fundraiser, Whitefield netted more money in some individual offerings than regular clergy earned in an entire year. He proved that revival could be a thriving business, not just for souls, but for cash too.[5]

In the summer of 1740, Whitefield went on a tour of New England where he drew enormous crowds. He started in Boston and then continued to Northampton. He had heard about Solomon Stoddard and Jonathan Edwards's revivals. Whitefield preached from Edwards's pulpit, and as he did, Edwards, along with much of the congregation, wept.

Spending time with Jonathan and his wife, Sarah, and their family affected Whitefield in more ways than one. "A sweeter couple I have not yet seen," he confessed in his journal. Sarah "is a Woman adorn'd with a meek and quiet Spirit, talked feelingly solidly of the Things of God, and seemed to be such a Help meet for her Husband." She inspired him, Whitefield continued, to "renew" his prayers that God "would be pleased to send me a Daughter of Abraham to be my Wife." Lest the almighty think Whitefield was getting randy, he assured God, "Thou knowest I only desire to marry in and for Thee."[6]

Whitefield had planned to remain celibate, allowing him to focus on his work. But when he started drawing the attention of women he wondered if he had chosen the right path. People found his crossed eyes and thick curls attractive. As his career took off, the evangelist decided that, as the Apostle Paul instructed, it was better for him to find a woman like Sarah to marry rather "than to burn"—to be overcome with lust.

A few days after the Northampton meetings, Whitefield traveled to Middletown, Connecticut. Farmer Nathan Cole documented the event. Like many others, Cole had read about the well-known evangelist. When the news spread that Whitefield was scheduled to preach in the area, Cole traveled several miles to attend. The farmer described the evangelist as "almost angelical; a young, Slim, slender, youth." Cole thought "he looked as if he was Clothed with authority from the Great God, and a sweet solemn solemnity sat upon his brow." Whitefield's sermon had the desired effect on Cole. "My hearing him preach gave me a heart wound; By God's blessing: my old Foundation was broken up, and I saw that my righteousness would not save me."[7]

In Middletown and in hundreds of other places, Whitefield's meetings changed lives and remade Christianity. Over time, his work gave new meaning to the term revival. Rather than marking a once-or-twice-a-generation event that occurred in a local church, revival came to refer to an experience outside of existing congregations, which competed directly with other forms of entertainment. To succeed, a minister did not need the backing of any kind of religious establishment nor of elites. But he did need broad appeal and popular support. Revivalists often circumvented traditional authorities and took their ministry—their show—to the masses. Their work directed colonists' attention away from traditional religious authorities and institutions and instead focused it on popular and entertaining evangelists.

Whitefield spawned many imitators, including Presbyterian Gilbert Tennent, who helped expand revivalist Christianity in the middle colonies. Tennent's father had established a "log college" in New Jersey (which eventually morphed into the College of New Jersey and then Princeton University) to train Presbyterian ministers to serve the large number of immigrants flooding into the middle colonies from the British Isles. Tennent graduated from Yale and then returned to New Brunswick, New Jersey, to pastor a Presbyterian church and to help his father with the new college. He occasionally joined Whitefield during his tours, which allowed him to study the revivalist.

On March 8, 1740, Tennent preached an infamous sermon called "The Danger of an Unconverted Ministry." In this address, which Benjamin Franklin printed and distributed, Tennent compared contemporary ministers to the Pharisees of Jesus's day, calling them "dead dogs, that can't bark." For the young preacher, only those who embraced revivalist Christianity found salvation. "Is a blind Man fit to be a Guide in a very dangerous Way?" he asked. "Is a possessed Man fit to cast out Devils?" Of course not. Then why did his fellow colonists attend churches with ministers such as these? "Isn't an unconverted Minister," he scolded, "like a Man who would learn others to swim, before he has learnd it himself, and so is drowned in the Act, and dies like a Fool?" He called rival ministers "blind as Moles, and as dead as Stones, without any spiritual Taste and Relish."[8]

The sermon exacerbated growing divides among Presbyterians between conservative institutionalists and innovative revivalists. Many church leaders appreciated the infusion of energy and converts that revivalist Christianity produced, but others wondered if revivalists had drowned the true faith in a sea of emotionalism. Tennent and his allies' brazen attacks against the character of their fellow clergymen left ministers in the leading protestant denominations with no option but to choose a side, for or against the new form of faith.

In the southern colonies, the top-down Anglican hierarchy asserted more control over religious life than in other regions, which allowed church leaders to rein in dissent more easily. Nevertheless, over the next few decades the revivalist movement grew in the South as well, eventually challenging the Anglican religious establishment.

What the revivalists began they could not control. The Holy Spirit seemingly led people in many new directions unmediated by the church or tradition. Allowing individuals to determine the boundaries of faith made possible the subversion of established norms. Educated preachers like Tennent and Davenport embraced Christian revivalism, but so too did a lot of people with more limited theological backgrounds and looser church affiliations. Revivalism created the opportunity for a radical reconstruction of leadership in North American religious life. It democratized the faith, making it more accessible to all regardless of race, gender, or education and also individualized it, making Christian practice independent of any necessary Christian community.

The revivals inspired some women to assume new positions of religious authority. One, Bathsheba Kingsley, made a public confession in the fall of 1741. She had in fact stolen a horse and rode away with it on the Sabbath. She explained that God had directed her actions, goading her to proclaim the gospel.[9]

A couple of years later she was again in trouble. A group of pastors including Jonathan Edwards came together to discuss Kingsley's extravagant religious behavior. She told the ministers that the Holy Spirit had made her "a proper person to be improved for some great things in the church of God; and that in the exercise of some parts of the work of ministry." God, she proclaimed, had called her to spread his word from house to house. "Dreams & sudden impulses," as well as "immediate Revelations from heaven" confirmed this calling.[10]

As Kingsley grew bolder, her husband tried to stop her, resorting to violence. She prayed that he would "go quick to hell." The ministers supported Kingsley and not her husband. According to Edwards, "Mindful of the complex workings of the Spirit at the time," the ministers "seek not to stifle Bathsheba Kingsley's zeal but to channel it." Their response to Kingsley revealed how the revivals had transformed some aspects of religion on the Atlantic Seaboard. Over one hundred years earlier, church and civic leaders in Massachusetts had banished Anne Hutchinson for claiming that God had spoken to her via divine revelation. Now, they trusted that the Holy Spirit inspired women like Kingsley to share his message. Colonists determined that God could and did work through people who many established religious authorities would never have permitted to speak from a pulpit. Although Edwards and his colleagues did not endorse Kingsley's actions, they did not want to obstruct her work either.[11]

Another New England woman, Sarah Osborn, also felt God calling her to minister. She had attended a Whitefield revival, which had "stirred" her up. Then she attended one of Gilbert Tennent's meetings, which further "roused" her. While the revivals inspired ecstatic, physical experiences in some, for Osborn they sparked turmoil and introspection. Upon hearing the revivalists' preaching, she wondered if

God had truly saved her. Experiencing the emotional individualism of revivalism was like sailing the ocean—moments of tranquility could instantly give way to storms. Feelings of freedom, exhilaration, and ecstasy could flip to chaos, fear, and doubt.[12]

Eventually Osborn determined that God had redeemed her. She spent the following decades sharing her experience of personal transformation in print and through religious meetings. She began a home Bible study with mostly women and both free and enslaved Black Christians. As word of her meetings spread, they grew to the point that some weeks more than five hundred people attended. When her Newport, Rhode Island, Congregationalist church fired its pastor for drunkenness, she even stepped in temporarily to help lead it.

With the limited records we have, we know that in the mid-eighteenth century about a dozen other women claimed to be public evangelists. They illustrated how revivalism could foster egalitarianism, creating space for new forms of ministry and new kinds of ministers.

The revivals also prompted some Indigenous men and women to reconsider the role of Christian faith within their communities. Native religious leaders had long trusted dreams, visions, and trances to provide spiritual insights. So when the revivals produced similar ecstatic experiences, they seemed to confirm and verify the integration of Christianity with contemporary Indigenous religious practices. Sometimes the revivals also inspired Indigenous leaders to give new Christian meanings to old rituals, such as dances and feasts.

Mohegan leader Samson Occom introduced revivalism to tribal groups in the Northeast. He converted in the 1740s and became an evangelist and a mediator between tribal and White communities. He adopted English dress, embraced White colonial culture, penned popular hymns, and received ordination with the Presbyterians. These moves allowed him to secure influence among White leaders, which he used to advocate for Indigenous rights. Occom spent two years in the British Isles, traveling from city to city and pulpit to pulpit raising money for church work and educational efforts in Indigenous communities in North America. The tour made him a celebrity and drew substantial positive press.

Late in his career, Occom believed that George Whitefield came to him in a dream. "I had been Preaching," Occom claimed, when Whitefield appeared and grabbed his hand. "I am glad that you preach the Excellency of Jesus Christ yet," the old revivalist told the minister. "Go on and the Lord be with thee." The dream served for Occom to legitimate his career. If Whitefield approved the ministry of the Indigenous leader, who could criticize it?[13]

Black Christians in North America also experienced bursts of revivalism. Because revivalist preaching emphasized personal conversion over theological complexity or formal church rituals, it offered a form of faith accessible across lines of class and education. By 1750, some Black converts had founded independent churches—spaces that became vital sites of community, resilience, and identity, offering a sense of dignity and spiritual autonomy in a society that denied them both.

White revivalists' concentration on winning hearts rather than reforming social structures led them to minimize the Bible's liberationist themes. Whitefield and other revivalists promised enslavers that revivalism not only didn't threaten slavery but also actually bolstered it. "Christianity," Whitefield assured his fellow enslavers, "will not make their negroes worse slaves" but encourage them to work harder.[14]

Accommodating revivalism to slavery offended many Black men and women. But some, including Phillis Wheatley, who had once been enslaved, appreciated Whitefield's efforts. After the evangelist's death, she eulogized him in a poem. It highlighted in part how Whitefield carried God's offer of salvation to Black men and women:

> *Take* HIM *ye Africans, he longs for you;*
> *Impartial* SAVIOUR, *is his title due;*
> *If you will chuse to walk in grace's road,*
> *You shall be sons, and kings, and priests to* GOD.

She saw Whitefield's work as empowering and emboldening those whom other Christian leaders ignored.[15]

While revivalism inspired many conversions, it also provoked passionate damnations. Charles Chauncy, the pastor of Boston's First Church and one of many critics, feared that revivalism sometimes upended racial, gender, and educational hierarchies. He found that "Men of all Occupations" and no "Learning, and but small Capacities" imagined they could "speak to the Spiritual Profit" of others. He fretted over the collapse of social roles and how revivals allowed women, children, and the enslaved to worship and preach equally. "Nay, there are among these Exhorters," he groused, "Babes in Age, as well as Understanding. They are chiefly indeed young Persons, sometimes Lads, or rather Boys: Nay, Women and Girls; yea, Negroes, have taken upon them to do the Business of Preachers." While many established and ordained ministers like Whitefield, Tennent, and Davenport helped oversee the revivals, they also created opportunities for people like Bathsheba Kingsley and Samson Occom to lead, threatening the established order.[16]

A century after the revivals overtook New England, historian Joseph Tracy named this surge in faith "the Great Awakening." His title stuck. In some ways "the Great Awakening" served as an apt description of the series of emotional revivals that touched tens of thousands of people regardless of race, ethnicity, or gender. However, to identify one set of revivals as "great" and distinct from others unnecessarily limits our ability to see that revivalist methods became a consistent part of North American religious life. Beginning in the 1740s, Christians permanently spliced revivalism into the North American religious DNA.

Although European Christians and their Christianities had structured most early colonial beliefs and practices, the new revivalism revealed that the nature of Christianity in the colonies was evolving. Out of the torrent of European Christianity, four distinct North American versions of the faith had started emerging. George Whitefield and his imitators helped craft a revivalist stream to promote an individualist focus and emphasis on heartfelt faith and a specific set of Christian morals. Churchly critics like Charles Chauncy drew on a reconfigured conservative stream to uphold decorum, tradition, and order. Rationalists like Benjamin Franklin drew from a third stream, the liberal stream, integrating European thought and the North American context to advocate for Jesus's ideals independent of what they saw as anti-intellectual, medieval superstitions. Meanwhile, those who sought to upend the status quo began working to redirect part of the main river of American Christianity into a new liberationist stream. As the colonies moved toward war with England, Christian activists positioned within every one of the developing streams sought to expand their role in the future of the nation.

5

REVOLUTION

Around one thousand members of the Continental Army, under the command of Benedict Arnold, amassed in Newburyport, Massachusetts, in September 1775. They could feel winter coming. The centuries-old maple trees had begun changing colors, and the days had started growing darker and colder. The smell of decay lingered in the air.

On the Sunday before the soldiers planned to begin an arduous march through Maine and on to Quebec to challenge a British regiment for control of the region, some attended a service at the First Presbyterian Church. As they listened to the sermon, they knew that below their feet lay dozens of tombs. After the worship service, the soldiers followed the sexton down to the crypt. One tomb held the body of George Whitefield. The soldiers pried open the tomb's lid, exposing the remains of the evangelist who had died five years earlier. Whitefield's body had decomposed, but his clothes still dressed his bones. The patriots removed the clerical collar and wristbands from the lifeless skeleton and sliced them into pieces. Each of the officers claimed a part of Whitefield's vestments. They believed the talismans would secure their victory. In that moment religious revivalism and political revolution melded together. Unfortunately for the Americans, the spirit of Whitefield did little to help them against the British in Quebec, who handily repelled the attack.

On the eve of the American Revolution, Britain controlled more than two dozen colonies across the Americas and Caribbean. In the thirteen colonies bracing for war, a conservative, communal, and church-centered strain of protestantism remained dominant. Puritan-descended Congregationalists, who shaped religious life in New England, accounted for about 20 percent of colonial worshippers. Presbyterians, concentrated mainly in the middle colonies, made up roughly 18 percent, while Anglicans, strongest in the South, comprised about 15 percent. Despite their differences in church governance, all three denominations upheld the ideals laid out in the Church of England's Thirty-nine Articles, which defined core Anglican doctrine and practice. Each group enjoyed the support of British imperial leaders, who viewed them as essential partners in maintaining religious and political order—and in rallying colonial loyalty to God and crown.

A variety of smaller protestant groups made up much of the remaining colonial churchgoing population. Baptists led among them, accounting for about 15 percent of congregants, followed by Quakers, who comprised just under 10 percent. Roughly 5 percent of colonial worshippers belonged to German Reformed churches, with slightly fewer adhering to Lutheran congregations, many of which were also German. Another 3.7 percent were Dutch Reformed. British authorities permitted these groups to organize freely, recognizing that they hailed from establishment protestant churches in their homelands and did not threaten the imperial religious order. Methodists, who still largely identified as members of the Church of England, made up about 2 percent of North American churchgoers. Catholics also constituted about 2 percent of the population, while about 1 percent worshipped in Moravian congregations. The colonies also supported sixteen Mennonite churches and five Jewish synagogues. Small communities of French Huguenots and other refugees from Catholic persecution likewise had settled in the colonies. Although most colonists remained loyal to their ancestral churches, the religious landscape of early America offered a remarkable diversity of Christian—and, to a small degree, non-Christian—possibilities.

In the years leading up to the revolution, North American ministers generally supported the imperial status quo while they tailored their messages to the unique context of the colonies and its many Christianities. They emphasized general concepts of religious liberty, Christ's offer of freedom from sin and spiritual captivity, and individual autonomy and rights. Although they focused their teachings primarily on the kingdom of God, their parishioners sometimes heard in their words secondary meanings relevant for the kingdom of man. As the colonies moved toward independence, patriots resurrected and reconfigured the old Puritan covenant. They renewed speculation that God might mold those living in North America into a peculiar people, fit to preside over a new empire poised to share his word with the world. Perhaps, they hazarded, out of the crucible of war God was erecting a new nation, a new Israel, a new chosen land.

The French and Indian War (1754–1763), known in Europe as the Seven Years' War, signaled the onset of new challenges for the North American colonists. The British had emerged victorious, gaining control of the Eastern Seaboard, which promised increased trade opportunities, enhanced security, and, for the majority protestant population, a significant victory over the Spanish and French Catholics. But as colonists moved into territory ceded by the French but still controlled by Indigenous groups, violence increased. Most battles had little to do with religion, but religion occasionally inspired conflict. Neolin, a Lenni Lenape (or Delaware) prophet, rallied tribes throughout the Ohio region to reject foreign technology and clothes, and to cease trading with the British. He claimed that if the tribes came together, the "Master of Life" would restore their communities and bring them material abundance. His invocation of a single omnipotent pan-Indian deity revealed how Indigenous leaders could appropriate Christian concepts and make them their own. An Odawa chief named

Pontiac took up Neolin's call and inspired Hurons, Potawatomis, Shawnees, Delawares, and Mingoes to join the fight. They attacked multiple colonial forts as well as settler outposts and killed approximately two thousand settlers. Leaders in Parliament determined that they needed to do more to protect the colonies, which required more revenue.

After the French and Indian War, Parliament had modified how it regulated and financed the colonies. When members passed the Stamp Act in 1765, a tax on paper goods, some colonists howled—Parliament had never before instituted a direct tax on the colonies. They objected to having leaders in Britain, where they believed they had no representation, making rules that affected them. They argued that only their local assemblies had the right to issue such taxes. In Virginia a young member of the House of Burgesses, the revivalist-leaning Patrick Henry, called for the passage of a series of resolutions denouncing the Stamp Act. In New England mobs began organizing protests and burned the figure of the stamp distributor in effigy. But for the most part protestant clergy in the colonies—theological liberals, conservatives, and revivalists alike—showed little interest in the 1760s in fomenting rebellion.

George Whitefield, who had returned home to London from his latest North American revivals amid the Stamp Act controversy, hoped that the empire's protestant establishment would hold. Nevertheless, the crisis forced him to make a choice, to pick a side. Unlike his Holy Club brother the Methodist pioneer John Wesley, he defended the colonies and not the crown. When his friend Benjamin Franklin, who had become one of the colonies' leading diplomats, spoke in Parliament on behalf of North Americans, Whitefield wrote that Franklin "stood unappalled, gave Pleasure to his Friends, and did Honour to his Country."[1]

Whitefield's decision to back the colonies underscored a growing realization among North American church leaders that their spiritual and civic freedoms were deeply entwined. The Church of England's Society for the Propagation of the Gospel in Foreign Parts oversaw much of the missionary work in the outposts of the empire. In

1762, Congregational leaders in Massachusetts sought to form their own missionary organization to work with local and regional tribes called the Society for Propagating Christian Knowledge Among the Indians of North America. The Church of England vetoed the New England plan. This action reminded New England Christians that they lacked true freedom and independence. British leaders, in their minds, had too much authority in the colonies, not just over economic policies, but over matters of faith.

A second controversy involved the question of a colonial bishop. For over a century, Anglican leaders in London hoped to place a bishop in the North American colonies, which would make it easier for the church to ordain new clergy without a transatlantic journey. In addition, while the Church of England had a good deal of power in the colonies, the number of dissenters had grown. Church authorities in England thought a bishop might bring order and discipline to North American Christianity.

Many colonists saw the idea of an Anglican bishop in their region as an infringement on their religious liberty. They did not want another representative of parliamentary power on their side of the Atlantic. Even the colonial Anglicans mostly opposed the idea, enjoying their autonomy and preferring the status quo.

Parliament never acted to place a bishop in the colonies, nor did members even debate it. However, many colonists believed that they intended to, and the very fact that Parliament did not discuss it led some colonists to fall back on conspiracy theories. Perhaps, they thought, the lack of deliberation indicated that Parliament had already made the decision.

Critics of Parliament saw an opportunity in the bishop controversy to foment further dissent. They published articles in colonial newspapers against a North American bishop, which drew counterarguments from Anglican leaders in England. Soon, however, Anglican leaders mostly dropped the issue. Nevertheless, some colonists, eager to keep momentum against Parliament going, continued stoking the controversy. They recognized that linking religious and political freedom together could support the revolutionary cause.

On March 5, 1770, Bostonians, angered by the presence of British soldiers occupying their city, began pelting soldiers with sticks and ice. The soldiers responded by firing into the crowd, killing five people. Colonists labeled the event the Boston Massacre. Whitefield, back in North America at the time, traveled to Boston shortly after the deadly protest. Poking at British leaders who, he insinuated, had broken their "charter" or agreement with the colonies, Whitefield observed "what a mercy, that our Christian charter" from God "cannot be dissolved."[2]

Demonstrations against Parliament's policies over the next few years inspired colonists from Georgia to Massachusetts to begin seeing their interests aligning. Some even began to consider themselves part of a larger entity beyond their individual colonies—part of an "America." However, they did not necessarily expect to break from Britain; they just wanted to reassert their political liberty and autonomy. Many leading clergy in England and around the colonies responded cautiously to the growing divisions. They hoped to maintain protestant unity in the empire.

Members of Parliament made matters worse in 1774 when they passed the Quebec Act to help regulate the province formerly controlled by the French. For many British colonials, the act's provisions represented another overreach. Parliament allowed colonists in Quebec to maintain their Catholic faith, to pay tithes to their churches, and to have a local, Catholic bishop. British authorities also granted rights to Catholics in Grenada, another colony they had just won from France. Catholics did not have such extensive rights in England. British leaders hoped to integrate the new colonies as seamlessly as possible while recognizing that they could not force French colonists to adopt English ways overnight. Just as they had allowed Scotland to keep its Presbyterian establishment and New England its Congregational establishment, they aimed to reduce and not exacerbate religious tensions in their newest territories. For members of Parliament, protecting Catholic rights represented their good-faith effort to support religious freedom and to maintain peace in the North American colonies.

While some North American colonial governments provided Catholics with specific rights, the majority feared that papist trickery had inspired the Quebec Act. They worried that Parliament had failed to recognize Catholicism as an ever-present threat, which indicated that perhaps the Antichrist was working through British leaders. As anger grew over multiple moves from Parliament, which colonists dubbed the "intolerable acts," over one thousand people gathered in Connecticut in the spring of 1774 for a protest. They claimed that Parliament, "being instigated by the devil, and led on by their wicked and corrupt hearts, have a design to take away our liberties and properties, and to enslave us forever." They listed their grievances on a handbill, which they posted around the region.[3]

Colonial church leaders did not necessarily anticipate war. The recent crises, however, led them to understand their rights and liberties as being more closely linked to other North American colonists than to their coreligionists across the Atlantic. Connecticut pastor and Congregationalist Samuel Sherwood believed in 1774 that the time had come for colonial leaders to act together to affirm their religious independence. If they did not, he predicted, "our charter and birth right privileges may be taken from us; that we may be ruled by the iron rod of oppression, and chained down to eternal slavery and bondage." They needed to share each other's burdens and to draw a hard line against London's overreach. He suggested that all protestants put aside their differences and "unite, and gather into one common interest." He wanted them to "stand or fall together: and not be devoured one of another; nor become an easy prey to foreign enemies who may seek our ruin."[4]

Some Anglicans, however, believed that Congregationalists like Sherwood concealed their true motives. They feared that the descendants of the Puritans, if empowered, would restrict religious freedom for all but their own members. "There would be no peace in the colonies," New Jersey priest Thomas Bradbury Chandler warned, "till we all submitted to the republican zealots and bigots of New-England; whose tender mercies, when they had power in their hands, have been ever cruel, towards all that presumed to differ from them in matters either of religion or government." The Congregationalists, he continued, would target the members of the Church of England, Presbyterians,

Quakers, Baptists, and the German and Dutch Reformed churches. The old Puritans, he decried, would "torment us with scorpions, whether we deserved it or not."[5]

Facing Parliament's heavy-handed tactics, political leaders from around the colonies organized the First Continental Congress, which met on September 5, 1774, in Philadelphia. The Congress began with a prayer from local Anglican minister Jacob Duché. Participants then made the strategic move of appointing Duché the chaplain of the group. Choosing a minister from the Church of England signified their efforts to maintain ties with Britain and their determination to legitimize their work by grounding it in the empire's protestant establishment. By invoking religion in the Congress, colonists also aimed to link their cause to God. Representatives including George Washington, Samuel Adams, John Adams, John Jay, and Patrick Henry sought ways to overcome their differences of government, history, and religious denominations in order to deal with common problems.

As the patriots debated how best to defend their interests, they recognized that linking their efforts to the Christian faith added legitimacy to their cause. But they also knew making such a move would generate controversy. The twelve participating colonies (Georgia did not initially join the Congress) had different religious establishments and different levels of toleration for dissent. Religion might unify, but it could also fracture. Leaders had to proceed carefully.

Continental Congress delegates designated July 20, 1775, as a national fast day, merging their religious convictions with their politics. They chose the date carefully—on that day Parliament planned to begin enforcing new restrictions on colonial trade. They aimed to "offer up our joint supplications to the all wise, omnipotent, and merciful Disposer of all events; humbly beseeching him to forgive our iniquities, to remove our present calamities, to avert those desolating judgments with which we are threatened." They asked God to "bless" King George with wisdom and to help him and colonial leaders find a peaceful resolution. They hoped that "virtue and true religion may

Political leaders from around the colonies opened the Continental Congress with a prayer from local Anglican minister Jacob Duché. In making this choice, the patriots positioned themselves and their cause on the side of God. When artist T. H. Matteson depicted the event in the 1840s, the era of manifest destiny and significant expansion, he hoped to remind Americans of what he viewed as their godly origins. (credit: New York Public Library)

revive and flourish throughout our land . . . and that her civil and religious privileges may be secured to the latest posterity."[6]

Churches all over the colonies observed the fast day with services and prayers. Jewish groups joined in with prayers as well. Continental Congress leaders claimed not just political authority, but moral authority. They aspired to use the protestant ideas and idioms that had shaped the British empire to define their own slice of it.

Loyalist ministers in the colonies struggled with how best to respond to fast days. One clergyman confided to a friend that "I absolutely refused either to read the order for Thanksgiving or to open the church on the day appointed." His decision, he continued, "was quickly represented as highly criminal. . . . My people who had hitherto been very moderate and happily united fell suddenly into the most violent commotions, I immediately lost my influence, was exclaimed against as a malignant Tory an enemy to my country and severely threatened." He felt his congregants "deceived, betrayed and persecuted" him for his "adherence to publick order and Tranquility."[7]

As colonial leaders struggled to craft a unified strategy and a religious justification for it, Anglican William Smith of Philadelphia preached a widely read sermon in 1775. The message, which he originally delivered to a group of militiamen, linked religious and political liberty, reinforcing the message of the Congress. The colonies had wanted to mend the breach with England, Smith explained, and "heal the wounds." But Parliament had failed them. "We know that our civil and religious rights are linked together in one indissoluble bond," he expounded. "Religion and liberty must flourish or fall together in America. We pray that both may be perpetual." Then Smith asked what kind of future the colonists wanted. Would this land be defined by "the Religion of Jesus, as it flows uncorrupted from his holy Oracles; or," he warned, if colonists abandoned their demands for Christian and political liberty, the continent would be "covered with a race of men more contemptible than the savages that roam the wilderness." The choice was theirs.[8]

As the North American colonies took ever more radical steps, most clergy in the British Isles stayed mum on the brewing conflict. They generally did not concern themselves with seemingly minor fracases in remote regions of the empire. However, Methodist leader and former missionary to Georgia John Wesley published *A Calm Address to Our American Colonies* in defense of Parliament's right to tax the colonies. The pamphlet focused mostly on political issues, but Wesley also challenged some of the patriots' religious assumptions, implying that neither side had a monopoly on God. "After all the vehement cry for liberty, what more liberty can you have?" he asked. "What more religious liberty can you desire, than that which you enjoy already? May not every one among you worship God according to his own conscience?" Wesley believed that anti-monarchists mostly in England drove the tensions between the colonies and Britain, hoping that rebellion would undermine the power of the king. Despite taking a position against the revolutionaries, Wesley would later have a tremendous influence on the early American republic. Americans forgave the vocal English cleric.[9]

In January 1776, Thomas Paine published *Common Sense*, making the case for the North American colonies to claim independence. "We have it in our power to begin the world over again," he promised. Paine took the intellectual justifications for revolution and made them accessible to a broad and diverse audience. While focused primarily on political arguments, Paine drew on the Bible to oppose monarchical political systems, which he called "the Popery of government."[10]

Ministers also crafted arguments for independence. The Presbyterian John Witherspoon used a fast day, May 17, 1776, to deliver a searing address. "This is the first time," he told his New Jersey congregation, "of my introducing any political subject into the pulpit. At this season however, it is not only lawful but necessary." He identified "the cause in which America is now in arms" as the "cause of justice, of liberty, and of human nature." He claimed that protecting Christian liberty required protecting political liberty. "There is not a single instance in history in which civil liberty was lost, and religious liberty preserved entire." He warned that if they "yield up" their political freedom, "we at the same time deliver the conscience into bondage." For Witherspoon and others like him, the fight against Britain represented a fight for the protection of Christianity.[11]

On July 4, 1776, the Continental Congress adopted the Declaration of Independence. The declaration embodied the political views of its drafter, Thomas Jefferson, and his allies. It also revealed how the colonies' leaders wove together Enlightenment political philosophy with religion. Jefferson opened the argument for independence by grounding the revolt in God-given individual rights. "We hold these truths to be self-evident," Jefferson began, "that all men are created equal, that they are endowed by their Creator with certain unalienable Rights, that among these are Life, Liberty and the pursuit of Happiness." Jefferson had chosen his words carefully. Rights did not come from kings or parliaments, but from nature and nature's God.

Jefferson's language drew on ideas circulating across the Atlantic among a small group of educated elites. European intellectuals Isaac

Newton and John Locke had transformed how some Europeans and North Americans understood both God and government. Extrapolating from the law of gravity, Newton hypothesized that a series of immutable laws controlled the universe. God established those laws, and then backed away to let the world mostly function according to them independent of divine intervention. Locke took a similar approach to describing human institutions such as government. They too, he believed, followed certain rules, and performed best when leaders adhered to them.

The words Jefferson sprinkled throughout the Declaration—nature's God, creator, supreme judge of the world, providence—illustrated that his deity was not the God of most traditional Christians but was far removed from the affairs of the world. Jefferson and those like him believed in a God who was like a watchmaker who built a timepiece, wound it up, and then mostly stepped aside to let it run. Jefferson aspired to build a government aligned with the natural laws that the watchmaker had put in place. Yet he and his allies believed that God's laws demanded justice, and that God would intervene when necessary to judge evildoers. Sometimes the watchmaker had to recalibrate the watch.

Many Enlightenment thinkers, including Jefferson, referred to the creator as "Deity." These so-called "Deists" stressed reason over emotion, and they placed significant emphasis on virtue and ethics. They criticized tradition and supernatural beliefs. They also had a very high view of themselves and of human potential. The Declaration symbolized their hope and optimism in humankind. People like Jefferson did not take seriously the old Puritan emphasis on the persistence of the sin nature. Many Enlightenment thinkers did not, however, go as far as Jefferson. Newton, for example, heralded science and simultaneously obsessed over the Bible's prophecies, convinced that the apocalypse predicted in the book of Revelation was imminent.

In justifying a war for independence, Jefferson tried to downplay religious controversies. He wrote nothing in the Declaration of Independence about Anglican bishops, or religious minority rights, or monopolies on missionary work. The men crafting the argument for revolution grounded their work in general Enlightenment ideas. Some, such as John Witherspoon, John Jay, and Patrick Henry, were devout protestants. One, Charles Carroll of Maryland, was Catholic. And many, like Jefferson, didn't think religion had a direct role to play in the form of government at all. But the signers shared a faith in human liberty and self-government for themselves and those like them—although not for those they enslaved or tribal nations or women or the poor.

After declaring independence, congressional leaders went to work crafting a document outlining their new national government. The Articles of Confederation, adopted on November 15, 1777, like the Declaration, ignored religion. The document's primary author, John Dickinson, had drafted a lengthy, murky, and contradictory paragraph on religious rights and liberties, but Congress struck it entirely from the articles.

The early architects of the new government knew that they could not easily regulate religion in such a diverse region. The kind of clear protestant establishment that had shaped the British empire was not going to work in North America. "No mechanism or political will existed to create a national American protestant establishment," historian Katherine Carté concludes, "in 1776 or, as Americans would find, at any time since." Too much diversity had flourished in the colonies for too long. Furthermore, since some colonies had established churches that differed from one another, and others did not have an establishment at all, political leaders had no way to forge a unified national religious establishment without undermining the colonies' own establishments. In leaving the British empire, colonists expected more freedoms. They refused to allow their new government to offer them fewer.[12]

With a declaration of independence and a plan of government undergoing debate in the colonies-turned-states, the new United States government now needed to win the war. The British army initially had the upper hand, with more equipment and well-trained men. Occasionally, the Americans stole a victory, but Washington's colonials mostly struggled against Britain's professional soldiers. In the South, thousands of enslaved men fled their masters and joined British regiments for the promise of freedom. American leaders did not offer them the same deal for enlisting.

In 1778, the patriots secured the support of Britain's long-hated enemy, the French. Spain also entered the war on the American side. Both countries hoped to gain territory from the conflict and to weaken Britain. Alliances with Catholic countries ensured that religious establishments in North America, whatever form they might take, would look very different than in Britain. Patriot leaders could not treat Catholics as religious rivals while maintaining their strategic partnerships. Loyalists, however, warned of the treachery of the popish French, claiming that the war had the potential to upend protestant power.

Once church leaders realized that war was inevitable, the majority supported the revolution. The leaders of the Congregationalist, Baptist, Presbyterian, and other reformed churches in the major coastal regions overwhelmingly backed the patriot cause. Those further from the coast remained more skeptical of the revolutionaries' agenda. Anglicans, meanwhile, sided with the crown in greater numbers than did other church members—the king remained, after all, head of their church. Yet some Anglicans, such as Washington and Henry, supported the cause of liberty. Over the course of the war about 75 percent of Anglican ministers left the colonies out of their loyalty to the king for other parts of the British empire. In some regions, patriots ransacked Anglican churches, tearing coats of arms and other imperial emblems from the walls.

The colonies also contained small but growing numbers of peace churches—Quakers, Moravians, Mennonites, and others. They believed that God never called his people to participate in violent acts. Neither patriots nor loyalists, they focused on building the kingdom of God and not battling to remake the kingdom of man. "Christians can have no interest in war," Philadelphia Quaker Anthony Benezet insisted. He warned that "he that leadeth into captivity shall go into captivity, and he that killeth with the sword, must be killed with the sword." Benezet believed that God had made all humans in his image, and killing would provoke his wrath. He also criticized colonial leaders for their treatment of tribes and for enslaving others. That patriots justified their war on the conviction that "all men are created equal and endowed by the creator with certain inalienable rights" struck Benezet as rank hypocrisy.[13]

Pacificists like Benezet who spoke out sometimes suffered persecution. Patriots pressured and occasionally abused pacifist Christians for their loyalty to their faith over the revolutionary conflict. Their testimonies remind us that the story of American Christianity is never just the story of the politically powerful and militarily mighty, of the unapologetic Christian nationalists. Indeed, some Christians from the very origins of the Republic understood their citizenship as in heaven rather than in a civil domain, and they viewed colonists' treatment of Black and Indigenous peoples as sins.

Overcoming early setbacks, the patriots eventually gained the advantage. In 1783 the British and Americans brought the conflict to a conclusion with the Treaty of Paris. Some North American Christians saw the victory as evidence of their unique destiny. Connecticut Congregationalist Ebenezer Baldwin predicted that the colonies would provide the "foundation of a great and mighty empire; the largest the world ever saw," with a commitment to the "principles of liberty and freedom, both civil and religious, as never before took place in the world." The United States would become "the principal seat of that glorious kingdom which Christ shall erect upon earth in the latter days."[14]

Another New England minister, Samuel Sherwood, also interpreted the conflict in biblical terms. In a sizzling apocalyptic sermon at the Continental Congress a few years earlier, he claimed that biblical prophecies "plainly relate to Great-Britain, and the American Colonies; and are fulfilling in the present day." On the eve of the revolution he thanked representatives for defending the Americans "whom God in his providence, has raised up to be his glorious instruments, to fulfil scripture-prophecies, in favour of his church, and American liberty, to the confusion of all her enemies." What the patriots witnessed, he explained, the Bible had foretold. Predictions about last days "trials and sufferings" and "wars and conflicts of the church with her anti-christian enemies and adversaries" revealed that North America served as ground zero for the conflict of the ages. "We may rationally conclude," he boldly claimed, that the biblical prophecies "reference to the state of Christ's church, in this American quarter of the globe; and will sooner or later, have their fulfilment and accomplishment among us."[15]

Sherwood's analysis revealed the challenges and possibilities of interpreting current events through the lens of biblical prophecy. During the French and Indian War, colonists had identified the British with the forces of good, and the French with the forces of the Antichrist, wedding the political and military victories of the colonies (and the British empire) with the unfolding of biblical revelation. Now they did the opposite. The British had become the allies of the devil while the French seemed positioned on God's side. Apocalyptic texts proved vague enough that American Christians in this war and those to come could read any number of current enemies into them, changing with the era. But they never stopped reading American wars into biblical prophecy.

Many of the theologians and ministers writing on millennial themes in colonial and revolutionary America saw a correlation between the United States and ancient Israel. As God had chosen the Hebrews to spread his truth to the rest of the ancient world, in more recent times he had chosen the new European settlers in North America (and not the tribes they displaced) to launch his next great work. To drive the colonies to war, the patriots had blended economic arguments against taxation without representation, Enlightenment arguments about the proper form of government, and religious arguments inspired by millennial hopes of establishing the kingdom of God on earth. They framed the conflict as a battle between good and evil, between Christ and Antichrist. Now in victory, they saw Americans as God's new chosen people and their nation as the new Israel. Meanwhile, far to the west, another group of Christians sought to conquer lands and the peoples who presided over them.

6

SANCTIFYING THE WEST

In 1620, the same year the first Pilgrims sailed to North America, a young woman living in Spain named María de Jesús de Ágreda took her vows and became a Franciscan nun. A fellow Franciscan described her as "a woman of about 29 years old, or a little less, of beautiful face, of White skin, but of rosy color, and large black eyes."

No typical nun, María had extraordinary experiences that included trances where she encountered God, saints, and angels. She wrote the autobiography of Mary, the mother of Jesus, which she claimed had come to her miraculously. Many Christians, including Spanish king Felipe IV, confident that the mystic fellowshipped with the almighty, reached out to María for advice. But serving as the Virgin Mary's amanuensis and the king's counselor paled in comparison to her greatest accomplishment.

María claimed that during trances she bilocated all over the world to minister to people who had not yet heard the Christian gospel. According to a priest who interviewed her, she traveled on the angelic wings of Saint Michael and Saint Francis to "personally preach to all those nations our Holy Catholic Faith." Some of her most extensive evangelistic work occurred among the Indigenous peoples of the North American Southwest. "These flights," a priest reported, "have been so continuous that there have been days in which there were more than three or four in less than 24 hours."[1]

María wrote about her ministry to North American tribes for a very specific purpose. She hoped to inspire others to continue the evangelistic work she had supernaturally begun. The spirit of Saint Francis promised her that since she had laid the foundations for others to build upon, many of "the Indians would only have to look upon our friars to be converted." María assured the Franciscans willing to go that when they arrived in New Mexico, large numbers of people would flock immediately to them for baptism. But unlike María, to traverse the Atlantic they would have to settle for lumbering ships and rough seas rather than the wings of angels.[2]

The nun also warned potential missionaries of the hazards that awaited them. She told a priest that some people would reject the Christian message "because the devil has them deceived." She claimed that

Seventeenth-century Spanish nun María de Jesús de Ágreda's claim to have ministered to tribes in the North American Southwest inspired subsequent generations of Catholic missionaries, including Father Junípero Serra, to engage in evangelistic work. (credit: Biblioteca Digital Hispánica)

Satan made them "believe that there is poison wherever there is the antidote, and that if they were to become Christians, they would be reduced to slavery instead of obtaining liberty and happiness in this life." María's claim that Indigenous conversion would produce freedom and not bondage revealed the limits of her ability to see accurately into the future. In reality many Indigenous people who joined the missionaries essentially became slaves. The devil may have been right.[3]

María provided compelling proof that she had bilocated to and ministered in North America. She reported seeing specific friars in New Mexico, and when those same people later visited her in Spain, she claimed to recognize them, and she described to them their New Mexican colleagues whom she had never met. She also seemed to know some of the local people, specific landmarks, and the geography of the region. Franciscan leaders believed that God used María, like John the Baptist, to pave the way for them to bring salvation to North America.

The stories of Indigenous men and women seemed to confirm María's supernatural presence in New Mexico. Early Franciscan missionaries working in New Spain heard tales of earlier visits from a person they described as the "lady in blue." This too seemed to prove the nun's ability to bilocate. María often wore a blue cloak over her brown Franciscan robe—she appeared as the lady in blue.

Spanish Franciscan Miquel Josep Serra Ferrer, growing up on the Mediterranean island of Majorca a century later, learned about María and her efforts in New Mexico. He believed that God had called him to do what Saint Francis and María commanded—to go to New Mexico and complete the work they had begun. He later went by the name Fray Junípero Serra.

Although Father Serra had limited success making converts, he transformed colonization in the North American West. The small but tenacious Franciscan literally imposed Catholicism on the California landscape through an elaborate and enduring mission system. While protestants on the East Coast sought to build one kind of Christian kingdom, he ensured that Catholics on the West Coast would build another kind, one that endures in part to this day.

After the Pueblo revolt in 1680 the Spanish made little effort to manage the Indigenous-occupied territory they claimed in the Southwest and California. But the loss of Florida during the Seven Years' War revealed the tenuous nature of their hold on their remaining North American colonies. Britain's protestant empire continued to grow, and its colonies expanded further west. Meanwhile, the Russians, with forts in Alaska, looked down the coast eager to secure more land to bolster trade. Spanish leaders knew that if they did not act, they would continue losing territory.

Unlike England, Spain never had many people willing to emigrate to North America and occupy new lands. Instead, government authorities dispatched relatively small numbers of mostly men to establish outposts. Soldiers led the way and used force to claim land from local people and to build presidios for defense. Once soldiers had secured an area, priests established missions to serve as the religious centers of the community, and small groups of citizens built pueblos and ranchos for growing crops and raising livestock. They often intermarried with local populations.

Spanish authorities in Mexico appointed Father Junípero Serra to build an extensive network of missions to run along the coast of California from San Diego to Monterrey. The missions eventually occupied the center of Spanish efforts in California, with religious leaders vying with government authorities for power and control over the colonization project. The Franciscans aimed to convert locals, teach them Christianity, and train them in European culture and lifestyles. They also expected the converts, called neophytes, to serve as a new class of laborers who would keep the mission system viable. They intended to remake the beliefs and values of California's people—they had little interest in partnering with or learning from Indigenous populations.

A mere five foot two, Serra did not immediately convey power and authority. He had feminine cheeks and a random tuft of hair that grew out of the top of his balding pate like a clump of dirty moss. He walked with a limp, and swarms of angry insects allegedly chased him, biting him mercilessly. Nevertheless, he commanded the attention of his fellow friars as well as that of Spanish leaders.

Serra joined the Franciscan order as a teenager. A smart and motivated student, he later earned a doctorate in theology. He encouraged men and women on Majorca to hear God's voice both within themselves and through the instructions of their ministers. Then he accepted a call to evangelize in New Spain. He had long dreamed of such an opportunity. Like his Franciscan predecessors, Serra had apocalyptic tendencies. He expected the world to end relatively soon and believed that signs of a heavenly war between Jesus, his angels, and Satan had started to appear. God had called him to share the gospel message as aggressively as possible before time ran out.

In 1750 Serra arrived at the Franciscan College of San Fernando in Mexico City. The college focused on serving the large Mexico City population and its parishes, and on training missionaries to evangelize Indigenous people and bring them under the tutelage of church and crown. Serra spent five months in the city and then moved north, seeking to minister to the Pame people in central Mexico. Over the next few years, he had some success baptizing Natives, but never as much as he had expected. In 1758 he returned to Mexico City, where he worked for the next decade.

While in Mexico, Serra participated as a *comisario* in the Spanish Inquisition. He tracked witches, demons, and those who might be partnering with them, and he investigated sorcery and heresy. Like those in Puritan New England who feared that any missteps might make them susceptible to heresy hunters, Spanish colonizers had to tread carefully around the small but powerful friar.

Serra aimed to emulate Francis of Assisi, the founder of his order. Like the thirteenth-century saint, he adopted a simple and humble lifestyle and often tortured himself, confident that pain would bring him closer to God. During devotions Serra routinely removed the clothes from his back and flogged himself with a small braided whip, which he embedded with shards of metal. He wore an undershirt made of coarse hair that chafed his skin. The irritation reminded him to renounce the sin of pride. He believed that his excessive devotion would inspire others to live more devout, godly lives.

Serra drew heavily on medieval mystics in constructing his beliefs. He viewed the boundaries between the natural and the supernatural worlds as fluid and thought that God constantly intervened and performed miracles for him and for others. On one of his travels, for example, he claimed that he and some companions had not made it to their destination by nightfall, so they stopped at the home of some strangers and asked for lodging. Back on the road the next day, they ran into a group of soldiers. The men asked the fathers how they had survived the night. They told them about the house. But the soldiers said no such home existed in the region. Serra determined that they had "without doubt" spent the night with "Jesus, Mary and Joseph." How did they know? Because of the "cleanliness and neatness of the house, in spite of its poverty and the affection with which they were lodged and entertained."[4]

During his years studying and teaching, Serra grew aware of developing Enlightenment thought, along with the kinds of Christian rationalist thinking that captivated some ministers like Jonathan Edwards. But unlike Edwards, who integrated rationalism into revivalism, Serra rejected it. He preferred the way of the medieval saints and mystics like María de Jesús de Ágreda over the philosophy of continental philosophers.

Nevertheless, he shared with the Atlantic coast revivalists a strong sense of the dramatic. Like George Whitefield, Serra was a showman. He understood the power of spectacle and emotion for conveying his messages. To depict the imminence of death, he waved a human skull about his audiences. To illustrate the horrors of hell, he lit fires. Francisco Palóu, one of Serra's closest allies, described how the Franciscan sometimes concluded sermons on divine punishment by touching "the great flame of the taper" to his bare chest, burning himself, "while his hearers were melted to tears." To illustrate the need for penance, Serra beat himself with irons. Such demonstrations shook audiences.[5]

On one occasion Serra's demonstration took an unexpected turn. Serra, Palóu recalled, "took out a chain" and "began to lash himself so cruelly that the whole audience broke out in sobs." This continued until "finally, one man rising up hurried into the pulpit, took the chain away from the penitent Father." He "stood up on the platform of the presbytery, and then, imitating the example of the Venerable preacher, he stripped himself to the waist" and began to beat himself. He told the crowd "with tears and sobs: 'I am the ungrateful sinner before God who should do penance and not the Father, who is a Saint.'" "He soon fell down," Palóu concluded, "before all the people who judged that he was dead." They were right—the man killed himself in front of the friars and the crowd.[6]

In 1768, Serra took up the new challenge of helping colonize and Christianize California. He believed that he would fulfill María de Jesús de Ágreda's prophesy of mass Indigenous conversions. He left Mexico City first for Baja, where the Jesuits had established a line of missions, but the locals in the sparsely populated region showed little inclination for allying with the uninvited colonizers. When the Jesuits got into trouble with the Spanish crown, the Franciscans took over their work but had no more success.

Opting against trying to resurrect a failing project, Serra looked north. He and Spanish officials devised a plan to establish a new line of missions along the coast of Alta California that would allow Serra to combine his leadership and organizational acumen with his zeal for evangelizing those who had not yet encountered the Christian faith. When the mission undertaking began, over three hundred thousand Indigenous men and women lived in the Alta region, with about 20 percent near the coast. They contended with not only the European invaders but also their diseases, including measles, smallpox, and influenza. Serra intended to build a new, Christian, Eurocentric world on top of their existing world. To prepare for the work, he raided the Baja missions for vestments, chalices, altars, and anything else that might be useful. Robbing Peter to pay Paul, Serra looted the Baja missions to make success in the North more likely.

In 1769 Serra performed his first baptism in the region. "This happy turn of events," he observed, "has come in fulfillment of the promise made by God, Our Lord, in these modern times—as the Venerable Mother María de Jesús de Ágreda asserts—that at the mere sight of his sons, the Franciscans, the pagans shall be converted to our holy Faith." He expected many more baptisms to follow. Initially, only children, often with health problems, came to the Franciscans for baptism. Their parents likely hoped that the Spanish would have medicine that might heal them. The pragmatic missionaries knew what the parents wanted. By enticing the Natives to come to them for aid, they could also share the Christian gospel. They offered a classic upsell if not a bait and switch. Get local people to the mission for one thing and offer them something else.[7]

Franciscans faced many challenges in converting Indigenous peoples. The missionaries vacillated between seeing their neighbors as ignorant and childlike and devilish and savage. They worried about Native "superstition," which they viewed as something entirely different from their own (superstitious) beliefs in bilocating nuns or bread and wine that transformed into Jesus's flesh and blood. Only by church leaders structuring Indigenous lives for them, the fathers insisted, could Natives remain safely in the faith. Otherwise, the temptations of the devil—of their old lives—would be too much.

Similar to other colonial missionaries, Franciscans expected converts to adopt European lifestyles. The fathers taught that joining the faith meant leaving old ways behind and embracing the new. For most of the locals, however, the Christians asked too much. Many would seemingly join the faith, but they would remain connected to their families, ancestors, and tribes. The Franciscans interpreted their actions as sin or backsliding.

The gulf between Franciscans and Natives on matters of sex and sexuality proved hard to overcome. Many tribes practiced elaborate rituals that included nakedness and sexualized movements and practices, which horrified the priests. Some California tribes also venerated transgender members of their community and same-sex relations. Franciscans expected those who joined them to repudiate their traditions. They aspired to control the most intimate parts of the lives of their acolytes.

Franciscans also had to contend with the actions of their fellow Spaniards. They expected all representatives of church and crown to serve as godly examples. But some soldiers took local women as lovers. Some also committed rape, had sex with Indigenous men, and molested children. Serra tried to remove from the region soldiers who had engaged in immoral behavior, but keeping up with the sins of the colonizers was a never-ending task.

As in other parts of North America, Indigenous men and women who allied with the friars had complex reasons for doing so. In some cases, they saw advantages in forming partnerships. They recognized the usefulness of Spanish technology and military might in times of war and conflict. They saw value in serving as intermediaries between tribes and the Spanish, which could lead to economic benefits. And some realized that the friars might have food and supplies they could trade for if local ecologies weakened.

Unlike in New England, where at the same time some Indigenous men and women had formed Christian towns, built Indigenous churches, worshipped with and followed Indigenous ministers, and translated Christian texts into Native languages, those on the West Coast seemed to have only the most rudimentary understanding of Christian faith and practice. Christianity remained a top-down religion led, directed, and enforced by Catholic Europeans rather than something that local people could make their own.

Once Indigenous men and women joined a mission, the Spanish considered them Christians for life and did not often let them leave the mission grounds. The fathers instituted strict rules in the missions and punished and humiliated those who violated them with beatings, whippings, and floggings. They showed little kindness to those they aimed to "save."

High mortality across California made building a stable, Native Catholic community difficult. Mortality rates spiked even higher among those who joined the missions. Neophytes lived in harsh, crowded environments and encountered even more disease living near Europeans. Very few neophytes progressed far enough for the Franciscans to allow them to take communion. But they participated in regular religious rituals including prayer, confession, and worship. The Franciscans believed that right practice would lead to right faith. Yet brutal life expectancy rates meant that by the time individuals came to understand and mature in the faith, they were likely close to death.

The Franciscans wanted to make their missions self-supporting and self-contained. They controlled tens of thousands of acres and housed populations in the hundreds. The priests taught neophytes European agricultural skills and practices and put them to work sustaining the mission community. Converts did not just expand the size of the Catholic church; they also proved instrumental to the survival of Spanish settlements by serving as the primary labor force. As more and more local people living in the areas around the missions—those who had survived disease—migrated away, Spanish soldiers working with the friars went on expeditions farther into the interior in pursuit of fresh labor. They claimed to search only for escaped Christians, but they sometimes returned with entire groups of new people, including many women and children. That Spanish law forbade forced conversions didn't stop such practices from happening. The Franciscans and the soldiers both depended on regular infusions of new workers to keep the missions sustainable. Some Spanish authorities accurately came to see the Franciscans' treatment of neophytes as a form of slavery.

The Franciscans' plans for California and its peoples differed from those of secular authorities. Political and church leaders split on fundamental questions regarding the role the Catholic Church should play in the empire, but they also diverged on more practical questions such as who should oversee soldiers, ranchers, converts, and priests. Serra aimed to organize the California mission system how he saw fit, which led to regular clashes with political authorities. He believed that he knew how best to establish settlements, foster productive agriculture, and bring people to salvation. He did not want bureaucrats getting in his way or jeopardizing his work.

Spanish leaders had established the mission system on a temporary basis. They believed that Indigenous people would become Christian, learn Spanish, and embrace European culture. Then they and the friars could break up the mission land and redistribute it to the colonized and converted neophytes, who would serve the Spanish crown. The mission itself would provide for the religious needs of the local community. But the Franciscans, and especially Serra, had little interest in ceding control or breaking up mission lands. Serra battled with colonial authorities to maintain his power. Spanish landowners, meanwhile, envisioned a future in which converts worked for them as cheap, dependent labor.

As much as the Franciscans hoped Spanish leaders would leave them alone to grow the church and minister to local people, traders continued visiting the region. The North American West Coast played an ever-growing role in global commerce. Missionaries simply could not bury their heads in the warm sands of California beaches and ignore the strategic importance of their work to the larger Spanish empire.

Spanish expansion in California and mistreatment of Native people led to resentments and sometimes conflicts. In 1775, as shots pierced the air at Lexington and Concord, another group of insurgents took up arms on the West Coast to overthrow those who claimed authority over them. The Spanish in San Diego had taken Kumeyaay land for their presidio, seized what food they could, and raped some Kumeyaay women. In response the Kumeyaay organized an attack on the San Diego mission, led by a group that included neophytes from numerous villages. In total about six hundred men participated in the assault. They slipped into the mission church, looted it, and then set it ablaze. They killed about a third of the Spanish soldiers and executed a priest.

According to the Franciscans' investigation, the Kumeyaay stripped the priest and "then they began to hack his naked body with their wooden sabres and to shoot at him innumerable arrows." After killing him, the investigators continued, "they bruised his head, his face and the rest of his body to such a degree that from his feet to his head there was not a single part untouched except his consecrated hands." The Franciscans interpreted the priest's unmaligned hands as a sign. "God willed it," they claimed, "that his hands should be preserved in order to show to all that he had not done evil, that his life should be taken away in such cruel fashion, but that he had labored in all purity to direct them to God and to save their souls." Rather than reflect on the causes of tribal anger, the Franciscans instead interpreted the attack as a Christian victory. They believed that the shedding of "martyrs'" blood sacralized the land, which was all the more justification to press on with their work.[8]

By the time of Serra's death in 1784, the friar had helped establish nine missions. He and his fellow Franciscans oversaw the labor of a few thousand converts and had baptized about six thousand people, most of whom were children. By 1800, the church's work had expanded to eighteen California missions with 13,500 people residing in them. Franciscans later built three more missions. During the mission period, 125 priests arrived from Mexico City to serve. Almost half died in California, and of those who survived, half failed to complete their ten-year commitment. The number of Spanish settlers in the West paled in comparison to the number of colonizers on the Atlantic coast, ensuring that Spain's ability to shape the area remained limited.

The mission system lasted until 1821, when Mexico achieved independence from Spain. The missions had served an important colonizing function by linking the North American West to the European imperial project of seizing the Americas from their occupants. The church fathers assimilated and Christianized some local peoples, although never as many as they hoped and expected, and brought death in the form of war and disease to many. In the decades that followed, hundreds of Indigenous people continued to return to the missions for worship. For them, the Christian faith had become an essential part of their lives. Although Serra may not have fulfilled María de Jesús de Ágreda's prophecies, Catholicism grew and eventually became central to identity in the North American West thanks in part to his work.

The missions Serra and his brothers built in California looked nothing like they do today. The pristine, whitewashed adobe, manicured gardens, vibrant roses, beautiful art, and cobbled walkways that draw hundreds of thousands of tourists each year took shape through major renovations in the early twentieth century. With the Spanish long gone,

Mexico driven from the region, Hispanics relegated to second-class citizenship, and the regions' Indigenous populations mostly subdued, White Californians recreated and reimagined the missions as romantic, paternal places of safety, education, and service that "civilized" local tribes. They ignored the history of disease, rape, slavery, and attempted cultural eradication.

For much of the twentieth century, government leaders and educators taught schoolchildren (like me in the 1980s) a warped history. The sparkling white sugar-cube mission that I built literally candy-coated a complicated and difficult period in North American Christian history, a period shaped far more by death than by redemption, by sinners more than saints, by hell more than by heaven. It's a history with which those of us in the West must still reckon.

As the Franciscans struggled to build a lasting mission system, leaders of the newly formed United States faced an even greater challenge: forging a stable government in a nation marked by deep religious diversity. With little historical precedent to follow, they set out to craft something unprecedented—bold, experimental, and, they hoped, exceptional. Whether their radical new vision could survive in practice remained an open and urgent question.

PART II

BUILDING A CHRISTIAN EMPIRE

7

DISESTABLISHING CHRISTIANITY

On June 10, 1797, President John Adams signed a treaty with Tripoli that contained a startling declaration. The United States, Article 11 of the treaty read, was "not in any sense founded on the Christian Religion." The statement, while accurate from a literal standpoint, did not reflect how most Americans understood their nation and its role in God's plan for the world.

The treaty represented the efforts of the Senate and of the John Adams administration to limit the exposure of American commercial ships sailing around North Africa and in the Mediterranean. For decades, bands of state-sponsored pirates roamed the seas, taking captives, plundering goods, and demanding ransoms. The United States, no longer assisted by the British Navy, needed to find a way to stop the looting. Government leaders opted to pay off the Bey of Tripoli and establish a treaty in exchange for protection for American ships. While most of the agreement focused on the rights of ships and sailors, it ended by affirming the United States' secular foundations and promised that Americans had no enmity against Muslims. US leaders pledged that "no pretext arising from religious opinions shall ever produce an interruption of the harmony existing between the two countries."[1]

Despite the explicit language the Senate wrote into the Treaty of Tripoli, most White Americans understood their nation as inherently Christian. But they could not agree on what that meant. For decades colonial leaders had struggled to balance their commitments to specific forms of protestantism with governing ever more religiously diverse populations.

With independence from Britain secured and a new national government to form, the role of religion in governance became a pressing issue. Many of the founders hoped to keep Christianity at the center of national life. Citizens empowered to rule in a new experiment in representative democracy, many leaders believed, needed Christian virtue to ensure that they would put the needs of the community and the nation above their own. But did the new nation need an established church to survive? To mold citizens fit for democracy? And if so, which church? The founders understood that they could not build a consensus around a single denomination. Nevertheless, they created a pathway for infusing faith into public life. Competing groups of Christians then took the opportunity provided by the founders to work to impose their version of Christianity on the government and laws of the new nation.

The Articles of Confederation had served the nation well enough during the revolution. They allowed the central government to craft foreign policy and establish treaties with other nations. But in otherwise granting significant autonomy to the individual states, they quickly proved inadequate for the challenges of peacetime.

In late 1786, leaders from six states met to address some core problems that the Articles seemed unable to solve. Internal rebellions, economic troubles, and disputes over Western territory all threatened the peace of the republic. The delegates convinced members of the

Continental Congress to call a Constitutional Convention with the goal of amending the Articles.

The convention, made up of thirty-five elite, highly educated White men, including George Washington, Benjamin Franklin, James Madison, and Alexander Hamilton, met in May 1787. Thomas Jefferson, abroad in Paris, could not attend. Almost immediately the delegates decided to abandon the Articles of Confederation altogether and replace them with a new governing document, a new constitution. They wanted Americans to have more freedoms and liberties than under monarchical systems, but they feared direct democracy as both impractical and too empowering of ordinary citizens.

Debates over what form the new government should take occasionally grew heated. A month into the convention Benjamin Franklin rose with a controversial and surprising suggestion. "How has it happened," the Deist and skeptic of orthodox Christianity asked his fellow delegates, "that we have not hitherto once thought of humbly applying to the Father of lights to illuminate our understandings?" He worried that the delegates had forgotten their "powerful friend" or imagined that "we no longer need his assistance." Then he turned to his proposal. "I therefore beg leave to move—that henceforth prayers imploring the assistance of Heaven, and its blessings on our deliberations, be held in this Assembly every morning before we proceed to business."[2]

The delegates tabled his request. They worried that adding prayer to their routine would make it look to those outside of the convention like they had grown desperate, that they needed God to solve their problems for them. They also balked at paying for a chaplain.

In September of 1787, the majority of delegates approved the final version of the Constitution. Although the Articles required unanimous agreement from the states for any amendments to pass, the Constitution's drafters decided that only nine of the thirteen states needed to ratify the document for it to establish a new American government. Then the real debate began. At the state level, discussions over ratification split those who wanted to see a stronger central government, called federalists, from those who did not, called anti-federalists.

The place of religion in the government—or more accurately its absence—became another flashpoint. The Constitution made no reference to God, not to a creator, a divine architect, a supreme being, a great governor of the world, or any of the other names for deity used in state constitutions, the Articles of Confederation, or the Declaration of Independence. A group of Presbyterians sent George Washington a letter complaining about the document's seeming atheism, but religion's absence in the document did not bother the war hero. "I am persuaded," Washington replied to the Christian group, "that the path of true piety is so plain as to require but little political direction." Washington did not believe that the American people needed magistrates to tell them to believe. Ministers, not government officials, he continued, needed "to instruct the ignorant, and to reclaim the devious." Meanwhile, the government in supporting "the progress of morality and science" would indirectly support "the advancement of true religion, and the completion of our happiness."[3]

The Constitution's only acknowledgment of religion came as a negative clause. Article VI specifies that "no religious Test shall ever be required as a Qualification to any Office or public Trust under the United States." This was a radical move for the time. Most states administered religious tests for government officials, and outsiders like Jews, Catholics, agnostics, "turks," and atheists could not hold government positions in many places. The founders could have put religious language into the Constitution, and they knew many Americans wanted them to. They consciously and explicitly chose instead to draft a godless Constitution.

The Constitution's lack of a bill of rights became another point of controversy during the ratification debates. Opponents of the new frame of government noted that many state constitutions had enumerated rights, and they worried that the federal Constitution did not. To them, the framers seemed to expect Americans to cede some of their independence to this new federal government without guarantees that the government would in turn protect core freedoms. To allay their fears, one of the leading proponents of the Constitution, James Madison, promised that the new Congress would amend the Constitution to better articulate liberties that the federal government could not infringe upon.

In 1788, a ninth state ratified the Constitution, meeting the requirement for adoption. The new government began operating in 1789. When the first Congress convened, James Madison, now a representative from Virginia, proposed a series of amendments to the Constitution. The House and Senate debated his proposals, rejected some, winnowed others, and reworded others still. Eventually the states ratified ten, which became the Bill of Rights. They prohibited the federal government from violating individual rights in key areas. They did not, however, restrict the power of state governments to limit the rights of individual citizens until the addition of new amendments in the 1860s.

One of the key amendment debates focused on religion. What religious rights did Americans have that the federal government could not or should not touch? The representatives who considered this question looked to state constitutions. They had many ideas from which to draw, but few consistent throughlines beyond relatively uniform support for mainstream protestant groups. Massachusetts, Maryland, New Hampshire, South Carolina, Connecticut, and the new state of Vermont all had established churches. Other states offered financial support to multiple protestant denominations. Most also limited political office to protestants. Of the fourteen state constitutions, eleven prohibited agnostics and Jews from holding political office, and seven banned Catholics from office.

Many American leaders claimed to support the concept of religious liberty, but they differed over what that meant. Religious liberty, historian David Sehat demonstrates, simultaneously "became a rallying cry for those who wanted to create a Christian commonwealth, and for those who wanted to establish a secular state." Both groups used the same language and the same terms but in very different ways. They agreed, however, that the nation should have no established national church. They also agreed that they did not want to inadvertently encourage the irreligious.[4]

Most conservatives and revivalists viewed religious liberty as an inherently protestant concept; they believed no liberty existed outside of Christ. They contended that those within the protestant faith should have the right to worship and practice as their consciences dictated, free of mandates from princes or priests. Such liberty would minimize intraprotestant conflict, ensure that the virtues taught by Jesus would shape the nation, and make Christianity richer and more vibrant. In other words, they believed Baptists and Presbyterians and Congregationalists and Episcopalians and Methodists should all have the freedom to worship as they wished and to maintain their own churches.

Christian liberals had a more extensive and inclusive view. They contended that upholding religious liberty involved safeguarding the rights of individuals, including those outside protestantism, to hold their own beliefs and worship freely without coercion or interference. This version of religious liberty protected religious minorities from the majority and provided space for Catholics, Jews, and dissenters. Liberals believed that by making religion a matter of individual conscience, they could avoid the kinds of religiously inspired conflicts and violence that had long dogged Europe and occasionally the North American colonies. None of the groups gave much thought, however, to the religious rights of those they enslaved.

James Madison embraced the broader, more liberal and inclusive view of religious liberty. Two of his proposed amendments to the Constitution addressed religion. The first originally read, "The civil rights of none shall be abridged on account of religious belief or worship, nor shall any national religion be established, nor shall the full and equal rights of conscience be in any manner, or on any pretext, infringed." The second read: "No State shall violate the equal rights of conscience, or the freedom of the press, or the trial by jury in criminal cases."[5]

In drafting these amendments, Madison used what he had learned in Virginia during a decade of debates over the relationship between government and religious liberty. The most populous state in the nation, Virginia had moderates and radicals, orthodox believers and heretics, mainstream groups and dissenters. Its citizens included the liberal Enlightenment rationalist Thomas Jefferson, the revivalist Patrick Henry, and the conservative Anglican George Washington, who each approached faith and its relationship to politics from a different angle.

Virginians' break from Britain had turned up the heat on a long-simmering debate over the role churches should play in public life. Colonial leaders had made the Church of England the established, taxpayer-funded, government-supported church. But during the war the legislature suspended its financial support because of the Anglican church's close ties to the British crown. Jefferson hoped this would mark the end of an established church in Virginia. In 1779 he introduced in the House of Burgesses a "Bill for Establishing Religious Freedom" to solidify the end of public funding for a religious denomination. "Our civil rights," Jefferson insisted, "have no dependance on our religious opinions, any more than our opinions in physics or geometry." He intended the bill to protect "the Jew and the Gentile, the Christian and Mahometan, the Hindoo, and infidel of every denomination."[6]

Jefferson believed that state establishments of religion inevitably corrupted both the churches they established and their members. "To compel a man to furnish contributions of money for the propagation of opinions which he disbelieves and abhors," he contended, "is sinful and tyrannical." An established church deprived an individual, Jefferson continued, "of the comfortable liberty of giving his contributions to the particular pastor whose morals he would make his pattern, and whose powers he feels most persuasive to righteousness."[7]

A few years later, in *Notes on the State of Virginia*, Jefferson succinctly summed up his views: "But our rulers can have authority over such natural rights only as we have submitted to them. The rights of conscience we never submitted, we could not submit. We are answerable for them to our God." Government, therefore, had no claim to religion or religious beliefs. "The legitimate powers of government extend to such acts only as are injurious to others. But it does me no injury for my neighbour," he explained, "to say there are twenty gods, or no god. It neither picks my pocket nor breaks my leg." Only "reason and free enquiry" could truly stop "error," not government coercion.[8]

Jefferson's approach appealed to both Enlightenment liberals and outsider religious groups. Virginia's Baptists, long struggling under the coercive power of the Anglican establishment, believed that minimizing the state's role in religion benefited them. They drew on the ideas of their fellow Baptist Isaac Backus, who had campaigned against establishment churches in Massachusetts. In 1778 Backus published a pamphlet entitled *Government and Liberty Described, and Ecclesiastical Tyranny Exposed*. Invoking the experience of Roger Williams, he insisted that governments should not compel minority groups like his Baptists to financially support other churches. His arguments resonated among dissenting sects in Virginia and across the Atlantic Seaboard.

Patrick Henry opposed Jefferson's propositions, but he understood that colonial leaders had to make some changes. After separating from Britain, it made little sense to subsidize only the Church of England. A few years after Jefferson made his proposal, Henry offered a new bill that would provide tax dollars to multiple denominations in the state—erecting a multi-church protestant establishment. "The general diffusion of Christian knowledge," he claimed, "hath a natural tendency to correct the morals of men, restrain their vices, and preserve the peace of society."[9]

Jefferson, out of the country at the time, missed the debate over Henry's bill. His young protégé, the pasty, five-foot-four James Madison, took up the fight. He published an anonymous pamphlet against Henry's proposal titled *Memorial and Remonstrance Against Religious Assessments*. "The Religion then of every man must be left to the conviction and conscience of every man," Madison began. "This right is in its nature an unalienable right." He believed that the law needed to limit the power of government and of the majority over the minority. Free societies, he continued, need not fear false religions. "Whilst we assert for ourselves a freedom to embrace, to profess and to observe the Religion which we believe to be of divine origin, we cannot deny an equal freedom to those whose minds have not yet yielded to the evidence which has convinced us." He saw no political downside to allowing people to believe what they wanted. "If this freedom be abused," he continued, "it is an offence against God, not against man: To God, therefore, not to man, must an account of it be rendered."

The history of state churches proved his point. "Ecclesiastical establishments," Madison argued, "instead of maintaining the purity and efficacy of Religion, have had a contrary operation. During almost fifteen centuries has the legal establishment of Christianity been on trial. What have been its fruits? More or less in all places, pride and indolence in the Clergy, ignorance and servility in the laity, in both, superstition, bigotry and persecution." At no time, he concluded, have religious establishments been "the guardians of the liberties of the people."[10]

As the debate over Henry's plan raged, Madison reintroduced Jefferson's "Bill for Establishing Religious Freedom." The House of Burgesses heeded Jefferson and Madison's arguments and in 1786 passed a bill called the "Statute for Religious Freedom." Although implementing the bill took time, and addressing the question of church property proved complicated, Virginia gave up its state church forever. Jefferson saw the bill as one of the three most important contributions of his life.

Madison's experience in Virginia with Jefferson and Henry influenced his understanding of religion as he helped draft and then amend the federal Constitution. As a member of Congress in 1789, he knew he needed to proceed cautiously. He wanted a secular state, but his vision was too radical for most Americans. While most congressmen understood the practical problems inherent in establishing a state church in a nation composed of dozens of protestant sects and other smaller religious groups, they continued to believe that the government had a right and an obligation to enforce Christian-based morality.

Congress debated Madison's proposed amendments, and other representatives floated alternatives. The majority agreed that the Constitution should not prohibit state establishments of religion, and because they aspired to cultivate in citizens virtue and godliness for the good of the republic, they also did not want to inadvertently provide protections for the irreligious. After much debate and negotiation, representatives produced an intentionally ambiguous new religion amendment. It began "Congress shall make no law respecting an establishment of religion, or prohibiting the free exercise thereof."

Madison and Jefferson believed that the amendment rendered the individual right to freedom of conscience nearly absolute, particularly in relation to federal government policies, and reinforced the Constitution's secular nature. Jefferson told a group of Baptists in 1802 that the amendment created "a wall of separation between Church & State." But it did not. "Separation between church and state" were his words, superimposed on a far vaguer amendment. They are not the words of the United States Constitution.[11]

Despite Jefferson and Madison's hopes, the Bill of Rights did not establish a secular public sphere or a government free of religion. Many of the Americans who supported the amendment, including government officials, read it differently from Jefferson. They believed that the amendment simply prohibited a federal establishment church. It did not outlaw state government churches, nor did it limit the federal government's ability to support the Christian religion. This ambiguity allowed the protestant majority to do exactly what Madison and Jefferson feared—they could use the federal government to encourage and promote their version of Christianity and what they viewed as Christian virtues. They just couldn't directly funnel money from the federal government to a specific denomination.

In choosing not to establish a state church, the architects of the new republic made a bold move. Knowing that in most Western governments the tight relationship between church and state inhibited rather than enhanced liberty, and that the diversity of beliefs in the United States made establishing a state church impossible, they opted for a relatively neutral new government framework on the question of religion. In the United States the people would rule. The people would decide how much religion they wanted in their government, institutions, and communities. And the people were mostly protestants.

After years of debate about the role of religion in the Articles and then the Constitution and then the Bill of Rights, little had changed in the minds of most Americans. They expected and wanted protestant Christianity to influence politics after the Revolutionary War, just as it had before. The Constitution might have forbidden a religious "test" for candidates for office, but the public made Christianity central to many political contests.

Jefferson's own campaign for the presidency revealed the ongoing power of protestant ideals to shape American politics. Having lost the presidential election in 1796 to John Adams, Jefferson focused on defeating his rival in 1800. But he had numerous obstacles to overcome. Some Americans believed that the man from Monticello aimed to destroy Christianity. Unlike the Anglican George Washington or the Congregationalist John Adams, Jefferson had heterodox ideas about God, Jesus, and the Bible. The founder believed that neither traditional trinitarian theologies nor Christian revivalism would survive for long. He even later created his own Bible—cutting with scissors the words of Jesus from the text and pasting excerpts together to form a new religious book void of miracles and the supernatural. He admired a philosopher Jesus who did not resurrect from the dead. But he mostly avoided discussing his beliefs in public. He had to suppress his views if he had any hope of winning national office. Privately he remained optimistic that the rest of the nation would eventually follow his lead in both politics and religion.

Jefferson's campaign corresponded with and helped define the rise of the first political parties in the United States, the Republicans and the Federalists. Confident in the people's ability to discern good religion from bad, and to understand right from wrong, Jefferson's Republicans encouraged freewheeling, localized, and independent forms of Christianity. Although they claimed to want to keep the state out of religion, Republicans infused national politics with their Christian convictions. Jefferson may have expected the First Amendment to create a strict wall, but his followers thought the amendment gave them carte blanche to entwine politics and faith. His campaign appealed to revivalists and other anti-institutionalist Christian groups, to rabble-rousers who hoped to challenge the old religious status quo.

Federalists like Adams hoped to build an orderly society run by strong, top-down authority. They wanted to limit average people's freedom and liberty, convinced that religion should bolster structured hierarchies. Their ideas tended to attract conservative Christians and some liberals. "The presidential election of 1800," historian Amanda Porterfield notes, "was the first time that voters made the choice between two different philosophies of government—and two different approaches to religion's role with respect to government authority."[12]

Adams's supporters sought to make Jefferson's personal, unorthodox views a central part of the presidential campaign. Alexander Hamilton warned John Jay that Jefferson should not serve as president since he was "an Atheist in Religion and a Fanatic in politics." Presbyterian minister William Linn claimed that although he respected the author of the Declaration of Independence, "my objection to his being promoted to the presidency is founded singly upon his disbelief of the Holy Scriptures; or, in other words, his rejection of the Christian religion and open profession of Deism." Linn argued that if Jefferson won, the United States might become "a nation of atheists."[13]

To prove his point, Linn flipped a Jefferson quote on its head. Where the Virginia statesman had said, "It does me no injury for my neighbour to say there are twenty gods, or no god. It neither picks my pocket nor breaks my leg," Linn responded, "But let my neighbor once persuade himself that there is no God, and he will soon pick my pocket, and break not only my leg but my neck." The minister cautioned that the new nation could not survive with a man like Jefferson at the helm. His election would "destroy religion, introduce immorality, and loosen all the bonds of society."[14]

Jefferson viewed the ideas of ministers like Linn as ignorant and backward. As a political candidate, however, he muted his opinions. Although he did not represent most Americans or even most of the Republican party in terms of religion, growing numbers of people embraced Jeffersonian ideas about liberty and democracy, and freedom of conscience, which helped the Virginian narrowly win the 1800 election. The campaign illustrated how Americans in the nation's earliest contested presidential elections wove their Christian ideas into their politics and how both of the first political parties made competing visions of Christianity central to their identities.

Most White Americans believed that the new United States was a Christian—a protestant—nation and that protestantism remained central to its ongoing success. They also agreed that they didn't want Congress determining right belief from wrong but thought that the federal government could and should encourage Christian morality. Church leaders and activists worked with legislators to craft laws and policies on the basis of Christian convictions, such as regarding the Sabbath, public days of prayer, and government-financed chaplains. Patrick Henry may have lost the specific battle over state support for churches to Thomas Jefferson, but his position—that the government should reflect the will of the people and in so doing promote mainstream Christianity—carried the day. Over time the First Amendment facilitated the rise of an unofficial, protestant establishment that most often functioned independently of the state but worked alongside it.

Over the next few decades, decisions by the courts and Congress helped build the unofficial protestant establishment. In the 1830s, Supreme Court Justice Joseph Story published a mammoth three-volume commentary on the Constitution. He focused in part on its approach to religion. Turning specifically to the meaning of the First Amendment, Story wrote, "The general, if not the universal, sentiment in America" at the time of the amendment's drafting was "that Christianity ought to receive encouragement from the state, so far as was not incompatible with the private rights of conscience, and the freedom of religious worship." The amendment did not, he insisted, "attempt to level all religions" or create state "indifference" to the matter of religion (as Madison and Jefferson wanted). That, he explained, would have "created universal disapprobation, if not universal indignation." Instead, "the real object of the amendment was, not to countenance, much less to advance Mahometanism, or Judaism, or infidelity, by prostrating Christianity; but to exclude all rivalry among Christian sects." The founders wanted to avoid an establishment church that would "give to an hierarchy the exclusive patronage of the national government."

The amendment "thus cut off the means of religious persecution (the vice and pest of former ages) and of the subversion of the rights of conscience in matters of religion, which had been trampled upon almost from the days of the Apostles to the present age."[15]

Story's description matched the observations of French traveler Alexis de Tocqueville, who was in the United States at about the same time. "Religion in America," he wrote, "takes no direct part in the government of society, but it must nevertheless be regarded as the foremost of the political institutions of that country." He felt "certain" that Americans held Christianity as "indispensable to the maintenance of republican institutions. This opinion is not peculiar to a class of citizens or to a party, but it belongs to the whole nation, and to every rank of society."[16]

The Senate may have promised the Bey of Tripoli that Americans had not founded the United States as a Christian nation, and Jefferson may have trusted that the First Amendment established a strict wall between church and state. But as Story and de Tocqueville recognized, by the 1830s few Americans actually believed such things. Christianity in the United States was political. In shutting down the possibility of a federal church, the First Amendment inadvertently opened the door for the rise of an unofficial protestant establishment that depended not on the government but on the people. While it blocked federal officials from foisting their views on churches, it did nothing to block religious activists from seeking to infuse the state with their beliefs. It provided Christian leaders with the freedom to channel the energy of their followers into remaking American life. Against Madison and Jefferson's hopes and expectations, the independent, protestant, quasi establishment proved more dominant and more powerful than any state church in the modern era. As its influence expanded, it became almost impossible to see. It didn't just fade into the background; it became the background, setting the parameters around which Americans shaped law, politics, foreign policy, the economy, education, and most other aspects of national life.

Building this unofficial establishment had required hard work. At the turn of the nineteenth century, church attendance was low, and religious leaders struggled to connect with a changing society. If churches hoped to survive and thrive, ministers and evangelists realized they would have to adapt, to reshape Christianity to meet the spirit of the age. They would have to maximize the opportunities the First Amendment provided them. They would have to reach the broader public in new ways. They recognized that what they needed, above all, was revival.

8

REVIVING THE NEW REPUBLIC

Connecticut congressman Joshua Coit worried about his wife, Nancy. While working in Washington, DC, he learned that back home she had grown enamored with the latest series of revivals to hit the young republic. He warned her to avoid religious enthusiasm. What people described as "awakenings of the Lord," he insisted, were "mere worship of the imagination." He believed that the "supreme being" made himself known through "our natural powers" and not through hidden truths or emotional fits. A few weeks later, he told Nancy that he hoped she "will not catch the religious frenzy which by your letters appears to be raging." He claimed to have no trust in any religion but that which was "consistent with and guided by cool and impartial reason." Coit represented the rational, mainstream, elite Christian faith of the era, while his wife rode the crest of something new.[1]

In the early years of the new republic, most Americans seemed to have better things to do than join churches. Although generic protestant sensibilities pervaded the culture, less than one in five Americans held a church membership. The flames from the 1740s and

1750s Atlantic revival fires had mostly burned out. Religious leaders worried about the future. For the American democratic experiment to survive, the nation needed more devout Christians, not fewer. Perhaps, some leaders thought, the churches bore responsibility for their decline. Ministers ran stifling and formal services and expected those who attended to listen in reverent silence. They had grown out of touch.

Inspired by the Revolutionary War's undermining of traditional institutions and social orders, a new generation of revivalists sought to topple religious hierarchies and revitalize American religious life. As the nation grew more democratic in its politics, some aimed to democratize the faith. Others played on the emotions of the public to gain power. In the first decades following the revolution, hundreds of people—men and women, Black, White, and Indigenous—repackaged Christianity as a populist religion that spoke to the demands of, and emerged from, the masses. They orchestrated sporadic, intense, emotional revivals that spawned widespread conversions, and then they organized the new converts into church communities.

But they had competition. A form of liberal Christianity, Unitarianism, grew as well, helping spread progressive versions of faith. Both groups, liberals and revivalists, expected to eventually vanquish their religious competitors and gain the upper hand in determining the trajectory of the new nation. But in the years immediately following ratification of the Constitution, no single group of Christians had the power, resources, and political allies to impose their will on the nation. In the free-for-all that followed the official disestablishment of religion through the First Amendment, Christians from every stream aimed to convince Americans of the truth of their ideas as they sought to instill their values on the broader culture.

The surge in revivalism in the early republic took initial root in places where traditional church ties proved weakest. It occurred most often in the Western states and territories, and away from both the longstanding conservative congregations and the elite liberal power bases. Many of those Americans living at the far ends of White settlement had no church to attend on a regular basis. To minister to the disparate White population, religious leaders organized summer sacramental meetings—multiday events where families living in remote locations could travel to a central town to celebrate communion together.

Late in the summer of 1801, minister Barton Stone organized a sacramental camp meeting in Cane Ridge, Kentucky. Perhaps as many as twenty-five thousand people attended in total, far outnumbering the entire local population. Seemingly overnight the meetings transformed the Cane Ridge region of rural Kentucky into a chaotic, pop-up urban space, a round-the-clock festival and celebration where campers became captives by choice. Organizers offered no starting or ending times for services, and since participants came from miles away, jobs and everyday responsibilities did not interfere with worship. Ministers erected crude platforms from which to preach. Some speakers had attended college and received ordination, but many had not. They exhorted sinners to accept salvation and to live holy lives. They harangued against the temptations of demons and called on listeners to flee the devil. They aimed to light a fuse in every participant, hoping to ignite powerful outbursts of religious ecstasy. They cheered the public display of wild and ecstatic behaviors. Some as young as eight years old experienced conversion, and teens exhorted adults to embrace the faith. Participants regardless of education, age, class, gender, or race routinely offered testimonies. The meetings thrived on chaos and disorder.

Thousands of people from multiple denominations attended the Kentucky revival. They included ministers and laypeople, citizens and immigrants, Black Americans and White Americans. Some enslaved individuals participated with their enslavers in White-led services, while others worshipped on the outskirts of the camp in segregated, Black-led gatherings. No Indigenous people seem to have attended. White settlers had driven most of the Shawnee, Cherokee, Osage, and other groups out of the region. Although the meetings challenged religious hierarchies, they did not challenge racial hierarchies.

Participants manifested the revival through their bodies. They experienced what Barton Stone described as "falling," "jerks," "dancing," "barking," "laughing," "running," and "singing." He later categorized and described the experiences, which had occurred periodically in Christian revivals in other eras. Those subject to the falling exercise, he explained, "with a piercing scream," would "fall like a log on the floor, earth, or mud, and appear as dead." The jerks occurred when a congregant's head "jerked backward and forward, or from side to side, so quickly that the features of the face could not be distinguished." Sometimes participants bent so far they could touch the floor with their heads, both forward and backward, as if their spines were rubber. What critics called "the barking exercise," Stone observed, "was nothing but the jerks. A person affected with the jerks, especially in his head, would often make a grunt, or bark, if you please, from the suddenness of the jerk." Holy laughter "was frequent," Stone recalled, which he described as "a loud, hearty laughter, but one sui generis; it excited laughter in none else."[2]

While exotic worship captured the attention of many attendees, camp meetings inspired more than spiritual experiences. In pop-up revival cities participants traded gossip and news, salesmen hawked goods, and confidence men swindled the gullible. The mingling of bodies, young and old, beautiful and ugly, hyped up on religious ecstasy meant, skeptics joked, that participants likely conceived as many souls at camp meetings as they saved.

Christian innovators replicated the Cane Ridge experience in smaller revivals around the country. The revivals helped those on the geographical margins of the new country become part of something bigger than themselves. They may not have had full-time ministers, beautiful sanctuaries, or colleges to attend for theological training, but the revivals allowed them to weave their lives into the fabric of a larger Christian story, one that offered unity to Americans in an era of strident political and class conflict.

The revivals inspired some participants to reject staid, institutional Christianity. They believed that they had rediscovered in the meetings a form of authentic, primitive faith. Stone broke away from

At early nineteenth-century camp meetings speakers preached from crude platforms and extolled and exonerated sinners to accept salvation and to live holy lives. Participants sometimes succumbed to such practices as holy falling, the jerks, dancing, barking, laughing, and running. (credit: J. Maze Burbank, *Religious Camp Meeting*, c. 1839, New Bedford Whaling Museum)

the Presbyterians to form a group he called simply "Christians." He believed denominations hampered true religion and that all Christians should leave their churches and unify as part of the single body of Christ.

Meanwhile, revivalist minister Alexander Campbell aimed to create a new, pure church that approximated New Testament fellowships. Like Stone, Campbell wanted independence from denominations and creeds and not to sully worship with anything that he could not trace back to New Testament practices. His followers formed a group called the Disciples of Christ. The Disciples and the Christians—and Stone and Campbell—eventually joined together to establish exactly what they had hoped to avoid: yet another American denomination.

Many groups and denominations benefited from the dynamic, explosive popularity of the rural, camp-meeting revivals, but none as profoundly as the Methodists. Methodist founder John Wesley had transformed how some protestants in England understood the conversion process. While listening to a sermon about faith, he felt his "heart strangely warmed." Salvation, the Oxford-trained minister realized, meant not only steady faithfulness but also feeling God's transforming touch on your life, usually at a specific moment. Wesley wanted to share his experience with others and help them discover it for themselves. As he embarked on this mission, he developed clear and straightforward methods to help believers live out the Christian life—hence Methodism. He focused on spreading Christianity, inciting conversions, and building the church.[3]

Wesley and other revivalist preachers helped accelerate a significant shift in American Christian theology from Calvinism to Arminianism, emphasizing that salvation was open to all, not just a select group. Most revivalists taught that individuals had the free will to accept or reject God's offer of redemption. This move toward Arminianism aligned with, and was influenced by, the disestablishment of official state churches. Ministers now had to attract congregants, so they broadened access to salvation—and, by extension, church membership. In this context, American men and women embraced the idea that they could shape their own moral destinies, becoming either self-made sinners or self-made saints. For many, the ideals of political democracy and religious democracy went hand in hand, reinforcing one another.

Many revivalist groups, including Methodists, Baptists, and Presbyterians, faced a shortage of ministers. The population was growing and expanding into new territories. To reach new communities, church leaders enlisted an army of "itinerant" preachers, or "circuit riders," who traveled from church to church or settlement to settlement, working to build faith among those who did not have regular churches and ministers. They did not sit and pray and wait for a group of elders to call them to the pulpit. They went out and constructed their own pulpits, organized congregations, and erected rudimentary church buildings.

In 1771, Wesley had sent young minister Francis Asbury to North America to travel the colonies, train new ministers, and build

Methodism. After the war, Asbury, like a Roman general, built an impressive army of itinerants willing to spread and cultivate the Methodist gospel. He admonished circuit riders to commit fully to the work. He advised his apprentices not to marry so that they might be free to travel wherever the Lord commanded. Jesus's apostles, he reminded them, did the same after his ascension.

Those who developed relationships felt conflicted. When one young Methodist minister decided to marry, his uncle, also a Methodist minister, wrote him with a warning. The nuptial, the uncle cautioned his nephew, "may produce some little sensation." Nevertheless, he noted, "Luther got married and so did Wesley and in both cases many wondered and some were displeased but soon all went on as before." He admonished his nephew to "only take care to 'walk by the same rule and mind the same things' you have committed all to God and he will take care of all never mind the persecution."[4]

Itinerants lived grueling lives, and many died young while engaged in their work. Many others could not endure the burden of the job and quit before completing their contracts. One itinerant wrote a supervisor complaining that ministers in "settled" regions have "but very faint ideas of the wants and sufferings of clergymen who live in the far west, or even new settlements." He described the job as more "painful than that of missionary in foreign lands." Circuit riders received substantially less pay than established ministers in coastal cities, which presented another challenge. "My labours in order to do much in revivals must be very arduous," one wrote his supervisor, "equal perhaps to the ordinary labour of two or three preachers, who labour as settled pastors." A few years' work "of this kind," he continued, and "I am worn out in my Master's service."[5]

The itinerant experience brought loneliness. Some men turned to their fellow ministers for companionship, and perhaps more. Historian Christine Heyrman analyzed letters between itinerants that contain powerful homoerotic yearnings. "None seems so much like my own flesh as yourself," one minister wrote to another. "I love you with a pure love fervently . . . I dream of you; I dream of Embracing you, in the fond arms of Nuptial love; I dream of kissing you with the kisses of my Mouth. I am Married to you; O that I could see you and spend a few moments in Heavenly Converse together." Whether florid language and sharing intimate dreams made celibacy more bearable or pointed toward same-sex physical acts, we don't know.[6]

Most Methodist itinerants faded into history, but Lorenzo Dow stood out for his creativity and innovative methods. A thin man with a long ginger beard, an ever-haggard look, and possessed eyes, he traveled the country preaching and admonishing sinners to seek salvation. He took the theatrics of predecessors like Whitefield and Serra to an entirely new level, earning the nickname "Crazy Dow" thanks to some of his more outrageous stunts. During sermons he pivoted from smashing chairs and gesticulating wildly like a caged animal to softening his voice and conveying the kind of serenity that could put a baby to sleep. He had aides planted in the audience to blow trumpets on cue or ring bells. He railed against elites and the wealthy, and against formalism in churches and overly theologized sermons. He mocked Calvinism and preached a religion of the people. His meetings, like those in Cane Ridge, often featured physical manifestations of the Holy Spirit, including the jerks. He published his messages in book after book, ensuring that his ideas—and his reputation—spread. More Americans named their children Lorenzo in the early republic than almost anything else in honor of the controversial itinerant.

When Asbury began his work, the colonies had fewer than one thousand Methodists. By the Civil War, the Methodist Church had become the largest protestant denomination in the nation. Asbury deserves much of the credit for its growth. He and his allies' message that all stood equal before God fit the times, and their ability to innovate, draw crowds, and deliver a faith and experience that many Americans craved launched them past their competition.

Just as in the 1740s, the surge in revivalism and demand for spiritual leaders provided fresh opportunities for those traditionally excluded from religious leadership. Some revivalist women insisted, along with the Apostle Paul, that in Christ there was neither male nor female. With souls needing to be saved, they claimed to have no choice but to obey God's call to spread his message. They did it by praying aloud, witnessing, and "exhorting." Few had the audacity to claim that their public speaking was actually "preaching," even when it was. They tended to find the most freedom working within Methodist, Baptist, and Presbyterian groups. Meanwhile, the wealthiest, most powerful, and influential denominations, including the Congregationalists and Episcopalians, reinforced their prohibitions against women leaders.

Some women preachers wrote about their experiences to defend their actions and as another method of spreading the faith. Elleanor Knight began her memoir with a justification: "God calls me to maintain the pure, unadulterated principles of the gospel, and also to proclaim them to the world." A heavenly guide had come to her in a dream insisting that she go into a meeting and speak. "I told him," she recalled, "that there was nothing but the Lord that could make me preach." When she awoke, "the impression came to my mind that it was my duty to preach the gospel." Another woman preacher, Harriet Livermore, also published a book defending women's ministry. She offered what she called *Scriptural Evidence in Favour of Female Testimony in Meetings for Christian Worship*. She led readers through the contributions of female figures throughout the Bible and concluded that in the modern era women should be free to pray, sing, and exhort in public meetings.[7]

Other women took even more radical positions: they went beyond preaching by serving communion and baptizing others. The women who spoke publicly of their faith challenged the male dominance of most American religious institutions. Although generations of historians ignored their contributions, women preachers always shaped the trajectory of North American Christianity, not just from the pews, but also from the platforms.

As the postwar revivals spread, some ministers labored to formalize the new work. In upstate New York, Charles Finney held wildly popular services and then systematized and explained what made them successful, ensuring that the techniques and practices he pioneered for making converts would endure long after he was gone.

Finney's parents had not raised him in the church. As an adult, he studied law and then embarked on a career as an attorney. After a dramatic conversion experience, he told a colleague that he now had "a retainer from the Lord Jesus Christ to plead his cause." Rather than seek a position in an established church, Finney initially hit the road as an itinerant, and he focused on persuading people to accept salvation. He claimed that until the millennium, "religion must be mainly promoted by means of revivals." His meetings were entertaining but restrained—unlike the emotional displays of camp-meeting revivalists. He presented a calm, lawyerly defense of Christianity, treating sinners as defendants accountable for their actions. Blending logic with occasional crude language, he laid out the evidence and built the case for Christ with the goal of convincing juries of unbelievers to side with him.[8]

Finney perfected a series of evangelistic tactics that other ministers later incorporated into their own work. He held protracted meetings—long, seemingly unending services. He set up what he called the "anxious bench"—a pew or open area at the front of the revival meeting. There sinners could sit and contemplate their own imperfections under the gaze of the entire crowd until they accepted salvation. Occasionally he called out specific people in his audiences, naming names and identifying their specific sins as he summoned them. Most of the time, the people on the bench had already started talking through salvation with Finney. This practice inspired later evangelists to call sinners to come forward to accept salvation.

Finney defended his controversial, revival-inciting "new measures." He argued that successful church leaders always modernized, always ensured that their work matched the times. He remained acutely aware that ministers had to compete for followers in a dynamic and ever-changing marketplace. "Without new measures," he claimed, "it is impossible that the church should succeed in gaining the attention of the world to religion." He knew what the church needed. "We must have more exciting preaching, to meet the character and wants of the age." Political and worldly excitements, he insisted, "can only be counteracted by religious excitements."[9]

A widespread revival of Christian faith that generates conversions, Finney told audiences, is not the product of some mysterious, divine "miracle." It was "a purely philosophical result of the right use of the constituted means." Ministers, not the Holy Spirit, were responsible for the success or failure of a revival. Finney argued that religious leaders must judge their effectiveness by their outcomes. If they were not inciting constant revivals, leading people to Christ, and growing their churches, they were worthless and had fallen for what Finney called "the devil's most successful means of destroying souls."[10]

Finney's work earned him support from many classes of people, including wealthy businessmen. Many probably believed in the attorney's message. But they were not stupid. They knew that Finney exhorted workers to be responsible, meet their financial obligations, abstain from drink and tobacco, and take care of their families. In other words, Finneyesque salvation produced not just ideal Christians but ideal workers for the evolving and growing market economy in the new republic.

Questions about what drove the revivals have dogged analyses of Finney's work and that of those like him ever since. Was Finney a populist religious innovator who took the beliefs and impulses of common people at face value and empowered them to see and experience God on their own? Or did the capitalist leaders who supported his ministry use him as a tool because they recognized how they could benefit financially from revivalist Christianity? Or both? Much of the discussion about revivalism's boosting of capitalist markets too often ignores the fact that the leaders of the most liberal protestant churches—those who sermonized against Asbury, against Dow, against Finney, against women preachers—also buttressed the market economy and usually even more overtly. Many more wealthy Americans could be found in established, conservative, or liberal urban churches than attending Western revivals. Christians in most American churches boosted the market economy and made peace with class divisions and capitalism.

While revivalist Christians differed on some issues, like the nature of baptism and the appropriate structure for church governance, from Asbury to Finney they all emphasized the individual and his or her relationship to God, instant and easy conversion accessible to all, the believer's ability to feel God's presence in their spirit, and the need to

live holy lives. Many claimed that they had restored the faith to its true New Testament, first-century, original form. The church, they insisted, had been corrupted over the years, and they wanted to strip it down to its essentials. The problem, then and now—in the fifth century and sixteenth and every other century—was that Christian leaders could not agree on what those essentials were. Christians' religious practices, all religious practices, reflected their historical context and cultural sensitivities. There was no faith independent of its time and place.

Just as Boston minister Charles Chauncy condemned the raucous revivals of previous generations, so too did New England minister Lyman Beecher pounce on some elements of the revivalist surge of the early nineteenth century. He criticized revivalists' lack of education and opposed their emphasis on quick and easy conversions. He thought their individual-centered focus undermined Christianity's power to transform the new republic. "It is not by preaching repentance and faith, exclusively," he insisted, "that the interests of religion are promoted. There is a state of society to be formed, and to be formed by an extended combination of institutions, religious, civil and literary, which never exist without the co-operation of an educated Ministry."[11]

Beecher's criticisms reeked of class snobbery. He worried that the wealthy would never submit themselves to an uneducated, poor pastor, and that without the wealthy, religious institutions would crumble. If that happened, then the culture and its political institutions would crumble as well. Conveniently forgetting about the contributions of Jesus's disciple-fishermen, Beecher groused that "illiterate men" have "never been the chosen instruments of God to build up his cause." Others expressed similar concerns. Revivalists' mix of democratic and Christian impulses agitated anti-revivalist ministers, who thought they threatened their churches, their power, and their nation's social stability.[12]

Some Black ministers had other concerns about revivalism. They worried that frenetic services could undermine the respectability they aimed for as they sought to build independent churches and compete with White ministers. "Many of our churches," Henry McNeal Turner wrote, "are cursed with the same moral miasma" that characterized dances and balls. "Let a person get a little animated, fall down and roll over awhile, kick a few shins, crawl under a dozen benches, spring upon his feet, knock some innocent person on the nose and set it bleeding, then, squeal and kiss (or buss) around for a while, and the work is all done." If instead "the individual had claimed justification under more quiet circumstances, its legitimacy would have been doubted." Turner determined that the path to cultural acceptance for Black Christians in a nation dependent on race hierarchies ran from and not to revivalism.[13]

Those seeking a more cerebral faith found it in a new movement that drew from the liberal stream. In some of New England's oldest Puritan-founded Congregational churches, anti-revivalist religious leaders developed a fresh version of Christianity they called Unitarianism. Unitarians remained committed to their churches and did not aim for schism but introduced new ideas into established traditions.

In their politics and mores, Unitarians upheld the conservative status quo. But in their theology, they pushed against convention. They championed dispassionate, reasoned, careful thought and did not trust emotions as tools for determining religious truth. They focused on humans' moral duties to each other and their societies. They believed in human potential and human responsibility. Individuals, they decided, worked out their own salvation over time, and Unitarians tried not to make a distinction between the saved and the lost. They saw most people as somewhere on the path toward a benevolent God who longed for them to choose to come to him. Their sermons often sounded more like academic lectures than camp-meeting entertainment.

Although Unitarians downplayed theology, in the first decades of the nineteenth century they nevertheless emphasized a few core convictions. Their name reflected their belief in the unity of God. They rejected the idea of the Trinity, which they understood as rooted more in Greek philosophy than the biblical text. They viewed God as personal, loving, and gracious, and not the angry and wrathful avenger of the revivalists. They saw Jesus as God's son, sent from the Father, but not as God. Jesus's life demonstrated human potential to do good, not the divine living among us. Unitarians viewed Christ's atonement as essential for changing hearts but not as a blood sacrifice required to quench God's wrath. For Unitarians, all people should aspire to live a Christian life. Faith should elevate humans into more perfect, more noble beings. They emphasized virtue and ethics and encouraged their fellow believers to build caring Christian communities.

Unitarians tended to be highly educated and at or near the top of the economic ladder. Although their numbers remained small, their social and economic power gave them disproportionate influence. Boston, the old Puritan city, and Harvard, the old Puritan school, morphed into Unitarian strongholds. In 1825 the leaders of Unitarian churches (mostly Congregationalists and Episcopalians) formed the American Unitarian Association. Many of the oldest Puritan churches in the region joined the group. The old quip that Unitarians supported the fatherhood of God, the brotherhood of man, and the neighborhood of Boston proved mostly accurate.

Rationalists like Thomas Jefferson encouraged Unitarian ideas. "The pure and simple unity of the creator of the universe," the former president wrote to a friend late in his life, "is now all but ascendant in the Eastern states; it is dawning in the West, and advancing towards the South; and I confidently expect that the present generation will see Unitarianism become the general religion of the United States." Liberal Christianity, he felt sure, would sweep over the land like a welcome rain.[14]

William Ellery Channing, the pastor of Boston's Federal Street Church, became the leading spokesperson for this updated version of liberal Christianity. Channing called the Bible as read through reason the foundation of the Christian faith. "I begin with the position," he preached, "that there is nothing in the general idea of Revelation at which Reason ought to take offence, nothing inconsistent with any established truth, or with our best views of God and Nature." All truth, then, was God's truth. When properly interpreted, the Bible would never negate reason.[15]

Although Jesus was not God according to Channing, he saw the Nazarene as central to Christianity. Channing affirmed the literal physical resurrection of Jesus from the dead and his miracles. Jesus, he taught, "was sent by the Father to effect a moral, or spiritual deliverance of mankind; that is, to rescue men from sin and its consequences, and to bring them to a state of everlasting purity and happiness." Channing called the "highest object of Christ's mission" the "recovery of men to virtue or holiness."[16]

Ecumenism and a greater toleration of religious difference characterized Unitarians in particular and liberal streams of Christianity in general. Liberals offered the faithful wide latitude in their convictions and beliefs about the nature of faith. Channing criticized preachers who "cast out professors of virtuous lives for imagined errors, for the guilt of thinking for themselves." He called for charity and forbearance with regard to doctrinal differences.[17]

As Unitarianism flourished in pockets of urban New England, another stream of liberal Christianity, called Universalism, gained currency. Universalists had many of the same presuppositions as Unitarians. However, they believed that reason and biblical revelation showed that God had destined all humankind for eternal salvation. Unlike the highly educated Unitarians, Universalists often had rudimentary educations. They criticized Unitarians for their elitism, entrenchment in the religious establishment, and commitment to traditional theological education. An old adage highlighted the difference between the two groups: Universalists thought God was too good to damn humans for eternity, while Unitarians thought they were too good for God to damn them at all.

A leading Unitarian, Ralph Waldo Emerson, aspired to push Americans even further from traditional Christianity. Emerson graduated from Harvard in 1829 and immediately moved into ministry, pastoring the Congregationalist (and Unitarian) Second Church in Boston. But three years later he quit. Emerson rejected core elements of the Christian faith and determined that truth could be found within the individual and not in the Bible. He saw intuition as more valuable than external revelation.

In 1838, the graduating class at Harvard Divinity School invited Emerson back to deliver the annual commencement address. "In this refulgent summer," Emerson began, "it has been a luxury to draw the breath of life." Focusing on the natural world, he observed, "The grass grows, the buds burst" and "the meadow is spotted with fire and gold in the tint of flowers. . . . Through the transparent darkness pour the stars their almost spiritual rays." The spiritual rays Emerson sought did not emanate from Christianity. Pointing his audience to truth found both within themselves and in the cosmos, he explained that "the moment the mind opens and reveals the laws which traverse the universe, and make things what they are, then shrinks the great world at once into a mere illustration and fable of this mind."[18]

Emerson insisted that most ministers, including those in the audience, failed to understand how far off track Christianity had become in the hands of its leaders. Rather than establish a "doctrine of the soul," the modern faith "has dwelt, it dwells, with noxious exaggeration about the person of Jesus." With their concentration on the Son of God, he implied, most ministers led their followers astray. Emerson counseled humans to focus instead on "first, soul, and second, soul, and evermore, soul." In retrospect, it may not have been wise for a bunch of ministers in training to invite the man who had bailed on his own calling to address them regarding theirs.[19]

Emerson joined a small group of elite American intellectuals, including a handful of Unitarian ministers, who met in the mid to late 1830s to discuss the "higher" issues of life. They believed that Unitarianism had become too cold—they viewed it as too reasonable and overly intellectualized. But they also feared and rejected the emotionalism of revivalism. The group, which came to be known as the Transcendental Club, included Emerson, Henry David Thoreau, and Margaret Fuller. Many transcendentalists embraced the Unitarians' celebration of the mind, but rather than letting it inspire them to look outward, to Christian service, their faith instead fostered a substantial self-analysis and self-examination. They saw God manifested in both humans and in nature, both imminent and transcendent. They aimed to find harmony with cosmic law, which inspired mystical convictions and practices. The transcendentalist movement led those disillusioned by Christianity, and organized religion more broadly, into a highly individualized spiritual experience found in nature and focused on the soul.

Churches in the United States experienced phenomenal growth in the early decades of the nineteenth century, considerably outpacing population growth. By 1850, 34 percent of Americans had become church members. Baptists and Methodists led this surge, followed by Presbyterians. The Catholic Church also expanded significantly, and by 1860, it had more churches than the Congregationalists or Episcopalians, the dominant denominations of colonial America.

In 1844, church historian Robert Baird reflected on the changes that had enveloped North American Christianity over the previous few decades. He divided the nation into two types of denominations: those he called "evangelical," and everyone else. The use of the term "evangelical" had a long history in Europe. Protestants since the Reformation who wanted to claim that their beliefs were truer, or that their faith was more real and active, than those they viewed as their religious competitors had described themselves as "evangelical." Baird used the term in the same way.

Baird, who considered himself an "evangelical," included in his evangelical tent most denominations—Congregationalists, Baptists, Methodists, Episcopalians, Presbyterians, the Reformed groups, and even Quakers. He listed among the other group Catholics, Mormons, Unitarians, and Universalists. He essentially used the term "evangelical" to describe all mainstream protestants, those whom he saw at the center of life in the early republic. For most of the next century, many different groups from every one of the major Christian streams claimed the term to position themselves as the supposed guardians of historic orthodoxy. "Evangelical" became so ubiquitous that it became nearly meaningless, and by the first decades of the twentieth century, it had mostly fallen out of use. Then during World War II a new group revived and redefined it.[20]

A better way to understand religion in this era is to focus instead on how competing groups drew from one of the four main streams emerging out of North American Christianity as they worked to build their churches and grow their influence. The conservatives included many Catholics, Episcopalians, Congregationalists, and Reformed groups. They maintained strong ties to tradition, had less flexible governing hierarchies, and emphasized the importance of education, especially for their leaders. Many attracted wealthier, more educated Americans and maintained close ties to the political establishment. Others served immigrant ethnic communities.

The second group, the revivalists, included Baptists, Methodists, and some of the newer denominations, including the Disciples of Christ. Located predominately in the West and South, they tended to attract some elite Americans but also people from the middle and lower classes. They downplayed community, tradition, and hierarchy, and instead emphasized revival, the individual, emotions, and religious feelings and excitements. Some Presbyterians fell within the conservative stream and others within revivalism.

The third group, the liberals, included some Congregationalists, Universalists, and Unitarians, the folks Jefferson expected to soon rule the nation. Most prominent in major cities and Northeast institutions like Harvard, they emphasized reason, science, and rationality. They too put a lot of emphasis on the individual, but more on the intellect and reason than on emotions.

In the early decades of the nineteenth century, conservatives and liberals still held most of the power. But revivalists, adopting in part the methods of Francis Asbury and Charles Finney, laid important foundations upon which future generations could build. Meanwhile, other Christians turned to a fourth stream for inspiration. Developing a liberationist form of Christianity, they aimed to upend the status quo and hoped to call their fellow Christians to account.

9

LIBERATED CHRISTIANITY

Two years into the Revolutionary War, Richard Allen attended a revival service led by a White Methodist itinerant in Delaware. "I was awakened and brought to see myself poor, wretched and undone, and without the mercy of God must be lost," he recalled. "I cried to the Lord both night and day. . . . All of a sudden my dungeon shook, my chains flew off, and glory to God, I cried." But the chains he lost and the dungeon he escaped were spiritual only. Allen was enslaved.[1]

Allen began attending Methodist meetings and participated in and led exhortation sessions. In the summer of 1783, Allen purchased his freedom from his enslaver. He was twenty-three years old. He had big plans for sharing the Methodist faith with other Black Americans. The egalitarian, democratic, populist gospel championed by some revivalist Christians initially drew those like Allen to the faith. But almost immediately Black Christians redirected it. Allen and his coreligionists refashioned Methodist ideas, recognizing that religious beliefs mattered both in this world and in the next. The Christian gospel, they determined, not only changed souls, but lives, and with them perhaps, the world. They worshipped not just the Jesus of the New Testament who offered individual salvation and a path to a blissful afterlife, but also the Old Testament God of the Exodus, the God of deliverance, the God who freed the enslaved and punished those who had abused his people.

The work of Allen and his allies helped form the liberationist stream of Christianity. They inspired those on the margins of American society to push back against the mainstream. They created an alternative religious politics and alternative vision for restructuring American society and laws, and they established the foundations that reformers would build upon for centuries to come. They tried to force those Americans who believed that the United States was God's chosen land to answer the question, Chosen for whom?

Africans brought to the colonies a variety of indigenous religions from their homelands, others carried Islam, and a small number had learned about Christianity from European missionaries. Christianity did not initially catch on among many enslaved women and men in North America. But the American Revolution and postwar revivalism sparked the expansion of more accessible and populist forms of Christianity. The revolution's rhetoric of freedom, liberty, and equality, combined with the egalitarian nature of the revivals, inspired numerous free Black leaders and enslaved men and women to embrace the faith. Significant numbers began converting to Christianity, and as they did, they remade it. Over time, Christianity in North America came to reflect the practices, ideas, and beliefs of not just Europeans but also of various African peoples. Practices and traditions blended, combined, and changed, creating a unique Christianity that fused elements from multiple continents.

Richard Allen helped remake North American Christianity. He ministered to Black Americans and also traveled side by side with White Methodist itinerants, preaching to people of all races. He impressed Methodist bishop Francis Asbury, who invited the young evangelist to join him in the 1780s on a preaching tour of the Deep South. Allen declined. He did not believe the precautions that Asbury outlined for him could guarantee his safety.

Like many other free Black men and women, Allen saw Christianity as incompatible with slavery. "I do not wish to make you angry," he told readers of his memoir, "but excite your attention to consider how hateful slavery is, in the sight of that God who hath destroyed kings and princes, for their oppression of the poor slaves." God, he argued, "was the first pleader of the cause of slaves."[2]

In 1786 Allen visited Philadelphia, where a White Methodist elder at St. George's Church invited him to help minister to the city's Black Christians. He planned to stay for only a few weeks, and then to move on. But once in Philadelphia, Allen later recalled, "I soon saw a large field open in seeking and instructing my African brethren, who had been a long forgotten people." He fretted that "few of them attended public worship."[3]

In 1787, Allen, another formerly enslaved Christian named Absalom Jones, and six others launched a mutual aid society—the Free African Society. They asked society members for annual contributions, which they used to help the poor and destitute. Black leaders like Allen, not far removed from enslavement, wanted to ensure that they built strong, independent communities that did not need or depend on the support of patronizing Whites. In launching the Free African Society, Allen demonstrated that religious action was not enough, that faith without works was dead. He aimed to serve Philadelphia's Black community by serving both bodies and souls. But his relationship with the society did not last. Most of the group's leaders wanted the organization to stay nonsectarian, and Allen remained doggedly dedicated to building Methodism.

When Allen joined St. George's, the church had only a few Black members. In good Methodist fashion, Allen, along with Jones, immediately went to work, preaching to Black residents on street corners and wherever they could find an audience. The evangelists brought dozens of people to St. George's and established new Black prayer meetings. As the number of Black folks attending the church grew,

Allen proposed starting a new church aimed specifically at ministering to them. St. George's White leaders dismissed the idea. They could not envision a world in which Black Americans did not need White support and oversight. Nevertheless, Allen and Jones and a few others began raising money in the early 1790s for an independent church.

Allen's success exposed the insecurities of the White Methodists at St. George's and demonstrated that Whites could oppose slavery without necessarily seeing Black congregants as their equals. White church leaders wanted to expand Methodism by converting Black individuals, but they did not want to fellowship side-by-side with former slaves and freemen. As the number of Black congregants grew, White leaders at St. George's began asking them to take seats in the back of the church or in the balcony, or to stand around the outside edges of the pews.

The conflict over race and seating came to a head at a Sunday morning service. As Allen and Jones walked toward their regular pews, the elder leading the service invited everyone to kneel and pray. Jones and Allen kneeled. Apparently, they were not in the section of the church where the White leaders wanted them. A White elder moved in and grabbed Jones, asking him to get up and move. He refused, asking the elder to wait until the prayers concluded. The elder and another White church leader physically pulled Jones up and dragged him away. When the prayer ended, Allen wrote, all the church's Black worshippers "went out of the church in a body, and they were no more plagued with us in the church." But the "Lord," he continued, "was with us."[4]

In March 1793, with Absalom Jones by his side, Allen drove a shovel into the ground on a piece of land at 5th Street and Adelphi, beginning the process of building a literal foundation for a Black church in Philadelphia and the metaphorical foundation for an independent Black Christianity in the new United States. On that spot Black Christians established the African Episcopal Church of St. Thomas and called Absalom Jones to serve as their minister.

The majority of Black congregants spurned by St. George's wanted to leave Methodism altogether. Allen, however, remained loyal to the denomination where he had discovered Jesus. He saw revivalist Methodism as more democratic and egalitarian than the conservative

Episcopal church preferred by Jones. "We are beholden to the Methodists, under God," he insisted, "for the light of the Gospel we enjoy; for all other denominations preached so high-flown that we were not able to comprehend their doctrine." He viewed revivalism as especially effective for reaching those with limited educations. "Sure am I," he declared, "that reading sermons will never prove so beneficial to the coloured people as spiritual or extempore preaching. I am well convinced that the Methodist has proved beneficial to thousands and ten times thousands."[5]

Allen built a new Methodist church a few blocks from Jones's church on land he had bought in 1791. When the congregation dedicated the building on July 29, 1794, with Francis Asbury on hand, it initially numbered only about forty people. But it grew over time. In 1796, Allen incorporated the church as the Bethel African Methodist Episcopal Church of Philadelphia. By the time of Allen's death in 1831, the congregation counted three thousand members.

As Christianity spread among people of African descent, so too did White efforts to control and shape it. Local White Methodist leaders refused to gracefully let Allen venture out on his own. They tried to assert control over Bethel, much as they had over Black bodies under slavery and the Black congregants at St. George's. At every step Allen and the Bethel leadership and congregants resisted. Eventually, White Methodists took Allen to court, seeking control of the church property. Black Philadelphians, though subject to harassment and discrimination, refused to stand down.

Allen understood that these events made schism necessary. White Methodists would not tolerate Black independence. In 1816, Allen and leaders from four other Black Methodist churches met together in Philadelphia and formed a new denomination—the African Methodist Episcopal Church. The group elected Allen to serve as the new AME denomination's first bishop. From the start, denominational leaders focused on the liberation of African-descended peoples around the world.

The growth of Black Christianity in Philadelphia reflected a larger trend occurring in many other parts of the new nation. A few years after Allen helped found the AME, James Varick, another Black Methodist minister, launched the African Methodist Episcopal Zion (AMEZ) Church in New York. Like the AME, leaders of the AMEZ adhered to Methodist ideas and doctrine but left the Methodist denomination in order to defend their autonomy and independence. They also condemned slavery, a necessary move since White Methodist church leaders, eager to expand their movement in the South, had begun softening their opposition to the slave system.

Building autonomous, Black-led congregations in the South proved more difficult. In 1776 a free man in Virginia named Reverend Moses tried to start a Baptist church. Local authorities arrested and assaulted him. A few years later in 1781 the people he had organized formed the First Baptist Church of Williamsburg. In Savannah, Georgia, free Black Christians established multiple Baptist churches where they worshipped independently of Whites. The new churches of the West, founded in the wake of revivals, sometimes had biracial congregations, and in some communities, enslaved people created their own congregations to worship with others like them.

In the early republic, some Black women heard the call of God to preach. Jarena Lee, born in 1783 to a poor family in New Jersey, spent her childhood working as a servant. At age twenty-one she converted to Christianity at a revival. The experience left her feeling conflicted. She had powerful dreams and visions that sometimes included appearances by Jesus, but she also worried about her sins and doubted that God had redeemed her soul.

In 1811, Lee attended one of Allen's services. She felt immediately at home. "This is the people," she recalled, "to which my heart unites." Allen didn't know when he welcomed Lee to his church that she believed that God wanted her to preach. Initially, she didn't tell him because she feared that no one would believe her. God, however, wouldn't relent. "Preach the Gospel," he promised, and "I will put words in your mouth, and will turn your enemies to become your friends." Still not convinced, she asked God to prove that he, and not the devil, had come to her. Confirmation came in the form of another vision. She saw a Bible lying on a pulpit and later dreamed that a great multitude listened to her preach. The signs could not have been clearer: God called her to minister.[6]

Lee told Allen about God's plan for her life. Allen, worried that women preachers would undermine his credibility and that of his church, told Lee that she must have misunderstood God's message. Unwilling to challenge Allen, Lee initially agreed. She spent the next eight years mostly abiding by Allen's dictate not to claim the mantle of preacher. During this time, she married a minister who led a small church outside Philadelphia. They had six children, but only two survived. Her decision not to answer God's call left her feeling abandoned by the almighty. The "holy energy which burned" as a "fire" within her, she remembered, "began to be smothered."[7]

When Lee's husband died suddenly, leaving her and the surviving children alone, she returned to Allen's Bethel church. During one otherwise mundane service in 1819, one of the ministers announced that he intended to preach from the second chapter of Jonah. Lee felt the Holy Spirit speaking to her through this text. Like Jonah, she had failed to obey God's call on her life; she had failed to deliver his message. But she could still repent. When the minister abruptly stopped his sermon, seeming to have lost his train of thought, Lee jumped to her feet and delivered the rest of the sermon, aided, she claimed, by God.

Lee's spontaneous sermon impressed Allen. He told the congregation that although he had forbidden her to preach, he now understood that God had chosen her for this good work. That day marked the beginning of Lee's career as a preacher. She later explained her actions in a memoir. "For as unseemly as it may appear now-a-days for a woman to preach," she wrote, "it should be remembered that nothing is impossible with God. . . . If the man may preach, because the Saviour died for him, why not the woman? . . . Did not Mary first preach the risen Saviour?" In addition to citing scripture, Lee also made a pragmatic argument: Her preaching induced people to salvation, so clearly God had blessed it.[8]

Lee preached mostly to Black audiences, but occasionally she preached to interracial crowds and Indigenous communities. Although she sometimes aroused opposition, from both within Methodism and without, she noted that Jesus had warned his disciples that he was sending them out as sheep among the wolves. She routinely walked many miles by foot to get from one meeting to the next. Poor and often hungry, she depended on strangers for shelter and to help care for her if she fell ill.

The Holy Spirit often seemed present at Lee's meetings. People wept, dropped to the floor, and displayed signs and wonders. In some extreme cases her work inadvertently summoned the angel of death as well. According to Lee, those who refused to repent and seek salvation sometimes perished within hours. God, she wrote, "wrought a judgement—some were well at night and died in the morning."[9]

In addition to advocating for women, Lee also sought freedom for the enslaved. "The wickedness of the people certainly calls for the lowering Judgements of God to be let loose upon the Nation and Slavery, that wretched system that emanated from the bottomless pit," she fulminated. She called slavery "one of the greatest curses to any Nation." Like so many other Black Christians, she viewed the Bible as a book of liberation that promised freedom to captives. For White Americans to countenance slavery revealed the shallowness of their faith.[10]

After the American Revolution, Christianity began spreading among those in bondage just as it had among free Black individuals. Enslaved men and women developed their own faith outside of formal church settings in what became a secret, Christian, "invisible institution." In clandestine gatherings, participants routinized religious forms and practices that drew directly on the Christianity of revivalists, which they combined with African religious practices and local folklore. Like the White folks of the era, they often believed in ghosts, and practiced magic, conjuring, divination, and various healing rituals. Some slaves incorporated into their Christianity the Islamic practices that their ancestors brought from Africa. On the South Carolina sea islands, for example, enslaved Christians bowed and prayed facing east. Christianity always reflected the integration of biblical ideas read through current cultural norms and practices.

The "ring shout" characterized some clandestine Black services, illustrating how enslaved men and women, who had supposedly forsaken African modes of dancing at Christian leaders' behest, reconfigured older traditions and blended them with Christian worship. The ring shout could run for hours, with singing, chanting, and calls and responses. Other practices, such as feasts, drum playing, and death processionals, also revealed a merging of older native cultures and traditions with the new.

Conversion was central to the invisible institution. Supplicants believed that they encountered Jesus as a real person who intervened in this world. He provided power, security, and, in the face of abuse or pain, comfort and healing. Converts also sometimes had out-of-body experiences.

Covert meetings often featured the singing of spirituals. Intensely personal songs, spirituals blended biblical narratives with visions of a better world. They included themes of liberation—the God who had once freed the slaves from Pharoah could do so again. Nineteenth- and early twentieth-century Black writers, including Frederick Douglass and W. E. B. Du Bois, saw in the spirituals the slave's most passionate cries for freedom.

A shift in White attitudes in the early decades of the nineteenth century had helped make Christianity more accessible to the enslaved. Enslavers recognized that for their labor system to survive, they needed to make changes. In part this required acknowledging to some extent the humanness of their workers. Enslavers developed a paternalistic ideology. They treated the enslaved as children whom they needed to care for, protect, and teach the ways of God. They also believed that they could use the Christian faith as a tool of social control, that it could help them inculcate a stronger work ethic and willingness to submit in those they held in captivity. Enslavers came to believe that the Christianization of those they exploited might further benefit them.

Many enslavers forced those they subjugated to worship in their churches on Sunday mornings, where Black Americans heard messages about duty and submission. They sat in segregated sections, usually in the back of churches, or in balconies. In regions with large enslaved populations, Black parishioners sometimes outnumbered Whites, especially in revivalist Methodist and Baptist churches.

A few Black individuals, including a small number of enslaved men, gained ordination in White-led churches. Several larger congregations in the upper South recognized that gifted enslaved preachers could better reach Black populations than could White ministers, so when enslaved spiritual leaders arose in their midst, they licensed and ordained them. But most African American ministers did not ask permission or seek approval of White church officials.

Despite enslavers' best efforts, they could not control the way Black North Americans interpreted and practiced Christianity. As the Romans recognized in the first century, Christianity could inspire revolution. It did not take long for enslavers who promoted the faith, expecting it to make their captives better workers, to realize that perhaps they had erred. Newspaper notices occasionally mentioned that a runaway thought of himself as a preacher, or that a missing person regularly sang hymns or talked about Jesus.

Others did more than run away in their quest for liberation. Born into slavery in the late 1760s, Denmark Vesey embraced Jesus's gospel of liberation. In 1799 he won a lottery and used the proceeds to purchase his independence. He hoped to secure the freedom of his wife and children as well, but their enslaver refused to release them. Losing his family reinforced Vesey's conviction that the slave system had to be destroyed along with the devil who had spawned it.

As a free man, Vesey found comfort in Christianity. He initially attended a biracial Presbyterian church in Charleston, South Carolina. In 1819, he and a group of Black Christians founded a new AME church. The Charleston church quickly became the second largest AME congregation in the nation. Local White leaders routinely harassed its members and interrupted its services. They realized that enslaved and free Black Christians found freedom and independence—they found liberation—in the autonomous space of AME churches, and they aimed to do everything in their power to undercut it.

Vesey's reading of the Bible inspired him to focus on this life as much as the next. Over the next few years, the Christian leader probably plotted a Black uprising—historians still debate what actually happened. He likely hoped to inspire enslaved and free men and women to take up arms, fight for their freedom, and then bolt for Haiti, where a few years earlier Toussaint Louverture had led a successful revolt, taking control of the island nation from White enslavers. Vesey apparently instructed his coconspirators to steal guns from their masters, as well as to secure swords and daggers so that, if necessary, they could kill in relative silence to avoid detection. But before the insurrection began, word of the plot leaked. Local White authorities armed themselves, organized intensive searches, and arrested Vesey and all suspected coconspirators. They executed thirty-five people, including Vesey. They burned down the AME church building and banished its free ministers to Philadelphia.

Much of Vesey's planning had supposedly occurred under the auspices of the church. According to trial transcripts, church "meetings, held usually at night in some retired building, avowedly for religious instruction and worship," occurred independently of White supervision. There, Vesey and his coconspirators preached "inflamatory and insurrectionary doctrines." Vesey's interrogators noted "the great impropriety of allowing meetings of any kind to be held solely by slaves." They lamented "the influence" of ordained ministers "over the minds of the ignorant blacks" and criticized Black ministers' efforts to enlist "into their cause perverted religion and fanaticism."[11]

Indeed, White South Carolinians saw Black Christianity as a threat to their own form of Christianity and to the economic system on which they depended. The Vesey plot provided them with a rationale for moving against it, or perhaps they exaggerated the threat as justification for attacking the independent religious work of Black Americans. Whatever Vesey did or did not plan, Whites determined that Black Christianity undermined the slave system and that they needed to wrest control of it from its Black leaders.

Nat Turner, a literate enslaved man living in Virginia, also embraced liberationist Christianity. Turner apparently had unique blemishes on his body from birth, and he believed that they marked him as a prophet. During his youth, he read the Bible closely and had visions in which God seemed to command him to use force to cleanse the United States of its sins. In perhaps his most dramatic supernatural experience, he saw himself walking into blood-drenched cornfields. The "Holy Ghost," he claimed, had "revealed itself to me" through this vision. The blood, he determined, came from Christ. "It was plain to me," Turner explained, "that the Saviour was about to lay down the yoke he had borne for the sins of men, and the great day of judgment was at hand."[12]

Turner would help execute that judgment. "I heard a loud noise in the heavens," Turner recalled, "and the Spirit instantly appeared to me and said the Serpent was loosened, and Christ had laid down the yoke he had borne for the sins of men, and that I should take it on and fight against the Serpent, for the time was fast approaching when the first should be last and the last should be first." Just as God had commanded Jarena Lee to preach, he commanded Turner to "slay" his "enemies with their own weapons."[13]

On August 21, 1831, Nat Turner and six fellow enslaved men launched an insurrection in Southampton County, Virginia. Beginning with Turner's enslaver, they killed every White person they encountered and urged enslaved people on each plantation they liberated to claim their freedom and join the uprising. The rebels killed around sixty White men, women, and children before local militias crushed the revolt. Turner was eventually captured and executed, along with fifty-five others accused of participating. White mobs retaliated by murdering roughly two hundred additional Black people, displaying their severed heads on posts as a brutal warning. The message to the enslaved was clear. Any rebellion would be met with overwhelming, unrelenting violence.

The slave revolts sent a clear message to White southerners. Christianity, if not handled carefully, could be a serious threat to the stability of the slave economy and even to their own lives. They believed they could no longer allow Christianity to flourish unchecked among oppressed communities. Harriet Jacobs, enslaved at the time in

Maryland, remembered the aftermath. "The slaves begged the privilege of again meeting at their little church in the woods," she wrote. "It was built by the colored people, and they had no higher happiness than to meet there and sing hymns together, and pour out their hearts in spontaneous prayer." Whites denied their request and "demolished" the church. But they didn't want to cut the enslaved off from the faith completely. "After the alarm caused by Nat Turner's insurrection had subsided, the slaveholders," Jacobs recalled, "came to the conclusion that it would be well to give the slaves enough of religious instruction to keep them from murdering their masters." Most required those they enslaved to attend church under their close supervision.[14]

The spread of liberationist Christianity among African American communities, both enslaved and free, across the North and South, laid a crucial foundation for shaping the emerging United States. Like Anne Hutchinson, Thomas Jefferson, and Francis Asbury, Richard Allen, Jarena Lee, and Nat Turner set the nation on its trajectory. The forms of Christianity developed by Black Americans highlighted how faith and action, power and liberation melded together inside and outside of churches. Yet despite the efforts of Black liberationists, slavery continued unabated, prompting questions about the nature of the God Americans worshipped and whether he expected his followers to submit to oppressive authority or to liberate those in captivity. As Christians White and Black sought to answer these questions, many understood that before they resolved them, more blood was going to flow.

While some Christians found reassurance in traditional churches, others responded to the turmoil of the age by striking out in bold new directions. Rejecting inherited institutions, they formed experimental communities of faith and practice—utopian visions meant to redeem both soul and society. But in testing the limits of religious liberty, these spiritual pioneers often collided with the realities of a still-maturing republic.

10

CREATING AMERICAN ORIGINALS

Just months after Thomas Jefferson put the last period on the Declaration of Independence, a twenty-three-year-old woman in Rhode Island named Jemima Wilkinson died. Her family did not put her into a coffin or lower her body into the ground. Her flesh seemingly came back to life, possessed by a divine spirit. Those around the resurrected Wilkinson called her the Public Universal Friend.

The Public Universal Friend, along with a handful of other pioneering religious leaders in the early republic, offered new, radical versions of the faith. Influenced by revivalism and the liberating messages of Jesus, they believed that they could interpret the Bible on their own, with little need to follow tradition or the wisdom and insights of established authorities. They challenged conventional norms and morals, especially on issues related to gender roles and sex. The almighty, they concluded, had used the revolution to mark the start of a new era, and the promised millennial kingdom of God seemed at hand. Just as God had used the Hebrews to share his plans for the ancient world, now he planned to use his new chosen people, Americans, and especially those leading new upstart Christian movements, to spread his message.

Utopian visionaries established new Christian communities, hoping that eventually the rest of the country would adopt their forms of faith. Yet their projects never generated the results they promised. The kingdom of God proved as elusive to early nineteenth-century believers as it has to every generation before and after. Rather than lead large numbers of Americans in new directions, utopian Christian pioneers generally drew more persecution than adulation. Their efforts to inaugurate the kingdom of God regularly inspired attacks from the hounds of hell. The harassment they faced demonstrated that in a new nation claiming to cherish religious liberty, those invoking the name of Christ could not preach a gospel that veered too far from the mainstream without finding their fellow Christians transformed into pitchfork-wielding mobs.

Innovators tried to push their fellow citizens to take seriously the First Amendment's free exercise clause, but their experiences demonstrated that Americans never had an absolute commitment to religious liberty. Mainstream American Christians tolerated a wide range of religious commitments from Methodism to Quakerism, but they did not tolerate all forms of faith. The First Amendment guaranteed disestablishment. It did not in practice provide for the free exercise of religion for those on the social and political margins.

In the early republic, Americans had a diverse array of Christian churches to explore and embrace. Yet some people saw the mainstream denominations as little more than fading, corrupt imitations of early Christianity. They questioned churches' support of the market economy and individualist values. They despised how most Christians embraced what they viewed as confining gender roles. And they wondered if traditional marriage, rather than bringing them closer to the divine, drove them further away. As they wrestled with these questions some ventured out in new directions, seeking to restore the "authentic" Christian faith. They promised Americans mysterious new rituals, true community, and liberation from stifling norms.

Born in 1752, Jemima Wilkinson grew up in the Quaker faith in Rhode Island. The Society of Friends fostered in her an openness to women's religious leadership. Smart and literate, she memorized large portions of the Bible and other important religious texts. She embraced revivalism and likely attended one of George Whitefield's final meetings before his death.

In the fall of 1776, Wilkinson came down with a terrible fever. Her health declined fast, and within a couple of days her family just about lost all hope for her recovery. But early one morning, Wilkinson surprised those around her by rising from her bed. She claimed that she was no longer Jemima, that Wilkinson had died and her soul had gone to heaven. In its place, God sent a spirit to possess Wilkinson's body and spread his message. Wilkinson now identified as the "Public Universal Friend," a prophet directed by God to start a new Christian movement.

The Friend's followers later claimed that their leader was neither male nor female, but they believed that a masculine spirit possessed the Friend's body, so they referred to the resurrected Wilkinson using "he/him" pronouns. I will do the same. While today we might be inclined to use the singular "they," to do so would be anachronistic.

Within days of resurrecting from the dead, the Public Universal Friend began preaching. Many of the Friend's followers believed that Jesus Christ had returned in the body of their leader. But others felt less sure. The Friend routinely called himself the "Comforter," the physical embodiment of the Holy Spirit. His messages often drew directly on biblical texts that emphasized imminent destruction. Like other revivalists of the era, the Friend prayed over the sick for miraculous healing, described divine visions, and engaged in prophecy. That signs and wonders followed his work served as evidence of Jesus's imminent return—or perhaps he had already come in the form of the Friend.

While the Friend preached a mostly orthodox message, the messenger, in the bodily form of a woman wearing loose-fitting men's clothes and claiming to be some kind of heaven-sent prophet, distinguished him, as did his views on sexuality and gender. The Friend seemed more focused on erasing signs of female identity than in repudiating gender writ large. The changes he made in his life, and his instructions to women in the movement about their behavior and dress, indicated that to exercise spiritual authority, women needed to suppress their gender identity. Yet he does not seem to have asked men to downplay or deny their masculinity. Rumors spread, however, that he attacked men's sexuality and maybe even their sexual organs. One French traveler, the Marquis de Chastellux, had heard that male followers of the Public Universal Friend literally followed Jesus's precept that his followers, if they were able, should make eunuchs of themselves. The Marquis had hoped to attend one of the Friend's services to study the movement firsthand but failed. "The crowd was so great," he reported, and "so turbulent, that it was impossible to get near the place of worship." Whether or not the Friend encouraged castration, he heralded sexual abstinence as an exalted spiritual discipline.[1]

As the Friend drew followers, he began to organize them into congregations called the Society of Universal Friends. Then, in the mid-1780s, he changed strategy. Rather than continue to amass converts as an itinerant evangelist, he launched a new religious community where followers could develop and practice their faith together free from the distractions and temptations of the secular world (which was a mostly protestant world). But for most followers, peace proved as elusive in utopian society as in their former lives. Conflicts, dissent, and scandals plagued the community. On July 1, 1819, the Friend died, and this time the body of Jemima Wilkinson did not resurrect. With no clear successor, no new spirit of God infusing the body of another human, Wilkinson's followers struggled to maintain the movement. By the time of the Civil War, they had mostly disbanded.

Ann Lee, another innovator with Quaker roots, offered a novel spin on Christianity. Lee claimed to have religious visions, and she spoke in unknown tongues. She fellowshipped in her hometown of Manchester, England, with a sect related to the Society of Friends known for whirling, dancing, and trembling called the United Society of Believers in Christ's Second Appearing. Outsiders dubbed them "Shakers."

In 1774 Lee emigrated to the United States with a few others, hoping that they might find religious freedom across the Atlantic. She traveled around New York and New England championing a liberationist gospel that emphasized the equality of the genders. She and her followers worshipped a God whom they saw as both male and female, a combination of both father and mother. Lee taught that when Jesus returned, he would appear in the form of a woman. As Lee's movement grew, she organized an American version of the United Society of Believers in Christ's Second Appearing. The millennium, she believed, had begun with the founding of this church.

During Shaker worship services, participants danced, sang, clapped, jumped in the air, fell to the floor, and sometimes moaned. Rejecting the rising tide of individualism and the expanding market economy, Lee demanded communal living and the shared ownership of all property among her followers. And, like the Friend, Lee encouraged celibacy. Sex, she claimed, represented the root of all sin dating back to Adam and Eve. Furthermore, if the kingdom was at hand, the faithful had no need or time for lovemaking. Lee counseled married couples who joined the movement to separate and embrace chastity. The path to salvation ran away from their partners' bodies.

To raise money for the community, the Shakers made and sold distinctive furniture characterized by simple lines and clean patterns. They used local woods, and rather than put flashy brass handles on their pieces, they carved basic nobs from lumber. In addition to their unique furniture, the Shakers crafted books, hymns, and pamphlets that emphasized and spread Lee's message.

While the Public Universal Friend and Lee had much in common, the latter provoked much more violence. Lee's embrace of her gender, worship of a female God, and expectation of a female Christ proved far more difficult for most Americans to tolerate than a messiah figure in the body of a woman who claimed to be sexless and acted and dressed more like a man. Lee and her allies faced beatings, stonings, and mobs. A string of attacks in New England weakened Lee, and she died in 1784. Following her death, the Shakers claimed that Christ had actually come in the person of Lee.

Lee's followers decided to establish a series of communities—nineteen in all from New England to Kentucky—where they could live independently of the outside world. The movement grew to about five or six thousand people, and members sought to expand their numbers through adoption of orphans. However, building a movement grounded on celibacy has never been popular or successful in the United States. Sex generates growth; abstinence leads to death.

Lee and Wilkinson demonstrated that women, often excluded from exercising religious power in traditional churches and movements, could find new opportunities for their gender outside of the mainstream. Their ability to attract followers showed that thousands of Americans felt dissatisfied with traditional ideas about sex and marriage and proved willing to choose celibacy as a religious virtue.

This era of religious experimentation and questing for new spiritual insights continued with William Miller. Sometime in the late 1810s, Miller, a Baptist and farmer from upstate New York, determined that he had cracked the Bible's prophetic code. He homed in on verses in Daniel 9, which listed a series of cryptic numbers and time spans. Based on these verses, he concluded that the countdown to Jesus's Second Coming began in 457 BCE when Persian conqueror Cyrus the Great ended the Babylonian captivity and freed the Hebrews. Moving forward from that date, Miller determined that Jesus would likely return on or sometime shortly after March 21, 1843, and no later than that April.

Miller was one of thousands of Americans scarred by the experience of serving as a soldier in the War of 1812. The war, combined with ongoing battles with Indigenous nations, drove some Christians back to the Bible's most violent, apocalyptic texts. They saw signs of the imminent end-times appearing everywhere, from combat to changing cultural mores to geopolitics to unusual weather. They strove to prepare themselves and their fellow Americans for Jesus's Second Coming.

For years Miller kept his calculations to himself. But after studying the scriptures from beginning to end, forward and backward, he started sharing his findings with friends and family. Inspired by their encouraging responses, in the early 1830s Miller began delivering sermon-lectures around the Northeast on his discoveries. In 1832, he published his interpretations in a book, claiming that Jesus would return in 1843. He challenged his readers to prove him wrong. "I have not yet," he explained, "by seventeen years study, been able to discover where I might fail." Moreover, he believed that his evangelistic successes demonstrated the truth of his message. In all his prophecy meetings, Miller boasted, "the church has been awakened, and the Bible has been read with more interest. In many, and I might say almost in every place, a revival of religion has followed, which has lasted for months."[2]

In 1839, Miller met minister Joshua Himes. A brilliant marketer, publicist, and business manager, Himes had participated in many of the progressive causes of the era, contending for women's rights and against slavery, among many other things. Intrigued by Miller's calculations, he joined the farmer preacher. They traveled the country organizing camp meetings and delivering lectures, and they bought a huge tent that held about four thousand people to use when they could not rent a meeting venue. To reach those who could not see them in person, they published two magazines, *The Midnight Cry* and *Signs of the Times*, and produced countless pages in tracts and booklets. Together they attracted a significant following of "Millerites" from many different denominations. In the 1840s, the duo began using the term "Adventist" to describe their particular version of Christian theology, but they insisted that they had no intention of fostering schism. With time so short, they had little interest in building a new movement.

In addition to attracting White Christians to the movement, Miller's ideas also appealed to Black Americans, both free and enslaved. Miller and Himes opposed slavery and joined abolitionist societies. Their theology, rife with judgment on the nation for its sins, drew Black followers. Millennial theology regularly proved popular with those seeking liberation from bondage.

Miller became a much-sought speaker, often giving multiple lectures per day primarily along the East Coast and into Canada. He also maintained a lively correspondence. He admitted to Himes that he had a hard time keeping up. "I must read all the 'slang' of the drunken and the sober," he explained. "And since 'hard cider' has become so popular, these publications are not few." But not to worry. "The polar star," he reminded himself as much as Himes, "must be kept in view, the Chart consulted, the compass watched, the reckoning kept, the sails set, the rudder managed, the ship cleaned, the sailors fed, the voyage prosecuted, the port of rest to which we are destined understood, the watchman to answer the call, 'Watchman, what of the night?'"[3]

As anticipation grew for Jesus's Second Advent, some followers, believing they needed to store up treasures in heaven and not on earth, gave up their jobs and let their fields go fallow. When Jesus did not return as expected in 1843, Miller determined that he had in fact erred. Nevertheless, he believed that Christians should maintain their hope in the second coming. If Jesus failed to return today, he might return tomorrow. If not this year, perhaps the next.

Some Millerites, refusing to concede defeat, reran Miller's numbers and developed a new calculation and date. Jesus, they surmised, would return on October 22, 1844. But they had many critics. One Presbyterian minister who in 1841 had published a book on the Second Coming wrote a fellow minister complaining that the Millerites, in shifting dates rather than admitting their mistaken calculations, undermined the study of prophecy. He claimed that they were bolstering "Satan's plan" to drive people to "excess and folly" and away from important millennial truths.[4]

As the new date approached, some of the faithful gave away their money and belongings, donned white robes, and climbed hills together to be closer to the heavens when Jesus appeared. But the Savior did not come. Journalists dubbed Jesus's failure to appear yet again the "Great Disappointment." Thousands of Miller's followers felt disillusioned, while writers in newspapers and magazines mocked them. One group returned to the scriptures and crafted yet another interpretation of biblical prophecy. They argued that rather than return physically to earth in October of 1844 Jesus had ascended at that time into the "holy of holies" in heaven. The end-times had thus begun and Jesus's physical return to earth was imminent. They forged these beliefs into the creation of a new movement and denomination, the Seventh-day Adventists.

While William Miller predicted the end of the world, and Ann Lee and Jemima Wilkinson preached celibacy, John Humphrey Noyes offered a different kind of utopia. Convinced that the kingdom of God was at hand, Noyes founded one of the most unique and controversial communities in North America. Like many religious innovators, Noyes believed that Americans misunderstood the relationship between Christianity and sex. He pushed against established norms and connected his understanding of faith and community with his understanding of sexuality, challenging mainstream social values.

Born in Vermont in 1811, Noyes grew up in privilege—his father served in Congress, and President Rutherford B. Hayes was a relative. In 1831, Noyes had a dramatic conversion experience at a revival. Noyes took away from his experience two things—a focus on the millennium and a conviction that true Christianity produced pure living. "The Millennium was supposed to be very near. . . . My heart," Noyes recalled, "was fixed on the Millennium, and I resolved to live or die for it."[5]

Noyes claimed that Jesus had already returned, spiritually, in the year 70, and his coming made it possible for Christians to live perfect, sinless lives. He described perfection as a "state in which *all* the affections of the heart are given to God" and "there is no sin." As evidence of his theory, Noyes offered his own life. He claimed that he had, in fact, eradicated all sin.[6]

Like Ann Lee, Noyes determined that Christians should practice faith in intentional community. He and his supporters settled on three properties in his hometown of Putney, Vermont. They dedicated themselves to searching the scriptures and growing their faith together. The group quickly ran into problems and in 1847 local authorities arrested Noyes, charging him with adultery. Released on bond, Noyes fled the state. The other members of the community followed him to the village of Oneida in upstate New York, where they purchased eighty acres and constructed a communal house—a utopia founded upon Noyes's theology. They financed their experiment by making excellent steel traps, travel bags, and, most famously, silverware.

Noyes established a series of religious rituals for the Oneida community. His most controversial teaching focused on "complex marriage." Jesus had told the Sadducees that "in the resurrection they neither marry, nor are given in marriage, but are as the angels of God in heaven." Since Noyes believed that Jesus's return had created the conditions for a heavenlike experience on earth, in his community, as in heaven, there would be no individual marriages. Yet unlike Lee, Noyes believed in sex. In his community, every man was married to every woman and every woman to every man. Community leaders taught new members that they must "abolish" sexual exclusiveness "by the express injunction of Christ and the apostles." Rather than treat sex as something secret or impure, Noyes taught his followers to celebrate it as an important spiritual act that demonstrated communal love.[7]

But in Oneida, Noyes did not preside over some kind of endless, free-love orgy. He established a few basic rules. First, to partner up, a community member needed to ask permission through a third party to ensure that both partners wanted to get together. And second, individuals could not discriminate. Noyes did not want members of the community getting too attached to other specific individuals.

The community practiced an early form of eugenics by deciding what pairs would make the "best" babies independently of parents' individual relationship with each other. The group also engaged in a form of communal childrearing, another radical innovation for the time. To control procreation and to limit unplanned pregnancies, Noyes instructed men not to "spill their seed" (ejaculate), which he called "male continence." His rules reduced unwanted pregnancies, freed sex from reproduction, and took women's sexual desires seriously in an era when men often treated women as asexual.

Noyes went to great lengths to explain and defend male continence in his writings. He attacked claims that "nature requires a periodical and somewhat frequent discharge of the seed," which he viewed as an unholy argument in favor of masturbation. "For it is obvious that before marriage men have no lawful method of discharge but masturbation." Then, after marriage, "it is as foolish and cruel to expend one's seed on a wife merely for the sake of getting rid of it, as it would be to fire a gun at one's best friend merely for the sake of unloading it. If a blunderbuss must be emptied, and the charge cannot be drawn, it is better to fire into the air than to kill somebody with it." Men did not need to ejaculate, he insisted.[8]

Young people at Oneida experienced complex marriage in ways their parents did not. Most had entered the community through their parents, not by choice—and they had not consented to a system that subjected them to sex with randomly assigned partners. Not surprisingly, those eager to form relationships looked to their peers, not the community elders, for companionship. But Noyes did not want young people pairing up with each other. Furthermore, teenage relationships might well lead to unwanted pregnancies.

To solve this "problem," Noyes developed another community innovation called "ascending fellowship," which proved traumatic to many of the community's young people. It served the dual purposes of trying to ensure that young people did not grow attached to each other and of helping young men learn male continence. Noyes paired older Oneidans with younger members to introduce the community's sexual practices. Older men chose young women, and older women chose young men. In the latter case, women past menopause proved ideal for training young men since they could not become pregnant. Noyes himself frequently served as young female virgins' first sexual partner, since he saw himself as the most enlightened, spiritual member of the community. His actions, he claimed, demonstrated that all were equal, and that he had time for even its youngest members. Critics rightly suspect that his motives may have been less pure.

Although the Oneida community never expanded beyond a few hundred members, for decades it remained relatively stable. But in the 1880s, facing both the challenge of replacing the elderly Noyes and continual opposition from some of those raised in Oneida as well as those on the outside, the community disbanded. One of the great American utopian experiments, based in revivalism, millennialism, perfectionism, and a form of sexual liberation, had survived for decades, but it came to an end without achieving its goals. The United States, and the world, had come no closer to seeing the kingdom of God on earth than it had been in the 1830s. The community's more lasting legacy continues, however, in the form of the Oneida brand silverware found on countless dining room tables.

Perhaps the most successful Christian group born on American soil was the Church of Jesus Christ of Latter-day Saints, founded by Joseph Smith Jr. Unlike Noyes, who saw a pure millennium approaching, Smith's reading of the Bible, like that of William Miller, taught him that history was moving in a different direction. Signs appearing all around indicated that rather than expecting a thousand years of peace, Christians should prepare for an imminent apocalypse. God had not blessed the United States but seemed on the verge of pouring his wrath upon the new nation for its many sins. As the tribulation neared, Smith believed that God had called him to separate from the mainstream churches and to provide an alternative community that ultimately aimed to restore the United States as God's Holy Land.

Born in Vermont in 1805, Smith grew up relatively poor. His family owned some land, but his father lost it in bad business deals. Smith had little formal education but could read and write. The Smiths moved to New York in 1816, where religion at the time seemed disorderly and chaotic. Conservative Christianity was losing its power, liberalism was on the ascent in urban areas, revivalism was prevalent in rural communities, and liberationists were pitching competing approaches to the faith.

In 1820, the fourteen-year-old Smith went out to the woods and prayed that God would reveal himself and direct Smith to the true church. God and Jesus Christ, Smith later claimed, appeared and told him not to join any of the existing churches. Smith determined that the true Christian faith had vanished long ago and that God had chosen him to recover it and to help believers prepare for the final age. Three years later, in 1823, Smith claimed that an angel called Moroni visited him and told him of ancient golden plates inside a steel box hidden under a large rock in the nearby hills.

Meanwhile, Smith also dabbled in folk magic. Like many others, he pursued secret or esoteric knowledge. Smith had discovered a stone that he thought would lead him to hidden treasure. Neighbors saw Smith as a con man who aimed to swindle people out of their money. In 1826 his work caused enough problems that the local police charged him with being a "disorderly person," and a magistrate dubbed him a "glass looker" (which was not a compliment).

The following year, Smith claimed that he had found the promised plates from a place he called the Hill Cumorah in upstate New York. They were covered in text that Smith identified as "reformed Egyptian." Concealed with the plates were two stones, the Urim and the Thummin (Old Testament seer-stone-like instruments), which he initially used to decipher and translate the ancient text.

Smith likely placed the stone or stones at the bottom of his hat and then put his face into the hat to block out all the light. By looking at the stones he could translate the golden tablets, which sat on a nearby table. Smith dictated what he saw written on the stones, with his wife, Emma, and later a few friends serving as his scribes. The translations of the tablets provided the text for the *Book of Mormon*, first printed in 1830. After Smith completed the translation, and a few other people claimed they had seen the plates, the plates vanished.

The *Book of Mormon*, broken up into books, chapters, and verses like a modern Bible, told an incredible story. It described the history of a group of ancient Hebrews who left Jerusalem around 600 BCE. They traveled to the bottom of the Arabian Peninsula and then sailed across vast oceans, landing somewhere in the Americas. Eventually, the descendants of the pioneering adventurers split into competing factions, called Nephites and Lamanites. But then Jesus, following his crucifixion and resurrection outside of Jerusalem, appeared in North America, where he brought a temporary peace to the warring groups. When the tribes later returned to war, the Lamanites gained the upper hand against the Nephites. A man named Mormon led the latter group and before he died, Mormon recorded the history of his people and of Jesus's extraordinary visit. Mormon's son, Moroni, the last Nephite, finished the text that became the *Book of Mormon* and buried it around 400 AD. Moroni later appeared to Smith in the form of an angel with instructions on how to recover his father's text. Meanwhile, the Lamanites, the Indigenous tribes of the Americas, lost all memory of their origins.

The discovery of the *Book of Mormon* provided the foundation for a new movement. Unlike other revivalists, Smith depended more on the revelation of a new holy text than on his own skill and charisma as a preacher. Further revelations led Smith to expand his modern canon. They included the *Pearl of Great Price*, *Doctrine and Covenants*, and other subsequent writings. Smith remained at the church's center, assuming the roles of seer, translator, prophet, apostle, and elder. He claimed to have restored the faith delivered once and for all to the saints, but what he produced was as American as George Washington. Once Smith printed the *Book of Mormon*, he incorporated his followers into a movement he called the Church of Jesus Christ of Latter-day Saints and began dispatching missionaries to spread the faith.

The United States played a central role in Latter-day Saints' origin story and in their end-times beliefs. Smith and other early members believed that God would use their nation to help fulfill last-days prophecy. Smith may have also prophesied that in the great days of tribulation the US Constitution would hang by a thread, and the saints would rescue it. Regardless of the authenticity of the prophecy, the conviction—that the Constitution was a sacred document that God had called the saints to protect—became an important tenant of the faith.

Initially, Smith's followers gathered in Kirtland, Ohio. As persecution for their unorthodox beliefs increased, Smith claimed that he received a new revelation instructing the saints to move to a spot near Independence, Missouri. This, he revealed, marked the location of the original Garden of Eden, and it would serve as the seat of Jesus's new kingdom, the new Jerusalem. But mobs and political adversaries chased the saints out of Missouri as well. They next settled in Illinois, in a place they called Nauvoo.

Smith became the mayor of Nauvoo, which grew quickly, with converts moving in from across North America and England. The saints' extensive missionary work had yielded good results. To protect the community, Smith organized a paramilitary unit. Violence, he knew, would continue to dog the faithful. The free-exercise clause of the First Amendment again proved almost meaningless to those on the margins of American religious power.

Latter-day Saints' beliefs diverged from more traditional Christian theologies in a handful of ways. Smith taught followers that God had called him to reinstitute the Old Testament practice of plural marriage, or polygamy. God told Smith in a revelation, "I the Lord justified my Servents Abraham, Isaac and Jacob; as also Moses, David and Solomon my Servents as touching the principle and doctrine of their having many wives, and concubines." Smith, he instructed, should do the same. This, God told him, represented "a new and an everlasting covenant" that Smith must obey for him and his wives to become "Gods." Smith obeyed.[9]

Smith believed that "sealing" in marriage assured partnerships in the afterlife and that men might have more than one wife to assist them. Smith had begun taking new wives before the revelation, and he married more than thirty women in all, ranging in age from fourteen to fifty-six, including some married to other men. His original wife, Emma, felt betrayed by the practice and had a hard time accepting it as God's will.

In 1840, Smith introduced the practice of baptism for the dead. He explained to the saints that baptism was essential for salvation, and that they could serve as proxies for their deceased ancestors, accepting the sacrament on behalf of their parents and grandparents and previous generations. For this reason, Latter-day Saints, more than any other American religious group, obsessed over genealogy. They needed to learn their family lineages to help bring those who had passed away with them into the celestial kingdom.

Had Smith chosen to practice this new Christianity quietly with a small group of adherents, perhaps he would not have aroused substantial opposition. Instead, in 1844 he ran for president of the United

States, demonstrating that the Latter-day Saints aimed to remake the nation. Smith demanded that Americans live up to their claims about religious freedom. He recognized, like the Shakers and many others, that Americans did not actually have the freedom to practice dissenting faiths, or to practice no faith at all. Mainstream protestants shaped every part of American politics and culture. Smith, however, called for Americans to embrace and honor the Constitution and the First Amendment's free-exercise clause.

At about the same time, a group of dissidents in Nauvoo published a newspaper critical of the church leadership. The Latter-day Saints–led city council shut down their presses. Outsiders, incensed by what they saw as Smith's willingness to suspend constitutional rights and fearing the prophet's growing power, arrested him and his brother Hyram Smith. While the Smiths awaited trial, a mob of 250 men stormed the jail and killed them. No one was ever convicted for the murders.

Smith's close ally Brigham Young took over as the church's leader and prophet. He told the saints that they must continue the work initiated by the group's founders, but not in Nauvoo. Perhaps the United States had fallen beyond redemption. He instructed the saints to leave for the Great Salt Lake basin in Utah, which Mexico claimed at the time. The Latter-day Saints, rather than remake the United States, chose to leave the country. In 1846, they began a great trek from Illinois to their new homeland among the Utes, Shoshone, and Paiutes. In Utah they established a new Zion and reimagined and reconfigured their apocalyptic visions of the last days, incorporating their sense of themselves as exiles in the "wilderness" awaiting the judgment of God to fall on the unfaithful. Although Smith had taught that regions in Missouri and then Illinois would serve as the base of their millennial kingdom, Young helped the saints come to see the new lands they inhabited in the West as sacred terrain central to the old stories contained in the *Book of Mormon*.

But the peace would not last. Not for Latter-day Saints, and not for other dissenting Christian groups.

Utopian visionaries sought to build the kingdom of God in North America, imagining a righteous Christian society that would serve as a model for the entire nation. But their dreams soon met fierce opposition. Mainstream religious and political leaders, threatened by these radical alternatives, moved swiftly to suppress them. Rival Christian factions clashed over what a godly society should look like, and over the boundaries of First Amendment protections. Their competing visions and power struggles exposed the deep tensions and contradictions at the heart of religious activists' efforts to forge a unified Christian America in a diverse and pluralistic nation.

Curbing the spread of alternative religious ideas was not the only concern of mainstream Christian leaders. They also believed that building God's kingdom on earth required that they establish clear moral standards and compel the public to abide by them. To make this possible, mainstream church leaders organized dozens of Christian-infused voluntary societies, each with its own mandates for Christianizing the early republic. Perhaps, they speculated, if Americans had the proper morals, they would find strange alternative religious communities less appealing.

11

BUILDING THE MORAL ESTABLISHMENT

After the revolution, church and state remained closely linked in many parts of the country. But that was beginning to change. Connecticut's representatives determined in 1818 that they needed to end their support for Congregationalists, enacting at the state level what the First Amendment had done at the federal level. Their move sent minister Lyman Beecher into what he called "a time of great depression and suffering." "It was the worst attack I ever met in my life," he confessed. "It was as dark a day as ever I saw." He described "the injury done to the cause of Christ" as "irreparable." The loss of an established church seemed to guarantee a falling away from the Christian faith and the end of God's blessings on the region and eventually the nation.[1]

To Beecher's surprise, separating church from state, rather than smothering Christianity, instead revitalized it. Disestablishment, the minister later realized, "cut the churches loose from dependance on state support. It threw them wholly on their own resources and on God. They say ministers have lost their influence; the fact is, they have gained."[2]

Like Beecher, many ministers felt anxious about the future. Church attendance during the revolutionary era had been low, and no one knew how having a godless constitution might affect American Christianity. Protestant leaders did not think any nation could prosper apart from God, and the stakes seemed higher for Americans than for any other people. "This nation," Beecher asserted, "has been raised up by Providence to exert an efficient instrumentality in this work of moral renovation." Every prior effort in history to build a godly commonwealth had failed. But Beecher, like his Puritan forebearers, believed that this time, faithful Christians would prevail.[3]

The resurgence of revivalism was one means for Christianizing the new nation. Social reform was another. Beecher and an army of religious activists from across the major denominations—conservatives, revivalists, liberals, and liberationists—sought in the first half of the nineteenth century to transform the United States into a moral empire. They believed that for republican government to work, the country needed virtuous citizens inculcated with particular kinds of generic Christian values. Since the government could not fund the nation's churches, the churches had to find other ways to raise and shape strong Christian men and women. Christian activists set out to enforce their beliefs through law and custom. They built dozens of voluntary societies with goals that ranged from educating children to keeping adults off liquor. God, they believed, demanded action. "The course which is now adopted by Christians of all denominations," Beecher asserted, "to support and extend, at home and abroad, religious and moral influence; would seem to indicate the purpose of God to render this nation, extensively, the almoners of his mercy to the world."[4]

To compensate for separating church from state, protestant leaders and reformers worked to erect a quasi-official religious establishment to promote and maintain a thoroughly protestant culture. They hoped to perfect humanity, and they modified their theology to justify their practices. Old understandings of original sin and humans' inherent depravity gave way to faith in the individual to overcome evil and live a godly life. They expected their work to redeem humankind and inaugurate the millennium kingdom of God. The United States, purified in the fires of revolution, might yet represent the new Israel if his faithful could create godly laws that would generate a godly society.

The architects of the new moral establishment faced many challenges in a rapidly changing nation. In 1803, President Thomas Jefferson purchased the Louisiana Territory from the French, doubling the geographic size of the United States, and, within a few decades, the number of states had doubled as well. The population expanded rapidly through both reproduction and immigration. The largest number of newcomers arrived from Ireland, with Germans and Scandinavians also coming in substantial numbers. The rising number of immigrants as a percentage of the overall population fostered anxieties among some native-born citizens who wanted to ensure that foreigners and their American-born children shared their goals and values. The traffic in human bodies continued as well. Due primarily to reproduction, the nation's enslaved population grew exponentially.

The shift away from the family economy to a larger market spurred the rise of clear economic classes distinguished by substantial disparities in wealth. Although ministers fretted over how people spent their time and money, few expressed any concerns with the overall economic system. While they sought to mitigate its excesses and support those affected by economic shifts, most religious leaders, aside from a few fringe visionaries, found little difficulty in reconciling capitalism with Christianity. They believed that if moral and religious growth kept pace with economic growth, everything would be fine.

As protestant leaders adjusted to these changes, they sought to restructure American culture around their ideals and beliefs. They claimed George Washington as inspiration. "Of all the dispositions and habits, which lead to political prosperity," the president had explained in his farewell address, "Religion and morality are indispensable supports." Washington claimed that "National morality" could not "prevail in exclusion of religious principle." Protestant reformers stepped up to offer the religious principles they found indispensable to political prosperity.[5]

Religious activists from across the country hoped to ensure that even without a state church, protestant beliefs and ideas would dominate every part of Americans' lives. Recognizing that making the United States a Christian empire required substantial consensus, the leaders of the major denominations rallied together around social reform. "God," Beecher claimed, "began to pour out his Spirit upon the churches; and voluntary associations of Christians were raised up to apply and extend that influence." He called reform groups "a sort of disciplined moral militia, prepared to act upon every emergency, and repel every encroachment upon the liberties and morals of the State."[6]

Education became a major focus of reformers. Many protestant leaders believed that building a Christian commonwealth began with the proper instruction of children. As the book of Proverbs explains, "Train up a child in the way he should go: and when he is old, he will not depart from it." Beecher believed that "the religious education of the family, and the moral culture of our schools and colleges must be secured" for the nation to thrive.[7]

Reformers saw the Bible as the foundation of American education. To meet the demands of the growing population for copies of the holy writ, a series of local Bible associations along the Atlantic coast banded together in 1816 to form the American Bible Society (ABS). Its leaders had two explicit goals: spread the Christian gospel and build a Christian "civilization" in the United States and then the world. They translated the Bible into foreign languages and printed and distributed it. In many rural areas, a Bible from the ABS might be the only book in the house of a White family. Enslaved families, however, did not usually receive ABS Bibles. Critics of slavery pushed ABS leaders not to discriminate as they worked to distribute their Bibles, but the organization's national leaders instead left it to their regional auxiliaries to determine if they should provide texts to those in bondage. Regional leaders usually opted not to, leading antislavery activists to view the ABS as complicit in the slave system.

In 1825, another group with related goals formed the American Tract Society. As in the American Bible Society, its leaders hoped to flood the nation with cheap literature that would attract converts, educate the public, and improve morals. These eager proponents of protestant Christianity embraced the latest technologies and, in the process, transformed mass communications. Within a few years, the society was publishing on average five pages of material for every person in the United States. The ecumenical editorial team included members from Baptist, Congregationalist, Dutch Reformed, Episcopalian, Presbyterian, and Methodist denominations. No tracts went out under the society's name that did not meet the unanimous approval of the full team. In the early years of the society, editors tended to gently criticize slavery. But as the organization's audience grew, editors sought to avoid offending Southern enslavers and therefore did not take on the institution directly. By the 1850s, critics viewed the American Tract Society, like the ABS, as bolstering human bondage.

Protestant activists used local public or common schools to spread their values. American community leaders approached education haphazardly; some communities provided good schools for their children, while others did not. Unitarian Horace Mann, a reformer active in the fight against a host of evils including slavery, tobacco, alcohol, profanity, lotteries, and dancing, opened a series of schools in Massachusetts that served as models for the rest of the nation. His ideals reflected those of the liberal, ecumenical stream—he hoped to inculcate children with Christian morals and values but did not want to get caught up in theological debates.

Mann's generic protestant Christianity and aversion to religious controversies drove some conservatives and revivalists to question the authenticity of his faith. His lack of dogmatism troubled them. Mann assured critics that Christianity remained central to his philosophy of modern education. He insisted that he had never "attempted to exclude religious instruction from School, or to exclude the Bible from school." He corrected those who called the public school system irreligious or anti-Christian. "Our system," he explained, "earnestly inculcates all Christian morals; it founds its morals on the basis of religion; it welcomes the religion of the Bible; and, in receiving the Bible, it allows it to do what it is allowed to do in no other system—to speak for itself. But here it stops," he continued, "not because it claims to have compassed all truth; but because it disclaims to act as an umpire between hostile religious opinions." He thought that public schools, to succeed, needed to teach protestant Christianity without falling into the kinds of theological debates that separated liberationists, revivalists, conservatives, and liberals.[8]

The nation's most popular public-school curriculum reflected Mann's generic protestant morals. Many common schools taught from the Eclectic Readers. These books, written by Presbyterian minister William Holmes McGuffey, eventually sold more than one hundred million copies. McGuffey wove protestant ideas into the text. His book for young readers included passages such as, "Oh! my God, let me do no sin. Aid me to do as I am bid. Our God can see all we do. Let all I do be fit for his eye." Another passage read, "Do you know who made the sun? God made it. God al-so made the moon, and all the stars. They give us light by night. God gives us all we have, and keeps us a-live. We should love God, and o-bey his ho-ly will."[9]

For slightly older readers, McGuffey drafted passages explaining the Christian faith, which he followed with corresponding questions. "Will little children be raised from the dead?" the minster asked his readers. "Where must we all appear after we are raised from the dead? Of what shall we then be judged?" Questions following a passage on the evils of profanity read, "What is it to swear? Is it a very foolish habit? Is it polite to swear? Is it very wicked?" To children in American public schools, the correct answers should have been obvious.[10]

McGuffey instructed students to practice their reading by studying the texts of the Lord's Prayer and the Ten Commandments. He also stressed a providential view of history that reinforced American views of the exceptional nature of the United States. He emphasized, for example, the heroics of Christopher Columbus and George Washington, and he highlighted the "savage" nature of Indigenous Americans (while also noting that they had been mistreated by White Americans).

As the number of schools expanded across the nation, so did the need for teachers. Lyman Beecher's daughter Catharine founded a seminary in 1823 with the express purpose of training women for work in schools. She believed that educating women would ensure that the United States realized its potential. "The formation of the moral and intellectual character of the young is committed mainly to the female hand," Beecher declared. "The mother forms the character of the future man; the sister bends the fibres that are hereafter to be the forest tree; the wife sways the heart, whose energies may turn for good or for evil the destinies of a nation." Women, therefore, needed good educations for more than themselves. "Let the women of a country be made virtuous and intelligent," she assured readers, "and the men will certainly be the same. The proper education of a man decides the welfare of an individual; but educate a woman, and the interests of the whole family are secured."[11]

Yet Beecher was no liberationist. She believed women should exert their influence through their children, or through training other people's children, and not through the ballot box. In one of her most popular books, she claimed that "in civil and political affairs, American women take no interest or concern." However, she noted a few exceptions where women should lead. Their wisdom is superior to men's, she claimed, on issues "pertaining to the education of their children, in the selection and support of a clergyman, in all benevolent enterprises, and in all questions relating to morals or manners." Like many reformers of her generation, Beecher challenged some of the restrictions that men had put on women, but she nevertheless continued to see men and women as inherently different and acting in separate spheres.[12]

Reformers saw a lack of literacy as one threat to the republic; the widespread consumption of alcohol represented another. In the first decades of the nineteenth century, Americans drank. A lot. On average they consumed seven gallons of hard alcohol per year—many drank throughout the day, every day. In previous generations, most Christians did not view drinking as a problem or a sin, unless excesses sparked other problems. Religious celebrations often featured alcohol. Even the Puritans drank, contrary to modern stereotypes. But there were exceptions. Quakers saw alcohol as evil, and revivalists warned that intoxicating spirits undermined the goal of sinless perfection.

As the economy shifted, drinking became a larger threat to the success of the republic. Drinking on a farm by yourself with only the swine to keep you company may not have been a good idea, but drinking in a factory near heavy equipment was much more dangerous. In addition, excessive drinking sometimes undercut families' economic stability, bred physical abuse, and could destroy a person's health.

To curtail alcohol consumption, Christian reformers in Boston in 1826 established the American Temperance Society. Initially they endeavored to reduce the amount of alcohol Americans consumed, but soon many reformers aimed for a more ambitious goal—they pushed legislatures to prohibit drinking altogether. They also asked individuals to pledge not to drink. Lyman Beecher, who had his hands in almost every reform pot, became one of the leading advocates of temperance. In a widely printed series of sermons, he called drinking "the sin of our land," and warned that it "is coming in upon us like a flood; and if anything shall defeat the hopes of the world, which hang upon our experiment in civil liberty, it is that river of fire."[13]

Over the next few years, new local and regional temperance societies sprung up all over the nation. In Philadelphia, Black Americans formed the Moyamensing Temperance Society, which counted over one thousand members who had pledged not to drink. In the 1830s some towns went "dry," meaning they banned the sale and consumption of alcohol within their limits. In 1846 Maine became the first state to ban the sale of alcohol.

Protestants believed that although they had no federally established church, they could and should use the law to impose their ideals on the nation. Ministers instructed their congregations on how to vote, seeking to spread their values. Beecher called on all Christians to "enforce reformation of morals by law" and to never cast a ballot for "an enemy to the Bible."[14]

In addition to shaping school curriculum and regulating alcohol, reformers sought laws focused on maintaining the Sunday Sabbath and against blasphemy, obscenity, profanity, dancing, and lotteries.

Others launched new societies focused on reforming jails, helping women escape sex work, caring for the poor, and serving those with mental illness, among many other things. Activists believed that through their voluntary efforts and political engagement, linking churches with reform ministries, they could perfect the United States and eventually humankind.

While many reformers worked to improve American society, others aimed to reform individuals. They emphasized Christians' need to perfect themselves as a means of perfecting their communities. Such convictions inspired the rise of a renewed "holiness" movement that looked both forward and backward, seeking to revive elements of John Wesley and Francis Asbury's emphasis on disciplined living while also rethinking and redefining what that meant for the life of the individual American Christian.

Methodist Phoebe Palmer helped spark the holiness revival. As she studied the Bible and sought to understand salvation and the Christian life, she kept returning to the biblical command "Be ye holy." How, she wondered, could any human truly be holy? The answer came to her through both the Bible and a dream. The "prize of holiness," she wrote, "had been presented by the dictations of the blessed word, as an attainment toward which, every redeemed one should not only aspire, but also possess—the rightful heritage of the believer." In other words, all true Christians could be holy.[15]

Palmer told followers that as she pursued holiness, supernatural forces clashed in the spiritual realm all around her. Angels appeared in dreams, and demons attacked her, tempting her to sin. Recognizing that her heavenly visions would make some Americans skeptical, she asked, "But are we to reject all manifestations from God, or answers to prayer, that may be given in dreams or visions of the night?" Since the early church, she concluded, "God hath spoken to his people in this manner."[16]

In 1837 Palmer believed she had discovered how to achieve holiness and entire sanctification. She simply needed to pledge herself totally to Jesus and he would cleanse her of all sin. She also needed to tell others what she learned. Married to a wealthy physician, Palmer had the resources to focus on ministry and to spread her ideas. She and her sister launched a weekly "Tuesday Meeting for the Promotion of Holiness" in her capacious and opulent New York City home. In 1843 Palmer published a book, *The Way of Holiness*, which Christians still read today. The book grew from her determination to explain how to be a "Bible Christian." As Palmer's popularity grew, she taught and lectured in churches in North America and the United Kingdom. While she did not offer a full-throated defense of ordaining women as preachers, she emphasized that in Christ there was neither "male nor female."

Palmer believed that holiness influenced both the individual's relationship with God and the development of a more virtuous society. Like her reformist counterparts, she spurned alcohol and worked for temperance, embracing the social side of her perfectionist faith. She dodged the issue of slavery, however, insisting that those attending her Tuesday meetings not discuss the issue. The application of holiness, apparently, had its limits when the issue of human bondage arose.

Through her holiness meetings and subsequent publications, Palmer became one of the most influential religious leaders of the nineteenth century. She inspired hundreds of thousands of people, and eventually millions, to dedicate themselves to godly living. Over time, however, tensions between Methodists who embraced her radical holiness beliefs and those who took more moderate positions led to schism, sparking the rise of a handful of new holiness denominations, including the Church of the Nazarene and the Wesleyan Church.

Like protestants, American Catholics also drank from the fountains of reform. The Catholic Church thrived in the early republic even as its members remained very much excluded from the centers of cultural and political power. As the country's borders extended to include former French and Spanish territories, a substantial number of Catholics were incorporated into the United States. Immigration from Europe, particularly Germany and Ireland, further increased the Catholic population in North America. The church also had numerous Black members, including some who remained enslaved. For the American Catholic leadership, establishing a unified church made up of Spanish, French, German, Irish, English, and African Americans represented a constant challenge.

Aiming to bring some order to the North American communion, in 1790 the pope appointed Maryland priest and Jesuit John Carroll to serve as the first bishop in the United States. His cousin Charles Carroll was the only Catholic to sign the Declaration of Independence. John Carroll worked to organize the church and expand its influence, and in 1808 the pope elevated him to archbishop. To keep up with the growing Catholic population, church leaders created additional dioceses in the major urban centers of Boston, Philadelphia, and New York. To help reach Western Whites, they also added a new diocese in Bardstown, Kentucky, about ninety miles from where the Cane Ridge revival fires had burned just a few years earlier. New Orleans had a large and important French Catholic population as well, which after the Louisiana Purchase became part of the American Catholic Church. Father Serra and his Franciscan brothers continued overseeing the church in the Spanish-claimed territory of the far West and Southwest. To train new clergymen in the United States, in 1820 Catholics opened St. Mary's Seminary in Baltimore. Church leaders also recruited priests from Europe and especially France, which led to challenges and some conflicts as French Catholic leaders tried to impose their ideas on predominately German and Irish congregants.

In 1808, adult convert Elizabeth Ann Seton accepted an invitation to help a group of French priests start a school at St. Mary's Seminary in Baltimore. While there she established a new religious community focused on serving poor children. Seton and the priests began recruiting other women to help with the growing project and in 1809 Carroll gave her the title "Mother Seton." Aided by a wealthy benefactor, Seton and her allies launched the Sisters of Charity of St. Joseph, the first women's religious community in the United States not tied to a European ministry. Over the next decade Seton and her allies in major East Coast cities established schools and orphanages and helped provide medical care to the needy. Their work laid the foundation for the Catholic parochial school system in the United States. In 1975, Pope

Paul VI canonized Seton, making her the first American-born Catholic saint.

As the influence of the Catholic Church expanded, protestant groups became increasingly concerned. They feared that Catholics aimed to eliminate the separation between church and state and establish a government led by Catholics. Protestants believed that, if given the opportunity, Catholics might persecute American protestants, as had occurred in different historical contexts and locations. Protestants fretted that if they failed to act, their dreams of an American millennium would vanish like sins expunged in the confessional.

Many protestant activists viewed staunching Catholic influence as a necessary part of their reform agenda. Samuel F. B. Morse, the inventor of the telegraph and Morse code, warned Americans in 1834 that they had failed to recognize the threat at their doorsteps. Catholics, Morse fretted, "are already the most powerful and dangerous sect in the country." Morse warned readers of a global Catholic cabal conspiring to take over the country's political system, make Catholicism the state church, and destroy everything White protestant Americans hoped to build. "All true patriots must wake to the cry of danger. They must up, and gird themselves for battle. It is no false alarm. Our liberties are in danger. The Philistines are upon us." Morse argued that curtailing Catholic influence required curtailing immigration.[17]

To rouse Americans against the Catholic Church, protestants spun incredible conspiracy theories. They used the hierarchal and somewhat secretive nature of the Catholic faith, along with priests' celibacy and nuns' cloistered lives, as the inspiration for salacious novels, memoirs, and exposés. The narratives of ex-nuns, real and fictional, had the greatest circulation.

As a young woman, Rebecca Reed had attended school at the Ursuline Convent in Charlestown, Massachusetts, just outside of Boston. She aspired to become a nun herself but the experience did not work out as she expected. She claimed that while living in the convent in 1832, the nuns and priests cut off all her communication with the outside world. After about six months as a virtual prisoner, Reed escaped out the back door never to return.[18]

Reed shared her story with protestant leaders in Boston and then wrote a book about her experience. As she drafted the book, rumors about its contents and the alleged abuse occurring at the Ursuline Convent grew. Anti-Catholic agitators decided to organize a protest in 1834. They believed that the nuns had either killed or secretly held captive another young nun who like Reed had supposedly tried to escape. The nuns and their students were eventually forced to flee from the mob, which burned down the convent.

Immediately after the fire, Boston leaders put together a committee to investigate what had happened. They condemned the riot, calling it "a base and cowardly act" against "defenceless females." The perpetrators "deserve the contempt and detestation of the community." The committee's findings confirmed in the minds of anti-Catholic agitators how deeply the church had penetrated into their community. Even city leaders, it appeared, had joined with the papists in defending the nuns.[19]

Just a couple of years later another memoir from another ex-nun appeared, which caused a much greater sensation. In 1836 a woman called Maria Monk, who claimed to have escaped from a convent in Montreal, published *Awful Disclosures of Maria Monk, or, The Hidden Secrets of a Nun's Life in a Convent Exposed!* Like Reed, Monk described entering the convent young and idealistic, only to have her dreams almost immediately shattered. As soon as she took her vows, her superiors told her that she must make herself available to priests for their sexual pleasure. She had no choice but to "live in the practice of criminal intercourse" with them. Then they informed her that if sex with priests resulted in pregnancy, nuns' newborns were "always baptized, and immediately strangled." Securing eternal life through baptism, the babies, the nuns told Monk, would be happy in heaven and would, if they could, thank those who had ended their lives. Monk even described the pit under the convent that held the corpses of dead infants.[20]

Monk also learned of—and participated in—the murder of a nun who had refused to sleep with priests. The nuns and priests smothered the insolent woman to death, smashing her with a mattress and their weight.[21]

Maria Monk's book shocked the nation. Investigators eventually revealed that Monk, with the help of a few leading New York protestant ministers, had made up her story. It was pure fiction. She and her allies hoped that *Awful Disclosures* would undermine Catholicism. Despite the book's fraudulent origins, only *Uncle Tom's Cabin* sold more copies in the mid-nineteenth century.

To corral and direct growing anti-Catholic fervor, some protestants organized a series of secret societies and then in the 1850s a new political organization, the American Party. Many Americans at the time feared that threats from abroad might undermine American security at home. They also worried about how immigrants might change the nation's identity and fretted that they might hurt the economy. The established political parties seemed unwilling or unable to address their concerns and so the organizers of the American Party stepped into the breech, creating a new alternative.

Members of the American Party were notoriously secretive. When questioned about their activities or rituals, they typically replied, "I know nothing." This evasiveness earned them the nickname "Know-Nothings." Their priorities, in contrast, were not a secret. Know-Nothing party leaders advocated for protestant-based Bible reading in the nation's public schools, eradication of parochial schools, stricter immigration and naturalization policies, affirmation of gender hierarchies and women's subordinate status, and a prohibition on Catholics holding political office. New York congressman Thomas R. Whitney argued, "AMERICANS ONLY SHALL GOVERN AMERICA." In the 1850s Know-Nothings managed to elect more than one hundred congressmen and numerous governors and other political leaders. The American Party's focus on foreign threats provided a brief moment of unity in an era defined by many internal political divisions centered especially on slavery. Party activists developed a framework that subsequent nativists utilized to redirect anti-immigrant sentiment into political allegiance.

Americans believed that for their experiment in democracy to work, they needed to eradicate foreign and subversive forms of Christianity. Roman Catholics and Mormons both seemed to threaten the American mission and were therefore unworthy of Constitutional protections, as this image illustrates. (credit: Thomas Nast, "Religious Liberty Is Guaranteed: But Can We Allow Foreign Reptiles to Crawl All Over Us?," Library of Congress)

Meanwhile, the Catholic press tried to flip the script on the protestants. Journalists documented protestant lies against the Catholic Church, exposed the falsehoods embedded in the salacious literature published by protestants, and highlighted anti-Catholic violence. In the process, they positioned themselves as the true Americans who championed democracy, church-state separation, and building a just and tolerant society. But protestants still maintained the upper hand. Although the Know-Nothing party soon faded, its core ideas endured. A populist, anti-immigrant Christianity has shaped American political life in profound ways ever since.

With the First Amendment prohibiting a national establishment of religion, and most states disestablishing their official churches, religious leaders worked to weave their ideals and values into American law, politics, education, and culture. They claimed that only through the privileging of their beliefs and the silencing of others—whether

Catholics, Latter-day Saints, or Shakers—could they secure the future of American democracy. In the process, protestant reformers helped erect a multi-denominational, unofficial, protestant-infused shadow establishment that dominated American life for more than a century. They had so much success that in 1835 Alexis de Tocqueville concluded, "There is no country in the whole world in which the Christian religion retains a greater influence over the souls of men than in America."[22]

Nevertheless, reformers never felt content focusing just on the United States. "If we look at our missionaries abroad," Beecher counseled his followers, "and witness the smiles of heaven upon their efforts, our confidence, that it is the purpose of God to render our nation a blessing to the world, will be increased." Indeed, American reformers working to erect the kingdom of God in the United States believed that their success depended on exporting their faith and values to the rest of the world, which is exactly what they set out to do.[23]

PART III

A NATION IN CRISIS

12

GOING INTO ALL THE WORLD

On a sweltering, humid summer afternoon in 1806, five students from Williams College in Massachusetts met together in a grove of trees to pray. As the meeting progressed, the sky grew dark, rain began to fall, lightning flashed, and the earth trembled. The students scrambled under a haystack to wait out the storm. While the heavens raged, one member of the group, Samuel Mills, the twenty-three-year-old son of a revivalist preacher, mentioned that he had been reading about British missionaries. He believed that Americans needed to join their fellow Christians in the ambitious work of spreading the gospel abroad.

Most American Christians at the time gave little thought to foreign missions. Going abroad with no invitation and little knowledge seemed dangerous. Until Western governments and their militaries had "civilized" foreign lands by force, many Christians believed, missionaries had little chance for success. But Mills did not hedge. He told the group that millions of "heathen" were lost and God wanted them to do something about it.

For the next few years Mills and his friends prayed and strategized. They believed that God wanted them to build an American foreign-missions movement but feared that if they shared their ideas they would look like fanatics. After Mills finished his studies at Williams, he and some classmates went to Andover Theological Seminary, a school that Congregationalist leaders founded in 1807. The first seminary in the nation, Andover served men who had already completed college work but who wanted or needed additional study in theology, the Bible, or other church-related disciplines. Its organizers believed that Harvard had drifted too far into liberal theology and Unitarianism. Andover offered an alternative theological education for those within the revivalist and conservative streams of the faith.

In 1810 Mills and some Andover friends believed that the time had finally come to share with church leaders their vision for global missions. They confessed that their minds had "been long impressed with the duty and importance of personally attempting a mission to the heathen." They aspired to fulfill Jesus's great commission, "Go ye therefore, and teach all nations, baptizing them in the name of the Father, and of the Son, and of the Holy Ghost: Teaching them to observe all things whatsoever I have commanded you" (Matthew 28:19–20).[1]

The "Haystack Prayer Meeting" marked the start of the American foreign missions movement. Mills and his allies worked with Congregationalist leaders to found the American Board of Commissioners for Foreign Missions (ABCFM). Soon many of the other major denominations either joined the ABCFM or launched their own similar missionary agencies. From that point on, foreign missionary work became a central feature of American Christianity.

As missionaries sought to fulfill the great commission, they helped shape the American empire and expand its global reach. They worked closely with diplomats to craft foreign policy in ways that served their interests. They also believed that it was their nation's destiny to expand across the continent and beyond, into new territories east and west. The more land the US government controlled, the more people missionaries could more easily reach. They drew on the state to support their labors, and in return they bolstered the power and influence of the American government around the world. Missionaries, historian Emily Conroy-Krutz demonstrated, "forced the government to articulate new conceptions of the rights of US citizens abroad and of the role of the United States as an engine of humanitarianism and religious freedom." They acted both as ambassadors for the gospel and as American imperialists weaving protestantism into American foreign policy, and they understood both roles as part of God's plan for building his kingdom.[2]

Jesus had promised that his followers would spread the gospel to all nations before the onset of the millennium. Reformers viewed the growing American missionary movement as a crucial step toward fulfilling that prophecy. "The long expected day is approaching," one ABCFM missionary advocate explained. "The Lord is shaking the nations; his friends in different parts of Christendom are roused from their slumbers; and unprecedented exertions are making for the spread of divine knowledge, and the conversion of the nations." Missionary leaders believed that the efforts of social reformers in the United States to perfect their communities meant little if they did not also carry the gospel to the rest of the world. God had not chosen Americans as his special people for the sake of the United States, but for the sake of the world.[3]

ABCFM executives hoped to send missionaries to locations where they had the greatest likelihood of success, places that in Jesus's words were "white already to the harvest." They aspired to spark faith among an interested population and then watch it spread like wildfire. They also promised to deliver an elevated form of "civilization." They did not separate Christian convictions from their White, American cultural identities and beliefs. "The Heathen are before you," two ABCFM missionaries admonished other Christians. "Their present miseries and their impending ruin call upon you to hasten to them the word of life." God wanted Christians to "go and pluck them as brands from the burning." Missionaries did not just prepare people for the afterlife but expected to save them from their supposed current sufferings, from their "backwards" cultures.[4]

Missionaries knew the work would challenge them. Veteran evangelist David Abeel delivered a characteristic sermon to commemorate the departure of new missionaries to Hawai'i and Africa. "You go where death may soon arrest you," he predicted, where illness, exhaustion, and bad climates "almost invariably produces some degree of bodily languor, and mental depression." The foreign people, he warned, were no better than the weather. They lacked religion and had "perverted notions of right and wrong," "blind attachment to their superstitions," and heaped "madness upon their idols." They practiced "dishonesty, deceit, treachery, cruelty, tyranny, and extreme selfishness." Such "evils" were "found, with some few modifications, in every heathen country." But no matter. The veteran told potential missionaries that God had called them to "toil" anyway, "and to toil under any circumstances, though it may often appear like labor thrown away." Despite such warnings of the inevitable hardships missionaries would routinely face, the ABCFM received hundreds of applications from eager men and women alike.[5]

The ABCFM sent its first missionaries to India in 1812, but the project quickly unraveled, and it took the Americans years to establish an effective mission in Bombay. The ABCFM also sent missionaries to the Middle East. Americans viewed Palestine as especially significant. Like Columbus hundreds of years earlier, they saw it as a sacred land whose people had forgotten their own history. They wanted to bring Jesus's gospel back to his homeland. Pliny Fisk, one of the earliest American missionaries to the Ottoman Empire, went forth to "besiege a great empire of sin, where Satan from ancient times has held undisputed possession of his strongholds, and erected his mightiest bulwarks," according to one ally. But Fisk had to proceed carefully. Ottoman leaders allowed missionaries to proselytize among Jews and other Christians, but did not want the foreigners targeting Muslims for conversion.[6]

ABCFM executives looked to Hawai'i as well. Due to the Hawaiian Islands' strategic location along Pacific trade routes, Hawaiians had long hosted foreign visitors. Occasionally young Hawaiian men would take jobs on merchant ships, and some settled in the United States. Of the latter group, a few converted to Christianity, including one named ʻŌpūkahaʻia ("Henry Obookiah" to the Americans). ʻŌpūkahaʻia, like other Hawaiians before him, sailed around Cape Horn and on to New York in search of work. He eventually made his way to New England, where he found a home with the family of Yale president and revivalist Timothy Dwight.

ʻŌpūkahaʻia drafted a memoir, which after his death missionaries selectively edited to use for their own purposes. It told the story of his "rescue" by White Yale students and his conversion to revivalist Christianity, which helped convince American mission leaders that God had primed Hawaiians for the gospel. They saw ʻŌpūkahaʻia's story as confirmation that a backward-seeming people just needed an honest encounter with true Christianity to find salvation.[7]

In 1820 the ABCFM dispatched its first missionaries to Hawai'i. Six of the seven missionary couples in the group had recently married. ABCFM leaders preferred not to send out male missionaries without wives. Missionary executives feared that seductive "heathen" women would overwhelm men if they could not channel their sexuality into a sacred marriage bed. Missionary courtships and marriages often happened fast, and partners barely knew each other before uniting over their shared commitment to missionary work. Yet they believed so much in their calling that they left their families behind for what they knew might be the rest of their lives.

Women signed on to the ABCFM knowing they could contribute to the mission in many ways beyond just as marriage partners. They brought substantial biblical knowledge as well as important diplomatic skills. They also believed that their gender better suited them for some kinds of humanitarian work. In the same way that nineteenth-century Americans generally believed that women could serve as teachers for children, so too could they teach supposedly childlike foreigners the Christian gospel, especially if they did it in partnership with male leaders. Although most missionary women did not claim the title of minister or evangelist, they essentially filled those roles.

The male missionaries in the ABCFM expected to take the lead in the missionizing effort, to serve as heroic evangelists carrying the gospel to heathens. But as historian Jennifer Thigpen noted, they did not encounter in Hawai'i what they expected. Powerful women, including Ka'ahumanu, ruled the islands. The Hawaiians quickly developed important relationships with missionary wives. The women, more than the men, Thigpen argues, directed "the future of the mission and the nature of Hawaiian-American interaction."[8]

ABCFM leaders viewed the mission to Hawai'i, unlike those in India and the Middle East, as a success. Missionaries inspired many conversions, and local chiefs, sensing an opportunity to build mutually beneficial partnerships, allowed the missionaries to set up schools and churches. Within a decade thousands of Hawaiians were regularly attending protestant worship services. In 1853, ABCFM executives declared the islands "Christianized" and began redirecting resources to other projects and places. The American foothold they established provided the foundation for the islands' eventual colonization and forced integration into the US empire.

As American reformers looked to Christianize peoples around the world, they had not forgotten those closer to home. With the United States government acquiring new territory, Christian leaders aimed to serve White settlers moving west as well as those peoples whose lands became part of the United States through conquest.

Continuing warfare set the context for missionary work and inspired activists' belief that only Christianity could bring permanent peace. Two Shawnee leaders, the prophet Tenskwatawa and his brother Tecumseh, called on their own tribe as well as others in the Ohio Valley region to join with them in defending their rights and their lands. In 1804 Tenskwatawa began having visions that spurred Indigenous peoples to mount a defense. He drew followers from among the Shawnee, Wyandot, Potawatomi, Odawa, and others. He called for total separation from White American habits, trade, and alcohol. According to one of Tenskwatawa's followers, the prophet taught that the "Great Spirit" had revealed the abominable nature of Whites. "The *Americans* I did not make," the spirit told Tenskwatawa. "They are not my *Children*. But the children of the Evil Spirit. . . . They are numerous—But I hate them—They are unjust—They have taken away your Lands which were not made for them."[9]

Tenskwatawa and his followers, which now included members of fourteen tribes, built a new community in 1808 called Prophetstown where the Tippecanoe and Wabash rivers come together in present-day Indiana. Worried about the prophet's growing strength, in 1811 Indiana territorial governor William Henry Harrison ordered soldiers to attack Prophetstown. In the ensuing Battle of Tippecanoe, American troops forced those living in Prophetstown to flee. Harrison then burned the settlement to the ground. The next year, in the War of 1812, multiple tribes and individuals, including Tenskwatawa and Tecumseh, joined the British against the United States. Once the Americans gained the upper hand over the British, they turned against those tribes that had fought against them. They waged a war of extermination and even attacked Indigenous groups that had previously allied with the United States. Tecumseh died in battle in 1813 and Tenskwatawa fled to Canada.

In the years that followed, church leaders sought to prevent further violence by acting as intermediaries between Native tribes and the US government. Protestant missionaries often enjoyed the backing of political leaders who believed Christianization and "civilization" could assimilate Indigenous peoples into American society. Early presidents like George Washington and Thomas Jefferson held that, given time and proper influence, Native communities could be integrated.

But such ideals were inseparable from settler colonial ambitions. Political leaders also coveted Indigenous land, and the rhetoric of "civilization" provided a moral justification for dispossession. If Native peoples abandoned communal landholding and embraced White agricultural practices, they would, in effect, make more land available to settlers. If they refused, officials claimed this refusal proved their "uncivilized" status and used it to legitimize land seizures. In either case, Native communities were trapped: Adopting "civilized" practices meant surrendering land; resisting them offered justification for its confiscation.

Missionaries' priorities largely matched those of the government. ABCFM leaders developed what they dubbed a plan for "civilizing and christianizing the Pagan tribes of American Indians," which they implemented around the country.[10]

Missionaries put significant work into the Cherokee Nation in the southeastern United States, hoping to make it a model for future efforts. In the early nineteenth century, Moravians and Presbyterians had helped establish schools for Cherokees. Then in 1817, ABCFM missionaries opened multiple churches and schools on Cherokee land. Baptists and Methodists sent missionaries as well.

Cherokees developed a written alphabet that Whites and their Cherokee partners used to translate the Bible and hymns into the native language. "Would it be chimerical to calculate," ABCFM leaders asked, "that in the course of years not very long, the tribe at large would become English in their language, Christian in their religion, and civilized in their general habits and manners?" Missionaries, like the government, aspired to eradicate Cherokee identity, to destroy Indigenous culture, and to replace it with their own, all the while confident that they had the best interests of those they "civilized" at heart.[11]

Cherokees understood the relationship differently. They aimed to build productive alliances, enlist advocates, and find useful skills and tools for working with Whites. While most had little interest in the gods of settler colonialists, they understood that schooling could help them survive and defend themselves. They sought their own independence and sovereignty, not to lose their identity.

By the late 1820s, most state and federal policymakers had given up on the idea of assimilating tribes into the American body politic. They grew more interested in controlling Indian Territory without the Indians. The Cherokees had, by the government's racist standards, "civilized." They had a republican form of government, a written constitution, and broad literacy. They had even gone to war as allies of the US government against the Creek Nation. Still, President Andrew Jackson lobbied Congress to pass the Removal Act of 1830. The act mandated that Indigenous peoples including the Cherokees sign new treaties relinquishing their lands.

Missionaries and protestant leaders joined the debate over the Removal Act. Catharine Beecher sent anonymous petitions to Congress opposing it. ABCFM secretary Jeremiah Evarts published a series of protests under a pseudonym, predicting that current policies would conjure God's retribution. "The great Arbiter of nations never fails to take cognizance of national delinquencies," he warned. "No sophistry can elude his scrutiny." Senator Theodore Frelinghuysen of New Jersey, who later served as president of the ABCFM, took to the Senate floor to protest the Removal Act. "I insist that, by immemorial possession, as the original tenants of the soil," the Cherokees "hold a title beyond and superior to the British crown and her colonies, and to all adverse pretensions of our confederation and subsequent Union. God, in his Providence, planted these tribes on this Western continent, so far as we know, before Great Britain herself had a political existence."[12]

But Congress ignored the protests, and the vast majority of White American Christians felt either indifferent to or supportive of removal. In 1831 the Georgia state legislature, seeking to curb missionary influence, began requiring all Whites living within the boundaries of the Cherokee Nation to swear an oath of allegiance to uphold the laws of the state (rather than the laws of the tribal nation on whose land they lived). Many missionaries refused and local authorities arrested two of them. The missionaries sued and eventually received a hearing before the US Supreme Court. In *Worcester v. Georgia* (1832) the court ruled that the State of Georgia could not impose its own policies on tribal lands and, therefore, had erred in punishing the missionaries. But the decision did little to change conditions on the ground.

Sensing that Cherokees would not prevail in their quest for autonomy, most missionaries changed tactics. They encouraged Cherokee leaders to get as many concessions as possible from the federal government in return for moving west. Most Cherokees did not want to move, and they lost faith in the missionaries. In the late 1830s, the US government forcibly relocated them to what is now Oklahoma, a region then designated as "Indian Territory." This forced migration became known as the Trail of Tears. Some White missionaries came out of the Cherokee crisis with less faith in their government and a sobering recognition that their goals and those of the US government did not always align, while the Cherokees who had embraced Christianity discovered that for their people, the United States was no Christian paradise.

At about the same time that the United States government worked to force Cherokees off their land, missionary groups began looking for converts among the peoples of the Pacific Northwest. In 1833, White East Coast Christians read a fantastic magazine story. A group of men including three Nimiipuu (Nez Perce), eager for instruction in the Christian faith, had supposedly traveled hundreds of miles in search of a Bible. Much as ʻŌpūkahaʻia's story had done for Hawai'i, their account inspired a generation of missionaries to dream of Christianizing the Pacific Northwest. The Natives, it seemed, desperately wanted the gospel and just needed missionaries to appear and deliver it.

In 1836 a small band of ABCFM missionaries, including Marcus Whitman and his new wife, Narcissa, Henry and Eliza Spalding, and William Henry Gray, moved to Oregon Territory. The Whitmans established a mission at Waiilatpu on Cayuse lands in what is now Walla Walla, Washington. The Spaldings went a bit to the north and settled among the Nimiipuu. Like many missionaries before them, they sought to compel the locals to adopt White American ways. The Whitmans believed that the Cayuse and Nimiipuu would soon face the inevitable encroachment of settlers on their lands, and so they aimed to "civilize" and prepare them for integration. They tried to teach White agricultural models and pushed their neighbors to adopt protestant views of sex, marriage, and morality. The missionaries had little success and made few converts.

In 1847 thousands of Whites passed through the region on their way to the lush Willamette Valley. Those who became sick on the journey sought help from Marcus Whitman, who had treated both White traders and Indigenous families when they became ill. The migrants brought with them to the mission measles and dysentery, which spread rapidly among the Cayuse, killing perhaps half of the tribe in just a few months. The Cayuse noticed that most White children recovered (they had more immunities), but Indigenous children did not, which they interpreted as an intentional, diabolical scheme by Whitman to clear the land of its peoples. They attacked the missionary compound, killing over a dozen people, including Marcus and Narcissa. The federal government responded to the violence by asserting control over Oregon Territory. Another missionary venture thus ended in failure for both the Christians and those they thought they could graft into God's kingdom.

While many Indigenous men and women like Tenskwatawa and the Cayuse rejected Christianity, others found it compelling. They took the gospel message introduced by Whites and, in making it their own, turned it into a tool of liberation and a cudgel useful for bashing White racism and hypocrisy.

Pequot William Apess had a difficult childhood. Born in 1798, Apess worked as an indentured servant and was often cold and hungry. During his late teens, Apess joined a multiracial Methodist congregation in Massachusetts where he had a conversion experience. "I heard a voice saying unto me in soft and soothing accents," he recalled, "Arise, thy sins that are many are all forgiven thee; go in peace and sin no more." God had "stooped," he believed, to save him. Soon thereafter he realized, however, that while the Bible may say all people are equal in Christ, this did not match his experience in North America. He recognized that White racism structured his world in ways that ensured that people of color would remain at the bottom of the socioeconomic scale. "How hard it is to be robbed of all our earthly rights and deprived of the means of grace," he lamented, "merely because the skin is of a different color; such has been the case with us poor colored people."[13]

In the late 1820s, Apess became an itinerant Methodist minister and activist. He denounced Indian removal and the mistreatment of tribal peoples. He wrote an autobiography and then in 1833 published a powerful essay entitled "An Indian's Looking-Glass for the White Man." Both provided damning indictments of White racism. "Can you charge the Indians with robbing a nation almost of their whole Continent, and murdering their women and children, and then depriving the remainder of their lawful rights, that nature and God require them to have?" Of course not. But you could, he accused, levy such charges against White Americans.

Then he extended his critique to White Christians' support of slavery. "And to cap the climax," he asked, who but White Christians had robbed "another nation to till their grounds, and welter out their days under the lash with hunger and fatigue under the scorching rays of a burning sun?" Judgment, Apess warned, was inevitable. "I know that when I cast my eye upon that white skin, and if I saw those crimes written upon it, I should enter my protest against it immediately." Taking pride in how God had made him, he continued, "And I can tell you that I am satisfied with the manner of my creation, fully—whether others are or not." He closed his argument by describing Jesus as "colored" and saying that modern American Christians would not welcome the savior into their own homes.[14]

While many White Christians believed that American greatness would define the future, Apess hoped to inspire repentance over the horrors of the past. His version of Christianity merged Methodist revivalism with liberationist themes. For him, as for so many outside the White mainstream, the true Christian faith could be found where Jesus had thrived—among the outcasts. They viewed the Whites who claimed to be delivering salvation to Indigenous people as practitioners of a false version of the Christian faith.

Church leaders also sent missionaries to non-Native peoples in the West. They called their work "home missions" to distinguish it from work among foreign peoples and tribes. In 1826 multiple denominations, including Congregationalists, Presbyterians, and Reformed groups, consolidated their efforts and formed the American Home Missionary Society (AHMS) to serve "frontier" regions. It aimed to do for unchurched (i.e., nonprotestant) areas of the United States what the ABCFM was doing for foreign nations. AHMS leaders sponsored the work of over a hundred and fifty missionaries in its first year, and by the 1830s the organization had over five hundred active missionaries. As the nation added new territory, AHMS workers proved eager to serve.

Home missionaries sought to ensure that the United States remained God's chosen land even as it expanded. They joined other Americans in envisioning a Christian nation stretching all the way to the Pacific Ocean. In 1845 editor John L. O'Sullivan coined one of the most famous phrases in American history when he stated that it was "our manifest destiny to overspread the continent." O'Sullivan saw manifest destiny not as a colonial power grab, or the move of an emerging empire seeking influence, but as part of the almighty's plan for his sacred people. Building on ideas preached by John Winthrop centuries earlier, O'Sullivan had been arguing for years that God had birthed the United States to bless the world. He had chosen it "to manifest to mankind the excellence of divine principles; to establish on earth the noblest temple ever dedicated to the worship of the Most High." A nation and not a church, he insisted, served as God's new earthly sanctuary.[15]

The year that O'Sullivan coined the term "manifest destiny," Texas joined the United States. The next year the US secured the rights to Oregon Territory from Britain, then in 1848 Americans seized California and the Southwest following war with Mexico. In 1854, through the Gadsden purchase, the United States took control of additional lands along the Mexican border. The United States now stretched from sea to shining sea with an army of missionaries eager to shape it.

By 1860, the ABCFM had dispatched thirteen hundred missionaries around the globe who served in forty-one locations. One-third were men ordained as missionaries; the rest were wives, doctors, farmers, printers, and teachers. Initially, most came from Presbyterian and Congregationalist churches (and often from New England), but over time the newer revivalist denominations joined the race for converts. American missionaries believed that God would reward them and their nation for their work. As one missionary recruiter promised, "Most happy, most blessed will be the individual, the church, the nation, who shall be earliest, longest and most faithful in this glorious work."[16]

Missionaries did much to spread American culture and Christianity to tribes and foreign peoples. But they also served as agents of American empire. When the ABCFM started sending people around the globe, the State Department had few diplomats positioned outside the United States. As the first Americans many foreign people encountered, missionaries often influenced foreigners' views of the United States. Missionaries served as cultural mediators, helping bring new peoples and regions into contact with one another. When they returned home, they shared their experiences, introducing diverse cultures to their fellow Americans. These ambassadors hoped to bring American values to all who would open their doors to them. Whether working with Cherokees, crafting laws in Hawai'i, educating Americans on Islam's significance in the Middle East, inspiring the government to crack down on tribes in the Pacific Northwest, or opening doors to India, the legacies of the first generations of missionaries long outlived them. They gave the expanding American empire a distinctive Christian hue.

The domestic debate over slavery, however, threatened to tear apart everything they were working toward.

13

SETTING CAPTIVES FREE

Isabella Baumfree was born into slavery in New York in 1798. She grew up on the estate of Dutch immigrants and learned to speak English only after being sold away from her parents to new owners around her ninth birthday. As a teen she experienced physical and sexual abuse. In 1826 she escaped and secured her freedom.

Not long after fleeing captivity, Baumfree saw Jesus in a vision. The experience led her to convert to Christianity, join a Methodist church, and start attending small revival meetings in New York City. Then in the early 1830s, she joined another religious innovator, Robert Matthews, and his short-lived utopian community, the Kingdom of Matthias. After that, Baumfree determined that God had called her to serve as an itinerant minister. "Her mission," her contemporary biographer wrote, was "to 'lecture' as she designated it; 'testifying of the hope that was in her'—exhorting the people to embrace Jesus, and refrain from sin, the nature and origin of which she explained to them in accordance with her own most curious and original views." Tall, unschooled, speaking with a Dutch accent, and usually appearing with her head wrapped in a scarf, she drew crowds but never quite seemed to fit in. Like Jesus.[1]

In 1844, Baumfree joined another utopian community where she and her fellow Christians focused on integrating their religious ideas with contemporary social issues. They advocated for pacifism, the abolition of slavery, and equal rights for Black Americans and women. As Baumfree added to her work as minister a commitment to abolition and women's equality, she took on a new name that fit the life she had crafted for herself: Sojourner Truth.

A few years later Truth gave a public address linking Christianity, abolitionism, and women's rights. "May I say a few words?" she asked. "I am a woman's rights. I have as much muscle as any man, and can do as much work as any man. I have plowed and reaped and husked and chopped and mowed, and can any man do more than that? I have heard much about the sexes being equal; I can carry as much as any man, and can eat as much too, if I can get it. I am as strong as any man." She defended women's equality and highlighted the unjust and inconsistent ways men treated her because of both her race and her gender.[2]

Sojourner Truth often preached on the intersections among Christianity, abolitionism, and women's rights, demonstrating the power of religious faith to offer liberation to the oppressed. (credit: Glasshouse Images/Alamy stock photo)

Truth represented a growing number of activists who invoked the Christian faith to fight for a more just and equitable society. They sought to apply their Christian ideals to all aspects of American life. But not all religious leaders shared their perspective. Americans read the Bible from many different angles as they wrestled with the great social and political issues of their time. Some saw in Christian texts the liberation of oppressed peoples, and they made securing equality central to their mission. Others insisted that God had established racial and gender hierarchies, and they viewed slavery as any other system of labor. As disagreements deepened, Christians on all sides, rather than throw up their hands and toss the Bible aside, redoubled their efforts to inject their version of the faith, their reading of the Bible, into American law and society. In their efforts to impose their moral vision on the United States, they split the nation's churches, and then the nation itself.

Americans' obsession with establishing a godly, pure, and just society inspired some reformers to challenge slavery. Sarah and Angelina Grimké, daughters of a South Carolina enslaver, witnessed the harsh realities of slavery on their plantation. As young adults, they converted to the Society of Friends, moved to Philadelphia, and joined the abolitionist movement.

In 1836 Angelina Grimké published *Appeal to the Christian Women of the South*, hoping that perhaps Southern White women might convince their husbands and brothers to end slavery. She based her argument on both the nation's founding documents and the Bible, insisting that "slavery is contrary to the declaration of our independence," to the "first charter of human rights given to Adam," and to "the example and precepts of our holy and merciful Redeemer, and of his apostles." She called on her women readers to "send petitions up to their different legislatures, entreating their husbands, fathers, brothers and sons, to abolish the institution of slavery."[3]

Perhaps nothing better highlighted the incompatibility of Christianity with slavery than how White enslavers treated Black women.

"The virtue of female slaves," Sarah Grimké wrote, "is wholly at the mercy of irresponsible tyrants, and women are bought and sold in our slave markets, to gratify the brutal lust of those who bear the name of Christians." Too often enslaved women became sexual objects, with no ability to protect themselves. "In our slave States," Grimké observed, "if amid all her degradation and ignorance, a woman desires to preserve her virtue unsullied, she is either bribed or whipped into compliance." She could not dare "resist her seducer," or she might be killed. "In Christian America," she concluded, "the slave has no refuge from unbridled cruelty and lust."[4]

As the Grimké sisters' reputation grew, a group of New England Congregationalist leaders issued a pastoral letter condemning their tactics. The ministers warned that women like the Grimkés defied God's order of creation and "threaten the FEMALE CHARACTER with wide-spread and permanent injury." When women properly exercised their "mild, dependent, softening influence" upon men, they suggested, "society feels the effects of it in a thousand ways." But when "woman assumes the place and tone of man as a public performer . . . her character becomes unnatural."[5]

With opposition to the work of the Grimkés mounting, Sarah offered a stinging critique of sexism in a series of published letters in which she dismantled her opponents' arguments one by one. "I ask no favors for my sex," she insisted. "All I ask of our brethren is, that they will take their feet from off our necks, and permit us to stand upright on that ground which God designed us to occupy." Grimké grounded her argument for women's equality first and foremost in Christianity. She vowed to "depend solely on the Bible to designate the sphere of woman, because I believe almost every thing that has been written on this subject, has been the result of a misconception of the simple truths revealed in the Scriptures, in consequence of the false translation of many passages of Holy Writ."[6]

Many influential women shared the ministers' perspective regarding women's "proper" roles. Even those who opposed slavery questioned the Grimkés' radicalism and defense of women's equality. Catharine Beecher, who continued to be one of the most prominent female reformers in the nation, lamented that in joining the abolition movement, some women pushed beyond what she saw as their natural domain. She instructed women not to seek political influence no matter how just the cause (even though she herself had recently petitioned Congress over Cherokee removal). She counseled women to focus on persuading the men in their lives to behave righteously. "Men are the proper persons to make appeals to the rulers whom they appoint, and if their female friends, by arguments and persuasions, can induce them to petition, all the good that can be done by such measures will be secured. But if females cannot influence their nearest friends to urge forward a public measure in this way," she concluded, "they surely are out of their place, in attempting to do it themselves." Only those who misunderstood God's order pushed for women's political equality.[7]

Beecher's younger half-sister, Harriet Beecher Stowe, provided another model for antislavery agitation. Her *Uncle Tom's Cabin* conveyed the horrors of enslavement through fiction. The main character in the book, an enslaved man called Uncle Tom, is a Christlike figure who experiences conversion, has a vision of Jesus, and helps others see the value of faith. Stowe contrasted the godly Tom with evil enslavers, who in the book clearly have no relation to true Christianity. Nevertheless, Stowe invoked negative racial stereotypes, and she did not believe in or promote racial equality but instead supported colonization projects to send formerly enslaved men and women to African nations. Her book also inspired a series of proslavery counternovels, presenting Whites as the Christian saviors of those they enslaved.

Most Americans, regardless of their position on slavery, rejected the Grimkés' argument for women's equality. Delegates at the 1840 American Anti-Slavery Society, for example, fought the election of a woman to the executive council. Then at the World Anti-Slavery Convention in London, organizers refused to seat six American women delegates, including Quaker Lucretia Mott. The trip across the Atlantic was not a total loss for the women, however. Mott met Elizabeth Cady Stanton, who had also traveled from the United States to London for the convention. The meeting inspired the women to launch a new movement to pursue gender equality.

In 1848 Stanton and Mott held a women's rights convention in Seneca Falls, New York, where delegates issued a "Declaration of Sentiments" grounded in part in Christian ideas. "The history of mankind," they began, "is a history of repeated injuries and usurpations on the part of man toward woman." Men, they argued, put women in "a subordinate position" in church and state, "claiming Apostolic authority for her exclusion from the ministry." Man, they continued, had "usurped the prerogative of Jehovah himself, claiming it as his right to assign for her a sphere of action, when that belongs to her conscience and her God." Having been totally disenfranchised, "aggrieved, oppressed, and fraudulently deprived of their most sacred rights," they concluded, "we insist that they have immediate admission to all the rights and privileges which belong to them as citizens of these United States." The declaration helped spur a new generation of activists to seek equality for women in American public life.

By the time Truth and the Grimkés joined the antislavery movement, it had already taken many twists and turns. When the American colonies declared their independence from Britain in 1776, most patriot leaders recognized the incompatibility of the ideals expressed in the Declaration of Independence and the continuation of slavery. Free Black individuals such as Prince Hall in Massachusetts petitioned government leaders to end the diabolical practice, emphasizing its incongruity with both the values of the war and Americans' self-professed Christian identity. Nevertheless, slavery remained deeply entrenched in many regions of North America and the founders refused to take it on.

Meanwhile, in England a movement to end slavery gained momentum, one that inspired a parallel effort to encourage free Black residents to relocate to African lands. White leaders on both sides of the Atlantic never envisioned integrating people with an African heritage into their social and political worlds. In the late eighteenth century, British leaders established a colony for British Black men and women in Sierra Leone. David George, a Baptist minister originally from Savannah, Georgia, who fled to Canada after the revolution, helped lead the colony. He believed that God intended North America's former slaves to evangelize the African continent.

Following the British lead, in 1816 a group of White protestant leaders organized the American Colonization Society (ACS). Its founders included Presbyterian minister Robert Finley, a handful of elite Virginia enslavers, and missionaries from the American Board of Commissioners for Foreign Missions (ABCFM). Finley believed that Black and White people could not live together as equals. Sending free Black individuals to Africa solved the problem Whites had created in enslaving their fellow humans. Plus, colonization, he asserted, would benefit the peoples of Africa. "Is it too much to believe it possible," he asked, "that He who brings light out of darkness, and good out of evil, has suffered so great an evil to exist as African slavery" in order that the descendants of the enslaved might take the Christian gospel to Africa?[8]

In the early 1820s, free African Americans founded Liberia with the support of the ACS. They hoped to build better lives for themselves outside the United States. But the colony proved difficult to protect and defend against both local inhabitants and European powers seeking to exploit African resources.

While on its surface the ACS seemed like another benevolent missionary organization, Black Americans called the reformers' bluff. AME founder and bishop Richard Allen, despite initially supporting some Black-led colonization projects, exposed the nefarious motives of ACS proponents. "Africans have made fortunes for thousands, who are yet unwilling to part with their services," he preached, and yet they insist on sending the free away and keeping the rest enslaved? "This land, which we have watered with our tears and our blood, is now our mother country, and we are well satisfied to stay where wisdom abounds and the gospel is free." Allen emphasized current and former slaves' rightful claims to American prosperity. They had built the nation's economy and yet White Americans denied them their just rewards.[9]

Rather than look to Africa for their salvation, many Black activists in the North worked ever more aggressively to end slavery in the

United States. In 1829 David Walker, the son of enslaved parents, published *An Appeal to the Colored Citizens of the World*, a radical document that condemned slavery and the American Christians who supported it. He predicted that God would avenge Africans for the cruelties they suffered. "The white Christians of America," he decried, "who hold us in slavery, (or, more properly speaking, pretenders to Christianity,) treat us more cruel and barbarous than any Heathen nation did." He interspersed with his call for abolition statements supporting Black pride and independence. Whites "think because they hold us in their infernal chains of slavery, that we wish to be white, or of their color—but they are dreadfully deceived—we wish to be just as it pleased our Creator to have made us."[10]

Walker did not simply provide an intellectual critique of Christian hypocrisy. He also called for action, for the enslaved to fight "under our Lord and Master Jesus Christ, in the glorious and heavenly cause of freedom and of God." He believed that the end of slavery was in sight, and that when people of color overthrew their oppressors, they would inaugurate the millennium. "It is my solemn belief," he confessed, "that if ever the world becomes Christianized, (which must certainly take place before long) it will be through the means, under God of the *Blacks*." Walker published his ideas in a pamphlet, which jittery Whites in the South banned.[11]

The burgeoning abolition movement had little success convincing political leaders in the 1830s and 1840s to reevaluate slavery. White Southerners had enough power in the Senate to block any effort to eradicate human bondage, and although most of the enslaved lived in the South, the North benefited in substantial ways from the slave economy too. Nevertheless, revolts, occasional calls from free Black Americans to overthrow the institution, and growing sectional tensions ensured that the issue would not go away.

A small number of White reformers followed the lead of Black abolitionists and demanded the instant and unconditional end of slavery. William Lloyd Garrison became the most famous (and for some the most notorious) White abolitionist. The scrawny, bespectacled intellectual scrapper was, like Sojourner Truth, a religious wanderer. He experimented with revivalist versions of Christianity, held utopian and perfectionist ideals, and eventually drifted into heterodoxy. Influenced by both Quaker friends and Black abolitionists, he viewed slavery as an intolerable sin.

Garrison called for the immediate emancipation of all enslaved people. To better spread his abolitionist sentiments, he founded a publication in 1831, *The Liberator.* In the very first issue he laid out his agenda. "I do not wish to think, or speak, or write, with moderation.... I am in earnest—I will not equivocate—I will not excuse—I will not retreat a single inch—AND I WILL BE HEARD." Many of his initial subscribers were Black Americans, but over time the paper grew popular with White reformers as well. Garrison saw himself as an Old Testament–type prophet and refused to relent no matter how much criticism came his way. He promised that "as long as there remains among us a single copy of the Declaration of Independence, or of the New Testament, I will not despair of the social and political elevation" of Black Americans.[12]

Garrison worked side by side with Black abolitionists. In 1831 he published an essay by Maria Stewart, a Black woman living in Boston. "O, America, America," she wrote, "foul and indelible is thy stain! Dark and dismal is the cloud that hangs over thee for thy cruel wrongs and injuries to the fallen sons of Africa." The God of the Bible would soon pour his judgment on the United States. "The blood of her murdered ones cries to heaven for vengeance against thee." For the next couple of years, Stewart gave public addresses—a rare thing for Black women in this era—linking Christian faith and abolitionism. Along with Jarena Lee, Sojourner Truth, and a few others, Stewart entwined Christianity, antislavery, and women's rights in her work. Black women, and especially Black women preachers, often understood better than most other Americans how race and gender intersected in ways that limited their opportunities.[13]

Garrison often used the Fourth of July holiday to denounce "slaveocracy." In 1838 he called for "a formal vote" to "repudiate the

Declaration of Independence as a rotten and dangerous instrument." Then he called on Americans to "brand Washington, and Adams, and Jefferson, and Hancock, as fanatics and madmen." On Independence Day in 1854, Garrison raised a copy of the notorious Fugitive Slave Act, which required Americans to return any escapees they encountered, lit it on fire, and shouted from the book of Deuteronomy, "Let all the People say 'Amen!'" He then waved a copy of the Constitution in the air, called it "a covenant with death and an agreement with Hell," and lit it on fire. His views and actions proved controversial even among many antislavery White Christians.[14]

As abolitionism moved from a priority of predominately Black Americans into a multiracial movement, it drew activists from across the religious spectrum. Presbyterian conservatives, Baptist revivalists, liberal Quakers, and liberationist African Methodist Episcopalians all provided leadership. Christian faith, the particular stream one swam in, or no faith at all seemed to have little bearing on who might champion or oppose abolitionism. Christians could easily find in their dogma justification for fighting slavery, and they could just as easily find reasons to defend it. And yet because Christianity remained so central to American identity, activists from every side tried to claim that their views aligned with God's.

In the 1840s, an even more powerful and effective abolitionist agitator joined the antislavery crusade. Frederick Augustus Washington Bailey was born enslaved in Maryland in 1818. His enslaver separated him from his mother and never named his father—it may well have been the enslaver himself. In 1838 he escaped slavery and settled in Massachusetts, where he changed his name to Frederick Douglass. He became a leader and ordained minister in the African Methodist Episcopal Zion Church.

Douglass hit the abolitionist circuit, giving lectures across New York, New England, and the Midwest. He and Garrison became friends and supported each other's work. Despite Douglass's overt Christian faith, even in the North many religious leaders refused to let him use their churches, forcing him to give lectures outdoors or in meeting halls.

Douglass relentlessly compared his understanding of Christianity with that practiced by those complicit in slavery. "I love the pure, peaceable, and impartial Christianity of Christ," he explained. "I therefore hate the corrupt, slaveholding, women-whipping, cradle-plundering, partial and hypocritical Christianity of this land." He doubted that those who supported slavery were even Christians at all. "For my part, I would say, welcome infidelity! welcome atheism! welcome anything! in preference to the gospel, as preached by those Divines!" Theirs was a "religion for oppressors, tyrants, man-stealers, and thugs. It is not that 'pure and undefiled religion' which is from above." He noted that most White Americans practiced a Christianity that inverted New Testament ideals, a faith "which favors the rich against the poor; which exalts the proud above the humble; which divides mankind into two classes, tyrants and slaves; which says to the man in chains, stay there; and to the oppressor, oppress on." But rather than just challenge the Christianity of slaveholders, Douglass also challenged their reading of the Bible. In one of his more popular addresses, "Dialogue Between a Slaveholder and the Bible," Douglass performed a two-person debate. He alternated between issuing the standard "Christian" justifications for enslavement and reciting scriptures that undermined those very arguments. He made the biblical text central to his work, a necessary move for any social reformer in the United States.[15]

Although Douglass discouraged violence, other Black American leaders believed that the time had come to overthrow slavery by any means necessary. Presbyterian minister Henry Highland Garnet delivered a speech to the National Convention of Colored Citizens in 1843 in which he invoked Denmark Vesey and Nat Turner as heroes and models to emulate. "The diabolical injustice by which your liberties are cloven down, neither God; nor angels, or just men, command you to suffer for a single moment," he preached. "Brethren, the time has come when you must act for yourselves." He saw little "hope of Redemption without the shedding of blood. If you must bleed," he counseled, "let it all come at once—rather die freemen, than live to be slaves." Douglass, who attended the convention with Garnet, vehemently disagreed. He thought such sentiments undermined their cause and he advised the organizers to remove Garnet's speech from the minutes of the meeting.[16]

Douglass, like many abolitionists, used Fourth of July celebrations to highlight the distance between American ideals and actual conditions. "This Fourth July is yours, not mine," he lectured in 1852. "You may rejoice, I must mourn." Then, building toward the climax of the speech, he asked, "What, to the American slave, is your 4th of July? I answer; a day that reveals to him, more than all other days in the year, the gross injustice and cruelty to which he is the constant victim. To him, your celebration is a sham; your boasted liberty, an unholy license; your national greatness, swelling vanity." Directly attacking American claims of righteousness, Douglass preached: "The existence of slavery in this country brands your republicanism as a sham, your humanity as a base pretense, and your christianity as a lie. It destroys your moral power abroad: it corrupts your politicians at home. It saps the foundation of religion; it makes your name a hissing and a bye-word to a mocking earth."[17]

As Douglass's work progressed, he broadened his agenda. He believed that abolitionists needed to focus not only on stopping slavery in the South but also on fighting racism in the North. Whites had beaten, ridiculed, and segregated him too many times in the "enlightened" North for him to believe that ending slavery would end injustice. He also added to his reform agenda a focus on issues including temperance, assistance for the impoverished, and advocating for full civil rights for both Black people and women.

Douglass, Garrison, and Garnet represented the most radical vanguard in the abolitionist movement. Many opponents of slavery took a more conservative approach. They determined that calls for the immediate and unconditional end to slavery caused more problems than they solved. They still wanted to end human bondage but determined that a gradualist path might draw more support and therefore be more effective. They also debated how best to work within the existing political system.

As the debate over slavery and its relationship to faith grew, church leaders disagreed over both theology and tactics. In some ways, the split over slavery marked a split over the relationship between reform and evangelism. Should Christian activists emphasize conversion, believing that if they changed hearts, those who entered the fellowship of Christ would repent of their sins and denounce human bondage? The revivalist tendency to focus first and foremost on souls and not actions inspired many in their camp to downplay the sin of slavery. Other Christian reformers believed that recognizing slavery as sin marked a first step in preparing for conversion. A person could not be saved while living with the illusion that God approved of enslaving others. A corollary debate emerged around the issue of Christian fellowship. Could a Christian worship alongside enslavers or even within denominations that countenanced slavery, patiently waiting for God to make all things right, or was enslaving people such an egregious sin that churches should disfellowship all who engaged in it?

Garrison eventually called on all true believers to leave their churches, a movement he dubbed "comeouterism." He added to the masthead of *The Liberator* the phrase, "No Union with Slaveholders." He saw all American congregations as complicit, whether directly or indirectly, in the slave system. The most radical abolitionists believed that all American churches had failed to live up to the gospel they preached.

While Black Americans from Nat Turner to Frederick Douglass saw in the Bible a call to liberate oppressed people, others believed that the scriptures supported slavery. Princeton theologian Charles Hodge published a "biblical" defense of human enslavement in 1836 in response to Unitarian William Ellery Channing's invocation of the Bible to condemn slavery. Channing had argued that the principles of the Christian faith made slavery's sinfulness obvious. Can the defender of slavery, he asked, "pretend, then, that in holding others in bondage he does to his neighbour what he would that his neighbour should do to him?" He added that if the Old Testament's support of slavery seemed reason enough to maintain the institution, then so too was the Bible's support of polygamy. "Why may not Scripture be used to stock our houses with wives as well as with slaves?"[18]

Hodge lamented how ministers such as Channing used the Bible. He claimed that both the Old and New Testaments supported slavery and that Jesus and the apostles, despite witnessing brutal forms of human bondage, never condemned it. "While they required the master to treat his slave according to the law of love, they did not command him to set him free." Hodge believed that only one conclusion was possible: "If the present course of the abolitionists is right," he insisted, "then the course of Christ and the apostles was wrong."[19]

Like Hodge, various ministers in both conservative churches and in the fast-growing revivalist tradition, including teachers at Andover Seminary and Yale, also published "biblical" defenses of slavery. Just as some abolitionists saw the Constitution as a proslavery document and others believed it could be the basis for overthrowing the institution, so too did the Bible serve as a text that people read in very different ways. While defenders of human enslavement criticized those who failed to introduce the enslaved to the Christian gospel, or who destroyed Black families and sexually exploited female slaves, they argued that such sins did not happen universally and that abuses did not make slavery inherently wrong.

Like their counterparts in the North, White leaders in the South developed elaborate biblical defenses of slavery. They insisted that the Bible emphasized submission to authority and the importance of divine hierarchies. In their view, denying that the Bible affirmed slavery circumvented its clearest and most literal readings. For critics to challenge the slave system, then, meant challenging the faith.

Presbyterian minister and theologian James Henley Thornwell used the dedication of a new Charleston church—built specifically for the enslaved to worship under White oversight—as an opportunity to defend slavery. In his sermon, Thornwell condemned abolitionists, whom he grouped with "atheists, socialists, communists, red republicans," and "Jacobins," accusing them of distorting the character of slaveholders. He then pivoted to proclaim the spiritual equality of all people, enslaved and free—while leaving the institution of slavery itself unchallenged. He insisted that White Southerners did not "own" those they enslaved, just their labor. "The plainest declarations of the word of God," he preached, "lead us to recognize" in an enslaved person "the same humanity in which we glory as the image of God. We are not ashamed to call him our brother." And yet those they called "brother" should never seek to escape their bondage, a role that God had appointed them to play. The enslaved "is an actor on the broad theatre of life." His "true merit depends not so much upon the part which is assigned, as upon the propriety and dignity with which it is sustained." In other words, the more faithfully the enslaved did their duty, the more they pleased God.[20]

As the abolitionist movement grew, slavery's Christian defenders knew they needed better and stronger defenses of their own practices. They offered a romantic view of slave life, affirming the position of theologians like Hodge and Thornwell that slavery could be a tool for bringing the lost to salvation. They presented those they enslaved as happy, docile, eager to serve, and members of the family. They ignored the brutality of the slave markets, the separation of children from their families, the rape, the torture, the violence. They also pretended that slaveholders did not abandon those they enslaved when they became ill or too old to work.

Apologists for slavery offered many rationales for their actions. George Fitzhugh claimed that the South embodied true Christianity in contrast to the North's infidelity. Too many people in the North, Fitzhugh argued, had succumbed to religious fanaticism, which explained their quirky religions and irrational abolitionist sentiments. Some join the Shakers, he explained, "and a select few to the saloons of Free Love; and hundreds of thousands find shelter with Brigham Young, in Utah; whilst others, still more frightened, go to consult the Spiritual Telegraph, that raps hourly at the doors of heaven and of hell, or quietly put on their ascension robes to accompany Parson Miller in his upward flight." They had abandoned the true faith and wanted to ruin the nation's traditional churches, while the South, in contrast, remained the land of order and Christian conservatism.[21]

White Southerner Christians focused on the conversions of enslaved people to justify their actions. Georgia Presbyterian minister Charles Colcock Jones published *The Religious Instruction of the Negroes in the United States* to inspire more Whites to take their evangelistic obligations seriously. He claimed that White Christians had a duty to "civilize" and Christianize enslaved populations. American Christians had sent "missionaries to the heathen, thousands of miles from us," built "Theological Seminaries" to train more ministers, introduced the gospel into "our public prisons," defended the Sabbath and launched Sunday Schools, promoted temperance, and printed "Bibles and tracts and religious works," yet they had forgotten those nearest to them. "But what have we done publicly, systematically and perseveringly for the Negroes, in order that they also might enjoy the gospel of Christ?" Jesus, he concluded, "will say to us, 'these ought ye to have done and not to leave the other undone.'" Jones countered arguments that the enslaved might use Christianity as a tool of rebellion by doubling down on the argument that if they, White Southerners, instructed slaves in the faith, they would produce better laborers and not rebels.[22]

Defenders of slavery claimed that they offered something greater than economic freedom: eternal salvation. Virginia Baptist minister Thornton Stringfellow argued that the Christianization of slaves represented all the proof needed to justify slavery's continuation. Enslaving people, he opined, "has brought within the range of Gospel influence millions of Ham's descendants among ourselves, who, but for this institution, would have sunk down to eternal ruin; knowing not God, and strangers to the Gospel." He claimed that in "their bondage here on earth, they have been much better provided for, and great multitudes of them have been made the freemen of the Lord Jesus Christ, and left this world rejoicing in hope of the glory of God." Such perspectives helped Southern Christian leaders defend the slave system.[23]

The debate among White Christians for and against slavery, combined with the searing critiques of Black abolitionists, forced religious schism. Among Presbyterians, the question of slavery exacerbated splits already occurring along other lines. Some leaders championed revivalism and a focus on individual conversion, and others believed that the movement should remain more focused on tradition, creeds, and church-community building. On top of this theological divide came the debate over human rights. In 1836 church leaders determined that they would not establish an explicit policy on slavery since the issue proved so divisive. The next year the denomination split. The divide occurred primarily between the revivalists and the conservatives, but the slavery question played an indirect role. The revivalists tended to oppose slavery, while conservatives most often supported it. Over the next few years, as Northern Presbyterians became ever more critical of the institution of slavery and White Southerners dug in, a reshuffling occurred so that by 1860 the Presbyterian Church had divided into a proslavery Southern branch and an antislavery Northern branch.

For Methodists, the slavery issue led directly to denominational rupture. Popular revivalist Peter Cartwright offered one of the most penetrating critiques of his fellow churchmen. He claimed that early revivalist preachers, even in slave states, had "denounced slavery as a moral evil." "But O, how have times changed!" he lamented. Methodism had grown and expanded, "and many Methodist preachers, taken from comparative poverty, not able to own a negro, and who preached loudly against it, improved, and became popular among slaveholders." As the Methodists' class status rose, "many of them married into those slaveholding families, and became personally interested in slave property." Once they developed a material connection to slavery, Cartwright argued, "then they began to apologize for the evil; then to justify it, on legal principles; then on Bible principles; till lo and behold! it is not an evil, but a good! it is not a curse, but a blessing!"[24]

Cartwright anticipated the coming split in the revivalist denominations. In the 1840s, Methodists determined that church leaders (ministers and missionaries) should not enslave people. When a bishop from Georgia inherited enslaved men and women, many Northern churchmen believed that he needed to free them or give up his ecclesiastical authority. Southerners disagreed. The next year, proslavery Methodists left and formed the Methodist Episcopal Church,

South. Similarly, in 1845 a debate among Baptists over the right of slaveholders to serve as missionaries led to schism. The proslavery faction formed the Southern Baptist Convention.

Despite the struggle over slavery, many Americans remained committed to the broader American mission. Novelist Herman Melville continued to see—or at least his fictional characters saw—the United States as the new Israel. "We Americans," he determined in the 1850s, "are the peculiar, chosen people—the Israel of our time; we bear the ark of the liberties of the world." God "has predestinated" and "mankind expects, great things from our race; and great things we feel in our souls." Despite its many imperfections, no nation, he insisted, could match the United States. "The rest of the nations must soon be in our rear," he continued. "We are the pioneers of the world; the advance-guard, sent on through the wilderness of untried things, to break a new path in the New World that is ours."[25]

In dealing with the question of human enslavement, White leaders in the protestant mainstream demonstrated again that race structured how they read their Bibles and how they sought to bring their faith into American life. If the most powerful churches in the nation could not champion liberty and equality and human rights, who could? Black liberationists had no choice but to continue developing an alternative Christianity, one independent from the White mainstream.

As slavery tore the largest American denominations asunder, Americans rightly feared that what happened in their religious communions was about to split their nation.

14

AN ALMOST CHOSEN PEOPLE

In November 1860, a divided country elected Abraham Lincoln president. Months before taking office, Lincoln promised to use his elevation to the White House to serve both God and the nation. "I shall be most happy indeed if I shall be an humble instrument in the hands of the Almighty, and of this, his almost chosen people." His use of the phrase "almost chosen people" was telling. Few other Americans would have employed such words. They believed that God had anointed them his chosen people. Lincoln's more humble recognition that the United States had not quite reached the status of a new Israel, a holy nation consecrated for epically biblical things, set him apart in an era in which most leaders claimed to know the mind of God and his plans for the world. And yet Lincoln committed to leading the people toward Christian righteousness, to serving as God's instrument.[1]

As the nation descended into civil war, Lincoln helped Americans make sense of the conflict and its role in God's plans for the nation. The man who revivalist Peter Cartwright a decade and a half earlier had accused of infidelity emerged as one of the most, if not the most, profound public theologians in the history of the United States. He led the nation, like a modern Moses, back to the promised land. And, like Jesus on a Good Friday, he gave his life as an exculpatory sacrifice for the sins of a people whose commitment to their mission had seemingly floundered.

Christian activists north and south used the Civil War to remake the case for how best to live up to their divine mandate, but they offered diametrically opposed visions of the future. Those in the North believed that slavery represented the nation's greatest transgression, that freedom in God meant both spiritual and literal freedom regardless of race. Those in the South viewed slavery as a benevolent means of Christianizing an unchristian people, and they thought that it modeled God's ideal, hierarchical social order. Both sides hoped that through the crucible of war, God would cleanse and purify the nation of its sins. They aimed to forge their fellow Americans into a new people recommitted to implementing God's will in North America and around the globe.

Perhaps more than the revolutionary generation, or even the early Puritans, the nation's Civil War–era religious leaders obsessed over signs of God's blessing and God's wrath. They read divine whisperings into every military victory and defeat, into every advance and retreat. God, they believed in both the North and the South, rewarded faithfulness with victories, and he also disciplined and chastised his people for their sins by permitting failures and losses. From the soldiers who carried Bibles onto battlefields, to the enslaved who saw liberation in the story of the Exodus and ditched their enslavers, to the justifications of violence espoused by US Army and Confederate generals, almost all participants in the American Civil War saw their cause as just. Most White Americans clung tightly to the conviction that God had destined North America as his chosen land, the new Israel, even as they drenched it in blood. Yet the war challenged some of their assumptions. Americans had to determine once again what it meant to be God's people and how to shape their city on the hill.

As the United States expanded westward, debates over slavery grew more intense. The Kansas–Nebraska Act of 1854 allowed settlers in those territories to decide for themselves whether to permit slavery. The law sparked a flood of both pro- and antislavery settlers into Kansas, turning it into a battleground. Among them was abolitionist John Brown, a devout Calvinist and Presbyterian who arrived from New York in 1855. Convinced he was on a divine mission to defend the oppressed and end slavery, Brown and several of his adult sons took up arms. In one of the conflict's most violent episodes, they led a surprise raid on a group of proslavery settlers, killing several.

A few years later, Brown rented land under a pseudonym in western Maryland, just across the river from the federal military arsenal at Harpers Ferry, Virginia. Brown hoped to arm abolitionists, ex-slaves, and eventually the enslaved with the arsenal's weapons. He and his allies believed that Southern slavery just needed a sharp blow against one of its load-bearing beams, a direct strike, and it would collapse. Their job was to swing the hammer. On the night of October 16, 1859, Brown and his interracial band of twenty-two guerrillas successfully captured the armory, the arsenal, and a handful of hostages. But the revolution never materialized. US Army Lieutenant Colonel Robert E. Lee and a battalion of marines easily put down the rebellion and captured Brown. Six weeks later, Brown hung to his death.

Brown quickly became a martyr in the eyes of many opponents of slavery. A Massachusetts minister called his hanging "the greatest death-scene in American history," which "will shine forth purer and nobler with every passing year, and passing age." His actions also inspired new lyrics for a popular song. In the mid-1850s, many revivalist camp meetings featured the chorus "Glory, glory, hallelujah!" sung with different verses. After the raid on Harpers Ferry, antislavery agitators reconfigured one of them to read, "John Brown's body lies a-mouldering in the grave, John Brown's body lies a-mouldering in the grave, John Brown's body lies a-mouldering in the grave, His soul is marching on!"[2]

As tensions mounted and violence occasionally erupted, Americans had to decide who might bring peace and stability to the nation.

Presbyterian John Brown believed that slavery proved that the United States remained far from a Christian nation. But he hoped he could purify the land of its sins. Although the revolution he envisioned never materialized, opponents of slavery viewed Brown as a martyr who gave his life for a righteous cause. (credit: Library of Congress)

The argument over slavery had inspired the rise of a new political party called the Republican Party. Abraham Lincoln, a member of that party, warned of coming trouble. "A house divided against itself cannot stand," he said, invoking the words of Jesus. "I believe this government cannot endure, permanently half slave and half free. I do not expect the Union to be dissolved—I do not expect the house to fall—but I do expect it will cease to be divided." Americans, he predicted, would soon have to choose between freedom and slavery.[3]

In 1860, Republicans chose Lincoln as their nominee for president. Party leaders viewed him as a moderate who could run on many issues besides slavery, and Lincoln vowed not to tinker with the institution where it already existed. He won the race, and his victory, Southerners knew, was no fluke. The tide had turned, and they would probably never again place a proslavery candidate in the White House. South Carolinian leaders, meeting in a Baptist church in December 1860, voted to secede from the United States rather than try to work with the incoming president. Shortly thereafter, six more states joined South Carolina. They united to form the Confederate States of America.

Secession raised immediate problems for those who understood the United States as the new Israel. Virginia minister B. F. Brooke hoped that his state would remain in the Union. He believed that more important than slavery was the "position of America in her religious mission and destiny—the influence of this great nation on the ultimate civilization and redemption of the world." He saw the founding of the United States as "the dawn of a day whose brightness was to usher in the Millennium of the Church, the Sabbath of universal peace, the jubilee of the nations!" Like generations before him, he insisted "that this country was discovered for Christ, and this Union built for the spread of his kingdom." A rupture threatened this longstanding millennial view.[4]

On March 4, 1861, Abraham Lincoln became the sixteenth president of the United States. He ended his inaugural address by calling Americans to heed "the better angels of our nature." Instead, Americans summoned their inner demons. Early on the morning of April 12, 1861, soldiers under the newly established breakaway Confederate government launched an attack on Fort Sumter, South Carolina, where US Army troops had holed up. Cannon fire marked the start of a war that lasted longer and proved far more brutal than anyone anticipated.[5]

As the crisis over Fort Sumter escalated, Henry Ward Beecher, the son of New England minister Lyman Beecher and brother of educator and reformer Catharine Beecher, took to his Brooklyn pulpit to remind his congregation of their obligation to fight for the United States and the end of slavery. He had no interest in a compromise with Confederate traitors. "It is time for every church to make its pews flame and glow with enthusiasm for freedom," he insisted, "and with hatred for oppression. While the air of the South is full of pestilent doctrines of slavery, accursed be our communities if we will not be as zealous and enthusiastic for liberty as they are against it!"[6]

Shortly after the conflict began, the leaders of the warring factions each beseeched God for his aid. Lincoln called for a day of national humiliation, prayer, and fasting as he attributed the unfolding of events to God's providence. With the nation at war, "it is peculiarly fit," he suggested, "for us to recognize the hand of God in this terrible visitation, and in sorrowful remembrance of our own faults and crimes as a nation and as individuals to humble ourselves before Him and to pray for His mercy." God, he believed, was chastising Americans for their sins.[7]

Confederate president Jefferson Davis made a similar move. He issued a proclamation seeking to frame the war as a battle on behalf of God. But unlike Lincoln, he did not acknowledge sin or fault or call for humility, but instead listed grievances and boosted the supposed righteousness of the Confederate cause. He claimed that the Confederates "prize the blessings of free government" and feel "aggravated" by "those whose enmity is more implacable." He called for his people to support "all the measures which may be adopted for the common defence, and by which, under the blessings of Divine Providence, we may hope for a speedy, just and honorable peace."[8]

Davis and other leaders of the Confederacy recognized the value of aligning their interests with the divine. Throughout the conflict they went further than US leaders in explicitly linking church and state, the Confederacy and God. The drafters of the Constitution of the Confederate States of America opened their text with the preamble, "We, the people of the Confederate States," invoking "the favor and guidance of Almighty God do ordain and establish this Constitution for the Confederate States of America." Southerners believed that naming God would help secure their victory. According to a South Carolina minister, the document "received the finishing touch of Christian statesmen, and reflects the accumulated wisdom of ages. It was not extempore. It was the slow crystallization of truth, justice, and benevolence into a massive bulwark for the defense of Christian liberty."[9]

At the same time, Confederates attacked the secular United States Constitution. New Orleans Presbyterian minister Benjamin Morgan Palmer saw the founding document as a symbol of the American people's declension from their colonial promise. "When this most religious people" who came to North American shores, he preached, "undertook to establish an independent government, there was a total ignoring of the divine claims and of all allegiance to divine supremacy." Nowhere in the Constitution could Americans "possibly infer that such a being as God ever existed." It is not, therefore, surprising, he concluded, that God "let fall the blow which has shattered that nation." The Confederate States of America, in contrast, righted this wrong and receded "from this perilous atheism." They now represented true Christianity on North American soil, while the Union represented godless secularism.[10]

Confederate General Stonewall Jackson sought to make the rebel government as Christian as possible. "I am persuaded," he wrote to a friend, "that if God's people throughout our Confederacy will earnestly and perseveringly unite in imploring His interposition for peace, we may expect it. Let our Government acknowledge the God of the Bible as its God, and we may expect soon to be a happy and independent people." Since the United States had erred in taking an "extreme position" in disestablishing Christianity, God's blessings would now fall on the Confederacy.[11]

In adding the word "God" to their Constitution, Confederates, despite their seditious actions, put Northern Christians on the defensive. New England Congregationalist minister and theologian Horace Bushnell recognized that Southern critics had a point. The government might, he advised, "insert in the preamble of our Constitution, a recognition of the fact that the authority of government, in every form, is derivable only from God; cutting off, in this manner, the false theories under which we have been so fatally demoralized."[12]

Building on Bushnell's sentiments, a group of reformers asked Lincoln to support their efforts to amend the US Constitution to directly acknowledge the almighty. The war, they told the president, represented God's judgment upon the nation, and fixing the Constitution might be a way to appease him. They speculated that omitting God from the founding document marked the "crowning, original sin of the nation." Their modified text, with their proposed insertion in brackets, read, "WE, the PEOPLE of the UNITED STATES, [recognizing the being and attributes of Almighty God, the Divine Authority of the Holy Scriptures, the law of God as the paramount rule, and Jesus, the Messiah, the Saviour and Lord of all] in order to form a more perfect union. . . ." Lincoln told the reformers that he "cordially approved" of their work but that he needed "time to deliberate." Although Congress never amended the Constitution to include a direct acknowledgement of God, Jesus, or Christianity, members of the executive branch did make some concessions. During the war the Secretary of the Treasury added "In God We Trust" to one- and two-cent coins.[13]

The debate over constitutional language illustrated how Southern Christian activists drew on their faith to explain the conflict. Minister Benjamin Morgan Palmer compared the secessionist states to the ancient Hebrews who sought exodus from oppression under godless leaders in Egypt. "Eleven tribes sought to go forth in peace from the house of political bondage," he preached. "But the heart of our modern Pharaoh is hardened, that he will not let Israel go." Another minister assured soldiers that their "cause is the cause of God, of Christ, of humanity. It is a conflict of truth with error—of the Bible with Northern infidelity—of a pure christianity with Northern fanaticism—of liberty with despotism—of right with might."[14]

A few Southern ministers even turned to prophecy to explain the war. One believed that he had uncovered in the Bible's prophetic books predictions about the rise of the Confederacy as God's end-times tool to spread his light around the world. He determined that the Confederacy embodied the godly "remnant" referred to in the ancient scriptures: "This reign is perpetual, everlasting . . . The remnant of Israel restored in the last days." In his reading, God had not made the United States the new Israel; instead, God carved out of the United States the Confederacy as his new Holy Land for fulfilling his end-times plan and bringing salvation to the world.[15]

Early battlefield triumphs inspired confidence in Southern pulpits. John T. Wightman, pastor of the Methodist church in Yorkville, South Carolina, saw victory as a sign of the fast-approaching end-times. "The 'seventh seal' is about to be broken, and the 'seventh trumpet' is about to sound," he assured his congregation. "With a heart beating with hope," he continued, "the Christian seer strains his eye through the misty future to catch the first glowing outlines of the kingdom of Christ. Auspicious dawn!"[16]

North Carolina Presbyterian minister J. W. Tucker felt confident that a string of Confederate successes confirmed God's design. "Our victories," he preached, "indicate the presence of God with our armies in this conflict. Who can read the reports of the battles of Bethel, Bull Run, Manassas Plains, Ball's Bluff, Springfield, Shiloh and Williamsburg, without being convinced that God gave us the victory, and that to him we should render thanksgiving for the glorious triumph of our arms." He reminded his congregation that "our cause is sacred. It should ever be so in the eyes of all true men in the South. How can we doubt it, when we know it has been consecrated by a holy baptism of fire and blood." Attributing victories to God is easy when things are going well. But as Southern ministers soon realized, explaining defeats proved more difficult.[17]

Like their counterparts in the South, Northern ministers in the first years of battle sought to make sense of the conflict's religious significance. Minister Horace Bushnell believed that the war served to purify the nation. "In these and all such terrible throes, the true loyalty is born," he preached. "Then the nation emerges, at last, a true nation, consecrated and made great in our eyes by the sacrifices it has cost!" For Bushnell, the conflict represented a divine opportunity that Americans should embrace. "And the victory, when it comes, will even be a kind of religious crowning of our nationality." The fight, then, represented part of God's larger plan to prepare Americans for their special duty.[18]

Lincoln approached the relationship between God and country with more humility than many of the nation's ministers. Artist Francis Bicknell Carpenter reported that when a minister told Lincoln he "hoped 'the LORD was on our side,'" Lincoln replied, "I am not at all concerned about that . . . for I know that the LORD is always on the side of the right. But it is my constant anxiety and prayer that I and this nation should be on the Lord's side." Indeed, Lincoln never seemed as confident that he could discern the will of God as the religious leaders around him. To discern the mind of God, to comprehend the meaning of the war and to communicate it to Americans, proved impossible. But rather than dodge the religious implications of the war, Lincoln worked to understand them, to seek to position his people on the side of the almighty.[19]

During the war, many soldiers experienced revival. With death all around them, they sought to get right with God. A Confederate captain felt that "the religious feeling in our regiment is very deep." His wartime soldiers who "were groping their way in darkness, are now the humble followers of the 'Lamb of God.'" After the war, he published accounts of religious revival as part of Southerners' continuing efforts to depict their cause as righteous even in defeat.[20]

Church services among the troops sometimes felt like old-time camp meetings. "It was a touching scene," one eyewitness recalled, to see the "stern" veteran "trembling under the power of Divine truth, and weeping tears of bitter penitence over a misspent life." Another soldier felt the Holy Spirit telling him that he was a "wretched sinner, standing on the verge of an awful hell." As this new reality set in, he conflated enemy soldiers with the devil. He "felt as if some one was after him with a bayonet, and soon found himself almost on a run, as he moved backwards and forwards on his beat." Desperate for salvation, the soldier turned his life over to Jesus.[21]

Chaplains regularly reminded soldiers that every sermon they heard might be their last. One asked "a packed house" of troops, "How know you but that ere tomorrow's sun shall rise the long roll may beat, and this brigade be called to meet the enemy?" He was right. The men who heard that particular sermon went to battle the following morning. "Poor fellows," the chaplain later concluded. "They had heard their last message of salvation; but it was sweet to believe that many of them were trusting in Christ, and that for them 'sudden death was only sudden glory.'"[22]

Comparisons of religiosity sometimes served as markers for the righteousness of the causes for which the warring armies fought. For Christian soldiers in the US Army, encountering equally devout Christians among the enemy could spark faith crises. According to Lincoln, "The rebel soldiers are praying with a great deal more earnestness, I fear, than our own troops, and expecting God to favor their side." He learned that a US prisoner of war reported that "he met with nothing so discouraging as the evident sincerity of those he was among in their prayers." Both sides had a difficult time believing that the other practiced a real faith. Evidence of enemy Christian devotion proved difficult to process.[23]

Chaplains in the North also chronicled revivals among troops. Black minister Henry McNeal Turner reported that US Army forces were "regularly fortifying ourselves as securely against the devil and his subalterns, or angels, as we are against the rebels," and he celebrated the "glorious revival" among soldiers. During evening services he heard "mourners" "groaning and praying in every direction for God's pardoning grace; and, thank God, several have not mourned in vain, having found the pearl of great price."[24]

Roman Catholic chaplains creatively adapted their practices to the conditions on the front. Father Peter Paul Cooney wrote to his brother about a group that came to him hoping to make their confessions. He and the soldiers stacked up bayonets and then, with the guns upright, they "got three blankets, two covering two sides hanging on the bayonets; the other covered the top, leaving the front open." The improvised confessional worked perfectly. "Here the poor fellows came," he recalled, "impressed with the idea that perhaps this would be the last confession of their lives. Some of the officers gave me their wills and then went to confession. But," he concluded, "it would take volumes to tell all."[25]

Catholics like Cooney understood that the war provided them with a new opportunity to demonstrate their Americanness. With the Know-Nothings and the horrors nurtured by fictitious nun Maria Monk still fresh in Catholic memories, New York priest Joseph Fransioli emphasized to his parishioners the importance of loyalty to the US government. "This duty of loving our country, which nature and society impose upon us, is more strictly enforced by Christian Catholic religion," he claimed. Jesus, he preached, came "not to dissolve the national and social duties, but to encourage and help us to their more perfect fulfillment. A Catholic that loves not his country does not understand his religion." Fransioli taught that "the true Christian patriot brings" everything "before the altar of his country," including

Leaders on both sides of the Civil War injected religion into every aspect of the conflict. Catholic leaders saw the war as an opportunity to demonstrate their faith, patriotism, and loyalty. In this photograph a Catholic priest leads mass for soldiers in the 69th Infantry. (credit: Library of Congress)

"his property and his life cheerfully ready for the sacrifice when it is demanded." Catholics, he insisted, needed to fight for the United States against the traitors.[26]

Bibles served as important commodities among soldiers, and stories often circulated that they could both lead one to heaven and stop bullets. The mother of one Confederate asked her son to keep his Bible close. "Since you desire it," he replied. "I will certainly wear the testament over my heart." Then, toying with his mother, he queried, "Did I tell you of the man whose life was saved by a pack of cards in his breast pocket?" Since many Americans viewed cardplaying as immoral, he knew full well that his mother would not find his sacrilegious joke amusing.[27]

Hymns became another tool for inspiring action and revealing how many Americans understood the conflict within their Christian identity. Philadelphia Presbyterian minister George Duffield Jr. had penned "Stand Up, Stand Up for Jesus" during the 1850s, which took on new meaning during the war. "Stand up, stand up for Jesus/ ye soldiers of the cross;/ lift high his royal banner,/ it must not suffer loss./ From vict'ry unto vict'ry/ his army he shall lead/ till ev'ry foe is vanquished/ and Christ is Lord indeed." The hymn grew popular among the troops, who took literally images Duffield had likely meant as metaphors.

The liberationist hymn "John Brown's Body" also became a favorite among troops in the North. Unitarian and abolitionist Julia Ward Howe heard the song while visiting the front. "We were about to see the grim Demon of War," she noted, "face to face." There she encountered soldiers singing the popular song. When she awoke the next morning, she felt inspired to write a new poem to fit the tune. She called it "Battle Hymn of the Republic."[28]

"Mine eyes have seen the glory of the coming of the Lord," she began. "He is trampling out the vintage where the grapes of wrath are stored; He hath loosed the fateful lighting of His terrible swift sword: His truth is marching on/ Glory, glory, hallelujah! Glory, glory, hallelujah! Glory, glory, hallelujah! His truth is marching on." Turning to the apocalyptic, Howe continued, "He has sounded forth the trumpet that shall never call retreat: He is sifting out the hearts of men before His judgment seat." Then, drawing on her abolitionist hope that the war would end slavery, she concluded, "As he died to make men holy, let us die to make men free, While God is marching on. / Glory, glory, hallelujah, &c. While God is marching on."

As sermons, songs, and prayer books all indicated, religious leaders had little trouble justifying the violence generated by the war. While a small number of ministers believed that Jesus had called his followers to be peacemakers, most Christians, in both the North and South, championed the use of force as a religious duty. New England Congregationalist William Barrows aimed to reconcile the seeming contradiction between serving the Prince of Peace and defending war by invoking the violence of the Bible. "We must not, then, require our religion to be more genial and gentle and tender toward evil and evil doers than its textbook, or God its author." And so they did not.[29]

The war challenged Lincoln in many ways as a strategist, politician, and Christian leader. When he took office, Lincoln promised not to end slavery in the Southern states. But over time, he had little choice but to adapt. Tens of thousands of enslaved men and women were claiming freedom for themselves. In the spring of 1862, the president ended slavery in the nation's capital. Daniel Payne, the pastor of the local African Methodist Episcopal church, preached a sermon commemorating the occasion. He encouraged the newly free men and women in the city to commit themselves to God and to supporting the government. Then he turned to the significance of Lincoln's act. If the nation "will do right," he counseled, "administering justice to each and to all, protecting the weak as well as the strong, and throwing the broad wings of its power equally over men of every color," then God will reward it. Only then will the US Army "be led to battle by the Lord, and victory secured by the right arm of our God."[30]

That summer, Lincoln decided to end slavery in the Confederacy. As he prepared to issue the Emancipation Proclamation, he sought a sign from God. According to one of his cabinet secretaries, Lincoln told advisors that "he had made a vow, a covenant, that if God gave us the victory in the approaching battle, he would consider it an indication of Divine will" for him to issue the directive. Lincoln received the sign he wanted at the Battle of Antietam in September, which allowed him to go forward from a position of strength rather than weakness. Lincoln determined, according to his confidant, that God had "decided this question in favor of the slaves."[31]

Lincoln pledged that on January 1, 1863, "all persons held as slaves within any State or designated part of a State, the people whereof shall then be in rebellion against the United States, shall be then, thenceforward, and forever free." Enslaved people in border states that had not joined the Confederacy had no change in status, and Lincoln had no authority over the Confederacy, which made the proclamation more symbolic than real. Nevertheless, AME minister James Lynch believed that emancipation turned the tide, that God intervened on behalf of the North once freedom for the enslaved and not just saving the Union became a priority. Americans had finally started to realize, he noted, that "Divine Providence had united the destiny of both races." God had "made the deliverance of the slave from bondage the sine qua non of the deliverance of the nation from the consuming fires of rebellion."[32]

As Lincoln presided over the conflict, he toggled between president and prophet. Seeking to remind the nation of its dependence on God, he called for another day of humiliation, fasting, and prayer on March 30, 1863. Based on his reading of the Bible and especially the story of God chastising the Hebrews for their sins, he wondered if the war may "be but a punishment, inflicted upon us, for our presumptuous sins, to the needful end of our national reformation as a whole People?" Despite Americans' many successes, "we have forgotten God. We have forgotten the gracious hand which preserved us in peace, and multiplied and enriched and strengthened us." Perhaps Americans needed to repent and turn back to the almighty, who had, in Lincoln's mind, made the United States exceptional among all nations.[33]

Many ministers agreed with the president. Presbyterian Thomas Brainerd used the president's declaration to warn his congregation that perhaps the war represented God's punishment for the collective sinfulness of the American people—and his list of sins was not short. It included "ingratitude, Sabbath-breaking, profanity, intemperance, gambling, under-mining and over-reaching selfishness, fraud and lying; lack of parental fidelity, and of respect for parents and for age; stinted charities, and prayerless and Godless lives; who doubts," he queried, "that all these cry to heaven for judgment against us? No wonder God is disciplining us." He hoped that the war would "lead to national reformation."[34]

As Confederate losses mounted at Gettysburg and beyond, Savannah Episcopalian minister and bishop Stephen Elliott sought to bolster the waning faith of his congregation by attacking Northern religiosity. US Army leaders, he preached, had "forsaken" God and "trampled upon his word and his immutable morality." But God would not let them prevail for long. "He is only biding his time while he chastens us for our sins and tries our faith, and while he ripens them for slaughter and vengeance." Rather than acknowledge defeats as testament to the unworthiness of their cause, the minister argued counterintuitively that military setbacks confirmed God's plan to transform the South into his chosen land. "Those of whom God is intending to make a nation to do his work upon earth, are precisely those whom he tries most severely. His purpose is to give them not merely victory, but character; not only independence, but righteousness; not peace alone, but the will to do good, after peace shall have been established." As the Confederate cause grew more hopeless, leaders refused to question the righteousness of their mission and found creative ways to account for both victories and defeats.[35]

In November 1863, the nation celebrated the first Thanksgiving holiday. Lincoln like his predecessors had on occasion declared days of prayer and thanksgiving. But early that fall, Sarah Josepha Hale, the editor of the popular *Godey's Lady's Book*, had written to the president, encouraging him to declare a reoccurring, annual day of Thanksgiving as a means of unifying the American people. She suggested they celebrate Thanksgiving on the last Thursday of November. Lincoln agreed. He asked Americans to pray on that day for the "Almighty Hand to heal the wounds of the nation and to restore it as soon as may be consistent with the Divine purposes to the full enjoyment of peace, harmony, tranquillity and Union."[36]

In 1864, with the nation still at war, Lincoln sought reelection. But the president had many critics, including Northern Democrats who believed that he had exceeded his constitutional authority in issuing the Emancipation Proclamation and in suspending habeas corpus. Some of his detractors published a satirical and racist pamphlet called *The Lincoln Catechism Wherein the Eccentricities & Beauties of Despotism Are Fully Set Forth: A Guide to the Presidential Election of 1864*. The document wove together issues of law, religion, and economics. The anonymous authors criticized Lincoln's eclectic religious sensibilities and they feared a postwar world defined by too much freedom and individualism. The president's vision for the republic, they fretted, made space for "abolitionists, mesmerisers, spiritual mediums, free-lovers and negroes." They did not know at the time that Lincoln's wife, Mary Todd, held occasional seances in the White House where she sought to communicate with her dead child. Lincoln may have participated in these seances, but he probably was not a true believer in the occult. Yet his lack of clear church commitment allowed critics to project onto him nefarious religious ideas.[37]

Nevertheless, in the North Lincoln had more allies than enemies, and he secured reelection. Slavery, Lincoln noted in his second inaugural address, "was, somehow, the cause of the war." Then the president transformed again into a prophet. Both US and Confederate, North and South, he reminded his audience, "read the same Bible, and pray to the same God; and each invokes His aid against the other. It may seem strange," he observed, "that any men should dare to ask a just God's assistance in wringing their bread from the sweat of other men's faces; but let us judge not that we be not judged. The prayers of both could not be answered; that of neither has been answered fully. The Almighty has His own purposes." Then he concluded on a note of grace directed more toward warring Whites than those suffering under enslavement. "With malice toward none; with charity for all; with firmness in the right, as God gives us to see the right, let us strive on to finish the work we are in; to bind up the nation's wounds; to care for him who shall have borne the battle, and for his widow, and his orphan—to do all which may achieve and cherish a just, and a lasting peace, among ourselves, and with all nations."[38]

On April 9, 1865, Robert E. Lee surrendered his army to Ulysses S. Grant. Less than a week later, on April 14, John Wilkes Booth assassinated Lincoln while the president watched a play at Ford's Theatre. That the president attended the theater and not church on Good Friday raised the eyebrows of the devout. Most ministers still went out of their way to praise the fallen president. Henry Ward Beecher reviewed Lincoln's significance for the Christian faithful. "Again," as in the days of Moses, he told his congregation, "a great leader of the people has passed through toil, sorrow, battle, and war, and come near to the promised land of peace, into which he might not pass over. Who shall recount our martyr's sufferings for this people!" Then he summed up the war: "God, I think, has said, by the voice of this event, to all nations of the earth, 'Republican liberty, based upon true Christianity, is firm as the foundation of the globe.'"[39]

The actions of seditionists and traitors, followed by the bullet of an assassin, demonstrated that religious leaders, at least in the short term, could not take the perpetuation of republican liberty or true Christianity for granted. As they set out to reconstruct the nation after the war, they worked to assess again their mission and to align it with God's ultimate plans for the United States and the world.

15

RECONSTRUCTING THE NATION

Charles Shelton, a "home" missionary in the Dakota Territory, penned an article in 1885 for a missions magazine titled "The Indians from a Christian Stand-point." He hoped to inspire more evangelistic efforts in the West. The nation's tribes, he warned, faced inevitable extinction. Yet Christians could play a role in determining how best to "exterminate" the "savage." "You can send to the Indian the rifle and exterminate him in this way," he wrote. "It is a slow and very expensive method." Or, he suggested, "we can send to the Indian this Gospel of Christ, this great power of civilization, and through its influence exterminate the savage, but save the man." Survival for Indigenous people, he told his White Christian audience, required their transformation. If tribes "continue to be pests to society, expense to our government, a blot upon our fair name, a reproach and a contradiction to every profession that we make of Christian love or of Christian conversation, the fault," he concluded, "rests with the churches."[1]

In the aftermath of the Civil War, federal leaders sought help from Christian groups like Shelton's as they sought to reassert their power across the entire United States. The US Army had won on the battlefields, and now governing authorities and their protestant collaborators sought to secure the peace. They aimed to reconstruct the nation, to rebuild Americans' shattered sense of their nation's exceptional history and manifest destiny, and to reinvigorate their commitment to the United States' Christian mission. But to succeed, policymakers knew they needed to limit dissent—including religious dissent.

Christian activists played key roles in every part of postwar reconstruction. In the South, Black ministers and White missionaries welcomed the formerly enslaved into the faith and worked with them to establish independent social and political lives. Defeated Southern Whites launched a multi-generation effort to defend their treason by reimagining the causes of the Civil War and God's role in it. In the West, a series of Indian wars led to the US government's creation of a comprehensive reservation system, where government-sponsored missionaries sought to Christianize tribes and "civilize" their children. In Utah Territory the US government cracked down on the Church of Jesus Christ of Latter-day Saints and its impressive theocracy, seeking to quell religious dissent.

Across the nation, Reconstruction policies provided new opportunities for church leaders in collaboration with the government to impose their ideas and values on the land and its peoples. Protestant activists believed that they alone had the tools and expertise to integrate Black and Native peoples, former Confederates, and religious dissenters into the body politic, while bringing healing and reconciliation to all Americans on their terms. Rocked by the split over slavery and then the war, they worked to build unity by identifying common threats and enemies and organizing Christians against them. Their actions demonstrated that after the conflict, just as before, the free exercise clause did not apply to all equally. But minority groups constantly challenged the power of mainstream Christian leaders.

Black Americans secured literal freedom in the 1860s and also discovered a new sense of spiritual independence. Black denominations in the North had rushed to send missionaries, ministers, and supplies into territories retaken by the US Army. Young African Methodist Episcopal preacher Theophilus Gould Steward traveled South from New Jersey to minister during the conflict. Black Americans, he noted in 1865, were "lying under an almost absolute physical and moral interdict. There was no one to baptize their children, to perform marriage, or to bury the dead. A ministry had to be created at once—and created out of the material at hand." He and his colleagues leapt into the work, building up churches where liberated African Americans could find refuge, spiritual instruction, and discipleship.[2]

Only about one-third of enslaved Americans considered themselves Christian at the start of the Civil War. But in the Reconstruction era Black churchgoing skyrocketed. And just about all of those who converted chose to attend Black-led churches. The days of Southern Black Christians submitting to second-class treatment in the house of the Lord had ended. In urban areas, African Americans could usually join churches that Black activists had founded before the war. In rural areas, they had fewer options. They sometimes had to settle for makeshift meetings in vacant buildings or arrange outdoor services until they could build rudimentary houses of worship.

Black clergy became some of the strongest advocates for full equality and rights in the postwar South. Seeing Jesus as a liberator, they aimed to make the egalitarianism of the gospel and the Declaration's line that "all men are created equal" the reality in the United States. Many engaged directly in politics, understanding that while slavery might have ended, securing political equality required vigilance. Formerly enslaved Baptist minister James Simms, who won election to the Georgia assembly, explained why so many of his fellow clergy engaged in politics. "In seeking out men to represent the colored people in the councils of the nation and State," he wrote, "the most competent men were to be found, with few exceptions, among the ministers of the gospel of Christ." He acknowledged that Black clergy's participation in politics might raise questions of the separation of church and state, but the context demanded it. "It was unavoidable," he insisted. "Many pastors and preachers necessarily had to leave their flock and legitimate field of labor to enter the arena of politics in order to secure right and justice for their people." They refused to separate political freedom from spiritual freedom.[3]

Black ministers' political engagement made them targets of violence. Members of the Ku Klux Klan, a terrorist organization founded by Southern Whites shortly after the war, burned down churches and threatened Black activists. A journalist testified to the US Senate about his interview with a minister. While "he had been preaching on the circuit," Klansmen dragged the preacher from bed in the middle of the night and "beat him severely." They "told him that if he returned to the county he would suffer for it." This was one example of many. As racial violence escalated in the South, serving as a minister proved dangerous.[4]

AME leader Henry McNeal Turner, like Simms, kept one foot in the world of politics and the other in the church. As a teenager Turner had joined the predominately White Methodist Episcopal Church, South, but he later transferred his membership to the African Methodist Episcopal Church. He served as the first Black chaplain in the Civil War. After the conflict, he worked with the Freedman's Bureau, an organization that supported formally enslaved men and women as they built new lives, he helped expand the Republican Party, and he planted new AME churches around the South. He also ran for office, winning a seat in the Georgia legislature.

In both his religious and civic life, Turner fought for Black equality. In 1875 Congress passed a civil rights act outlawing racial discrimination, but in 1883 the US Supreme Court invalidated the law. The decision had profound implications for voting. "It has made the ballot of the black man a parody," Turner excoriated, "his citizenship a nullity and his freedom a burlesque." Furthermore, like slavery before it, segregation made a lie of claims that the United States represented in any way God's chosen land. "And as long as the accompanying decision remains the verdict of the nation, it can never be accepted as a civil, much less a Christian, country."[5]

Frustrated by White Americans' propensity to cloak their racism in their religion, Turner drew on the liberationist stream of Christianity to defend Black rights. He made the radical claim in 1896 that "God is a Negro." "We have as much right biblically and otherwise to believe that God is a Negro," he wrote, as Whites "have to believe that God is a fine looking, symmetrical and ornamented white man." Many Americans, he recognized, believed that God is a "white-skinned, blue-eyed, straight-haired, projecting-nosed, compressed-lipped and finely-robed *white* gentleman, sitting upon a throne somewhere in the heavens." But for Black Christians, this image proved destructive. "Why should not the Negro believe that he resembles God as much so as other people? . . . *God is a Negro*." Having lost hope in the United States, Turner eventually called for North American people of African descent to emigrate to West Africa in search of true freedom.[6]

Historian, sociologist, and Black activist W. E. B. Du Bois summarized in 1903 the role that churches played in Black life, especially in the postwar South. "The Negro church of to-day is the social centre of Negro life in the United States," he wrote, "and the most characteristic expression of African character." Postwar Black churches, as Du Bois understood, represented the heart of Black efforts to secure social, political, and religious equality. Church leaders had engineered the Christian faith into a tool of liberation, which made them a threat to the White Christians of the South and much of the rest of the United States.[7]

In addition to working to suppress Black political and religious power, many Southern Whites launched a quasi-religious campaign to reshape the memory of the Civil War. Rather than acknowledge their deep investment in slavery, they recast the conflict as a tragic clash between two honorable forces—the North fighting to preserve the Union, and the South struggling to defend local autonomy and states' rights. The authors of this revisionist account reduced slavery to a secondary issue, incidental to the "real" causes of the war. As a result, by war's end, many White Southerners felt they had no reason to repent, no moral reckoning to face, and no obligation to embrace Black equality or suffrage. For them, the war had simply preserved the Union and, almost as an afterthought, ended slavery. Nothing more.

Christianity became central to this new Southern narrative. In defeat, White Southerners cast themselves in the role of Christ, imagining their suffering as redemptive. They claimed they had sacrificed for the greater good of the nation, their values—chivalric protection of White women, paternalistic care for those they enslaved, and Christian devotion—positioned them as the rightful moral leaders of the country. In their view, God had chosen them to guide the nation toward righteousness, but first he had humbled and purified them through the bloodshed of war.

White Southerners perpetuated this myth of the "Lost Cause" by honoring people like Stonewall Jackson and Robert E. Lee, whom they viewed as the nation's greatest martyrs. At about the same time that ministers like Henry McNeal Turner proclaimed God a "Negro," many Southerners began erecting statues and monuments to Confederate traitors as symbols of their supposed virtues and heroic sacrifices. White Southerners reimagined the very men who in the 1860s led their states into a brutal and horrific war, only to lose, as ideal Christian citizens and true American patriots. For White Southerners, the statues and monuments became symbols of Southern White pride; for Black Americans, they represented perpetual reminders that despite the South losing the war, White Southerners continued to believe in the righteousness of the Confederate cause.

While White Southerners grappled with the legacy of the Civil War, many Americans looked westward. Government leaders and their protestant activist allies focused on subduing and remaking the West as they had the South. Two major obstacles stood in their way: Latter-day Saints and Indigenous tribes. In 1885, President Grover Cleveland highlighted the ongoing challenges of each. He vowed that "the Indians within our boundaries shall be fairly and honestly treated as wards of the Government and their education and civilization promoted with a view to their ultimate citizenship." Then he shifted to the other supposed impediment to Western development. "Polygamy in the Territories," he continued, "destructive of the family relation and offensive to the moral sense of the civilized world, shall be repressed."

Fulfilling dreams of a White protestant nation achieving its manifest destiny demanded that the government and Christian activists partner to remake the West.[8]

The discovery of gold and silver in the West and the expansion of the railroad drove more and more people onto tribal territories, which led to escalating conflicts. Hoping to curtail violence, the federal government established a reservation system that authorized the allocation of large swaths of land to tribes, but the program never worked as well as Congress had promised. The government and the nation's original inhabitants periodically battled each other to shape the direction and makeup of the region, with each offering competing visions of the land, its use, and who should care for it.

President Ulysses S. Grant had turned to Christian leaders for help in implementing a new post–Civil War "peace policy" for the West. He partnered first with the Society of Friends. Quakers had long lobbied government leaders to modify their treatment of Indigenous peoples, and who better to implement a "peace" policy than those running "peace" churches? Quakers blamed their fellow Christians for neglecting their duty to the nation's tribes. Failure "to convert these heathen," they claimed, resulted from "the corruption and unfaithfulness of men whose examples have dishonored the Christian name." Friends leaders promised Congress that "the faithful exercise of the principles and commands of our Lord Jesus Christ will be found sufficient to solve the Indian question without military aid."[9]

Quakers and other like-minded religious reformers convinced Grant to establish the Board of Indian Commissioners (BIC), which was dominated by Christian activists. Congress authorized the board in 1869 to help bring Natives onto reservations and then ensure that the reservations ran smoothly, much as the Freedman's Bureau helped administer Reconstruction policies with the formerly enslaved. Tribes, many religious reformers believed, needed land away from White settlers for their own protection, which would give them time to assimilate and Christianize. On reservations they could learn the Christian faith, the value of private property, and White agricultural methods.

Reformers resurrected the pre–Civil War plans of missionaries like the Whitmans, who aimed to bring Indigenous people into the kingdom of God and into the United States at the same time.

Neither Grant, nor Congress, nor religious leaders worried about the First Amendment's disestablishment clause when crafting Indian policy. The promises of freedom and liberty enshrined in the US's founding documents generally did not apply to noncitizens, including Indigenous people. Reservation missionaries celebrated how church and state worked hand in glove. "The prospects of the Nez Percés are now assuming a very hopeful aspect," one missionary in Lapwai, Idaho, wrote, "and, with the harmonious action of the representatives of the Government and the missionaries, the christianization and civilization of these Indians will speedily be placed beyond question." Protestant reformers rarely saw any conflict between their actions and the Constitution. They only objected when practitioners of minority faiths tried to assert their will on others—when mainstream protestants faced competition.[10]

The BIC assigned specific Christian denominations to oversee individual reservations, and it empowered church leaders to appoint reservation agents. Missionaries became the symbols of federal presence on reservation lands, while the military remained outside reservation borders, always present in the shadows. The missionaries offered a carrot in the form of Christianity and "civilization," but if tribal citizens refused it, the army had the stick in hand.

Leaders of the Bureau of Indian Commissioners made the religious nature of their government-funded work explicit in their first report to the president. They sought to "protect" Indigenous people, "to educate them in industry, the arts of civilization, and the principles of Christianity; elevate them to the rights of citizenship, and to sustain and clothe them until they can support themselves." Moving into passive voice, they added, "The establishment of Christian missions should be encouraged, and their schools fostered." Reformers saw the imposition of faith on Native peoples as essential to their success. The religion "of our blessed Saviour is believed to be the most effective agent for the civilization of any people."[11]

Missionaries made the reeducation of reservation families a top priority. "It is absolutely essential," Congregationalist missionary leader George Whipple insisted, "to educate a heathen people in order to perpetuate Christianity among them." While preaching might make converts, education sustained them and prevented backsliding. Missionary agencies had learned this lesson, Whipple told Christian leaders, "among the freedmen of the South."[12]

Reformers also used boarding schools to instill in Natives the values championed by White Christians. They believed that separating Indigenous children from their families and training them away from their tribes would help "Americanize" and integrate the next generation. And some Indigenous parents agreed, seeking a better life for their children than what they might find on reservations.

In Carlisle, Pennsylvania, hundreds of students each year from many different tribes studied together at a boarding school that Richard H. Pratt founded in 1879. Pratt complained that missionary-run schools located on reservations had not facilitated the transfer of people off reservations and into mainstream society but instead encouraged students' continuing ties to their people. "A great general has said that the only good Indian is a dead one," Pratt told a group of activists. "In a sense, I agree with the sentiment, but only in this: that all the Indian there is in the race should be dead. Kill the Indian in him, and save the man." Pratt and others started new boarding schools for exactly this purpose.[13]

The nation's leading White denominations all hoped to grow their influence through their reservation work. By 1872, Christian groups oversaw more than seventy reservations. The Quakers led the way with jurisdiction over sixteen reservations, Methodists had fourteen, Presbyterians nine, Episcopalians eight, Baptists and Reformed Dutch had five each, Congregationalists three, the restorationist "Christians" and Unitarians had two each, and Lutherans and the American Board of Commissioners for Foreign Missions oversaw one each. "Indian" policy and Christian policy had become interchangeable.[14]

Catholics controlled only seven reservations, which frustrated church leaders. In the years after the Civil War, they made up one of the largest denominational groups in the nation (and by some counts the largest). Furthermore, the peace policy explicitly undermined the long-standing efforts of their missionaries by putting protestant groups in charge of some reservations where Catholics had long labored. Rather than abandon generations of work, some individual Catholics ignored the religious boundaries established by the BIC and continued their outreach.

Catholic priest Luciano Osuna had started preaching among local tribes in California in 1864. In the early 1870s, the Round Valley Reservation, where Osuna often worked, came under Methodist jurisdiction. Methodist leaders had no interest in competing with Catholics for the loyalty of the Yuki people, so they tossed Osuna off the reservation multiple times. When Osuna maintained that as a Catholic priest he had a right to go where he pleased to minister, a Methodist reservation leader struck him with a cane. This did little to stop Osuna. He continued to visit the reservation, and eventually the Methodists had Osuna arrested and charged with insanity. A group of physicians declared him sane, and Osuna went free.

Frustrated by the government's policies and the experiences of those like Osuna, Catholics pushed for more access to Indigenous peoples with whom they had long-standing ties. They established a Bureau of Catholic Indian Missions in 1874 in Washington, DC, to lobby the government. Their efforts paid off. Government leaders granted Catholics access to several more reservations. Catholics, some protestants warned, had slyly outmaneuvered their religious rivals to gain the upper hand in ministry and to secure tax dollars to use for their religious purposes.

Many Indigenous people had little interest in submitting to the wishes of faraway policymakers and their missionary collaborators. They decided that to protect their way of life, they had to defend their lands and their cultures. At about the same time that missionary Charles Shelton aimed to drum up support for expanded missionary work in the West, the federal government moved in the 1880s to restrict the religious freedoms of Indigenous men and women.

Policymakers wanted to dispense with the old and replace it with the new.

Secretary of the Interior Henry M. Teller laid out a new list of policies and regulations for reservation life. He hoped to quash "old heathenish dances, such as the sun-dance, scalp-dance, &c," which he thought undermined assimilation efforts. "If the Indians now supported by the Government are not willing to discontinue them," he asserted, "the agents should be instructed to compel such discontinuance."[15]

Commissioner of Indian Affairs Hiram Price agreed with Teller. In 1884 he established the Code of Indian Offenses, which was complete with punishments. "The 'sun-dance,' the 'scalp-dance,' the 'war-dance,' and all other so-called feasts assimilating thereto, shall be considered 'Indian offenses,'" he decreed. He also targeted Indigenous spiritual leaders. "The usual practices of so-called 'medicine men,'" he warned, "shall be considered 'Indian offenses' cognizable by the Court of Indian Offenses."[16]

Yet the concerted efforts of federal agents to root out traditional Indigenous practices and the corresponding work of missionaries to replace them with Christianity never achieved the goals both aimed for. Religious revitalization movements—movements focused on restoring traditional Indigenous habits, customs, and beliefs—continued to characterize life on many reservations. During the winter of 1888–1889, a Paiute in Nevada named Wovoka claimed that performing a new sacred ritual later called the "Ghost Dance" would hasten the day when Whites would vanish from the earth, the buffalo would return, and the world would be restored. Wovoka's message spread and evolved rapidly among the tribes in the West. As the Ghost Dance morphed, many participants began to anticipate the coming of a new messiah, a savior for Indigenous people.

Troubled by the Ghost Dance and its growing popularity, White authorities sought to suppress it. Their crackdown revealed again the precarious nature of religious liberty in North America. Policymakers and the military did not hesitate to limit the religious practices of minority groups. The vast majority of Americans believed that for the good of the nation they needed to eradicate faiths outside of the Christian mainstream.

In November 1890, President Benjamin Harrison directed the army onto the Standing Rock Indian Reservation in South Dakota in order to crush the Ghost Dance movement. Many Lakota in the region had embraced the ritual and Harrison feared that this unusual religious practice might spawn rebellion. Reservation police sought to arrest the renowned warrior Sitting Bull, accusing him of allowing millennial fervor to sweep through his community. When one of Sitting Bull's followers opened fire on the police, chaos erupted, and an officer shot and killed Sitting Bull. His death sent shockwaves through the Lakota. What, they feared, would the government do next?

Many Lakota fled the reservation, hoping to evade government authorities. But they struggled to survive as the weather worsened, and that December a group of Lakota surrendered to the army at Wounded Knee, in South Dakota. While the soldiers collected weapons from the tribal members, a gun went off. The bullet did not hit anyone, but the shot caused a panic among the soldiers who began firing from an elevated position into the Lakota encampment. Lakota returned fire and army soldiers battled until hundreds of Lakota lay dead. The tragedy revealed that debates over religious freedom were far more than academic. For minority groups to choose to dissent from mainstream Christianity could mean death.

By the late 1880s, the battles between the US government and Indigenous tribes had mostly waned. Nevertheless, countless Indigenous peoples found ways to resist White efforts to overtake their land and to decimate their cultures, while others embraced Christianity, discovering value in the faith. And some did both at the same time.

A different kind of challenge to the nation's concept of religious liberty came with the growing power of the Church of Jesus Christ of Latter-day Saints. In 1846 saints began settling by the thousands on

Indigenous territory in the Salt Lake region. They believed that, like the Hebrews, God had led them into a new promised land.

At the end of the Mexican-American War a couple of years later, the United States seized Mexican lands including Utah. The Mormons had returned to the United States without having moved an inch. Brigham Young proposed that Congress establish a huge "State of Deseret" carved out of the massive Western territory. In the era before the Civil War, states had substantial autonomy, and Young saw this as an opportunity to build his own Christian kingdom within the United States.

Had Congress agreed, Young would have presided over the largest state in the nation. But instead, Congress made Utah a territory as part of the Compromise of 1850, a major legislative agreement that sought to maintain the balance of power between pro- and antislavery states. President Millard Fillmore named Young the territorial governor, and the Mormon prophet used his position to build a powerful church hierarchy that controlled just about every aspect of life in the region—from the militia to local law enforcement to the courts. The territorial legislature, dominated by saints, organized the church as a corporation, empowered it to oversee marriages in the territory, and authorized its control of far more land and resources than churches typically received in other states.

Utes, Shoshones, Paiutes, and Navajos all lived in the region—people the Mormons identified as the descendants of the ancient tribe of Lamanites featured in the Book of Mormon. Young hoped to find allies among the tribal nations, but the growing Mormon presence put pressure on fisheries and threatened Indigenous autonomy, which led to sporadic fighting.

By the 1850s, Young had established a thriving theocracy around the Great Salt Lake basin. But as more and more White gentiles (non-Mormons) settled in and near Utah, and as thousands of emigrants moved through Mormon country every year on their way west, the saints' dreams of a peaceful and separate existence began to crumble once again. Young's authoritarian rule provoked significant opposition from non-Mormons, and his form of Christianity offended many Americans.

The saints' practice of plural marriage elicited widespread criticism from outsiders. The Republican Party declared in its 1856 platform that "it is both the right and the imperative duty of Congress to prohibit in the Territories those twin relics of barbarism—Polygamy, and Slavery." That spring, President James Buchanan, a Democrat, moved into the White House. He believed that if he appropriated half the Republican agenda, the crusade against polygamy, he could focus attention away from the other half, the quest to end slavery. He moved to replace Young as territorial governor with a non-Mormon. Knowing Young would resist, he dispatched the army to Utah to oversee the transition. The Utah legislature warned Buchanan that it would not allow federal officials to impose their will on the region, which the president interpreted as an act of war. He declared the territory in rebellion, illustrating the real-world limitations that leaders of the protestant establishment and their political allies placed on dissenting groups' religious liberties.

Young prepared for battle. "Woe, woe," he declared, "to that man who comes here to unlawfully interfere with my affairs. Woe, woe to those men who come here to unlawfully meddle with me and this people." He instructed the saints to stockpile weapons and cease trading with emigrants, and he called up the Nauvoo Legion, the nation's only religious militia. He also encouraged the regional Indigenous tribes to seize cattle and supplies from wagon trains coming into the territory.[17]

In September 1857, over 120 emigrants on their way from Arkansas to California stopped in southern Utah. Threatened by local Paiutes, the migrants formed their wagons into a haphazardly constructed fort and prepared for a siege. Local Mormon leader John D. Lee, the "spiritual son" of Brigham Young, intervened. Waving a white flag of truce, Lee promised the emigrants safe passage out of Utah. But then he covertly arranged for Paiutes to attack the women and children while the LDS men killed every one of the unarmed men. The attackers used guns, knives, stones, and clubs to carry out the devilish deed. They spared the lives of only seventeen children, thought to be too young to remember what happened. Brigham Young then covered up the saints' role. As other Americans had inflicted violence upon the Mormons, so too in the Mountain Meadows Massacre did the saints unleash violence against others.

Later that year the saints and the US government reached a compromise. Young allowed the president's new territorial governor to move in, ending Utah's theocratic rule under a self-proclaimed LDS prophet. But politicians and legislators had not finished targeting the twin relics of barbarism. As the Civil War raged, President Lincoln signed the Morrill Anti-Bigamy Act, prohibiting polygamy in federal territories. The act further targeted the saints by establishing limits on the amount of property religious organizations could own.

After the war, polygamy continued to inspire anti-LDS vitriol, and the church showed no signs of abandoning the practice. LDS women became some of the staunchest defenders of plural marriage. One Mormon woman, who had seven sister wives, explained her theological reasoning to her skeptical New England family. She drew on the Old Testament patriarchs to show that God condoned polygamy, and then she tied this to Jesus's claim that God had woven true believers into the line of Abraham, a polygamist. "According to Jesus Christ and the Apostles, then," she wrote, "the only way to be saved, is to be adopted into the great family of polygamists, by the gospel, and then strictly follow their examples." This meant repudiating her biological family. Latter-day Saints also noted that many so-called Christian men had affairs and kept mistresses. Better, they argued, to join in marriage and ensure that men treated women with kindness and support rather than use and discard them.[18]

In 1874, Mormon leaders decided to challenge the constitutionality of the Morrill Act. They grew tired of dodging the government, and the act made it difficult for church representatives to build power in Washington. They argued that under the First Amendment's free-exercise clause they had a right to plural marriage. Eventually the case reached the US Supreme Court. In *Reynolds v. United States*

The Latter-day Saints' practice of plural marriage, which the US Supreme Court determined was not protected by the First Amendment, inspired vehement persecution. This cartoon, in which the devil plays the violin while a Latter-day Saint dances with his wives, illustrates the kinds of propaganda the saints endured. (credit: Maria Van Dusen, "A Mormon and His Wives Dancing to the Devil's Tune," 1850, Beinecke Rare Book and Manuscript Library, Yale University)

(1879), the justices ruled that the First Amendment did not provide protection for plural marriage. To "permit this," the court argued, "would be to make the professed doctrines of religious belief superior to the law of the land, and in effect to permit every citizen to become a law unto himself." They argued that the saints could believe what they wanted, but they could not act on those beliefs if those actions violated the law. Most Americans agreed with this reading of the amendment. As interpreted, the Constitution mostly protected the rights of mainstream protestant groups to worship as they saw fit. Although many of the founders had intended the Bill of Rights to protect the rights of minority groups, judges often proved reluctant to defend those rights.[19]

The saints remained defiant and pledged to obey God and not the courts. Even Catholics, often victims of persecution themselves, piled on. Archbishop James Cardinal Gibbons wrote, "Every man that has the welfare of his country at heart, can not fail to view with alarm the existence and the gradual development of Mormonism, which is a plague-spot on our civilization, a discredit to our Government, a degradation of the female sex, and a standing menace to the sanctity of the marriage bond." Catholic leaders hoped that American officials would recognize their church as part of the religious mainstream, and some saw distancing themselves from other minority faiths as a shrewd strategy.[20]

Once the court determined that the Constitution did not protect plural marriage, federal authorities started cracking down on saints who engaged in the practice, and they threatened to seize church property, including temples. Many saints, seeking to avoid persecution, went into hiding, some as far away as England. Others moved across the border to Mexico. Polygamous church leaders who remained in Utah relocated frequently, moving from home to home, always hoping to stay one step ahead of the authorities.

Mormon President Wilford Woodruff opened the new year of 1886 with an ominous entry in his journal. "Persecution" by the government, he wrote, "against the Latter Day Saints has commenced in the year 1885 And there is a prospect of its being very severe during 1886." The next year Woodruff felt even more pessimistic. He believed that American leaders were "depriving the Latter day Saints of all Civil Religious & political rights which the Constitution guarantees unto us" and "for our religion." In his estimation, "Earth & Hell with the priests & people of this Nation are uniting together to try to destroy the Church of Christ & the Zion & Kingdom of God from off the Earth."[21]

To keep hell and the priests and people of the United States from prevailing, Woodruff finally shifted positions. "I have arived at a point in the History of my life as the President of the Church of Jesus Christ of Latter Day Saints," he recorded in his journal on September 25, 1890, where "I am under the necessity of acting for the Temporal Salvation of the Church." He worried that if he did not change course, moral crusaders might destroy American Mormonism. After prayer and counsel, he issued a new proclamation, which for the LDS faithful proved nearly earth-shattering. The church, he vowed, would no longer conduct plural marriages. "We are not teaching poligamy or plural marriage nor permitting any person to Enter into the practice" any longer. "I hereby declare my intention to submit to those laws and to use my influence with the members of the Church over which I preside to have them do likewise." And, he added, "I now publicly declair that my advice to the Latter Day Saints is to refrain from contracting any Marriage forbidden by the Law of the land."[22]

Six years later, in 1896, Utah achieved statehood.

In 1893, at the annual meeting of the American Historical Association, Professor Frederick Jackson Turner delivered a speech entitled "The Significance of the Frontier in American History." The West, Turner lectured, had fostered democracy and served as a safety valve, absorbing legions of immigrants and native-born Americans and providing them with land, opportunity, and independence. He emphasized the crucial role of religion in the federal government's conquest of the region. Churches served not only to provide religious support—they established the civil, social, and moral frameworks that helped transform the "frontier" from a potential backwater into an integrated and vital part of the United States. "The most effective efforts of the East to regulate the frontier came through its educational and religious activity, exerted by interstate migration and by organized societies," he summarized. The major churches "strove for the possession" of the West. "The multiplication of rival churches in the little frontier towns had deep and lasting social effects. The religious aspects of the frontier make a chapter in our history."[23]

The "frontier," however, had supposedly closed in 1890, when the census revealed that the nation had no more "free" land. "And now, four centuries from the discovery of America," Turner concluded, "the frontier has gone, and with its going has closed the first period of American history." Although his conclusion presumed that Indigenous people never had any rights to land, he was right in one sense: The United States government allied with mainstream protestant churches had imposed its will and its version of the Christian faith on many of the peoples of the American West. Christian missionaries and activists, perhaps more than any other group, had shaped the region as it evolved.[24]

But the future was far from certain. Turner warned that with the closing of the "frontier" and the exhaustion of "free" land, the United States was heading into an unpredictable new era. Without the safety valve of the West to absorb restless populations, how would the nation manage the waves of immigrants now flooding its shores? For many protestant leaders, the answer was clear: They would take up the mantle of Americanizing and Christianizing the newcomers, determining the nation's identity in the process.

PART IV

THE CHALLENGES OF THE MODERN WORLD

16

IMMIGRATING FAITH

In 1893, the World's Columbian Exposition, commonly known as the World's Fair, opened in Chicago, drawing tourists from all around the globe. The most popular area of the fair, the Midway Plaisance, consisted of a strip of hodgepodge exhibits that stretched nearly a mile long, where fairgoers could supposedly encounter distinctive and alluring "heathen" cultures and religions. Music and the chatter of dozens of languages filled the section with a vibrancy and dissonance. Turkish bazaars, a Cairo market, and an enormous Ferris wheel drew fair goers to the Midway day and night, as did Hungarian "gypsies," South Seas islanders living in thatched huts, and a belly dancer called "Little Egypt." One visitor noted that he had heard that some of the exhibits revealed "the worst violations of decency and virtue he ever heard of: vile dens, revolting performances, etc." He chose to skip the Midway and yet, somehow, he knew what it displayed.[1]

Liberal protestants made the most of the fair, hoping to use it to expand their influence in the United States and abroad. They organized the World's Parliament of Religions, which met in conjunction with the exposition, bringing together Buddhists, Taoists, Hindus,

Zoroastrians, Jains, Catholics, protestants, Jews, and an (American) Muslim to discuss their common beliefs and practices. Organizers invited one African Methodist Episcopal minister to represent Black churches both in the United States and in all of Africa. He joked that he gave "color to this vast Parliament of Religions." The most popular speaker at the meeting was Swami Vivekananda, an Indian guru, who introduced yoga and Vedanta to the United States.[2]

The organizers made room on the stage for many global faiths, but they established outer limits. They excluded North American Indigenous spiritual leaders as well as members of the Church of Jesus Christ of Latter-day Saints. The liberal protestants did not want the two groups, both of whom had suffered tremendous persecution at the hands of American Christians, telling their stories to an international audience.

The liberal protestant organizers had mixed ideas about what they hoped to accomplish. Some aspired to see the globe's major religious leaders tear down the boundaries that separated them and identify a set of core universal religious truths that might bind all faiths together. But most of the American protestants at the event believed that they held the ultimate truth. They felt confident that all people would or should embrace Christianity, and they viewed the parliament as a means of helping achieve this goal.

One of the organizers, Chicago Presbyterian minister John Henry Barrows, envisioned the parliament as a showcase for the "simple faith in Divine Fatherhood and Human Brotherhood" offered through Jesus Christ—the "Asiatic Peasant who was the Son of God." Barrows hoped the gathering would help those engaged in "the work of Christian evangelization" identify common ground before emphasizing divisions. For Barrows and his allies, the better Christians understood other religions, the more effectively they could convert their followers.[3]

Many of the foreign representatives at the parliament had very different priorities and expectations. Near the end of the conference Vivekananda told the audience that "much has been said of the common ground of religious unity. But if anyone here hopes that this unity will come by the triumph of any one of these religions and the destruction of the others, to him I say: 'Brother, yours is an impossible hope.'" Vivekananda had no interest in conversions or in seeing Christianity overtake the world. "If anybody dreams of the exclusive survival of his own religion and the destruction of the others," the guru concluded, "I pity him from the bottom of my heart."[4]

Disagreements among faith leaders over religious expansion and conquest represented one part of a larger debate about empire, which raged in the 1890s in the press and among politicians, church leaders, and ordinary Americans. The world was shrinking, and national boundaries were changing. Peoples and ideas and resources intersected in new ways. With European countries expanding their territory and claiming new colonies, Americans from political leaders to missionary executives wondered if they too should further commit to the race for empire. Men and women argued about the role of the US in the world and about the kind of nation they wanted to build. How large could the nation grow while maintaining its divine mission? Should it seal its borders, or expand further, seeking new territory? Should Americans welcome strangers and aliens into their midst, or build a wall?

As Americans wrestled over these issues, immigration surged. Many newcomers arrived with deep commitments to Catholicism, Judaism, and other religions. They had to determine how best to accommodate their beliefs to the heavily protestant nation. Some sought isolation, hoping to be left alone, but others acculturated. They painted a protestant veneer over their traditional faiths. They recognized that even as the nation grew more diverse, the protestant establishment still set the rules by which all other groups had to play. For the protestants themselves, "christianizing" and "Americanizing" immigrants became a top priority. They worked with their partners in the government to ensure that newcomers adapted to their Christian values and their understanding of the nation.

In the late nineteenth century, railroads and steamships made it much easier for people to travel far greater distances than in any previous generation. The United States had relatively open immigration policies and millions of men and women, looking for fresh opportunities, arrived on American shores from all over the world. The surge in immigration benefited the Catholic Church more than any other religious group. Between the Civil War and the turn of the century, the percentage of Americans identifying as Catholics doubled from about 8 percent of the population to 17 percent. Catholics overtook Methodists as the largest denomination in the nation.

American Catholic leaders faced the daunting task of unifying a diverse constituency in a predominantly protestant nation. Poles, Germans, Italians, Irish, Hispanics, and others brought unique religious and cultural practices to their new homeland. The Irish dominated church leadership, comprising half of the bishops in the 1880s and two-thirds by 1900. They promoted a standardized faith and worked to integrate Catholicism into the American context.

Germans sought to preserve their old-world languages and practices, believing that isolation from broader American culture best protected their faith and their children's. In the upper Midwest, they established German-speaking parishes and schools. Poles, like Germans, aimed to maintain their homeland's worship styles and set up national parishes. Frustration with Irish leadership led one group to form the Polish National Catholic Church.

Italian immigrants brought a suspicion of church hierarchy and power, having lived near the Vatican. They knew the church's public image concealed flaws visible only to insiders. Italians viewed the church as central to life's milestones—baptism, first communion, marriage, death—but were less committed to regular mass attendance.

Hispanics and especially Mexicans had their own unique experiences in the United States. In the late nineteenth century, Mexico experienced a shortage of clergy, particularly in rural regions, which led lay leaders and local communities to develop their own folk religious practices. They made veneration of Our Lady of Guadalupe the center of their devotional life. Around the turn of the century over a million people moved north across the border from Mexico. In the West and Southwest, Hispanics filled church pews, yet the vast majority of their priests had Irish or French roots. Unlike in the East and Midwest, where the Catholic hierarchy initially permitted immigrants to organize national congregations around their culture and language, in the West church leaders sought to speed Hispanic assimilation into White American culture through English-speaking parishes.

Yet even as church leaders pushed for assimilation, they faced urgent practical challenges. In East Coast cities, the number of orphans was growing. Catholic leaders tried to place those they could with Catholic families, hoping that if parents reared children in the faith, they would stay in the faith. Church leaders turned to Mexican Catholics for help with this project. In 1904, a group of nuns from New York City traveled with forty Irish orphans to a mining town in Arizona, where they placed the children with Catholic Mexican families. The White residents of the mining town exploded in rage. They did not believe that Catholics should ever place White children with Mexican families. Among other things, they claimed that the Mexicans' beans and tortillas would make the White children sick. In the "great Arizona orphan abduction," some local White families kidnapped the children at gunpoint from their Mexican homes and threatened to lynch the nuns who had brought them, as well as the local Catholic priest. A series of lawsuits followed, and the courts determined that placing White children with Mexicans constituted a form of child abuse. The children never returned to the Mexican American homes. The event illustrates how even in communities in the Southwest where Whites and Mexican Americans worked side by side, a huge cultural chasm created a nearly impenetrable wall between them.

Immigrants brought new life and vitality to the church, but American-born leaders continued to shape much of its overall trajectory. A Catholic convert from Methodism, Isaac Hecker, became one of the church's most important innovators. The pope permitted him to launch a new order in the United States, the Missionary Society of St. Paul (the Paulist Fathers). To spread his message, he founded a magazine, *The Catholic World*. Hecker hoped to evangelize American protestants and to draw them into the Catholic fold.

Hecker repackaged the faith in terms that native-born Americans understood. He aimed to reconcile Americans' commitment to what they perceived as the exceptional nature of their country with what global Catholic leaders viewed as the church's core, universal essentials. Navigating the separation of church from state was one of his greatest challenges. Vatican leaders had long believed that countries should aim to make Catholicism their established religion and use the power of the state to root out heresy. Many American Catholic leaders knew the Vatican's position challenged core American ideas, which made Catholics vulnerable to criticism. Leaders like Hecker had to proceed carefully.

Rather than parrot Catholic teaching, Hecker instead made the case that Catholicism best represented American ideals. He offered an alternative, and mostly invented, history, crediting the Catholic Church with inspiring foundational American ideas about religious freedom. He called separation "the keystone of the arch of American liberties, and Catholics of all climes can point to it with special delight." Protestants, Hecker insisted, represented the true opponents of religious freedom. "Protestant religious dogmas," not Catholic beliefs, "are foreign to republicanism and lead to a theocracy in politics."[5]

Hecker and his fellow believers worried especially about the next generation of Catholics. They knew that protestants aimed to convert as many people as possible and that public schools had long served as one of protestants' most effective state-funded tools for indoctrinating children. "The so-called American public-school system," Hecker alleged, "is a cunningly-devised scheme, under the show of zeal for popular education, to force the state, in violation of American principles of liberty, to impose an unjust and heavy tax on its citizens, with the intent of injuring the Catholic Church." Not only did modern education hurt Catholic children, he continued, but it was "sapping in the minds of the American youth the foundations of all religion and driving them into infidelity."[6]

Convinced that Catholic children needed their own schools, Americans bishops, meeting in Baltimore at the Third Plenary Council

in 1884, called on local priests to expand their educational efforts. "For thirty years and more the Catholic population of this country has been forced to pay tribute to a system of godless education of which not one can conscientiously take advantage," one Catholic leader lamented, echoing Hecker. "Millions of money are annually taken from Catholics for the support of schools in which they have no interest," he protested. "The Catholic considers it unfair to tax him for the support of schools from which all ideas of religion are excluded, nor can he accept those in which a false religion is taught." Abandoning any hope in the public schools, bishops recommended that within two years every priest in the United States ensure that his parish had its own Catholic school.[7]

The work of American Catholics like Hecker to adapt the faith to the American context troubled some church leaders. Conservative clergy in the United States, Europe, and at the Vatican worried that too many American Catholics had erred in championing religious freedom, that they had embraced a new heresy. In 1895, Pope Leo XIII issued the encyclical *Longinqua*. After praising the United States and the growth and success of the church in North America, he clarified that Catholics should not emulate or champion the American model of government. "It would be very erroneous," he warned, "to draw the conclusion that in America is to be sought the type of the most desirable status of the Church, or that it would be universally lawful or expedient for State and Church to be, as in America, dissevered and divorced."[8]

The encyclical did not quell the debate. In the early 1890s a new biography of Hecker celebrated the convert's accommodating of Catholicism to its political context. Radical clerics in the US and Europe used the Paulist Father's example to defend their efforts to modernize the faith and to adapt it to their particular national environments. Once again, Pope Leo intervened. He sent a letter to Archbishop James Cardinal Gibbons entitled *Testem Benevolentiae Nostrae* to address what became known as the "Americanism" controversy. "From the foregoing it is manifest," he wrote, "that we are not able to give approval to those views which, in their collective sense, are called by some 'Americanism.'" The pope did not want the members of his global church to undersell their differences with protestants, and he rejected the American principle of the separation of church and state. The pope believed that, ideally, governments and the Catholic Church should rule nations together.[9]

Many native-born protestants, like the antebellum Know-Nothings decades earlier, looked down on Catholics and especially Catholic immigrants. In some cities in the urban North, they formed anti-immigrant groups such as the American Protective Association (APA), which had over one million members in the 1880s. Its leaders aimed to restrict further immigration, to curtail the rights of those who had already arrived, and to drive Catholics out of politics. The group also criticized large corporations for attracting immigrant workers to the United States and complained that immigrants undercut White laborers' earning power. The potent combination of fears of immigrants and anger at the wealthy for employing them merged in this era into a new expression of populist nativism that has lingered in American culture ever since.

Jews, like Catholics, worked to preserve their faith in a nation dominated by protestants. In the late nineteenth century, more than one million Jews immigrated to the United States. Some maintained their old-world traditions, practicing what they described as the traditional Orthodox faith. Others innovated. A group of American and European Jews in the mid-nineteenth century developed a new expression of Judaism they called Reform. American Rabbi Isaac Mayer Wise argued that the "principle" of Judaism "must develop new forms corresponding to the new conditions which surround its votaries who live among the civilized nations." Reform Jews worshipped on Sundays instead of on the traditional Saturday Sabbath, let men and women sit together at worship, rejected circumcision, turned bar mitzvahs into confirmations, and downplayed traditional dietary laws. They aimed to update the faith to match the realities of the modern world.[10]

For some Jews, Reform had gone too far. They developed a third branch in the United States called Conservative Judaism. Adherents focused on maintaining Jewish culture and tradition, but they spurned the dogmatism of their Orthodox counterparts. Conservatives wanted to maintain their connection to the historic Jewish faith but did not necessarily accept the most narrow and literal interpretations of it. They engaged with modern scholarship, including textual criticism of the Torah and the Talmud. Jews' relative freedom in North America allowed them to launch new traditions and remake old ones to suit their particular needs and desires.

Despite their increasing numbers in the United States, Jews around the turn of the century mostly maintained a low profile. Facing anti-Semitism nearly everywhere, they did not yet push back against protestant hegemony but instead worked to carve out decent lives for themselves and their families in a nation organized around protestant values and ideals.

Millions of protestants also immigrated to the United States in the nineteenth century. They helped breathe new life into conservative ethnic churches. In the upper Midwest and especially Michigan, immigrants from the Netherlands built the Dutch Reformed Church. At mid-century some members split away to start the Christian Reformed Church (CRC). While the CRC remained small, it became an intellectual powerhouse, launching new Christian presses and institutions of higher education, including Calvin College. During the twentieth century, the CRC exercised disproportionate influence on both the revivalist and conservative streams of North American Christianity while essentially straddling the two. Meanwhile, millions of Germans and Scandinavians poured into Lutheran pews, especially in the Midwest. By World War I, only Catholics, Baptists, and Methodists outnumbered American Lutherans.

While White Americans living in the East fretted about European immigration, some in the West feared the ships arriving from Asia. White American Christians had varying responses to the newcomers. Some missionaries saw potential in the Chinese and wanted to bring as many as possible to the United States where they might convert them to Christianity. Others hoped to curtail immigration. They preferred that missionaries carry on their work ministering to the Chinese in China, not in the American West.

As the number of immigrants swelled, the California state legislature reconsidered its immigration policies. Sacramento Congregationalist Minister S. V. Blakeslee told senators that the arrival of "heathens" would shake the nation from its Christian foundations. People will craft a government in their own image, he claimed, either "noble, righteous, peaceful, Christian; or, base, corrupt, iniquitous, heathenish." Rather than make the Chinese Christians, Blakeslee worried that the Chinese would make Americans godless. "Where Americans have converted one Chinaman to Christianity, the Chinese," the minister claimed, "have converted ten Americans to real heathenism. Their dens of infamy, and of gambling, and of opium, are numerous in our cities and country towns, and various efforts are made for filling them with victims." Unless the state halted immigration, Blakeslee warned, the persecution of Christians at the hands of Chinese was "inevitable."[11]

Ultimately, the federal government intervened. In 1882 Congress passed the Chinese Exclusion Act, which banned Chinese immigration altogether. For the first time, the US government barred an entire racial group from entering the United States.

Nevertheless, anti-Chinese sentiment continued to grow. The popular national magazine *North American Review* published dueling articles in 1887 about the immigration debate. The first, by journalist and activist Wong Chin Foo, made the case that "heathen" Chinese were nothing to fear in a "Christian" country. "We do not," he sarcastically noted, "organize into cowardly mobs under the guise of social or political reform, to plunder and murder with impunity; and we are so far advanced in our heathenism as to no longer tolerate popular feeling or religious prejudice to defeat justice or cause injustice." Wong noted that Chinese immigrants faced many forms of discrimination and violence. To survive they created their own small, segregated "Chinatowns" on the outskirts of western cities. Wong ended his article with an inverted altar call. He "earnestly" invited "the Christians of America to come to Confucius."[12]

The next month *North American Review* printed a rejoinder from Yan Phou Lee, a graduate of Yale and a revivalist converted under popular preacher Dwight Moody, entitled "Why I Am Not a Heathen." He insisted that Christians were Chinese immigrants' best friends. While he acknowledged the discrimination immigrants faced in the United States, he attributed xenophobia and anti-Chinese riots to the godless rather than the godly. "I was intelligent enough to know that Christians had no hand in those outrages," he wrote. "If there is any sentiment in this country in favor of the Chinese to-day, it is only to be found in the Christian church." He ended his essay, like Wong, with an altar call. "Do you wonder that I am a Christian? I cordially invite all heathen, whether American, or English, or Chinese, to come to the Saviour."[13]

Lee and Foo both recognized that many White protestants held nativist prejudices. White Americans believed that a Christian country could remain Christian only if its leaders blocked immigration from the non-Christian parts of the globe. Those who did arrive discovered the power of the unofficial protestant establishment. The United States was not, in any real sense, a nation that practiced church-state separation. Immigrants had no choice but to modify their faiths to their new contexts, to become like protestants if they hoped to thrive. Yet no matter how hard they tried, they could never adapt enough to mollify the fears of nativist crusaders.

As millions of immigrants sought refuge in the United States, American protestants continued to look abroad to make converts and enlarge their kingdom. Serving as the new chosen people required them to take Jesus's gospel to the ends of the earth. The nation's growing army of missionaries represented the first foot soldiers of American overseas expansion. In 1860, the United States had sixteen missionary societies. By 1900, this number had surged to over ninety organizations sending missionaries abroad. Many of these societies were founded and operated by women, who by the early twentieth century constituted the majority of American missionaries.

Missionaries worked in many different capacities. Presbyterian executive Robert Speer estimated in 1902 that the "Christian" nations of the world ran 558 missionary societies, 7,319 mission stations, 14,364 organized churches, 94 colleges and universities, 20,458 schools, 379 hospitals, 782 dispensaries, 64 missionary ships, and 152 publishing houses that printed Bibles in 452 languages. His numbers indicated the evolving nature of the missions enterprise. For much of American history, missionaries had generally focused on converting unbelievers to the Christian faith. Their work, at least as they understood it, focused first and foremost on spiritual transformation. By the turn of the twentieth century, however, many missionary organizations had evolved alongside changes in the protestant faith. Seeking to remain relevant in a rapidly changing world, they adopted a more socially oriented gospel that emphasized saving bodies along with souls.[14]

Missionaries often viewed the gospel and American values as interdependent. Popular minister Josiah Strong advised a missionary group to export with Christianity "Anglo-Saxon" faith and "civilization." The "two great needs of mankind," he contended, were "a pure, spiritual Christianity" and "civil liberty." White Christians needed, for the sake of the world, to follow God's directive to be their "brother's keeper." They had a burden to "save" the rest of humankind.[15]

By the late nineteenth century, American church leaders had developed a comprehensive vision of foreign missions. John R. Mott, the most influential missionary organizer of the era, published a book in 1900 with a self-explanatory title: *The Evangelization of the World in This Generation*. Building on the work of longtime missionary organizer A. T. Pierson, he believed that missionary societies should ensure that all people had the opportunity to convert to Christianity, but their methods might take different forms in different places. He encouraged missionaries to integrate four approaches—educational, literary, medical, and evangelistic—as they introduced every tribe and nation to Christianity. Although he used more tempered language than Strong, his ideas had similar implications. God had tasked missionaries with not only transforming souls but also whole persons, remaking the lost in the image of Americans.[16]

Missionaries' work had transformative effects in many parts of the world, sometimes intentionally, and sometimes not. Just as American religious leaders justified the conquest of North American Indigenous lands as part of God's plan for the United States, so too did they view the expansion of the nation beyond its coasts as divinely orchestrated.

The 1898 Spanish-Cuban-American War, sometimes called the Spanish-American War, allowed missionaries to realize some of their dreams. Expansionist-oriented Americans had long viewed the Philippines as a strategic site for facilitating Pacific trade. When the US declared war on Spain, Commander George Dewey, leading the Pacific fleet, sailed from China to the Philippines, where he engaged the Spanish navy. In just seven hours the Americans secured the victory. The Americans now had control over a new, important, and predominately Catholic region in the Pacific with more than seven million people.

Protestant missionary leaders rejoiced. Two executives with the American Board of Commissioners for Foreign Missions noted, "It was not ambition, or greed for territory, or any human impulse that brought our flag to Manila and has held it there these five months, the glorious symbol of liberty and a Christian civilization; it was the will of God, and we stand in awe as we think of it." Liberal protestant minister Washington Gladden agreed. He believed that the United States was "divinely called" to intervene in the Caribbean and Pacific against Catholic Spain. He argued that taking Spanish territories "means that we shall give the people a thousand times more liberty than they ever dreamed of possessing." "If this is imperialism," he added, "I am an imperialist."[17]

President William McKinley claimed that God had instructed him to seize the Philippines. "I went down on my knees and prayed Almighty God for light and guidance more than one night," he told a group of religious leaders. "And one night late it came to me this way—I don't know how it was, but it came." What had God told the president? "That there was nothing left for us to do but to take them all, and to educate the Filipinos, and uplift and civilize and Christianize them and by God's grace do the very best we could by them, as our fellow men for whom Christ also died." McKinley, like the missionaries who preceded him, believed that Americans had an obligation to bring protestant Christianity and American values to the rest of the world.[18]

Many American Christians believed that God had directed McKinley's hand. They saw American imperialism as part of God's divine plan and as an ideal tool for spreading the protestant faith. Baptist theologian William Newton Clarke claimed that "the attitude of the religion that bears the name of Jesus Christ is not one of compromise, but one of conflict and conquest. It proposes to displace the other religions." The "intention to conquer," he asserted, "is characteristic of the gospel."[19]

Others read the gospel differently. In accepting the Democratic nomination for president for a second time in 1900, Presbyterian William Jennings Bryan asked, "If true Christianity consists in carrying out in our daily lives the teachings of Christ, who will say that we are commanded to civilize with dynamite and proselyte with the sword?" Imperialism, he continued, "finds no warrant in the Bible. The command 'Go ye into all the world and preach the gospel to every creature' has no gatling-gun attachment."[20]

Black activist and reformer W. E. B. Du Bois believed that religious leaders had become the tools of colonizers. He called "the problem" of the twentieth century "the problem of the colour line," which White Christians exacerbated. "Let not the cloak of Christian missionary enterprise be allowed in the future," he argued, "as so often in the past, to hide the ruthless economic exploitation and political downfall of less developed nations, whose chief fault has been reliance on the plighted faith of the Christian church."[21]

The American occupation of the Philippines presented a particular challenge for American Catholics. While they did not necessarily oppose imperialism, they didn't want protestants moving by force into Catholic regions. Just as they objected to protestant missionaries' invasion of the Indigenous territory in the West that they had dominated, so too did they look skeptically on protestant designs for the formerly Spanish Philippines. "I cannot approve," Archbishop John Ireland fretted, "of any efforts of Protestants to affect the religious duties of the inhabitants of the islands. Catholics are there in complete control; they have a thorough church organization; the inhabitants are Catholic. . . .

Protestantism will never take the place in their hearts of that faith." He rightfully worried that Filipinos would conflate American protestant missionaries with the American government and official US policy. Appealing to the nation's colonial ambitions, he continued, "Do your Protestant missionaries realize that they are doing the greatest harm to America by making her flag unpopular?"[22]

Even further west, in China, Americans again confronted questions over the relationships among imperialism, missionary work, and business. Missionaries had invested heavily in Asia beginning in the 1830s, and their growing influence inadvertently threatened local Chinese cultures, economies, and political systems. Some Chinese men and women saw the missionaries as a front for dangerous European and American imperial and capitalist designs. In the 1880s and 1890s, groups of Chinese men and women periodically launched anti-Western riots that targeted missionary property. They also harassed and sometimes killed missionaries and native converts. Anti-foreign riots climaxed in 1900 with the Boxer Uprising, during which anti-foreign Chinese killed thirty-two American missionaries and hundreds of Chinese Christians.

Missionary agencies as well as their supporters in the US asked the government to intercede on behalf of the Americans in China. Their request was not unique. American diplomats had previously intervened in various parts of the world on behalf of missionaries. The State Department offered missionaries privileges not normally extended to Americans traveling abroad, and the government negotiated with foreign powers to protect not just the missionaries themselves but also their property.

American protestants sought to apply their understanding of the Christian faith to every major American policy directive, foreign and domestic. They thought they had little choice. "We will not renounce our part in the mission of our race, trustee, under God, of the civilization of the world," Senator Albert Beveridge vowed on the floor of the

United States Senate after the Spanish-Cuban-American War. God, he declared, "has marked us as His chosen people, henceforth to lead in the regeneration of the world."[23]

To fulfill this divine mandate, protestant activists tried to shape immigration policy and force those who came to the United States to conform to mainstream White protestant norms. But they could not stop the inevitable. Immigrants made the nation more diverse. Christian leaders also looked outside of North America, venturing into all the world carrying the flag in one hand and the Bible in the other. Maintaining their role as God's peculiar people and ensuring that the United States remained his chosen land required nothing less.

But as the globe shrank and demographics shifted, protestant activists and their allies in government faced a daunting question: How best could they fulfill their mission in a changing world? In the near term they redoubled their efforts to root out the many sins that threatened to unravel the nation. They also sought to minister to the physical needs of those they hoped to convert and to keep them in the fold.

17

SAVING AND PURIFYING BODIES

Carry A. Nation intended to carry the nation to righteousness. The religious wanderer wanted Americans to purge their bodies and their communities of sin. She used both a Bible and a hatchet to attack demon rum and to compel Americans to obey her directives. While reformers had always worried about Americans' spiritual lives, in the late nineteenth century activists like Nation placed a new emphasis on their physical bodies as well.

Born Caroline (Carrie) Amelia Moore in 1854, Carry married Disciples of Christ minister David Nation in 1874. Carrie later changed the spelling of her first name to "Carry." Like Sojourner Truth, she used her name to convey her sense of mission.

Frustrated by Kansas leaders' indifference to booze, Nation established a local branch of the Woman's Christian Temperance Union (WCTU). Then she tried to enforce prohibition laws herself. The six-foot-tall crusader stood directly outside saloons, where she prayed out loud for God to close them down, sang mocking songs about the consequences of drink, and pounded on a hand organ to draw attention.

Convinced that God had called her to escalate her protests, in 1900 Nation started attacking the inside of saloons with rocks and bricks. An early incursion, she recalled, did not go as planned. "I threw a brick at the mirror, which was a very heavy one, and it did not break, but the brick fell and broke every thing in its way." Then she saw what she needed. "I was standing by a billiard table on which there was one ball. I said: 'Thank God,' and picked it up, and threw it and it made a hole in the mirror." She also attacked paintings of nude women.[1]

As controversy over Nation's tactics grew, the temperance activist claimed that God told her to "smash the saloons." He reinforced this violent directive through scripture. In Nation's Bible, next to Jeremiah 1:10, which reads, "See, I have this day set thee over the nations and over the kingdoms, to root out, and to pull down, and to destroy, and to throw down, to build, and to plant," she scribbled "smashing." But she knew smashing was unorthodox and worried that people thought she was "partially insane." Like many religious zealots, and especially women religious zealots, Nation's unwavering passion for improving her community led people to question her mental acuity.[2]

As Nation fine-tuned her smashing approach, she developed a unique method she called "hatchetation"—using hatchets to bust up saloons. To finance her efforts, she sold small pewter hatchet pins. Savvy saloonkeepers fought back. They had her arrested, and some hired women to attack Nation when she appeared. In more than one instance, they badly beat the religious crusader. Bars and saloons even began hanging signs that read, "All Nations Welcome Except Carry!"

In the last decades of the nineteenth century, Christians like Nation sought to minister to the whole person, to demonstrate that Christianity was a religion of the body and not just the soul. God cared not just about heartfelt conversions, but also about the condition of peoples' actual hearts (and livers). The Civil War had left hundreds of thousands of men maimed, and Americans looked for healing in all kinds of places. Christian leaders recognized that they needed to take a page from their missionary colleagues and focus on the physical and not just the spiritual. Revivalists, mavericks, spiritual seekers, and iconoclasts recalibrated the faith to match the context, making

Carry A. Nation wanted Americans to purge their bodies and their communities of sin. Like the woman depicted here, she used a hatchet to attack demon rum and the saloons that sold it. (credit: Currier & Ives, *Woman's Holy War*, ca. 1874, New York: Currier & Ives, Library of Congress)

Christianity relevant in new ways to the changing needs of the American people.

Activists pursued a range of strategies to minister to the body. Some worked to pass laws that would compel Americans to purify their lives—censoring speech, regulating sexuality, and curbing alcohol consumption. Others embraced a theology of physical healing, renewing attention to Jesus as the great physician. Together, these efforts urged Americans to turn not to secular authorities but to the savior who could heal both body and soul; and to his self-appointed agents on earth. Many Christians believed that by cleansing individual bodies, they could help cleanse the nation itself.

Living through the turmoil leading up to and during the Civil War, some Americans suspected that the end-times had begun. Although Jesus had not returned as Baptist preacher William Miller predicted, some of his followers, including Ellen G. White, continued matching up Bible prophecy with current events as if they were assembling a puzzle with new pieces that seemed to appear every day. White had converted to revivalist Christianity through Methodist camp meetings and then grew enamored with Miller's end-times predictions. When Jesus did not return to earth as Miller and his followers expected, White claimed that Jesus had instead entered the holiest part of heaven in preparation for his still-imminent return.

In 1863 White and a few others formally organized the Seventh-day Adventist Church, a new denomination, hoping to spread the message of Jesus's Second Coming. Their name reflected their conviction that Christians should observe and keep holy the original, Jewish seventh-day Sabbath (Saturday) as they awaited Christ's return. Although Adventists maintained that the Bible was their only authority, they regarded White—who claimed that God gave her thousands of revelatory visions—as a modern-day prophet who was instrumental in shaping, reforming, and purifying the faith.

After the war, White received a new revelation: God wanted her to open a home for healing. Her church sanitarium would provide the faithful with prayer and holistic medical treatments in an environment that protected them from practices—both medical and moral—to which Christians like White objected. In an era in which the doctor's cure might be as dangerous as the disease, thousands of Christians turned to the great physician to restore their bodies.

The Adventists' launch of the Western Health Reform Institute in 1866 in Battle Creek, Michigan, marked the start of what became an expansive, worldwide effort by the church to establish medical clinics that integrated healthy diets, natural cures, and prayer. To help run the growing Battle Creek sanitarium White recruited John Harvey Kellogg. Kellogg's father had served as an Adventist health reformer, and as a teen John had worked in the church's publishing department. A voracious reader, he educated himself on all manner of Adventist beliefs and reforms. Kellogg continued his studies in more orthodox (for the time) medical schools. In 1875 he returned to Battle Creek and with White sought to update, perfect, and oversee practices at the institute. He convinced church leaders to build a massive, state-of-the-art medical and surgical sanitarium. Kellogg wanted to integrate naturalist cures with the best scientific medical practices of the day.

In Battle Creek the Adventists sought to cook meals that were as healthy as possible. God did not want Christians, White believed, consuming meat, alcohol, or tobacco. Such messages often paralleled the ideas promoted by other reformers at the time. They recognized that Americans ate too many fatty foods and drank too much alcohol. Adventists championed instead whole grains, plain fruits, and vegetables, and they used little salt and other seasonings. Seeking to attract people to their movement rather than repel them with tasteless, flavorless meals, the Adventists created appetizing substitutes. Kellogg developed granola and breakfast cereals including Corn Flakes.

Adventists believed that care for the body also meant restricting sexual activity. White and Kellogg both identified masturbation as a major problem of the age. In a small publication called *An Appeal to Mothers*, White warned that children "experienced" in masturbation "seem to be bewitched by the Devil." She claimed that "everywhere" she looked, she witnessed the brutal effects of this act. "I saw imbecility, dwarfed forms, crippled limbs, misshapen heads, and deformity of every description."[3]

Kellogg also published a book warning Americans about the effects of masturbation. One of his cases illustrated the danger. A "bright boy," he wrote, "kind, affectionate, active, intelligent" could not give up the solitary pleasure. Eventually "his mind had sunken to driveling idiocy. His vacant stare and expressionless countenance betokened almost complete imbecility." To avoid such results, he offered a buffet of cures for young masturbators. "Bandaging the parts has been practiced with success," he counseled. "Tying the hands is also successful in some cases," although some will "continue the habit in other ways, as by working the limbs, or lying upon the abdomen." Another option included "covering the organs with a cage," which, he noted, "has been practiced with entire success." You could also cut boys' penises. "A remedy which is almost always successful in small boys," he explained, "is circumcision." The "operation should be performed by a surgeon without administering an anesthetic," so as to associate the penis with pain and punishment. "The soreness which continues for several weeks interrupts the practice, and if it had not previously become too firmly fixed, it may be forgotten and not resumed." Kellogg also advised young people to avoid certain stimulants, including tea, coffee, and tobacco, which he thought drove people to fondle themselves.[4]

In 1902 the Battle Creek Sanitarium burned down. Rather than totally rebuild, White established a series of smaller, more rural sanitariums spread throughout the country, including the College of Medical Evangelists in Southern California (now Loma Linda University). The Adventist movement continued to grow in the United States and, thanks to an extensive missionary movement, around the world as well, eventually drawing millions of people to the faith.

Kellogg, however, broke with Adventism. After the fire, he had wanted to rebuild the hospital, making it bigger and better than ever. White disagreed, and after a series of conflicts church leaders disfellowshipped the doctor. He left the church and took with him the rights to the Corn Flakes empire. White didn't believe she needed them. After all, who needs money when Jesus is coming back at any moment?

Adventists and others like them had to fight popular Christian ideas about health and wellness. In the eighteenth and first part of the nineteenth century, most American Christians believed that they should simply endure physical ailments and suffering. They assumed that the world of miracles they read about in Jesus's day had ceased with the end of the apostolic age. Pain and disease represented the inevitable consequences of sin. Like Job, Christians could and should endure misery with good cheer to demonstrate their faithfulness. Such views led earlier North American Christians like Junípero Serra to self-flagellate.

After the Civil War, revivalist Methodists, Congregationalists, Baptists, and Presbyterians, like White's Adventists, rethought the relationship between the body and faith. They believed that just as God could heal and perfect the soul, he might also heal and perfect the body. They determined that Jesus, in taking the sins of the world upon himself on the cross, had also taken on the physical effects of sin, including sickness. They read James 5:14 literally: "Is any sick among you? let him call for the elders of the church; and let them pray over him, anointing him with oil in the name of the Lord." They concluded that with enough faith, God could and would heal people of their physical afflictions. Jesus made miracles available for the taking.

African American Sarah Mix became one of the nation's most popular faith healers in the late 1870s and early 1880s, traveling the country and holding revivals. As her reputation grew, so did criticism from skeptics and rival ministers about faith-healing beliefs and practices. Unwilling to back down, she published a book defending her work. "I feel it my duty," she wrote, "to lay my experience before the public." She hoped to "increase the faith of some poor suffering ones, who are beyond the reach of aid from the arm of flesh, and are willing to trust in God for deliverance." Like all other women taking on leadership roles in American protestantism, Dix positioned herself as both humble handmaiden and divinely appointed agent of God's word.[5]

Carrie Judd Montgomery read accounts of Mix's healing work. The wealthy and educated Episcopalian, suffering from a severe back injury, had struggled to get out of bed for nearly two years. She wrote Mix seeking advice and perhaps healing. Mix told Montgomery that even though hundreds of miles separated them, at a given time and date they would pray together for healing. She then counseled Montgomery to believe that God had healed her and to get out of her bed. Montgomery did. The healing did not happen all at once, but over several weeks Montgomery's strength gradually grew. When she finally felt well, like Mix she traveled the country preaching and praying for the sick. In 1890 she married a wealthy Scotsman, and they settled in Northern California, where she built ministry houses for religious training, for the sick to seek healing, for the care of orphans, and for sex workers trying to redirect their lives.[6]

Faith-healing revivalists debated exactly when and if they or their followers should visit medical professionals for help. Most healers did not entirely discount the importance of doctors. After all, God could heal a person through conventional medicine just as he could through prayer. But human medicine had its limits, and some argued that those who fully trusted God could and should expect divine healing. For those of unwavering faith, God could restore a body just as easily as he could save a soul.

Yale-educated Congregationalist R. A. Torrey struggled to discern the relationship between faith and modern medicine. The pastor of a large Chicago church—and later one of the primary architects of fundamentalism—Torrey prayed in late 1886 for healing for a nineteen-year-old woman suffering from leukemia. The prayers initially seemed to work. But the next day the woman died. Torrey blamed the victim's lack of faith. Making the failed cure even worse, an autopsy found that the woman was not actually dead when she arrived at the morgue, but in a coma, and she slowly froze in the morgue's refrigerator. The woman's mother claimed the body and felt sure that her daughter would resurrect from the dead. She did not.

This experience did little to chasten Torrey. When the minister's eight-year-old daughter, Elizabeth, grew ill from diphtheria, Torrey chose faith rather than use a well-regarded antitoxin. He initially thought his prayers had been effective, but then his daughter, began struggling again to breathe. At that point he called a doctor, who administered the antitoxin. But the medicine came too late, and Elizabeth died. Torrey blamed himself—for losing faith and for calling a doctor. He determined that had he simply trusted God and not a medical professional, his daughter would have rebounded.

Torrey wrote John Alexander Dowie, another faith healer in Chicago, about his experience. "For twelve or more years," Torrey told Dowie, "none of our children had taken medicine and they had all been healed in God's way, this one included." But as Elizabeth gasped for air, he continued, "my faith failed and ultimately I went for a physician." He feared he had gone "the way of unbelief, not the way of faith." He sought Dowie's counsel and prayers and wondered if Dowie thought Torrey had undiagnosed sins in his life that had inspired God to let his daughter die.[7]

Dowie was hardly a reliable advisor. A flamboyant faith healer, he'd staged headline-grabbing revivals near the Midway at the World's Fair and founded healing homes where the sick sought cures without the help of doctors. His defiance of growing medical regulations led to more than a hundred arrests, yet no court ever convicted him. To escape relentless police harassment, Dowie eventually founded an interracial theocratic commune outside Chicago, where he ruled with near-absolute authority—until his own followers overthrew him. Unsurprisingly, Dowie was unable to offer Torrey the comfort or peace the grieving father so desperately sought.

Most faith healers tried to link their ideas with relatively mainstream protestant beliefs, but a few pushed further afield. Like Ellen G. White, Mary Baker Eddy struggled with poor health through much of her life, and she found the Congregationalism of her childhood insufficient for meeting real-world needs. She sought different types of cures, but nothing proved effective until she encountered Phineas P. Quimby. Quimby claimed clairvoyant powers, which allowed him to identify and diagnose the diseases of strangers. He also healed through mesmerism, putting his patients into trances. Over time he determined that real healing lay in the power of suggestion, creating in patients a positive mental attitude. He offered them a mental cure for their physical ailments.

Eddy believed that Quimby had healed her. She worked with him for a few years, adopting many of his ideas, which she blended with Christianity. But in 1866, shortly after Quimby died, Eddy slipped on some ice and suffered serious injury. "I then withdrew from society about three years," she recalled, "to ponder my mission, to search the Scriptures, to find the Science of Mind." She focused on the New Testament accounts of Jesus's healings, which led her to what she called "Christian Science."[8]

Eddy published a series of books laying out her new version of Christianity, which integrated the ideas of Quimby with those of Christian healers. Eddy did not believe that her ideas reflected a move away from the true faith but instead signified a proper rediscovery of it. Jesus, she contended, taught "the Principle and rule of spiritual Science and Metaphysical Healing—in a word, Christian Science." Disease did not exist but resulted from mental misunderstandings. True believers needed to war against the idea of matter, to ascend above it to truth and principle. "Spirit," she wrote, "I called the reality; and matter, the unreality." She taught Christian Scientists to reject their senses and seek the divine outside of them. The properly trained mind could overcome disease. Jesus had shown the way by demonstrating that God alone was real, and the Bible served as testament to this fact. Christian Scientists did not seek to improve material lives but to help people move beyond them.[9]

To train others in her ideas, in the 1870s and 1880s Eddy published her teachings, founded a college, and launched a new religious denomination that became the Church of Christ, Scientist. Church leaders established reading rooms for the public, where people could peruse, study, and contemplate Christian Science literature. The reading rooms became ubiquitous in cities around the United States. The movement remained small but attracted wealthy New Englanders and especially New England women, who provided substantial funding.

By the turn of the century, the healing fad had slowed. Many mainstream Christians from both conservative and revivalist traditions shifted and began downplaying faith healing. Not coincidentally, rapid improvements in medicine sped the change. More competent doctors meant Americans felt less compulsion to turn to faith healers, miracle cures, and quacks for help. But the healing tradition endured on the protestant fringes and in unorthodox groups, seemingly providing occasional, spectacular evidence of God's supernatural intervention in the world.

White and Eddy built comprehensive, alternative versions of Christianity complete with their own religious fellowships that aimed to minister to the whole person. Other activists had a narrower concentration, working through existing churches and religious organizations to focus on specific bodily ills and their cures. Like the reformers in the early republic, they believed that by healing individuals of specific social sins, they could redeem the nation.

The movement to limit alcohol consumption gained significant traction in the late nineteenth century. It drew support from both ministers who worried about their congregants polluting their bodies and business leaders who depended on a reliable, sober workforce. They imagined a Jesus who smashed saloons, and not one who turned water into fine wine.

The antiliquor crusade also attracted women concerned about the nation's families. The Woman's Christian Temperance Union (WCTU), founded in 1874, became the nation's largest reform organization. Its members focused first on reducing the amount of alcohol that Americans drank and then on curbing its influence. Methodist Frances Willard, who led the group in the 1880s and 1890s, called the WCTU's work "home protection" because she understood that alcohol, in draining people's bank accounts and sometimes energizing certain men's violent and abusive tendencies with their wives and children, represented a danger to the family. In an era in which Americans did not often discuss issues of domestic abuse, "temperance" became a proxy for advocating for women suffering under violent men.

Willard had a comprehensive view of social reform. She and her fellow WCTU activists aimed to establish "a religion of the body which for the first time in history shall correlate with Christ's wholesome, practical, yet blessedly spiritual religion of the soul." They supported free public education, rights for workers, prison reform, laws to end prostitution, and many other initiatives. Willard described the WCTU's mission as helping to "forward the coming of Christ into all departments of life." But its focus did not extend to civil rights. Although Black women joined the WCTU, union leaders generally ignored issues of race and racism and occasionally traded in racist stereotypes.[10]

Willard emphasized the "woman's" in Woman's Christian Temperance Union, joining an ongoing debate over gender roles. She believed that God had made women as a sex more capable than men of leading the kinds of improvements the nation needed. But for women to succeed in cleaning up the United States, they needed equality and the right to vote. She argued that if White women had the ballot, they could legislate proper Christian morality through the democratic process.

Along with temperance, moral crusaders focused on sex reform. In the 1870s and 1880s, some Americans, working mostly outside the protestant mainstream, sought to liberalize social norms and to challenge traditional ideas about gender and sexuality. But other reformers worried that new ideas about sex and personal freedom undermined old ideas about virtue and character. They pushed back, seeking to further limit Americans' bodily autonomy, confident that their work served God and country.

Victoria Woodhull became one of the nation's most famous advocates of new approaches to sex, sexuality, and marriage. A religious experimenter, Woodhull had done some fortune-telling and faith healing, dabbled in spiritualism, and claimed clairvoyant powers. She wanted to change how Americans thought about marriage. She emphasized the centrality of "love" rather than duty as the basis for relationships, and she insisted that what people enjoyed in marriage they could still have sans the legal institution. Healthy relationships did not require binding contracts, nor permanence. "I am a 'Free Lover,'" Woodhull acknowledged. "I have an inalienable, constitutional and natural right to love whom I may, to love as long or as short a period as I can; to change that love every day if I please, and with that right neither you nor any law you can frame have any right to interfere." Knowing that her opinions generated controversy, Woodhull tried to ground them in the teachings of Jesus. "When Christian ministers are no longer afraid or ashamed to be Christians they will embrace this doctrine," she argued. "Free Love will be an integral part of the religion of the future."[11]

But most ministers and reformers were not prepared for the revolution. Government investigator Anthony Comstock hoped to silence Woodhull and those like her. As a young person working with New York's Young Men's Christian Association (YMCA), Comstock came to believe that "vice" represented a grave threat to Americans. In 1873, he established the New York Society for the Suppression of Vice, an organization that aimed to regulate Americans' sexuality, prohibit birth control, and limit access to materials about sexuality. He took stands against abortion, pornography, contraception, and masturbation. He also fought the sale of "rubber goods"—condoms, diaphragms, and sex toys. He believed that such things could ruin family and home, and if the family fell, then the nation would fall. He had many supporters and helped convince Congress to pass legislation, later dubbed "Comstock laws," that made it a federal crime to send or disseminate "obscene" materials, including those discussing or providing birth control or abortion, through the US mail.

Comstock worried about youth, and especially young men. He warned that they faced all kinds of temptations from free lovers, liberals, prostitutes, and religious skeptics. "It may not be pleasant or popular to speak of a devil," Comstock wrote, "or of his having a kingdom and power; but I doubt if any man could go through the experiences of my past eleven years and not be thoroughly persuaded that there is one." Seeking to censor reading material, he warned Americans that "vile books and papers are branding-irons heated in the fires of hell, and used by Satan to sear the highest life of the soul. The world," he insisted, "is the devil's hunting ground, and children are his choicest game."[12]

Robert Ingersoll, an Illinois attorney and the son of a Presbyterian minister, challenged Comstock directly as well as the policies that he sponsored. He traveled from city to city, holding popular lectures where he attacked vice crusaders. Although many states still had laws against blasphemy, Ingersoll relentlessly mocked Christianity and its grip on American life. "When I read the bible I found that God in His infinite wisdom couldn't control the people He had created and that He had to drown them. If I had infinite power and couldn't make a people that I could control and had to drown them, why I'd resign." Addressing a group of Presbyterians, Ingersoll declared that he too had a "missionary spirit." "When I see my fellow men trembling with fear, thinking that they are to be clutched by an ogre of the sky—it is not only my duty, but my pleasure, to convince them that the ogre does not exist." One fan thanked him for exposing "Christianity as rather humbugry in such plain language."[13]

Never one to cower from a fight, Comstock attacked "Ingersollism." "In some respects," Comstock wrote, Ingersoll and his allies were "worse" than other peddlers in sin, "in that while they pretend to be far above religion and laws, they undertake the defence of all the foregoing evils."[14]

Comstock also attacked Ingersoll's First Amendment rights. "The freedom sought by our forefathers to worship God did not mean to serve the devil," the protestant activist opined. "Freedom to speak or print does not imply the right to say or print that which shocks decency, corrupts the morals of the young, or destroys all faith in God." His response illustrated once again how many government authorities understood the First Amendment. In their minds the Constitution did not provide space for religious dissenters.[15]

The challenges freethinkers faced as they squared off against moral reformers revealed how Americans still struggled to tolerate those who veered too far from religious orthodoxy. Yet in the long run, Christians' efforts to intimidate supposed infidels and agnostics often had the opposite effect from what they intended. Their protests generated more publicity for iconoclasts like Ingersoll, who relished the opportunity to use his speeches to trigger Christians and undermine their efforts to impose their convictions on the broader public.

As reformers like Comstock worked to police Americans' sexuality and speech, the nation's most famous preacher was entangled in some vice of his own. Henry Ward Beecher, son of Lyman and brother of Catharine Beecher and Harriet Beecher Stowe, served as the pastor of the Plymouth (Congregational) Church in Brooklyn. He leaned liberal in terms of theology and emphasized God's love for humanity more than his judgment of sin. Like many of the nation's best ministers, his sermons took the form of theatrical performances—he used slang, humor, and impersonations from the pulpit.

With long, flowing hair, the cravat-wearing parson captivated many women, including one church member, Elizabeth Tilton. Her husband, Theodore, suspected that Elizabeth was having an affair, and when Theodore confronted Elizabeth, she admitted she had indeed slept with their minister. This was likely not the first time Beecher violated his marriage vows.[16]

A small group of people in the church knew about the relationship. But they suppressed rumors about it until 1872, when Victoria Woodhull published an article on the tryst. Some of the nation's leading moral crusaders, including Beecher's sisters, had subjected Woodhull to scorn and ridicule for her free love views (and her history of acting on those views). She wanted revenge and so she exposed the corruption within the moral establishment.

Although Woodhull buried the story on page nine of her weekly newspaper, she knew what she was doing. "I intend that this article," Woodhull admitted, "shall burst like a bomb-shell into the ranks of the moralistic social camp." Beecher's hypocrisy—not his sexual proclivities—troubled Woodhull. The minister had defended women's rights and supported suffrage, but he denounced Woodhull's advocacy of free love. She called on him to embrace his promiscuity and to blaze a new trail for Christians everywhere. She told a reporter that she chose to reveal the scandal because "I am a prophetess—I am an evangel—I am a Saviour, if you would but see it; but I too come not to bring peace, but a sword." Federal marshals working for Comstock arrested Woodhull for violating obscenity laws by publishing and distributing her article.[17]

Embarrassed by the story, Theodore Tilton attacked Beecher in the press. When a church-run investigation led by Beecher's allies exonerated the minister, Tilton took him to court. The trial focused Americans' attention on kissing, among other salacious acts. Many witnesses had seen Beecher kiss Elizabeth. Beecher admitted it. And then he added that he also kissed Theodore exactly the same way that he kissed Elizabeth. The Tiltons, in turn, when pressed by attorneys acknowledged that they often greeted their friends with a "holy kiss." The testimony exposed how members of leading Brooklyn families swapped kisses, caresses, and holy love, with everyone trying to justify everything as no more than the physical manifestations of godly affection, while in reality they titillated each other. This did not surprise Woodhull, who saw the entire scandal as vindication.

The sensational affair and trial, splashed across the press, exposed Americans to a world of sex, scandal, and partner swapping—the very forces Comstock fought to suppress. Battles over morality laws, masturbation, free love, and birth control, in courtrooms and popular culture alike, revealed deep divisions over sex, family, and virtue. Most Americans wanted stable families, but they clashed over how to build them. Alarmed by shifting attitudes, mainstream protestant leaders with the aid of Congress turned to the law in a desperate bid to restore old moral boundaries, to put the genie back in the bottle, to hide the sex toys from public view.

In the last decades of the nineteenth century, Christians gave substantial attention to the body, and they treated the Bible as its diagnostic manual. They sought to instruct their fellow Americans on how to prevent sickness, and they experimented with new formulas for healing. They passed laws and worked to regulate Americans' consumption of alcohol, sex, and erotic materials. Christian activists strove to convince their countrymen that abiding by the dictates of the holy scriptures, even though they never entirely agreed on the nature of those dictates, served as the key to personal and national success. Many of their achievements faded over time, but others, like Anthony Comstock's laws, remained (and remain) front and center in the culture wars.

As moral crusaders railed against sex and drink, critics asked a sharper question: Why fixate on private vices when people were poor, hungry, and desperate? Christian activists realized they couldn't address the body without confronting deeper issues of poverty and social justice. But they soon discovered that offering satisfying answers was far harder than raising alarms.

18

CHRISTIANITY, CAPITALISM, AND THE SIGNS OF THE TIMES

On May 1, 1886, workers nationwide went on strike to demand an eight-hour workday. To celebrate and publicize the event, they held huge parades and organized community picnics. In Chicago, one of the nation's fastest growing and most important industrial cities, eighty thousand workers protested. A few days later a group of labor activists held an outdoor rally in Chicago's Haymarket Square to denounce police violence and worker deaths at the local McCormick Reaper Works. Someone in the large crowd tossed a bomb at a group of police, which killed one officer and wounded others. The police responded by firing into the crowd, killing four bystanders and injuring many more. Police never identified the bomb thrower. They did, however, arrest a handful of political dissidents who had attended the rally and charged them with inciting a riot. Juries convicted eight of them. Although no evidence linked the radicals to the bomb, half of the group hanged for the crime.

One of the convicted, August Spies, saw his imminent death in religious terms. During his sentencing hearing he condemned the hypocritical Christianity of the city's elite and their refusal to recognize injustice. Then he wrote his wife with a story that he thought paralleled his own. It focused on "the crucifixion of a young, bright, generous and noble hearted Jew, by the name of Jesus." Jesus, he said, "overthrew the tables of the money changers (bankers)," which precipitated his "legal" murder.

Jerusalem's leaders, Spies determined, could not stomach Jesus's criticism of their greed. And when they "saw their 'respectable business' thus exposed by this 'foreign, half-distracted, wild eyed, ranting agitator,'" they "formed a conspiracy, 'drummed up' some charges against the 'lawless fiend' and—crucified him as a 'convicted felon.' You will readily see," Spies ominously concluded, "the analogy of this and our own case." Spies, and workers like him, tried to push middle-class Christians to take more seriously the radicalism of Jesus's message, to see their savior as a liberator and not an ally of business tycoons.[1]

Throughout the nation's history, mainstream protestant leaders, rather than challenge the American market economy, mostly accommodated their faith to capitalism. Revivalists' focus on individual conversion paralleled capitalist ideas about the free market. Just as anyone could choose salvation and strive to live a holy life, so too could they choose to work hard and achieve prosperity. Many in the liberal stream also embraced capitalism. The market economy kept money flowing into their ministries and provided the nation with stability. Beautiful churches did not build themselves, and someone had to pay elite ministers' salaries.

But in the last part of the nineteenth century, changes in the American economy exposed some of the long-term flaws in capitalism, inspiring different groups of Christian activists to pioneer new approaches to ministry. In parts of urban America, religious leaders developed a new form of Christianity, a social gospel that aimed to meet the needs of poorer Americans. They did not call for revolution; they simply sought to reduce the pain caused by capitalism. In rural regions, where farmers often felt exploited by banks and railroads, a different group of activists worked to build political power to challenge corporations and the overwhelming influence of the cities. A third group, assessing the nation's problems, viewed ultimate reform as futile. They saw in the nation's troubles signs that the end-times had begun, which inspired them to work even more relentlessly to impose their version of Christianity on American life before Jesus returned in judgment. Ever eager to keep faith relevant, church leaders responded to great challenges by redoubling their efforts to apply it in practical ways to the issues of the age, and to shape law and policy with their ideals.

By the late nineteenth century, the United States had become the world's leading industrial nation. An elite investor class, a growing white-collar middle class, and an impoverished working class provided the structure for the new economic order. Corporations including Standard Oil, US Steel, Coca-Cola, General Electric, and the National Biscuit Company (Nabisco) drove the economy through roller-coaster-like cycles of boom and bust that included multiple serious depressions. Some Americans grew fabulously rich, and others lived precariously on the edge of failure.

Mark Twain labeled the era the "gilded age." While the nation looked glitzy on its surface, it had a grimy core. The satirist believed that Americans chased wealth like they had once pursued salvation. Some church leaders even encouraged this. Baptist minister Russell Conwell told Christians around the country that they "ought to get rich." He claimed that money served as one of God's greatest tools; the more a Christian had, the more he or she could do with it. Jesus had loaves and fishes; his modern disciples needed fat wallets. "Money is power," the minister insisted, "and you ought to be reasonably ambitious to have it. You ought because you can do more good with it than you could without it." He reminded his listeners that "money printed your Bible, money builds your churches, money sends your missionaries, and money pays your preachers, and you would not have many of them, either, if you did not pay them."[2]

The message preached by Conwell and those like him resonated with countless middle-class Americans seeking to reconcile their faith with the new economy. It affirmed their values and ideals. But it made little sense to working-class Americans struggling to survive in dirty, unsafe, overcrowded cities. By 1890, more than a third of the nation's residents lived in urban areas, including many new immigrants. Religious leaders had to develop new tactics for reaching them, especially if they didn't want the poor organizing into revolutionary movements that challenged elite leaders and their religious partners.

Congregationalist Washington Gladden remade his ministry to meet the needs of the era and to serve those seemingly left behind by the changing economy. In the 1880s, he answered a call to pastor the First Congregational Church in Columbus, Ohio, an important industrial town at the time, where he spent the next three decades. Gladden focused especially on the rights of working people of all colors and nationalities. He denounced racism and condemned lynching. During labor conflicts he advocated for workers and their unions and sided against wealthier members of the community, including those in his own congregation. Gladden publicly criticized leaders of the American Board of Commissioners for Foreign Missions for accepting a $100,000 donation from John D. Rockefeller—he didn't want missionaries washing the Standard Oil tycoon's dirty money. "If the churches of Christ are to separate themselves from the iniquity of conscienceless and predatory wealth," he insisted, "there can be no better place than this to begin."[3]

From his pulpit and in dozens of books, the bald minister with the Santa Claus beard demonstrated that the Christian faith had tremendous relevance for modern concerns. He helped develop a social gospel, an application of Christianity to modern problems, and he criticized those who focused on individual salvation from sin or on conversion without working to improve their communities. "It is the religion of politics, of economics, of sociology that we are to teach," Gladden wrote. "Nothing else. We are to bring the truths and the powers of the spiritual world, the eternal world, to bear upon all these themes." Jesus, he argued, came to remake the culture and not just

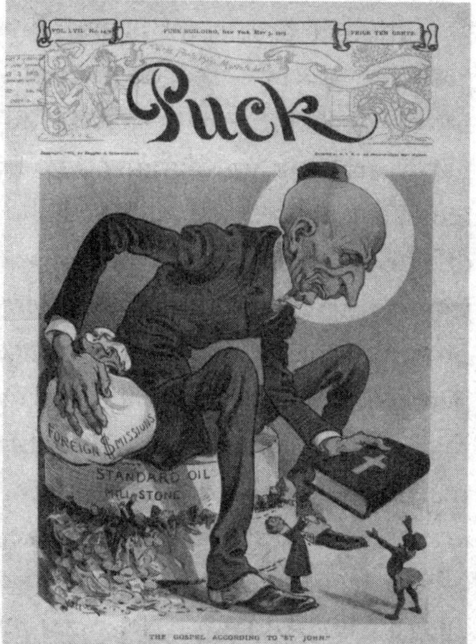

Puck magazine depicted John D. Rockefeller grinding money out of the bodies of his workers, which he used to support foreign missions. The Rockefeller family subsidized many liberal protestant causes. (credit: "The Gospel According to 'St. John,'" *Puck*, May 3, 1905, Library of Congress)

to save souls from it. "There can be no adequate social reform," he preached, "save that which springs from a genuine revival of religion; only it must be a religion which is less concerned about getting men to heaven than about fitting them for their proper work on the earth." But it was religion, nonetheless. Ministers like Gladden knew they were competing against more radical labor movements for the loyalty of the working class.[4]

Like Gladden, Baptist minister Walter Rauschenbusch strived to make the gospel relevant to real-world problems. His church, located in New York's Hell's Kitchen, exposed him to the many challenges of city life, from hunger to crime to unemployment to disease. He eventually moved into academia, mentoring future ministers with his activist theology at Rochester Theological Seminary. "The essential purpose of Christianity," he argued, "was to transform human society into the kingdom of God by regenerating all human relations and reconstituting them in accordance with the will of God." In many lengthy tomes, Rauschenbusch used history, theology, and modern thought to make the case that the primitive church had served the common person, and so it should again.[5]

Another protestant liberal, Jane Addams, sought to embody the gospel in one of Chicago's poorest and toughest communities. In 1889 she opened a settlement called Hull House to minister primarily to the newly arriving immigrants who packed into unsafe and unsanitary tenement houses. She believed she was adding "a new impulse to an old gospel." Hull House quickly grew into a major, multifaceted institution where community members could attend concerts, lectures by prominent academics, and language and job-training classes, as well as peruse a public library and an art gallery. "I believe that this turning, this renaissance of the early Christian humanitarianism," Addams reflected, "is going on in America, in Chicago, if you please, without leaders who write or philosophize, without much speaking, but with a bent to express in social service, in terms of action, the spirit of Christ." For Addams, settlement houses represented modern churches in action. She inspired other reform-minded women living in Western cities—including Denver, San Francisco, and Seattle—to establish their own settlement houses, where they educated immigrants, worked to rescue women from prostitution, and fought for better schools.[6]

A few activists offered direct critiques of the market economy. Born in India to missionary parents, Wellesley professor Vida Scudder eventually viewed the approach of activists like Addams and many of the social gospel ministers as too conservative. She didn't want only to minister to those struggling with poverty; she wanted to transform the economy to prevent poverty. She hoped to build a truly equitable society by preaching a gospel that integrated socialism with the Christian faith. Jesus occupied the center of Scudder's vision. "Realizing the dangerous, the revolutionary elements in the teaching of Jesus," she argued, "one hardly knows what to say to those who all down the centuries try to find in the Gospels and in the Christian religion, a defense of the status quo." She explained to readers of the socialist magazine *The Masses* that churches' championing of capitalism revealed a failure to truly understand Jesus. "For among those who know an interior union with the Living Christ (pardon the strange language)," she wrote, "He is manifest more and more as the Christ of the Revolution."[7]

Yet few Christians and few socialists saw Jesus this way. Most economic radicals viewed Christianity in Marxist terms and saw religion as little more than a tool of class oppression, which frustrated Scudder. Nevertheless, she acknowledged, "the ultimate source of my socialist convictions was and is Christianity. Unless I were a socialist, I could not honestly be a Christian." Scudder spent her long career as an activist, writer, and professor trying to bridge the yawning gap between socialists on the one side and Christian reformers on the other.[8]

As activists' books and articles influenced a generation of seminary students, a small, easy-to-digest publication brought the social gospel into countless churches and family parlors. Author Charles Sheldon wrote a bestselling novel in 1896 called *In His Steps*, in which a young minister encouraged everyone in his congregation to ask themselves, "What would Jesus do?" before deciding on any course of action. As members of the congregation sought to respond to this question, they transformed their community. The book sold millions of copies. Sheldon simply asked the question, and Christians ever since have argued over how to answer it. Would Jesus lead a socialist revolution? Or run a major corporation that provided jobs for thousands of people and financed missionary work? Would he champion civil rights for racial and ethnic minorities? Or seek to separate the races and cut off immigration? Would he run for president, or volunteer in an urban school? American Christians could not agree. Then or now. But the question stuck.

For generations, Christian reformers had integrated social concern with their ministries. Theologians and activists like Rauschenbusch, Gladden, Addams, and Scudder went a step further, however, by prioritizing good works over doctrine and by reading the latter through the lens of the former. They joined a broad base of activists and contributed to and drew on the latest social science research as they focused on alleviating the destructive social and environmental conditions that caused so much of the poverty and despair they witnessed around them. Downplaying individual sin, they called on Christians to serve Jesus not by preaching the gospel but by transforming their communities. To solve the nation's problems, they advocated structural over individual solutions, which often called for substantial transformations of social relations and the economy. They developed new partnerships with community activists and academics, realizing that enacting the types of reforms they envisioned required time and political mobilization.

For Black Americans, the Christian gospel often had a social component. Members of liberationist churches saw the gospel as by definition about community improvement and social justice, which ministers emphasized both in the preached word and in the voluntary actions of their congregations. In the South, middle-class African American women engaged in a variety of reforms, usually with little to no support from the White community. They established parks and playgrounds, found housing for the elderly, organized schools for the poor, and sought to expand health care.

Baptist and Republican Party activist Nannie Helen Burroughs blended social gospel ministry, demands for racial justice and women's rights, and political agitation in her work. In 1900 she helped organize the Women's Convention for the largest Black denomination in the country, the National Baptist Convention. "For a number of years there has been a righteous discontent," she told her Baptist brothers, "a burning zeal to go forward in his name among the Baptist women of our churches and it will be the dynamic force in the religious campaign at the opening of the 20th century." She spent the rest of her long career organizing Black women to seek the betterment of their communities and their race.[9]

Meanwhile, attuned to the changes engulfing the nation, some White revivalists rejected the liberal theology of social gospel architects yet nevertheless emphasized social reform. Methodist ministers William and Catherine Booth founded the Salvation Army in London in 1865, and in the 1880s their army of boisterous, uniformed activists invaded New York City. The army, according to its charter, sought to provide "the spiritual, moral and physical reformation of all who need it; the reclamation of the vicious, criminal, dissolute and degraded; visitation among the poor and lowly and sick, and the preaching of the

Gospel and the dissemination of Christian truth by means of open-air and indoor meetings."[10]

Army activists took the Christian message of individual salvation to the people. They preached on street corners, in brothels and saloons, in parks, at parades, and just about anywhere else they could find a crowd. They beat drums and shook tambourines and used drama to convey the power of faith. But preaching represented just the start of their efforts. They opened soup kitchens, employment offices, and health care centers. They helped the poor stay warm in the winter and cool in the summer. They wrestled faith from the churches and took it directly to the people. They became one of the world's largest and most respected Christian charities.

A handful of new ministries focused specifically on reaching the many working-class men who had little interest in stepping through a church door. The transition of people away from farms and into urban offices and factories seemingly produced soft and effeminate bodies. American leaders worried that men had lost their manliness. Yet men still supposedly had innate energy and wild natures that needed an outlet, which some found in fighting, illicit sex, or alcohol. Christian reformers sought to channel male vigor in positive directions.

Hoping to attract men to the Christian gospel, a group of Christian leaders opened the first American branch of the Young Men's Christian Association (YMCA) in Boston in 1851. Reformers in London had founded the group a few years earlier. The ministry sponsored the work of evangelists and distributed Christian literature. Over the next few decades, YMCA leaders built multiuse complexes in the nation's urban areas, which often included lecture halls, libraries, and study rooms.

YMCA leader Fred B. Smith understood that many laborers saw traditional religious institutions as allies of the middle class and the rich. "We dare not minimize the seriousness of the fact that the great mass of laboring men feel themselves estranged from the Church," he concluded, "and sometimes feel the Church to be an active opponent. I repeat that the continuance of the Church as a universal influence depends in no small measure upon her ability to win these laboring men."[11]

In the late nineteenth century, YMCA activists adopted a new tactic. They embraced sports as a tool for generating religious growth. They sought to provide young men with healthy ways to spend their free time and improve their bodies and minds, all the while avoiding saloons and brothels. They found that basketball, a sport YMCA leaders developed to keep men active during cold winters, alongside other sports, could direct men's energy in positive ways, channeling it into healthy competition and teamwork. As the focus of the YMCA evolved, leaders made building gymnasiums a new priority. At the Y, evangelicalism, Christian discipleship, and physical training mixed and merged.

Groups like the YMCA worked across denominations and traditions to reestablish Christianity as a hypermasculine, muscular faith. They depicted Jesus as a "he-man," the most manly of modern men. One YMCA writer insisted that "the sentimental Christ has had his day and ceased to be." In the context of a growing feminist movement and an ever-expanding fight for women's suffrage, many church leaders countered with a male-centric Christianity emphasizing power and conquest.[12]

As the nation fixated on the problems of urban America, farmers warned that they were bearing the brunt of economic change. The rise of railroads and corporations, widening class divides, and the steady drain of people to the cities were battering rural economies. In the early 1890s, frustrated by politicians' deference to urban business interests and powerful investors including railroad barons, farmers launched a new political movement: the People's Party, whose members became known as Populists. They championed direct election of senators, the initiative process to propose new laws, and a graduated income tax (at a time when the US had no federal income tax at all). Populists pushed for public ownership of key industries like railroads, telegraphs, and utilities, and they condemned land grabs by speculators and large companies, insisting that land should belong to those who worked it. They also demanded an end to the gold standard to expand the money supply and ease the economic squeeze on ordinary Americans.

Populists couched their demands in the language of common sense and core Christian principles. One of the movement's leaders, Kansan Mary Elizabeth Lease, saw populism as "an echo of the life of Jesus of Nazareth, a movement that means revolution." She located Populist priorities in "the Sermon on the Mount, and that other command, that ye love one another. We seek to put into practical operation the teachings of Christ, who was sent to bring about a better day." In the future utopia that Populists envisioned, she promised, "there shall be no more coal kings nor silver kings, but a better day when there shall be no more millionaires, no more paupers, and no more waifs in our streets." For Lease and many other Populists, the egalitarian nature of Christianity had direct political ramifications that both Democrats and Republicans had ignored.[13]

Populist and Baptist minister Isom P. Langley echoed Lease's sentiments in an early statement of party principles. "Theologians," Langley lamented, "boast of the Christian government of the United States; but where is the spirit of Christ in our national and State governments? Is that government Christian," he asked, "which creates millionaires and palaces on the one hand, and paupers and miserable homes on the other?" He felt sure that no serious follower of Christ could mistake the United States for a Christian country. Then Langley turned his sights on the nation's religious leaders. "If the Christian ministers of the United States had the moral courage to preach the religion of Jesus Christ instead of yielding to the influence of Mammon-worshippers, our political organizations would not dare to neglect the demands of the people." Populists like Lease and Langley understood that the political establishment and the protestant establishment walked hand in hand with corporate leaders. Turning to the democratic process, integrating faith with activism, they hoped to remake the country.[14]

The 1892 elections produced relatively impressive results for the People's Party. Four years later, Populists even dreamed of capturing the presidency. But they faced an unexpected challenge in the form of Democrat and former Nebraska congressman William Jennings

Bryan. A conservative Presbyterian, Bryan championed the rights of rural Americans and committed to applying the principles of Christianity to politics and economics. The Populists decided to join forces with the Democrats and make Bryan their nominee as well.

At the 1896 Democratic National Convention, Bryan delivered one of the most spellbinding speeches in American history. He argued that the nation's cities could not survive without the nation's farms. "I tell you," he bellowed, "that the great cities rest upon these broad and fertile prairies. Burn down your cities and leave our farms, and your cities will spring up again as if by magic. But destroy our farms and the grass will grow in the streets of every city in the country." Then, as he concluded his speech, he stretched out his arms like Jesus on the cross, absorbing the sins of America. He promised to answer the Republicans' "demands for a gold standard by saying to them, you shall not press down upon the brow of labor this crown of thorns. You shall not crucify mankind upon a cross of gold." As he finished, the packed auditorium remained silent for a few seconds. Then it exploded into cheers and applause. At only thirty-six years of age, Bryan ranked among the nation's rising political stars and the youngest major party candidate ever to run for president. But he lost to Republican William McKinley.[15]

In 1905, leaders of thirty protestant denominations, including those overseeing the largest Black churches, met in New York to discuss ways to address the nation's problems together. Almost a century earlier church leaders from many denominations had come together to build an ecumenical missions movement; now they assembled to focus on a new set of issues and challenges. Church leaders vowed to unite "the great Christian bodies in our country" to "stand together and lead in the discussion of, and give an impulse to, all great movements that 'make for righteousness.'" Then they turned to the major issues they hoped to attack. "We believe that questions like that of the saloon, marriage and divorce, Sabbath desecration, the social evil, child labor, relation of labor to capital, the bettering of the conditions of the laboring classes, the moral and religious training of the young, the problem created by foreign immigration, and international

Conservative Presbyterian William Jennings Bryan championed the rights of rural Americans and committed to applying the principles of Christianity to politics and economics. *Judge* magazine spoofed his sanctimonious insertion of religion into the 1896 presidential campaign. (credit: Grant E. Hamilton, "The Sacrilegious Candidate," *Judge*, September 14, 1896, Library of Congress)

arbitration—indeed, all great questions in which the voice of the churches should be heard—concern Christians of every name." These issues demanded "united and concerted action if the Church is to lead effectively in the conquest of the world for Christ."[16]

In 1908, protestant leaders officially launched the Federal Council of Churches (FCC), a new ecumenical organization, for this purpose. The nation's most influential church leaders aspired to shape public policy and imprint their beliefs on a rapidly changing society.

The creation of the FCC marked an important moment in the history of American protestantism. It revealed that while theology and tradition still separated one protestant denomination from another, the nation's most powerful churches—from all four streams—felt willing to put aside their differences in order to grow their collective influence. "The Federal Council of the Churches of Christ in America," socialist Vida Scudder summarized, "expresses again the deepening conviction that the scope of the gospel and the program of the churches must include the creation on earth of a Christian civilization, organized upon the ethical teachings and controlled by the spirit of Jesus Christ." Indeed, the ecumenical FCC leaders sought to ensure that as the nation grew more diverse, it would, at least in part, remain securely in their hands. Building a Christian civilization in the United States grounded in Christian nationalism remained one of American church leaders' highest priorities.[17]

The social gospel drew substantial support from many of the nation's liberal-stream activists, but some revivalist and conservative religious leaders fretted that the movement had gone too far. In focusing on real-world reform, they believed, ministers and leaders of the FCC had neglected the essence of the gospel—they had forgotten that reform without individual salvation served no long-term, eternal purpose. Critics of the FCC agreed that the nation, and the world, faced enormous problems; they just looked to different sources and offered different kinds of solutions.

While social gospelers sought to redeem society, another group of ministers and theologians, gripping newspapers in one hand and the prophetic books of the Bible in the other, looked to the end of history itself. Reviving and reshaping the ancient Christian doctrine of premillennialism, they preached that Jesus would return before the millennium, not after. For these believers, the task was not to build a better world but to ready souls for God's imminent judgment.

Irishman John Nelson Darby helped lay the foundations for the post–Civil War surge in American apocalyptic thinking. During a series of evangelistic tours in North America in the 1860s and 1870s, Darby sought to convince Christians that exceedingly dark days loomed ahead. His ideas spread among small numbers of Presbyterians, Baptists, Methodists, and Congregationalists. "All through the States the truths are drawing attention," Darby reported to his brother. "Ministers come here to see what it is." As the Irishman's influence grew, he provided American millennialists with a pallet of ideas from which they could pick and choose as they called for their fellow Christians to reject modern trends and embrace the apocalypticism of the early church.[18]

Darby and his followers helped develop and explain a relatively new idea in Christian theology—the concept of the "rapture." Identifying and explaining the rapture, a dramatic experience in which all living Christians mysteriously vanish from the earth and the dead rise to heaven, represented one of their great theological innovations. The word "rapture" does not appear in the Bible, and it was not a well-developed theological concept prior to the nineteenth century. Most premillennialists taught that after the rapture, those left behind will undergo a seven-year tribulation. A new leader—who is actually the Antichrist—will take power in this period, assuming control over a ten-kingdom confederacy established within the boundaries of the old Roman Empire. Premillennialists' preoccupation with identifying possible enemies drove them to become serious students of geopolitical developments.

Growing interest in premillennialism led ministers and theologians to organize a series of prophecy conferences that, combined with the rise of a handful of popular publications, helped define the parameters of what was emerging in the United States as a new, distinctive, interdenominational premillennialist movement.

It was also a White movement. White premillennialists had no interest in making common cause with like-minded Black Christians. Nevertheless, a handful of Black leaders offered new interpretations of the Bible's prophetic books. Liberationist minister T. G. Steward used Daniel and Revelation to discuss the coming apocalypse. But rather than affirming the White premillennialist view that the Antichrist would soon take power over a restored Roman Empire in Europe, he saw the devilish tyrant assuming control of the United States. "We may quite safely identify," he wrote in *The End of the World*, "the successors of this Roman kingdom with all those European nations which have developed the current civilization, whose people blended together in a common citizenship make up the population of America." For Steward, the restoration of the Roman Empire predicted in Daniel signified the restoration of the people of the old Roman Empire into a new empire—the United States. Americans, he warned, had provoked the wrath of God because they substituted for the true gospel a White-centric message that applied "great ideas of liberty, fraternity and equality" only to people of their own race. Meanwhile, "it was Christian America that robbed Africa of millions of her population and committed unheard of horrors," and "representatives of all Christendom in America have Christianized the Red man off the face of the earth." Under White rule, the tribulation predicted in Revelation had already begun for Indigenous and Black Americans. But destruction would soon come to White Americans as Jesus set all things right.[19]

Steward emphasized the prophetic significance of Psalms 68:31, a passage widely heralded by Black Americans (and African Christians) but mostly ignored by Whites, which reads, "Princes shall come out of Egypt; Ethiopia shall soon stretch out her hands unto God." According to some Black theologians, this passage indicated that at the end of the age, a holy remnant of Africans will rule with Jesus. "The bloody wave will soon have spent its force," Steward wrote, "and then shall the end come—the end of war and oppression; the end of the insolence of white pride and black contempt, and the ushering in of a new era in which righteousness shall prevail, and the peaceful, loving spirit of the Lord Jesus Christ shall reign over all the earth." With the US and other Western nations rendered powerless, Christians like Steward expected "the church of Abyssinia" to inaugurate the new millennium.[20]

Black minister James T. Holly also recognized the significance of the "princes of Egypt" passage. He preached that Christians of African ancestry will play a special role in the coming kingdom. "The African race has been the servant of servants to their brethren" during "the Hebrew and Christian dispensations. And it is this service that they have so patiently rendered through blood and tears that shall finally obtain for them the noblest places of service in the Coming Kingdom. . . . The crowning work of the will of God," he emphasized, "is reserved for the millennial phase of Christianity, when Ethiopia shall stretch out her hands directly unto God." While most White American Christians continued to look to their own country as God's chosen land, the descendants of enslaved men and women believed it was anything but.[21]

Most premillennialists incorporated their eschatology (or study of the end-times) with mainstream protestant revivalist or conservative views, but a few forced schisms. Haberdasher Charles Taze Russell formed a Bible study group in Pittsburgh, Pennsylvania, that focused especially on prophecy. "We have no apology to offer," Russell maintained, for focusing on "many subjects usually neglected by Christians," including "the coming of our Lord, and the prophecies and symbolism of the Old and New Testaments." He criticized the nation's most powerful institutions, including government, businesses, and churches, which he thought had conspired to oppress the poor and keep power in the hands of the rich. Because members of the group believed that their citizenship lay in heaven, they refused to participate in war or pledge allegiance to a national flag. They taught a conservative morality, including no drinking or smoking.[22]

In 1879, Russell launched *Zion's Watch Tower*, a magazine dedicated to sharing his theological insights. A few years later, he united his followers under the Zion's Watch Tower Tract Society, solidifying their community and mission. Russell had inherited and then sold a valuable family business, and he used the proceeds to fund his ministry and its extensive printing operations. Russell's group later adopted the name Jehovah's Witnesses. Almost immediately, mainstream premillennialists in the major denominations saw the Jehovah's Witnesses, like the Latter-day Saints and the Christian Scientists, not as co-laborers, but as heretics. They represented yet one more sign that the great apostasy had come and that the devil masqueraded as an angel of light.

A comprehensive reference work became the most successful means of spreading the new premillennialism among mainstream protestant audiences. In 1909 Oxford University Press published the *Scofield Reference Bible*, which introduced millions of readers to the premillennial Second Coming. The Bible's editor, Cyrus Ingerson Scofield, a Civil War veteran (he had fought for the Confederacy), lawyer, and a bit of a scoundrel, had experienced a dramatic conversion and became a minister. He wrote extensively about premillennialism and established a correspondence course focused on biblical interpretation, but the reference Bible became his greatest achievement.

The Bible included Scofield's notes on the bottom of almost every page, which helped readers interpret verses within a premillennial framework. Scofield occasionally inserted notes into the text itself as well, blurring the lines between the scriptures and his interpretations. The book, with millions of copies in circulation, is probably the best-selling book in the history of Oxford University Press. While many historians have credited Darby with the revival of American premillennialism, Scofield deserves most of the credit.[23]

The prophecy conferences, a small number of new premillennial-focused magazines, and the publication of books by Scofield and others helped create a loose, disparate, interdenominational premillennialist network. Despite the diversity of adherents and the many traditions from which they came, the faithful had begun to identify the key themes that would drive their movement for decades to come: Jesus was coming soon; signs of the imminent end had appeared in popular culture, social movements, politics, and in various international events; and the religious apostasy predicted in Revelation—which included the denial of premillennialism—had come upon them. Christians in turn felt that God had called them not to neglect their duties in this world but to help prepare for the coming judgment, to be wary of state power and global alliances that would serve the devil's agenda, and finally, to look to the Middle East for signs that armies were preparing for the battle of Armageddon.

In the last decades of the nineteenth century, shoe salesman turned preacher Dwight Moody became the nation's most popular evangelist. The three-hundred-pound, Chicago-based Congregationalist integrated apocalyptic revivalism with a conservative version of social activism that appealed to middle-class White Americans. He focused primarily on personal, individual salvation. "I look on this world as a wrecked vessel," Moody declared. "God has given me a life-boat, and said to me, 'Moody, save all you can.'"[24]

During the second part of the 1870s and through most of the 1880s, Moody traveled from major city to major city holding multi-week revivals. He preached in a dark business suit and used a conversational tone. His simple sermons revealed his lack of education and theological training—he had only attended school through fifth grade.

Moody recruited fellow revivalist and talented musician Ira Sankey to stir the crowds before he preached. At Moody's services, Sankey played lively, crowd-pleasing hymns that set the emotional tone for the sermons. Sankey's musical performances, one observer noted, combined "a circus quick-step, a negro minstrel sentimental ballad, a college chorus, and a hymn all in one." His creative efforts added a new staple to revivalism; music became central to evangelistic services.[25]

Editors for the popular magazine *The Nation* tried in 1876 to explain the success of Moody and Sankey, whose services they described as "an old-fashioned revival with the modern improvements." They viewed the positive focus of Moody's sermons as a key reason for his popularity. Moody's God, they informed readers, was "mild and loving," "forgiving and pardoning to the last; a God who cares little for correctness of dogma so that the heart be pure—the God of the ignorant no less than the wise." Revivalism had come a long way from the days of educated, erudite Jonathan Edwards warning sinners that God held them in his angry hands, to Moody and Sankey leading a happy band of comfortable middle-class believers to the pearly gates. Christian leaders always understood how to calibrate their messages to their audiences, but perhaps no group in the United States did it better than those in the revivalist stream.[26]

As Reconstruction collapsed, Moody ignored the crushing of Black rights and instead urged White Northerners and Southerners to reconcile. He saw revivalism as a tool for sectional healing. During most of his career, Moody, like most White revivalists, refused to challenge Jim Crow or to call out racism and discrimination. He prioritized regional peace over justice for Black Americans, and he segregated his Southern revivals.

Black ministers felt betrayed by this former Union veteran. AME preacher B. T. Tanner declared that Moody "could not preach in a barn of mine, and certainly not in my church. He has gone South, and in so far as his influence could he has crystallized the worst phase of caste prejudice that the world has ever seen." Frederick Douglass also criticized Moody's efforts with an unflattering comparison to famed agnostic Robert Ingersoll. "Infidel though Mr. Ingersoll may be called," Douglass acknowledged, "he never turned his back upon his colored brothers," as had White Christians during Moody's visit to

Washington, DC. "The negro can go into the circus, the theatre, and can be admitted to the lectures of Mr. Ingersoll, but cannot go into an evangelical Christian meeting." In cities where Moody appeared, Black newspaper editors relentlessly criticized the evangelist for upholding Jim Crow.[27]

In 1886 Moody founded the Chicago Bible Institute (renamed the Moody Bible Institute in 1899) to recruit and train a new army of workers dedicated to urban revivalism. A handful of prominent businessmen led by Quaker Oats mogul Henry Parsons Crowell served on MBI's board of trustees. They ensured that the mission of the school aligned with their market interests, promoting a gospel of salvation that celebrated individual attainment and the free market. Moody also won the support of corporate tycoons George Armour, Cyrus McCormick, and John Wanamaker, among many others. Businessmen loved Christian ministries, whether liberal, conservative, or revivalist, so long as they directed the energy of working people into religion rather than labor activism. Crowell ensured that like his Quaker Oats, the gospel disseminated at MBI was guaranteed pure.

Facing a grim future, at least in the short term, premillennialists never faltered. They believed that while they were living in the shadow of the Second Coming, they could remake the world.

The work of Gladden, Rauschenbusch, Addams, Scudder, Burroughs, Moody, the Salvation Army, the YMCA, Populist activists, and apocalyptic revivalists represented the diverse array of Christian responses to the problems of capitalism. A handful of prominent religious leaders denounced the market economy and its exploitation of their fellow Americans, but few Christians had ears to hear. Working people, radicals, and outsiders constantly invoked the Christian faith to critique injustice, to call out "Christian" America for its lack of authentic Christianity, but their words mostly fell flat. Ministers across the theological spectrum understood that churches needed to be more accommodating to working people if they hoped to maintain their relevance, but few had any interest in overthrowing the economic system.

They focused instead on working within it and softening capitalism's hardest edges. Mainstream protestant leaders knew that to maintain their power and influence, they could not afford to alienate the rich and powerful and the politicians who served them.

For most White Americans, despite the work of many church leaders to address current social problems, Christianity and the emerging consumer-driven middle-class American way of life proved nearly indistinguishable. But for another group of Christians, including those at the bottom rungs of society, a new form of revivalism offered hope for change.

19

NEW CHRISTIANITIES FOR THE NEW CENTURY

"Breathing strange utterances and mouthing a creed which it would seem no sane mortal could understand," wrote a journalist in 1906, "the newest religious sect has started in Los Angeles." At the time, the City of Angels was a small and inconsequential outpost in the far West—no Hollywood studios, no UCLA, no Disneyland. Little did the readers of the *Los Angeles Times* know that this story, titled "Weird Babel of Tongues," foreshadowed the global transformation of the Christian faith.

Black preacher William J. Seymour led the new Los Angeles "sect." The *Times* condescendingly identified the thirty-five-year-old as "an old colored exhorter, blind in one eye." The meetings occurred "in a tumble-down shack on Azusa street," where "devotees of the weird doctrine practice the most fanatical rites, preach the wildest theories and work themselves into a state of mad excitement in their particular zeal." The multiracial makeup of the participants proved almost as surprising to observers as the religious rites. At the small, dilapidated mission, Black, White, Asian, and Latine worshippers, alongside European immigrants, communed together. The "color line," one participant wrote, "was washed away in the blood."[1]

The Azusa Street meetings, which harked back to the wild and tumultuous Cane Ridge revivals a century earlier, lasted nearly three years and drew Christians and curiosity seekers from around the country. Because Seymour and other leaders believed that the Holy Spirit should control the direction of the meetings, they had no formal, organized service schedule or explicit leadership. Men and women prayed, preached, exhorted, spoke in tongues, wept, trembled, and convulsed as they believed the Spirit commanded, often late into the night.

Rather than sparking a revival within established churches, these Christian innovators—who called themselves "pentecostals" in reference to the New Testament story about the Holy Spirit coming to Jesus's followers on the day of Pentecost—launched a new form of Christianity that operated outside the mainstream religious establishment. They offered Americans a tangible gospel, something they could witness, feel, and experience, bringing them back in spirit if not in body to the first-century church. The movement, which combined elements from the revivalist stream and, especially in its early years, the liberationist steam, empowered the powerless, including women, racial and ethnic minorities, and the poor.

As pentecostals reshaped the faith for the new century, other Christians adapted their beliefs to the changing times. Some leading protestant liberals underwent what one advocate called an "awakening." They consciously incorporated new knowledge and new ideas into their theologies and churches, downplayed classic doctrines, and redirected part of the liberal stream, crafting a version of Christianity they called "modernism." Meanwhile, conservatives and old-school revivalists sought to suppress change by urging Americans to reject theological innovation and return to the "fundamentals" of the Christian faith. Yet despite growing differences, liberals, conservatives, and revivalists still often worshipped under the same denominational roofs, while pentecostals broke away to launch new churches. With the nation growing ever more religiously and ethnically diverse, the faithful in every stream developed fresh strategies to win American hearts, influence the culture, and realize their vision for the country's future.

According to pentecostal tradition, the modern tongues movement began on January 1, 1901, in Topeka, Kansas, when minister Charles Fox Parham laid his hands in prayer on a student, Agnes Ozman, who began babbling in a foreign language she did not know. Speaking in tongues had occurred in the early church and intermittently throughout Christian history. In North America, the phenomenon appeared occasionally in revivals and among outsider groups such as the Latter-day Saints and Shakers. Until the early twentieth century most American Christians did not emphasize the gift or subject it to careful theological analysis.

Parham joined other preachers—many from the old holiness tradition that Phoebe Palmer had helped inspire—in questioning whether the modern church had relinquished its power and authority by neglecting some of the most extravagant New Testament gifts of the Holy Spirit. In seeking a return to first-century practices, Parham was not unique. Those worshipping at John Alexander Dowie's utopian community in Chicago, Alma White's Pentecostal Union in Denver, A. J. Tomlinson's Church of God in Cleveland, Tennessee, and Charles H. Mason and Charles Price Jones's Church of God in Christ in Mississippi, among many others, also experienced New Testament gifts of the spirit. At Frank Sandford's Shiloh compound in Maine, some believers claimed to speak in other tongues. Meanwhile, they all read hazy reports about new revivals with exotic manifestations of the Holy Spirit occurring in Wales and India.

As Parham and his students followed news of revivals and delved into scripture, they homed in on Acts 2:1–4, a passage in which Jesus's followers began to speak in other tongues. Parham's students concluded that God intended to restore not only the gift of healing but also tongues. Ozman experienced it first, and then Parham spoke in tongues as well. He believed that speaking in tongues marked the baptism of the Holy Spirit, a secondary experience that followed salvation. It served as the essential evidence of the fullness of faith, and Christians who failed to experience tongues did not experience total Christianity.

Over the next few years, Parham and his students preached their new "apostolic" faith and opened new "assemblies" (a term they preferred over "churches"). In 1905, Parham organized a Bible school in Houston, Texas, where he met William Seymour, a promising student. The child of former slaves, Seymour had grown up Catholic but converted to a version of holiness, revivalist Christianity. In 1903 he contracted smallpox, which destroyed his sight in one eye.

Seymour, intrigued by Parham's teachings on spiritual gifts, began studying with him. Parham, however, embraced a racist theology, seeing Anglo-Saxons as superior humans, and he abided by local Jim Crow ordinances. While willing to train Black and Mexican students, Parham made all of them, including Seymour, sit outside the classroom door at his makeshift school rather than with the White students.

In 1906, Seymour moved to California where he worked with a holiness congregation and then started a home Bible study. Under his guidance some participants spoke in tongues. Frank Bartleman, an early chronicler of the pentecostal revivals, noted that the spirit was moving "outside ecclesiastical establishments as usual." Seymour's Bible studies quickly grew too large to continue in a private residence. He and his followers rented an old, abandoned AME church building at 312 Azusa Street, where the revival began in earnest. News of the religious manifestations spread through the press, drawing ever-larger crowds consisting of both true believers and what Bartleman dubbed "religious sore-heads and crooks and cranks." While Seymour nominally oversaw the revival, the leadership varied. "We had no pope or hierarchy," Bartleman recalled. "We had no priest class, nor priest craft." Exhorters earned the respect of the congregation based on their "spiritual gifts" and not their social class or education, which many of them lacked. "We did not even have a platform or pulpit at the beginning," Bartleman continued. "All were on a level."[2]

The day the *Los Angeles Times* broke the story about the revival, a massive earthquake struck San Francisco, destroying wide swaths of the city and sparking tremendous fires. Azusa Street pilgrims saw a sign in this calamity. When Jesus's disciples had asked him for signs of his Second Coming, he replied, "There will be great earthquakes, famines and pestilences in various places, and fearful events and great signs from heaven" (Luke 21:11). The return of apostolic gifts and a huge and deadly natural catastrophe together signaled the imminent return of Christ. Pentecostals knew that God was shaking the world.

Upon learning of Seymour's success, Parham traveled to Los Angeles to try to seize control of the revival. He objected to the wild and chaotic nature of the services and to the race mixing and intermingling that characterized them. However, Seymour stood his ground, and Parham lost the fight for the newly christened Apostolic Faith Mission. The next year, police in San Antonio arrested Parham along with a twenty-two-year-old man and charged them with committing an "unnatural" offence—of having sex. Authorities later dropped the charges, but the scandal haunted Parham for the rest of his life.

As the pentecostal movement grew and evolved, several characteristics distinguished it from other revivalist movements. Pentecostals emphasized the New Testament gifts of the Holy Spirit, including the gift of tongues, which some viewed as a heavenly language while others interpreted it as a human dialect unknown to the speaker (which missionaries sometimes used to communicate with those who did not speak their language). Pentecostals linked this gift with their faith in an imminent apocalypse, drawing upon Peter's sermon in Acts 2:17–18. As pentecostals understood this text, Peter, quoting the prophet Joel, explicitly connected the outpouring of spiritual gifts with signs of the last days. Summing up what had been happening at the Azusa mission, Seymour wrote, "O the time is very near. All the testimonies of His coming that have been going on for months are a witness that He is coming soon."[3]

Peter had also predicted in his sermon that in the last days women would "prophesy." Pentecostals used the passage from Acts to justify including women in leadership positions at a time when most other

Christian groups did not treat women as capable leaders, which gave the movement a liberationist tinge. Beginning at Azusa and continuing through the rest of the century, pentecostals proved more willing to ordain women as ministers than most other large Christian groups, although in practice they often fell short of their egalitarian ideals.

A small number of pentecostals also emphasized Mark 16:17–18. Jesus told his disciples (in a text that, in part, early biblical editors likely added to the original manuscript): "And these signs shall follow them that believe; In my name shall they cast out devils; they shall speak with new tongues; They shall take up serpents; and if they drink any deadly thing, it shall not hurt them; they shall lay hands on the sick, and they shall recover." In the Appalachian South, some pentecostals used this passage as a command to introduce poisonous snakes into their worship services, and others drank small amounts of toxins. Some died, and most pentecostals quickly refuted such practices, but they continue in some congregations to this day.

In this depiction of a rural Southern pentecostal church, a woman preacher seeks healing for a young child. The practices of female preaching and faith healing were both controversial. Those on the margins of American society often reconfigured Christianity to meet their real-world needs. (credit: Thomas Hart Benton, *Lord, Heal the Child*, 1934)

The Azusa Street revivals and the manifestation of New Testament signs and wonders set the stage for the explosive growth of pentecostalism. With the very little money they could raise, pentecostal leaders almost immediately sent missionaries around the world. Meanwhile, the pilgrims who visited Southern California spread the message of Pentecost through their holiness networks across the United States, northern Mexico, and into Canada. Yet their flamboyant and exotic practices, coupled with their seeming egalitarian worship, proved a bridge too far for most revivalists, who often treated members of the movement with disdain. Despite early pentecostals' desire to avoid institutionalizing the movement, many built new churches and then new denominations.

In the era of Jim Crow the interracial and liberationist hopes of Azusa quickly faded as the movement formalized, both in Southern California and throughout the country. The largest group of Black pentecostals worshipped in the Church of God in Christ (COGIC), a denomination that had its origins before the revivals. Baptist ministers Charles H. Mason and Charles Price Jones established COGIC in 1897 in Mississippi as an independent holiness denomination. In 1907 Mason visited Azusa Street, where he spoke in tongues. Upon returning home, he encouraged others in his network to seek spirit baptism. He also championed the idea of interracial Christian fellowship, confident that breaking down racial divides represented the will of God, although building an enduring multiracial community proved nearly impossible in practice.

White pentecostals launched their own new denomination, the Assemblies of God, at a meeting in 1914 in Hot Springs, Arkansas. They wanted to coordinate missionary activity, start a school for training new ministers, and establish a publishing house to aid in spreading their message. Within a few years, the Assemblies had solidified creeds and institutional hierarchies, laying the groundwork for rapid expansion, which its members' tireless evangelistic work further fueled.

Latines also embraced pentecostalism. Many Mexicans had attended the Azusa revivals, and they disseminated the faith through their protestant churches. Mexican-born Francisco Olazábal grew up immersed in the world of folk Catholicism, where both God and spirits abounded. When his mother converted to Methodism and became a lay evangelist, Olazábal followed her into revivalist Christianity. In 1911, fleeing the Mexican Revolution alongside hundreds of thousands of others, he moved to Texas where he took a job pastoring a local church. After a few years he relocated to Chicago to attend the Moody Bible Institute and then to California, where he pastored Spanish-speaking Methodist churches. In 1916 he visited some old friends who had been at Azusa Street, and they converted him to pentecostalism.

Olazábal joined the Assemblies of God and played a pivotal role in building a Spanish-speaking ministry within the denomination. However, he soon grew tired of the racism in the movement and his second-class citizenship. In 1923 he founded the Interdenominational Mexican Council of Christian Churches, a new, independent pentecostal group. Working primarily in Texas, California, New York, and Puerto Rico, Olazábal converted thousands to the pentecostal faith, helping spark the tremendous expansion of Latine pentecostalism.

Other Mexican Americans took a different route. Their pentecostal-driven obsession with returning to the New Testament led them to question the trinity, a doctrine they knew was likely unfamiliar to most early-church Christians. In the rural West, they created a distinctive version of revivalism called "oneness" pentecostalism. Their skill at integrating pentecostalism with their local culture and music helped them draw migrants to the revivalist faith.

Just a few years into the twentieth century, pentecostalism had emerged as a major new force within global Christianity. Its leaders believed they had restored the church to its original, primitive form. They were building schools, launching media ministries, and aligning themselves with those in power. As historian Grant Wacker wrote, pentecostals balanced "the most eye-popping features of the supernatural with the most chest-thumping features of the natural," and they did so "without admitting it." They sparked a religious revolution that continues to transform the nature of faith in North America and around the world.[4]

At the same time that hundreds of thousands of North Americans grew preoccupied with the apostolic-era gifts of the Holy Spirit, Christians in the liberal stream began exploring a different set of ideas and theories. Most Americans believed that God had directly revealed timeless and unchanging truths about life and society through the Bible or nature. But in the 1880s and 1890s, new developments in sociology, anthropology, economics, philosophy, and psychology revealed that many truths once considered immutable reflected specific times and places. This inspired in some Americans a growing sense of historical consciousness that led them to rethink their assumptions about the nature of truth and its relationship to Christianity.

Changes in higher education helped facilitate an American intellectual renaissance. Harvard, along with two new universities, Johns Hopkins and the University of Chicago, borrowed from German models to revamp academia in North America. They mimicked Germans' emphases on specialized research and intellectual freedom and inquiry, and they separated scholarship from faith. Other leading American universities followed suit, moving away from a focus on classical learning and the promotion of virtue toward an emphasis on scientific discovery and technological innovation.

University leadership also shifted. Institutions with Christian roots downplayed their sectarian ties and replaced clergy presidents with secular scholars. Wealthy donors gained influence through seats on trustee boards.

Andrew Dickson White, the founding president of Cornell University, embraced many of the new trends. He made clear that at his school the war between science and religion had ended: Science had won. "I simply try to aid in letting the light of historical truth into that decaying mass of outworn thought which attaches the modern world to mediæval conceptions of Christianity," he wrote, "and which still lingers among us—a most serious barrier to religion and morals, and a menace to the whole normal evolution of society." He and communications tycoon Ezra Cornell, the patron of Cornell University, explicitly differentiated their school in its charter from sectarian colleges. They pledged never to inquire into the religious beliefs of their faculty, preferring to let God assess hearts and souls. White boasted that he and Cornell had helped inspire the nationwide shift away from clergy-led colleges and toward the rise of the laity-led university. He failed to acknowledge, however, how in the process academics ceded power to the extremely wealthy like Cornell. Big business replaced big religion as a primary driver of American higher education.[5]

Changes in scientific thought posed the greatest challenge to traditional Christianity. Many American theologians had long sought to integrate religion and science, confident that all truth represented God's truth. But as Charles Darwin's theories of evolution, described in his 1859 book *On the Origin of Species*, gained acceptance in the following decades, reconciliation became increasingly difficult. Most theologians in the nineteenth century did not fret too much about the age of the earth, and some squared old earth geology with the book of Genesis. But theories of species transmutation, along with Darwin's argument that humans emerged via natural selection and the survival of the fittest, posed far greater challenges. Christians maintained that God created humans in his image, separate from animals. Darwin indicated otherwise. "Never since the scientific revolution completed by Newton," church historian Sydney Ahlstrom observed, "had the humanistic and religious traditions of the West been confronted by a greater need for adjustment and reformulation." Some American theologians outright rejected evolution, while others attempted to reconcile faith and science through hybrid theories of theistic evolution in which God orchestrated a Darwinian process. Their efforts marked the beginning of a long-running battle in American churches and schools about how to teach science and its relationship to Christianity.[6]

Another challenge to Christianity emerged from the worlds of history and literature. Some Christians, responding to new textual scholarship, questioned the nature and authority of the Bible. In the late nineteenth century they adopted a literary-critical approach to interpreting the sacred text called "higher criticism," which raised significant doubts about the traditionally accepted authorship, historical accuracy, and dating of certain biblical books. They also recognized that core beliefs were usually (and to some always) culture dependent.

Christian theology, they noted, changed over time and reflected the eras in which it developed. Their conclusions undermined traditional trust in the accuracy and authority of scripture and the belief in an essential, timeless, unchanging Christian faith. More liberal Christians came to view the Bible as a work of great literature that they could apply to the human condition in specific eras and contexts rather than a book of scientific or historical truths presented in a propositional form. Their ideas led to another subtle but significant shift: Some Christians realized that they could no longer limit their arguments to specific elements of Christian theology; they placed religion as a whole under scrutiny.

Most of the Christian engagement with the intellectual currents of the age—whether higher criticism or evolution—occurred in universities and theological seminaries. Biblical scholars and theologians wrestled with new ideas and theories and corresponded with their European counterparts. Theological innovation happened not in churches but in classrooms, where aspiring ministers and missionaries had the freedom to accept those ideas they found compelling, reject those they didn't, and determine how best to translate academic scholarship to church life.

Several influential preachers embraced liberal ideas and incorporated them into their sermons, translating them in ways that made them relevant to everyday parishioners. In the process they revitalized part of the liberal stream. They preached compelling, captivating sermons that centered on Jesus, portraying him as warm, friendly, and affirming rather than angry, vengeful, stoic, or long-suffering. Their Jesus wanted people to grow spiritually and lead productive, useful lives guided by moral truths. He was the smart and humble guru who delivered the Sermon on the Mount and taught people how to live righteous lives in the service of others. They rejected the concept of original sin and focused instead on ethics, convinced that with the proper training and education, humans could do good. They dismissed religious dogma and minimized the importance of sacraments like baptism and communion. Positive and hopeful about the future, they believed that humans, society, and religion all evolved in positive directions. They rejected doom and gloom apocalyptic teachings and irrational physical exuberance.

Around the turn of the century, many liberal theological intellectuals, including the architects of the social gospel, began calling themselves "modernists." Drawing inspiration from the broader modernist movements in art, literature, and culture, they focused on the process of being Christian. They saw God as present in and speaking through the flow of history. They critically examined their faith, aiming to make it relevant to the contemporary world. They abandoned notions of an absolute, objective, external, orthodox religion. Instead, they emphasized the practice of believing, of asking questions of themselves and of their faith and then embarking on an intellectual journey in search of answers. This process of actively pursuing faith rather than passively accepting it became the essence of modernist protestantism. "Although Protestant modernism was largely a movement waged among scholars and seminarians, scribbling in their austere enclaves," scholar Kathryn Lofton summarizes, "there was nothing passive about Protestant modernism. It was an aggressive, demanding process of cross-examination and inquiry" that transformed the nature and language of "Christian faith within universities, Protestant churches, and American culture." Perhaps unwilling to honestly fess up to the dramatic effects their work might have on what passed at the time for traditional orthodoxy, these theologians emphasized process and method rather than conclusions and ends. Take the right road, they believed, and you'll inevitably get to the right destination. They just didn't name the destination.[7]

Shailer Mathews, the dean of the new University of Chicago Divinity School (financed by John D. Rockefeller), celebrated what he viewed as the revolution underway in Christianity. In a 1913 article titled "The Awakening of American Protestantism," he wrote that prominent theologians were reinterpreting faith "in the terms and under the influence of evolution and democracy." He envisioned the emergence of a new Christianity that embodied "not a theory about the Bible but the actual religious experience and ideals which are recorded in the Bible." American believers, he hoped, would abandon "the formal legalistic principle of Protestantism" dating back to the Reformation and instead focus on the "normative worth of the Christian experience that gave birth to Protestantism and the Bible itself." This new faith, he believed, would "in the long run" present a "gospel of a saved society as well as of saved individuals." For modernists, just as for revivalists, transforming American society into their version of the kingdom remained a top priority.[8]

In making his views so explicit, Mathews gave conservatives and revivalists a gift. Rather than claiming to represent the historic faith, he explicitly taught that faith had evolved over time and that Christians needed to catch up. He admitted exactly what his opponents had been claiming all along—that liberal protestants had discarded the traditional, historic Christian religion and replaced it with something entirely new. Those who disagreed with his ideas wondered if they still shared the same faith with the modernists worshipping in the pews next to them.

Mathews understood that not everyone would embrace this "awakening." On the other side of the revolution, he wrote, stood those who had "little sympathy with the evangelization of social evolution." He called them "earnest Christians who, in the spirit of" ancient church father Tertullian, "repudiate all efforts at re-thinking Christian faith and prefer a bald literalism in the treatment of the Scriptures."[9]

Indeed, as liberal ideas continued to gain ground in the major American protestant denominations, many Christian leaders and laypeople wanted to do what they could to combat them. Presbyterian oilmen Lyman and Milton Stewart had established Union Oil in the 1880s. It became one of the nation's most successful oil companies, making the brothers millionaires. Like Rockefeller, and especially John D. Rockefeller Jr., the Stewarts used their wealth to support religious work. But while the Rockefellers subsidized the growth of liberal protestantism, the Stewart brothers financed apocalyptic revivalism.

In an effort to reinforce the core tenets of traditional Christianity, Lyman Stewart financed publication of a series of books on the Christian "fundamentals." For the project he brought together anti-modernist conservatives and revivalists from many different denominations, trusting that "more can be accomplished through interdenominational" collaboration. The editors solicited essays from respected scholars, influential ministers, and evangelists from around the English-speaking world. They were all White men. The editors never considered how women, or racial or ethnic minorities, might enrich the movement or broaden its appeal.[10]

The Fundamentals covered a range of topics, including personal testimonies, the virgin birth, the deity of Christ, the inspiration of the Bible, higher criticism, Catholicism, and newer religious movements such as Mormonism and Christian Science. While the essays addressed science and Darwinism, opinions on evolution varied. Scotland's James Orr, for example, indicated that Christians could accept some forms of theistic evolution. The series generally avoided political topics apart from socialism, which Princeton theologian Charles Erdman attacked directly while acknowledging that socialists had in some cases shown more compassion for the poor and the oppressed than many of the faithful. "Christian doctrines and Christian duties cannot be divorced," he wrote. The "social teachings of the Gospel need a new emphasis today." But "this does not mean," he stressed, "the adoption of a so-called 'social gospel.'" He criticized postmillennial promises of an earthly utopia and called for renewed attention to the ramifications of biblical prophecy for addressing social problems. "The real blessedness of the Church and of the world," he concluded, "awaits the personal return of Christ."[11]

Stewart sent *The Fundamentals* to every (presumably White) English-speaking protestant minister, evangelist, professor, theology student, YMCA and YWCA leader, Sunday school superintendent, and religious periodical editor in the world. Between 1910 and 1915, Stewart distributed three million copies of individual volumes of *The Fundamentals* at a cost of about two hundred thousand dollars, funding the project with help from his brother Milton. The brothers chose to remain anonymous, referred to only as "two Christian laymen."[12]

The publications exposed new fault lines developing at the base of American protestantism. Mainstream conservatives and revivalists, along with pentecostals, believed that modernism represented a threat to the Christian faith, that perhaps it did not represent a form of real Christianity at all but a false faith. Maybe, they speculated, it signified that the end-times had commenced. Jesus had predicted the last days' rise of false prophets and a falling away from the true faith. Perhaps modernism fulfilled this prophecy?

Conservatives and revivalists found it increasingly difficult to join in fellowship with liberals. Nor did they want to partner with pentecostals, whose populist and working-class roots and exotic worship styles they found embarrassing. Within mainstream protestantism, differences over theology and the practical application of the faith proved harder and harder to surmount.

Amid the escalating theological tensions, some Christians returned to Matthew 24:3–8, wondering if Jesus had foreseen their era. As the Galilean sat on the Mount of Olives his disciples asked him, "What *shall be* the sign of thy coming, and of the end of the world? And Jesus answered and said unto them, Take heed that no man deceive you. . . . And ye shall hear of wars and rumours of wars: see that ye be not troubled: for all *these things* must come to pass, but the end is not yet. For nation shall rise against nation, and kingdom against kingdom." The growing splits among conservatives, revivalists, and liberals represented one kind of developing war. But another kind loomed on the horizon as well, one that placed new demands on the nation's protestant leaders and exacerbated their differences with each other. Theological disagreements quickly turned into political and policy fights. Rather than unite to face one of the nation's greatest crises together, protestants instead battled each other to define the United States' role in the world and what it meant to build God's kingdom in North America.

PART V

SHAPING THE AMERICAN CENTURY

20

MAKING THE WORLD SAFE FOR DEMOCRACY

Presbyterian revivalist Billy Sunday loved to preach both Armageddon and Americanism. He had gained fame in the 1880s as a gutsy base runner for the Chicago White Stockings, but when he converted to Christianity he abandoned the ballpark for the revival tent. He would no longer be stealing bases from other teams, but souls from the devil.

By the early twentieth century, Sunday's revivals filled the largest auditoriums in the country's greatest cities. In part his success—like that of most revivalists in American history—derived from his populist style. Like his predecessor Dwight Moody, he had little formal education. He was a common guy, a man of the people. He described himself as "proud" to be from the "corn rows of Iowa." "The mal-odors of the barnyard are on my feet," he boasted. "I have greased my hair with goose-grease; I have blackened my shoes with a cob; I have wiped my proboscis with a gunny sack; I have drunk coffee out of my saucer and eaten peas with a knife. . . . I am a graduate from the University of Poverty and Hard Knocks." *The Atlanta Constitution* praised the evangelist's form. He preached to his audience "in the vernacular; he exhorts them in the style of vigorous directness common to the baseball diamond and the street; he translates the Bible into the slang of the day and paraphrases the sacred text with a freedom that is startling in its realism." Sunday's populist impulses inspired some revivalists to better connect with the public, while they embarrassed others as uncouth.[1]

As Christians debated their obligations to the state during World War I, Sunday rallied hundreds of thousands of Americans behind the military. "If you turned hell upside down," Sunday famously preached, "I'll bet you'd find 'Made in Germany' stamped on the bottom of it." He promised that the United States would "back the old Kaiser off the map." According to a *New York Times* reporter, he concluded a Manhattan revival service by leaping "up on top of his pulpit" and "wildly waving a flag with both hands while every soul in the audience was on his feet cheering." During his wartime sermons he often "went off at a tangent" to "flay 'Kaiser Bill' and 'his dirty bunch of pretzel-chewing, limburger-eating highbinders.'" When invited to give a benediction before the US Congress, Sunday concluded, "We pray thee that thou wilt bare thy mighty arm and strike that great pack of hungry, wolfish Huns, whose fingers drip with blood and gore." Congressmen broke decorum by responding to the prayer with yells, cheers, and clapping.[2]

Many Americans lacked Sunday's enthusiasm for war. For over a century, American leaders had steered clear of direct involvement in European conflicts, relying on the Atlantic as a natural barrier. But as ties between the US and the wider world deepened, Americans were forced to reconsider their stance. The outbreak of war sparked intense debate. Some argued for maintaining neutrality and isolation, while others urged the US to step forward and help shape a new global order.

The debate over intervention broke the protestant establishment. Once Wilson committed the nation to war, Christian leaders in every stream grappled with their positioning. Should they rally behind the president like Billy Sunday and work to make the world safe for

Few evangelists could entertain a crowd like Billy Sunday. He wove calls for salvation along with commentary on the latest social and political issues of the day from war to temperance to women's rights into his messages. (credit: George Bellows, *Metropolitan* Magazine, May 1915, Boston Public Library)

democracy, or should they adopt the position of the Old Testament prophets, serving as outsiders calling the people to repent for their sins? Was the war going to help refine humanity and set the stage for the implementation of a global social gospel, or was this conflict speeding the world to Armageddon?

The battle forced Americans to wrestle with profound theological questions on the nature of, and relationships among, religion, politics, and citizenship. It demonstrated once again that in the United States, Christian leaders never compartmentalized their faith but applied it to every aspect of domestic life and foreign policy. Many sought to convince themselves and the world that the nation remained God's chosen land, but their differences over what that meant and how God wanted them to act ultimately split the nation's churches and denominations. As a result of the war, the fractures that had started appearing in previous decades grew into deep and nearly impassable chasms.

Woodrow Wilson brought with him to the White House a Calvinistic faith in God's sovereignty along with a commitment to social Christianity. He believed in the value of democracy, people's right to self-determination, and the importance of cooperation through global organizations. He also espoused a racialized and patriarchal understanding of the "proper" social order. Like generations of social gospelers, he expected the White race to rule over everyone else and thought that God wanted great nations like the United States to "rescue" weaker ones. American leadership could make the world more orderly, just, and peaceful. But building that better world, he reasoned, might require sacrifice. The US had to be willing to suffer in order to clear a path to righteousness.

As Wilson settled into office, problems mounted in Europe. A series of alliances crafted over many decades had produced two major coalitions. The first, the Triple Alliance (or Central Powers), included Germany, Austria-Hungary, and Italy; and the second, the Triple Entente (or Allies), included Great Britain, France, and Russia. The precarious balance of power began to unravel in the Balkan countries of southeastern Europe where Serbian nationalists hoped to annex Bosnia, a province of the Austro-Hungarian Empire. On June 28, 1914, a Serbian assassinated Archduke Franz Ferdinand, heir to the Austro-Hungarian throne, in the Bosnian capital of Sarajevo. Germany encouraged its alliance partner to respond decisively while Serbia appealed to Russia for help. Russia, in turn, looked to France for support. In late July, Austria-Hungary declared war against Serbia, and before long most of Europe was embroiled in the conflict.

In the early years of the war, Americans found comfort in the fact that the wide Atlantic seemingly protected them. Reaffirming the long American tradition of keeping free from European entanglements, Wilson pledged the United States to neutrality. But what neutrality meant in practice remained far from clear. Should the United States substantially enlarge its military in a show of strength and defense, or would military preparations more easily draw the country into Europe's war? Eventually the president chose expansion.

Many protestant leaders initially opposed enlarging the military, even for defensive purposes. Liberal minister Henry Sloane Coffin, pastor of New York's Madison Avenue Presbyterian Church, like other political progressives, worried that business leaders had goaded politicians into the move. "The gravest danger to our peace at present," Coffin preached, "lies not in the attack of some foreign power jealous of our wealth, but in our own imperialistic commercialism eager to pre-empt for its selfish advantage the markets of the world." The editors of a revivalist magazine asked why "cool-headed statesmen, brought up in the atmosphere of American traditions, should advocate such schemes for a colossal navy and a colossal army?" Why would they "squander the money that ought to go into schools and reforms and other social improvements," and "rob our young men of some of the best years of their life?"[3]

Chicago Presbyterian Martin D. Hardin delivered a scathing sermon about the European conflict, which a representative entered into the *Congressional Record*. "If every cabinet and council" in Europe, he claimed, "had been made up of members taken from their lunatic asylums it is doubtful if they could have wrought such havoc and universal misery." He saw two possible paths forward. Either "real Christianity" will "spread until it embraces the nations in their intercourse," or the United States will be "dominated by its suspicious military minds." The two "are in absolute and irreconcilable conflict." He argued that only maintaining American neutrality and combating militarism would legitimate American claims to postwar leadership.[4]

A minority of religious leaders believed that the US should join the conflict, but they generally did not express their views publicly. Baptist A. C. Dixon, one of the editors of *The Fundamentals*, lamented the United States' isolationism. "I wish that the United States would join the Allies and thus help to bring it to an end," he confided from London to his daughter. "The English," he groused, "are beginning to look upon President Wilson's policy as a very shilly-shally affair and I rather share their feelings."[5]

As the war progressed, neutrality became increasingly difficult for Wilson to navigate. On May 7, 1915, a German submarine torpedoed the British liner *Lusitania*, killing more than one thousand people including 123 Americans. The ship also carried war supplies. When Wilson issued an ultimatum warning Germany to cease U-boat attacks, Secretary of State William Jennings Bryan warned his boss that the directive undermined their chance to play "the part of a friend to both sides in the role of peace maker." Bryan's allies in the State Department encouraged the Great Commoner to rein in the president. A friend reminded the cabinet secretary that as "the most conspicuous follower of the Prince of Peace" in government he should obey Jesus rather than achieve "victory carrying the bloody banner of war."[6]

A few weeks later, Bryan resigned from the cabinet. In a letter to conservative Seattle Presbyterian minister Mark Matthews, Bryan wrote that he had quit the administration in order to organize a fight against "the President, the entire Metropolitan Press, the financial interests, the munition manufacturers and the militarists" who, he believed, intended to drive the nation into the conflict. But one minister, writing to Bryan, worried that his decision, righteous as it was, marked a "national calamity and a blow at civilization in its progress toward a Christ-future."[7]

During the 1916 presidential campaign, Wilson ran on the slogan, "He kept us out of war." He intended, however, as Bryan well understood, to move the nation toward intervention. For Wilson, securing a "Christ-future" meant victory over Germany and its allies. Once securely reelected, the president had a free hand to deal with the ongoing European crisis and Germany's increasing provocations. Almost immediately he worked with Congress to pass the Selective Service Act, which presented yet another challenge to American Christians. Jesus had told his disciples to love their enemies, turn the other cheek, and pray for those who persecuted them. He had also told them at the Last Supper to buy swords. So which was it?

Unlike in the Civil War era, many revivalists preached pacifism and denounced compulsory military service. "To try to imagine Peter, James, John and Paul, or other true disciples in the trenches shooting each other," wrote minister P. A. Klein, "or charging each other with fixed bayonet is a thing I cannot comprehend. And that a law which would create such a state of things can be right is likewise to me unthinkable." "There is no greater inconsistency extant than for the Church of Jesus Christ to go to war," wrote pentecostal Frank Bartleman. "Her business is to preach, not murder. . . . War is not God's way for the Church." He lamented what he viewed as Americans' imperial ambitions and greed. "It is all for gold. We are in the game of war," he determined. "We want the dollar." In reference to the transfer of American matériel to the allies, he warned, "Chickens come home to roost. And so will much of our ammunition, with interest."[8]

Black leader and head of the Church of God in Christ Charles H. Mason, like other pentecostals, struggled to demonstrate loyalty while following his conscience. His explicit pacifism as well as the fact that some of his White followers were of German descent captured the attention of the newly formed Bureau of Investigation. Federal officials arrested Mason during the war and temporarily jailed him for denouncing military service. "I cannot understand," he admitted, "after preaching the gospel for twenty years and exhorting men to peace and righteousness, how I could be accused of fellowshipping the anti-Christ of the Kaiser."[9]

Traditional peace churches stuck to their guns, metaphorically speaking. The Quakers launched a new organization, the American Friends Service Committee, to help its people and members of other peace churches navigate the draft. The committee provided conscientious objectors with nonmilitary service opportunities. Christians on the political Left launched the Fellowship of Reconciliation to seek peaceful solutions to conflict and to aid those opposed to the war. They drew support from progressives, including Jane Addams and socialist Norman Thomas. Both groups claimed to follow the principles of Jesus.

In contrast to revivalists, most liberals in the 1910s rejected pacifism. Hardened by the ugliness of trench warfare in Europe and focused on addressing the problems of corporate and institutional evil, they spurned what they viewed as the unrealistic idealism of some of their fellow believers. Theologian and dean of the University of Chicago Divinity School Shailer Mathews worried that peace activists had become naive instruments played by isolationists. They were "led astray by an active propaganda conducted by those who wished to keep us in a state of military unpreparedness in the interest of their own programs and policies." He hoped that entering the conflict would create an opportunity for modernists to impose their vision of the kingdom of God not just on the United States but on other parts of the globe.[10]

In response to increasing provocations from Germany, Wilson appeared before Congress on April 2, 1917, to ask for a declaration of war. Building to the lines that would define the rest of the conflict, he demanded that "the world must be made safe for democracy." A few days later Wilson received a telegram from a leading apocalyptic revivalist. William Blackstone warned the president that the rapture was imminent—probably just weeks away—and encouraged him to "watch and be ready . . . to meet our Lord in the air." He concluded by assuring the president that he was "praying that this may be your experience and that God will provide a fit Successor to guide our nation through the Tribulation Period."[11]

Armageddon or not, the United States was at war.

Following Congress's declaration, Christians from every stream worked to define their obligations to the state and to articulate how their faith intersected with American foreign policy. Navigating American entry into the conflict proved especially challenging for religious and racial minorities. Wilson and his allies had segregated the federal government and the military, and it made little sense for Black Americans to risk their lives to make the world safe for democracy abroad while not experiencing democracy at home. Yet like most other religious, ethnic, and racial minorities, they understood the importance of demonstrating patriotism. They generally lined up with their churches behind the war effort. Leaders of the largest denominations partnered with the Federal Council of Churches to provide chaplains and ensure that Black soldiers and sailors had the religious support they desired.

Some Black ministers saw potential in the outcome of the war. Seattle minister James Morris Webb blended criticisms of Germany with visions of a Black Jesus and African nationalism. He expected the Kaiser's plans for world rule to come to naught, yet they reinvigorated his millennial dreams. "As the Kaiser failed through his efforts to establish himself as a Universal King," Webb preached, "his career caused my mind to be lifted to a summit and view some Biblical prophecy, that there shall come a Universal King." But this was not the king so prevalent in the White imagination. "According to Biblical History," Webb continued, "he will be a black man with wooly hair." Then taking a jab at Wilson, he concluded, "His ruling will be safer than Democracy. For there will be no discrimination and segregation under his dominion." Webb used biblical history to argue that Jesus, through Mary, had "Black" blood, which will be apparent at the time of the second coming.[12]

American Catholics, who like Black Americans often had their loyalty questioned, generally supported the commander in chief. Many had worked for decades to better integrate their church into the mainstream of American life, and the conflict generated new opportunities. When the war initially began in Europe, church leaders had supported Wilson's position of neutrality. Then, shortly after Congress declared war, Archbishop James Cardinal Gibbons delivered a message to Wilson pledging the church's "most sacred and sincere loyalty and patriotism toward our country, our Government, and our flag." "We stand ready," he assured Wilson, "to cooperate in every way possible with our President and our national Government, to the end that the great and holy cause of liberty may triumph."[13]

Even though millions of American Catholics had come from lands now at war with the United States, they worked hard to demonstrate their patriotism. The conflict allowed more recent immigrants and their children to better assimilate. Walking a fine line, church leaders rallied their members to fight for the United States rather than against particular enemy nations. Sometimes they even sided more with the president than the pope on issues of foreign policy. When Benedict XV offered a problematic peace plan, Wilson ignored him, and so did most American Catholic leaders.

In the summer of 1917, church leaders launched the National Catholic War Council to oversee the church's wartime actions. Leaders of the group aimed to "promote the spiritual and material welfare of the United States troops during the war wherever they may be." They wanted to ensure a large Catholic presence in training camps and on military bases, print and distribute religious literature to soldiers and sailors, and coordinate relief efforts. The Knights of Columbus, a social service arm of the church, helped as well.[14]

Catholic leaders, like protestants, prayed that the war would drive global leaders to the church for guidance. They created a subcommittee in the war council "to prepare the public mind by writing and publishing the teachings of the Catholic Church in regard to the true social welfare of mankind." They hoped that belligerent nations, seeking to avoid another calamity, would reconstruct geopolitics "upon the Eternal principles of religion and morality which the Catholic Church has been commissioned by Almighty God to teach to the world in all places and at all times unto its consummation." Like their American protestant counterparts, they believed that God wanted them to impose their convictions on the rest of the world.[15]

The conflict raised different issues for liberal protestants. During the first decade of the new century, progressive idealists in the United States and abroad, including many Christians in the liberal stream, had organized dozens of peace movements. Some even sought to remake international relations along new lines, including steel baron Andrew Carnegie, who financed the creation of a Peace Palace at The Hague and then established the Church Peace Union (later called the Carnegie Endowment for International Peace). Millions of Americans and Europeans, most often working through their churches and religious organizations, hoped, prayed, and labored to make the brutal warfare of the nineteenth century a thing of the past. According to many protestants, such work could help usher in the kingdom of God.

Although the outbreak of war in Europe represented a serious impediment to liberal ideals, activists didn't skip a beat. The Federal Council of Churches created the General War-Time Commission, which helped oversee chaplains and lobby the government on religious issues. The YMCA and Salvation Army ministered to soldiers on the front, ensuring that they had Bibles and other religious literature. While none of the groups relished war, they believed in the justness of the cause.

Just as Catholics had big plans for leading postwar reconstruction, so too did liberal protestants. Having worked across national boundaries to build peace coalitions, they saw the world's nations as mutually dependent. They trusted that the more cooperation they could facilitate, the better the outcome. The war might serve as a refining fire to purge evil and help advance humankind. The moral and ethical Christianity they had been developing could serve as the basis for a new world order.

Manhattan minister Harry Emerson Fosdick saw the war as little more than a temporary roadblock on Christians' world-perfecting itinerary. The Christian, he preached, "determines to play his part, that this war may impede the Divine Purpose as little as possible and that out of it may come indeed a world made 'safe for democracy.'" Fosdick believed that Jesus would approve the use of force for moral ends, and that the war might ultimately reveal the futility of nationalism and patriotism and replace them with a sense of global harmony and universal citizenship. He believed that fostering international Christian unity could achieve these outcomes. But as was often the case with liberal protestants of that era, he assumed the world's peoples would find peace through the adoption of liberal protestantism. He expected those of other religions as well as his fellow Christians in the conservative and revivalist streams to conform to liberal ideals.[16]

Other leading liberals shared his hopes. Henry Sloane Coffin also believed that the war created the opportunity to raise out of the world's ashes a new global Christian civilization. He thought God "divinely created" the church to provide "for the world's reconstruction into a universal fellowship." Social gospel leader Walter Rauschenbusch claimed that humans worldwide were "demanding a christianizing of international relations. The demand for disarmament and permanent peace, for the rights of the small nations against the imperialistic and colonizing powers, for freedom of the seas and of trade routes, for orderly settlement of grievances—these are demands for social righteousness and fraternity on the largest scale." The social gospel, he explained, had evolved: "Before the War the social gospel dealt with social classes; to-day it is being translated into international terms."[17]

Christians in the revivalist stream, and especially those who over the previous few decades had embraced a revitalized apocalyptic premillennialism, did not expect to see a more Christian, fraternal, or just postwar world. They viewed the conflict as proof of the sinfulness of humanity and the hopelessness of the immediate future. The conflict represented for them another step toward the ultimate battle of Armageddon that would mark the end of history as described in the book of Revelation. For decades they had argued that, contrary to the claims of social-gospel liberals and political progressives, humankind had not improved. Premillennialists could not help but find some satisfaction in international turmoil. They used the war to promote their gospel and their movement. Their ability to anticipate conflicts around the rapidly changing world with total confidence and to explain their meaning on the basis of ancient prophecies captured the attention—and then the souls—of thousands of Americans.

Apocalyptic revivalists, more than any other mainstream group of Christians, provided a consistent critique of Wilson's justification for entering the conflict. They saw democratizing the world as neither a worthwhile nor a sustainable goal. "We are reminded by the inspired prophets," the editors of *Christian Workers* cautioned readers, "that the ascendency of democracy, though certain, is not lasting." In fact, the editors believed that the Bible foretold an era of democracies ruling over much of the earth just before totalitarian governments took power and opened the door for the Antichrist. The editors of *King's Business* complained that American leaders had encouraged citizens' full participation in the conflict by promising "that the result of this awful war will be that all tyrannical government will end and that there will never be another war." But they thought this outcome was as likely as Billy Sunday turning pacifist. "This is a pleasant hope, but it is absolutely without warrant either in what we know of man or what we know of the teachings of the Bible."[18]

Apocalyptic revivalists worried about Wilson's consolidation of federal power and his interventions into the economy as well. "The way is being paved," Frank Bartleman wrote, for the Antichrist. "Men must obey. They must take the 'mark of the Beast.' They are to be simply the separate parts of a great State machine to be used up as ordered for the wild Beast's glory." Christian writer and lawyer Philip Mauro had a similar response to changes on the home front. "The principles of Socialism," he wrote, "which were utterly opposed to monopoly, have led to the greatest monopoly that has yet appeared in the world. . . . We have seen the establishment of Government control of public-service corporations, Government control of incomes (both of corporations and individuals), Government control of food and fuel, and Government control of the persons of individuals themselves, for life or death—so far as their lives are supposed to be required in order 'to make the world safe for democracy.'" Mauro saw this consolidation as inevitable. He had little reason to object to what he thought the prophets had predicted thousands of years earlier in the scriptures. In fact, Mauro felt grateful that the "adoption of socialistic principles" in the United States had occurred without the kind of bloodshed paralyzing Russia at the time.[19]

During World War I some protestants joined President Woodrow Wilson's crusade to "make the world safe for democracy" and did what they could to support the war effort. Others embraced pacifism and focused on building the global Christian church rather than cheering on nationalistic conflicts. For Catholics, the war provided another opportunity to demonstrate their loyalty. (credit: Library of Congress)

And yet in one crucial area, revivalists, joined by Christians in each of the other streams, called for a major expansion of federal power. Building on the work of prior temperance crusaders Carry Nation, Frances Willard, and other members of the WCTU, activists pressured President Woodrow Wilson to ban booze. The government, they argued, should force Americans to stop wasting resources, including valuable grain, on the production of alcohol. With little debate, Congress passed a Prohibition amendment to the Constitution in 1917 as a wartime measure, which the states soon ratified. The Eighteenth Amendment, which took effect in early 1920, prohibited "the manufacture, sale, or transportation of intoxicating liquors." Americans could drink alcohol without fear of punishment—they just could no longer sell, manufacture, or transport it. The move electrified Christian activists, who believed that the implementation of Prohibition meant that once again they could transform the trajectory of the nation. After decades of hard work, they had inspired a change to the Constitution. This confirmed for them that they could remake the nation's government and dictate the nation's morals based on their own protestant convictions. But it proved to be a pyrrhic victory.

The war renewed apocalyptic revivalists' obsession over the fate of Palestine, a land that played a central role in their end-times schemes. They did everything in their power to influence American foreign policy in the Middle East. Premillennialists had long expected a substantial emigration of Jews to Palestine to precede the battle of Armageddon, which inspired them to take up the Zionist cause before almost any other groups of Americans. They looked especially to Matthew 24:32–33: "Now learn a parable of the fig tree; When his branch is yet tender, and putteth forth leaves, ye know that summer is nigh: So likewise ye, when ye shall see all these things, know that it is near, even at the doors." Interpreting the fig tree as a symbol of the Jewish nation, they believed that for the remaining last-days prophecies to be fulfilled, Jews needed to return in significant numbers to Palestine, the land that God had established for them. Without a major Jewish migration, there could be no Second Coming.

The reestablishment of Israel, however, would not end well for Jews, according to premillennialists. Those who had refused to accept Jesus as savior would encounter horrific persecution. Meanwhile, the Antichrist would face a series of enemies who sought control of the supposedly vast untapped resources yet to be discovered in Palestine. Near the end of the Antichrist's seven-year reign, he would engage in a series of wars culminating in a great battle at Armageddon, a literal valley in Israel. There Christ and his army of saints would vanquish the Antichrist, inaugurating Jesus's millennial reign on earth.

Chicago businessman William Blackstone, who wrote a best-selling book on Jesus's imminent Second Coming and the fulfillment of prophecy, helped focus Americans' attention on the Middle East. His wealth and connections with prominent Americans provided him with substantial influence despite his somewhat controversial theological beliefs. In 1891 he had penned a "memorial" advocating the creation of a new homeland for Jews in Palestine. It included the signatures of over four hundred American leaders, including the chief justice of the Supreme Court, the speaker of the House of Representatives, future president William McKinley, the editors of the country's major newspapers including *The New York Times* and the *Chicago Tribune*, and corporate barons J. P. Morgan and John D. Rockefeller. He presented it to then-president Benjamin Harrison. In a letter accompanying the petition, Blackstone explained to Harrison that prophecy guaranteed that Jews would return to Palestine. He also cited Genesis 12:3, "I will bless them that bless thee," promising the president that God would favor the United States if the president supported the Zionist cause. In this way Blackstone both predicted the return of Jews to Palestine and worked to facilitate it.[20]

Some American Jews also began envisioning a restoration of Israel, and in 1897 a small group founded the Federation of American Zionists. Many Jews, however, viewed Zionism as a distraction. They focused on integrating into American society, not reclaiming a historic homeland. For those Jews who embraced Zionism, however, apocalyptic revivalists proved natural if awkward allies.

During the war, Blackstone resurrected his memorial with the hopes of persuading President Wilson to support the creation of a Jewish state. He also developed friendships with important American Jewish leaders, including Louis Brandeis, the first Jew to serve on the US Supreme Court and the president of the Federation of American Zionists. Brandeis purportedly remarked that Blackstone was the true "father of Zionism" since his work "antedates" that of Theodor Herzl. Remarkably, Blackstone never hid from any prominent Zionist leaders his belief that in the end-times Jews would face horrific persecution at the hands of the Antichrist unless they accepted Jesus as the Messiah.[21]

The Blackstone–Brandeis relationship took a strange turn in 1917. Blackstone oversaw a trust for world evangelism established by revivalist millionaire oilman Milton Stewart of *The Fundamentals*. Wanting to ensure that the money was used effectively in the event of Blackstone and Stewart's rapture, Blackstone asked Brandeis to help him draw up legal documents to transfer the trust to Brandeis to use for the Zionist cause. Apparently Brandeis agreed to help. The justice maintained a safe deposit box with Blackstone's legal papers, copies of his premillennial tracts, and sealed documents that Blackstone instructed Brandeis to open only after the rapture. These documents would further instruct Brandeis on how to find salvation in a world ruled by the Antichrist.[22]

In the late fall of 1917, British troops under the command of General Edmund Allenby engaged in a series of battles against Ottoman regiments in the Middle East. As the Allies neared Jerusalem, British Foreign Secretary Arthur Balfour wrote Lord Rothschild, the most prominent Jew in Great Britain, to inform him that "His Majesty's Government view with favour the establishment in Palestine of a national home for the Jewish people, and will use their best endeavors to facilitate the achievement of this object." Just a few weeks later, Allenby marched into Jerusalem, making Balfour's promise a reality. Brandeis recognized that limited, British-led supervision of Palestine was the likely outcome of the war rather than the independent Jewish state that Blackstone wanted. Nevertheless, Brandeis wrote a friend that he still hoped to use the "Blackstone crowd" to support his agenda. The Blackstone–Brandeis friendship marked the beginning of an apocalyptic revivalist–Zionist partnership of mutual opportunism, a relationship that continues to this day.[23]

The war accelerated the developing theological schism between modernists on the one side and apocalyptic revivalists on the other. Moderates and conservatives fell somewhere in the middle. Leaders of the warring theological camps all sought to impose their agendas on American foreign and domestic policy, but they differed on their goals and how they understood the nation's role in the conflict and in the postwar future.

Apocalyptic revivalists did not see the United States as God's chosen land, which reflected their increasingly marginalized position in American life during the conflict. While journalists and clerics often lamented that all Christendom had gone to war, they insisted that a Christian was a redeemed individual, not a governing entity, a national group, or a state. "There is not, and never has been," minister Leonard Newby preached, "such a company of people as a Christian nation, and never will be until the Lord comes." *King's Business* made a similar point. Editors defined "a Christian nation" as a nation that "has accepted Christ as its Saviour and as its Lord" in commerce, politics, international relations, "and in all the departments of its life." But "such a nation does not exist on earth, and never has existed, and never will exist until our Lord comes again." Assemblies of God leader Stanley Frodsham characterized Christian nationalism as an "abomination" and encouraged fellow believers to "renounce their loyalty" to their "former king"—their nation—upon joining God's spiritual kingdom. Such sentiments irritated more mainstream protestants who still aspired to use the power of the state to Christianize and Americanize the world.[24]

Apocalyptic revivalists' conflicted views on military service and democracy, as well as their lack of faith in ultimate victory, raised questions among many Americans about their loyalty. Leading modernists carped on these issues. The University of Chicago's Shirley Jackson Case insisted that while the United States needed "every ounce of the nation's energy," premillennialists "were advocating a type of teaching which is fundamentally antagonistic to our present national ideal." He accused apocalyptic revivalists of "primitive thinking" and "mythological interpretation," claiming that they represented a tremendous danger to the nation. "Under ordinary circumstances one might excusably pass over premillenarianism as a wild and relatively harmless fancy." But not during the war. "In the present time of testing it would be almost traitorous negligence to ignore the detrimental character of the premillennial propaganda." Painting premillennialists as cold and heartless, he continued: "The retention of a vain hope of catastrophic world-renewal begets indifference, if not actual hostility, toward all remedial agencies designed to improve the present order of existence." Because premillennialists viewed Wilson's efforts to make the world safe for democracy as unattainable, Case believed that they indirectly, and maybe even directly, aided the enemy. A minister and Bible scholar writing in the liberal protestant magazine *The Christian Century* agreed, warning that the "most serious menace of millenarianism is its inevitable effect upon the loyalty, courage and devotion of our citizenship in the present world war."[25]

Chicago dean Shailer Mathews condemned premillennialism during the war for its social and political implications. "Partly because of the war, partly because of the extensive circulation of its literature, partly because of its literalistic appeal to the Bible, partly because of the lack of theological education on the part of active Christian workers, premillenarianism," he warned, "is a danger." It "forces men to choose between the universally accepted results of modern culture, and diagrams from the book of Daniel, elevations of church members into the sky, and interpretations of the prophets which reach the heights of absurdity in aeroplanes, tanks, and the Kaiser." He accused revivalists of drawing on faulty apocalyptic expectations about the coming Messiah that undermined the United States' role in the world.[26]

As the controversy grew, additional modernists jumped into the fray, supporting and reaffirming the positions of Mathews and Case, while apocalyptic revivalists responded in kind. Methodist James Allen Geissinger complained that premillennialism "paralyzes every impulse to Christianize the world" and that its adherents ignored "unjust wages, bad housing conditions, child labor, and every other social and moral problem." *The Christian Century* and *The Biblical World* each published lengthy series disparaging premillennialism as well. George Preston Mains, in his unimaginatively titled book *Premillennialism: Non-Scriptural, Non-Historic, Non-Scientific, Non-Philosophical* attributed the success of the movement to the "unprecedented world war" which incited "a new expectation of the imminent coming of Christ for the ending of the world," a period of "systematic, persistent, and even audacious propaganda of this faith." He added that the modernist attack on apocalyptic revivalism revealed the "growing conviction that the movement no longer should be allowed to pass unchallenged." Mains was certainly right. The war verified in a way that nothing else could that Christians from all streams had to take seriously premillennialist doomsday scenarios and their implications for current affairs.[27]

Apocalyptic revivalist T. C. Horton relished liberals' obsession with and anger at premillennialists. "Our Postmillennial brethren are on the warpath," he wrote. "For forty years or more they have held their peace. They had but one text book on the subject. . . . Now they are everywhere on the alert, writing books, declaiming from the rostrum, sounding the alarm from pulpit and press. 'Beware of the Premillennialists!'" Then he cut to the heart of the controversy: "What's the matter, brethren? Why the sudden arousement?" His answer: "Now these good brethren are finding fault because the dear saints are flocking to hear the preachers and teachers who are premillennialists."[28]

But his assessment told only half the story. The war exacerbated the theological divide because it transformed an obscure intellectual debate primarily among theologians over the Bible's millennial teachings into one about patriotism, nationalism, citizenship, and war, generating conflict among Baptists, Presbyterians, Methodists, and others. The debate spoke directly to questions of the nature of the protestant establishment, who should lead it, what direction they should take it, and America's role in God's eternal scheme.

While apocalyptic revivalists objected to modernists' efforts to portray them as bad citizens, they also scrambled to reframe the debate. Postmillennialism, the Moody Bible Institute's James Gray asserted, represented the true threat to the nation. "The whole theory of postmillennialism is pregnant with the idea that the world is morally growing better all the time, the corollary of which is that military armaments are a menace and to be discouraged at every point." He blamed postmillennialists for playing into Germany's hands by earlier supporting superficial peace movements and discouraging American armament. The premillennialist, in contrast, sets his mind "on the surest methods of winning the war." Turning back to the larger religious issues at stake, he argued that his theological opponents "have little real familiarity with what God is doing in the world, and the place which this war occupies in His plan." Just as the international military conflict began winding down, in the United States a political-theological war started ratcheting up.[29]

On November 11, 1918, the Central Powers officially surrendered. The war had devastated much of the world. Establishing the peace proved to be almost as challenging for the Americans as helping to win the war. Woodrow Wilson had always hoped and planned to play a major role in shaping the postwar world. During the conflict he delivered a speech to Congress identifying "Fourteen Points" that he thought would set the parameters for the reconstruction of Europe, define postwar international relations, and prevent another world war. Among his many proposals, the president made the case for religious liberty abroad. He believed that people should have the right to worship according to their consciences. Since many European governments still supported establishment churches, this was a somewhat controversial proposal. This did not mean, however, that Wilson saw all faiths as equally valid. He believed that the conservative-stream protestant Christianity he practiced would ultimately win over the world.

Wilson's proposal of a League of Nations, like his rationale for intervening in the war itself, split the nation's protestant leaders. Liberals strongly supported it. They viewed the League as another tool for establishing international unity and a vehicle for enacting a global social gospel. Apocalyptic revivalists hated the concept of what seemed to mark the start of a movement toward the creation of a global superstate. They expected the League to facilitate the rise of the Antichrist by bringing together the major nations of the world under the command of a single leader.

The United States never ratified the Treaty of Versailles or joined the League, striking a major blow to Wilson's crusade to make the world safe for democracy. But the president's call for the United States to impose its ideas about religious freedom on the rest of the world endured. Meanwhile, the war for control of the protestant establishment and the nation's major White denominations between modernists and apocalypticists—who after the war began calling themselves fundamentalists—had just begun.

21

THE RISE OF FUNDAMENTALISM

In May 1919, some six thousand White revivalist ministers, theologians, and evangelists gathered in Philadelphia for the weeklong World Conference on Christian Fundamentals. The war had ended, and they wanted to ensure that their version of Christianity shaped the peace, in the United States and through their missionaries abroad. They heard sermons on everything from "Christ and the Present Crisis" to "Why I Preach the Second Coming." The men and women in the audience believed that God had chosen them to build on the ideas embedded in *The Fundamentals*, to challenge religious liberalism, to go on offense. They aimed to call Christians back to the essentials of the faith, and to prepare the world for one final revival before Jesus returned.

Minneapolis Baptist preacher William Bell Riley planned the meetings, hoping to build what he described as a "confederacy of conservatives." A tall, austere, and uncompromising man, Riley was a natural-born crusader who rarely saw a religious fight he did not expect to win. "The hour has struck," Riley declared, "for the rise of a new Protestantism." He described the inauguration of this movement as more significant than Martin Luther's posting of the ninety-five theses on the church door in Wittenberg, Germany, four hundred years earlier. While Riley was no Luther, the conference helped mark the launch of a new, vibrant, organized, and politically adept form of apocalyptic revivalism.[1]

But what to call this burgeoning new movement?

The following year Baptist minister and editor Curtis Lee Laws helped organize another "fundamentals" conference. As participants discussed their differences from their liberal counterparts, leaders of the group decided that they needed a clear term to distinguish them. They rejected "conservatives," Laws explained, as "too closely allied with reactionary forces in all walks of life," and they discarded "pre-millennialists" as "too closely allied with a single doctrine and not sufficiently inclusive." In fighting liberalism within their churches and seminaries, they hoped to draw as many allies as possible. "We suggest," Laws concluded, "that those who still cling to the great fundamentals and who mean to do battle royal for the fundamentals shall be called 'Fundamentalists.'"[2]

Revivalists and conservatives had been wrestling with theological liberalism for a couple of decades, but they had not intended to build a new, separate Christian movement. Then the Great War began, accentuating the real-world ramifications of what had started as a somewhat esoteric theological controversy. It pushed theological differences into debates over patriotism and citizenship, which proved disruptive to the nation and the nation's protestant churches. Apocalyptic revivalists and liberals disagreed about their obligations as Christian citizens to the state, about the role the US should play in global conflicts, and about the reconstruction of the postwar world. Their differences had ramifications for the American people as a whole, which brought substantial outside attention to the controversy. The fundamentalist-modernist controversy evolved from an abstract theological fight waged primarily in wartime religious publications to one that expanded much further in the 1920s, eventually splitting the nation's major denominations, undermining the influence of the protestant establishment, and initiating a generations-long struggle for control of religious life in the United States.

On Sunday, May 21, 1922, modernist Harry Emerson Fosdick, perhaps the most influential minister of his generation, stepped up to the pulpit of Manhattan's First Presbyterian Church to deliver a sermon entitled "Shall the Fundamentalists Win?" His well-heeled congregation listened as Fosdick narrated the revolution underway in American religious life. The emerging fundamentalist movement had Fosdick, like many other modernists, on the defensive. He challenged apocalyptic revivalists' faith in the historicity of biblical miracles, the virgin birth, the inerrancy of the Bible, and the sacrifice of Christ as a total payment for human sin. Revivalists' obsession with the Second Coming of Jesus particularly baffled him. Fosdick believed that only the widespread disillusionment of the "chaotic" and "catastrophic" war years could explain the rise of what he saw as an obscure doctrine, one that he claimed he had never encountered in his youth. He attributed apocalypticists' success to Americans' distress over "new knowledge" about the origins of the universe, human history, and comparative religions, each of which seemed to threaten Christian belief. "You cannot fit the Lord Christ," he asserted, "into that Fundamentalist mold."[3]

While Fosdick dissected fundamentalism, an ally of the New York preacher worried that modernists had failed to develop an attractive program of evangelism. They needed to do more than criticize; they needed to offer a positive alternative to the fundamentalists. "We are having a great deal of discussion in the South about Fundamentalism and Modernism," the minister wrote to Fosdick. "I am about the only evangelist who does not preach the so-called Fundamentalism. . . . I wish that the Modernists could outline a campaign on Evangelism that would show the nation the real vital power of a modern interpretation of Evangelism."[4]

Fosdick mostly agreed. "Christian liberalism," he admitted, had failed "to achieve a successful evangelistic method and appeal."

Liberals had become complacent. "I presume," he replied, that since fundamentalists made liberals "fight on the defensive so much," they had failed to "realize" liberalism's "positive potentialities." He and his allies knew that if they wanted to maintain their influence over American culture and politics, they needed to do better.[5]

Unlike modernists, fundamentalists put substantial effort into evangelism. They invested heavily in schools focused on training workers to disseminate their message of instant and eternal redemption. Fundamentalists did not necessarily intend to compete with more established colleges, but rather to offer something different that fit the times.

In the first decades of the twentieth century, fundamentalists and their pentecostal allies opened Bible institutes all over the nation. William Bell Riley launched the Northwestern Bible and Missionary Training School in Minneapolis in 1902; Lyman Stewart opened the Bible Institute of Los Angeles in 1908; Colorado fundamentalists opened the Denver Bible Institute in 1914; C. I. Scofield started the Philadelphia School of the Bible in 1914; the Assemblies of God launched Central Bible Institute in Missouri in 1922; Aimee Semple McPherson opened the Echo Park Evangelistic and Missionary Training Institute in Los Angeles in 1923 (renamed Lighthouse of International Foursquare Evangelism, or L.I.F.E., Bible College in 1926); Robert C. McQuilkin founded Columbia (South Carolina) Bible School in 1923; Lewis Sperry Chafer opened Evangelical Theological College in Texas in 1924 (later Dallas Theological Seminary); Bob Jones began the school that bears his name in Florida in 1927; and Edmund Ironside opened the Dallas Colored Bible Institute in 1928, where he and his White colleagues trained dozens of Black Americans in the fundamentalist faith. These schools tended to attract working people who didn't have the time or money for a traditional college education. Riley interpreted the success of the many Bible schools as proof that God was preparing a faithful remnant for the final days.

Two other schools played important roles in fundamentalism. Wheaton College, founded just outside Chicago in 1860 by revivalists and abolitionists, had always stood apart from other fundamentalist institutions in that it offered a full liberal arts curriculum and emphasized classical studies rather than just training for ministry. Nevertheless, Wheaton became a mainstay of apocalyptic revivalism and one of the fundamentalist movement's most intellectually respectable colleges. Yet despite the school founders' progressive views on race, in the first half of the twentieth century Wheaton enrolled very few Black students.

A second significant training camp for fundamentalists was Princeton Theological Seminary. Affiliated with Princeton University, the seminary had long been a bastion of old-school Presbyterianism and conservative protestantism, where at the turn of the twentieth century eminent theologians including Charles Hodge and B. B. Warfield challenged liberal approaches to the scriptures. In the 1920s, J. Gresham Machen served at Princeton as professor of New Testament. Dubbed "Dr. Fundamentalist" by acerbic journalist H. L. Mencken, Machen taught some of the most important fundamentalist ministers of the interwar era, including Harold Ockenga, Donald Grey Barnhouse, and Carl McIntire. But as Princeton began to liberalize, Machen led an exodus of conservatives and apocalyptic revivalists out of the school and formed Westminster Theological Seminary in Philadelphia as an alternative Presbyterian school. Administrators had passed him over for a promotion, and he disagreed with school leaders' efforts to reorganize the seminary, a move intended to take power away from conservative members of the faculty. In making the decision to separate from Princeton, conservative protestants ceded to moderate and liberal Christians one of the most intellectually respectable seminaries in the nation and one of the few places where fundamentalists could receive a top-tier graduate education that did not directly challenge their faith.[6]

As Machen realized firsthand in losing the fight for Princeton Seminary, the growing fundamentalist-modernist controversy had substantial institutional and economic implications. Fundamentalists believed they represented true Christianity, that the blood of centuries of revivalists, reformers, and institution builders circulated in their veins. They thought American protestants' established churches, seminaries, mission stations, hospitals, and schools belonged to them.

"Nine out of ten" dollars, "if not ninety-nine out of every hundred" invested in Christian ministries, William Bell Riley lamented, "were given by Fundamentalists."[7]

Fundamentalists believed they could hold on to the power and resources of the old protestant establishment. Convinced that modernists had abandoned the true faith, they assumed modernists would abandon their positions in mainstream religious institutions as well. Hoping to avoid Machen's fate, fundamentalists initially refused to separate from their churches. But they miscalculated. In the end liberals and moderates won control of most of the nation's major denominations. The United States' core religious institutions, Riley lamented, were "filched by modernists. It took hundreds of years to collect this money and construct these institutions. It has taken only a quarter of a century for the liberal bandits to capture them."[8]

Much of the mainstream press tended to sympathize with and promote modernism over fundamentalism, which forced fundamentalists to find alternative ways to disseminate their message. They quickly grasped the power of the newest media, radio. A small number of Christians feared that when the Apostle Paul dubbed Satan "the prince of the power of the air" he had foreseen the new technology, but most fundamentalists and pentecostals saw radio as a useful tool. Leaders of the Moody Bible Institute and the Bible Institute of Los Angeles built radio stations in the 1920s, and evangelists including Aimee Semple McPherson, Harold Ockenga, Donald Grey Barnhouse, John Roach Straton, Louis Talbot, J. Frank Norris, Lightfoot Solomon Michaux, and Paul Rader took to the airwaves with great success. McPherson called radio "a beautiful priceless gift from the loving Hand of our Father God." It presented a "most unheard of opportunity for converting the world, and of reaching the largest possible number of people in the shortest possible time." These ministers effectively preached apocalyptic revivalism over the air, assessing the relationship between faith and culture, and delivering end-times diatribes into countless living rooms throughout every part of the country.[9]

In radio's early years, preachers sometimes got into trouble. For example, audiences could hear McPherson all over the FM band rather than on her assigned frequency. Secretary of Commerce Herbert Hoover started cracking down on the many broadcasters engaged in this practice. To force McPherson's compliance, he decided to temporarily shut down her station. The devil may have captured the film industry, but McPherson intended to put up a fight before he commandeered her radio station. Hoover claimed that she telegrammed him in response: "Please order your minions of Satan to leave my station alone. You cannot expect the Almighty to abide by your wave length nonsense." Shortly thereafter, she complied with his directives.[10]

Evangelist Charles Fuller took Christian broadcasting to new heights. He began broadcasting from the Bible Institute of Los Angeles's studio in 1924 and then gradually expanded his ministry. In 1936 Fuller formed a partnership with a new national network, Mutual Broadcasting, and soon thereafter he preached his first coast-to-coast sermon on the newly dubbed *Old Fashioned Revival Hour*. Americans loved the show. By the mid-1940s, it had an audience estimated at twenty million. A typical broadcast included upbeat hymns, his wife's reading of inspirational letters from listeners, and then a short sermon from Charles delivered in simple, plain language on the fundamentals of the Christian faith. His program succeeded by blending the best of the nineteenth-century revival tradition with the latest twentieth-century technology.

Conservatives, like revivalists, also made excellent use of radio. Lutheran minister Walter Maier, who had a doctorate in Semitic languages from Harvard, built a popular on-air ministry. Maier vacillated between conservative, Bible-oriented sermons and commentary on news and international events. Although he called his show *The Lutheran Hour*, he did not often focus on specific Lutheran doctrines but instead emphasized the importance of salvation. He urged all unbelievers to attend church, regardless of their choice of denominations. By the end of the 1930s he had the largest national radio audience of any minister in the era.

Fundamentalists proved much better at integrating mass media into their ministries than their liberal counterparts, which played an important role in building the movement and spreading its doomsday messages. They compressed the Christian faith into small, compact messages and packaged them in entertaining wrapping using drama and music. Their sense that time was running out made them willing to gamble and experiment with new technologies and to invest without thinking too far into the future. Without necessarily realizing it, they laid the foundations for a revolution in religious mass media.

With schools peppered across the country churning out new evangelists, ministers, and missionaries, and radio stations broadcasting revivalist ideas, the fundamentalist movement grew rapidly. National magazines, annual conferences, and the airwaves provided vital links that melded fundamentalists into a national network. At a time when more Americans were on the move, many into cities, fundamentalist leaders downplayed their denominational affiliations and distinctive theological positions. They made it easy for people from traditional Baptist, Presbyterian, Methodist, Disciples of Christ, and Congregational fellowships to church shop in pursuit of ministers who affirmed their preexisting values, who entertained them, or who seemed to preach the "old time" gospel.

The liberal *The Christian Century* in 1924 summed up the state of the fundamentalist-modernist controversy: "The differences between fundamentalism and modernism are not mere surface differences, which can be amiably waved aside or disregarded, but they are foundation differences, structural differences, amounting in their radical dissimilarity almost to the differences between two distinct religions." "The God of the fundamentalist," the editor concluded, "is one God; the God of the modernist is another. The Christ of the fundamentalist is one Christ; the Christ of the modernist is another. The Bible of fundamentalism is one Bible; the Bible of modernism is another." Fundamentalists could not have agreed more.[11]

The fundamentalist-modernist controversy, like the prophecy conference movement that preceded it, originated among Whites. While many Black protestants embraced the "fundamentals" of the faith, and others saw hope in modernism, they mostly remained on the sidelines as public debate raged in the leading White religious denominations and periodicals. At no point did the White factions consider reaching out to the nation's Black churches. Despite fundamentalists' talk of doctrinal purity as the foundation for Christian fellowship, the color line always trumped theology. White fundamentalists had no interest in cultivating Black allies or bringing them into the fundamentalist network, even if some African Americans shared fundamentalist beliefs. Meanwhile, Black churchgoers understood that racism was a feature of the White fundamentalist faith.

Leaders of the predominately Black National Baptist Convention made their commitment to fundamentalist doctrine clear. "All colored Baptists are fundamentalists," a Black editorialist in the *National Baptist Union-Review* claimed, "except a half-dozen imitators of Ingersoll, Darrow, Fosdick, and Dieffenback, the so-called 'Intellectuals' of our race." The paper called modernism a "cancer on the body ecclesiastic" and then proudly noted that "the infection of false teachings afflicting white Baptist churches, schools, and homes balks at the color line because Colored Baptists will have none of it." Church leaders counseled young ministers not to spend time studying "Evolution" or "Liberal Religion," but instead they "should be devoted to prayerful, strongly mental meditation of the Word of God as held and taught by Baptists throughout the ages."[12]

Black leaders who advocated for the "fundamentals" interpreted them differently than their White counterparts. E. C. Morris, the president of the National Baptist Convention, emphasized the importance of clinging to the historic doctrines of the Christian faith. However, he simultaneously denounced lynching and justified African Americans' pursuit of their civil and social rights as integral to authentic Christianity. His seamless shift from criticizing modernist theology to expressing concerns about social justice revealed a substantial divide between White fundamentalists and Black liberationists. Whites simply did not—and did not have to—think about how their faith related to issues of injustice and discrimination.[13]

Former Civil War chaplain and AME preacher T. G. Steward wrote his son in 1923 near the end of his long life, reflecting on the

state of Christianity in the United States. The growth of liberalism and modernism worried him. "We have got to drop the white fetish; the whites have failed—completely failed; and their overthrow is nigh. They have lost their gift of self government as will soon be apparent. Europe is going to the bow-wows; and America will follow. The colored people must give them up and hold on to GOD." White Christianity, he believed, lacked power and effectiveness. He felt particularly concerned about the social gospel. "The whites are throwing away their religion which has been their ballast and guide, and are discarding the supernatural, and worshipping an abstraction—teaching social service, and social salvation, and ignoring personal character and conduct."[14]

Other Black religious leaders opposed both fundamentalism and modernism. Minister A. B. Adams, who had a regular column in the *Pittsburgh Courier*, emphasized the importance of what he saw as the classic faith. If "the worn out theological conceptions of the white man have not sufficiently benefited the Negro youth," then ministers should "impart to them the teachings of God. . . . Proclaim the Word of God. We have too many man-made faiths in the world." He flayed modernists, including ministers like Fosdick, whom he accused of abandoning the scriptures. But lest anyone mistake him for a fundamentalist, he concluded by asserting his independence. "Please do not misunderstand me being a fundamentalist. I am not, although the fundamentalists are a little better than the modernists."[15]

Others did not think that fundamentalists were better at all. Some Black leaders feared that fundamentalism could erode decades of hard work and rights activism. In a pointed editorial, journalist Ernest Rice McKinney warned in the *Amsterdam News*, "A Fundamentalist is nothing more than the same old reactionary strutting forth in a brand new robe. . . . The Negro race is filled to overflowing with these 'Fundamentalist' gentlemen. They are everywhere and in everything. They keep us poor, ignorant and weak. But, some day, we will revolt." He lamented the stereotype that African Americans naturally had a "childlike religious faith," worrying that if fundamentalism spread among Black Christians, it would reinforce this stereotype. Only ignorance, he wrote, could explain White or Black predispositions to such simple versions of Christianity.[16]

Black writers feared that if ministers clung to the fundamentals in the face of modern advances, they risked making religion irrelevant to young people. An article in the *Pittsburgh Courier* blamed the decline in church attendance among younger Black Americans in part on church leaders' "fundamentalism" and lack of engagement with the social gospel and current thought.[17]

While many Black religious leaders took sides in the controversy, others hoped to stay out of the increasingly vitriolic war raging among White protestants. In a series of news summaries, Roscoe Simmons warned African Americans to keep their distance. "American white people are still fighting over religion," he told readers of the *Chicago Defender*, "Maybe the Modernists and Fundamentalists arguing about creeds will stumble up on true religion." A few weeks later, he quipped, "No doubt as to our white people having religion. Getting them to use it every day is something else." Then, in another column, he advised, "Don't follow our smart white people off in this religious war. . . . Our white people are tangled up. Pray for them; don't follow them." Nevertheless, Simmons and other Black leaders saw a potential opportunity in the fundamentalist-modernist war, one that echoed the sentiments of generations of Black millennialists. "Keep up the controversy," he wrote. "Fifty years hence the priesthood of the New World will be children of the New World's slaves."[18]

The idea that Black Americans could emerge from the White church controversy as the nation's spiritual leaders also appeared in a *Pittsburgh Courier* editorial. "The layman stands aghast while he listens to this bitterness as it belches forth from the mouths of professing Christians—and more, men called of God." The paper then demanded a return to a simple faith in Jesus and his teachings and an acknowledgment of the mysteries of God. "We must look to another than the Caucasian Church," it concluded, "for a true and reliable exemplification of the life of our common brother." White Christian leaders, however, remained oblivious to the ways that race structured their theology.[19]

The fundamentalist-modernist controversy proved extraordinarily divisive in the world of missions as well. In some ways, missionaries served on the front lines of the battle. Just about every missionary had to determine for himself or herself how much emphasis to place on individual salvation versus the social gospel. A Presbyterian working at Peking University worried that fundamentalists had started trying to purge more liberal missionaries and teachers (like him) from the denomination's foreign work. "I had to hold the pass against them almost single handed," he told modernist Henry Sloane Coffin. But he feared the problem would grow worse before it got better. He hoped to return to the United States to defend liberalism and to have a part "in the struggle to stop these floods of obscurantism, and to help to hold the educated and scientific people for the church." Should the modernists fail and "a split becomes inevitable," he concluded, "I would throw in my lot with the liberal wing, and perhaps take a part in its missionary work."[20]

At the start of 1930, a group of laymen from the leading White denominations conducted a major survey of American missionary work funded by John D. Rockefeller Jr. Harvard philosopher and modernist William E. Hocking led the project. The group set out to reassess the missionary enterprise, questioning whether American churches should continue overseas missions, and, if so, to craft updated goals and methods for their work.

The report they produced shocked, or perhaps more accurately, horrified conservatives and revivalists. It served as a brutal indictment of American missions, critiquing both missionary organizations and individual missionaries. It presented the majority of missionaries as naive and shallow, and concluded that perhaps missionaries did more harm than good in the cultures in which they worked.

The authors of the report did not seem to think salvation in Jesus was the world's ultimate hope, which more than anything else had been at the root of evangelistic efforts for generations. Instead, they advised missionaries to find common ground in other cultures and religions to build international understanding, cooperation, and partnerships. Hocking and his team saw little value in converting foreigners to Christianity. Instead "ministry to the secular needs of men in the spirit of Christ," Hocking contended, "is evangelism, in the right sense of the word." The fundamentalist editor of *The Sunday School Times* called the Hocking study a "strange, sinister, Satanic document."[21]

The report symbolized a massive shift underway in American missions that would accelerate after World War II. Over the next few decades, the number of liberal and modernist missionaries gradually declined, while the number sent around the globe by conservative, pentecostal, and fundamentalist organizations expanded rapidly. Many liberal protestants did not abandon foreign work altogether, they just moved into more secular-oriented humanitarian nongovernmental organizations (NGOs). As Hocking advised, they represented their faith through their work and not their words.

In the first decades of the twentieth century, pentecostals mostly charted their own path and generally worked independently from other apocalyptic revivalists. Issues of race, class, and education, as well as pentecostals' less restrictive views of gender, kept the movements somewhat divided. Pentecostals generally occupied a slightly lower economic rung than many other revivalists and tended to have more rudimentary educations. But members of both groups drew deeply from the revivalist stream, they exchanged ideas, and at times their work overlapped.

Canadian-born pentecostal Aimee Semple McPherson started her career with the Assemblies of God and then launched her own independent ministry. She became the most popular revivalist of the 1920s, blending fundamentalism, apocalyptic revivalism, and Hollywood theatrics to make Christianity relevant and enticing to a new generation. During World War I, McPherson crisscrossed the nation in a "gospel car" painted with the slogans "Jesus Is Coming Soon—Get Ready" and "Where will you spend eternity?" She settled in Los Angeles in late 1918, and after a couple of years of traveling back and forth to revivals around the country decided to buy a piece of property on which to build a new church for local meetings. On January 1, 1923, she dedicated Angelus Temple (the building is now a federal historic landmark), which sits on prime real estate across the street from Echo Park. The church served as the foundation for a new denomination, the International Church of the Foursquare Gospel.

McPherson's fame derived from her Sunday evening "illustrated" sermons. Utilizing her dramatic talents, the evangelist embodied the gospel before her audience with props and costumes in theatrical displays. These sermons gave "full vent to her showman's genius," journalist Sarah Comstock wrote in a profile for *Harper's*. They took the form of a "complete vaudeville program, entirely new each week, brimful of surprises for the eager who are willing to battle in the throng for entrance." McPherson's sermons displayed the "novel and highly original use that she makes of properties, lights, stage noises, and mechanical devices to point her message. Heaven and Hell," she wrote, "sinner and saint, Satan, the fleshpots of Egypt, angels of Paradise and temptations of a bejazzed World are made visual by actors, costumes, and theatrical tricks of any and every sort."[22]

Having worked with the Salvation Army, an organization well known for its crowd-arresting spectacles, McPherson found no contradiction in her rejection of the values of Hollywood while employing show business techniques. She would not hesitate to use the devil's tools to tear down the devil's house.

Like colonial evangelist superstar George Whitefield, McPherson knew what she was playing at. Early in her career, she realized "that the methods so often used to impart religion were too archaic, too sedate and too lifeless ever to capture the interest of the throngs." She promised to be different. "I developed methods," she recalled in her 1927 autobiography, "which have brought hundreds of thousands to meetings who otherwise would never have come. . . . Religion, to thrive in the present day, must utilize present-day methods. The methods change with the years, but the religion remains always the same." According to her daughter, McPherson believed that "the best sermon in the world was no good without an audience. The recipe for rabbit stew is to catch the rabbit."[23]

McPherson took on modernism in some of her illustrated sermons. In "Trial of the Modern Liberalist College Professor Versus the

Lord Jesus Christ," the evangelist played the role of prosecutor in a mock trial that focused on the infiltration of liberalism into American churches. The judge charged the faux jury with determining how leading institutions of revivalism in previous centuries, such as Yale and Princeton, currently stacked up next to the word of God. As exhibits, McPherson quoted modernist professors and preachers including social gospel architect Walter Rauschenbusch and modernists Harry Emerson Fosdick and Shailer Mathews, among others. The evangelist's case rested simply on the Bible, the words of leading fundamentalists, and the views of George Washington and Abraham Lincoln. By citing American presidents along with theologians, McPherson intentionally associated fundamentalism with patriotism and theological liberalism with un-Americanism. Her actions anticipated the marriage of faith and patriotism that later became a hallmark of the fundamentalist movement.[24]

McPherson used her power to advocate for women's equality, especially through her LIFE Bible College. "The Lord is calling the handmaidens today as well as the servants; the daughters as well as the sons," she preached at a baccalaureate sermon. "There are some who believe that a woman should never witness for Jesus Christ—that her lips should be sealed. This is not according to the Word of God," she insisted. "I would bring a message to my sisters just now: 'Go on with the Word of God!' God has used the womenfolks!" McPherson cited Florence Nightingale, Frances E. Willard, Carry A. Nation, and Catherine Booth as proof of God's anointing women to accomplish a divine agenda.[25]

As famous as McPherson's sermons made her, sex made her even more famous. In the spring of 1926, she vanished from a local beach and after an extensive search, her family and local authorities concluded that she had drowned. A month later she reappeared in Arizona claiming that members of the Los Angeles "underworld" had kidnapped and held her for ransom in Mexico. Rumors quickly spread that the divorced evangelist had actually been vacationing with a secret lover—her radio station engineer—in the beach town of Carmel-by-the-Sea. A yearlong media frenzy ensued, initially fueled by the district attorney's decision to convene a grand jury to investigate the truth of her kidnapping tale. A preliminary criminal hearing followed in which the district attorney accused McPherson of perpetrating a hoax. He believed that in fabricating a kidnapping, she had corrupted public morals, obstructed justice, and conspired to manufacture evidence. A grand jury agreed, issuing criminal indictments.

As McPherson prepared to go to trial in 1927, she learned a titillating bit of gossip of her own. While media mogul William Randolph Hearst's newspapers and magazines relentlessly criticized the evangelist over her supposed tryst, she discovered that Hearst was simultaneously having an affair with popular actress Marion Davies. She got word to the newspaper tycoon that if he did not intervene on her behalf, she would aim her mass media weapons at him. Hearst spoke to the district attorney, and he dropped the charges, leaving the mystery of McPherson's whereabouts that spring unresolved. Despite occasional struggles, McPherson succeeded in bringing a vibrancy and Hollywood style to the modern faith she called "old time."

From Aimee McPherson to William Riley, apocalyptic revivalists proved their movement was no wartime fluke. Yet modernists held the upper hand in the 1920s and 1930s, largely retaining leadership in the major denominations. Many fundamentalists, unwilling to associate with those they saw as apostate, gradually left to form new Baptist, Methodist, Presbyterian, and independent churches—much like the pentecostals before them. Determined to reshape American culture around their beliefs, they built a movement with far-reaching ambitions. To much of the nation, the answer to Fosdick's famous question—Shall the fundamentalists win?—seemed to be no. But time would tell a different story.

For fundamentalists, holding power within the old churches was never the only goal. They were equally driven by the conviction that their values could redeem the nation. Even as they battled liberals inside the church, they launched a broader campaign to claim the culture for the fundamentalist Christ.

22

RELAUNCHING CULTURE WARS

In the 1920s, tens of millions of Americans attended movies every week. As the popularity of films grew, sociologists wanted to understand their influence on young people. What they discovered horrified many Americans. Teenagers confessed that movies taught them how to date, kiss, and "pet." One high school woman told an interviewer, "I also like to see them kiss, love, drink, smoke, and lead up to sex relations. It makes me get all stirred up in a passionate way." Her favorites were "Love pictures, Wild West pictures," and "murder cases," she acknowledged, because "I like to love, myself, and I know others want to do the same. After I see them I go out and love and have sexual relations and go on parties and only do worse." Christians leaders in every stream worried that this "juvenile delinquent" represented teenagers in general. They attacked Hollywood for undermining the nation's morals and values.[1]

Following a series of off-screen scandals, Hollywood studio bosses recognized that their success depended on an approving public and the goodwill of politicians. They walked a fine line, keeping enough titillation to entertain their audiences while also working to keep critics mollified. Hoping to head off government oversight, the studios required actors to sign morals clauses (German shepherd Rin Tin Tin was exempt), and they issued guidelines to regulate film content. They also hired former postmaster general and Presbyterian Will Hays to coordinate their efforts. Hays helped the studios evade censorship and appease skeptics. He eventually created a code for the film industry, which he worked with Catholic Joseph Breen to enforce, outlining the kinds of messages studios should promote and those they should avoid, all the while living on a lucrative studio contract. He advised filmmakers not to glorify crime, sex, or vulgarity, and not to mock faith. He also forbade nudity, profanity, and obscenity.

Despite the studios' efforts, most Christian groups, Catholic and protestant, remained skeptical of Hollywood. "Don't be deceived," a minister wrote Federal Council of Churches leaders, "the movie industry is simply using Mr. Hays to blind the Christian forces in this country." Then shifting to common anti-Semitic tropes, he added, "Even if he were ever so honest, and kindly disposed toward reform, that 'Jew bunch' that he represents will surely not stand for it one moment." Fundamentalist T. C. Horton quipped, "Given the moron audience and the moron picture, the moron actor and the moron director are inevitable." An editor at the modernist *Christian Century* told readers, "Since time began men of unclean minds have tended to commercialize recreation and entertainment. . . . The world of pleasure-seeking will not automatically clean up the movies. It will have to be done by the pressure of public conscience." Protestants working through the FCC, later joined by Catholics acting through the church's National Legion of Decency, kept up the pressure on the studios. Although they never got everything they wanted, their efforts ensured that American filmmakers had less freedom than their European counterparts.[2]

The Hays Code was the equivalent of using a fig leaf to cover a sex organ. Journalist Frederick Lewis Allen summed up at the time the superficial nature of the Presbyterian's influence. Hays, he wrote, made the "moral ending" "obligatory," smeared "over sexy pictures with pious platitudes," and blacklisted "many a fine novel and play" that questioned "the traditional sex ethics of the small town." Yet in hiring Hays, the studios had achieved their goals. "Mr. Hays, being something of a genius, managed to keep the churchmen at bay," Lewis concluded. "Whenever the threats of censorship began to become ominous he would promulgate a new series of moral commandments for the producers to follow."[3]

Hollywood represented just one challenge that religious leaders encountered in the wake of World War I. Leaders of the protestant establishment faced substantial competition as they aspired to maintain their position as the caretakers of American culture. At the same time that those in the different religious streams battled each other, they also fought changes in American life. They worked to articulate a position on the evolving economy in the era of the first Red Scare, with some activists championing capitalism and others trying to democratize the workforce. They responded to the passage of woman suffrage by trying to quell new ideas about gender and sexuality. They watched with mixed feelings as Darwinian theories of evolution trickled into school curriculums. Then, near the end of the decade, they mobilized voters to prevent the election of a Roman Catholic president. Despite their theological differences, White conservatives, modernists, and fundamentalists saw eye to eye on many important social issues and worked to have their ideas reflected in American culture. But they sensed their power waning. As the nation grew more religiously diverse, Americans proved less willing to defer to protestant leaders on many social issues.

American workers hoped that World War I would permanently transform the economy, making it more democratic, fair, and equitable. When the war ended, however, business leaders sought to roll back many of the wartime compromises they had made on hours and wages. Their backtracking sparked the nation's largest-ever wave of strikes, which in 1919 paralyzed much of the economy. Over four million people walked off their jobs. Many protestants opposed the strikes, noting that labor leaders were disproportionately Catholic and Jewish. But those with social gospel sympathies hoped that unions could play a role in creating a more just society and building the kingdom of God in the United States.

In trying to quash workers' demands, business leaders exploited recent news from abroad. American corporate executives linked groups that challenged the capitalist system with the Bolshevik Revolution. They claimed that what had happened in Russia could happen in the United States if workers had their way. They accused those who sought to organize the poor, including Christian groups, of disloyalty.

Years before the Bolshevik Revolution, Presbyterians in New York had opened the Labor Temple on Manhattan's Lower East Side to minister to working-class Americans of all races and nationalities. They hoped to bridge the gap between middle-class churches and the poor and to draw working people to nontraditional religious services and activities. They also saw the temple as a way for church leaders to check the pulse of immigrants and labor organizers to assess how best to translate the gospel into relevant terms. The work of the temple grew during the war and especially in its aftermath.

Kenneth Miller, a Labor Temple leader, warned that "social injustice takes its toil in the well-being of the people" and drives them to "all sorts of theories of social radicalism." He believed that capitalist abuses and not communist intrigue caused unrest. Yet traditional Christianity had failed to provide an alternative to the cutthroat economy. Workers, he noted, "are suspicious of the Church as an ally of capitalism." He wanted Christians to promote a "better understanding and a truer vision" of Jesus. "How," he asked, can the church "show her love of social justice free from the bitterness and materialism of much radical thought?" He thought the Labor Temple provided the answer. It "is trying to unite the religious activities of a Christian church with a wider social work, thoroughly imbued with the spirit of Christ," to reach and serve "a non-Christian community."[4]

The war, however, and then the communist revolution made the actions of Christian ministries like the Labor Temple and its explicit support of organized labor controversial. Woodrow Wilson's

Department of Justice orchestrated a series of investigations during what historians call the first Red Scare. Many states did their own parallel inquiries. They targeted those groups that government officials believed represented a threat to the nation. In New York, the state legislature held a series of hearings on radicalism in which legislators scrutinized the Labor Temple. An attorney who helped lead the New York investigations warned that the Labor Temple "is not a Christianizing center." He fretted that temple leaders had allowed communists and radicals to rent space for meetings and claimed that its programs made it "a travesty of religion," "subversive of public morals," and "designed to undermine the confidence of its audiences in the government under which we live."[5]

Kenneth Miller pushed back. "Every Sunday night," he testified, "we have an open forum at Labor Temple" which serves as "a center for Christianizing influences" in a very diverse and pluralistic working-class community. He argued that Christians had to adapt their messages to their contexts and audiences. In the "very heart of the congested, polyglot East Side," he continued, "the home of strong labor unions and of social radicalism," the "Christian approach must be unconventional, friendly, obviously sympathetic with human problems." The church, he believed, "which is so often charged with undue alliance with capitalism, has had here a rare opportunity to show her sympathy with the working class." Another leader explained that those at the temple were "blazing a trail. Just as the foreign missionary uses methods differing from those of the traditional Church in our own land so in this Home Missionary field we must adopt such methods as will best accomplish our tasks." But such Christian experiments happened only rarely, and as at the Labor Temple, they often took fire from all sides.[6]

In contrast to organizations like the Labor Temple, Christian ministry looked very different on the Upper East Side, where identifying too closely with labor could imperil religious leaders. There John D. Rockefeller Jr. recruited Harry Emerson Fosdick to take the pulpit of his church, Park Avenue Baptist (even though Fosdick was a Presbyterian), and then began plans to build a major new nondenominational church for the minister on the other side of Central Park near Union Theological Seminary.

Fosdick occasionally ran into trouble with his patron. Rockefeller took personal offense at one sermon the minister gave in which he chided industrial leaders. "As you know," the oil baron told the modernist preacher, "all my life I have sought to stand between labor and capital . . . seeking to modify the extreme attitude of each and to bring them into cooperation." Rockefeller worried that when Fosdick lumped business executives together, failing to distinguish between the supposedly benevolent men like the Rockefellers and the scoundrels, he risked losing his influence among the wealthy. "I covet so much the preserving of your powerful influence with all classes of men," Rockefeller claimed, "that I am particularly sensitive to anything which may even to a minute degree lessen that influence."[7]

Fosdick replied immediately, seeking to dig himself out of the hole he had fallen into. "You say that the businessman is sensitive to public criticism. I often wonder at his being so very sensitive. I say far more critical things about my own realm, the ecclesiastical, than I ever dream of saying about the industrial realm." Noting that he ran a "powerful church" loaded with "powerful men," Fosdick pleaded for Rockefeller's sympathy. He must, he said, deal honestly with "industrial problems" just as he dealt with "international, ecclesiastical, and theological problems." Then he returned to the requisite groveling. "I sincerely trust," he assured Rockefeller, "that the idea did not at all get into your mind that I thought you not a liberal in your industrial attitude." He advised Rockefeller "that if ever in the pulpit I shoot off a gun on the industrial question, I am thinking of you as behind the gun and not in front of it." Rockefeller didn't have much reason to fret. Americans at the time skewed politically conservative and pro-business. No one, and certainly not protestant leaders, was coming for Rockefeller and his friends' money and power.[8]

Some religious leaders even doubled down on the supposedly capitalist nature of Christianity. Bruce Barton, the son of a preacher, took what he learned in church, combined it with what he had learned as an advertising executive, and produced a new synthesis of Christianity and capitalism. He published his ideas in 1925 in *The Man Nobody Knows*, which became the top-selling nonfiction book in the United States. He called Jesus the founder of modern business and he extracted from the New Testament economic "truths." Jesus's parables, Barton contended, were in fact sleek, succinct, and sophisticated advertisements, and he credited Jesus with building a corporation from the ground up. Jesus "picked up twelve men from the bottom ranks of business and forged them into an organization that conquered the world," he observed. Barton called on Americans, like Jesus called on his disciples/business partners, to maximize their profits.[9]

While many critics saw Barton's philosophy as an unholy bastardization of religion, others embraced it. They believed that Barton properly applied ancient truths to the current condition. More than any other individual in the 1920s, Barton took capitalism and baptized it in the waters of a generic Christianity to produce a new consensus that merged traditional religious values with modern consumer culture.

Another revolution in morals occurred within American families as growing numbers of men and women began to challenge traditional views of sex and gender. For many protestants, especially those committed to the idea that God had designed distinct male and female roles, this shift felt like a direct assault on the Christian faith. Determined to defend what they saw as a divinely ordained order, these Christians combatted the new attitudes spreading through popular culture, politics, and even some of their own homes.

Following the lead of progressive reformers like Victoria Woodhull, women continued battling stifling ideas about gender. Nineteenth-century activists such as suffrage leader Elizabeth Cady Stanton taught that Christianity, rather than emancipating women, smothered women's efforts to seek full equality. While male clergy credited the Bible for "all the blessings and freedom" women enjoyed, Stanton believed that the Bible also limited women's opportunities. Biblical authors treated "the demands for political and civil rights" as "irreligious" and "dangerous to the stability of the home, the state and the church." Stanton alleged that too many women stood "with bowed heads" and "accepted the situation." She criticized those who "clung" to the Bible "with an unreasoning tenacity, like a savage to his fetich."[10]

And yet she recognized that in the United States there was no getting around the centrality of the Bible. So rather than discard it, she sought to reinterpret it. Stanton put together a committee of women to write new essays and interpretations of the Bible to expose its misogyny while also highlighting its liberationist passages. In 1895 Stanton and her committee published the first volume of *The Woman's Bible*, which covered the Pentateuch, the first five books of the Old Testament. The first pages of Stanton's book focused on the creation account in Genesis, which she and her cowriters used to deny the maleness of God. "The first step in the elevation of woman to her true position," Stanton wrote, is "recognition by the rising generation of an ideal Heavenly Mother, to whom their prayers should be addressed, as well as to a Father." Three years later she published her committee's commentary on the rest of the Bible.[11]

Although the book became a bestseller, Stanton had misjudged the cultural landscape. Establishment Christianity and its adherents dominated the nation. For any reform movement to succeed in the United States, activists needed to align their efforts with the mainstream protestant faith, rather than criticize it as the problem.

More typical was Southern Baptist reformer Annie Armstrong. Despite making substantial contributions to her community, she believed that women like herself should remain in the background. She wrote a church executive with some ideas for improving the Sunday School curriculum but prefaced her letter by warning that he need not reveal the source of the suggestions. "I have heard so much about 'women's sphere' and her going beyond proper bounds," she began, "that I think I am beginning to feel on this point as the children do when they are told 'children should be seen and not heard.'" Nevertheless, she hoped he would allow her to minister "a little outside of my 'proper sphere.'" Women like Armstrong made immeasurable contributions to their denominations while working to downplay and hide their efforts.[12]

During World War I, suffrage leaders pushed President Wilson to support women's right to vote. Eventually the president encouraged Congress to pass a suffrage amendment to the constitution, which he claimed was vital to winning the war. In the summer of 1920, enough states finally ratified it to make it law.

Riding the wave of momentum from the suffrage movement, a new generation of women in the 1920s pushed boldly against the boundaries that traditionalists had long sought to preserve. At the forefront of this cultural shift stood the "flappers"—young women whose daring fashion, carefree attitudes, and public presence became iconic symbols of rebellion against convention. With their short skirts, bobbed hair, and embrace of Jazz Age nightlife, flappers became popular culture icons and rattled social conservatives, who saw in them a threat to the moral and social order. "The average little frizzle-headed, fudge-eating, ragtime flapper who can't turn a battercake without splattering up the kitchen," Billy Sunday preached, "knows more about devilment than her grandmother did when she was 75 years old. . . . Yes sir, woman is the battleground of the universe." The ballplayer was right—many Christians had identified women and their bodies as a significant battleground.[13]

Church leaders reacted by trying to bolster rather than erase traditional gender differences. Calling "the woman question" the "burning question of the day," missionary and fundamentalist Peter Z. Easton outlined a very specific sex hierarchy. "Man," he claimed, "represents the Creator, and woman the creature." To challenge this hierarchy meant challenging God. "All the evidence, therefore, goes to show that emancipated woman, trampling under foot the laws of God in nature and revelation," was "herself an incarnate demon, with nothing womanly in her but the name." That the women's movement had moved from the domain of "short-haired women and long-haired men" to the "noblest men and women in the church" made it all the more necessary, he believed, for true Christians to "sound the alarm."[14]

Social conservatives believed that changes on the outside reflected changes on the inside. Pentecostal Frank Bartleman's tract *Flapper Evangelism: Fashion's Fools Headed for Hell* warned that "every bobbed head is a token of rebellion against God's decree," while Texan and Baptist John R. Rice denounced the bob as part of a triumvirate of evil in his infamous *Bobbed Hair, Bossy Wives, and Women Preachers.* Many ministers encouraged women to dress "modestly" and not to tempt men into sexual sins, and when extramarital sex did happen, ministers often blamed women.[15]

With the economy growing, more middle-class women sought jobs outside the home. They most often found employment in sex-segregated professions, serving as teachers, nurses, retail clerks, and office secretaries. Choosing to move beyond the "traditional" role of mother and homemaker—regardless of the reason or need—provoked strong criticism. Moody Bible Institute administrator Harold Lundquist complained that "the American home is not what it was a generation ago. . . . There can be no doubt that the Scriptures teach that a woman's place is with her family in her home." His sentiments were typical. "Women as a rule should be trained for motherhood," *King's Business* sermonized, "motherhood in its highest and best sense, rather than for the various forms of public life." Seattle Presbyterian Mark Matthews, never afraid to speak bluntly, instructed wives to "go home." But unlike many ministers he did not lay the blame for American decline at the feet of women alone. "The average husband," he preached, "is a coward. The average wife is a bully. . . . Women ought to be forced to go home. But their husbands are too cowardly to force them."[16]

The liberal *Christian Century* recognized the shifting nature of the family and the challenges such changes raised for Christians. That the church "has succeeded, so far as it has, in keeping the Christian home intact is one of its greatest achievements," the editor wrote. "The home is now in unusual peril, owing to the increased knowledge and freedom of sex life. This throws an obligation upon the church to face the problem, not only with faith but with understanding, for it is one of extreme difficulty."[17]

The successful fight for the ballot and wartime changes inspired some women to push for additional reforms, including more information on and access to birth control. Although Americans had practiced various forms of birth control for centuries, information about safe, reliable, and effective contraception proved hard to get. Activists like Gilded Age reformer and crusader Anthony Comstock had ensured that Americans rarely discussed birth control in public. Margaret Sanger changed that. Not only did she talk openly about sex and sexuality, she also encouraged women to take control of their reproductive lives without necessarily seeking the advice or consent of their doctors. Her efforts supported broader progressive goals of improving health and cutting poverty. But many Americans believed that discussions of sex should remain in the bedroom and that only God should determine how many children a married couple produced.

Few church leaders discussed abortion in the first half of the twentieth century. Most protestants believed that married Christians did not sin in using artificial birth control and they had few qualms about early-term abortions, which they saw as a form of contraception. But a few ministers equated abortion with murder. Billy Sunday alluded to the issue in a women-only revival meeting. According to *The Atlanta Constitution*, Sunday "painstakingly" went into "detail" regarding the many pitfalls that could ensnare women and declared "the murder of unborn babies the curse and damnation of America." New York Baptist and Manhattan vice crusader John Roach Straton received numerous letters encouraging him to take on the practice. One distraught mother begged him to expose a clinic where "criminal operations" had been performed on her daughters, while another described abortion as "the shedding of innocent blood, the sin of blood-guiltiness, the unpardonable sin, the MURDER OF THE UNBORN." Fundamentalist John Rice also called abortion "murder" and made the case for life at conception. Editors of the Moody Bible Institute's magazine even found common ground with Catholics on the topic. They supported the pope's 1930 encyclical on the sanctity of marriage and against artificial birth control and abortion, although editors hoped they would "not be accused of going over to Roman Catholicism."[18]

In the 1920s gay men and women in cities like New York and San Francisco began forming visible subcultures, frequenting clubs, and pursuing relationships more openly. Their public presence signaled a growing if uneven tolerance for sexual diversity among some Americans. At the same time, the term "homosexuality" became widely used to describe same-sex desire.

Many Christian leaders taught that gay relationships were certain to provoke God's wrath. Conservative Presbyterian Donald Grey Barnhouse criticized what he interpreted as the celebration of "homosexuality," and he lamented the rise and spread of "unnatural vice." Journalist and evangelist Dan Gilbert called same-sex relations "one of the ugliest blotches upon American civilization" and identified it as "one of the surest signs that the days of Noah are closing in upon us." Fretting that "well-financed and highly-organized" "cults of homosexuals" "sponsor all sorts of propaganda to woo and win new addicts to their horrible vice," he called on the public to "stamp out this plague in our midst." Moody Bible Institute professor Wilbur Smith called same-sex relations "another dreadful tendency of our time." "It is the curse," he preached, "of all large penal institutions, of all concentration camps, internment areas, and great bodies of soldiers kept within military areas for long periods of time. . . . Our Lord Himself said that Sodomic conditions would again be manifest before the coming of the Son of Man." Although few Christian activists publicly discussed abortion or same-sex relations in the interwar era, those who did often viewed both as problems God called Christians to fix.[19]

Americans worried about changing ideas of sex and sexuality sought scapegoats to blame. Perhaps children were learning the wrong values in school. Some thought that the root of the problem was the introduction of Charles Darwin's theories of evolutionary biology into American education. If biology teachers taught students that they were animals, activists asked, why should we be surprised when they acted like animals? To stem the nation's moral decline, then, meant stemming the teaching of Darwinian theories of evolution.

In the early 1920s, activists, many inspired by religion, began stoking popular resentment against evolutionary theories. In Tennessee the state legislature passed an explicitly religious bill prohibiting the teaching of "any theory that denies the story of the Divine Creation of man as taught in the Bible, and to teach instead that man has descended from a lower order of animals." Violating the law could result in a misdemeanor fine ranging from $100 to $500.[20]

The Tennessee bill caught the attention of the young American Civil Liberties Union (ACLU), whose leaders questioned the constitutionality of all anti-evolution bills. Local city boosters in Dayton, Tennessee, sensed an opportunity to bring attention to their city. They recruited twenty-four-year-old John Thomas Scopes, a high school science teacher and football coach, to confess to teaching evolution and to serve as the ACLU's defendant in a test case.

As Scopes and local prosecutors prepared for trial, events quickly spiraled out of their control. The law's defenders recruited William Jennings Bryan for the prosecution. After dropping out of Wilson's cabinet during the war, Bryan had dedicated his twilight years to hawking Florida real estate and advocating conservative protestantism. He challenged theologically liberal approaches to the Bible, believing that modernist interpretations had wreaked havoc among both his fellow Presbyterians and Christians more generally. He had little interest in apocalyptic revivalism but simply defended what he saw as the classic faith. As he honed his message, he began to view Darwinian evolution as a primary symbol of the dangers of modern thought. In response to those who questioned why he had plunged into a religious controversy, the Democratic leader explained that his anti-evolution campaign did not represent a career change. "I have not turned aside from politics," he forthrightly declared. Instead, he viewed the battle against evolution as part of his long battle for good government and a healthy nation.[21]

Famed criminal defense attorney Clarence Darrow volunteered for Scopes's team. He later explained that he aimed not just to defeat the bill but to challenge "religious fanaticism." Darrow saw himself as a crusader for truth and righteousness, just a different truth and a different righteousness than Bryan professed. "To me it was perfectly clear that the proceedings bore little semblance to a court case," he recalled, "but I realized that there was no limit to the mischief that might be accomplished unless the country was roused to the evil at hand." Darrow publicly offered his services to Scopes and the ACLU, leaving the organization little choice but to accept. This was the only time Darrow ever worked for free. Those with much larger agendas quickly overshadowed the ACLU's goal of overseeing a narrow test case. Scopes would no longer really be on trial. Instead, Bryan and Darrow planned to debate the facts of evolution, the nature of true religion, and the proper balance between individual liberty and majority rule.[22]

Journalists from around the nation descended on Tennessee for the trial, where they framed the controversy as a contest over the intellectual legitimacy of fundamentalism. H. L. Mencken, like Darrow, labeled just about everyone who disagreed with evolutionary theory a "fundamentalist" regardless of his or her actual religious affiliations. His imprecise reporting helped decouple the term "fundamentalism" from the movement that had made it. The rest of the nation's leading journalists followed suit, linking opposition to evolution with fundamentalist Christianity even though evolution did not play a significant role in the rise of the fundamentalist movement and many Americans besides fundamentalists disliked Darwin's theories.

Darrow opened the defense's case with a dramatic speech that linked the anti-evolution movement with religious ignorance and intolerance. "Hard as it is for me to bring my mind to conceive it, almost impossible as it is to put my mind back into the sixteenth century," he told the packed courtroom, "I am going to argue" the case "as if it was serious, and as if it was a death struggle between two civilizations." He claimed that evolution became an issue only when "the fundamentalists got into Tennessee" and warned that "fires . . . have been lighted in America to kindle religious bigotry and hate."[23]

One of Darrow's scientist-advisors pleaded with the attorney not to frame the case as science versus religion. "I gave Darrow and the other lawyers," he wrote his wife, "to understand that I nor any of the other biologists would allow ourselves to be exploited as enemies of Christianity, for we are all in sympathy with the essential spirit of Christianity though we cannot accept many of its theological concepts." Darrow mostly obliged when it came to his witnesses, but he thought the case ultimately exposed the larger question of science versus religion. He saw the two as irreconcilable.[24]

Bryan's courtroom performance did not impress Mencken. "He can never be the peasants' President," Mencken wrote, "but there is still a chance to be the peasants' Pope. . . . It is a tragedy, indeed, to begin life as a hero and end it as a buffoon."[25]

The jury took nine minutes of deliberation to find Scopes guilty. (The verdict was later overturned on a technicality.) Even Darrow had asked for a guilty verdict so that he could appeal the case to the state supreme court. Bryan responded with a short but prescient speech about the significance of the trial, noting that eventually the "people," the ultimate jury, would rule on the issues fueling the controversy. Darrow, never one to cede the last word, interpreted the case differently. He believed that it represented the rebirth of religious bigotry. "I think this case will be remembered because it is the first case of this sort since we stopped trying people in America for witchcraft."[26]

The Scopes trial inspired a redefinition of fundamentalism. Before Scopes, "fundamentalism" referred to a well-defined, close-knit, apocalyptic revivalist movement. After the trial and its coverage in the national media, fundamentalism still referred to a specific network of revivalists, but the meaning of fundamentalism in the popular imagination had shifted. Thanks to the work of Bryan, Darrow, Mencken, and many others during the anti-evolution crusade and Scopes trial, "fundamentalism" became a pejorative term applied to groups that seemed socially conservative, anti-modernist, anti-science, anti-education, anti-intellectual, anti-progressive, rural, intolerant, and Southern. Fundamentalists would spend the next decade and a half trying to reclaim the term before mostly abandoning it.

While some Americans thought Darwin jeopardized the future of the United States, others worried about immigration. The war deepened many White protestants' concerns about foreigners in their midst. They felt suspicious of religious and ethnic groups that during the conflict had seemed perhaps less than 100 percent American. Labor unrest and the Red Scare compounded their fears. They also recognized that as the number of immigrants from nonprotestant nations grew, the power of the protestant establishment diminished. Large numbers of Americans called for an overhaul of the nation's immigration laws with the goal of reducing the number of "undesirables." They hoped to limit the number of Catholics and Jews coming to the United States.

The reborn Ku Klux Klan helped spearhead the crusade against immigrants. By the mid-1920s the Klan boasted a membership of approximately four million. Unlike the Reconstruction-era Klan, which used violence and intimidation to maintain White supremacy over newly freed African Americans, the 1920s Klan had a more comprehensive agenda. Committed to "one hundred percent Americanism," Klansmen feared that immigrant, Catholic, Jewish, urban, and Black Americans, along with intellectual elites, threatened the power of small-town, White, rural protestantism. The organization drew members from the revivalist, conservative, and liberal streams by strategically tapping into the major issues of the era.

In the pages of the popular *North American Review*, Klansman and dentist Hiram Wesley Evans lamented the nation's supposed moral breakdown and tied together many of the concerns of social conservatives. "One by one all our traditional moral standards went by the boards, or were so disregarded that they ceased to be binding. The sacredness of our Sabbath, of our homes, of chastity, and finally even of our right to teach our own children in our own schools fundamental facts and truths were torn away from us. Those who maintained the old standards did so only in the face of constant ridicule." The Klan promised to make America great again by focusing on "Native, white, Protestant supremacy." Protestantism, Evans claimed, "is an essential part of Americanism; without it America could never have been created and without it she cannot go forward." The Klan grew rapidly until a series of financial and sexual scandals in the second half of the 1920s brought it down.[27]

Anti-Semitism also grew after the war. Many protestants questioned Jews' loyalty and associated them with labor radicalism and various un-American movements. Copies of the fraudulent *Protocols of the Elders of Zion* circulated widely, claiming to reveal the plans of a secret Jewish cabal scheming to overtake the world. Presbyterian Mark Matthews sent a copy to Woodrow Wilson and asked the president to use it to purge the government of Jews. "They are today antagonistic to our principles of government," he wrote. They are "willing to produce a collapse in government and in finances in order that they might bring out of the collapse a Jewish Government over all." A series of articles titled "The International Jew" published in Henry Ford's virulently anti-Semitic *Dearborn Independent* reinforced the *Protocols*' message of a secret Jewish group scheming to rule the globe.[28]

In response to growing anti-immigrant sentiment and waves of postwar labor strikes, Congress in 1921 passed an emergency immigration law that severely limited immigration and created national quotas. Three years later Congress passed the Immigration Act of 1924 (also called the Johnson–Reed Act), which structured American immigration policy for the next four decades. It sharply curtailed immigration from southern and eastern Europe and from Africa and cut it off almost entirely from Asia. Many of the act's advocates believed the law was necessary to "protect" the White race from supposed racial suicide and to guarantee the survival of White protestant "civilization." Congress also established the Border Patrol to help oversee immigration and to guard against the illegal importation of alcohol. Congress and the public made clear that they considered only certain races and religions from select parts of the world worthy of American citizenship.

Arguments over Prohibition, immigration, and Catholicism took center stage as activists looked ahead to the 1928 presidential campaign. Well before most Americans had thought about the election, rumors circulated among political insiders that leaders of the Democratic Party planned to nominate Al Smith. That the New York governor could possibly win the election troubled protestants from all streams. A Roman Catholic grandson of immigrants, Smith owed his career to New York's infamous political machine, Tammany Hall. He opposed Prohibition and he drank and smoked. Some protestants feared that a wet Irish Romanist in the White House would assuredly bring down the judgment of God on their nation.

In the spring of 1927, *The Atlantic Monthly* published an open letter to Smith from attorney Charles Marshall. Despite Americans' admiration of Smith, Marshall began, "there is a note of doubt, a sinister accent of interrogation . . . as to certain conceptions which your fellow citizens attribute to you as a loyal and conscientious Roman Catholic." The Episcopalian lawyer asserted that many Americans worried that the Catholic Church and the American Constitution contained contradictory principles, especially regarding church and state. Marshall concluded by asking Smith to declare where his ultimate loyalty as president would lie—to his church or his nation.[29]

Marshall received a flood of mostly positive letters thanking him, but some readers objected to the hit piece. A Catholic critic who had spent a year as a student in a New York City public school called out Marshall's, and America's, hypocrisy, noting how school leaders wove protestantism into the curriculum. A self-identified Jew also thrashed Marshall. "Funny how all these Gentiles believe in a low Jew who didn't even know his father, he was a Bolschiwick of the first water and he just got nailed to the Cross. . . . But we all must admit that for a Jew he was a darned good Faker and he slipped one over on millions of boobs." "Put this in your Pipe," he signed off, "and smoke it."[30]

Smith published an immediate reply to Marshall's letter. He pledged himself to American ideals and claimed that they did not conflict with the tenets of his church. "I believe," he wrote, "in the worship of God according to the faith and practice of the Roman Catholic Church. I recognize no power in the institutions of my Church to interfere with the operations of the Constitution of the United States. . . . I believe in absolute freedom of conscience for all men. . . . I believe in the absolute separation of Church and State." He could not have expressed his convictions any more clearly. But it didn't matter.[31]

Most fundamentalists opposed Smith, and modernists split on his campaign. Writers in *The Christian Century* criticized the governor for undermining Prohibition, and editor Charles Clayton Morrison told readers they should have no qualms about voting on religious grounds against Smith. A voter who opposed the "ultimate ascendancy of the Roman Catholic church in the United States," a "medieval church, dominated by a Latin mentality and controlled by a foreign oligarchy," he wrote, and instead preferred the system erected by our

"Protestant-minded, Anglo-Saxon fathers," should not be "stigmatized as a bigot."[32]

New York Baptist John Roach Straton became one of Smith's most vocal opponents, and he tried to organize a fundamentalist political lobby to counter the Catholic threat. His unapologetic political activism during the campaign provoked many critical responses. One anonymous correspondent called the minister an "old dog" and warned "we will get you." The writer also told Straton he was "not clean enough to wipe Smith's ass." Another barely literate correspondent denounced Straton in the strongest language he could muster. He called him a "Cocksoaker" and "hipogrit" and then offered "for Chists seek, let me give you a tip . . . why don't you and all other cocksoackers ceep your moth shot when you are in your Church." He concluded: "I hope the Devil get you S. of a b. befor long." The letter was signed, "A 200% AMERICAN."[33]

The 1928 election resulted in a tremendous victory for Herbert Hoover and the Republican Party. The secretary of commerce garnered twenty-one million votes to Smith's fifteen million. Hoover swept most of the North and won a handful of Southern states, including Florida, Texas, North Carolina, Tennessee, and Virginia. The American people's unbroken record of electing only protestants to the presidency remained intact.

Despite occasional victories, protestants felt a tremendous sense of anxiety in the 1920s. More and more Americans challenged their preeminence while others simply abandoned the faith. New groups like the ACLU defended the civil liberties of religious minorities and dissenters, pushing Americans to honor their commitment to religious freedom, and protestant activists could no longer count on the courts to defer to them as they had so often in the nineteenth century. Even Prohibition by the end of the decade seemed in many ways to have failed. While the amendment had curbed Americans' drinking, it also fueled organized crime and a thriving underworld.

The postwar era better reflected the values of F. Scott Fitzgerald's Jay Gatsby than those of morals crusader Anthony Comstock. Journalist Walter Lippman noted that the "acids" of modernity had for many Americans dissolved religious life. "The irreligion of the modern world," he observed, "is radical to a degree for which, I think, there is no counterpart." Protestants, however, had no intention of surrendering. In fact, they had just begun the fight to lead their nation back onto the path of righteousness. What they could not have anticipated at the time, however, was how a global economic depression was about to transform the nation and challenge them in new ways.[34]

23

THE POPULIST REVOLT

When Herbert Hoover accepted the Republican nomination for president in 1928, he promised that with divine aid he would fulfill an elusive American dream. "We in America today are nearer to the final triumph over poverty than ever before in the history of any land. . . . We shall soon, with the help of God, be in sight of the day when poverty will be banished from this nation." Little did the candidate realize that his world was about to turn upside down.[1]

By the mid-1930s many Americans faced serious economic challenges. They struggled to understand what had caused the economic meltdown and how to survive it. Some believed that their fellow citizens had angered God. "Business depressions," economist and popular writer Roger Babson argued, "are caused by dissipation, dishonesty, disobedience to God's will—a general collapse of moral character." As Americans' faith declined, he asserted, so too did their economy. He believed that only "moral awakening, spiritual revival and the rehabilitation of righteousness" could bring recovery. Many Americans shared Babson's views, convinced that religious renewal could save the day. Rather than treat financial catastrophes as symptoms of economic problems, they reverted to a version of the old Puritan idea of the covenant. God rewarded nations financially for their faithfulness and punished them financially for their collective sins.[2]

In blaming Americans' fading faith for the Great Depression, Babson drew attention to a spiritual crisis that had been building since World War I. The United States' churches had been struggling for over a decade to maintain their authority and influence. Religious leaders floundered in their efforts to attract and hold members and to navigate new social and cultural trends. Meanwhile, both the fundamentalist-modernist controversy and the Scopes trial drew negative headlines. By the mid- to late 1920s, a religious depression had engulfed the nation. Church attendance flagged, Sunday Schools shrunk, fewer people volunteered for missionary work, and Americans' giving to churches dropped.

Then the economy crashed. As the financial crisis worsened, so too did the anxieties of religious leaders. To their dismay, there were no signs of a religious revival. This was unusual. Economic depressions usually sparked renewed religious fervor. A study by the Social Science Research Council (SSRC) observed that, unlike past economic recessions, the Depression had failed to drive "men to God." *The Christian Century*'s Charles Clayton Morrison believed he knew why. For too long, he argued, church leaders had cozied up to corporate and political elites, sacrificing their moral authority in the process. To many, the clergy now resembled the money changers Jesus had driven from the temple, not the prophetic voice of Christ. Morrison hoped the crisis would jolt Christian leaders into breaking free from their entanglements with business and government, allowing the church to reclaim what he called its "full prophetic authority in an hour like the present when the social order is undergoing radical reconstruction."[3]

Morrison represented one among thousands of Christian leaders seeking to recalibrate the relationship among Christianity, American institutions, and the broader culture. With the protestant establishment under siege and church leaders fighting with each other, dozens of new religious innovators appeared on the scene, promising

Americans alternative paths to security and salvation. But in the end, a messiah in a wheelchair named Franklin Delano Roosevelt would save the American people. Over the course of the 1930s, the biggest threat to protestant power turned out to be not Catholics or Jews or agnostics, but a competent and efficient New Deal state.

During the 1932 presidential campaign, Roosevelt promised to provide a "new deal" for the American people. What he had in mind, however, remained a mystery. At his inauguration, he guaranteed that the nation "will endure as it has endured, will revive and will prosper." Then he assured his audience that "the only thing we have to fear is fear itself—nameless, unreasoning, unjustified terror which paralyzes needed efforts to convert retreat into advance." Elected with an overwhelming mandate, the president pledged to use his office to redefine the relationship among the federal government, the economy, and the American people.[4]

When the Depression hit, the United States did not have an adequate welfare infrastructure. Aimee Semple McPherson's Angelus Temple illustrated the challenges that churches faced. McPherson had built one of the most expansive and effective welfare ministries in the nation. Los Angeles residents could call on McPherson's church twenty-four hours a day, seven days a week, for food, first aid, blankets, and clothing. The staff included a social service worker and nurses who could care for minor health problems. The church also had a day nursery for the children of working mothers, a dispensary, a fumigation room, a laundry, an employment office, and numerous sewing and food-storage rooms. As the crisis worsened, McPherson converted a twenty-four-thousand-square-foot warehouse into a soup kitchen and employment office. Once opened, the kitchen served 2,100 meals a day.

McPherson had an inclusive vision for her humanitarian programs. Since the Los Angeles County Board of Supervisors determined that publicly funded charities could aid only those who had entered the state before the stock market crash of 1929, McPherson filled the gap, boldly advertising free assistance to all comers—

including the area's Latines. Mexican American actor Anthony Quinn benefited from the commissary. "The one human being that never asked you what your nationality was, what you believed," he recalled, "was Aimee Semple McPherson. All you had to do was pick up the phone and say, 'I'm hungry,' and within an hour there'd be a food basket there for you." He credited her for "literally" keeping the Mexican community alive, adding, "and for that I'm eternally grateful." But as demand increased, Angelus Temple welfare leaders began restricting aid. They determined that they could afford to help a family only once. After that, the family needed to seek assistance from a government agency.[5]

Utah's Latter-day Saints also dramatically expanded their social welfare services during the 1930s. They recognized that with the state taking over ever more responsibility for providing for people's basic needs, Americans might look to the government and not churches for assistance. Church leaders established an extensive welfare network, which anti–New Deal conservatives then championed as a valuable alternative to government programs. The Saints built what may have been the only private welfare program that came close to meeting the needs of its religious community, but to succeed church leaders required substantial investment from parishioners.

Churches around the country replicated the work of McPherson's revivalists and Utah's Latter-day Saints on much smaller scales. Yet religious volunteerism could not stem the crisis. Churches, county governments, and community agencies failed to keep up with the tremendous demand for their services. The federal government's construction of a new social safety net, led in many cases by people who had trained in social gospel ministries, brought some relief. "For the first time," historian Alison Collis Greene observed, "the state rather than the church led the way," with reform coming from government and not Christian organizations. Activists' "decision to work through secular rather than religious avenues meant that the churches not only lost influence over charity and reform in the aftermath of the Great Depression, but that they also lost their most visionary reformers." Churches' inability to provide for their parishioners' most basic needs undermined their authority. Since the 1930s, religious leaders have waged a mostly losing battle to regain a prominent role in American welfare and social services.[6]

The economic crisis exacerbated a demographic crisis occurring in the American Catholic Church. World War I and the Immigration Act of 1924 significantly curtailed new Catholic immigration to the US, facilitating the rapid Americanization of church members and the decline of ethnic parishes. Hoping to hold on to their members, Catholics, like protestants, pivoted to meet the needs of the day.

As the global economic depression worsened, Pope Pius XI issued a new encyclical, *Quadragesimo Anno*, which attacked concentrations of wealth and instructed Catholics to work toward a healthier, more just social order. Although many reform-minded American Catholics embraced the document, their application of the encyclical varied. Some interpreted it as the pope's rejection of free market capitalism and a call to organize the poor. Others believed that God wanted Catholics to drive the American church to the political right, even if that meant working outside the democratic process.

Dorothy Day viewed Catholicism as incompatible with capitalism. Born in Brooklyn in 1897, Day grew up in a home without much religion. But she was curious about God. At age twelve she insisted that her parents let priests in the local Episcopal church baptize her, and in high school she studied Greek in order to better understand the New Testament. After two years of college, she moved to New York, where she began writing for left-wing papers. She fought for suffrage and against American intervention in World War I. She rejected establishment morals and values, took multiple lovers, and had an abortion. In 1926, she gave birth to a child, and she asked a Catholic nun to baptize the baby. The nun mentored Day in the faith, and Day soon converted. Her leftist friends could not believe that she had really joined Catholicism. "The mass of bourgeois smug Christians who denied Christ in His poor," she revealed, "made me turn to Communism." Then working with communists on social justice issues "made me turn to God." Day felt called to bridge the gap between radical social activism and Catholicism.[7]

In 1932 Day met Frenchman Peter Maurin, another Catholic radical. The next year they began publishing and distributing copies of a new magazine, *The Catholic Worker*, which integrated religious faith with radical politics. They explained their purpose in the first issue: "It's time there was a Catholic paper printed for the unemployed. The fundamental aim of most radical sheets is the conversion of its readers to Radicalism and Atheism. Is it not possible to be radical and not atheist? Is it not possible to protest, to expose, to complain, to point out abuses and demand reforms without desiring the overthrow of religion?" Yes, they believed. Like many other reformers on the margins of American religious life, they denounced the close relationship between institutional Christianity and capitalism.[8]

Another Catholic, Father Charles Coughlin, garnered substantial attention for his very different approach to the nation's problems. The bishop of Detroit had recruited Coughlin to build a new church in a new parish in the new suburb of Royal Oak, in the heart of industrial America. Coughlin dedicated the church to Saint Thérèse of Lisieux and established the Shrine of the Little Flower in her honor.

Coughlin, like the conservative Lutheran Walter Maier and various revivalist ministers, sensed that the new technology of radio had the power to draw people to faith. The priest bought time in 1926 and began preaching over the airwaves. In 1930 CBS syndicated his show, providing him with a national audience. His velvety, vibrant speech lured listeners to their speakers as sirens did for enchanted sailors to the open sea. Between thirty and forty million Americans, mostly from the industrial Midwest and Northeast, tuned in to Coughlin's show. Many responded to his messages with letters, sending more mail to Coughlin than to any other American in the early 1930s. Listeners also sent money, usually small donations. One morning the priest supposedly arrived at the bank carrying twenty thousand one-dollar bills for deposit.

As the effects of the economic collapse grew clearer, Coughlin complemented his usual sermons on Jesus with new messages highlighting the nations' challenges. The crash had decimated Detroit's labor market, and Coughlin feared that if ministers and political leaders did not act, communists would draw additional converts to their movement.

During the 1932 presidential campaign, the priest endorsed FDR, warning the nation that it must choose between "Roosevelt or ruin." After the election, Coughlin did his best to saddle up to the president and his staff. Roosevelt, although privately skeptical of the Royal Oak radio man, flattered the priest. Better to have a nut with a microphone on your side than on your opponents', he reasoned.

When not condemning the "moneychangers," Coughlin floated a series of unorthodox and harebrained policy proposals. In 1934 the priest launched a new political movement called the National Union for Social Justice to try to influence public policy. "I am not boasting," he boasted, "when I say to you that I know the pulse of the people." He called for a "just, living, annual wage," abolition of the federal reserve, economic reform, reduced taxes, support for organized labor, and "nationalizing" important "public resources." That year a journalist for *The New Republic* called Coughlin "one of the few success stories to come out of the depression."[9]

A few months after launching the National Union, Coughlin demonstrated his power. Roosevelt had lobbied the Senate to support American membership in the World Court. Coughlin, an isolationist, claimed that the court would undermine American sovereignty. He demanded that the Senate not "jeopardize our freedom," "barter our sovereignty," or "entangle us with the religious, the racial, the economic and the martial affairs of the Old World." He called on every "solid American who loves democracy, who loves the United States," and "who loves the truth" to flood Congress with telegrams opposing the treaty. And they did. Coughlin claimed that over two hundred thousand of his followers contacted their senators. Even if he exaggerated his numbers, tens of thousands sent messages. The Senate defeated the treaty, giving Roosevelt one of his first major setbacks and Coughlin a major victory.[10]

Coughlin's intervention did not amuse the president. After the World Court stunt, savvy New Deal operatives brought some of Coughlin's economic proposals to the Senate floor, where they knew they had no chance of passing. The "process of letting the air out of Father Coughlin," one critic noted, "is already well advanced." The administration engaged in a "deliberate attempt to humiliate Father Coughlin, and to show how little power he has left." By the next year he had lost perhaps a half dozen "bondslaves" in the Senate and fifty congressmen who no longer agreed to do his bidding.[11]

Over the next few years, Coughlin's sermons grew more unhinged. His criticism of international and American economists, policymakers, and bankers evolved into vile anti-Semitism. The church hierarchy eventually forced the priest off the airwaves. Nevertheless, his success demonstrated the growing influence of American Catholics in national political life as well as a strong, continuing isolationist attitude among some of the nation's most powerful religious leaders. It also illustrated the latest version of technically sophisticated, entrepreneurial showmanship by an American cleric. Catholics had taken a page from the revivalist playbook and made it their own.

In contrast to Coughlin, Father John Ryan, a priest, academic, and longtime reformer, became one of Roosevelt's greatest champions. Ryan spent his entire career laboring to integrate Catholic theology with progressive economic theory, arguing that Americans needed to improve their economic system and provide workers with more just wages. Ryan admired Roosevelt and in 1936, while Coughlin worked to undermine the president's reelection campaign, Ryan entered the fray on FDR's behalf. He delivered a pro-Roosevelt radio broadcast, entitled "Roosevelt Safeguards America," which the Democratic National Committee printed and distributed. Ryan denounced those who smeared the president, including Coughlin, and argued that New Deal policies mirrored the pope's directives. He ended with a request: "In this critical hour, I urge you to use every effort at your command among your relatives, friends and acquaintances in support of Franklin D. Roosevelt." Ryan's efforts earned him the nickname Right Reverend New Dealer, and to reward the priest for his loyalty FDR invited him to offer one of the prayers at the 1937 inauguration.[12]

Like Ryan, many Catholics felt at home in the New Deal. Roosevelt recognized the power of the Catholic vote, and he appointed more

Catholics to important positions in his administration than had any previous president. They helped the president mobilize predominately urban and working-class Catholics behind his efforts to reshape the federal government.

A handful of creative visionaries used the social and economic turmoil of the Great Depression to offer alternatives to mainstream Christianity. What, they asked, were establishment churches doing to meet people's needs? Not enough. Many Americans concluded that religious leaders failed to provide a thorough interpretation of the global economic crisis or serious solutions for solving it. They sought new religious communities that spoke to their practical needs.

On the East Coast a Black preacher of mysterious origin called Father Divine competed with more traditional ministers for adherents. He offered converts a sense of equality and community in an era that often lacked both. After World War I, he had settled on Long Island, where he turned his house into an interracial commune and started building a new religious movement. To accommodate those followers who did not live in his group home, Divine held banquets, which essentially became boisterous block parties. In the fall of 1931 police arrested the minister and charged him with being a public nuisance.

The trial judge made little effort to even appear objective, and he sentenced Divine to a fine and a year in jail (an appeals court later overturned the verdict). Four days after issuing the original sentence, the judge dropped dead. "It was obvious to all of Father Divine's followers," *The New Yorker* reported, "that Father Divine had struck down the Justice." Publicity over the trial, and the minister's seeming ability to channel divine retribution against his enemies, made him a celebrity and accelerated the growth of his movement. As the economic depression worsened, Divine moved to Harlem.[13]

Father Divine's growing fame and brush with the law presented a challenge for FBI director J. Edgar Hoover. Americans kept writing the FBI asking for information on this "cult" leader, but Hoover had little to offer. The job of the bureau, he explained to one enquirer, was not "to keep an eye on Father Divine." Another wrote Hoover that Divine used his "I'm God tactics" to lure "white girls" to the movement like the "Chinese use drugs to get the white girls." Meanwhile, Hoover also received at least one letter from a Divine acolyte who assured Hoover "we are all at work in and for the same cause," converting "thousands and thousands of the underworld characters." He hoped Hoover would visit the mission to show his support.[14]

Divine crafted a unique theology that placed himself at its center—as God incarnate. When an FBI agent met with him, the agent dryly reported having "difficulty" collecting basic details like Divine's height, weight, or identifying marks, noting that Divine "sets himself up to be 'God.'" Divine also refused to provide a birthdate or acknowledge any human relatives, further blurring the line between man and deity in his public persona.[15]

Divine dubbed his interracial ministry the Peace Mission movement, which in the 1930s had bases in Long Island, Harlem, and Philadelphia. His interracial group of followers usually lived, worked, and prayed together in semicommunal settings. The group hosted enormous banquets and launched a handful of businesses, which included barbershops, restaurants, grocery and clothing stores, laundromats, "huckster wagons" (which delivered groceries), farms, newspapers, and hotels. The businesses provided jobs for followers, served the local community, and helped finance the movement.[16]

Unlike most Black religious leaders, Father Divine taught that the United States was the chosen land. He called the Declaration and Constitution divinely inspired and believed that the United States served as the foundation for the coming kingdom of God. He championed international disarmament, the end of capital punishment, and pacifism. "Though we believe America through a New Birth of freedom under GOD is destined to be the Saviour of the nations, the use of force," he preached, "is strictly against our religious conviction." He refused to identify with any race, taught that all humans were the same, and criticized Jim Crow. He called for the abolition of all segregated neighborhoods and demanded that authorities prosecute anyone who practiced discrimination in hotels, schools, colleges, churches, theaters, and other public spaces.[17]

Political activists occasionally courted Divine. Members of the American Communist Party, which explicitly taught racial equality, sometimes partnered with the minister. Democrats also tried to win him over, but Divine had little faith in FDR or the New Deal. He taught a classic self-help philosophy, opposed the welfare state, and encouraged his followers not to take government assistance. He also criticized the president for doing too little for Black Americans. Although Divine's influence declined somewhat after the Depression, he led the Peace Mission movement until his death in 1965, when his wife Edna Rose Ritchings, known as Mother Divine, took over.

During the Depression a handful of small, far-right, fascist-leaning Christian organizations expanded their influence. Their leaders generally drew on racist and anti-Semitic tropes and admired how foreign dictators such as Adolf Hitler, Francisco Franco, and Benito Mussolini had seemingly brought economic recovery and political stability to their countries. They believed that the US could also benefit from a blending of Christianity with fascism.

In the 1920s, minister Gerald Winrod joined the fundamentalist movement in his home state of Kansas and launched a new ministry called the Defenders of the Christian Faith. Rather than serve as a traditional pastor, he hit the road as an itinerant and took to the airwaves, warning all who would listen against the dangers of religious liberalism. Like Father Coughlin, he traded in anti-Semitism. He believed that the Antichrist secretly led a massive global conspiracy orchestrated by a Jewish cabal.

In the 1930s, Winrod's messages evolved to fit the context. "The time has now come," he preached, "when the Christian element of our citizenry must be stirred out of its lethargy." He worried that the New Deal secretly introduced communism into the United States. He called on his audience to "stamp" it "out of our Land" and for "organized, concerted, Christian action against the Red menace."[18]

In 1938, Winrod launched a campaign for the Republican Senate nomination in Kansas, using it as a platform to spread his fringe views. He blamed Jews and ecumenical Christians for the nation's economic woes, accusing the Federal Council of Churches (FCC) of pushing "left-wing radicalism and Socialism" from church pulpits. Winrod's campaign exposed how fundamentalist extremists could spin conspiracy theories about hidden enemies, counterfeit Christianity, government overreach, and demonic forces—and then weaponize those fears for political gain. It also highlighted a striking divide in public opinion: While left-leaning Americans saw the FCC as captive to capitalist interests, conservatives viewed the same organization as a mouthpiece for socialism.[19]

Just as Coughlin's activism worried Catholic divines, Winrod's growing influence worried protestant leaders. Trying to make sense of the revivalist's appeal, FCC General Secretary Samuel McCrea Cavert contacted a Kansas minister seeking information. Knowing of Winrod's "bitter and grossly unfair attacks upon the Federal Council of Churches," Cavert wrote, "his anti-Semitic utterances and his illiberal spirit generally, I find it difficult to believe that the churches of the State would rally to his support, but I hear rumors which tend to indicate that this is the case." Much to Cavert's relief, Winrod did not really have the backing of most of the state's Christians. Voters resoundingly defeated the fundamentalist minister. Nevertheless, in this moment of national crisis, his mix of political activism with apocalyptic theology drew many admirers.[20]

Rather than look to a charismatic minister or a utopian dreamer as the nation's potential savior, millions of Americans turned instead to Episcopalian and vestryman President Franklin Delano Roosevelt. By the first decades of the twentieth century, Episcopalians ranked as the nation's wealthiest Christians. The church counted among its leaders both conservatives, who aimed to protect their power and upper-class status, and liberals, who hoped to use the social gospel to improve their societies. Roosevelt had a foot in both worlds—he was very rich and very committed to progressive change. Yet he treated individual convictions and beliefs as private matters. While he talked about religion a lot, he rarely spoke of his own specific faith.

Although religion had not played as prominent a role in the 1932 presidential election as in 1928 (when the Democrats had nominated a Roman Catholic), it did influence some votes. Fundamentalists saw an especially ominous sign during the Democratic National Convention. On the first set of convention ballots, Roosevelt received 666 votes. Six-six-six was the number long associated with the Antichrist (Revelation 13:18). For the rest of FDR's tenure, some apocalypticists suspected that the president secretly served Satan.

Some of Roosevelt's policy positions troubled Christians. Many objected to his seeming disregard for Prohibition. Texan J. Frank Norris and Seattle minister Mark Matthews, both longtime Democrats and pastors of two of the largest churches in the nation, despised FDR. "What are you going to do about this infernal wet issue?" Matthews wrote Norris after the Democratic convention. "Roosevelt is worse than Smith." "I quite agree with you on Roosevelt's being worse than Smith," Norris responded, "and in addition to being wet, he is a Communist." As the ministers expected, shortly after taking office FDR laid the foundation for repeal of the Eighteenth Amendment. When administration officials later polled clergy on their reaction to FDR's initiatives, many respondents complained bitterly about his undermining of Prohibition. A Baptist warned the president, "God can not bless a Rum-soaked, dancing, nudist nation with total prosperity."[21]

Radio evangelist Lightfoot Solomon Michaux had a different assessment. The Black preacher believed that if ministers spent less time harping on the president and more time leading their churches in righteousness, "they might be able to say as I can about my parish . . . as far as we are concerned, America is still dry. Our slogan is, If the world wants liquor, let them have it, and the church stay dry that it may be a light and an example."[22]

The president also moved to undercut the power of reservation missionaries, further alienating church leaders. FDR recognized the challenges faced by the nation's Indigenous peoples, who ranked among the poorest of Americans, and he wanted to undo some of the wrongs that the federal government had perpetuated for generations. He appointed John Collier as Commissioner of Indian Affairs to start the process of reconfiguring Indian policy.

A longtime progressive, Collier had worked in the 1920s to expose the government's mistreatment of Native peoples. He argued that the

Fundamentalists did not trust Franklin Roosevelt and fretted about his expansion of the size and power of the federal government. The owner of this prophecy truck apparently hoped Congress would stop Roosevelt's "dictatorship," cut taxes, recognize the United States' unique role in biblical prophecy, and heed the message of the soon-coming return of Jesus. (credit: John Vachon, *Gospel Car at Capitol (1939)*, Library of Congress)

true goal of government suppression of Indigenous spirituality, and particularly federal agents' efforts to eradicate Pueblo dances, was securing Indigenous property for Whites. "The war against Pueblo religion," Collier told readers of *The Christian Century*, "is a war to expropriate the Pueblos from their lands in the cheapest way. That is the whole story." Pueblos had organized against the government and in defense of their rights, and Collier sought to convince White Christian audiences of the righteousness of the Indigenous cause.[23]

Under FDR, Collier oversaw the 1934 Indian Reorganization Act, which sought to restore land, autonomy, and rights to Indigenous tribes. Policymakers shifted away from forcing Natives to assimilate and instead offered them more freedom to maintain and celebrate their unique cultures and identities as they saw fit. As Collier assumed his new position, he issued a circular to government bureaucrats overseeing reservations. "No interference with Indian religious life or ceremonial expression will hereafter be tolerated," he instructed. "The cultural liberty of Indians is in all respects to be considered equal to that of any non-Indian group. . . . The fullest constitutional liberty, in all matters affecting religion, conscience, and culture, is insisted on for all Indians. In addition, an affirmative, appreciative attitude toward Indian cultural values is desired in the Indian Service."[24]

Some missionaries took to the pages of *The Christian Century* to object to Collier's new policy. But the New Deal reformer dismantled their arguments. "This administration," Collier concluded, "will continue to try to admit Indians to the most important of all human birthrights—affirmative liberty of conscience." The debate, unfolding in the pages of the liberal-stream magazine, illustrated how little had changed in hundreds of years. Protestants still believed that the Constitution guaranteed mainstream protestants' religious liberty and not necessarily anyone else's.[25]

With multiple religious controversies brewing, Roosevelt, looking ahead to the 1936 presidential election, reached out to religious leaders. He understood the important role they played in American politics and the power they wielded. "Because of the grave responsibilities of my office, I am turning to representative Clergymen for counsel and advice," he wrote in a letter that went to more than one hundred thousand ministers, priests, and rabbis. "Tell me where you feel our government can better serve our people. . . . We shall have to work together for the common end of better spiritual and material conditions for the American people."[26]

The letter generated a huge response. Apocalypse-obsessed revivalists proved especially critical of the president's policies, and they eagerly shared their thoughts. They worried that as more Americans turned to the federal government for help, the fewer rights they would retain. Eventually, they would be powerless when the government ceded control to the Antichrist. "In my humble judgment," Wheaton College president J. Oliver Buswell told the president in less than humble terms, "you are seriously in error. In fact, the socialistic or communistic tendencies of your administration" were "entirely contrary to the spirit and the detailed teachings of the Word of God." Percy Crawford, the leader of the Young People's Church of the Air, warned the president that his failure "to honor Jesus Christ will result not only in the downfall of your administration, but of the country as a whole." One Florida man complained that the president had "added every letter of the alphabet to the New Deal except G-O-D."[27]

Conservatives also expressed frustrations. Presbyterian J. Gresham Machen called the Social Security Act "inimical (1) to liberty and (2) to honesty." "In our collective national life," another Presbyterian leader wrote FDR, "God is even more forgotten than your 'forgotten man.'" Conservative religious leaders recognized that the federal government, in taking over some of the services Americans used to look to churches to provide, might inspire in citizens a new faith in the New Deal while undermining their faith in their seemingly impotent ministers.[28]

Some theological liberals shared the political views of their conservative and revivalist counterparts. Los Angeles Congregationalist minister James W. Fifield Jr. founded Spiritual Mobilization in 1935 to organize ministers and business leaders to combat the New Deal. He believed that the government had undermined individual rights as well as the authority of churches. Manhattan Presbyterian Norman Vincent Peale contrasted New Deal policies with the Constitution. "President Roosevelt is not getting a square deal from the country," he sarcastically preached. "The President obviously holds a philosophy of government which cannot be reconciled under the constitutional system under which he lives." Americans must choose, he advised, "either to change the Constitution or to change Mr. Roosevelt. The latter course would probably be wiser for the years have proven that the Constitution is rather sound intellectually."[29]

Other liberal Christians praised Roosevelt's approach to solving the nation's problems. *The Christian Century* identified FDR's "ability to strike the spiritual note unerringly" as the basis of his success. "In a fundamental sense, the Roosevelt personality has grown on the nation because it has been revealed as spiritually deep and spiritually sound. The American people find in their President a religious leader."[30]

The president routinely invoked religion as a political tool that could lift up all Americans. He delivered a radio address in 1936 to mark the new "Brotherhood Day" sponsored by the ecumenical National Conference of Christians and Jews. "The very state of the world is a summons to us to stand together," he asserted. "For as I see it, the chief religious issue is not between our various beliefs. It is between belief and unbelief." He wanted more faith, more religion in American life. "No greater thing could come to our land today than a revival of the spirit of religion," he proposed. "I doubt if there is any problem—social, political or economic—that would not melt away before the fire of such a spiritual awakening."[31]

Although many American Christians embraced the president and his ecumenical message, Black ministers were more skeptical. They had a complicated relationship with the New Deal and especially the Democratic Party. Many remained loyal to the party of Lincoln.

Editors for the *National Baptist Union-Review*, which primarily served a Black readership, printed article after article condemning the New Deal. "The American people," they admonished, "should hold tightly to their constitutional heritage—it has been tested by the years, and has been found good. If the people fail to do this, all that our forefathers gave to us will be destroyed." J. G. Robinson, editor of the influential *A.M.E. Church Review*, wrote the president directly. He called FDR a hypocrite for taking communion before his inauguration and then resurrecting the sale of liquor shortly thereafter. He criticized the Democratic Party's "attitude towards the Negro race" and advised FDR to "more thoroughly and earnestly consider the rights of the American Negro, and instead of pushing the 'New Deal,' give to them the principle of the 'Square Deal.'" Black Americans recognized that FDR aimed to do more for their communities than previous presidents, but in many areas he fell short.[32]

Civil rights activists were also leery of Roosevelt. Baptist activist Nannie Helen Burroughs had long backed the GOP. In 1932 she told a friend that she wanted to help reelect Herbert Hoover over Roosevelt even though it was "a bear cat of a job." Reporting on conditions in the nation's capital, where she lived, she claimed that the New Deal "for negros will be the usual raw deal and everybody with any sense knows it." A few years later she wrote Roosevelt a scathing letter demanding that he take racism and the needs of Black Americans seriously. "Living as they are, under relentless, demoralizing, soul-destroying race prejudice, discrimination and injustice of every conceivable kind—material help for the Negro is not enough." She demanded that the president stop ignoring "the question of race discrimination, undemocratic practices, un-American attitudes, and unsound and unfair government practices in dealing with colored citizens." FDR had spoken out for the rights of those facing oppression in Europe and Asia. Why, she asked, did he ignore prejudice at home? "We cannot accept," she told him, "without question, the reason for your unbroken silence regarding the mistreatment of colored citizens in your own country."[33]

Yet over the course of the 1930s, some Black leaders and voters shifted their loyalty to FDR and the Democrats, marking the start of what eventually became a major political realignment. Pentecostal minister Smallwood Williams, the leader of a growing church in Washington, DC, looked past the Democrats' long history of racism and support for Jim Crow to praise the president. He criticized the GOP as "insensitive to the economic needs of poor people." Its leaders had become "bedfellows with Big Business, making empty promises to poor people and fat provisions for the rich." Lightfoot Solomon Michaux wrote Roosevelt an encouraging note: "If you are to be called a socialist and a wrecker of the Constitution because of your administration taking the bull of depression by the horn to throw him out of America in whatever way possible, you rejoice and be exceedingly glad, for great will be your reward in heaven." Baptist minister Adam Clayton Powell Jr., a future congressman, supported FDR and advised other African Americans to do the same. He adopted apocalyptic language to challenge those men and women who viewed the president as "the anti-Christ" and naively voted Republican "for Lincoln's and Jesus' sake." The Harlem minister predicted that the wheelchair-bound Roosevelt will "break the tape at the Pearly Gates before the rest of the field." "Brothers," he concluded, "the Lord will not smite thee by day nor your forefathers turn over in their graves by night just because you have voted for Roosevelt."[34]

Black leaders hoped the crisis would awaken White Americans to the wrongs they had committed, seeing it as God's judgment on their chosen land. Minister R. C. Lawson believed that the Depression represented God's punishment for "the terrible, atrocious things that happen down south, jim-crowism, lynching and prejudice to the darker brothers." He believed that survival required repentance. "Only by turning back to God," Lawson surmised, "will He lift His hand off the neck of the people." Few White Americans, however, believed this.[35]

American Christians of all races and classes and religious traditions had mixed feelings about FDR. Many from liberal, social gospel–oriented churches cheered his efforts to use the federal government to aid the American people. Religious conservatives fretted that FDR's actions undermined American traditions, classic liberalism, and the role of religion in social services. Revivalists worried that the spirit of the Antichrist had duped FDR into inadvertently preparing the United States for the end-times. Liberationists recognized that the president did more for the poor and marginalized than prior American leaders, but they also recognized that he did not do enough. The one thing they all agreed on was that American Christians should continue to play a significant role in American politics, getting their people into positions of power, and effecting national policy. As the power of the federal government expanded, they sought to influence and control its trajectory.

Between 1926 and 1936, the overall number of churches in the United States declined by 14.2 percent. Liberal churches took the greatest hit as they struggled to keep their theology both relevant and distinctly Christian. Seminary professor and theologian John C. Bennett called the "disintegration of liberalism" the "most important fact about contemporary American theology." Modernist icon Harry Emerson Fosdick sought to make sense of the liberal crisis. In a widely circulated sermon, he celebrated modernism's success in reconciling faith with reason, and religion with contemporary knowledge. But like Bennett, he worried that culture was shaping Christianity more than Christianity was shaping culture. "We have already largely won the battle we started out to win," he exulted. "We have adjusted the Christian faith to the best intelligence of our day and have won the strongest minds and best abilities of the churches to our side." Yet that, Fosdick insisted, was not enough. "Let all modernists lift a new battle cry: We must go beyond modernism!" Rather than accommodating the churches to culture, he argued, they needed to return to a time when they could "stand out from it and challenge it!" as Christ had done. Fosdick feared that Christian liberals had lost their prophetic edge and recognized that little separated liberal Protestant mainstream leaders from the nation's political and economic elites.[36]

Those in the conservative stream seemed less affected by the crisis. Researchers for the Social Science Research Council noted that "very little change in the form of worship" appeared during the Depression. Conservative groups "are long lived and have forms which extend over the centuries." The Missouri Synod of Lutherans, for example, like many conservative-stream denominations, grew in the 1930s.[37]

In contrast to conservative churches, the SSRC found that revivalist churches dramatically adapted their worship styles and service orders to meet the crisis. At the time, many Americans viewed fundamentalists as drifting toward irrelevance. After all, fundamentalists had lost, or would soon lose, control over most of the traditional levers of protestant establishment power. They surrendered denominational boards, missionary leadership positions, and seminary professorships to moderates and liberals. Yet moving with the flow of history, making quick pivots as circumstances demanded, proved an effective strategy for those steering the fundamentalist movement. Revivalist ministers sought to apply faith to culture and address real-world concerns. To visit a revivalist congregation, SSRC investigators found, was to be "made very conscious of the times in which we are living." Many updated their apocalyptic premillennialism to align with the latest headlines, effectively using calamitous events to drive people to Jesus.

By the early 1940s, fundamentalist leaders could legitimately claim to speak for over one million Christians in the United States. Yet many religious observers failed to grasp how the tides of American religion had already begun shifting toward fundamentalism.[38]

As Americans watched the New Deal response to the Depression unfold, most understood that Roosevelt's programs had inadvertently transformed Americans' relationships with both their churches and their government and further undermined the power of the already-reeling protestant establishment. Churches no longer competed just against each other; they now competed against the federal government for the loyalty of the American people. Meanwhile, the specter of an even greater crisis had begun to materialize on the horizon, one that would eventually allow American Christians to make anew the case for American exceptionalism, which they tied to a new form of Christian nationalism.

24

WARS OF FAITH

As madmen lit the fires of war around the globe in 1939, Franklin Roosevelt took to the airwaves like a pulpit pundit. Aware of Americans' strong isolationist tendencies, he wanted the public to recognize how international turmoil could affect their own nation. "Storms from abroad directly challenge three institutions indispensable to Americans, now as always," he warned, naming them as religion, democracy, and international good faith. He listed religion first, he explained, because it provided the foundation for the American character, democratic government, and international peace. That devilish foreign enemies now threatened Christianity required Americans to "prepare to defend, not their homes alone, but the tenets of faith and humanity on which their churches, their governments and their very civilization are founded."[1]

Christian leaders seeking to build a godly nation engaged in a kind of endless dialogue with the outside world, seeking to shape the course of events while outside events shaped them. World War II forced Christians to wrestle anew with questions of peace and violence, justice and equity, and religion and nationalism. It required believers to determine what obligations they owed the state and their fellow humans living in other parts of the world, and what roles they should play in trying to influence American foreign policy. Most important, it compelled them to reassess their devotion to the United States as God's Holy Land, and to determine if God had chosen their nation to lead the rest of the world to salvation, during the 1940s and beyond. Some looked to erect global, supranational ecumenical alliances, while others used the war to justify building a new Christian nationalism that entwined faith and policy.

In the years after World War I, Americans watched Europe and Asia with wary eyes. American legislators wanted nothing to do with the world's problems, and the League of Nations, which the United States had never joined, had little power. During the 1930s, Congress passed a series of neutrality acts intended to keep the US free from the kinds of entanglements that had drawn the nation into World War I. The acts inspired public debate, driving religious leaders to explain and defend how their beliefs intersected with their citizenship.

Protestant liberals generally supported American neutrality. Chastened by World War I and their failed crusade to make the world safe for democracy, they determined that perhaps the Prince of Peace did not sanction violence. Walter W. Van Kirk, the head of the Federal Council of Churches' Department of International Justice and Goodwill, wanted to revive historic pacifism. He published a book in 1934 intending to "throw a modest light upon the heroic struggle now in progress among Christians everywhere to recast in the language of the twentieth century the pacifist witness of the early church." Pacifism had come back into vogue among many liberal Christian groups, and he found a receptive audience.[2]

Yet as conditions deteriorated in Europe and Asia, liberals began to divide. In contrast to the pacifists, another group believed that Christians needed to intervene in global politics, using force if necessary, in pursuit of justice. Their most influential leader, Union Theological Seminary professor Reinhold Niebuhr, championed a philosophy of "Christian realism." Niebuhr had embraced pacifism as a young man, but in the late 1920s his thinking evolved. While most of his liberal-stream protestant colleagues advocated international cooperation and demilitarization, Niebuhr felt less sure that Americans could avoid violence. His groundbreaking 1932 book, *Moral Man and Immoral Society*, outlined how Christians should make sense of and respond to the challenges of racism, economic injustice, imperialism, and war. He argued that individuals could be just—they could prioritize the needs of others and sacrifice for the greater good. But when organized into groups, humans could not act in Christlike ways. Christians, he believed, must "recognize that when collective power, whether in the form of imperialism or class domination, exploits weakness, it can never be dislodged unless power is raised against it." Individuals may have moral characters; communities never do.[3]

Niebuhr grounded his philosophy in original sin. He argued that the fall made it impossible for Christians to build the kingdom of God on earth or redeem society. Forthrightly and somewhat pessimistically recognizing human imperfection, he called on Christians to get their hands dirty in politics, even if doing so meant supporting "lesser" evils or using the coercive power of the state for the ultimate good. In Niebuhr's view, the utopian optimism of the social gospel failed to grasp the practical realities of how power operates.

In shaping a Christian realist political philosophy, Niebuhr drew on neoorthodoxy, a new development in European liberal theology. The father of neoorthodoxy, the Swiss-German theologian Karl Barth, spent most of his life witnessing near continuous tragedies on the continent. Like Niebuhr, he recognized the pervasiveness of original sin. He believed that the ultimate hope for humanity lay in faith in a transcendent God and the redemptive power of Jesus. He chided modernists for their naive optimism and failure to take sin seriously. Yet he rejected fundamentalism. Neoorthodox Christians embraced both the latest science and biblical criticism. They saw fundamentalists as nitpickers who missed the forest for the trees.

The growth of neoorthodoxy linked with Christian realism sparked an internecine war within the liberal stream. For years

Niebuhr had worked with Charles Clayton Morrison and *The Christian Century*, the magazine of record for liberal protestantism. But as Morrison redoubled his commitment to pacifism, his differences with Niebuhr became more transparent. In response to Germany's invasion of Poland in 1939, and of Denmark, Norway, and France in 1940, Niebuhr called for a strong American response and for Christians to support US military intervention in Europe. He argued that placing a "premium" upon pacifism "is a very sentimentalized version of the Christian faith and is at variance with the profoundest insights of the Christian religion."[4]

Niebuhr's position earned him tremendous scorn. One person accused the theologian of abandoning "for the time being the Gospel of Jesus." "Cannot a Christian," he asked, "everlastingly hold for an entirely different way of organizing political units of the world than through this continual resort to killing?" Another wrote him, "God damn this brand of American Christianity." A *Christian Century* writer also condemned Niebuhr's views, claiming that Niebuhr seemed "in an utterly new and wholly dangerous mood."[5]

In 1941, Niebuhr launched a new magazine called *Christianity and Crisis* as an alternative to *The Christian Century*. He hoped to convince Americans, and especially Christians, that they could not remain on the sidelines as the world descended deeper into war. The board of editors included a who's who of Christian realists and ecumenical leaders. Pulling no punches, Niebuhr accused liberal ministers of indirectly helping expand the influence of racist and nativist isolationists like those leading the America First Committee, the nation's most prominent group lobbying against American intervention in the European war. "Only vegetables," Niebuhr quipped, "are completely rooted to their own soil. All higher forms of life create and destroy, live in mutual dependence and in mutual conflict in areas of geography on land and sea, which are not strictly their own."[6]

Niebuhr's defense of military intervention earned him fan mail from an anxious modernist who fretted that Americans had conflated isolationism with protestant liberalism. "The striking thing," the correspondent wrote, was that "those who are commonly rated as patriotic belong almost exclusively to the Fundamentalist set, and it has become one of the worst incriminations against Modernism. Your article coming as it does is most welcome in showing that not every liberal theologian is taking to the woods." The writer was right. As the war expanded, many Americans doubted liberal protestant leaders' ability to properly diagnose and respond to real-world issues.[7]

Catholics, like liberal-stream protestants, initially hoped the United States would stay out of the conflict. Right Reverend New Dealer Father John Ryan took away from World War I the belief that Americans should oppose all war. To build a Catholic anti-war movement, in 1927 he had launched the Catholic Association for International Peace. Although many Catholics—apart from radicals such as those in the pacifist Christian Workers' movement—acknowledged the possibility of just wars, most American Catholics did not believe the conflicts in Europe and Asia met historic just war criteria.

Ryan maintained a noninterventionist position into the early 1940s. At the same time that Niebuhr and Morrison debated pacifism in the pages of *The Christian Century*, the Catholic leader claimed that Christians' "immediate obligation is to help in keeping our own country out of war." But, he added, "this does not imply the advocacy of a cowardly, un-Christian and impossible isolation." He insisted that "America should refrain from participation in any of the wars now raging because such participation would not only be injurious to herself but in the long run would not benefit the other countries of the world." Like Ryan, most American Catholics hoped that the United States could serve as peacemaker rather than belligerent, but they also remained open to the possibility of intervention if the cause proved just.[8]

Global wartime chaos drove revivalists' anticipation of the apocalypse to all-time highs. And for good reason. Jesus's sermons on the Second Coming and the prophecies of Daniel, Ezekiel, and Revelation all seemed to converge in the late 1930s almost exactly as fundamentalists had outlined decades earlier. The faithful had long believed that Jews would reclaim Palestine in the last days, a process that began during World War I and accelerated during the 1930s. They had also spent generations anticipating the rise of rival empires—identified in this era as the United Kingdom, Russia, Germany, and Japan—which now seemed to be taking shape before their eyes. "For the first time in history," theologian Alva McClain wrote, "four great world powers are appearing contemporaneously in the precise quarters of the world as specified by prophecy *with the Jew back in his own land.*" Popular radio evangelist Charles Fuller saw the same signs. "The Bible," he preached on New Year's Eve 1939, "gives us a very vivid, clear, comprehensive word-picture of the days in which we are now living, and the remarkable thing about this word picture of the last days, of this age—the days in which we are now living—is that it was written some 1900 years ago." Armageddon, fundamentalists determined, had to be imminent.[9]

But unlike during World War I, they were ready to engage in the fight. Religious liberals had exploited fundamentalists' lack of involvement in the Great War, painting premillennialists as subversive and un-American. They did not want this to happen again. Most fundamentalists hoped for the chance to launch some mortars at the global surrogates of the Antichrist.

By late 1940 the Allied powers teetered on the verge of defeat. Hitler controlled most of Western Europe, and he had England reeling. Once Roosevelt secured reelection in 1940 for an unprecedented third term, he committed fully to helping the Allies defeat the Axis powers. In his January 1941 State of the Union address Roosevelt laid out his vision of what an Allied victory would accomplish. "We look forward to a world," he pledged, "founded upon four essential human freedoms." He identified them as freedom from want, freedom from fear, freedom of speech, and freedom of worship. Once again, he placed religious liberty at the heart of American policy. He promised Congress that he envisioned no "distant millennium. It is a definite basis for a kind of world attainable in our own time and generation." Roosevelt, like Wilson before him, wanted to reshape the world in the image of the United States.[10]

FDR claimed that only an Allied victory could protect American religious freedom. "Today," he told a radio audience, "the whole world is divided between human slavery and human freedom—between pagan brutality and the Christian ideal. We choose human freedom—which is the Christian ideal." In another speech he claimed that the Allies had discovered a secret Nazi plan "to abolish all existing religions—Catholic, Protestant, Mohammedan, Hindu, Buddhist, and Jewish alike." The regime aimed to seize church property, outlaw religious symbols, and intern church leaders. "And in the place of the Bible," the president warned, "the words of *Mein Kampf* will be imposed and enforced as Holy Writ," and the swastika will replace the cross. For Americans, the stakes could not have been higher.[11]

On Sunday morning, December 7, 1941, Japanese planes dispatched from aircraft carriers hidden in the vast Pacific surprised the United States by attacking the American naval base at Pearl Harbor, Hawai'i. Enemy planes damaged or destroyed much of the western fleet, and three thousand Americans lost their lives. The "date," Roosevelt proclaimed the next day, "will live in infamy."[12]

Some of Roosevelt's closest advisors believed that the president needed to continue emphasizing the religious nature of the conflict as he mobilized the American people. Harold Ickes, the Secretary of the Interior, wrote an unsolicited letter to the president shortly after the declaration of war. "Formerly there were more wars for religion than for anything else and the religious conviction is a deep one." He suggested that the government lead "a carefully planned campaign . . . to explain the religious implications in this war." Religion, he knew, made for excellent propaganda, especially in a country as Christian as the United States, with its sense of divine mission.[13]

Government leaders understood, however, that they had to proceed cautiously. The religious makeup of the nation had changed in recent decades. They worked to downplay differences and to emphasize commonalities, especially among Catholics, Jews, and protestants. A government-produced training film, *For God and Country*, treated chaplains from each of the faiths as essentially interchangeable (Ronald Reagan played the Catholic chaplain). The message of the film mirrored the one Roosevelt had been preaching for years. It didn't matter what your faith was, so long as you had faith.

Military leaders made religion manifest on dog tags, which allowed soldiers to list their religious identities as "P" for protestant, "C" for Catholic, and "H" for "Hebrew." The government made few accommodations for those outside of these faiths. The army provided no "B" for Buddhists or "A" for atheists, and leaders lumped alternative Christianities, such as Mormonism and Christian Science, in with protestants. The army buried those who perished on the battlefield under grave markers in the forms of either crosses or stars of David.

GIs experienced far fewer religious revivals than in previous wars. Perhaps this was not surprising, considering the government's emphasis on religion rather than Christianity. Nevertheless, many wartime soldiers found prayer to be helpful during the conflict, stating that it prepared them for battle. Meanwhile, their families back home could sing along to Irving Berlin's "God Bless America" and Frank Loesser's "Praise the Lord and Pass the Ammunition," both huge hits that linked the United States' war effort with God's aims.

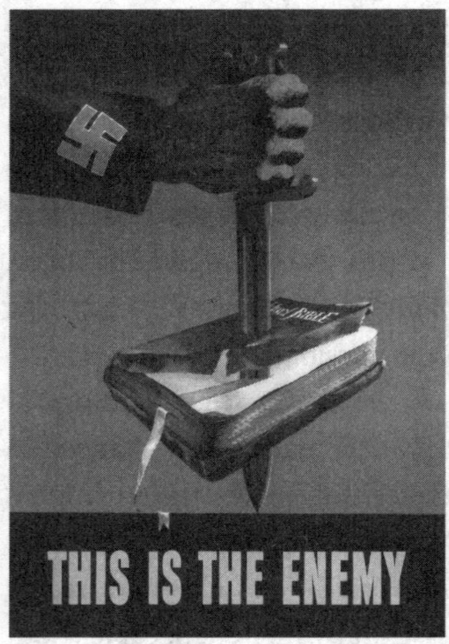

American leaders made religion central to their campaign to shape how the public understood what was at stake in World War II. Victory was not just about defeating the Axis powers but also about securing freedom of worship in the United States and around the globe. (credit: National Archives and Records Administration)

Liberal protestant leaders used the global conflict to try to expand their influence and remake the world according to their values. As Europe and Asia plummeted into violence, a group of religious leaders and laypeople working through the Federal Council of Churches had formed the Commission on a Just and Durable Peace. Its leadership represented the establishment elite, and they appointed Republican attorney and Presbyterian layman John Foster Dulles to head the commission. The group hoped to shape and influence Roosevelt's foreign policy, secure international peace though religious ecumenism, and champion individual rights and social justice. They believed that a robust international ecumenical movement might keep another global war from happening ever again.

The American declaration of war galvanized the commission's work and its commitment to integrating activism and Christianity. In late 1942, the commission published a pamphlet with essays from an all-star list of American clergymen and ecumenical leaders. "Our purpose," Dulles clarified, "is that the American people be filled with a righteous faith and sense of mission in the world. It is lack of such a faith which has made us weak." The writers called on Christians around the world to unite with those of other religious traditions. The head of the National Conference of Christians and Jews encouraged all people who believed "in the Fatherhood of God and the Brotherhood of Man" to "act in concert." Summing up the essays, Manhattan's Harry Emerson Fosdick claimed that "until the nations come to grips" with Jesus's "principles and make earnest with them in their political structures as well as in the personal lives of their citizens, we will suffer one debacle of our social hopes after another."[14]

The next year, Dulles published a new book on behalf of the commission: *Six Pillars of Peace*. He and his colleagues again demonstrated that they expected liberal, ecumenical protestants to reshape the postwar word. It was a presumptuous document by a presumptuous group. They called for an effective international peacekeeping organization, centralized economic planning, autonomy for colonial peoples, limits on militarization, and a defense of individual and religious liberty. The book received major media coverage in North America and Britain, much of it very positive. Dulles even used the leverage he gained to secure multiple meetings with FDR and other political leaders to discuss postwar reconstruction.[15]

Not to be outdone, Catholic theologian and priest Fulton J. Sheen published his own *Seven Pillars of Peace*. When it came to peace, Sheen believed more was more. If the protestants proposed six core principals, the Catholics would offer seven. He called for "the unity of religious groups for social purposes" and "the primacy of the moral law over force and expediency." Like his protestant counterparts, he expected his church to play a role in shaping the postwar world.[16]

The nation's major religious organizations agreed with many of the Dulles commission's recommendations. In 1943 the FCC released a joint statement alongside the Social Action Department of the National Catholic Welfare Conference and the Synagogue Council of America. The declaration, which signers claimed was the first American interfaith pronouncement on world order, marked a new phase in American ecumenism. Rather than emphasize differences, many of the nation's religious leaders sought common ground and a means for influencing American foreign policy. They championed individual rights as well as rights for colonial peoples and religious and ethnic minorities. They also demanded a just global social and economic order.

As liberal, ecumenical protestants worked to remake the world in their image, and occasionally to bring Jews and Catholics onboard, they often failed to understand the limits of their own perspectives. As much as they wanted to build a global interfaith peace movement, Christian ideas about truth, justice, and ethics defined their liberalism. The hierarchy they built assumed that White ecumenical protestants would enlighten the rest of the world. Wartime liberals failed to achieve many of their objectives, and they lacked the self-awareness to fully understand why.

The war challenged liberal leaders in other ways as well. Their refusal to sanctify Allied total-war tactics, their relentless focus on postwar peace, and their unwillingness to wrap themselves in the flag led critics to question their loyalties. Journalist Stanley High lamented in a *New Republic* cover story entitled "The Church Unmilitant" that the conflict for Americans had failed to become "a Holy War." He blamed Americans' "spiritual immobilization" on "a large and exceedingly influential element of Protestant clergy" whose pacifism had shaped their approach to the conflict. He singled out *The Christian Century* for particular blame. Its editors had sent the December 10, 1941, issue to the presses before Pearl Harbor, but it appeared in mailboxes after the attack. The issue echoed the magazine's position over the previous few years. Its writers criticized American leaders and blamed the US government for fomenting war. High blamed church leaders for either not believing or failing to communicate to their congregations "that religion and the church have a stake in an American victory." This, he feared, marked a dangerous new juncture in American history that would undermine the power and influence of establishment Christianity for years to come.[17]

Unlike liberal and modernist leaders, many revivalist ministers rallied to the flag. Shortly after Pearl Harbor Aimee Semple McPherson vowed to "fight the good fight of Faith"—and she meant fight. "It is the Bible against 'Mein Kampf.' It is the Cross against the Swastika. It is God against the antichrist of Japan," she preached. "This is no time," she insisted, "for pacifism." During the annual meeting of the International Church of the Foursquare Gospel, McPherson interrupted what the *Los Angeles Times* called the "old-time hallelujah-singing, hosanna calling, speaking-in-tongues camp meeting" to call down a plague on Adolf Hitler and Emperor Hirohito. "How many of you," she asked her audience, "would like to see Hitler covered with boils from head to foot?"[18]

Most fundamentalist leaders took similar positions and attacked their liberal-stream counterparts. "Certainly our New Testament does not teach believers to be slackers," Bible Institute of Los Angeles teacher and minister Keith Brooks insisted, "when their government calls upon them to defend their homes and country." Then he impugned the motives of pacifists. "It is not for us to say," he smirked, "which of these may be unconsciously seeking in Scripture something to justify a cowardly quirk in their own hearts." New York Methodist minister Arno

Gaebelein called for an unapologetic, aggressive response to Pearl Harbor. "Our country has been ruthlessly and viciously attacked by a heathen nation." He called "so-called *Christian objectors*" either "cowards or shallow thinkers or both." Revivalists masterfully used the war as a means of building the credibility of their movement, portraying themselves as the most loyal and American of Christians and the most manly of men. In the process they breathed new life into Christian nationalism by wedding revivalist Christianity with American independence and world power.[19]

Liberals and Catholics could get away with promoting pacifism and isolationism without facing too much acrimony, especially before the US entered the war, but those on the religious margins faced significant persecution for refusing to support the war effort. Members of the small, fringe apocalyptic sect the Jehovah's Witnesses endured assaults, harassment, and discrimination for objecting to military service and for their lack of nationalism. When some local schools punished Witness children who refused to stand for the pledge of allegiance, the organization fought back, which sparked a debate that led to the United States Supreme Court. In *Minersville School District v. Gobitis* (1940) the court determined that students must stand and pledge allegiance to the flag regardless of their religious beliefs. It was a bad look for American schools and courts to persecute schoolchildren for exercising their religious convictions, especially when in Germany Hitler was persecuting and interning Jehovah's Witnesses.

Three years later in *West Virginia State Board of Education v. Barnette* (1943) the court reversed course, finding that the First Amendment's prohibition against a state-established religion meant that Witnesses' children should be free to remain in their seats during the pledge of allegiance. "If there is any fixed star in our constitutional constellation," Justice Robert H. Jackson determined, "it is that no official, high or petty, can prescribe what shall be orthodox in politics, nationalism, religion, or other matters of opinion, or force citizens to confess by word or act their faith therein." The experience of Jehovah's Witnesses highlighted the limits of Americans' tolerance for dissenting religions and especially those that challenged the authority of the state. But as the nation grew more religiously diverse, the *Barnette* case also demonstrated that courts had started to think more broadly about the First Amendment.[20]

Roosevelt used the war to craft global, ecumenical religious alliances, and there was no alliance he coveted more than with the Roman Catholic Church. He knew that Vatican City had become a hotbed of wartime activity. The pope's commitment to official neutrality led diplomats from most of the warring powers to establish offices near the pontiff. American policymakers wanted, needed to know what was happening within those medieval and Renaissance walls, where foreign diplomats and spies worshipped, schmoozed, and strategized. But Roosevelt wanted more than just buzzy intelligence. He believed that partnerships with international religious organizations could contribute to the attainment of American goals.

To facilitate a potential alliance, the president dispatched Myron Taylor as his "personal envoy" to the Holy See. The move angered many Americans. They believed that having a political representative at the Vatican confirmed what they had claimed all along: the Catholic Church was a political rather than a religious institution. Leaders of the Federal Council of Churches warned that if Taylor's appointment "should unfortunately prove a stepping-stone to a permanent diplomatic relationship, we should feel obliged in good conscience to oppose it, as a violation of the principle of separation of governmental function and religious function, which is a basic American policy and which both history and conscience approve, and as an ultimate injury to all faith." FDR brushed off the criticism. His move, he assured church leaders, had nothing to do with "the functions of church and state, and it is difficult," he wrote, "for me to believe that anyone could take seriously a contrary view, or that the action taken could interrupt in any way the necessary and healthy growth of inter-faith comity." Always the pragmatist, Roosevelt believed that if sending a delegate to Rome could help American foreign policy, he was going to send a delegate to Rome.[21]

Another group of unofficial American envoys—missionaries—struggled to maintain their religious outreach during the war. Most of those living near the front lines returned home for the duration. But a small number of missionaries took on new and surprising roles during the war: They became spies and intelligence operatives imbedded in global hotspots. Many worked for the Office of Strategic Services (OSS), which FDR established in 1941 as the nation's first independent foreign intelligence–gathering agency. Due to the agency's late start, its leaders had to scramble to find well-qualified operatives. They did not have well-planned or centrally coordinated recruiting efforts. Instead, through a series of fits and starts, they discovered that missionaries proved to be ideal agents. More than just about any other group, missionaries had excellent language skills, knew how to build the trust of local populations, and had mastered the various geographies of the regions in which they had labored.

Missionaries who served the OSS had many different motives for exchanging the cross for the sword, but each hoped that in serving the United States, they served God. They sought to build a new global order that blended a generic, ecumenical, protestant Christianity with American power. But first they had to win the war. They had to defeat the evil that threatened them before they could get back to the good work of expanding God's kingdom. "To make the devil flee," one missionary-spy had determined years earlier, "it is sometimes necessary to resist him."[22]

A handful of leaders working for the major missionary organizations cut secret deals with the OSS, often through the State Department. The government gave cooperating missionary agencies priority transportation to and from mission stations and ensured that supplies made it to missionary schools and hospitals abroad. In return, a very select number of missionaries did fieldwork for the government. One, fundamentalist John Birch, volunteered in China for army intelligence and then the OSS. While continuing to seek Chinese converts and run Bible studies for natives, he scrambled back and forth across enemy lines, led guerrilla attacks against the Japanese, and helped American bombers identify high-value human targets. Another, Lutheran Stewart Herman, who had served as the pastor of the American Church in Berlin from 1935 to 1941, worked from the OSS's London station.

He partnered with members of the Confessing Church, the German religious underground, to identify and recruit agents to penetrate Nazi Germany.

Perhaps the most effective missionary agent was William Eddy. During the war he served the OSS in North Africa, where American generals George Patton and Dwight Eisenhower relied on him for advice as they planned Operation Torch, the invasion of the region. Eddy had been on the ground actively recruiting allies among the locals and scoping out incursion points. He also hatched assassination plots against high-level enemies.

The war seemingly changed everything for religious activists-turned-spies. Or maybe it didn't. Maybe double-crossing, deceiving, and even assassinating those who did the devil's handiwork represented the logical culmination of their sense of global Christian mission, how they planned to bring peace and charity back to earth. They never felt quite sure. Men like Dulles and Fosdick could wax eloquent about postwar reconstruction, but without agents like Birch and Eddy there might not be peace.

The war also inspired some revivalist Christians to organize in new ways. The Federal Council of Churches, since its founding decades earlier, had included among its member denominations Christians from every stream and its leaders claimed to represent all American protestantism. By the 1940s, however, liberals and modernists ran the organization, setting its priorities and shaping its mission. They had the ear of Roosevelt and others in government, which frustrated revivalists.

Missionary executive Ralph T. Davis began talking to ministers around the country about creating a fundamentalist alternative to the FCC. Fundamentalists had long battled the government over rules governing the airwaves, and as the nation mobilized for war, they also fretted about the draft, the war's impact on their missionary stations, and the selection of military chaplains. "The functions of the proposed council," Davis suggested, "should be to deal with problems which are common to us all. Perhaps the headquarters should be located in Washington." Davis was not advocating another evangelistic society;

he wanted to shape the fundamentalist movement into a mainstream organization with its own political lobby to represent its interests in the nation's capital.[23]

Davis and his allies initially planned to call their group the "Fundamentalist Council" as an alternative to the Federal Council. But as their ambitions expanded, they settled on "National Association of Evangelicals for United Action" (NAE). Replacing the label "fundamentalist" with the term "evangelical" was a canny move. For five hundred years countless protestants had used the term "evangelical" to assert that their beliefs were truer, or that their faith was more real and active, than those they viewed as their religious competitors. Yet the term had mostly fallen out of use by this period until they resurrected and redefined it.

In 1942 the United States' most powerful White fundamentalists descended on St. Louis to organize the NAE. The group included members from both the conservative and revivalist streams, and they represented the political ideologies of the broader fundamentalist movement. They leaned conservative and anti–New Deal but wanted the organization to remain nonpartisan. Boston Congregationalist Harold Ockenga served as the association's first president. In his keynote address at the conference, he identified Roman Catholicism, theological modernism, secularism, and New Deal liberalism as the nation's greatest threats. His ideas represented the decade-long cross-fertilization of conservative political ideology with fundamentalist theology, which helped set the trajectory of the new "evangelicalism."[24]

After Ockenga finished his sermon, William Ward Ayer, pastor of Manhattan's Calvary Baptist Church, reminded the group of its self-appointed role in God's divine mission for North America. "It is not boasting to declare that evangelical Christianity has the America of our forefathers to save. . . . Millions of evangelical Christians, if they had a common voice and a common meeting place, would exercise under God an influence that would save American democracy." He argued that revivalist and conservative Christians should unite to reclaim the nation, advocating for a new and effective form of Christian nationalism.

While NAE leaders did not speak explicitly about race, de facto racial segregation prevailed. Their inclusion of vocal segregationists among the leadership and their courting of explicitly segregated denominations guaranteed that Black Americans were not welcome. They did not intend to represent historic Christianity writ large, but to represent the interests of White, middle-class, politically conservative fundamentalists.

As the NAE pursued its remaking of Christian nationalism, the broader political landscape shifted dramatically. On April 12, 1945, Franklin Roosevelt died of a cerebral hemorrhage. Harry S. Truman, vice president for only a few months, moved into the Oval Office. He had just learned of the development of the atomic bomb, and once it was ready, he decided to use it. On August 6, 1945, a B-29 Superfortress, the *Enola Gay*, dropped an atomic bomb that detonated over Hiroshima, Japan. A few days later the United States dropped a second atomic bomb over Nagasaki. Truman credited God for the weapon. "We thank God that it has come to us," the president told the American people, "instead of to our enemies; and we pray that He may guide us to use it in His ways and for His purposes." On August 15, the Japanese surrendered. The war had finally ended.[25]

Truman's decision to use atomic bombs proved as controversial among churchgoers as among the general public. Some American religious leaders had already questioned the morality of the United States' total-war strategy. A group of liberal clergymen, including Harry Emerson Fosdick, issued a statement in 1944 protesting the "carnival of death" that the American military had unleashed on German cities. In a symbol of how far things had come since World War I—when the modernists assumed the role of warmongering crusaders and fundamentalists the aloof peacemakers—NAE president Harold Ockenga published a rejoinder in *The New York Times* defending firebombing. "We Protestants repudiate the un-American pacifism of Dr. Fosdick and associates," he opined. "Protestant Christian patriotism endorses and supports the use of force to free the world of the menace of German militarism and Japanese barbarism. We want the men at arms to know that the church is praying for their complete victory." The new "evangelicals" wanted the American public, the government, and the military to understand that they, not their liberal counterparts, represented true, unapologetic patriotism.[26]

Many Christians wrote their leaders expressing anger and sadness toward their government over the use of atomic weapons. One lamented to the head of the Presbyterian denomination, "This is not war, it is mass murder." *Christian Century* editors called for the "churches of America" to "disassociate themselves and their faith from this inhuman and reckless act of the American government." Leaders of the Federal Council wrote Truman directly, criticizing his decision. "Many Christians," they claimed, felt "deeply disturbed over use of atomic bombs against Japanese cities because of their necessarily indiscriminate destructive effects and because their use sets extremely dangerous precedent for future of mankind." Most American Catholic leaders, including the editors of the nation's leading Catholic magazines, agreed.[27]

Some Christians, however, especially from the revivalist tradition, saw atomic weapons as part of God's divine plan for American supremacy. Revivalist Clarence Benson described the bomb's use as a fitting end to this war of "religion." "The conflict between these two unconquered nations was a battle of the gods," he opined. "God accepted the challenge and placed in the hands of His people the mysterious weapon which was to bring overwhelming devastation without the loss of a single American." Editors of the National Association of Evangelicals' new magazine hoped that the bomb would remain in Christian hands only. "Our concern is not so much about the atomic bomb as about the people who control it. If the people are saved Christians, it will do the world no harm. If they are pagan, beware!"[28]

The United States' role in the new United Nations also divided Christians. Liberal, ecumenical protestant elites saw the UN in part as the fulfillment of their dreams. They hoped it might ultimately lead to permanent peace and a one-world government, providing a potential silver lining at the end of an otherwise horrible era. Fosdick had relentlessly advocated for such an organization. "The world," he claimed, "cannot be saved from war to any decent chance at equity and peace without some kind of world organization that will governmentally represent and serve its common interests." Leaders of the Commission on a Just and Durable Peace called for "a duly constituted world government of delegated powers: an international legislative body, an international court with adequate jurisdiction, international-administrative bodies with necessary powers, and adequate international police forces and provision for enforcing its worldwide economic authority." Individual nations should, they insisted, even cede their militaries to the global organization. Although the UN ultimately had a more limited scope than many liberal protestants had anticipated, they nevertheless hoped it would set the world on a path toward lasting peace.[29]

For evangelicals, however, the establishment of the UN, like the establishment of the League of Nations before it, confirmed their belief that increasing internationalism represented the loss of American sovereignty and one more step on the road to Antichrist rule. The UN, they speculated, could potentially serve as a tool for the devil to use to assert his power. "Whatever clever foreign diplomats or bungling American politicians may tell us," *Moody Monthly* editors wrote, "we help the world best by guarding our own interests." Returning to the classic American anti-entanglement mantra, they counseled national leaders to "keep America out of the pest house of European diplomacy." Influential Black minister and radio broadcaster R. C. Lawson predicted that the new international organization would ultimately facilitate "the Ten-Toe Kingdom of Daniel headed by the anti-Christ." Journalist and minister Dan Gilbert called on "Christian Americans" to "let their members of Congress know that they oppose the use of tax-funds of the American people to finance this Christ-rejecting, God-dishonoring propaganda arm" of the Antichrist.[30]

Wartime evangelical leaders crafted an absolutist politics that framed their position as the only righteous one, while simultaneously implying that those who disagreed with them were anti-American and inadvertently serving as pawns of Satan. Such sentiments appealed not only to the members of their churches but also to those Americans who still embraced Christian nationalism and believed that it was possible for the US to maintain absolute sovereignty and return to a position of isolation from European affairs.

The war marked the start of a new stage in the history of American Christianity. Those in the conservative stream continued to thrive but did not often play a significant role in American public life. Liberationists had only limited opportunities during the conflict to challenge the status quo, although they would later use American wartime commitments to freedom and democracy and human rights as the justification for a new crusade for civil rights.

For revivalist and liberal leaders, the war marked a significant pivot. Those in the revivalist stream resurrected and reshaped Christian nationalism, positioning themselves as the true guardians of the nation. Led by fundamentalists newly rebranded as "evangelicals," they claimed to be loyal patriots and heirs of the founders. Their new political lobby became a springboard for postwar influence. They continued to defend the United States as God's chosen land, a Christian nation.

Liberal leaders, by contrast, looked beyond US borders, turning to international organizations to preserve peace. To spread their beliefs, they partnered with global ecumenical bodies like the new World Council of Churches rather than focusing on national churches. Rejecting American exceptionalism, they sought to build new supranational institutions.

As believers from all four streams offered Americans competing visions of faith and governance, the looming Cold War promised to test them once again.

PART VI

UNRAVELING THE RELIGIOUS ESTABLISHMENT

25

ONE NATION UNDER GOD

The United States emerged from World War II as the world's foremost superpower. The American military ranked as the strongest in history, with a navy larger than the rest of the world's fleets combined. Yet American policymakers knew that they could not afford to celebrate for long. The world lay in ruins: Economies had collapsed, industries were shattered, cities reduced to rubble, and fields lay untended. Revolution filled the air as colonial peoples readied to overthrow their prewar overlords.

Americans believed that victory in World War II had reaffirmed their exceptional nature, that God still destined the United States to lead the world forward on religion, human rights, democracy, and freedom. Yet just as the United States moved to cement its influence around the globe, so too did the Soviets. The destruction of empires and rise of newly independent former colonies created a power vacuum that both the US and USSR hoped to fill.

Soviet leaders had long schemed to spark a global communist revolution. Many Americans believed that Russians sought not only a world without capitalism but also a world without religion. To them, communism was more than a competing economic system—it was dogmatic atheism. Marx had famously called religion the "opium of the people," viewing religious faith chiefly as a tool of oppression. American policymakers came to see the communism of Lenin and Stalin as a false faith, complete with its own dogma, sacred texts, converts, and missionaries, bent on world conquest.

To counter communism, American leaders positioned religion at the heart of their developing Cold War strategy. They established a new generic, ecumenical, theistic religion that entwined God and country. They believed that a rekindling of religious faith—in faith—would ease the public's anxiety over the threat of nuclear war, neuter the communist menace, help them win the fight against the Soviets, and sanctify postwar economic abundance. The more the nation's leaders could inject God into public life, the better. And the American people responded. A massive revival of religion, which religious leaders had hoped to see during the Great Depression, and then during World War II, finally arrived, just a little later than anticipated. Americans renewed their confidence in their nation's chosenness, sure that as long as they stayed true to their divine heritage, the United States would remain God's instrument ready to deliver freedom to the rest of the world.

To win the Cold War abroad, Americans believed they first had to win it at home. Diplomats and policymakers expected the Soviets to try to disrupt domestic life in the United States, so they looked for signs of communist subversion. In Congress, Joseph McCarthy used the Senate Committee on Government Operations and its Permanent Subcommittee on Investigations to launch a communist witch hunt.

One of McCarthy's top advisors, J. B. Matthews, focused on the communist infiltration of churches. A Methodist missionary in the 1910s, after the Great War Matthews joined numerous left-wing organizations. In the 1930s he grew disenchanted by the spread of communism and took a job as the House Un-American Activities Committee's director of research. His prior experience in liberal groups made him especially suspicious of progressive religious leaders. In 1953 he caused a sensation when he published an article entitled "Reds and Our Churches," accusing liberal churchmen of being communist stooges. "The largest single group supporting the Communist apparatus in the United States today," he declared, "is composed of Protestant clergymen." He painted progressive ministers and socially active Christians as unwitting allies of the nation's enemies. "A partial explanation of these thousands of clergymen who have collaborated in one way or another with the Communist-front apparatus may be found in the vogue of the 'social gospel,'" he insisted. "Many graduates of the 'liberalized' Protestant seminaries abandoned religion altogether in favor of the 'social gospel.'" For Matthews, a former social gospeler himself, to view God as working through Christians to build a better, more just and equitable society was to serve the spirit of Lenin.[1]

Many moderate and liberal religious leaders from across the Christian spectrum denounced the anti-communist hysteria. Reinhold Niebuhr responded directly to Matthews's accusations. "These charges are indiscriminate, and they are designed to hit every 'liberal' even if he has valiantly fought communism." Even the president intervened, condemning sweeping, misleading attacks. "The churches of America," President Dwight Eisenhower insisted, "are citadels of our faith in individual freedom and human dignity. This faith is the living source of all our spiritual strength. And this strength is our matchless armor in our world-wide struggle against the forces of godless tyranny and oppression." Nevertheless, the damage had been done by Matthews and many others with similar views. Liberal leaders had seemed insufficiently patriotic during World War II, and now during the Cold War it seemed that the communists had duped them.[2]

Navigating the Red Scare was a challenge for American Catholics. Joseph McCarthy was Catholic, and many Catholic groups backed his efforts. FBI director J. Edgar Hoover, who fought communism with a little more finesse than McCarthy, elevated Catholics to top bureau positions while embedding a broad, generic Christianity into the FBI's ethics and practices. Meanwhile, more politically liberal Catholics, like their protestant counterparts, often ended up on the defensive against the era's zealous Cold Warriors.

The anti-communist hysteria inspired entrepreneurs to launch timely new ministries. Australian preacher Fred C. Schwarz founded a wildly popular organization he called the Christian Anti-Communism Crusade, which attracted hundreds of thousands of followers in the United States who praised its blend of faith and politics. "I believe in God and His love, Christ and His redemption," he told all who would listen, "and the great commission to go into all the world and preach the gospel. Communism is the enemy of God and of Christ and His gospel. These two facts have motivated me to do everything within my power to stay the advance of Communism." Billy James Hargis, a pioneer in religious television, launched Christian Crusade with the twin goals of fighting communism abroad and cultural changes at home. His star rose until a young couple from his Bible college confessed to each other before their wedding, a ceremony they had invited Hargis to conduct, that neither was a virgin. Both had slept with Hargis.[3]

The recording industry and Hollywood even got in on the red-scare action. Lowell Blanchard and the Valley Trio recorded "Jesus Hits Like an Atom Bomb" (1950), fretting that "Everybody's worried 'bout the Atomic Bomb, but nobody's worried 'bout the day my Lord will come when He'll hit—Great God Almighty—like an Atom Bomb when He comes, when He comes." Some Hollywood studios produced films that reinforced the mainstream status quo and squelched dissent. Two blockbusters, *The Robe* (1953) and *Ben-Hur* (1959), presented Christians as heroes and religion as a saving force for the world. The OSS's successor, the new Central Intelligence Agency (CIA), even tried to fund production of a film on the life of the Buddha, hoping to convince Asians to ally with the US against communism.[4]

American policymakers knew that they could not defeat the Soviets and their growing global communist network without substantial help. Who better to enlist in the crusade, some reasoned, than the world's religious leaders. Truman picked up where Roosevelt had left off, seeking to unify the world's Orthodox Christians, Catholics, protestants, and Jews together in the struggle against godless totalitarianism. The president made religious faith, or the lack thereof, a tool of Cold War diplomacy.

Pope Pius XII did not trust communist leaders, and Truman wanted his help in waging the Cold War. In 1947 Truman reached out to the Holy Father. "I am privileged," he wrote, "to pledge full faith to you once again to work with Your Holiness and with every agency of good the world over for an enduring peace." He assured the religious leader that Christian principles provided the foundation for peace, and he reminded the pope that the United States "is a Christian Nation." "The greatest need of the world today," he concluded, "fundamental to all else, is a renewal of faith." The pope agreed, eager to work with Truman.[5]

A few years later, Truman sent an official American diplomat back to the Vatican. Protestants across the theological spectrum threw tantrums just as they had during the Roosevelt administration. Harry Emerson Fosdick sent a blistering note to the president. "This is a tragic blunder, abandoning the American principle of separation between church and state and singling out for preferential honor and influence a particular church," he lectured Truman. "This deplorable appointment will, I am sure, prove to be as imprudent and ill-advised as it certainly is false to the traditional principles of our Republic." Catholic Cardinal Francis Spellman had called such critics "unhooded Klansmen sowing seeds of dissension and disunion." Dismissing protestant opposition, Truman and American Catholics moved ahead in partnership with the pope.[6]

Truman made an even bolder, and perhaps even more unlikely, move in seeking another important alliance. On May 14, 1948, a triumphant David Ben-Gurion announced the creation of the State of Israel. Minutes later, Truman recognized the new nation, stunning his advisors. Revivalists felt sure that God had inspired Truman's actions. They had long believed that the return of Jews to Palestine marked a necessary precursor to the Second Coming. "Do you realize what this means?" Bible Institute of Los Angeles Professor Louis Talbot asked on his radio program. "This could be the beginning of that train of events which will not end until the Lord Jesus Christ Himself returns and sets up the everlasting Kingdom." The editor of the *Pentecostal Evangel* enthusiastically told readers that events in the Middle East had aligned so closely with biblical prophecy that "we may well wonder whether we are awake or . . . merely having a very exciting dream." *King's Business* called the rise of Israel "the greatest piece of prophetic news that has appeared in the twentieth century." Evangelicals' prophetic expectations once again seemed to match world events. Over the next couple of decades, revivalists often returned to the 1948 creation of Israel as the principal event that validated their prophecy and marked the beginning of the end.[7]

Eisenhower, like Truman, used religion to bolster his administration and policies. He adopted the role of high priest over the nation, overseeing the maturation of a revised form of generic American religion that linked God with the state and American patriotism. The president believed that Americans' dedication to equality and democracy stemmed from their Christian convictions. After meeting with a leading Soviet politician just weeks after winning the presidential election, he claimed that "our form of government is founded in religion. . . . Our form of Government has no sense unless it is founded in a deeply felt religious faith, and I don't care what it is. With us of course it is the Judeo-Christian concept but it must be a religion that all men are created equal." He insisted that the founders, in establishing the United States, had aimed to "translate" a religious concept "into the political world."[8]

Eisenhower used the term "Judeo-Christian" strategically. It represented a change in how Americans understood the roots of their religious identity. Beginning in the 1930s, some American leaders, both political and religious, had shifted from referring to the United States as a Christian nation, or as having been built on Christian foundations, to instead using "Judeo-Christian." Leaders of Christian-Jewish interfaith dialogues had developed the term to counter far-right Christian nationalists and Nazi anti-Semitism. The use of the term spread after the war. Americans, troubled by the Holocaust, wanted to acknowledge that the Christian tradition grew upon deep Jewish foundations. They also wanted to find inclusive ways to express American religiosity vis-à-vis the secular communist threat. After the creation of Israel, the term allowed Christian Zionists to bolster their connections between the land of Israel and the United States.

Eisenhower practiced what he preached, and he worked to set an example for the people. On January 20, 1953, he opened his inaugural address by reading a prayer he had composed himself rather than inviting a clergyman to offer the invocation. A few weeks later, a Presbyterian minister baptized the president in the National Presbyterian Church in Washington, DC.

Eisenhower, like Roosevelt, made ecumenical theistic religion central to his government. Niebuhr explained Eisenhower's work this way: "The President seems quite sincere in the espousal of the some-what vague religion which he expresses. It is 'faith' itself which he advocates and not faith in any particular religion." It was bland and generic, nothing for anyone to pick a fight over or be insulted by, as long as you didn't actually believe that you had a claim to any kind of exclusive truth. In an increasingly pluralistic nation, American leaders shifted from promoting a particular faith to championing religion itself.[9]

As the Cold War heated up, some Americans determined that the flag salute needed revising. They considered it too secular and wanted to add the words "under God." The pastor of the New York Avenue Presbyterian Church in Washington, DC, Scottish immigrant George M. Docherty, loved the idea of adding religion to the pledge. He counted among the members of his congregation President Eisenhower. At a special service in February 1954 in honor of Lincoln's birthday, Docherty told his audience that the American verses seemed little different from those pledged by Soviet children to their flag. "Indeed," he preached, "apart from the mention of the phrase, the United States of America, it could be the pledge of any republic. In fact, I could hear little Muscovites repeat a similar pledge to their hammer and sickle flag in Moscow with equal solemnity." Docherty believed that adding God to the pledge would distinguish it from those of communist nations. Eisenhower quietly absorbed the message from his seat in the same pew where Lincoln had once worshipped.[10]

As word of the minister's suggestion spread, Americans flooded Congress with letters of support, which led *The New York Times* to conclude that "a religious revival of significance" must be underway. Protestants and Catholics, political liberals and conservatives all sang the praises of Docherty's proposal. Most of those who opposed the idea, fearing that it violated church-state separation, kept their mouths shut rather than provoke the scorn of their friends and neighbors.[11]

On June 14, 1954, Congress passed legislation adding "under God" to the pledge. "From this day forward," Eisenhower declared as he signed the bill, "millions of our school children will daily proclaim in every city and town, every village and rural school house, the dedication of our nation and our people to the Almighty." He believed that the pledge provided an antidote to the dark times in which Americans were living and the perennial fear of nuclear annihilation. "In this way we are reaffirming the transcendence of religious faith in America's heritage and future; in this way we shall constantly strengthen those spiritual weapons which forever will be our country's most powerful resource, in peace or in war."[12]

God also secured a spot on American currency. In 1955, Congress mandated that the Treasury Department add "In God We Trust" to American money. The line had appeared on some coins since the Civil War, but never consistently. When the Treasury minted new gold coins in 1907, President Theodore Roosevelt caused an uproar when he opted not to include the phrase. "To put such a motto on coins," he argued, "not only does no good but does positive harm, and is in effect irreverence, which comes dangerously close to sacrilege. . . . It seems to me eminently unwise to cheapen such a motto by use on coins." But cheapen it Cold War Americans would.[13]

In 1956 Eisenhower approved another bill making "In God We Trust" the official motto of the United States. While a few groups groused that government leaders' actions violated church-state separation and even added an indirect religious "test" to those who aspired to hold office, the elevation of God in American public life generated little controversy. Most Americans believed that the founders had built the United States upon Christian foundations, and they wanted to be sure that every time they pledged allegiance to the flag or dropped some cash on a lunch counter for a Pepsi-Cola, they would remember that in God they put their trust.

Yet God remained absent from the Constitution. Congress debated but did not approve a revived "Christian" amendment that read, "This Nation devoutly recognizes the authority and law of Jesus Christ, Saviour and Ruler of nations through whom are bestowed the blessings of Almighty God." Even in the Cold War era, this proved a bridge too far.[14]

Although Americans rejected a constitutional amendment, most embraced the Cold War revival of religion. References to the nation's Judeo-Christian heritage and the phrase "In God We Trust" appeared everywhere. Corporate leaders, the Advertising Council, the Chamber of Commerce, and hundreds of religious leaders worked on dozens of projects to educate and inform the public about the importance of religion and to link it to their belief in American exceptionalism.

The Supreme Court, however, didn't follow the tide. In contrast to the executive and legislative branches, justices had been questioning how and when government institutions should provide support for religion. Church and state, they determined, had grown too cozy. A debate in New Jersey allowed the court to clarify and update the rights and boundaries established by the First Amendment. The New Jersey legislature had passed a bill reimbursing parents for the bus fares they paid to send their children to public schools. The bill also reimbursed parents who sent their children on public buses to private Catholic schools. Critics howled that the reimbursement of Catholic parents represented government support of religion. The debate over the government policy and its relationship to religion eventually wound its way to the Supreme Court in 1947 as *Everson v. Board of Education.*

Justice Hugo Black wrote the majority opinion defending the policy. In his first draft, he spent little time assessing the historical context undergirding the First Amendment. He emphasized instead how getting children safely to schools, including private schools, served a public purpose. However, a dissenting draft opinion, written by Justice Wiley Rutledge, probably with the help of Justice Felix Frankfurter, used history to make its case against the state policy. Rutledge made much of James Madison's *Memorial and Remonstrance* and Thomas Jefferson's letter to the Danbury Baptists.

Black, afraid that he might lose votes, revised his draft and added a significant history section in which he too invoked Jefferson and Madison. Even though the justices did not agree on the specific issue at hand, their competing opinions led them to concur that the establishment clause had an expansive application. "In the words of Jefferson," Black claimed in his majority opinion, the clause "was intended to erect 'a wall of separation between church and State.'" The First Amendment, he continued, "requires the state to be a neutral in its relations with groups of religious believers and non-believers." It "has erected a wall between church and state. That wall must be kept high and impregnable. We could not approve the slightest breach."[15]

Everson established a new precedent. The justices codified Jefferson's interpretation of the amendment as the new law of the land, although his was only one of the many ways the founders understood its meaning.

The following year, a new case required the Supreme Court to further clarify the intent of the First Amendment. The board of education in Champaign County, Illinois, had created a religious "release time" program. Students in the district could voluntarily attend privately funded classes of their choice taught by religious leaders during school hours. The classes focused on religious instruction—either protestant, Catholic, or Jewish. Atheist Vashti McCollum, who had a child in the county, claimed that her son's opting out of religion classes led to his ostracization. She sued the school board.

Black once again drafted the majority opinion. In *McCollum v. Board of Education* (1948) the justice described the school policy as "beyond all question a utilization of the tax-established and tax-supported public school system to aid religious groups to spread their faith." For the courts to quash the program, he continued, does not "manifest a governmental hostility to religion or religious teachings." He argued that "the First Amendment rests upon the premise that both religion and government can best work to achieve their lofty aims if each is left free from the other within its respective sphere." Then, returning to the new precedent, he concluded, "Or, as we said in the Everson case, the First Amendment has erected a wall between Church and State which must be kept high and impregnable."[16]

Many protestants criticized the court's new interpretation of the establishment clause. They correctly recognized that through its recent decisions, the court aimed for genuine religious neutrality, which threatened to chip away at protestants' long-held advantages over minority sects and religions. A group of liberal churchmen including Reinhold Niebuhr and Harry Fosdick published a statement condemning the high-wall metaphor. "This hardening of the idea of 'separation' by the Court will greatly accelerate the trend toward the secularization of our culture," they wrote. "We contend that Jefferson's oft quoted words, 'wall of separation,' which are not in the Constitution but which are used by the Court in the interpretation of the Constitution, are a misleading metaphor."[17]

The courts, perhaps more than the Constitution itself, had erected a high and impregnable wall of separation. Protestant leaders suddenly found themselves on the wrong side of that wall. While the Cold War emphasis on battling godless atheism seemed to encourage Christian nationalism, beneath the surface leaders of the judicial branch encouraged Americans to compartmentalize faith and to move in more secular and pluralistic directions. Christian activists learned an important lesson: They could no longer count on the courts to bolster their power.

A handful of celebrity ministers helped drive religion's revitalization in the 1950s. Catholic and protestant, liberationist and revivalist, they aimed to direct Cold War Christian fervor using radio, print, and the new medium of television. They offered an anti-communist gospel of self-help that reinforced capitalism, individualism, and the ability of all people to succeed, which brought comfort to the millions of Americans purchasing record numbers of new suburban houses, cars, boats, televisions, barbeques, and pink flamingo lawn ornaments.

Norman Vincent Peale served as the pastor of Fifth Avenue's Marble Collegiate Church in Manhattan. Peale preached an upbeat faith that used cheery stories and anecdotes to counter Americans' anxieties over nuclear Armageddon. Fred and Mary Trump, along with their son Donald, were among the members of his congregation. In addition to his pastoral work, Peale launched *Guideposts*, a kind of *Reader's Digest* of religion, and he helped found a faith-infused therapy clinic.

Peale gained national fame through his 1952 bestseller *The Power of Positive Thinking* (one of the forty-six books he wrote). In this book, Peale offered a unique blend of traditional Christian concepts, ideas from psychology, and elements of New Thought positive thinking. He encouraged readers to discover self-confidence and pursue worldly goals. Laying out his aims on the first page, Peale bluntly told readers that he wrote the book to help them understand that "you do not need to be defeated by anything, that you can have peace of mind, improved health, and a never-ceasing flow of energy. In short, that your life can be full of joy and satisfaction." In other words, the Christianity he pitched to the masses promised his upwardly mobile Manhattan congregation middle-class bliss.

Peale proposed "a system of simple procedures" to improve his readers' lives. Anyone who followed the minister's plan would become more "popular, esteemed, and well-liked." Readers, he advised, should "picturize, prayerize, and actualize" their dreams and goals. This was "a curious formula," he admitted, "but I have practiced it and personally know that it works. I have suggested it to many people who also found real value in its use. It is recommended to you." Millions of Americans read the book, seeking the fulfillment that the minister guaranteed.[18]

The Catholics also had a 1950s celebrity superstar, New York Bishop Fulton Sheen. A brilliant scholar and theologian from Peoria, Illinois, Sheen held multiple advanced degrees from major European universities. During the 1920s and 1930s, his influence within the American Catholic Church grew as did his skill at using radio and print media to bridge the gap between Catholic theology and American life. After World War II, he joined the crusade against communism. In 1950, church leaders appointed him national director of the Society for the Propagation of the Faith, making him one of the church's top evangelists.

Like Peale, Sheen sensed Americans' anxieties and offered them solace through the written word. He published *Peace of Soul* in 1949, in which he called on "the modern man" to return "to God and happiness."[19]

Happiness.

It's hard to imagine Junípero Serra or the early Jesuit missionaries preaching happiness, but the times had changed. Like every other successful American religious leader, Sheen tailored the faith to meet the needs and expectations of his era and audience. To reach middle-class White Americans, a cheery saccharine gospel seemed essential. Sheen emphasized Americans' debilitating bondage to anxiety, fear, and depression, and he offered the Catholic faith as an alternative. While he grounded his ideas in traditional church teaching, he understood that Americans wanted, needed, affirmation.

In 1951, Sheen launched a television show, *Life Is Worth Living*, which earned him an Emmy. By the end of the 1950s, 87 percent of Americans had televisions in their homes and religious leaders like Sheen knew they had to compete with popular entertainments to grab Americans' attention. As Sheen's fame grew, the editors of *Time* magazine visited him at his television studio to assess his appeal. They called him "perhaps the most famous preacher in the US, certainly America's best-known Roman Catholic priest, and the newest star of US television." Sheen had mastered the message, blending anti-communism, pop psychology, and Catholicism, and he also mastered the most powerful new medium, the television. In an era in which Americans downplayed religious differences, millions of people of all faiths welcomed the priest into their living rooms.[20]

Those in the White revivalist stream also had their own religious celebrity, a charismatic Southerner named Billy Graham. Born in 1918 in North Carolina, Graham spent his early career working as an evangelist for a fundamentalist Christian youth ministry. In September of 1949, he organized a major evangelistic campaign in Los Angeles. Just two days before the first services, President Truman revealed to the world that the Soviet Union had conducted a successful test of an atomic bomb, which set the tone for the meetings.

On the revival's first night, the handsome, lanky thirty-one-year-old stepped up to the podium in a makeshift tabernacle erected on a vacant lot in Southern California. "I think that we are living at a time in world history when God is giving us a desperate choice, a choice of either revival or judgment," the preacher blustered in a Southern twang. "There is no other alternative! . . . God Almighty is going to bring judgment upon this city unless people repent and believe—unless God sends an old-fashioned, heaven-sent, Holy Ghost revival."[21]

Graham made combatting the "religion" of communism a top priority. "Throughout the entire world at this moment Christianity and communism are battling for the minds of men," he preached over the ABC radio network. "Communism is far more than just an economic and philosophical interpretation of life. Communism is a fanatical religion that has declared war upon the Christian God." Communism "carries with it all the indications of anti-Christ. Almost all ministers of the gospel and students of the Bible agree that it is master-minded by Satan himself who is counterfeiting Christianity."[22]

But he did not despair. Throughout Graham's career he reminded his listeners of God's promise to the Hebrews in 2 Chronicles 7:14: "If my people, which are called by my name, shall humble themselves, and pray, and seek my face, and turn from their wicked ways; then will I hear from heaven, and will forgive their sin, and will heal their land." Like most other revivalists, Graham did not see this verse as a promise just to ancient Israel. He also believed it applied to the modern United States. Judgment was coming, but it was never too late to repent and find redemption.

Like other new "evangelicals," Graham sought to influence culture, politics, and foreign policy with faith. He worked across denominational lines and often partnered with those in more liberal denominations, seeking to lure them into the revivalist stream. He helped found *Christianity Today* as an alternative to the liberal *Christian Century.* The magazine proved to be an ideal venue for promoting evangelicals' efforts to bring Christian revival to the United States, reminding the nation of its supposed Christian foundations, and promoting a political conservatism that exalted individual faith, free markets, and anti-statism.

The publishers located the *Christianity Today* offices in Washington, DC, to make the magazine "a symbol of the place of the evangelical witness in the life of the republic." In a letter to the board of directors, the magazine's editor, Carl Henry, made the periodical's conservative political presuppositions explicit: "The magazine is committed to neither party, but it is committed to specific principles." He identified those principles as limited government, the free enterprise system, and church-state separation (meaning keeping Catholics from gaining any advantages). He routinely criticized the welfare state, arguing that it had assumed the role that churches should fulfill. Among Christian groups, liberals continued to have the most economic and political power. But revivalists, motivated by the conviction that time was short, had started catching up.[23]

Men like Peale, Sheen, Graham, and their many imitators, in focusing on congregants' depression and anxiety, addressed problems mostly affecting the White middle class. Many Black preachers prioritized other issues. In 1954, the leaders of the Dexter Avenue Baptist Church in Montgomery, Alabama, called Martin Luther King Jr., a PhD student in his mid-twenties, to serve as their pastor. Not long after King moved to Montgomery, National Association for the Advancement of Colored People (NAACP) activist Rosa Parks refused to give up her seat for a White rider on a local bus. The police arrested her. The local NAACP office quickly mobilized, launching a boycott of the city's public transportation. Protest organizers invited King to serve as leader of what they knew was a huge undertaking.

King explained the purpose of the protest at a mass meeting, declaring, "We are determined here in Montgomery to work and fight until justice runs down like water, and righteousness like a mighty stream." He called on the oppressed to reach for "the daybreak of freedom and justice and equality," urging them to "be Christian" in all their actions. Yet he reminded them, "It is not enough for us to talk about love," but they needed justice as well. "Justice is really love in calculation. Justice is love correcting that which revolts against love."[24]

Like other ministers of the era, King worried about the communist threat. But he had a different take on it compared to his White counterparts. In a sermon entitled "Communism's Challenge to Christianity," he agreed that Marxist ideas were incompatible with the Christian faith. But he also suggested that the global appeal of communism revealed weaknesses in White American Christianity. Communism "should challenge us," he preached, "to be more concerned about social justice." He pointed out that communists welcomed all to the party regardless of race or ethnicity. Christianity and not communism, he continued, should serve the poor and lead the way on racial integration, but too often in the United States this was not the reality.[25]

In building a ministry and a movement, King blended the liberationist and revivalist theology he learned from his minister father. He also drew on the social gospel and a neoorthodox understanding of evil. While academic theologians in urban seminaries of the 1950s might talk about original sin, King experienced it in the form of racial violence. He understood in very personal ways humans' capacity for depravity. Like generations of liberationists before him, he reminded his audiences that Americans needed a redeemer. A racist and segregationist nation was not a Christian nation.

As King confronted the nation's moral failings on race, White protestant leaders were also grappling with what they saw as another threat to their cultural dominance: the rising prominence of Catholics in American public life. The same year that the Supreme Court issued the *Everson* decision, a group of White protestant leaders established a new organization to renew the fight against this "foreign" faith. Rather than resurrect the old nativist tropes of the previous century, they adopted the language of the day. They simply aimed, they claimed, to defend the separation of church and state, not to promote intolerance and bigotry but to counter it. They called themselves "Protestants and Other Americans United for Separation of Church and State" (POAU).

The group included *The Christian Century*'s Charles Clayton Morrison, liberal Methodist bishop G. Bromley Oxnam, and leaders of both the Federal Council of Churches and the National Association of Evangelicals. Conservative, liberal, and revivalist groups did not unite on much, but their shared disdain for the Catholic Church brought them together. If state governments could help underwrite the transportation of children to parochial schools, what next? Subsidies or vouchers for the schools themselves? What would happen if a Catholic somehow landed in the White House? How might he further undermine the power of protestants?

Leaders of POAU outlined their beliefs in a manifesto. They claimed that Catholicism "holds and maintains a theory of the relation of church and state which is incompatible with the American ideal." Catholics, they argued, had taken advantage of Americans' religious tolerance to undermine the very constitutional foundations that had established that tolerance. They had used American freedom to try to destroy American freedom. It was time to curtail Catholics' influence.[26]

In the 1950s, POAU members kept a vigilant watch on the Catholic Church and what they feared was its growing sway over American political leaders. They voiced alarm over Truman's and later Eisenhower's Cold War outreach to the Vatican and staunchly opposed any move to appoint a US ambassador to the Holy See. When rumors spread in 1956 that the Democrats were considering Senator John F. Kennedy, a Catholic, for the vice-presidential ticket, POAU leaders mobilized quickly against his nomination.

Although the party passed over JFK, protestant leaders had correctly sensed that Kennedy had White House ambitions. In 1960, Kennedy decided to make his own run for the presidency. From the start of his campaign, Kennedy tried to dispel protestants' concerns about his religion. He addressed his faith multiple times, promised to support the separation of church and state, opposed funding for parochial schools, and even decried his predecessors' decisions to send official representatives to the Vatican. Some Catholic leaders worried that Kennedy might actually roll back some of the church's gains in an effort to appear neutral. Powerful leading protestants required as much.

The protestant press gave substantial space to the religion issue. Most writers praised Kennedy's specific positions on church-state separation—he took a more absolutist position than most protestants—but they traded in the same old stereotypes about all Catholic politicians being under the thumb of a foreign prelate, and they continued to insist on the incompatibility of Catholic theology with American democracy. They also fretted that Catholic voters would blindly support JFK based solely on his religion, or even that church leaders might coerce them into voting Democratic.

As Kennedy gained ground in the campaign against Republican nominee and vice president Richard Nixon, a group of about twenty-five American protestant leaders secretly conspired against him. In August 1960, evangelist Billy Graham organized a clandestine meeting in Montreux, Switzerland, where he was conducting a European religious crusade. The meeting included the leader of the National Association of Evangelicals, the leader of Protestants and Other Americans United, minister Harold Ockenga, *Christianity Today* editor Carl Henry, and Norman Vincent Peale. What exactly they discussed is not clear. No one seems to have kept notes at the meeting, and participants proved reluctant to discuss it. In his autobiography, Graham claimed that the meeting focused on evangelicalism and not the presidential campaign. But shortly after the meeting Peale sent Nixon a letter indicating that Graham had called them together to strategize about the election and its "religious issue."

Building on the momentum from the Montreux meeting, many of the same activists, along with about 150 clergymen from 37 denominations, gathered that September in Washington, DC, for another closed-door meeting focused on the election. Graham was vacationing at the time in Europe with his wife, which proved fortuitous for him.

The press crashed the gathering. As the meetings concluded, Peale met with journalists and read a public statement. "The key question" in the presidential election, the Manhattan minister determined, "is whether it is in the best interest of our society for any church organization to attempt to exercise control over its members in political and civic affairs." Although the Vatican had no role in the Kennedy campaign, the nation's top protestant ministers told Americans that papal prelates called the shots among Catholic voters.[27]

Protestant leaders' ham-fisted efforts on behalf of Nixon provoked widespread condemnation. Catholics who may have otherwise voted for Nixon felt the attacks against the senator for his faith represented attacks against them. Many other Americans, shocked by the actions of church officials, did not want to be perceived as religious bigots, which in turn made them more open to a Kennedy presidency.

As the religion issue reached a crescendo, Kennedy addressed it in a major speech in the heart of the Bible Belt. "I believe in an America where the separation of church and state is absolute," he told a Texas minister's association, "where no Catholic prelate would tell the President (should he be Catholic) how to act, and no Protestant minister would tell his parishioners for whom to vote—where no church or church school is granted any public funds or political preference—and where no man is denied public office merely because his religion differs from the President who might appoint him or the people who might elect him." He assured the nation, "I am not the Catholic candidate for President. I am the Democratic Party's candidate for President who happens also to be a Catholic." He vowed to resign if an irresolvable conflict between his faith and the presidency ever arose. For Kennedy, religion was a private matter that the leaders of a diverse nation should—must—compartmentalize and separate from their public life. Those with deep, immoveable religious convictions need not apply for the position of president. In the end, Kennedy won the election by a minuscule one hundred thousand votes out of sixty-eight million cast. It was the closest election since 1884.[28]

As Kennedy settled into office, the courts continued revisiting the relationship between church and state. In 1962 the Supreme Court heard a case challenging the New York legislature's recommendation that public-school students recite the following prayer: "Almighty God, we acknowledge our dependence upon Thee, and we beg Thy blessings upon us, our parents, our teachers and our Country." In *Engel v. Vitale*, Justice Hugo Black struck down the government-composed prayer. The establishment clause, he argued, required that "in this country, it is no part of the business of government to compose official prayers for any group of the American people to recite as a part of a religious program carried on by government." Anticipating backlash and charges of hostility toward religion, Black insisted that the court was not promoting rigid secularism but was instead safeguarding genuine, uncoerced faith.[29]

Black's decision triggered substantial grousing. Conservatives, revivalists, and liberals alike sensed that the *Engel* decision threatened their power and supremacy in public education. Kennedy encouraged Americans to heed the court and then added that the decision provided "a welcome reminder to every American family that we can pray a good deal more at home, we can attend our churches with a good deal more fidelity, and we can make the true meaning of prayer much more important in the lives of all of our children."[30]

The court had another religious knot to untie the following year in *Abington School District v. Schempp* (1963). The state of Pennsylvania required schoolchildren to participate in daily Bible reading. "At least ten verses from the Holy Bible shall be read," the law mandated, "without comment, at the opening of each public school on each school day." Once again, the court opted for strict separation. Justice Tom Clark wrote for the majority, dismantling the practice of official Bible reading in public schools. "The place of religion in our society is an exalted one," he insisted, which grew out of the home, the church, and "the inviolable citadel of the individual heart and mind." The government, he continued, should not "invade that citadel, whether its purpose or effect be to aid or oppose, to advance or retard. In the relationship between man and religion, the State is firmly committed to a position of neutrality."

Justice William Brennan added a long concurrence that pussyfooted around the many ways that the United States government was anything but neutral on religion. He did not want this decision to threaten every public practice of Christianity. Activities that may have begun as explicitly religious acts, he argued, did not violate the

First Amendment if they had "ceased to have religious meaning." In other words, government officials could use religious words, symbols, and practices in public as long as they didn't really take them too seriously. "The reference to divinity in the revised pledge of allegiance, for example," Brennan opined, "may merely recognize the historical fact that our Nation was believed to have been founded 'under God.' Thus, reciting the pledge may be no more of a religious exercise than the reading aloud of Lincoln's Gettysburg Address, which contains an allusion to the same historical fact." Sometimes a prayer was not a prayer, and the Bible was just a book.[31]

Many protestant leaders, frustrated by the new limits the court set on public expressions of religion, discovered in the men in black robes a new enemy. For generations they had fretted about the power of the presidency and nefarious papist plots from abroad, all the while failing to see a revolution coming in the judiciary. While some made their peace with the argument that the First Amendment established a high wall of separation between church and state, others shifted from primarily criticizing the power of the executive branch to griping about the actions of judges. They attributed to the courts the erosion of traditional American freedoms. Eventually, savvy political operatives channeled the anger of protestant activists against the courts into partisan politics.

During the Cold War attendance at religious services skyrocketed, enrollments at seminaries surged, and construction of new houses of worship boomed. The religious depression, like the economic depression, was over. Polling data from the period showed that the percentage of Americans who claimed church affiliation reached an all-time high in 1960 of 69 percent. The growth occurred across the four streams (and among non-Christian religions as well). Nevertheless, it did not occur uniformly among protestants. Revivalist churches grew exponentially faster in the two decades after the war than those in the liberal stream.

Some worried, however, about what they saw as the shallowness of Americans' renewed faith. Niebuhr acknowledged that the nation had undergone a revival of religion affecting Catholics, protestants, and Jews. But what leaders revived, he complained, were not the historic faiths but vapid, self-help therapeutics. "The themes of 'peace of mind' and 'positive thinking,'" he wrote, "either express a religion of self-assurance or they are pious guides to personal success. They cannot be taken seriously by responsible religious or secular people because they do not come to terms with the basic collective problems of our atomic age, and because the peace which they seek to inculcate is rather too simple and neat." The religion of the 1950s, the theologian argued, was fleeting. It drove people away from deep reflection on core theological issues, and fostered indifference toward the social and communal aspects of faith.[32]

Self-trained sociologist Will Herberg, in his now-classic book *Protestant-Catholic-Jew*, tried in 1955 to explain the change in American religious life. After noting that the nation had evolved from a protestant-dominated culture to one that made some room for Catholics and Jews, he shifted to criticizing the nature of postwar faith. "Religion has become part of the ethos of American life to such a degree that overt anti-religion is all but inconceivable," he wrote. "Yet it is only too evident that the religiousness characteristic of America today is very often a religiousness without religion, a religiousness with almost any kind of content or none, a way of sociability or 'belonging' rather than a way of reorienting life to God." Like his friend Niebuhr, he worried that "it is thus frequently a religiousness without serious commitment, without real inner conviction, without genuine existential decision." Americans in this era, he concluded, had rejected the "radical demand of faith."[33]

And yet the books focused on finding personal peace by Graham, Peale, Sheen, and others, including Rabbi Joshua Loth Liebman, had become bestsellers for a reason. The detonation of atomic bombs, the onset of a nuclear arms race, and the growing realization of the horrors of the Holocaust compelled Americans to wrestle anew with the problem of sin and evil and to seek therapeutic solutions. For some, the popular and widely prescribed antianxiety sedative Miltown brought comfort. Others turned to two-martini lunches and copies of the glossy new magazine *Playboy*. Others still renewed trust in God, American exceptionalism, and faith in faith. But as much as Americans longed for peace, peace was not what they would find in the 1960s.

26

STILL SEEKING LIBERATION

Minister Albert Cleage Jr. had agitated for equal rights for Black Americans for decades. In the 1950s he founded a new Congregationalist church in Detroit, where he blended faith with activism and community organizing. The congregation met in a building that a previous congregation had constructed in the 1930s. As the civil rights movement expanded, Cleage commissioned an artist to cover over a stained-glass window at the center of the church. It depicted White Pilgrims landing at Plymouth Rock. In its place the minister hung a huge painting of a Black Madonna holding a Black Christ child. He dedicated the painting on Easter Sunday 1967. "Now we have come to the place," he preached, "where we not only can conceive of the possibility, but we are convinced, upon the basis of our knowledge and historic study of all the facts that Jesus was born to a black Mary, that Jesus, the Messiah, was a black man who came to save a Black Nation." He renamed the church the Shrine of the Black Madonna.[1]

Just a few months later, the city exploded in violence. That summer police raided a predominately Black nightclub. For decades police had been hassling Detroit's Black residents, and shortly after the police left, people on the street began breaking nearby windows and rioting, which led to a full-scale rebellion. By the end of five days of unrest, forty-three people lay dead.

Amid the chaos, activists took paintbrushes to a white statue of Jesus located at the Catholic Sacred Heart Seminary. They colored all of the savior's visible skin—his face, hands, and feet—black. Their Jesus looked very different than the most ubiquitous image of Jesus in the United States at the time, Warner Sallman's lily-white, Anglo-looking *Head of Christ* (1941). Sallman's painting had no relation to what the historical Jesus may have looked like, yet millions of Americans decorated their homes with it. Once Americans encountered a Black Madonna and a Black Jesus, the racial overtones of worshipping a Jesus who looked like *Head of Christ* became impossible to ignore. How people depicted Christ in the 1960s and 1970s reflected how they consciously and sometimes subconsciously understood the relationship between race and religion.

Cleage believed that the violence that engulfed Detroit in 1967 demonstrated the need for a total transformation of religion and society, and a new theology to match. "We reject the traditional concept of church," he wrote. "In its place we will build a Black Liberation movement which derives its basic religious insights from African spirituality, its character from African communalism, and its revolutionary direction from Jesus, the Black Messiah." He pledged to "make Black Christian Nationalism the cornerstone of the Black man's struggle for power and survival."[2]

In the decades after World War II, the movement for civil rights gained momentum. Black activists had different approaches and different tactics, but in their struggles, many drew on reconceptualized versions of liberated Christianity. They envisioned building a kingdom of God in North America free of violence and bigotry—a Black Christian nationalism. Their success inspired other groups to fight for civil rights as well, and together they tried to push churches across all four streams to make justice central to their mission.

As the civil rights movement expanded, minister Albert Cleage Jr. pushed Americans to rethink the relationship between race and Christianity. He commissioned an artist to paint a Black Madonna holding a Black Christ child, shown here with the church's caretaker, to challenge popular perceptions of Christianity. (credit: Graham Bezant, *Toronto Star*, Getty)

In 1936, Morehouse graduate and Baptist theologian Howard Thurman traveled to South Asia where he met anti-colonial Indian activist Mohandas Gandhi. The two men discussed the principles of Jesus, how Americans practiced Christianity, and the race problem in the United States. During the trip, one Indian asked Thurman if defending Christianity made him a traitor to his race. The question stung. Thurman returned home dedicated to helping Black Americans build a Christian theology of nonviolent resistance. "Why is it," he asked, "that Christianity seems impotent to deal radically, and therefore effectively, with the issues of discrimination and injustice on the basis of race, religion and national origin?" To answer this question he offered a new kind of liberationist Christianity that integrated philosophy, the ethical teachings of multiple religions, and the ideas and experiences of Gandhi.[3]

Thurman's work inspired the next generation of activists including Martin Luther King Jr. The young civil rights leader, like Thurman, saw both Jesus and Gandhi as models to emulate. But putting the philosophy of nonviolence into practice, King well knew, could be difficult.

During the Montgomery bus boycott, King received ominous warnings and threatening messages against his family, causing his faith to waiver. After one particularly menacing phone call, King recalled bowing his head over the kitchen table and praying aloud. "I am here," he told God, "taking a stand for what I believe is right. But now I am afraid." Ready to give up, he felt God in a new way. "At that moment I experienced the presence of the Divine as I had never experienced Him before." " 'Stand up,' " God told him, "'for righteousness, stand up for truth; and God will be at your side forever.' Almost at once," he realized, "my fears began to go. My uncertainty disappeared. I was ready to face anything. The outer situation remained the same, but God had given me the inner calm to face it." This encounter gave King the confidence to fight on.[4]

Building on the success of the Montgomery bus boycott, King, his allies in the Southern Christian Leadership Conference (SCLC), and other civil rights activists enlarged their efforts. The Supreme Court had sided with the NAACP in overturning the principle of separate but equal in *Brown v. Board of Education*, but Whites refused to integrate without a fight. Activists marched, protested, launched sit-ins, and organized freedom rides to secure the equal rights that the Constitution promised.

In the spring of 1963, King chose Birmingham, Alabama, one of the largest segregated cities in the nation, for a civil rights campaign. The police were ready. Officers responded to peaceful marches by arresting hundreds of adult activists and even the children and teens who had skipped school to participate. Then, when the protests did not stop, police sicced German shepherds on marchers and used the fire department's high-pressure water hoses to pummel them with dangerous force. Media crews captured the events, and Americans saw on television horrific images of White officers brutally attacking peaceful protesters. This shocked many Americans, and it played poorly for the United States abroad. While the Kennedy administration fought for the support and loyalty of the developing world at the height of the

Cold War, massive resistance to integration made American ideals of justice and liberty look like a sham.

During the protests, authorities arrested King. While incarcerated, he saw a letter from local religious leaders published in *The Birmingham News* that criticized the demonstrations as unwise, untimely, and lacking common sense. King drafted a response from his cell that illustrated his evolving convictions. The letter combined his own ideas, the theologies of liberationists, and the practical, Christian realism of neoorthodox thinkers including Reinhold Niebuhr.

King began by aligning himself with the biblical prophets. "I am in Birmingham because injustice is here," he wrote. He then challenged his critics, arguing that the greatest obstacle to Black freedom was not extremist groups like the White Citizens' Councils or the Ku Klux Klan, but the White moderate, more committed to "order" than to justice and preferring a "negative peace" marked by the absence of tension over a "positive peace" defined by the presence of justice. American Christians and especially White Christians had let the minister down. They stood "on the sideline" merely offering "pious irrelevancies and sanctimonious trivialities." In the midst of a fierce struggle against racial and economic injustice, he had heard countless ministers dismiss these as mere "social issues" unrelated to the gospel, while churches retreated into an otherworldly faith that drew a sharp and, to King, false line between body and soul, the sacred and the secular.

King did not believe they would escape punishment for their complicity. "The judgment of God is upon the church as never before," he warned. "If the church of today does not recapture the sacrificial spirit of the early church, it will lose its authentic ring, forfeit the loyalty of millions, and be dismissed as an irrelevant social club with no meaning for the twentieth century." King understood that churches remained central to the rights movement and simultaneously represented the greatest obstacles that organizers faced.[5]

A few months later, King told Americans at the March on Washington for Jobs and Freedom that he had a dream that one day "this nation will rise up and live out the true meaning of its creed: We hold these truths to be self-evident, that all men are created equal."

But back in Birmingham, the violence continued. Just a few months after the marches, Klansmen placed more than a dozen sticks of dynamite in a stairwell behind the 16th Street Baptist Church, an epicenter of the protests. In the previous couple of years terrorists had bombed multiple Birmingham churches. Black houses of worship often served as prime targets for those seeking to threaten activists. This bomb killed four young girls, Addie Mae Collins, Denise McNair, Carole Robertson, and Cynthia Wesley. It also blew Jesus's face out of a stained glass window that depicted the Savior as a shepherd caring for his flock. In that instant Jesus's whiteness shattered. God had seemingly punished White Jesus for standing by as Black children gave their lives for the cause of equality.

Responding to the tragedy, organizer Anne Moody asked God to explain himself, to come down from heaven and talk to her. His silence

A bomb killed four girls and blasted the face of Jesus from a stained glass window that showed him as shepherd to his flock. In that moment, Jesus's whiteness cracked. It was as if God struck down White Jesus for watching silently while Black youth gave their lives for equality. (credit: Birmingham Public Library Archives, Birmingham, Alabama)

made her indignant. "You know something else, God?" she declared. "Nonviolence is out." It had served its purpose, but no more. "If you don't believe that, then I know you must be white, too. And if I ever find out you are white, then I'm through with you. And if I find out you are black, I'll try my best to kill you when I get to heaven." Over the course of the 1960s, more and more activists, especially younger ones, wondered if they could worship a God who let such horrors continue.[6]

While Martin Luther King Jr. is the singular civil rights movement icon carved in granite on the National Mall, thousands of everyday activists like Moody, many of them young, had provided much of the momentum for change. In 1942 a group of students affiliated with the University of Chicago's modernist Divinity School founded the Congress of Racial Equality (CORE) to focus on challenging racism and segregation. They worked in the 1950s with King and the Southern Christian Leadership Conference.

In the spring of 1960, a new group of young activists organized by the SCLC's Ella Baker formed the Student Nonviolent Coordinating Committee (SNCC). Drawing on the nonviolence they saw embedded in the "Judeo-Christian" tradition, they worked to create "a social order of justice permeated by love." SNCC and CORE activists often joined forces in the early 1960s, organizing direct confrontations, mass protests, and civil disobedience campaigns as they sought to highlight inequalities in the United States.[7]

SNCC activist Mary King put her group's ideology into its larger Christian context. Her fellow activists' "fortitude, determined action, and fearlessness" stemmed, she asserted, "to a great degree from the Protestant upbringings of most of its workers. Even if one were in rebellion against a church that provided insufficient witness or failed to challenge the status quo, still at work was the fundamental influence of the Christian tradition."[8]

Activist Fannie Lou Hamer saw in SNCC and other civil rights organizations an authentic version of Christianity that served as an alternative to the churchly variety. Churchgoers of all races, she believed, had failed to embody the true faith, forcing activists to look for it in extra-ecclesiastical contexts. "You know," she told an interviewer, the church "failed to do what the church should have done." Too many ministers, she believed, preached a social conservatism, especially regarding race issues. They were too comfortable and too complacent. For this reason, Hamer more often saw Jesus represented in the activists working outside of religious institutions rather than within church doors. "It's young people today," she concluded, "that really is the Christian church instead of all these big fine buildings that's so-called churches." She believed that the nation's indifference to civil rights guaranteed that "one day America will crumble. Because God is not pleased. God is not pleased at all the murdering, and all of the brutality, and all the killings for no reason at all." Like so many Black activists before her, she viewed the United States as a hellish carnival of evil that fell far short of what God expected from those claiming to be his chosen people.[9]

While civil rights activists most often partnered with churches rooted in the liberationist tradition, some also hoped to win over White revivalist-stream Christians. Black evangelist Tom Skinner, drawing on American history and Black Power principles, offered a sharp critique of racism within White revivalism. In a sermon to a largely White Christian college audience, Skinner condemned revivalists who preached that Jesus was the answer to Black Americans' problems while never daring to set foot in a Black neighborhood. In contrast, he praised the work of Black nationalists, whom he called witnesses for God. "It was not the evangelical who came and taught us our worth and dignity as black men," he reminded his listeners. "It was not the Bible-believing fundamentalist who stood up and told us that black was beautiful. It was not the evangelical who preached to us that we should stand on our two feet and be men, be proud that black was beautiful and that God could work his life out through our redeemed blackness. Rather, it took Malcolm X, Stokely Carmichael, Rap Brown and the Brothers to declare to us our dignity."

Moving to perhaps the most controversial part of the sermon, Skinner slammed Christian nationalism. "As a black Christian I have to renounce Americanism. I have to renounce any attempt to wed Jesus Christ off to the American system," he preached. "I disassociate myself from any argument that says a vote for America is a vote for God. I disassociate myself from any argument that says God is on our side. I disassociate myself from any argument, which says that God sends troops to Asia, that God is a capitalist, that God is a militarist, that God is the worker behind our system." He ended the sermon declaring, "The liberator has come." A testament to Skinner's unique influence, Jesse Jackson, Maya Angelou, Betty Shabazz (Malcolm X's widow), and Louis Farrakhan, along with many prominent revivalists, attended his funeral in 1994.[10]

Despite the efforts of Skinner and a small handful of others like him, White revivalists proved nearly immoveable on issues of race. In fact, some of the nation's most prominent evangelists and ministers opposed much of the civil rights movement. Billy Graham was the epitome of the Southern White "moderate" minister who so disappointed King. Early in his career, Graham seemed like a promising partner for activists. Despite facing substantial blowback from other Southern Whites, he famously integrated his crusades and brought Black ministers onto his staff. For Graham the move was both theologically correct and good politics in the Cold War context. "After traveling all over the world," he wrote, "I am convinced that one of the greatest black eyes to American prestige abroad is our racial problem in this country." In the late 1950s, as King's star ascended, Graham befriended King. The Black minister even gave an invocation at Graham's 1957 Manhattan crusade, one of the most important in the White evangelist's career. But over time Graham cooled to the movement, concluding that activists had pushed too hard. In 1963, within days of the publication of King's "Letter from a Birmingham Jail," Graham told reporters that King and his allies should "put the brakes on a little bit."[11]

The following year, President Lyndon Johnson signed the Civil Rights Act of 1964 into law, with King and other activists by his side. The law outlawed discrimination in commercial establishments on the basis of race, color, religion, national origin, and sex, required equal access for all individuals to public places and to employment, further enforced desegregation of schools, and bolstered voting rights.

The category of "sex" was added to the bill at the last minute. It provided a new legal foundation from which women could challenge discrimination.

Many prominent White revivalists criticized the bill. Jerry Falwell, a young and ambitious preacher from Lynchburg, Virginia, defended the South's autonomy on race issues. When Johnson asked clergy across the nation to support the legislation, Falwell, like many other White ministers, refused. "It is a terrible violation of human and private property rights," Falwell claimed. "It should be considered civil wrongs rather than civil rights." The next year Falwell preached one of the most famous (or infamous) sermons of his career in response to King's march in Selma, Alabama. He began by telling the men and women at his Thomas Road Baptist Church that their citizenship resided in heaven, not on earth. "Preachers," he declared, "are not called to be politicians but to be soul winners. . . . If as much effort could be put into winning people to Jesus Christ across the land as is being exerted in the present civil rights movement, America would be turned upside down for God." He called King a communist and claimed that the civil rights movement did far more harm than good. Meanwhile, conservative Presbyterian Carl McIntire wrote Johnson claiming that the Civil Rights Act contradicted "the clear and unmistakable teaching of the Bible." Johnson's expansion of federal power and advocacy of civil rights intensified evangelicals' growing distrust of the Democratic Party.[12]

While leaders like Thurman, King, and Hamer found redemption in Christianity, other activists saw Christianity as part of the problem and not the solution. Malcolm X helped lead a small, controversial American religious group called the Nation of Islam (NOI). He delivered a scathing critique of both Christianity and the Black believers who embraced it. "Brothers and sisters," he thundered, "the white man has brainwashed us black people to fasten our gaze upon a blond-haired, blue-eyed Jesus! We're worshiping a Jesus that doesn't even look like us! . . . The white man has taught us to shout and sing and pray until we die, to wait for some dreamy heaven-in-the-hereafter, when we're dead, while this white man has his milk and honey in the streets paved with golden dollars right here on this earth!" Convincing people to worship a White Jesus, Malcolm taught, was one of Satan's greatest tricks.[13]

Although most Christian activists kept their distance from the Nation, a new generation of liberationists embraced Malcolm's critique of White Christianity. They crafted a Christian theology of Black power and Black nationalism. They believed Black Americans could reject the White Christ without rejecting the true Jesus. Harking back to the days of Henry McNeal Turner who had espoused in 1896 that God is a "Negro," they reconstructed the faith to empower the civil rights movement.

A couple of years after Cleage unveiled his Black Madonna, theologian James Cone published *Black Theology & Black Power*. He identified the "desperate need for a black theology, a theology whose sole purpose is to apply the freeing power of the gospel to black people under white oppression." He hoped to answer that need. "Black Power," he summarized, "even in its most radical expression, is not the antithesis of Christianity, nor is it a heretical idea to be tolerated with painful forbearance. It is, rather, Christ's central message to twentieth-century America."[14]

Cone called the White church the contemporary manifestation of the Antichrist. For White Christians to find true salvation, he argued, they must give up not just their privilege, but also their neutrality. To join Christ, they must join the oppressed, they must be oppressed themselves. Nor did Black ministers escape Cone's jeremiads. Too often Black leaders encouraged their flocks to endure subjugation in this world in exchange for freedom in the next. He viewed this as sin. "Except in rare instances," he concluded, "the black churches in the post-Civil War period have been no more Christian than their white counterparts."[15]

In developing a Black theology of liberation, Cone, like Cleage and Malcolm, emphasized the problem of Jesus's perceived Whiteness. "The 'raceless' American Christ has a light skin, wavy brown hair, and sometimes—wonder of wonders—blue eyes," he wrote. For Whites to find Jesus "with big lips and kinky hair is as offensive as it was for the

Pharisees to find him partying with tax-collectors. But whether whites want to hear it or not, Christ is black, baby, with all of the features which are so detestable to white society." Cone explained that to be faithful to the Bible, Jesus's "present manifestation must be the very essence of blackness." He maintained that "Christ is black because he is oppressed, and oppressed because he is black. And if the Church is to join Christ by following his opening, it too must go where suffering is and become black also."[16]

Cone and Cleage sought to reframe Christianity as an effective tool for championing rights. They knew that as violence escalated and activists like Medgar Evers and Martin Luther King fell to the bullets of White assassins, many people lost faith. They wanted to provide them with a new version of Christianity, a liberated Christianity, a Christianity for the disinherited.

Many of the nation's Latine civil rights organizers also worshipped a Jesus of the disinherited. Yet the battle for racial equality took different forms among the nation's Latine population. For generations Black protestants had their own independent churches that served as staging grounds for civil rights activism, while the vast majority of Latine Christians often worshipped under White Catholic leaders. Nevertheless, they understood the importance of their faith to the civil rights struggle and the role that their churches could play in it. They hoped and believed that the recovery of the authentic gospel would inspire church leaders to join them in their work.

Mexican American labor organizer César Chávez blended Catholicism with his determination to expand the rights of immigrants. The child of migrant farmworkers, Chávez spent his youth bouncing from school to school—he attended over forty schools in eight years—as his parents followed the harvest in search of work. In the 1960s, Chávez began organizing field-workers, seeking to secure for them better pay and treatment. To bring people together he drew on the tactics of the Black civil rights movement as well as on his own Catholic faith. He studied the papal encyclicals that had previously inspired Dorothy Day and others to link Catholicism with social reform in the United States. He partnered with sympathetic priests and reached out to other marginalized groups, including Catholic Filipinos, as he sought to erect a broad labor coalition.

Another Catholic, Dolores Huerta, also worked to unionize Mexicans and Mexican Americans. She ran voter registration drives and sought to improve working-class neighborhoods. In 1959, she organized Latine, Filipino, Black, and White workers into the Agricultural Workers Organizing Committee, and then she joined forces with Chávez to launch the United Farm Workers (UFW). Huerta and Chávez ensured that their organization focused on more than just labor. UFW leaders helped farmworkers and others establish financial credit, get insurance, and ensure that their children received proper educations, among many other things.

In their fight for justice, many Latine activists drew on Catholic faith and symbolism. They made religious iconography such as depictions of Our Lady of Guadalupe, the "patroness of the Americas," central to their public presentations to demonstrate God's role in their cause. Chávez routinely incorporated spiritual fasts into his protests, as well as communion. At the end of one twenty-five-day fast, Senator Robert Kennedy knelt with Chávez and they received the sacrament together, along with eight thousand activist workers.[17]

Chávez likened his protest marches to holy pilgrimages. "In every religious oriented culture 'the pilgrimage' has had a place," he taught, "a trip made with sacrifice and hardship as an expression of penance and of commitment—and often involving a petition to the patron of the pilgrimage for some sincerely sought benefit of body or soul." Such pilgrimages remained central to Mexican culture. Sometimes the pilgrimages marked a celebration, and other times repentance. In some instances, Chávez said, "the penitents would march through the streets, often in sack cloth and ashes, some even carrying crosses, as a sign of penance for their sins, and as a plea for the mercy of God." He followed their model. He wanted marchers to focus on "their own personal sins as well as their yielding perhaps to feelings of hatred and revenge in the strike itself." He believed that in marching, strikers would "set themselves at peace with the Lord, so that the justice of their cause will be purified of all lesser motivation."[18]

Chávez believed that churches in general, and the Roman Catholic Church in particular, occupied an important position in the struggle. But before Christian leaders could truly help, they needed to understand their role. "What do we want the Church to do?" he queried. "We don't ask for more cathedrals. We don't ask for bigger churches of fine gifts. We ask for its presence with us, beside us, as Christ among us. We ask the Church to sacrifice with the people for social change, for justice, and for love of brother. We don't ask for words. We ask for deeds. We don't ask for paternalism. We ask for servanthood." Chávez envisioned a different kind of Christianity, one grounded in people's material, lived existence rather than one focused on spectacle and symbolism.[19]

Chávez wanted Christians from every tradition and stream working in solidarity with him. As a member of a religious minority, he knew that he needed cross-denominational alliances. "When we refer to the Church we should define the word a little," he told his allies. "We mean the whole Church, the Church as an ecumenical body spread around the world, and not just its particular form in a parish in a local community." He hoped to get protestant churches on board with the farmworkers' movement. Yet Catholic imagery and symbolism became so prominent in Chávez's efforts that one ally of the organizer had to march separately from the main group. Abby Flores Rivera told an interviewer that her Baptist father fully backed the movement but refused to let his daughter rally behind a banner depicting Our Lady of Guadalupe. Instead, she found other ways to support the protests.[20]

Inspired by Chávez, King, and others, younger activists sought to compel church leaders to pay more attention to racism within Catholicism. In 1969 Ricardo Cruz organized Catholic students in Southern California into the group Católicos por La Raza. They focused on spurring the church to engage more deeply with social reform and civil rights efforts, and they criticized investment in ostentatious new buildings rather than in helping the poor. That same year a group of Latino priests formed Padres Asociados para Derechos Religiosos, Educativos, y Sociales (PADRES). For hundreds of years Latines in the West and Southwest had worshipped under the direction of White priests. These men of the cloth sought to end discrimination in the Catholic hierarchy and to push the church to diversify its leadership.

Meanwhile, during the 1960s, more radical forms of Catholicism developed in parts of Latin America. In 1971 the Peruvian theologian Gustavo Gutiérrez published *A Theology of Liberation*, an important book that blended Marxism and Catholic theology. An American Catholic press translated the book into English in 1973, and it circulated among Catholic radicals. "My purpose," Gutiérrez began, is "to let ourselves be judged by the word of the Lord, to think through our faith, to strengthen our love, and to give reason for our hope from within a commitment that seeks to become more radical, total, and efficacious." This, he said, "is the goal of the so-called theology of liberation." As Gutiérrez's influence grew, some in the United States embraced his ideas. They espoused a reconceptualized Christianity that, in seeking to follow in the footsteps of Jesus by serving the poor and oppressed, adopted Marxist critiques of North American capitalism.[21]

Indigenous peoples continued to face overwhelming challenges as well. Widespread poverty, underfunded schools, and insufficient medical care characterized life on reservations. In 1968, a group of Indigenous men and women formed the American Indian Movement. Its members, who lived mostly in urban areas, sought to build a pan-Indigenous political movement to support tribal communities. They established networks across community centers, churches, and various social organizations.

Writing in the heyday of the American Indian Movement, Standing Rock Sioux scholar Vine Deloria saw Christianity as mostly an enemy of civil rights to be vanquished rather than as a tool to be redirected. Instead of calling for justice within Christianity, and finding themes of liberation in the scriptures, he saw Christianity as a mark of oppression that perpetuated great harm on Indigenous lands and communities. "Who will find peace?" he asked. "Who will listen to the trees, the animals and birds, the voices of the places of the land?" he continued. "As the long-forgotten peoples of the respective continents rise and begin to reclaim their ancient heritage, they will discover the meaning of the lands of their ancestors. That," he argued, "is when the invaders of the North American continent will finally discover that for this land, God is Red." Although many Indigenous Americans worshipped in Christian churches, Deloria pushed them to resurrect old practices and ideas. He believed that church leaders' efforts to merge Christianity with Indigenous beliefs would fail to bring the liberation and equality Indigenous communities needed.[22]

The work of King and Chávez, Hamer and PADRES, and Gutiérrez, Cone, and Deloria helped Christians understand how their institutions had contributed to the American racial nightmare. They also provided Americans with multiple paths toward redemption. They knew that in the first century, Jesus walked among those suffering under Roman domination. Jesus's people in the twentieth century, these theologians and activists insisted, were the dispossessed living under White domination. To truly understand the Christian gospel, then, one had to live it from within marginalized communities. White America, with its racism and materialism, misconstrued the true Christian faith. One Black revivalist summed it up: To be faithful, Christians needed to reject the "honky Jesus" and embrace the "funky Christ." As civil rights activists and their followers rediscovered Jesus, they achieved some of their goals but left much work still to do.[23]

In 1969 a group of civil rights activists led by James Forman interrupted services at Manhattan's Riverside Church—the church built by Rockefeller for Harry Fosdick, and still one of the most prominent, progressive protestant congregations in the nation. Forman walked up to the altar, turned, faced the crowd, and read a statement asking for reparations for Black Americans from the nation's churches and synagogues. The protest highlighted the divide between young liberationists and members of established liberal churches. Forman demanded that White liberal Christians not only support the civil rights movement but recognize their complicity in racism, that they see not just the sins of their fathers, but their own.

Most Americans preferred not to scrutinize their lives for sin. Instead, the turmoil of the era stirred in many ancient longings and apocalyptic fears, sparking a growing fascination with the end-times. As American Christians watched their nation not only grapple with civil rights but also then descend into a quagmire in Southeast Asia, they were once again forced to confront a defining question: If time was running out, would they rally behind Christian nationalism or stand as prophetic voices against injustice?

27

APOCALYPSE NOW

To many Americans in the 1970s, the United States seemed to have lost its way. The North Vietnamese Army and Vietcong had the US military reeling in Southeast Asia. Students challenged every kind of authority, from their parents to college administrators to draft boards. Some civil rights activists, frustrated by the pace of change, abandoned hope in the possibility or even desirability of integration. For many people, the future looked as bleak as the nation's smog-filled skies and polluted waterways.

Minister and former Mississippi River tugboat captain Hal Lindsey believed that what the Bible described as the end-times had commenced. In 1970 he published *The Late Great Planet Earth*, a book in which he linked contemporary events with ancient biblical prophecies to argue for Jesus's imminent Second Coming. In chapters with ridiculous puns for titles and subtitles, including "Scarlet O'Harlot" and "Sheik to Sheik," Lindsey highlighted the many global events that he believed marked the fulfillment of specific biblical predictions. They included the expanding power of communist China and the Soviet

Union, the rise of Arab nationalism, and the creation of the European Common Market.

Changes in the Middle East had prophecy watchers especially excited. As the world moved toward the Battle of Armageddon, Lindsey claimed that the biblical prophets had predicted that three specific events would occur. "First," he wrote, "the Jewish nation would be reborn in the land of Palestine. Secondly, the Jews would repossess old Jerusalem and the sacred sites. Thirdly, they would rebuild their ancient temple of worship upon its historic site." The first of these steps occurred in 1948 with the creation of the State of Israel. The second happened in 1967 when Israel captured Jerusalem during the Six-Day War. All that remained was the reconstruction of the Jewish temple. Many revivalist Christians believed that the temple would rise again on the land currently occupied by the Dome of the Rock, a major Muslim holy site. The most radical among them gleefully anticipated the day when this Muslim sacred space would be destroyed.[1]

Lindsey offered a rough date for the rapture based on Jesus's promise that when certain signs appeared the "generation" that witnessed them would not "pass till all these things be fulfilled" (Matthew 24:33–34). The "rebirth of Israel," the evangelist informed readers, marked the fulfillment of this prophecy. "A generation in the Bible," Lindsey continued, "is something like forty years. If this is a correct deduction, then within forty years or so of 1948, all these things could take place." The countdown had begun, and Lindsey expected it to conclude with the rapture by 1988. *Late Great* is still in print and has not been updated or revised, although as Lindsey went through multiple marriages and divorces his acknowledgments changed accordingly.

Late Great was a cultural phenomenon. It became the best-selling nonfiction book of the 1970s, with seven and a half million copies purchased that decade and nearly twenty million copies in print today. In 1979, Orson Welles narrated a popular film version of the book.[2]

Apocalyptic ministers like Lindsey tapped into Americans' growing unease. They had come out of World War II and then launched a Cold War brimming with confidence that they were presiding over what *Time* and *Life* publisher Henry Luce called "the American century." By the end of the 1960s, they no longer felt so confident. The war in Vietnam divided the nation and the nation's churches, young people spurned traditional religious authority and formed alternative Christian communities, and one charismatic minister offered a new, multiracial version of the social gospel that eventually ended in tragedy. Whether anticipated by biblical prophets or not, many Americans saw a reckoning on the horizon. The United States had lost its luster and now seemed far from a city on the hill for the world to emulate. This gave some Christians a sense of resignation, but others saw it as a call to action. They believed that living their faith meant battling to set the nation back on the right trajectory.

As American involvement in Southeast Asia increased in the mid-1960s, religious leaders used the conflict to reiterate their particular visions for building a promised land in the United States that offered salvation to the rest of the world. Evangelical leaders saw the Vietnam War as an essential part of the United States' campaign against the twin threats of communism and atheism. Evangelicals continued to be the nation's most promilitary religious group. National Association of Evangelicals founder Harold Ockenga wrote to President Lyndon Johnson in 1966 to encourage him to "fight to win the war and thus to end it" using "whatever weapons and fire power necessary to win." Billy Graham advised Nixon to consider using defectors to bomb North Vietnamese damns—a tactic that would have wiped out villages and killed hundreds of thousands of civilians. Presbyterian Carl McIntire organized numerous marches and public demonstrations in support of the war. Revivalists viewed the conflict as yet another opportunity to demonstrate their patriotism, commitment to Christian nationalism, and what they saw as God's plan for them to disseminate their values around the globe. But their nation had to prevail.[3]

Most American Catholics also supported the United States' efforts in Southeast Asia. They saw the war as an important fight in the global crusade against atheistic communism and, in predominately Buddhist South Vietnam, many political leaders were Catholic, which helped them garner sympathy among their coreligionists. Furthermore, the focus on religion during the Kennedy campaign had again demonstrated that Catholics always needed to work to prove their patriotism—protestants never assumed it. Supporting the war helped them do that. All the way to the end of the conflict, polling revealed greater Catholic than protestant support for the war.

Yet the Catholic Church also provided some of the war's most influential critics, including priests Daniel and Philip Berrigan. To bring attention to what they saw as the injustices of American intervention in Vietnam, the Berrigan brothers devised many stunts. They broke into government offices, destroyed draft cards with napalm, and doused government records with animal blood and red paint. They also protested American nuclear policy. They used their Catholic faith to critique what they saw as American imperial arrogance. Their efforts bolstered the work of traditional peace churches and groups like the American Friends Service Committee and the Fellowship of Reconciliation.

Liberal protestant leaders, more than the congregants they served, expressed doubts about the war. South Vietnamese president Ngô Đình Diệm had been restricting the rights and freedoms of Buddhists, which undercut American leaders' claim that the conflict represented a Cold War defense of religious liberty. A Vietnamese Buddhist monk immolated himself in June of 1963 to protest Diệm's repressive policies. A few more monks followed his example. A group of American protestants including Harry Fosdick and Reinhold Niebuhr, along with some prominent rabbis and an American Buddhist, responded with an ad in *The New York Times*. They described as "fiction" any characterization of the conflict as a fight for freedom. Their ad illustrated that even early in the war, well before the Gulf of Tonkin Resolution and Lyndon Johnson's bombing campaigns, some of the nation's religious leaders had serious reservations about American Cold War policy in Asia.[4]

As the war expanded, opposition deepened among some prominent ecumenical clergy. In the mid-1960s, a group of protestant,

Jewish, and Catholic leaders formed Clergy and Laymen Concerned About Vietnam (CALCAV). The group's protestant leaders mostly hailed from what journalists had begun describing as the "mainline" denominations—the old, classic, established, elite church groups that exercised substantial influence in American life. The term encompassed both conservative- and liberal-stream denominations, including the United Church of Christ (the descendants of the Congregationalists and other liberal denominations who had merged in 1957), Methodists, Presbyterians, Episcopalians, Disciples of Christ, and some Lutheran and Baptist groups. Journalists and other observers of American religion contrasted the "mainline" with revivalist groups such as the Assemblies of God as well as the Baptists, Presbyterians, and Methodists who had formed their own revivalist-oriented denominations.

Almost all CALCAV leaders lived in the North, except for Martin Luther King Jr., and most resided in major coastal cities. They worked in academia, in journalism, or as denominational executives. Few members of the group served local congregations, and they tended to be well removed from average churchgoers, both physically and in spirit. They criticized the nation's wartime tactics and strategies and consistently called for a negotiated peace.

One group, which included Harvard theologian Harvey Cox, Father Daniel Berrigan, and Lutheran minister and historian Martin Marty, encouraged young men in 1967 to avoid conscription. In a public statement they declared, "We hereby publicly counsel all who in conscience cannot today serve in the armed forces to refuse such service by non-violent means. We pledge ourselves to aid and abet them in any way we can. This means that if they are now arrested for failing to comply with a law that violates their consciences, we too must be arrested, for in the sight of that law we are now as guilty as they."[5]

The anti-war movement received a boost when Martin Luther King Jr. publicly condemned American actions. Over the course of the 1960s King increasingly connected problems at home with events abroad. "We were taking the black young men who had been crippled by our society," he preached at New York's Riverside Church, "and sending them eight thousand miles away to guarantee liberties in Southeast Asia which they had not found in southwest Georgia and East Harlem. So we have been repeatedly faced with the cruel irony of watching Negro and white boys on TV screens as they kill and die together for a nation that has been unable to seat them together in the same schools." The conflict became another opportunity for the liberationist minister to highlight how Americans' entwining of faith with nationalism too often contradicted the gospel they claimed to cherish.[6]

King was not alone. By the late sixties, editors at *The New York Times* noted that many of the leaders of the mainline churches, as well as publishers of the major liberal protestant and Catholic periodicals, had turned on the Johnson administration. The *Times* also highlighted how the war divided those in the pulpit from those in the

As the Vietnam War expanded, opposition deepened among some prominent clergy, including Martin Luther King Jr. The conflict inspired the liberationist minister to highlight how Americans' entwining of faith with nationalism too often contradicted the gospel they claimed to cherish. (credit: John Goodwin)

pews. Disillusionment with the conflict had grown "rapidly among clergymen—and especially among seminarians," journalist Edward B. Fiske reported. Fiske noted that most congregants, in contrast, even in the mainline churches supported the war and lined up more closely with the Christian-nationalist evangelicals than their own ministers.[7]

In 1970, President Richard Nixon, having failed to produce peace with victory, expanded the conflict into Cambodia. Presbyterian minister George Chauncey, who led the denomination's Office of Church and Society, believed he could accomplish what the president hadn't. He and a group of ministers traveled to Paris where he hoped to negotiate an end to the war. The move infuriated one of the denomination's chaplains. "I sometimes find it hard to acknowledge that I belong to the Presbyterian Church US," he wrote, "in the face of this type of activity." Another member called on church leaders to repudiate this "interference with United States foreign policy" and accused the peace group of "playing the communist game." A third warned that ministers' social activism tended to further "weaken us as a denomination at a time when there is already much dissatisfaction and concern in our churches."[8]

Instead of dodging the growing controversy, in 1971 a group of Presbyterian leaders called for an anti-war peace march to coincide with their annual denominational meeting. Once again, church executives had outpaced their congregants and many of their local ministers. Rather than register for the march, one pastor returned his invitation with a message typed across it: "I protest the so-called Witness for Peace in the name of the church in the behalf of the radicals and the communists and against the government, our service men, and real peace." Another minister wrote Senator Robert Byrd, clarifying that the march did not represent the views of all clergy. "This demonstration is highly embarrassing to a great many of us in our church," he said. "It is not the type of ecclesiastical conduct that is becoming to the church nor that with which we wish to be identified." A third wrote to President Nixon: "We want you to know that this group of zealous but misguided churchmen do not represent our sentiments." It is "indeed a sad situation when clergymen, instead of looking after the spiritual welfare of our countrymen as they should be doing, are instead giving aid and comfort to our enemies by their meddling interference in military affairs."[9]

Angry local ministers and congregants also balked at denominational leaders' request that they sign a pledge calling for unconditional US withdrawal. One minister rewrote his card: "I pledge my loyalty to my duly-elected president and to his sincere efforts to extricate us from a conflict he did not initiate, but one that perhaps mistakenly but sincerely sought to defend an invaded nation from Communist aggression." Another minister scrawled across the pledge, "President Nixon is getting us out of Indochina—why don't you get behind him? Why not help to unite this nation—rather than divide it like you are doing in our church."[10]

Like Presbyterian leaders, Methodist executives spoke out against the war. At the general conference of the United Methodist Church in 1972 churchmen called for Congress to kneecap the president by cutting off funding for the conflict. They also issued a statement calling the war an "intolerable monstrosity" and confessed that they had sinned by not doing more to end it. Episcopalian and United Church of Christ leaders made similar moves. As they had during World War II, liberal church executives and ministers' hesitancy to fully support an aggressive, militaristic American foreign policy cost them the support of many congregants who continued to embrace the Christian nationalism that had run through much of American history.[11]

In 1973, Nixon signed a ceasefire agreement with the North Vietnamese. For many Americans, Vietnam represented a horrible mistake that brought little peace and little honor. Unlike the celebrations that marked the end of World War I and World War II, Americans did not pour into the streets, organize parades, or stage massive homecomings. Two years after the ceasefire, in 1975, the North Vietnamese took control of the entire nation.

The American catastrophe in Vietnam forced all Americans to question the future of their country. World War II had seemed to reaffirm Americans' belief in their nation's exceptionalism. What happened? Had the United States become just one more corrupt imperial nation-state among many? Didn't God want the US to serve as the base for ushering his kingdom to earth, or had it forfeited that role? Debates over the war represented not just the split between pro-war evangelicals and mainline critics, but also a growing divide between elite mainline leaders and their congregants. Liberal church leaders—especially those in coastal cities or working in theological seminaries—had run too far ahead of those in many mainline pews.

Meanwhile, for revivalist evangelicals the war provided a welcome opportunity. It gave them yet another chance to pledge their loyalty to their nation and to the United States' mission in the world. They continued to beat the drum of Christian nationalism, and many Americans, including some who had traditionally worshipped in mainline churches, seemed willing to fall into line behind them.

The war and threat of conscription drove young people in the Age of Aquarius to reassess their values. Tens of thousands turned to Jesus, the "first hippie," to find meaning in their lives. They blended the counterculture's criticism of mainstream American society with calls for a return to a New Testament type of Christianity. Disgusted by the consumerism seemingly at the heart of American life, the complacency of their nation's churches, and most churches' embrace of middle-class values, they built alternative communities. They had long hair and wild, shaggy beards, wore beads and bell-bottoms, wandered cities and beaches barefoot or in sandals, and talked about being high on Jesus. Dubbed "Jesus people" and sometimes "Jesus freaks," they rejected the trappings and demands of the modern world and looked forward to a postapocalyptic Christian utopia.

The young people who made up the Jesus-people movement drew on the revivalist tradition. They focused on individual encounters with God and the need for a conversion experience. "Their lives," a journalist writing for *Time* magazine observed, "revolve around the necessity for an intense personal relationship" with the supernatural Jesus "and the belief that such a relationship should condition every human life." Like others in the revivalist stream, they sought converts using innovative methods that fit the times. They spread their message through underground newspapers and set up urban coffee shops with names like the Way Word in Greenwich Village, the Catacombs in Seattle, and the Carpenter's Shop in Southern California, where people could chill, caffeinate, and gab about religion. Some also used drugs, seeing marijuana and psychedelics as gateways to authentic Christian experiences.[12]

Southern California became an epicenter of the Jesus-people movement. Charismatic young people evangelized in Venice and Hollywood and even in suburban Orange County, where Christian squares and the countercultural came together in surprising ways. In Costa Mesa, minister Chuck Smith had launched Calvary Chapel with the goal of offering a biblically focused, theologically rigorous pentecostalism. Smith's daughter introduced the balding, middle-aged Smith to Jesus freak Lonnie Frisbee, a hippie who looked like the White Jesus so prominent in the American imagination. Frisbee kept his sexuality hidden from church elders—he was gay or perhaps bisexual.

Impressed by Frisbee, Smith teamed up with the Jesus-aping evangelist. Frisbee worked the streets, making converts among the region's young people and bringing them to Calvary Chapel where Smith mentored them in the faith. As the church filled with unkempt young people, its leaders bought a house and then an old hotel in the area to serve as communal living spaces for those needing shelter. With the number of conversions increasing, church leaders found unique venues for mass baptisms. Smith dunked thousands of new Christians in the Pacific Ocean, while another ally of the Jesus freaks, crooner Pat Boone, baptized new converts in his Beverly Hills pool.[13]

Jesus people obsessed over the apocalypse and the imminent Second Coming of Jesus. Hal Lindsey, who wrote *Late Great Planet Earth* while living in a communal home near UCLA called the JC Light & Power House (JC for Jesus Christ), helped them articulate their convictions and connect them to world events. Robert Ellwood, a scholar who studied the movement as it unfolded, noted that *Late Great* was "one of the few volumes besides the Bible" he saw in "virtually every movement commune, home, and church parlor." Larry Eskridge, a participant in the movement and later its historian, asked Jesus people what book other than the Bible had the greatest influence on them. The vast majority said *Late Great.*[14]

The Jesus-as-hippie apocalyptic revival movement reached a climax in Dallas in the early summer of 1972 with a music and ministry festival called Explo '72. Organized by a more buttoned-up youth ministry called Campus Crusade for Christ (now simply Cru), the event lasted five days and drew more than one hundred thousand youth to seminars and workshops. The conference ended with a music festival at the Cotton Bowl dubbed "Godstock." It featured a message from Billy Graham and musical performances by Johnny Cash, Kris Kristofferson, Andraé Crouch, Larry Norman, Barry McGuire, and a band called "Armageddon Experience." Perhaps as many as two hundred thousand people attended the festival.

That Graham and other leaders of the new evangelical movement championed Christian rock and roll marked a major reversal. During the 1950s and the first part of the 1960s, the era of Elvis and the Beatles, many Christian leaders viewed rock as the devil's jam. They made racist claims that its rhythms and beats derived from African pagan rituals and contended that it inspired rebellion and godlessness. But a handful of talented musicians pushed back against these tropes. Jesus-people coffee shops often offered live musical performances that blended pop music styles with Christian lyrics. By the time of Explo, ministries focused on the nation's youth had come to see popular music as a tool they could exploit.

The same year that Larry Norman played Explo, he released a new album with a song that said it all: "Why Should the Devil Have All the Good Music?" "Some people," Norman began, "say rock 'n' roll is of the devil, I don't believe that/It came from the church, belongs to the church." Getting to the heart of the matter, he opined, "And there ain't nothing wrong or satanic or communistic with blues licks." Wrapping up his song, which focused more on defending his musical tastes than on reaching potential converts, he sang, "All I'm really trying to say is/ Why should the devil have all the good music?/There's nothing wrong with what we play."[15]

Norman's album symbolized the rise of a new genre called "contemporary Christian music" that over the next decade became increasingly distinctive. Christian musicians crafted songs that mimicked popular styles but included lyrics that seemed safe for teenagers and their parents. No sex, no profanity, no hedonism, and no rebellion, at least not in the verses. What happened backstage and in roadside motels was sometimes another matter.

The apocalyptic messages conveyed by revivalist musicians, writers, and preachers found another innovative expression in the 1972 Armageddon-themed film *A Thief in the Night*. The movie scared a generation of young baby boomers into preparing for the rapture. Larry Norman's track "I Wish We'd All Been Ready" haunts the film. Swelling violins add a sense of impending doom, as does the melancholy sound of Norman's vocals. The low-budget film has become a cult classic, reportedly seen by over three hundred million people. But the producers of *Thief* and its three sequels wanted to do more than simply entertain audiences. They claimed that the films sparked thousands of conversions. They also published *Finding God in the Final Days*, a study guide that offered proof texts to support the major plot points of the production. The book warned readers of the looming rise of the real-life Antichrist.[16]

While explicitly Christian artists worked to inject their beliefs in music and film, in the theater others from less churchly perspectives also found inspiration in the "first hippie." In 1971, Andrew Lloyd Webber and Tim Rice opened the rock opera *Jesus Christ Superstar* on Broadway. It told the story of the passion of Christ through a 1970s lens. That same year the musical *Godspell*, which told a series of Christianity-inspired parables, opened off-Broadway. In 1966 John Lennon had quipped that the Beatles were more popular than Jesus, but by the mid-1970s Jesus once again had the upper hand.

In places like Orange County, California, the Jesus people successfully navigated the prevailing currents of the era to craft a timely version of Christian utopia. In Indianapolis, minister Jim Jones offered another. Like many charismatic leaders before him, Jones set out to build a pure religious kingdom on earth, promising Christians a very different kind of community grounded in social justice and racial reconciliation. He also hoped to become part of the civil rights revolution, tying faith to progress on human rights.

As a young man, Jones gravitated toward pentecostalism, with its exuberant worship styles and its more socially and racially inclusive tendencies. After graduating from high school, he bounced around, working odd jobs while taking college courses. He grew enamored with Marxism and in the late 1940s became an atheist. But his 1949 marriage to a Methodist led him back to church. There he discovered the social gospel. Perhaps, Jones speculated, Christianity could serve as a tool for building a racially integrated, socialist movement in the United States.

In 1956, Jones established his own Indianapolis church, the Peoples Temple. During services he practiced divine healing, and sometimes he claimed to raise people from the dead. Occasionally a bloody stigmata appeared on his hands, serving as another sign of God's favor. Only his closest allies knew that the minister staged most of the church's supposed miracles using sleight of hand, plants in the audience, and, as evidence of "passed" cancers, chicken entrails.

As the church grew, Jones made social activism and especially championing civil rights its primary focus. To demonstrate his commitment to racial integration, Jones and his wife adopted children of different races (Korean, Indigenous, and Black). He took a part-time job leading the Indianapolis Human Rights Commission and worked to integrate many of the city's core spaces. His efforts gave him access to the city's leading Black organizations, which he used to line up invitations to speak at Black churches. Those opportunities allowed him to troll for new members for the Peoples Temple.

In 1965 Jones moved the Peoples Temple to Redwood Valley, California, more than one hundred miles north of San Francisco. Jones told his followers that a nuclear weapon would soon strike the United States, and they would be safer in Northern California than in Indianapolis. Hundreds of his followers moved with him to a state that had long proved particularly fertile for growing new religious movements. Meanwhile, he preached that the US government, via the CIA and FBI, monitored his actions and sought to undermine his socialist-religious-communal experiment.

Despite Jones's conspiratorial claims about nefarious government agents lurking outside his church doors, in California he ingratiated himself with the political elite. He saw himself as among the vanguard of the rights revolution—someone akin to civil rights leaders César Chávez, Angela Davis, or Huey Newton. In reality, he was a White man who, Democratic Party leaders recognized, could influence the votes of thousands of people. Candidates for office either visited the temple or invited Jones for meetings. By the mid-1970s, his allies included Governor Jerry Brown, vice presidential candidate Walter Mondale, and even Rosalynn Carter, the wife of Jimmy Carter, who Jones had met during Carter's 1976 presidential campaign. Popular State Assemblyperson Willie Brown regularly heralded Jones's work.

Although Jim Jones may never have really believed in the Christianity he preached, he started a new church focused on social reform and civil rights. He hoped to influence American leaders and politicians. (credit: *Peoples Temple Bus Trip: Washington, DC*, 1974, Peoples Temple Publications Department Records, MS 3791, California Historical Society)

As critics started to dig in to rumors surrounding the temple, journalists reported on the nature of politicians' relationships with Jones. "While it appears that none of the public officials from Governor Brown on down knew about the inner world of Peoples Temple," they wrote, "they have left the impression that they used Jones to deliver votes at election time and never asked any questions. They never asked about the bodyguards. Never asked about the church's locked doors. Never asked why Jones's followers were so obsessively protective of him. And apparently," they concluded, "some never asked because they didn't want to know."[17]

Jones never developed a comprehensive or consistent theology. He drew on Eastern ideas about reincarnation, criticized the "Sky God" of traditional Christianity, and for a while called himself "God Socialism." What he lacked in explicit doctrine he made up for in discipline. He demanded absolute loyalty, established strict rules, and policed the behavior of his followers. He berated those who sinned and forced the faithful to confess their shortcomings, especially if they involved sex. He knew information was power and wielded it to discourage dissent and to threaten those who questioned him. He had members beaten for their sins, sometimes with a huge wooden paddle, like a frat party hazing ritual.

Jones denounced the nuclear family structure and sought to convince his followers to pledge themselves to the larger Peoples Temple movement and not to an individual husband, wife, or child. The group raised children collectively, including many they fostered or adopted (for which it received government stipends). Jones slept with multiple women in the community, and a few men too. *New Yorker* journalist Lawrence Wright later wrote that Jones's followers "made allowances" for him. "Their leader's alleged psychic gifts so charged him with sexual energy that he was constantly in need of release. He claimed to masturbate thirty times a day." The minister often wore large, black sunglasses, especially during his healing "trances." They shielded the fact that he was reading information off index cards, making it look like he had psychic abilities. He also became ever more dependent on drugs to help him sleep, and then amphetamines to energize him while awake. The glasses hid his bloodshot eyes.[18]

Ever afraid of being exposed, Jones put money into building a new community beyond American borders. In the mid-1970s, he leased 3,800 acres of remote jungle in Guyana, then sent a team of Peoples Temple members to begin preparing a site to house his religious community. The country, its new, independent socialist government, and its multiracial, English-speaking society impressed him. To the minister, Guyana represented heaven on earth.

Reporters in the Bay Area, intrigued by Jones's unique religious experiment, started digging into the community and tracking down ex-members for interviews. But anytime journalists tried to publish a critical story, Jones used his connections to quash it. His luck, however, ran out in August 1977 when the magazine *New West* published an exposé based on interviews with defectors. The series emphasized church leaders' abuse, intimidation, and coercion of members, and Jones's staged healings.

With the jig finally up, Jones fled to South America with hundreds of members, about 70 percent of whom were Black. In the new "Jonestown" community, the minister maintained absolute control. Jones censored mail and mostly cut off members' communication with the outside world. Meanwhile, he lied to his followers about what was happening in the United States, claiming they had escaped just in time. The country, he said, had descended into chaos. Neo-Nazis had gained power and race riots had devastated the nation's major cities.

As Jones's conspiracies and fearmongering deepened, he developed a doctrine of revolutionary suicide. He instructed followers that rather than suffer arrest or death at the hands of their enemies, they should prepare to take their own lives. He forced followers to prove their faith in him by drinking Flavor Aid (a cheaper, generic version of Kool-Aid) that he claimed to have poisoned. Armed guards supervised the mock-suicide drills. Jones and his closest allies also staged attacks on the compound to make residents believe that they faced constant threats from the outside world. Meanwhile, his drug problem worsened. He became more controlling, more paranoid, and more strung out.

With most communication cut off, some of the families of Jonestown members grew concerned. They lobbied Congress to investigate Jonestown. In late 1978, Congressman Leo Ryan of California traveled to Guyana to assess this rogue American community. The visit started well enough, but near the end, Ryan offered to take anyone who wanted to leave back to the United States. Fifteen people chose to go. As they waited at the airstrip to depart, a group of Jonestown residents acting on Jones's orders opened fire on the group, killing the congressman and four others, and shooting almost a dozen more.

Back at the compound Jones told his followers that the time for revolutionary suicide had arrived. "We are sitting here waiting on a powder keg," he told them. "If we can't live in peace then let's die in peace.... There's no way, no way we can survive.... The best testimony we can make is to leave this goddamn world." He claimed that the CIA intended to destroy their socialist experiment and that they needed to embrace death over returning to supposedly fascist America. "It's the will of Sovereign Being that this happened to us," he continued. "That we lay down our lives in protest against what's been done." He ended with a proclamation: "We didn't commit suicide, we committed an act of revolutionary suicide protesting the conditions of an inhumane world." On November 18, 1978, Jones directed his followers to serve children and elderly members Flavor Aid laced with cyanide. Once they had collapsed, the adults lined up for their own cups of Flavor Aid. That day more than nine hundred people died, including Jones, who investigators discovered with a gunshot wound to his head.[19]

The Jonestown mass suicide forced Americans to grapple with the power of faith. Jones didn't believe in the Christianity he so often preached to outsiders and potential recruits. From early on, he saw people as puppets and himself as the puppet master, uniquely gifted to pull their strings. While Jones rejected the God of the Bible, he understood that most Americans embraced Christianity. To achieve his social and political ambitions, he seized on its language, rituals, and symbols. The separation of church and state gave him room to operate. But ultimately, it wasn't enough. In the end, Jones led his followers not to the interracial utopia he had promised, but to a self-fashioned Armageddon.

For generations, Americans had been gripped by biblical visions of Armageddon. In the turmoil of the 1960s and 1970s—with Vietnam, Watergate, and social upheaval—many came to believe the end was near. Enterprising revivalist Christians stoked these fears, weaving global events into ancient millennial prophecies and tapping into a deep sense of American Christian destiny. They worked to keep the United States at the heart of millennial hopes, urging believers to prepare for Judgment Day while pushing to shape American law, culture, and policy around their Christian ideals. Time, they warned, was running out.

Meanwhile, mainline churches faced a different challenge. As church leaders grappled with the era's most divisive social issues, they unwittingly drove many from their pews—sparking an exodus that reshaped the American religious landscape.

28

THE TERMINUS OF THE MAINLINE

On April 8, 1966, the editors of *Time* magazine put the question "Is God Dead?" on the cover of their magazine. The corresponding article focused on the rise of a new group of scholars of religion who aspired to draft a novel kind of theology, one without a god. *Time* editors used their innovative and paradoxical school of thought to probe larger changes in American religion. The Enlightenment and the Copernican Revolution centuries earlier had provided natural explanations for what many humans had previously considered supernatural events. As Enlightenment-era thinkers adapted to the scientific revolution, these contemporary theologians argued, those with more liberal tendencies had remade God into the image of a human. They now believed that religious liberals should take this philosophical evolution to its logical conclusion by dispensing altogether with the idea of a supernatural deity. "Slowly but surely," cover story author John Elson wrote, "it dawned on men that they did not need God to explain, govern or justify certain areas of life." The combination of secularization, science, and urbanization, he determined, "made it comparatively easy for the modern man to ask where God is, and hard for the man of faith to give a convincing answer, even to himself."[1]

Magazine publisher Bernhard M. Auer knew that the cover would generate controversy. "After months of searching for a work of art suggesting a contemporary idea of God," he wrote, "the editors came to the conclusion that no appropriate representation could be found. In designing the first TIME cover ever to use only words, they decided that the ferment in modern theology was best suggested by the startling question hurled at a baffled world by the new theologians." The publisher, perhaps hoping to dispel the idea that *Time* intended to attack Christianity, noted that Elson began his research for the cover story "quite literally" in prayer.[2]

The cover generated more letters from readers than anything in the magazine's history; most Americans emphatically rejected the death of God and found the question offensive. And yet the *Time* story hinted at a larger crisis faced by American Christians. The nation had seemingly lost its Christian consensus, or at least its mainstream leaders had lost their power. Ideas that less than one hundred years earlier had put Robert Ingersoll on the far fringes of American life had gone mainstream, and not just among skeptics, but now even among some leaders in Christian institutions.

Ministers and theologians reacted to increasing secularization by trying to explain anew the benefits of faith to the individual and the nation, remaking Christianity once again to fit the times. Some White liberal leaders, perhaps unintentionally, accelerated secularization—not by urging Americans to abandon faith, but by encouraging them to privatize it. Religion, they argued, should be personal and individual, not public and authoritative. Unlike their revivalist counterparts, they had little interest in building a Christian republic. The "city on a hill" they envisioned was pluralistic, tolerant, and ecumenical.

Other White liberals, stirred by the civil rights movement and second-wave feminism, began centering social justice in their ministries. They sought to steer their churches and denominations toward the liberationist stream. But as with their stance on the Vietnam War, many charged ahead of their congregations—often leaving average churchgoers behind.

Conservative and especially revivalist church leaders, in contrast, reminded Americans that they could have a heartfelt, personal relationship with Jesus. With their unapologetic embrace of Christian nationalism, consumer capitalism, conservative politics, and "traditional" social mores, they welcomed disillusioned White mainliners with open arms. They capitalized on cultural divisions to begin the process of displacing the mainline and building a new kind of protestant establishment. They tried to demonstrate to the nation that in their churches, God remained far from dead.

Time's controversial cover story spotlighted a new wave of radical theologians. Unlike earlier generations of social gospel advocates, modernists, and neoorthodox ministers, who saw Christian ideas as essential for transforming individuals and society, these leaders argued in the 1960s that the real solution to the world's problems was not more Christianity, but more secularization.

In 1963 Anglican Bishop John A. T. Robinson published *Honest to God*, a controversial book that launched debates not just in his native United Kingdom but also in the United States, where it became a bestseller. Robinson believed that humans had become so secular in their thinking that appeals to the supernatural proved nearly worthless. Theism and the traditional Christian concept of God no longer provided the answers humans sought. Rather than work to build the church, Christians, he advised, should focus their efforts on creating a just, secular society. "For a prominent cleric to characterize as downright dishonest the sincere God talk of the average churchgoer," historian David Hollinger explained, "exposed as never before the gap between the people in the pew and the increasingly cosmopolitan church leaders." Robinson blurred the line, Hollinger continued, "between what most people took Christianity to be, and the enlightened, humane dispositions of the left-liberal intelligentsia."[3]

Harvard theologian and Baptist minister Harvey Cox added a new ingredient to the simmering theology soup with his 1965 publication *The Secular City*, which sold more than a million copies. Cox believed that religion still mattered, just not in the ways we traditionally thought. "The forces of secularization," he wrote, "have no serious interest in persecuting religion. Secularization simply bypasses and undercuts religion and goes on to other things. It has relativized religious world-views and thus rendered them innocuous. Religion has been privatized." Cox both described and advocated. "Fewer and fewer" people, he concluded, expected religion to "provide an inclusive and commanding system of personal and cosmic values and explanations."[4]

Robinson and Cox were just two of dozens of church leaders from within traditional, liberal-stream Christian institutions who sought to remake religion into a secular force for good. Although the vast majority of American Christians had little interest in a godless theology, Cox and Robinson correctly observed that Christians had in recent decades begun to compartmentalize their faith, separate their individual religious commitments from their public lives, and operate more from shared secular rather than shared Christian assumptions. Their work complemented the kinds of secularization and privatization of religion suggested by recent court decisions, such as *Engel* and *Schempp*, ending official prayer and Bible reading in public schools.

While mainline church leaders worked to fend off intellectual attacks from the new theologians, they faced a different kind of challenge from some rogue pastors and their followers in the pews. In the spring of 1960 Episcopal priest Dennis Bennett shared some startling news with his well-educated, upper-middle-class, 2,500-person congregation in the Los Angeles suburb of Van Nuys. He had spoken in tongues. His confession split the congregation and garnered national headlines. Dozens of church members followed Bennett's lead and experienced the gift of tongues, which scandalized those who didn't. "We're Episcopalians," one parishioner told *Newsweek*. "Not a bunch of wild-eyed hillbillies."[5]

For decades those who experienced a pentecostal-type baptism in the Holy Spirit often left traditional denominations and joined pentecostal churches. Or they practiced the gifts of the spirit quietly, without drawing attention to themselves. Bennett's acknowledgment of the integration of pentecostal practices with mainline worship marked the rise of a new "charismatic" revival. Tongues-speaking and a focus on faith healing began occasionally appearing across the nation's mainline protestant denominations.

Many of the participants in the new charismatic revival exercised their gifts at retreats, through parachurch ministries, or in designated spaces set aside for practices such as anointing with oil or praying for physical healings. The average Methodist or Episcopalian service did not morph into a holy rolling, swinging from the chandeliers, pentecostal party. Nevertheless, as the phenomena spread, denominational boards investigated and then debated how to respond. Most mainline groups quickly made their peace with what they surmised might be the authentic work of the Holy Spirit. A handful of nonpentacostal revivalist denominations, in contrast, wanted to maintain a clear boundary between their worship styles and those of pentecostals, who they still treated as their embarrassing country cousins. They denounced tongues-speaking and other manifestations as fabrications, if not demonic.

The charismatic revival affected the Catholic Church as well. Just as with the Episcopalians, when Catholic laypeople began speaking in tongues in the late 1960s, Vatican leaders generally did not object. They sought new ways to attract converts, and some believed that ecstatic religious experiences might help.

The charismatic renewal represented for Catholics one small part of a growing openness to new ideas and practices that had begun a few years earlier. Pope John XXIII convened the Second Vatican Council in Rome, a series of meetings that lasted from 1962 to 1965. "Vatican II" focused in part on making the faith more relevant to the changing world. Church leaders settled on a long list of changes and recommendations. They called for an expanded role for laypeople in directing church life, replaced Latin mass with services led in local languages, encouraged parishioners to participate in worship through hymn singing, and perhaps most important, counseled the faithful to read the Bible for themselves rather than depending on a priest to mediate between them and God.

Church leaders vowed to engage better with modern scholarship and to adjust the church to democratic norms and religious pluralism. They even embraced ecumenism by inviting non-Catholic observers to the council and setting guidelines for interfaith dialogue. The church did not, however, revise its traditional prohibition on women becoming priests, and Catholic leaders continued requiring priests to remain celibate. Although the changes troubled traditionalists, they addressed concerns that many congregants shared. In encouraging a new ecumenical openness, church leaders also facilitated Catholic-protestant collaborations on social and political issues.

While the Catholic Church continued to bar women from the priesthood, some protestant denominations began rethinking long-standing restrictions. Since the earliest days of Christianity, maverick and iconoclastic women had demanded equality with men, but most churches in most times and most places structured their fellowships around patriarchy. But early in the twentieth century some of the nation's Black denominations started ordaining women, as did various holiness and revivalist groups. The largest, most powerful White denominations generally acted more slowly. As a renewed feminist movement gained momentum after World War II, the Methodists and Presbyterians began ordaining women. Then in the 1960s, some Lutheran women joined the clergy. In the 1970s, a few Episcopalian bishops ordained women, and in 1976 denominational executives officially allowed women to join the priesthood. Policy reforms did not, however, generate widespread changes. Women have never made up more than a small minority of mainline pastors and priests. In the 2010s, they represented just 11 percent of US clergy.

Pauli Murray, who in 1977 became one of the first Episcopalian women to receive ordination, challenged her fellow Christians and fellow Americans in all kinds of new ways. Born poor and reared by her grandparents, Murray's birth certificate identified her as a girl, but, living in an era before the term "transgender" was common, she believed she was male. She earned a college degree in New York City and applied to law school at the University of North Carolina in the late 1930s, but the school rejected her because she was Black. She later applied to Harvard Law School. Harvard rejected her because of her gender. She ended up earning her law degree at Howard University, a historically Black college in Washington, DC. She aimed to tear down all forms of segregation and discrimination. She coined the term "Jane Crow" to describe how discrimination against women paralleled "Jim Crow" discrimination against Black Americans. First as an attorney and then as a priest, she focused academic and church leaders' attention on how racism and sexism intersected and reinforced each other.

The issue of women's ordination was especially fraught among Southern Baptists. In 1964 a local congregation in Durham, North Carolina, called a woman as their pastor and ordained her to the ministry. During the 1970s, additional Baptist congregations ordained women. Meanwhile, religious conservatives in the Southern Baptist Convention began criticizing liberal trends in theology and the denomination's approaches to cultural issues, including feminism. In the late 1970s, conservative male leaders in the SBC initiated a multiyear effort to capture the most important leadership roles in the denomination.

Once in power, the conservatives made invalidating female ordinations a priority. In 1984 they finally succeeded, getting a resolution through their annual meeting that read: "Therefore, be it Resolved, That we not decide concerns of Christian doctrine and practice by modern cultural, sociological, and ecclesiastical trends or by emotional factors; that we remind ourselves of the dearly bought Baptist principle of the final authority of Scripture in matters of faith and conduct; and that we encourage the service of women in all aspects of church life and work other than pastoral functions and leadership roles entailing ordination." They linked women's ordination to the culture wars and then rolled back women's ecclesiastical equality. While many denominations grew more inclusive, Southern Baptist leaders sought to reinstitute patriarchy.[6]

Many people in the convention felt devastated. One connected the group's abysmal race record to its revised stance on women's ordination. "The Southern Baptist Convention came into existence," a Kentucky pastor wrote church leaders, "because of its refusal to acknowledge the equality of all persons in Christ. Thus we built a rationale for slavery on a foundation of biblical texts. We did the same with the issue of racial segregation in the 1950s and 1960s. It is long past time that Southern Baptists got on the right side of history for a change. We believe sexism is no more acceptable to the Gospel of Jesus Christ than racism." A Southern Baptist woman couldn't believe that the news was true. "We might not ordain women, but we can certainly work them to death. Give them all kinds of jobs to do, but for heaven's sake don't call them 'Pastor' or 'Deacon.' Who's kidding who?" But the critics lost the battle.[7]

White church leaders found that addressing race, racism, and the evolution of the civil rights movement proved even more challenging than navigating debates over gender or secularism. Many ministers understood that their churches had for centuries been complicit in establishing and perpetuating racist hierarchies. In responding to the civil rights and Black liberation movements, some sought significant change and even repentance. Others preferred to maintain the status quo. How best to deal with the nation's sins divided church from church and parishioner from parishioner.

In the Southern Baptist Convention, the 1954 *Brown* decision emboldened some pastors to voice support for integration—at least in principle, if not always in practice. Hoping to head off a divisive debate, SBC leaders urged congregants to respect the courts and love their neighbors across racial lines. The response was swift and fierce: A flood of angry letters poured in, revealing deep resistance within the pews. "I had rather spend my tithes buying alcohol and distributing it among the people affected by integration (both races) than to spend my tithe advocating the integration of races," one deacon wrote. "God has NEVER favored a race as much as He did the Negro when He permitted him to be brought out of savagery and cannibalism into slavery (and rigid discipline)." Another telegrammed, "If your members wish their wives and daughters to mix with Negros, why not have them set the example?" A pastor from Dallas asked SBC leaders to "please quit brainwashing our Southern Baptists with this communist-inspired, UN-promoted propaganda."[8]

White mainline leaders also struggled to articulate a clear position on civil rights. Many church executives, in their efforts to build solidarity with systemically marginalized groups, focused on combating racism. The Presbyterians, to better support the civil rights movement, created a new Council on Church and Race. Members of the council, conscious of the church's past sins and historic indifference to racial justice, worked to right past wrongs. But not all Presbyterians believed their approach made sense.

A controversy over radical activist Angela Davis proved emblematic of the challenges Presbyterian leaders faced. In January of 1970, California's Soledad State Prison descended into chaos. A White guard had shot and killed three Black prisoners. Black inmates, furious about their mistreatment at the hands of White authorities, rebelled. In the ensuing mayhem an inmate beat a White guard and then threw him to his death three floors below. Prison authorities accused George Jackson, Fleeta Drumgo, and John Clutchette of the murder. All three had been active in the civil rights movement. The media dubbed them the "Soledad Brothers." Civil rights activist, academic, and Marxist Angela Davis organized a campaign to free the men.

A few months later, hoping to free the Soledad Brothers, George Jackson's brother took hostages from a courtroom while brandishing a gun that belonged to Angela Davis. In the melee that followed, the judge was killed. California authorities charged Davis with first-degree murder. The Presbyterians' Council on Church and Race pledged $10,000 to Davis's defense fund. In May, Lois Stair, the first woman ever to hold the position of moderator (or chairperson) of the General Assembly, the denomination's ruling body, defended the donation. "Miss Davis has been actively involved in the struggle for justice, freedom and equality for black people," Stair told her fellow Presbyterians. "We strongly support this struggle. We are also aware that Miss Davis has repeatedly acted and spoken in protest against mistreatment of black people in our penal institutions. We, too, share these concerns."[9]

As the Presbyterian moderator certainly realized, many churchgoers did not share her perspective. The committee's support of Davis infuriated many White Presbyterians. Some individual churches withheld their contributions to the denomination, costing the organization over $700,000. Angry individuals also suspended their tithes-giving to their local congregations. One pastor reported that parishioners withheld all their offerings except those specifically earmarked for the church "pipe organ fund."[10]

The debate over the Council on Church and Race's support of Davis highlighted the growing chasm between a group of White, social justice–oriented church leaders, who wanted Christians to help lead the nation toward equality and righteousness, and those in the pews who often proved more conservative. Critics contended that their church's endorsement of Davis revealed deeper, systemic issues. One layperson identified a series of church leaders' supposed misjudgments that went well beyond the issue at hand, and accused Presbyterian authorities of "an incredible display of unmitigated stupidity." Another angry congregant asked, "Are you people simply stupid and incompetent, or has the communist party taken over the United Presby. church?" Another told church leaders, "To support an avowed communist and Anti-Christ is the last thing that I want."[11]

Correspondents sometimes invoked scripture to justify their fury. "I do not remember any place in the Bible where the Lord says we should protect the murderer, the revolutionary, the rioter, the blasphemer. I don't recall His ever saying it was okay to burn buildings, destroy property, defy authority, or wantonly kill." This, she concluded, "is the final straw." A church elder accused Presbyterian executives of failing to follow "God's word." "I promise to bother you no more," she swore. "As soon as my term of being elder is out, we plan to seek a church of the Bible, as do so many of my friends."[12]

Most of letters that arrived in the denomination's Philadelphia headquarters criticized leaders' actions. But a few praised church executives for prioritizing social justice. "As a member of a minority group, Sioux Indian," one member wrote, "I felt the response of the General Assembly in an instance growing out of repression, and having wide repercussions in the movement towards racial equality was most appropriate. It is my deepest wish that the Commission on Church and Race continue to work in this vital area for our denomination."[13]

The American context made it extraordinarily difficult for church leaders to act out of conviction rather than pragmatism. Unlike in countries with establishment churches, in the United States, parishioners—the consumers—were almost always right. If leaders failed to represent the views of their rank and file, their churches could not survive. The editors of *Christianity and Crisis* correctly noted that "a minister of prophetic conscience may find himself in a squeeze within the political structure, between a conservative congregation below him and a cautious officialdom above him." The editors understood that for a minister to champion an unpopular political cause usually meant generating blowback from all sides. In the specific case of civil rights and social justice, as on Vietnam, many White parishioners believed that their leaders had veered too far from their own beliefs and priorities, forcing leaders to decide with whom their ultimate loyalties lay.[14]

The gay rights movement, like civil rights and the second wave of feminism, presented yet another challenge and opportunity for church leaders. Most American Christians believed that same-sex attraction and especially same-sex acts represented serious sins. To be openly gay and seek Christian fellowship in the United States was difficult if not impossible. Revivalist minister Troy Perry pushed Christians to reassess their prejudices as he sought to build a Christian community in which gay men and women would feel welcome.

Perry had spent his late teens and early twenties ministering in various Baptist, holiness, and pentecostal churches. In the mid-1960s, when leaders at the church where he worked discovered that he was gay, they immediately booted him from his position. Over the next few years, Perry grew increasingly frustrated that gay men did not have a space where they could worship without hiding their identity. God, he determined, wanted him to build a new church to meet this need. He placed an ad in *The Los Angeles Advocate* announcing the start of a new, queer-friendly congregation.

On October 6, 1968, Perry and eleven others met in his Southern California living room for their first service. They prayed and sang hymns, then Perry preached, and finally the group took communion. The launch of the church, *The New York Times* observed a year later, "reflects both the growing willingness of American homosexuals to assert themselves as a distinct minority group and the emergence of a more liberal attitude toward homosexuals among religious bodies." It was certainly the former, but perhaps not the latter. That Perry had to establish a new church reflected the ongoing prejudices of establishment religious bodies.[15]

Perry published an autobiography in 1972, which he opened by asserting, "God created homosexuals and homosexuality." Then he turned to his own role in God's work: "I am a minister of the Gospel. I have been licensed and ordained. I have finally found my mission in this life. And I am a homosexual, a happy homosexual." Perry hoped that in telling his story he might destigmatize nonconforming sexual orientations.[16]

Shortly after launching his ministry, Perry began officiating same-sex marriage ceremonies. In this he jumped far ahead of the rest of the nation's religious leaders. "No confessional family or denomination," *The Christian Century* reported in 1971, "has moved a single centimeter toward sanctioning marriage of members of the same sex, and probably none will in the near future." Church leaders worried rather that should the government sanction gay marriage, religious leaders might have to conform.[17]

Perry's new church flourished, growing to over four hundred members within just a few years. Together with his fellow believers, Perry founded new congregations across the nation and incorporated them as the Metropolitan Community Church (MCC). Church leaders skillfully combined pentecostal practices, traditional revivalism, and elements of high-church liturgy, creating a unique and vibrant worship experience. The denomination also ordained women. Perry

Revivalist minister Troy Perry confronted religious prejudice and built a new church community where gay men and women could truly belong and worship freely. He aligned his mission with the broader gay liberation movement, demanding full social equality not merely within religious spaces, but across American society. (credit: courtesy of Troy Perry)

linked his work with gay liberation, seeking full social equality, not just in the church, but in all parts of American life.

Perry's gay-affirming movement attracted new converts as well as exiles from churches in every stream. MCC leaders saw their work as temporary—they did not intend to build a permanent denomination defined by members' sexual preferences. They prayed that the nation's established churches would repent of their prejudices, see the error of their ways, and welcome back their lost sheep. They hoped in vain. Mainstream churches not only refused to support gay rights, but the leaders of the revivalist National Association of Evangelicals and the more liberal National Council of Churches both passed on the MCC's request for membership.

Episcopal priest Gene Robinson, like Perry before him, fought for gay rights. Ordained in 1973, Robinson led the conventional life of a typical minister during the first part of his career—he married, had children, and served his parish. But he was gay, which he confessed to his wife early on in their relationship. In the mid-1980s, they divorced, and he made his identity public. He continued to serve as a priest in the Episcopal Church and in 2003 denominational leaders made him their first openly gay bishop.

By the end of the 1980s, rights activists had compelled the mainline denominations to assess the relationship between sexual orientation and Christian ethics. The Presbyterians took up the issue in a multiyear study on human sexuality. That church leaders were even considering gay equality stoked outrage among many parishioners. "If the General Assembly adopts the position that practicing homosexuals may be ordained as ministers in one or more of our Presbyterian churches," one layperson wrote church executives in response, "we may need to withdraw from the church and look elsewhere for moral guidance for ourselves, our children and our society. We fail to see why the Presbyterian Church (USA) should put up a sign authorizing vulnerable young people to choose active homosexuality and bisexuality as acceptable habits." Another thought that her Presbyterian ancestors likely did "some real flip-flops in their graves to see Sodom and Gomorrah come to America." Finally, one noted, "I would like to express my violent opposition to the Presbyterian church becoming a Church of SIN, SEX, SATAN, AND SODOMY!!!!!!!"[18]

Presbyterian leaders at the time decided not to endorse gay marriage or ordination. But in recent years the consensus has shifted. Today, Presbyterians, alongside most other mainline denominations, recognize and will often bless same-sex marriages. Yet as these churches have embraced greater inclusivity, they have also faced deep divisions, marked by schisms and the departure of both individuals and entire congregations.

By the end of the 1960s, historians, sociologists, and journalists recognized a great re-sorting occurring among American churchgoers. Revivalist church growth accelerated while the White mainline had begun a slow death spiral. The great events of the century hastened the church shuffling. As the most prominent and outspoken leaders within the liberal stream grew more ecumenical and less nationalistic, they lost followers. But the shadows hinting at their coming demise had been cast decades earlier. In the 1930s, prominent and well-connected mainline church leaders had rejected American militarization despite the fascist threat, and in the 1940s they proved reluctant to support total war against the Germans and Japanese. During the Cold War, they preached peace to such an extent that their opponents labeled them communist sympathizers, which their opposition to the Vietnam War seemingly reinforced. Then in the 1960s they embraced the rights movements, seeking not just salvation in the afterlife but justice in a deeply flawed American society.

In mainline leaders' efforts to serve the Prince of Peace and right long-term wrongs, they abandoned many of those in the pews. They made excellent prophets but poor church builders. The typical congregant simply did not share the views of these predominately Northern, urban, and coastal elites. Average churchgoers did not want to spend their Sundays exploring their own sexism and racism or understanding how the United States had built an empire at the expense of others around the world.

In 1969 sociologist Jeffrey Hadden addressed these issues in *The Gathering Storm in the Churches*. He argued that an unprecedented crisis had overtaken Christianity. Most parishioners viewed the church as "a source of comfort and help in a troubled world." Their ministers, in contrast, used the church to "challenge men to put an end to social injustice in this world." He believed that "the increasingly bold stance of clergy on civil rights and other social issues has left a large proportion of the laity bewildered and resentful." The widening divide did not auger well for the future. These changes, he predicted, put "clergy and laity" on "a collision course. . . . It seems hard to avoid the conclusion that the conflict that has been witnessed in recent years is only a prelude to what seems almost inevitably to be a much more serious conflict in the years ahead."[19]

The data proved Hadden right. In the second half of the twentieth century, the United Methodists, Presbyterians (USA), and Episcopalians all lost between 50 and 60 percent of their church members. The United Church of Christ lost almost 80 percent. God might as well have been nearly dead in the mainline. Meanwhile, in this same era, Southern Baptists grew by 37 percent, and the Assemblies of God grew by over 200 percent. The pentecostal and predominately Black Churches of God in Christ grew by over 1,000 percent.

In the 1970s, a new generation of revivalists recognized that on many cultural and political issues the views of the average mainline churchgoer did not align with those of the religious elite. Sensing an opportunity to highlight the contrast between their own convictions and those of the mainline, revivalist leaders went to war. Culture war. They launched a new form of Christian nationalism. They positioned race, gender, and sexuality at the center of their resurrected and refashioned crusade to once again remake the United States as God's chosen land.

PART VII

REMAKING AMERICAN CHRISTIANITY

29

THE RELIGIOUS RIGHT

The chaos and upheaval of the 1960s and 1970s led revivalist Christians to question the fate of their nation. If the sins of the American people became too great, they surmised, perhaps the United States would lose its anointing as God's chosen land. And it looked like their sins were indeed becoming great.

Amateur historians Peter Marshall and David Manuel summed up revivalist views in a 1977 book that promised to tell the long history of American exceptionalism. "This nation," they preached, "was truly to be one nation under God," and for most of its history they believed that it had lived up to its promise. But since the New Deal era, the nation had lost its moorings. According to Marshall and Manuel, the reason that "we Americans are in such trouble today is that we have forgotten" God's design in shaping the United States. "We've rejected it. In fact, we've become quite cynical about it. We, as a people, have thrown away our Christian heritage."[1]

How had American Christians abandoned the true faith? They had grown numb to the signs of moral decline—abortion, sex education, divorce, pornography, and the unraveling of the "traditional" family—all made worse by a seeming indifference to the erosion of godly authority in American life. But American Christians could still act. "God's call on this country," Marshall and Manuel insisted, "has never been revoked. . . . Our forefathers have broken the trail for us, and shown the way. Their call is our call." If Christians obeyed, "America would yet become the citadel of light which God intended her to be from the beginning!" They could restore the covenant that God had made with John Winthrop and renewed with the founders.[2]

Along with other evangelicals, Marshall and Manuel believed that Americans could and should return the nation to its supposed Christian foundations. They envisioned a revival of faith, where the country would once again become God's chosen land. However, to truly reclaim their position as the people of God, they first needed to cleanse the nation of its many sins. In the 1970s and 1980s, revivalists embarked on a series of new culture wars, driven by the goal of redeeming what they perceived as a fallen people and a corrupt nation. They aspired to guide the country back to the path of righteousness, believing that only through purification could the United States fulfill its divine destiny. They sought to awaken the hearts and minds of their fellow citizens, urging them to strive for a nation that reflected their values and principles. Along the way they found a new savior not in their churches, but in the White House and in the reconstituted Republican Party.

Sex took center stage in the new culture wars, capturing attention and sparking debates across the nation. Americans' ideas about sex had been evolving for decades, and even many faithful churchgoers had started questioning traditional sexual prohibitions. Reinhold Niebuhr received a letter from a woman in her twenties seeking his advice. "My problem," she wrote, "is to understand the relation of sex to religion. To me, love is the core of the Christian religion. . . . I cannot see clearly how pre-marriage relationships would necessarily flout that religion and yet this is the deeply ingrained viewpoint of my social background." Although the pipe-smoking theologian liked to tweak many of the pillars of established orthodoxy, Niebuhr didn't budge on sex. Premarital intercourse, he replied, could do real damage. "The woman is much more endangered in finding a marriage partner by previous sexual relations than the man is in danger," he advised her. "I would not regard any sexual relations outside of marriage as a mortal sin, but I think the prohibition of them corresponds to the true facts of human nature and is not arbitrary."[3]

Although Niebuhr may not have been ready for change, in the 1960s large numbers of Americans began more routinely separating sex from marriage and procreation. Recognizing the onset of a sexual revolution, school leaders sought tools and resources to help young people navigate evolving ideas and practices. They revised and updated their health curriculum, placing greater emphasis on human sexuality.

Many Christians objected to the introduction of a more comprehensive sexual education into public school curriculum. The courts had driven prayer and Bible reading out of education, and now sex had seemingly replaced them. God was out, sex was in, and the collapse of civilization was seemingly at hand. Billy James Hargis's Christian Crusade ministry published a book titled *Is the School House the Proper Place to Teach Raw Sex?* Obviously not, he thought. But trying not to sound too preachy, the book's author joked, "The young high school student who made a collage of contraceptive devices should at least be awarded a booby prize."[4]

San Diego Baptist minister Tim LaHaye published a pamphlet in 1969 decrying sex ed. "If you look at the curriculum instead of the high sounding propaganda some educators put out about it," he wrote, "you will find that it is really radical information that often borders on pornography and smut." He claimed that sex ed leaders launched an "anti-God, anti-Christian and anti-Bible movement" and "are bent on the degeneration of today's young people." Educators, he warned, expected high schoolers to know such terms as "promiscuity, Prophylactic, incest, adultery, homosexuality, syphilis, Lesbian, rape, transvestite, abortion, conception, arousal, chastity, climax, coitus, copulation, ejaculation, erection, frigidity, hymen, genitals, heterosexuality, mistress, venereal, prostitute and virgin." But Hargis, LaHaye, and their allies lost the battle. To avoid sex education, Christian parents had to find alternatives to their local public schools.[5]

In the 1970s and 1980s, revivalists suffered another school-related setback—this time in the courts. Although the central issue at hand was racial segregation, evangelicals feared the Supreme Court might clear a path for the government to challenge their understanding of sex and gender and how they applied that understanding to their educational institutions.

The Internal Revenue Service (IRS) had determined that educational institutions practicing racial segregation were by definition not charitable and therefore not tax-exempt. The IRS then sought to apply this ruling to Bob Jones University (BJU), a revivalist university in South Carolina that had denied admission to Black Americans until 1971 and was still prohibiting interracial dating in 1975. BJU challenged the IRS policy and ultimately lost at the Supreme Court in an 8–1 decision announced in 1983. That the IRS had the power to use its tax codes to shape Christian university policies (and their budgets) provoked a significant backlash among Christian supporters of Southern segregation, as well as among people who simply believed that the government should not dictate policies to private religious institutions.

Leaders of the National Association of Evangelicals (NAE) saw the Bob Jones case as marking the start of a long war, waged by and through the federal government with the help of the courts, against revivalist ideas about race, gender, and sexuality. Attorneys for the NAE admitted that most evangelicals did not agree with the BJU policy against interracial dating. Yet the policy, they argued, was "based not on personal bias or prejudice, but sincere religious belief." Furthermore, much larger groups of evangelicals held other beliefs that made them equally susceptible to losing their tax-exempt status. "What the Government might view as a violation of the public policy against sex discrimination," they wrote in an amicus brief, "evangelicals would consider faithful adherence to Scriptural teaching with respect to the proper roles of women within the church. For example, many evangelical churches do not believe in the ordination of women as pastors or elders. Left intact, the decision of the court below will inevitably be used to justify subordination of religious belief to current notions of public policy." The attorneys behind the brief, like the churchgoers they represented, wanted the courts to protect their ability to practice discrimination on the basis of "sincerely held" religious beliefs in their churches, schools, and, more recently, their businesses.[6]

Battles over sex and gender accelerated in 1972 when Congress passed a new equal rights amendment (ERA) to the US Constitution. The amendment read: "Equality of rights under the law shall not be denied or abridged by the United States or any State on account of sex." As innocuous as this statement may seem, revivalists and other social conservatives believed that adding such language to the Constitution would undermine what they saw as the fundamental differences between men and women, and that it would open the door to a host of "alternative" lifestyles, including government support for gay and lesbian rights. When Congress sent the amendment to the states for ratification, social conservatives—many of them women—organized a powerful grassroots campaign against it.

Attorney, Roman Catholic activist, and mother of six Phyllis Schlafly, who had long worked to drive the Republican Party to the right, led the anti-ERA crusade. Linking her model of the family with God and country, Schlafly helped kill the momentum behind ratification. She told an interviewer that "the ERA is designed to convert us into a unisex society. It would prevent us from making any distinction between men and women." If the ERA became law, she speculated, women would be drafted into the military and forced into combat. The amendment also meant "you couldn't give any preferential treatment to wives, mothers, and widows. You wouldn't be able to make reasonable, common sense separation of treatment such as in single sex schools, fraternities, or athletics; or in other areas such as prison regulations and insurance regulations." She claimed that the "ERA also makes it impossible to have any laws against homosexuals. They would have to be treated with the same rights as husbands and wives because you couldn't discriminate on the basis of sex." She convinced legions of followers that the ERA would create the appearance of a sexless society that subjected women to all kinds of abuse.[7]

Many revivalists agreed with Schlafly. They believed that the "traditional" family was under siege, being attacked from countless angles. James Dobson, an expert on child development with a doctorate from the University of Southern California, founded Focus on the Family in 1977 to bolster the White, middle-class, Cold War nuclear family ideal. Through publications, videos, and radio shows, Dobson examined how politics, public policy, and legislative decisions affected families. Blending evangelical Christianity and conservative activism, he immediately began to shape the broader culture as well as the rhetoric of politicians. He helped make "family values" the mantra of the pre-Trump Republican Party.

Revivalists recognized that they could not just criticize feminism and blame the sexual revolution for undermining the family; they also had to provide attractive alternatives. Christian author Marabel Morgan taught women to embrace both submission to their husbands and kinky sex to strengthen their marriages. She wrote an advice manual called *The Total Woman* (which sold more than three million copies in its first years of publication) that encouraged women to tell their husbands how much they "admired" them and to yield to their authority. "The biblical remedy for marital conflict," she advised, "is stated, 'You wives must submit to your husbands' leadership in the same way you submit to the Lord.' God planned for woman to be under her husband's rule." Morgan and many other revivalist leaders at the time likely didn't realize how their instructions set women up for violence and cruelty. Giving husbands a biblical mandate to lead as patriarchs, and counseling wives that God expected them to submit to men's authority, made it difficult for women to challenge abuse. As recent investigations have revealed, in many cases pastors even counseled women to return to violent spouses as part of their duty to God.[8]

Morgan saw sex as a tool revivalist women could use to strengthen their marriages. To keep husbands from wandering, she encouraged Christian wives to spice things up (the onus was always on the women). "You can be lots of different women to him," she counseled.

"Costumes provide variety without him ever leaving home. I believe that every man needs excitement and high adventure at home. Never let him know what to expect when he opens the front door; make it like opening a surprise package. You may be a smoldering sexpot, or an all-American fresh beauty. Be a pixie or a pirate—a cowgirl or a show girl. Keep him off guard." One enthusiastic reader of the book gave her own spin to Morgan's advice. She greeted her hubby at the door wearing only Saran wrap.[9]

Like Morgan, several other Christians drew on the sexual revolution to construct a revivalist alternative. Tim and Beverly LaHaye's 1976 book, *The Act of Marriage: The Beauty of Sexual Love*, served as a kind of how-to manual for sex, complete with sketches that placed God at the center of coitus. The LaHayes taught that the almighty endorsed the missionary position and they cautioned that masturbation and fellatio were the devil's candy. "It is readily apparent," they wrote, "that oral sex is on the increase today, thanks to amoral sex education, pornography, modern sex literature, and the moral breakdown of our times." The book sold over a million copies and spawned many imitators.[10]

Arguments over gender, sexuality, and family set the context for an even more acrimonious debate regarding abortion. During the 1950s and into the 1960s, the number of botched back-alley abortions across the United States rose substantially, creating a health crisis. In response, leaders of the American Medical Association, joined by leaders of the burgeoning feminist movement, lobbied Congress, state legislatures, and the courts to loosen restrictions. The debate over abortion did not initially align with partisan divisions. Supporters and opponents of the issue could be found within both major political parties. In the late 1960s, some governors, like California's Ronald Reagan, began easing abortion restrictions.

The Catholic Church had long opposed all efforts to loosen abortion laws. Pope Paul VI reiterated the church's position in 1968, issuing a new encyclical entitled *Humanae vitae*. Despite fears of overpopulation and the development of new, safer birth control technologies, he counseled the faithful not to use artificial birth control of any kind.

Furthermore, he instructed, "We are obliged once more to declare that the direct interruption of the generative process already begun and, above all, all direct abortion, even for therapeutic reasons, are to be absolutely excluded as lawful means of regulating the number of children." While many American Catholics agreed with the pope on abortion, fewer agreed on preventative birth control. Substantial numbers of American Catholics bought condoms and used the pill, quietly but directly defying a clear papal directive.[11]

In states with strict laws, women turned to the courts for justice. In 1971 "Jane Roe" sued the State of Texas for denying her constitutional rights by prohibiting her from getting an abortion. The Supreme Court took the case. In *Roe v. Wade*, issued in 1973, the court legalized abortion across the country during the first trimester of pregnancy and part of the second. During the third trimester, states had the option of restricting women's right to an abortion. Once the Supreme Court issued its decision, the United States' religious communities divided. Catholics who accepted the church's teaching on birth control criticized the decision, while protestants and Jews had mixed responses.

Roe did not particularly trouble many revivalist Christians, who saw early-term abortions as akin to preventative birth control. But in the years after the decision, a few activists—including Francis Schaeffer, a long-haired, goatee-sporting, knickers-wearing evangelical guru—began to rally evangelicals to the antiabortion cause. Schaeffer drew thousands of young revivalist students and intellectuals in the 1960s and 1970s to a retreat in the Swiss Alps he called L'Abri (meaning "the shelter") to participate in a unique Christian community. He encouraged his disciples to engage better with Western culture and to bring the arts, philosophy, and literature—essentially all of life—under the lordship of Christ. He wanted them to stem the tide of what he called "secular humanism" and to return the United States to its supposed biblical foundations.

To spread his ideas, Schaeffer wrote numerous books whose sales eventually totaled in the millions. In *How Should We Then Live?* (1976), he criticized the *Roe* decision and the practice of abortion. The following year he produced a documentary film espousing his ideas, which he showed on college campuses throughout the United States. Then he partnered with medical doctor C. Everett Koop to produce a new film entitled *Whatever Happened to the Human Race?* It graphically described and sensationalized the process of terminating a pregnancy. While Schaeffer never achieved the public notoriety of some ministers, he laid many of the intellectual foundations for evangelical engagement with modern politics.

Inspired by Schaeffer and others, revivalist activists began partnering with Roman Catholics, their traditional archenemies, to build a "pro-life" movement. They pressured political candidates on the issue and worked to amend the Constitution to invalidate *Roe*. They moved abortion to the center of their "family values" politics, making it a litmus test for candidates seeking election to office, and hatched a strategy to transform the makeup of the Supreme Court to undo *Roe*.

In the 1980s, some antiabortion activists turned to extreme tactics. Randall Terry, an evangelical who later converted to Catholicism, founded Operation Rescue to draw national attention to the issue. Leading protests at abortion clinics, Terry often likened his acts of civil disobedience to those of the civil rights movement. His followers stormed clinics, blocked entrances, and staged provocative stunts, at times even displaying dead fetuses for the media to amplify the shock. Terry's efforts pushed the abortion debate into a far more heated and polarizing phase.

Many of the leaders of the burgeoning "family values" crusade faced yet another challenge in the form of the ongoing gay rights movement. "Family values" leaders believed that same-sex relations, like abortion and feminism, threatened to provoke God's wrath. The gay rights movement had received national attention in 1969, when police raided a Greenwich Village gay bar, the Stonewall Inn. In response to the raid, activists graffitied "Gay Power" around the city. Over the next few days, several demonstrations took place. Stonewall helped launch the Gay Liberation Front (GLF), which called for the sexual liberation of all people.

Despite growing calls for change, in the aftermath of the Stonewall uprising, Congress mostly ignored gay and lesbian demands for equal treatment. Local municipalities, in contrast, began to address activists' concerns. In 1977, the Dade County Commission, whose jurisdiction included the city of Miami, passed an ordinance protecting gay men and women from discrimination. Evangelical Anita Bryant objected to the statute. The former Miss Oklahoma, Christian singer, and popular spokesperson for Florida orange juice started an organization called Save Our Children (later renamed "Anita Bryant Ministries") with the goal of overturning the local ordinance and building a national campaign against gay rights. If "homosexuals" are a "legitimate minority group," she claimed, "so are nail biters, dieters, fat people, short people, and murderers." She especially feared the influence of gay schoolteachers, who she claimed discussed their sexuality with their students. What, she asked, "gives the homosexual any more right to stand up in front of children and talk about his sexual preferences than a man who has a great Dane as his lover?"[12]

Although Bryant seized the national spotlight, she was not well informed. At the start of her crusade, she didn't even understand how people of the same gender had sex. "What can they do as two men in bed or two women in bed?" she asked. "I didn't really know the nitty-gritty of the thing." When she found out what some gay men actually did in bed, she recalled, she "about fell through" her chair. She told an interviewer for *Playboy* magazine that gay men's eating of "the forbidden fruit of the tree of life" (sperm), made them an "abomination" in the eyes of God. "Why do you think the homosexuals are called fruits?" she asked. "It's because they eat the forbidden fruit of the tree of life." When pressed, she acknowledged that heterosexual "eating" of the forbidden fruit was also popular. "The abomination," she admitted, "is spreading."[13]

Revivalists like Bryant opposed gay rights by framing "homosexuality" as a sinful choice, not as a core part of a person's God-given identity. From this belief, they spun fear-driven slippery slope arguments. "If the homosexual's lifestyle must be accepted," warned Texas minister James Robison, "what will be next—the thief's, the murderer's, the rapist's?" For Robison and others, "homosexuality" was nothing less than "the most severe symptom of a sin-sick society."[14]

The nation's focus on issues of gender and sexuality inspired some revivalist leaders to establish new political advocacy groups. In 1978 Beverly LaHaye launched Concerned Women for America to defend what she called traditional family values. Her organization grew rapidly in size and power, quickly dwarfing liberal organizations like the National Organization for Women in terms of membership. Its leaders called for a return to a mostly imagined heyday in which men were men, women were women, and the nation cherished the group's preferred model of family. They had remarkable success in mobilizing voters in support of their issues, which gave them significant clout in policy circles.

While most revivalists moved further to the right as the family values debates escalated, a small number in the 1970s tried to push back against the social conservatism that characterized their movement. A group of young Black and White, male and female revivalists from multiple denominations met at a Chicago YMCA in 1973 to discuss the future of their movement. Together they drafted a new manifesto called the "Chicago Declaration of Evangelical Social Concern" and created a new group called Evangelicals for Social Action (ESA)—they dropped the "evangelical" label in 2020 and are now called Christians for Social Action.

Their declaration touched on the many social issues of that generation. They began by acknowledging that although "God requires justice" for all people, evangelicals had not "proclaimed or demonstrated his justice to an unjust American society." They took what they understood to be an all-encompassing pro-life position—they rejected not only abortion, but also the nuclear arms race, the death penalty, and war. Turning to race, they confessed, "We deplore the historic involvement of the church in America with racism and the conspicuous responsibility of the evangelical community for perpetuating the personal attitudes and institutional structures that have divided the body of Christ along color lines. Further, we have failed to condemn the exploitation of racism at home and abroad by our economic system." ESA activists did not, however, acknowledge that the state could play an important role in reducing racism though civil rights legislation—on this issue they remained divided. Nor did they support gay rights.[15]

In addition to raising issues of race and poverty, the "Chicago Declaration of Evangelical Social Concern" also called for revivalists to rethink their movement's historic treatment of women. "We acknowledge," the declaration read, "that we have encouraged men to prideful domination and women to irresponsible passivity. So we call both men and women to mutual submission and active discipleship." Out of ESA came the Evangelical Women's Caucus, which challenged the hierarchical views so deeply embedded in revivalism. The conference and declaration, with its attention to issues of race and gender, marked the rise of a small progressive wing within modern White revivalism. Its impact on the larger movement, however, proved negligible.[16]

While White revivalists in the mid-1970s had zeroed in on a handful of social issues, they had not yet linked those issues to the success of a particular political party. When Southern Baptist Sunday school teacher Jimmy Carter campaigned for the presidency in 1976, a *Newsweek* cover story entitled "Born Again!" indicated that the increasingly important evangelical vote remained up for grabs. The Georgia governor hoped to beat incumbent Gerald Ford. When reporters on the campaign trail asked Carter about religion, he responded using typical revivalist language, explaining that he had a "personal relationship" with Jesus Christ. To the press, this sounded bizarre. Kenneth Briggs of *The New York Times* recalled that "many reporters reacted to Jimmy Carter's unabashed espousal of 'born again' Christianity with about as much befuddlement as if Mr. Carter had said he had ridden in a flying saucer." But to his supporters, Carter seemed to embody exactly what the country needed. After all, as one Southern minister famously exclaimed, his initials even matched those of Jesus Christ.[17]

The Carter presidency disappointed many evangelicals. Carter's sponsorship of the White House Conference on Families backfired when social conservatives claimed that liberals had rigged the conference, set the agenda to reflect their beliefs, and refused to let "pro-family" activists speak. The president's support of the ERA and gay rights and his conviction that *Roe* had settled the abortion debate (even though he personally opposed the practice) further quenched many revivalists' enthusiasm for the Georgian.

Political activists within the right wing of the Republican Party sensed an opportunity. They had long wanted to push their party in a more conservative direction, and they knew they had much in common with the religiously oriented social conservatives that Carter and Ford had competed for. They hoped to tap into the energy that had recently led evangelicals to establish new public policy groups, including the Religious Roundtable and the Christian Voice. In June 1979, new-right architects Paul Weyrich and Richard Viguerie reached out to popular revivalist preacher Jerry Falwell for a meeting. During a break, Weyrich and Falwell discussed their mutual interests. "Jerry," Weyrich said, "there is in America a moral majority that agrees about the basic issues. But they aren't organized. They don't have a platform. The media ignore them. Somebody's got to get that moral majority together."[18]

Falwell agreed and later that year the three men incorporated the Moral Majority. The initial board of directors boasted prominent ministers including Tim LaHaye. "This was war," Falwell remembered. He believed that "to win the war against crime and immorality, to save the American family, to stop the killing of 1.5 million unborn infants every year would take everyone willing to take a stand regardless of his or her race or religion, social class or political party." Falwell told Christians around the nation that they had a threefold mission: to get people saved, to get them baptized, and to get them registered to vote. He believed that if he could lead revivalist Christians to the polls, they would turn the tide in the nation. Within a couple of years, the Moral Majority represented nearly seven million (mostly White) people dedicated to pro-life, pro-family, pro-Israel, and pro-strong-national-defense causes. Through church-based voter registration drives, Moral Majority leaders motivated hundreds of thousands of previously apolitical Christians to cast votes, most often on behalf of the GOP. Meanwhile, a handful of other prominent ministers, including Pat Robertson, reinforced Falwell's message, encouraging White revivalists to engage in partisan politics.[19]

Going into the 1980 presidential election, incumbent Jimmy Carter courted evangelicals. But Carter's actions were too little, too late. His opponent, Ronald Reagan, a former actor and divorcé who did not regularly attend church, claimed to believe in many of the issues that socially conservative, revivalist Christians cared about. Reagan took a hard anti-communist line, denounced the supposed decline of the family, praised the "old-time religion," and criticized the permissiveness of the sixties generation. He questioned the science behind evolutionary theory and supported the teaching of creationism in the public schools. Despite having signed a bill as governor that dramatically expanded abortion rights, Reagan flipped and took an anti-choice position in 1980. He believed that the federal government had been overreaching for decades and that states and local communities should reclaim power. Reagan, Falwell concluded, "seemed to represent all the political positions we held dear. . . . So we threw our growing political weight in his direction."[20]

Journalists and political scientists credited the newly energized conservative religious activists, including Falwell's Moral Majority and numerous smaller, lesser-known evangelical organizations, with helping give Reagan his margin of victory over Carter. An ABC News/Harris Poll survey concluded that the Moral Majority had played a large part in getting conservatives to the polls and in swinging the South from Carter's column to Reagan's. Perhaps more important, Falwell helped turn evangelicals into a voting bloc that the GOP could not ignore. In every election since 1980, the Republican Party has crafted platforms specifically designed to appeal to the religious right, and as a result it has carried ever-larger majorities of the White revivalist vote.

Reagan understood how to galvanize White Christians and use them to help achieve his policy goals. In 1983 he delivered a speech to the National Association of Evangelicals in which he wove religion, domestic issues, and foreign policy together. The president began by defending the need to have religious leaders in government. "Freedom prospers," he emphasized, "when religion is vibrant and the rule of law under God is acknowledged." Then he attacked the Supreme Court's understanding of the First Amendment: "When our Founding Fathers passed the first amendment, they sought to protect churches from government interference. They never intended to construct a wall of hostility between government and the concept of religious belief itself." He denounced secularism and abortion and called for Congress to pass a "prayer in schools" amendment. Turning to foreign policy, he linked his opposition to a nuclear freeze with faith in God. Then as he reached the climax of his speech, he famously identified the USSR as an "evil empire." Reagan knew that when it came to aggressively and unapologetically fighting communism, he had no more loyal allies than the evangelical audience hosting him on that day. Media mogul Norman Lear complained that Reagan had become the religious right's "evangelist in chief."[21]

The AIDS crisis became a defining challenge of the Reagan presidency and one that intensified deep divisions over gender and sexuality. As Reagan largely sidestepped the issue, wary of drawing attention to the gay rights movement, some religious leaders responded with cold indifference, showing little compassion for those suffering from the disease. Catholic political activist and syndicated columnist Pat Buchanan, who later worked for Reagan, notoriously declared, "The poor homosexuals. They have declared war on nature and now nature is exacting an awful retribution." Charles Stanley, president of the Southern Baptist Convention, preached that same-sex relations represented "a sinful life style, according to Scripture, and I believe that AIDS is God indicating His displeasure and His attitude toward that form of life style, which we in this country are about to accept." A South Carolina pastor wrote Stanley thanking him for speaking out. "Dogs and lesbians," he said, "are the direct result of men denying their Creator. The world has seen an explosion in deviant sexual activity in step with its criticism and denial of God's word. Faithful preaching is the finest antidote to sodomy and AIDS!"[22]

The president preferred to focus on the economy. Reagan not only gave Americans "family values" and the religious right, but he also bequeathed to the nation the "yuppie." Although most Americans could not partake directly in the consumption of pricey consumer goods that defined yuppie culture, many participated voyeuristically.

They obsessed over the wealthy and tried to crack the code to their success. They purchased best-selling advice books written by affluent Americans on how to build prosperity, such as real estate tycoon Donald Trump's *The Art of the Deal*, and they studied self-help guides such as Mormon businessman Stephen Covey's enormously popular *The 7 Habits of Highly Effective People*. And by "effective," he meant rich.

The fervor for wealth even seeped into the realm of religion. In the 1980s, a novel protestant movement gained traction, captivating the masses with its "prosperity gospel." Charismatic preachers proclaimed to their congregations—and to millions of television viewers—that divine favor was synonymous with financial abundance. They preached that God desired for them to be wealthy, and that unwavering faith was the key to unlocking this divine prosperity.

Traveling evangelist and pentecostal faith healer Oral Roberts helped establish the prosperity gospel. In 1947 Roberts published a collection of essays focused on the relationship between faith and money. He opened his book by writing that Jesus's "highest wish is for us to prosper materially and have physical health equal to His peace and power in our soul." He and other ministers drew their ideas in part from Psalms 1:3, which reads, "And he shall be like a tree planted by the rivers of water, that bringeth forth his fruit in his season; his leaf also shall not wither; and whatsoever he doeth shall prosper." To prosperity ministers this text was crystal clear. The godly person will prosper in all ways. During the 1950s Roberts led huge healing-tent revivals and in 1963 he opened a Bible college in Tulsa, Oklahoma, where he trained a new generation of prosperity leaders.[23]

Alongside Roberts, Oklahoma-based Assemblies of God minister Kenneth Hagin helped grow the nascent prosperity movement. The Bible, Hagin preached, was akin to a legal document—it provided certain guarantees, such as health, happiness, and financial security, to Christians who properly lived by its principles. He emphasized Mark 11:24: "Therefore I say unto you, What things soever ye desire, when ye pray, believe that ye receive them, and ye shall have them." Christians, he advised, could attain what they desired by claiming them in "Jesus's name." Over the next couple of decades, Roberts, Hagin, and

others trained thousands of ministers who blended pentecostalism with prosperity theology. They drew both Black and White leaders to the movement.

Prosperity preachers made excellent use of technology and especially television to spread their gospel. The most popular ministers had shows in which they preached, prayed, and groveled for donations. They encouraged their audiences to send in prayer requests, and to drop what money they could into their envelopes. Rumors abounded that bank tellers and not prayer warriors were the only folks who ever handled the incoming mail.

Christians' use of and access to the airwaves evolved rapidly. In the 1970s, pentecostal Pat Robertson started buying up local television stations and with them formed the Christian Broadcasting Network (CBN). In 1977 Robertson made an even bolder move, launching a satellite into space that allowed him to create a national Christian cable television network. Revivalists no longer had to depend on local stations willing to sell them airtime but laid the foundations for their own alternative media universe.

Robertson recruited ministers Jim and Tammy Faye Bakker for his network. Naturals both in front of and behind the camera, the young couple produced a popular children's puppet show. They also proved to be excellent fundraisers during the network's telethons. Jim could seemingly cry on cue, and when he did, the donations flowed like manna from heaven. In late 1972 the young couple left CBN and formed a new nonprofit corporation, the Trinity Broadcasting Network. They hired Los Angeles–based prosperity ministers Paul and Jan Crouch to help run the new ministry. The partnership quickly unraveled, and the Bakkers ventured out on their own again, starting the PTL (Praise the Lord) Network.

In the Reagan era, prosperity preachers reached peak influence. Their gospel matched the times, and their use of state-of-the-art cable and satellite technology brought them and their ideas into millions of American homes. Then a series of scandals rocked the movement.

Oral Roberts had by the 1980s overextended his ministries. God, he said, commanded him to build a new medical school and hospital

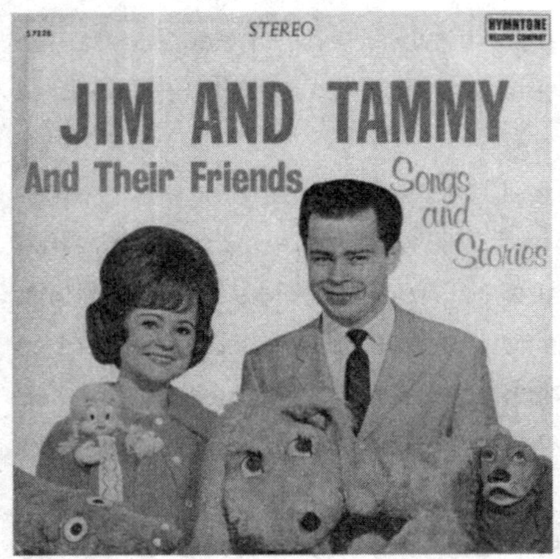

Naturals both in front of and behind the camera, Jim and Tammy Bakker produced a popular children's puppet show. In late 1972 the young couple formed the Trinity Broadcasting Network and later the PTL (Praise the Lord) Network. Living out the new "prosperity gospel," the Bakkers used donations to their ministries to live extravagantly, and they made little effort to hide their wealth. (credit: unknown)

where he aimed to combine prayer, the laying on of hands, faith in divine healing, and traditional medicine. While building the enormous new medical center, he ran short of cash. Roberts claimed that a colossal nine-hundred-foot Jesus appeared to him and assured him that the money would come. "I have only seen Jesus once before," he told his followers. "But here I was face to face with the King of Kings. . . . Oh! I will never forget those eyes!" The two talked for an hour and a half. Roberts promised followers that if they donated a "precious seed" to the hospital, God would bless them, returning to them more than they gave. But the project turned into a financial boondoggle. Deep in the red, in 1987 Roberts claimed that if followers did not donate another $8 million to help him run his ministry, God would "call him home." The money poured in, and God spared Roberts. However, the reprieve was temporary. Roberts closed the hospital in 1989, and God called him home two decades later in 2009.[24]

Jim and Tammy Faye Bakker's fundraising tactics and lavish lifestyles raised alarms as well. Beginning in 1979, federal agencies including the IRS began quietly investigating the couple. The Bakkers used donations to the ministry to live extravagantly, and they made little effort to hide it. Then in 1987 a new story broke. Jessica Hahn, a former church secretary, claimed that when she was twenty-one years old Jim Bakker and another minister raped her. To buy her silence, they paid Hahn over a quarter of a million dollars of ministry money.

The government's inquiries combined with the work of investigative journalists brought to light Jim's bisexuality and all kinds of corruption in the Bakkers' Christian empire. Jim Bakker eventually went to jail for fraud.

Financial scandals among some of the nation's most high-profile prosperity-gospel preachers stretched into the new millennium, reinforcing the public image of these ministers as con artists swindling poor grandmothers out of their Social Security checks to fund mink coats, Bentleys, and private jets. Yet despite the backlash, the prosperity gospel has not only survived—it has thrived, attracting followers both in the United States and around the world. In many American churches, as in much of American life, greed still seems to be good.

Reagan's efforts to court White revivalists, coupled with the organizational prowess of new-right activists and the prosperity preachers' theology that sanctified capitalist greed, significantly bolstered the right wing of the GOP. However, this success came at a steep price. In some religious institutions, politics began to overshadow faith, with ministers exchanging divine favor for political clout. As debates over social issues grew increasingly partisan, the resulting fractures splintered churches, parishes, and synagogues.

Sociologist James Davison Hunter used the metaphor of "culture war" in a 1991 book to describe the changes underway. The United States, he observed, "is in the midst of a culture war that has and will continue to have reverberations not only within public policy but within the lives of ordinary Americans everywhere." He defined culture war "as political and social hostility rooted in different systems of moral understanding." He saw this as a zero-sum conflict. "The end to which these hostilities tend is the domination of one cultural and moral ethos over all others."[25]

Hunter argued that the modern American culture war differed from those of the past. Rather than protestants fighting Catholics or Jews as they had in previous eras, conflict now occurred among protestants, among Catholics, and among Jews. Culture war soldiers fought within their own established groups and not between groups. Old alliances had broken down and new ones had replaced them. Furthermore, new forms of media intensified and aggravated differences in ways that exacerbated the culture war—which the Republican Party and its religious-right partners adeptly exploited. Loyalty to denominations crumbled, and Christians re-sorted themselves in what sociologist Robert Wuthnow dubbed the "restructuring of American religion," choosing fellowship based more on political affinities than on historic beliefs and practices. Rather than religion shaping one's political preferences, savvy Republican operatives and their religious-right allies ensured that politics shaped the churches many Christians chose to attend. Evangelicalism and the Republican Party began to merge and morph into a single entity in which the term "evangelical" signified as much about one's partisan politics as about one's version of Christianity.[26]

In the years since Hunter published his book, the culture wars and the divisions they wrought within American churches have swelled. Perhaps the religious right will succeed in remaking the nation along revivalist lines, as Marshall and Manuel hoped when they called Americans to return the nation to its Christian foundations. Or perhaps in the alliances revivalists built with secular politicos as they grasped for power, they sowed the seeds of their own destruction, guaranteeing that no one will ever again think of the United States as a particularly Christian nation. American Christians are still asking what Jesus would do, and they are still having a hard time answering the question.

With the new millennium on the horizon, Christians in the United States faced a sobering challenge: In a country being reshaped by diversity and global uncertainty, unity over faith and purpose seemed more elusive than ever. Revivalists wanted more Americans to embrace Christian nationalism, but they could not reach consensus on what it meant to be God's people, in God's land, in the modern age.

30

LIVING AT THE CLOSE OF THE MILLENNIUM

By the turn of the millennium, the United States had become a place of tremendous religious diversity. The tri-faith protestant-Catholic-Jew nation that sociologists described in the 1950s had evolved into one teeming with Muslims, Buddhists, Hindus, Taoists, Sikhs, Jains, Zoroastrians, and adherents of many other faiths and no faith at all.

Revisions to immigration policy helped facilitate the nation's growing diversity. In 1924, Congress had passed the Johnson-Reed Act, severely limiting immigration to the United States from much of the world. The act stood until 1965, when President Lyndon Johnson championed and Congress passed a new immigration and naturalization act. The new rules ended the old, racist quota system and made it possible for immigrants to enter the United States from any part of the globe.

Many Americans found the nation's growing diversity attractive. Immigrants brought countless new faiths that Americans could try out, assess, and plunder, like any other consumer product. Upper-middle-class Whites appropriated what they liked, especially from Eastern religions, and repackaged them to meet their needs. Yoga, Zen Buddhism, Transcendental Meditation, and more recently mindfulness became popular religious practices among urban, college-educated White Americans. Others turned to gurus from abroad for inspiration and enlightenment.

Nevertheless, immigration reform helped Christians more than any other group. Since at least the mid-1990s, the majority of legal immigrants to the United States have identified as Christian. Most undocumented immigrants have too. Christian newcomers arriving from all over the world filled the gap left by the large number of native-born Whites abandoning the faith. As historic, elite churches in the nation's cities hemorrhaged members and sometimes had to close their doors, and middle-class folks moved to the suburbs, taking their tithes with them, new immigrant churches took over urban church buildings. Meanwhile, rather than White Americans sending missionaries to the "heathens in the darkness" abroad, Christians from ethnic minority communities began evangelizing White Americans. Koreans, Mexicans, and Argentines, among many others, led evangelistic campaigns across the United States.[1]

At the dawn of the new millennium, Christian innovators sought to rekindle revival amid mounting competition. One faction aspired to "reconstruct" the nation into a Christian commonwealth akin to Calvin's Geneva, while others employed apocalyptic jeremiads to galvanize Christians to action. Some propagated their end-times beliefs through fiction, and one group even amassed weapons for the ultimate battle. Religious leaders worked to reassert their authority, but revelations of clergy sex abuse undermined their efforts. In response to the September 11, 2001, terrorist attacks, President George W. Bush launched a new crusade, echoing the ambitions of his predecessors to reshape the world in the image of the United States.

In the late 1990s Americans occasionally read stories about sexual abuse in churches. Sometimes a victim came forward and told their story, and authorities charged a ministry leader with a crime. But for the most part stories about abuse received little sustained attention. Reporters for *The Boston Globe*, however, sensed a pattern. Suspecting that the few stories that appeared in the press represented more than isolated incidents, a team of journalists launched a major investigation into the Boston archdiocese. In early 2002 they began publishing what they found.

The *Globe*'s first stories focused on Father John J. Geoghan. Across at least three decades, one hundred and thirty people accused the priest of rape and child abuse. By the mid-1980s, church leaders knew that the priest was preying on young people. Victims' families had begged Geoghan's superiors to intervene to ensure that no more boys suffered. But rather than report the abuse to the police, church leaders simply shuffled the priest from parish to parish, where he continued harming children. "Why," the *Globe* asked, "did it take a succession of three cardinals and many bishops 34 years to place children out of Geoghan's reach?"[2]

Globe journalists discovered that in the previous decade leaders of the Boston archdiocese had settled molestation cases against at least seventy priests who had abused more than two hundred individuals. They had paid out millions of dollars in settlements to bury victims' stories. "For a church that celebrates mystery and often speaks in whispers," one reporter summarized, "it was the most closely held secret of all. Catholic priests were molesting children, crimes so unspeakable that the Archdiocese of Boston went to extraordinary—and expensive—lengths to cover up the scandal."[3]

The *Globe*'s revelations sparked investigations in many other dioceses that continue to this day. Journalists learned that the Boston stories revealed just the tip of the iceberg, and that sexual abuse marred churches in every part of the world. Since then, the global Catholic Church has made substantial changes and now has clearer, stricter, and more transparent policies. Catholic leaders, including the last three popes, have all apologized for clerical abuse and for how the church mishandled it.

Many Catholics, however, saw the church's response as too little, too late. Two decades of revelations undercut the authority and prestige of the church and especially its leaders. A 2019 poll revealed that about eight in ten Americans believed that clergy sexual abuse remained an ongoing problem. It also showed that the scandal drove congregants to quit their churches and to reduce their tithes.[4]

Investigations into the Catholic Church prompted subsequent inquiries into protestant religious communities. The *Houston Chronicle* documented how leaders of the nation's largest protestant denomination, the Southern Baptist Convention, like the Catholic Church, paid victims, quashed their stories, and failed to report sex crimes to local authorities. In many other denominations, executives also ignored and covered up abuse, silenced victims, and shuffled predators from congregation to congregation. Such revelations have inspired younger generations to look for spiritual fulfillment outside of organized religion.

In the 1990s, a different kind of tragedy unfolded in Texas. Vernon Howell, born in 1959 to a teenage mother in Houston, Texas, endured a challenging childhood and struggled at school. Raised in the Seventh-day Adventist tradition, Howell left the church in the early 1980s to join the Branch Davidians, a small splinter group that had separated from the main church in the late 1920s and early 1930s.

Davidian Adventists preached imminent judgment. They expected to face horrific persecution and to go through an intense tribulation that would ultimately lead to the premillennial—but post-tribulation—return of Christ. They preached that at Jesus's return he would cleanse the earth of all impurities in a bloody apocalypse.

In the 1980s, Howell reorganized the Davidian movement. He believed that God had given him, like Adventist founder Ellen G. White, prophetic visions and revelations, which he shared with the community. He also believed that God had anointed him the new King David, a leader chosen to preside over the holy remnant of true believers as the world careened toward Armageddon. This conviction led Howell to change his name to David Koresh, an amalgamation of "David" for the ancient king and "Koresh," the Hebrew form of "Cyrus," an Old Testament figure that God had used to protect his people and execute his judgment on evil.

As Koresh grew in power, his theological proclivities moved beyond the apocalyptic. He determined that God wanted him to father as many children as possible. With the consent of the community, he began sleeping with Davidian wives and teenage daughters.

Koresh taught his small remnant of righteous saints that since God had chosen them to represent him on earth during the tribulation, the forces of evil would try to destroy their movement. To prepare for the inevitable confrontation, Branch Davidians began stockpiling guns and other weapons in their "Mount Carmel" compound outside Waco. Koresh also warned his followers that the devil's soldiers would likely take form as agents of the American government. Like many other premillennialists, Adventists—both in the mainstream movement and in splinter groups, including the Branch Davidians—believed that when the tribulation began, the leaders of the US government would move against the true church.

Almost completely oblivious to Koresh's theology and beliefs, agents from the Bureau of Alcohol, Tobacco, Firearms and Explosives (ATF) tried to storm Koresh's compound on February 28, 1993. They believed that Koresh had violated federal weapons laws and sexually abused children. Koresh had cooperated openly for years with local law enforcement and child protective services, and government agents could have arrested him while he was outside the compound, but they opted for a raid instead. Rather than surrender, the Davidians hunkered down. As agents swarmed the compound, a bloody ninety-minute gun battle ensued, which left four ATF agents dead and at least twenty agents wounded. The invading army shot Koresh twice, but he survived. Six Davidians died in the initial confrontation. The battle ended with a ceasefire followed by a fifty-one-day standoff.[5]

From the beginning the ATF and then the FBI had refused to take Koresh's Christian apocalyptic views seriously. Shortly after the raid began, Koresh called 9-1-1 begging for help and for the government to call off the attack. He tried to tell law enforcement authorities how the raid had fulfilled Branch Davidian prophecy, but they had little interest in listening to or trying to understand Koresh's worldview. "This is life and death," Koresh told them. "Theology . . . is life and death."

David Koresh believed that God had anointed him to preside over the holy remnant of true believers as the world careened toward Armageddon. Almost completely oblivious to Koresh's theology, agents from the Bureau of Alcohol, Tobacco, Firearms and Explosives (ATF) tried to storm Koresh's compound in 1993. Many Americans saw the siege as an assault on their religious liberty. (credit: Steven Reece, Getty)

Despite Koresh's efforts to explain himself, he found it impossible to negotiate with agents who refused to engage with him on a theological level.[6]

As the siege continued, Koresh claimed that God wanted him to open the "seven seals" from the book of Revelation, which would herald the apocalypse. "We believe," he preached to a negotiator, "that America is a great nation and that it, like Assyria and Nineva of old, can hear the message of Jonah and it can have a chance to say hey, you know, this, this—what this guy's teaching out of the book is straight out of the Bible, it's in harmony, it's perfect. Maybe there's a misunderstanding here." Essentially at war with the United States, Koresh still believed that God could use the nation to serve a righteous purpose.[7]

While Koresh hoped his enemies would repent, he had no intention of backing down to the agents of the Antichrist. "You got to do the truth no matter what they do to you," he insisted. Nor was the government going to relent. On April 19, the FBI attacked the compound with tear gas, hoping to drive the Davidians out. Within a few hours, horrific fires consumed the complex and killed many of those inside. The standoff ended with the deaths of Koresh and more than eighty Davidians, including many children.[8]

Koresh had promised negotiators that once he had written up his interpretation of the seven seals, he would exit the compound. FBI agents, who had mostly ignored the counsel of religious studies scholars, had not taken Koresh seriously. They believed that he was stalling (stalling for what was not clear). Federal agents had no sense of Koresh's powerful apocalypticism. "From the very beginning," Congressional investigators later wrote, "negotiators failed to take seriously the point of view of the Davidians." After the tragedy, the FBI found evidence that Koresh was working on an interpretation of the seven seals, just as he had promised.[9]

Koresh's apocalyptic views emerged from a rich tradition. Like millions of Christians before him, he believed in the imminent Second Coming of Christ. He saw in the Bible evidence that some Christians would live through the tribulation and that during that time God wanted the small remnant of saints to battle physically the forces of the Antichrist. When the ATF launched a heavily armed raid against the Branch Davidian compound, this theology produced truly cataclysmic results. The US government, naively and inadvertently, attacked the Davidians' community with overwhelming firepower, playing directly into the Davidians' apocalyptic expectations. As Koresh explained, theology was indeed life and death.

Horrified by what seemed like the government's overreach in Waco, a few people on the far right tried to punish members of the federal government. In 1995, on the anniversary of the Waco tragedy, Gulf War veteran Timothy McVeigh drove a rental truck with explosives up to the Alfred P. Murrah Federal Building in Oklahoma City. He ignited the bomb, which blew off the front of the building and killed 168 people. The Oklahoma City bombing was the most violent act of domestic terrorism in American history. McVeigh claimed to want revenge for the deaths of the Branch Davidians. Journalists and investigators discovered in the wake of the bombing a broad network of far-right militias and White supremacist groups dotting the nation, many of whom grounded their political ideology in visions of apocalyptic White Christian nationalism.

As the millennium approached, the appeal of end-times fantasies grew. In the 1990s, revivalist Tim LaHaye gave premillennialism a modern makeover. Already a bestselling author on prophecy, sex, gender roles, and education, LaHaye set his sights on fiction. Teaming up with novelist Jerry Jenkins, he turned his outline for an end-times drama into *Left Behind*—the first installment in what became a blockbuster sixteen-volume series.

The *Left Behind* books explain through fiction American premillennial eschatology from beginning to end. The first novel opens with the rapture, where all true Christians suddenly vanish from the earth, plunging those left behind into chaos. Only the intervention of the UN secretary-general, a good-looking Romanian named Nicolae Carpathia, brings stability to the global situation. Carpathia turns out to be the Antichrist. To consolidate his power, he organizes a one-world government, a one-world currency, and a one-world religion. Meanwhile, a small remnant of new Christian converts—a "tribulation force"—works to get as many people saved as possible while challenging Carpathia and his henchmen. Eventually, the Antichrist amasses his armies in Israel near the valley of Armageddon for one final attack on Christian and Jewish rebels. But before he can succeed, Christ returns and vanquishes evil.

With over eighty million copies in circulation, the *Left Behind* series has become a cultural juggernaut. It was the best-selling series of novels in US history until *Harry Potter* dethroned it. The franchise spawned a few awful feature-length films starring outspoken evangelical and former teen star Kirk Cameron, which were so bad that LaHaye tried to sue the producers for the damage they did to the books' reputation. Later, when Cameron had moved on to protesting COVID-19 lockdown orders and mask mandates, producers cast Nicolas Cage to try to revive the film series.

Journalists, policymakers, and academics have tried to understand and explain the success of the novels as well as assess their influence on the culture. "In this volatile moment," *Time* magazine claimed after the 9/11 attacks, "many people are starting to read the Left Behind books not as novels but as tomorrow's newspapers." Such was the goal of premillennialists since the late nineteenth century. Former Secretary of State Madeleine Albright even claimed that the books had affected the US's international relations. She fretted that the surge in apocalyptic ideas in the 1990s undermined her ability to work with the United Nations and destabilized the Middle East peace process. Yet most readers of the novels had no idea that the *Left Behind* authors intended to do anything more than tell a good story.[10]

Despite Tim LaHaye and David Koresh's differences, they shared the conviction that the kingdom of God would not appear on earth before the great battle of Armageddon. Another group of protestants, called reconstructionists, had a different view of the end-times. Beginning in the 1960s and working mostly from within the conservative stream, they resurrected and reconfigured classical Calvinism for the modern world with its emphasis on establishing a Christian society based on biblical law. Reconstructionists believed that God ultimately intended to restore Old Testament ideals on earth, which meant among other things the death penalty both for blasphemers and for those engaged in same-sex relationships.

Rousas John Rushdoony was the leading political theologian of reconstruction and the movement's most significant early organizer. The son of Armenian immigrants, Rushdoony attended the University of California, Berkeley, and then earned a divinity degree at the Pacific School of Religion and ordination from the Presbyterians. He embarked on a career as a missionary to the Shoshone and Paiute peoples in the US West. Driven by what he saw as the government's overreach, he called for more independence for tribes. In 1952 he left missionary work to serve as pastor of a small Presbyterian church in Santa Cruz, California. He began partnering with different groups of right-wing political activists against what they saw as an overbearing federal government.

In the mid-1960s, Rushdoony raised enough money to establish the Chalcedon Foundation, which became the epicenter of his work and of the reconstruction movement. Through the foundation, Rushdoony sought to educate Americans about the dangers of the state, to develop a group of like-minded disciples to spread his message, and to engage in various kinds of advocacy. They reshaped homeschooling in the United States, influenced various politicians (mostly libertarians) including Senator Rand Paul, and inspired the work of some far-right religious militias. They also engaged in regular legal advocacy, waging numerous battles in defense of Christian "rights." Rushdoony's massive two-volume *Institutes of Biblical Law* served as the defining text of the reconstruction movement.

In recent decades reconstruction has taken hold in many places around the United States. For example, in the college town of Moscow, Idaho, home to the University of Idaho, and just seven miles east of Washington State University, self-taught minister Doug Wilson launched a new church in the late 1970s and then a new denomination, the Confederation of Reformed Evangelical Churches. Members of the group later changed their denomination's name to "Communion of Reformed Evangelical Churches" because some people thought the denomination might have links to the Civil War–era Confederacy, the Confederate States of America. This was not a stretch. Wilson liked to emphasize what he saw as the benefits of chattel slavery to people of African ancestry.

Wilson claimed that his movement grew out of the classical reformed tradition. He and his allies placed significant emphasis on cultivating the life of the mind, the Western canon, and rigorous intellectual debate. They established a small college, located on prime real estate at the center of downtown Moscow. They recruited fellow believers to the region, and church members now own many of the businesses and restaurants in the area. They also run a K–12 school. Their stated goal is to make Moscow a "Christian town."

Starting locally, Wilson aspired to train a new generation of Christian leaders to infiltrate and eventually take charge of the nation's most powerful institutions. His disciples graduate from his school, scatter across the country, and open new churches to spread his theology. In recent years, however, Wilson and his allies have strayed from their original mission. Their decision to go all in on the culture wars overshadowed their focus on classical Christian education. COVID-19 lockdowns, civil rights for trans Americans, and gender-neutral restrooms have Wilson spitting mad and firing up flamethrowers (literally) in silly YouTube videos.

The Doug Wilson of the 2020s morphed from a wannabe Francis Schaeffer, a pseudo-intellectual guru with acolytes worshipping at his feet, to a sad, diminished echo of the culture-warring Jerry Falwell rambling about gays, abortionists, and Anthony Fauci, the former director of the National Institute of Allergy and Infectious Diseases. Wilson loves to provoke, to hear himself speak, and to go viral by making the most outlandish and hateful of comments. Like Falwell, he enjoys picking on the powerless. Few people living in the greater Palouse region around Moscow see anything that resembles Jesus in Wilson or his ministry. But the White nationalist militias in northern Idaho love the minister and what he represents. Meanwhile, through the publishing arm of his ministry and the new churches joining his network, his ideas are spreading, influencing among others Donald Trump's Secretary of Defense Pete Hegseth.

At the same time that Wilson was building his ministry, Americans discovered a new threat in the form of al-Qaeda, an organization that championed an extreme form of Islam. In the 1990s, al-Qaeda leaders worked to purge Muslim counties of Western influence, and they wanted to establish and promote Islamic governments that shared their views. Al-Qaeda had many enemies, but leaders of the group particularly resented United States influence in the Middle East. On the morning of September 11, 2001, nineteen al-Qaeda terrorists highjacked four US commercial airplanes and crashed them into the World Trade Center buildings in Manhattan, the Pentagon, and into a field in Pennsylvania, killing nearly three thousand people.

The events of 9/11 stunned the nation. Influential revivalist Christians claimed that the attacks exposed a hidden war for global dominance between Islam and Christianity. Some also saw the tragedy as a sign of God's judgment. Appearing on Pat Robertson's television show, Jerry Falwell claimed that the "sins" of the United States had so angered God that he withdrew his protection from the country. "I really believe," Falwell admonished, "that the pagans and the abortionists, and the feminists, and the gays and the lesbians who are actively trying to make that an alternative lifestyle, the ACLU, People for the American Way, all of them who have tried to secularize America. I point the finger in their face and say 'You helped this happen.'" He later apologized for his words, but this kind of over-the-top rhetoric made Falwell one of the most controversial leaders in the nation.[11]

Once again, revivalists rallied for a new crusade, convinced that God had set the United States apart as his chosen instrument to halt the spread of Islam and reestablish moral and political order across the globe. They saw America not merely as a nation, but as a divinely appointed force—a bulwark against chaos and a beacon of righteousness in a world they believed was teetering on the brink.

The president at the time, George W. Bush, had made the Christian faith central to his political career. His revivalist convictions, combined with his mainline roots and Methodist Church membership, helped him appeal to political conservatives across the protestant spectrum and many Catholics too. During a Republican presidential primary debate in Iowa in 2000, a moderator asked the candidates to name their favorite philosopher. Bush didn't hesitate; it was Jesus Christ "because he changed my heart." When the moderator pushed the candidate to elaborate on what he meant, Bush replied, "If they don't know, it's going to be hard to explain. When you turn your heart and your life over to Christ, when you accept Christ as the savior, it changes your heart."[12]

Bush infused Christianity into his policy agenda more overtly than any of his post–World War II predecessors. In an era in which the nation grew less religious, he made the presidency more religious. Bush launched the Office of Faith-Based and Community Initiatives, advocated for vouchers for parents to send their children to private schools, and went full in on the culture wars, attacking reproductive choice, stem-cell research, and the campaign for marriage equality. Ron Suskind, writing in *The New York Times Magazine*, credited Bush with creating a "faith-based presidency."[13]

Almost immediately after 9/11, Bush used Christian language to describe the conflict against al-Qaeda, calling it a "crusade." "We need to be alert to the fact that these evildoers still exist," he told the American people. "This is a new kind of—a new kind of evil. And we understand. And the American people are beginning to understand. This crusade, this war on terrorism is going to take a while, and the American people must be patient." White House aides realized Bush had stumbled. Calling the American response to al-Qaeda and the war in Afghanistan a "crusade" gave the conflict a hyper-religious connotation in an era when many Americans claimed to value religious tolerance and pluralism. But his words were authentic. Bush's rhetoric of an axis of evil, of black and white, good and bad, you-are-for-us-or-against-us ultimatums, and the president's vision for transforming the Middle East, reflected his ideals and those of modern evangelicalism.[14]

In 2003, Bush expanded the war beyond Afghanistan and into Iraq. Leaders of the largest White protestant denomination in the nation, the Southern Baptist Convention, had encouraged the move. "We believe that your policies concerning the ongoing international terrorist campaign against America are both right and just," Richard Land, the head of the SBC ethics commission, wrote before the invasion. "Specifically, we believe that your stated policies concerning Saddam Hussein . . . are prudent and fall well within the time-honored criteria of just war theory as developed by Christian theologians in the late fourth and early fifth centuries A.D." When *The Wall Street Journal* profiled some religious leaders who criticized the war, Bush's evangelical surrogates rallied behind him. Land, along with James Dobson, Albert Mohler, D. James Kennedy, Jay Sekulow (who later served as one of Donald Trump's impeachment trial lawyers), and other leaders of the religious right, wrote the newspaper's editor to publicly reaffirm their support for the president and the war.[15]

Within a few weeks, the US military took control of the Iraqi capital of Baghdad. When speaking to French President Jacques Chirac about the conflict, Bush may have invoked Ezekiel's end-times prophecy. "Biblical prophecies are being fulfilled," the American president apparently determined. "This confrontation is willed by God, who wants to use this conflict to erase his people's enemies before a new age begins." Premillennial convictions did not drive Bush's decisions. Nevertheless, he well understood that the neoconservative ideals undergirding his foreign policy meshed almost perfectly with the ideas of evangelical apocalypticism.[16]

Under Ronald Reagan and later George W. Bush, revivalists steadily expanded their influence over American politics, leading many to see the Republican Party as the party of Christian faith. During this era, evangelicals became a key pillar of the GOP coalition, but their ambitions didn't stop there. Religious leaders aimed not just to support the party, but to reshape it in their own image. Meanwhile, Americans increasingly viewed the Democrats as the party of secularism and atheism. Yet on the horizon stood a young, charismatic Democratic politician from Illinois, molded by the liberationist tradition, who set out to change that.

31

THE END OF CHRISTIAN AMERICA OR A NEW BEGINNING?

In 1846, the protestant establishment exercised significant influence in the United States. To win elections, aspiring politicians needed to adopt mainstream Christians' ideals and values. Abraham Lincoln learned this lesson when he ran for Congress. He suppressed his true feelings about faith, calibrated his speeches to the pious sensitivities of his audiences, and aligned himself with orthodox Christian thought.

By 2008 so much had changed.

Or had it?

During the primaries that year, Senator Barack Hussein Obama sought the Democratic Party's nomination for president. Rising in the polls, he seemed positioned to beat his main rival, Hillary Clinton. Then a religious controversy erupted. Journalists for ABC News had scrutinized decades of sermons delivered by Obama's Chicago pastor and spiritual mentor, Jeremiah Wright.

Obama had stumbled his way into Wright's fellowship and into liberationist Christianity. His mother did not raise him in church, and as a young man he had little interest in religion. "In our household," Obama remembered, "the Bible, the Koran, and the Bhagavad Gita sat on the shelf alongside books of Greek and Norse and African mythology." But while working as a community organizer, he encountered a world built by the social gospel, the Christianity of the civil rights movement, and Black liberation theology. Curious about the religious vibrancy he saw in the lives of those with whom he worked, in 1988 he attended a service at Wright's Trinity United Church of Christ. Wright's sermon that morning focused on the "audacity of hope." Obama described how the message inspired him, how Wright helped him see the merging of "the stories of ordinary black people" with biblical epics. "Those stories—of survival, and freedom, and hope—became our story, my story; the blood that had spilled was our blood, the tears our tears; until this black church, on this bright day, seemed once more a vessel carrying the story of a people into future generations and into a larger world."[1]

Unlike Obama, Wright was more prophet than politician. During the campaign, producers for ABC News highlighted the most incendiary clips they could find from the minister's long career. Wright's most controversial messages focused on American foreign policy and the war on terror. Immediately following 9/11, Wright claimed that the attack on the United States represented the judgment of God. The American government, he observed, had taken Indigenous land, dropped atomic bombs on civilians, and interfered in Latin American politics.

A 2003 sermon on the US government proved even more controversial. In this message Wright mixed crank theories with examples of American leaders' lies, such as the Bush administration's claim that Saddam Hussein helped orchestrate 9/11. Wright stated, for example, that federal scientists developed HIV to commit mass genocide. The government, he concluded, "wants us to sing 'God Bless America.' No, no, no, not God Bless America. God damn America—that's in the Bible—for killing innocent people. God damn America, for treating our citizens as less than human. God damn America, as long as she tries to act like she is God, and she is supreme. The United States government has failed the vast majority of her citizens of African descent."[2]

With the "God damn America" clip playing around the clock on cable news, Obama felt compelled to address the controversy. To achieve mainstream success, he needed to espouse mainstream (read: White) Christian ideals and not the prophetic critique of the nation so prominent in the liberation stream. "The profound mistake of Reverend Wright's sermons is not that he spoke about racism in our society," Obama lectured. "It's that he spoke as if our society was static; as if no progress has been made. . . . But what we know—what we have seen—is that America can change. That is [the] true genius of this nation. What we have already achieved gives us hope—the audacity to hope—for what we can and must achieve tomorrow."[3]

Like Lincoln putting up his handbills in 1846 to signal his orthodoxy, Obama withdrew his membership from Trinity and ended his relationship with Wright. Politics demanded it. The people demanded it. Those using religion to propel culture war demanded it. Obama hoped that the United States might finally be ready for a Black president, but he learned it was not ready for a Black president driven by liberationist Christianity.

Obama absorbed a lesson that American political leaders kept learning well into the twenty-first century. Despite the nation's seeming secularization and the fracturing of protestantism, Christianity remained central to American public life. The old protestant establishment may have foundered, but powerful activists sought to remake it and impose their faith and will on the nation. Republican leaders including George W. Bush and later Donald Trump understood this, and they made religion central to their campaigns. Democrats like Obama and Joe Biden struggled to catch up.

At the same time, the Supreme Court began overturning long-held precedents, reversing course and loosening the boundaries between church and state. A majority of justices allowed twenty-first-century Christians, like their nineteenth-century predecessors, to resurrect a form of Christian supremacy, to impose their beliefs on the rest of the nation. The court determined that Christians' religious convictions deserved more protections than other civil rights.

In the new millennium, Christianity remained deeply entwined with American identity—not as a fading legacy, but as a living force shaping the nation's laws, politics, and culture. The United States may not be the city on a hill, but it remained distinct among its peers. Even as formal religious adherence declined, the struggle between those seeking to build a Christian nation—a chosen land—and those defending secularism, pluralism, and democratic inclusion has endured. Both sides continue to frame their visions in religious terms, underscoring the profound and persistent role Christianity plays in structuring America's most urgent social and political debates.

From the start of his career, Obama integrated faith with his political aspirations. He determined that Democrats should stop allowing Republicans like President George W. Bush to claim Christianity as theirs alone. He encouraged his fellow party members to wear their religions on their sleeves. While running for the US Senate in 2004, Obama delivered a primetime address at the Democratic National Convention on behalf of presidential candidate and Roman Catholic John Kerry. Obama's speech was brilliant, both in terms of its content and in demonstrating his rhetorical power. "There are those who are preparing to divide us," he warned, "the spin masters and negative ad peddlers who embrace the politics of anything goes. Well, I say to them tonight, there's not a liberal America and a conservative America—there's the United States of America. . . . We worship an awesome God in the Blue States, and we don't like federal agents poking around our libraries in the Red States." In referencing the "worship" of an "awesome God," he alluded to an extremely popular evangelical chorus. He knew exactly what audiences he aspired to win over.[4]

In 2006, Barack Obama laid out his vision for the relationship between faith and politics. He pointed to polling data showing that religious identity, or its absence, had become one of the strongest predictors of political allegiance, with religious voters overwhelmingly leaning Republican. This pattern frustrated Obama, who urged Democrats to embrace and speak openly about their own faith commitments, challenging the party's growing reputation as secular or disconnected from religious life. "I think we make a mistake," he wrote, "when we fail to acknowledge the power of faith in people's lives—in the lives of the American people—and I think it's time that we join a serious debate about how to reconcile faith with our modern, pluralistic democracy." His argument was both practical and ideological. "And if we're going to do that then we first need to understand that Americans are a religious people. 90 percent of us believe in God, 70 percent affiliate themselves with an organized religion, 38 percent call themselves committed Christians, and substantially more people in America believe in angels than they do in evolution."[5]

Democrats had allowed their opponents to "fill the vacuum" in peoples' lives, he contended, "cynically" manipulating Christianity to "justify partisan ends." Meanwhile, "secularists" and party operatives "are wrong when they ask believers to leave their religion at the door before entering into the public square." He believed that history justified his position. "Frederick Douglass, Abraham Lincoln, William Jennings Bryan, Dorothy Day, Martin Luther King—indeed, the majority of great reformers in American history—were not only motivated by faith, but repeatedly used religious language to argue for their cause. So to say that men and women should not inject their 'personal morality' into public policy debates is a practical absurdity." American law, the former president of the *Harvard Law Review* argued, "is by definition a codification of morality, much of it grounded in the Judeo-Christian tradition."[6]

Obama's efforts to inject more religion into Democratic politics guaranteed that it would play an unusually large role in the 2008 primary. The contest pitted the first-term Illinois senator against fellow senator Hillary Clinton. For years Clinton had acknowledged her deep and abiding Christian faith, which helped fuel her passion for social and economic justice. She grew up in a mainline Methodist church, where she developed a strong commitment to the social gospel. But like many mainliners, she felt uncomfortable speaking about faith in public, and when asked about her convictions she rarely used the word "Jesus." She symbolized the prototypical Democrat who so frustrated Obama, reticent to inject religion into her politics despite her fervent and enduring Christian convictions, thereby ceding by default questions of religion to the GOP.

Obama, in contrast, talked a lot about religion, which nearly backfired when the media discovered Jeremiah Wright's old sermons. Obama made things even worse during a private campaign fundraiser in San Francisco in which he seemed to depict religion as a crutch heralded by those too dumb to know any better. Previous administrations had failed rural voters, he claimed. "And it's not surprising then they get bitter, they cling to guns or religion or antipathy to people who aren't like them or anti-immigrant sentiment or antitrade sentiment as a way to explain their frustrations." Speeches like these fueled the skepticism of Obama critics, who believed that his faith talk was merely a strategic ploy to advance his political career. Yet Obama persevered, defeating Clinton and then Republican candidate John McCain.[7]

In the early years of his presidency, Obama routinely talked about his conversion, about Jesus dying for humans' sins, and about the power of the resurrection. In fact, he mentioned Jesus far more often than Bush had. He also often linked his policy proposals to his Christian values. On health care, for example, he claimed to have "one final idea today that will help break the cycle of poverty—affordable health care for every American. Our God is big enough for that now."[8]

Nevertheless, Obama did not preach the Christian nationalism or Christian supremacy of the religious right but instead championed American religious pluralism and even the value of unbelief. Although his faith guided him, he did not seek to impose his beliefs on others. During his inaugural address he described the United States as "a nation of Christians and Muslims, Jews and Hindus and nonbelievers." At a news conference in Turkey, he told a predominately Muslim audience that despite the United States' "very large Christian population, we do not consider ourselves a Christian nation or a Jewish nation or a Muslim nation; we consider ourselves a nation of citizens who are bound by ideals and a set of values." Yet like Bush before him, Obama believed that all governments should prioritize American concepts of religious liberty. "People in every country," he asserted in a speech in Cairo, "should be free to choose and live their faith based upon the persuasion of the mind and the heart and the soul. This tolerance is essential for religion to thrive." In other words, tolerate all except those whose religious convictions tell them not to be tolerant.[9]

Obama often invoked his Christian faith as he navigated some of the most divisive culture war battles of his presidency, including the long-running debate over same-sex marriage. As both a candidate and president, he supported full legal equality for the LGBTQ+ community and sought new legislation to better track and prosecute hate crimes. He also signed the repeal of the Clinton-era "Don't ask, don't tell" policy, allowing gays and lesbians to serve openly in the military. Yet, like Bill Clinton before him, Obama initially opposed marriage equality.

Prodded by Vice President Joe Biden during their 2012 campaign for a second term, Obama finally shifted his position. "We are both practicing Christians," he said during an interview alongside his wife, Michelle, "but, you know, when we think about our faith, the thing at root that we think about is, not only Christ sacrificing Himself on our behalf, but it's also the golden rule, you know, treat others the way you would want to be treated." When Obama finally threw his support behind same-sex marriage, he did it in the language of Christianity.[10]

Three years later the Supreme Court made same-sex marriage the law of the land in *Obergefell v. Hodges* (2015). The majority of justices concluded that the Fourteenth Amendment of the Constitution safeguarded the rights of same-sex couples to marry with the same rights and benefits as other couples. Same-sex couples now had a president who endorsed their right to marry and a court that appeared ready, in certain instances, to provide them equal protection under the law.

Obama hoped that Hillary Clinton would succeed him in 2016 as president and that she would solidify his legacy. The Democrats mostly rallied behind her. The GOP had a harder time selecting a nominee.

After a wild and chaotic primary, Republicans settled on Donald Trump, a hedonistic Presbyterian who drew on the business-friendly positive thinking of his one-time pastor Norman Vincent Peale. Although most of the traditional leaders of the religious right expressed little faith and confidence in Trump, a handful of Christian ministers believed that God was working in surprising and miraculous ways through the reality television star.

Jerry Falwell Jr., who had taken over his father's university, became one of the first major religious-right leaders to endorse Trump during the primary. But more lay behind his endorsement than anyone at the time knew. Falwell had an ongoing business partnership with an attractive young man, a former pool boy from Miami named Giancarlo Granda. In 2014 sexually explicit pictures of Jerry's wife, Becki, had fallen into the hands of some of Granda's other business partners who aimed to use them to shake down the Falwells for cash. Meanwhile, Becki Falwell and Granda were in the midst of a seven-year sexual relationship that Jerry encouraged (he sometimes watched their sexual acts). Faced with the threat of Becki's pics going public, Falwell turned to Trump attorney and fixer Michael Cohen for help. Cohen made the pictures vanish. Falwell may well have endorsed Trump during the 2016 primaries even if Cohen did not have compromising pictures of his wife, but it didn't hurt Trump that he had blackmail material at the ready.[11]

Pentecostal minister Frank Amedia also backed Trump earlier than most other Christian leaders. During the campaign he served as Trump's "liaison for Christian policy." Amedia claimed that a secret, spiritual battle raged between good and evil, light and dark, Christ and Antichrist. "If we could see into the heavenlies right now," Amedia claimed in an interview about Trump, "we would see a skirmish going on that I believe is the beginnings of the preparation of the way of the coming of the Lord." Amedia told all who would listen that a Trump victory over Clinton would ensure that the United States "stays under the favor of God," that it remained his chosen land. To refuse to support Trump, then, meant defying God and putting the nation at risk.[12]

Along with Amedia and Falwell, Trump found an even more important ally in the person of Paula White-Cain, a minister whom he appointed to lead his evangelical advisory board. Focus on the Family founder James Dobson claimed that White-Cain converted Trump to revivalist Christianity during the campaign, which allowed leaders like Dobson to assert that Jesus had washed away all of Trump's many, many past sins. If God had forgiven Trump, why shouldn't Christian voters?

White-Cain did not have close ties to the old guard of the religious right. Instead, she served as a leader in the little-understood New Apostolic Reformation (NAR). Many of the leaders of the NAR emerged from nondenominational churches rooted in pentecostalism. They believed that God had begun a fresh work through their loosely linked cell networks independent of established denominations. The men and women at the helm of NAR churches claimed that the Holy Spirit blessed them with spiritual gifts, which gave them apostolic authority and empowered them to plant and lead churches.

Fuller Theological Seminary Professor C. Peter Wagner participated in and helped chronicle the rise of the NAR in the late 1990s. In an era characterized by the implosion of the mainline, and stagnation among many revivalist denominations, Wagner had grown enamored with independent pentecostalism and sought to explain its ability to buck trends, attract followers, and speak to people around the world. In a book entitled *Churchquake!* Wagner gave the New Apostolic Reformation its name and described its characteristics. He called it "an extraordinary work of God at the close of the twentieth century, which is, to a significant extent, changing the shape of Protestant Christianity around the world." Most of the nation's churches, he believed, had lost their way. "Structures that were originally developed to facilitate evangelism, Christian nurture, worship, social service and ministry in general," he wrote, had become "the causes of much inefficiency and ineffectiveness in these same areas. Dysfunctionalism has been setting in." Reading the same demographic data as everyone else, he surmised that "the old-line denominations are losing their market share of the American public, so to speak. The newer denominations, including the Pentecostals, have flattened out; and an increasing share is being served, at least in part, by the heretofore semi-invisible New Apostolic Reformation."[13]

New Apostolic Reformation leaders fostered a strong Christian nationalist strain within their flocks. They taught that the United States would help establish God's kingdom in the world. To make this happen, they followed what NAR leader Lance Wallnau dubbed the "seven mountain mandate." They sought to wrestle control of seven core American institutions—family, religion, education, media, arts and entertainment, business, and government (and sometimes they included science and technology as one of the mountains)—from the demons they believed controlled them. "We are entering a bigger battle than most of us appreciate," Wallnau instructed followers. Encouraging believers' political activism, he proclaimed, "God loves the idea of nations, and nations are designed to reveal His glory. . . . Jesus intends that you and I, as modern day kings and priests, teach nations His wonderful secrets. We are to make disciples, not of people only, but of nations." Like so many before him, he believed that American Christians played a special role in God's plan. "You are about to pioneer the last great chapter of the journey of the Church—into the Kingdom Age," he told followers.[14]

Just a few years after writing these words, he found a leader to assist NAR Christians in their efforts to overtake American institutions. God chose Donald Trump, Wallnau and his allies believed, as the vehicle for helping them achieve their goals. They saw him as a modern incarnation of Old Testament king Cyrus, a non-Jewish king whom God used to aid the Hebrews, his chosen people.

Since many of the traditional leaders of evangelicalism had endorsed other candidates in the 2016 primary, the famously vindictive Trump showed little interest in working with them. Instead, he allowed White-Cain to introduce him to dozens of more fringy ministers. They included shady-seeming televangelists, faith healers, and messianic rabbis. Pentecostal prophets and apostles, long ostracized from the centers of protestant power, suddenly had a friend who might win the White House. Eventually leaders of the religious right began to fall into line behind Trump's oddball collection of tongues-speaking, prosperity-preaching, Gucci-wearing, sun-tanned evangelists.

The menagerie of ministers and evangelists Paula White-Cain assembled, combined with the enthusiasm of the evangelicals in the pews, delivered for the New Yorker. Despite Trump's clear lack of Christian character and his short-lived "conversion," in the general election he won 81 percent of the White evangelical vote, a higher percentage than previous GOP frontrunners George W. Bush, Mitt Romney, and John McCain.[15]

Trump's vow to appoint antiabortion justices to the Supreme Court galvanized revivalist and conservative Catholic support behind him, and the new president followed through. First, Trump nominated and the Senate confirmed Neil Gorsuch to the seat that Senate Majority Leader Mitch McConnell had blocked Obama from filling in the last year of his presidency. In 2018, Trump nominated Brett Kavanaugh to replace the retiring Anthony Kennedy. Then on September 18, 2020, the liberal and feminist icon Ruth Bader Ginsburg died. With just over six weeks until the next presidential election, Trump rammed a new justice, Amy Coney Barrett, through the Senate. The president presided over the swearing-in of the conservative Catholic mother of seven on October 26, 2020, one week before Election Day. The ceremony turned out to be a COVID-19 super-spreader event. Under Trump, conservatives gained a supermajority on the court. Decades of hard work had brought conservative activists the ultimate prize—a supermajority of justices sensitive to their priorities and willing to overturn multiple precedents they didn't like (a move that critics point out is not at all "conservative").

As Trump campaigned for reelection in 2020, he worked to hold on to the White evangelical vote. Frustrated by the Black Lives Matter movement and the broader fight for racial justice, Trump had riot police deploy tear gas to forcibly remove protesters from Lafayette Square, across the street from the White House. He then marched through the square, and over to the front of St. John's Church. With photographers at the ready, he raised a Bible over his head. Although he did not speak, his message was clear. He represented

Christianity, church, and the good book, while those agitating for racial justice did not. He choreographed the move in part to appeal to evangelicals, who he knew needed to turn out for him again that November.

To challenge Trump, the Democrats nominated Joe Biden. A lifelong Catholic, Biden regularly went to mass, took communion, and prayed the rosary. During the campaign, Biden ran multiple advertisements touting his Christianity. Like Obama before him, he wanted to remind Americans that they did not have to choose between faith and secularism, but among competing forms of Christianity. Biden offered a modern, Catholic version of the old social gospel, while Trump seemed to many Americans to represent an angry, intolerant, irrational form of patriarchal White Christian nationalism that was grounded more in political rhetoric than sincere conviction.

In the 2020 election, Trump secured the votes of 85 percent of those Americans who both self-identified as evangelicals and attended church regularly, and 81 percent of those who claimed to be

On June 1, 2020, President Donald Trump walked from the White House to St. John's Church. There, posing for cameras, he held a Bible aloft. Though he said nothing, the symbolism was unmistakable: he stood for Christianity, church, and America—while those demanding racial justice threatened God's chosen land. (credit: Brendan Smialowski, Getty)

evangelical but rarely attended church. It was not enough. Biden won the election.[16]

Trump, however, refused to concede. Instead, he traded in conspiracy theories and encouraged his followers to "take back" the country. Christian supporters descended on the Capitol in early January, where they engaged in multiple "Jericho Marches." They circled the Supreme Court and the Capitol, praying and blowing shofars, old Jewish horns, replicating the Old Testament Hebrews' siege of Jericho. On January 6, the day that Congress met to certify the electoral results, Trump's supporters attended a rally on the National Mall where the president encouraged them to "fight like hell." Then they marched to the Capitol and violently forced their way inside, beating Capitol police along the way. The evangelical faithful mixed in amid the QAnon adherents, anti-Semites, neo-Confederates, and revolutionary cosplayers. They carried signs that read "Jesus Saves," "In God We Trust," "Jesus 2020," and "Jesus is My Savior, Trump is my President." One man marched through the halls of Congress carrying a Christian flag, and another waved a Bible. Some groups chanted, "The blood of Jesus covering this place."

These Christians believed they had no choice but to try to overthrow the Congress. For more than a month, various evangelicals had claimed in sermons, on social media, and during protests that malicious forces had stolen the election, conspired to quash Christian liberties, and aimed to clamp down on their freedom to worship and spread the Christian gospel. They felt sure that the final days of history had arrived and that the Capitol marked the site of an epochal battle. As one evangelical from Texas told *The New York Times*, "We are fighting good versus evil, dark versus light."[17]

Like their predecessors who championed the *Protocols*, this group of Christians eagerly embraced Trump's conspiratorial lies, and social media became an ideal venue for getting their ideas into the mainstream. They believed that Barack Obama was born in Africa, making him an illegitimate president, and that he was a Muslim too. They partnered with QAnon activists in accusing Democrats and Hollywood stars of secretly committing atrocious immoral acts that include cannibalism, pedophilia, and sex trafficking. They drew on anti-Semitic tropes to argue that billionaire philanthropist George Soros used his vast wealth to construct a one-world, anti-God government. They saw lies as truth and truth as lies.

And in their world, Joe Biden had stolen the 2020 presidential election from Donald Trump. A fake election pushing Trump out of the way meant that Satan could bring his plans for globalization and world domination to fruition. Revivalist talk radio host and Trump ally Eric Metaxas summarized their views on Facebook right after the insurrection. "When the left is THIS desperate, be sure their end is nigh," he wrote. "They have pushed their narrative as far as it can go & many have been blinded to anything else. BUT GOD IS ABLE TO DELIVER. This is a spiritual battle. God alone can deliver from this Satanic conspiracy. He will do it."[18]

When Biden took the oath of office fourteen days after the insurrection, many pro-Trump Christian activists, as well as members of the NAR who claimed that prophecy foretold a second Trump presidency, had to pivot. They resurrected and reconfigured a new version of the Lost Cause for a new era. They depicted Trump as a Jesus figure, a martyr to the cause of Christian righteousness, who may have suffered an electoral death but who was destined to have a political resurrection.

In the meantime, savvy activists ensured that Christianity continued to saturate American life. Politically conservative Christians had recognized decades earlier that many Americans disagreed with them on many of their fundamental cultural priorities. On gay rights, sexual norms, abortion, and feminism they lost ground every year. Having ceded their ability to compel most Americans to support their policies through the democratic process, they instead turned to the courts, where decades of patient work bore fruit.

Religious activists working to restore elements of nineteenth-century Christian nationalism found a receptive majority on the Supreme Court ready to advance their cause. The Roberts court supported their efforts to undermine the strict separation of church and state that earlier courts had upheld since the landmark 1947 *Everson* decision. The justices began prioritizing the religious rights of Christians over other kinds of rights.

In 2014, the court ruled in a 5–4 decision that a for-profit corporation could essentially be "Christian" (which might be a surprise to Jesus). The case centered on Hobby Lobby, whose owners, the evangelical Green family, objected to an Affordable Care Act mandate requiring employer-provided health insurance to cover contraceptives for their thirteen thousand employees. Claiming their business was run according to biblical principles, the Greens argued that providing such coverage violated their religious liberty. The court sided with them, allowing corporations to deny contraceptive coverage based on the owners' personal religious beliefs. The justices effectively granted religious rights to corporations and restricted employees' access to federally mandated healthcare.[19]

Another case involved school prayer. It originated in Bremerton, Washington, where high school football coach Joseph Kennedy routinely invited his players to join him in prayer at the end of games. They knelt together at the fifty-yard line in a public demonstration of Christian faith. Sometimes Kennedy also led prayers during official school activities. School administrators wanted the coach to stop the public prayers to ensure that the school did not run afoul of the establishment clause. The court disagreed. Writing for the majority, Justice Neil Gorsuch argued that prohibiting the postgame prayers "would be a sure sign that our Establishment Clause jurisprudence had gone off the rails. In the name of protecting religious liberty," he claimed, the school district "would have us suppress it. Rather than respect the First Amendment's double protection for religious expression, it would have us preference secular activity." In a dissenting opinion Justice Sonia Sotomayor argued that the decision hindered Americans' religious liberty. In this case a school authority indirectly compelled his players to join him in his chosen religious activity, not theirs. "As much as the Court protests otherwise, today's decision is no victory for religious liberty."[20]

In addition to defending evangelicals' public worship in taxpayer-supported institutions, the court also picked up another longtime part of the religious right's agenda, moving to limit gay rights. In late 2017 the court heard a case about a business owner and baker in Colorado who refused to design and bake a cake for a same-sex couple. He claimed that "to create a wedding cake for an event that celebrates something that directly goes against the teachings of the Bible, would have been a personal endorsement and participation in the ceremony and relationship that they were entering into." The court sided with the baker. But Justice Kennedy, who wrote the majority opinion, dodged the question of discrimination and instead focused on how the State of Colorado had inconsistently applied its antidiscrimination laws. The court's move failed to settle the controversy.[21]

The issue of antigay discrimination came up again in 2022. In this case, an evangelical woman wanted to open a new wedding web-design business that denied service to same-sex couples. The court's majority upheld her right, and that of Christians more generally, to discriminate. "Today," Justice Sotomayor noted in a dissenting opinion, "the Court, for the first time in its history, grants a business open to the public a constitutional right to refuse to serve members of a protected class." She warned that little distinguished this case from one that might arise if a business owner tried to discriminate against people in mixed-race marriages by citing her religious beliefs, which just decades earlier Southern White Christians had tried to do.[22]

As enthused as religious-right activists felt about the preferential treatment they received from the Roberts court, the ultimate prize remained overturning *Roe v. Wade*. The issue of abortion had in part helped draw revivalist evangelicals and Catholics into common cause in the late 1970s, and it had provided a significant part of the foundation for their alliance with the Republican Party. But GOP policymakers never seemed to take ending abortion all that seriously, and political leaders recognized that most Americans supported *Roe*. The idea that the court would overturn reproductive choice seemed like a pipe dream. But Donald Trump had promised to appoint justices who would do the job in exchange for votes, and, with the help of Senate Majority Leader Mitch McConnell, he delivered.

On June 24, 2022, the Supreme Court overturned *Roe* in *Dobbs v. Jackson Women's Health Organization.* Writing for the majority, conservative Catholic Justice Samuel Alito framed the decision as one based in a generic "morality." He went out of his way to insist that Americans should read the decision narrowly and that the justices had no intention of overturning other rights that the court had historically upheld based on similar reasoning. But this distinction rested on a weak foundation, and his ally, another Catholic, Justice Clarence Thomas pounced on it. "In future cases," Thomas wrote in a concurrence, "we should reconsider all of this Court's substantive due process precedents," and then he named the three he thought most in need of reassessment: *Griswold* (which protects Americans' right to contraceptives), *Lawrence* (which protects Americans' right to sexual freedom including same-sex acts), and *Obergefell* (which protects Americans' rights to same-sex marriage). He noted that the court had a "duty" to "correct the error" established in these similar "privacy" cases. Thomas, who is in a mixed-race marriage, did not mention *Loving v. Virginia*, another similarly reasoned case that affirms Americans' constitutional right to marry who they want regardless of race.[23]

In overturning *Roe*, the court gave the states the authority to determine their own abortion policies. The Alabama Supreme Court applied Dobbs in exactly the way leaders of the pro-life movement had hoped. Alabama justices determined that life began when the sperm and egg came together—in effect putting an embryo, even one outside of the womb, under the protection of the state constitution. State Supreme Court Chief Justice Tom Parker cited the Bible and his own Christian views in an opinion to argue that life began at conception. The principle that human life is distinct from that of other animals "has deep roots," he wrote, "that reach back to the creation of man 'in the image of God.' Genesis 1:27." He then went on to quote church fathers Augustine, Aquinas, and Calvin, among others, to justify his decision. "Human life cannot be wrongfully destroyed without incurring the wrath of a holy God, who views the destruction of His image as an affront to Himself," he wrote. Parker saw no problem in using his personal Christian theological views—claiming that they represented the views of the people in his state—as a basis for determining law.[24]

The same week that the Alabama court released its decision, Parker gave an interview in which he affirmed the New Apostolic Reformation's "seven mountain mandate." He believed that his position on Alabama's highest court allowed him to do his part to reclaim the United States for Jesus and for his interpretation of the Christian faith, revealing how the NAR had moved from the margins to the center of American political-religious power.[25]

The end of *Roe* promised to shake up American politics. According to polls, Americans were more pro-choice than ever. Meanwhile, leaders of the pro-life movement scoured old laws that *Roe* had invalidated but that Congress and state legislatures had never overturned. Some even sought to resurrect the Comstock Act. Congress passed the act in the 1870s, making it a federal crime to send or disseminate "obscene" materials, including birth control, through the US mail. Did this law still apply?

Conservative Christian activists believed that it did, and some members of the US Supreme Court took them seriously. Antiabortion medical providers argued a case in 2024 hoping to curtail if not prohibit the use of pills routinely prescribed for inducing an abortion. During the arguments, Justices Alito and Thomas both invoked the Comstock Act. "Shouldn't the FDA have at least considered the application of 18 U.S.C. 1461?" Alito asked, referring to the act. Thomas was even more direct: "So how do you respond to an argument that mailing your product and advertising it would violate the Comstock Act?" Were Americans still bound by the moral prohibitions of Anthony Comstock and his fellow Gilded Age Christian vice crusaders? If the men and women seeking to refashion the United States into a nineteenth-century version of a Christian nation had their way, then yes.[26]

As Americans approached the 2024 presidential election, critics of the latest version of Christian nationalism assumed that they would finally bury the religious right once and for all. A majority of Americans disagreed with religious activists on a series of social issues, from abortion to gay rights to separation of church and state. They felt confident that the presumptive Democratic nominee, Joe Biden—and later, after he stepped aside, his vice president, Baptist Kamala Harris—would prevail.

On the Republican side, Donald Trump easily secured the nomination of the Republican Party for the third time in a row. He again emphasized immigration during his campaign. When LBJ signed the 1965 Immigration and Nationality Act, over 80 percent of the country identified as White. Since then, the number of White Americans had dropped while the proportion of other racial and ethnic groups steadily grew. The most recent census data showed that 60 percent of the country now claimed to be White, 18 percent of Americans identified as "Hispanic or Latino," and 13 percent as "Black or African American." Almost 6 percent of Americans identified as Asian, and over 1 percent as Native American. Almost 3 percent of Americans identified as mixed race. The nation had become more diverse, with projections indicating that Whites would lose their majority status no later than 2050 and probably sooner.

Assessing all this data alongside the decline of protestant church membership, scholar Robert P. Jones had forecast the imminent end of "White Christian America." Christian nationalists had studied the same data as Jones. But what Jones saw as a fait accompli, White Christians saw as a mandate for action. In promising to radically curtail immigration, Trump offered White Christian Americans a lifeline, a chance to reverse the trendline, a chance to bolster White Christian America. Perhaps, they thought, the battle was not yet over.[27]

However, the Christian nationalists who had long cheered Trump worried in 2024 that the candidate had gone soft on abortion. Trump had pivoted during the campaign, recognizing that a majority of voters supported some reproductive choice. He moved the party away from its long-standing goal of eradicating abortion. Instead, he insisted that states should decide the issue for themselves. "Republicans," the GOP platform read (with Trump's penchant for random capitalization),

"Will Protect and Defend a Vote of the People, from within the States, on the Issue of Life. . . . After 51 years, because of us, that power has been given to the States and to a vote of the People."[28]

Cognizant that the party had backed down from a national abortion ban and no longer defended a "human life" amendment, pro-life activists felt betrayed. However, the platform drafters offered them a significant concession. They promised to "support a new Federal Task Force on Fighting Anti-Christian Bias that will investigate all forms of illegal discrimination, harassment, and persecution against Christians in America." The Republican Party, as it had for decades, made privileging Christianity in American public life a top priority. In many ways the Republican Party had finally become an appendage of American evangelicalism and its conservative Catholic allies rather than the other way around.[29]

Religion proved once again decisive in the election. Eighty-five percent of White evangelicals voted for Trump, with Harris garnering only 14 percent. Sixty-four percent of Protestant Latines voted Trump, 59 percent of White Catholics, and 57 percent of nonevangelical White protestants. Among evangelicals and Catholics who regularly attended church or mass, Trump's numbers were even higher. In the mainline, the opposite was the case. Those who regularly worshipped tended to vote in higher numbers for Harris compared to those Methodists and Episcopalians and Presbyterians who spent their Sunday mornings in bed or watching football. Harris received the most support from Black protestants (83 percent) and from Americans with no religious affiliation (72 percent).[30]

When Donald Trump returned to the White House in January 2025, he did so not just as a politician, but as a self-anointed messiah. In his inaugural address, he cast his survival of an assassination attempt as divine intervention. "Just a few months ago, in a beautiful Pennsylvania field, an assassin's bullet ripped through my ear. But I felt then, and believe even more now, that my life was spared for a reason. I was saved by God to make America great again." For Trump and his most fervent supporters, the election was not merely a political victory but providential proof. They saw his return as part of God's plan to reclaim America, not just as a nation, but as his chosen land.

Trump's inauguration was a fitting coda to a long and turbulent story. In the United States, the struggle over faith and power had never been merely symbolic—it was, and remains, a battle for power in order to define the nation's soul through its politics, policy, and culture.

CONCLUSION

Preachers and prophets. Charlatans and chiselers. Politicians and peaceniks. Cathedrals and camp meetings. Revivals and racism. Choirs and choruses. Sex and abstinence. Love and hate. Sanctuaries and strip malls. Tongues-speaking and drug-taking. Abstaining and indulging. Groping and embracing. Fighting and forgiving. Liberating and repressing. Organizing and dividing. Advocating and assailing. Damning and deifying. Reforming and revolutionizing.

All of it—the holy and the profane—doesn't just describe American Christianity; it defines it.

It's what makes American Christianity.

And it's what makes America Christian.

For centuries the Christian faith has structured Americans' sense of national identity. Even as pews empty and institutions crack, its power lingers, embedded in the country's culture and politics.

Today, fewer than one in four Americans regularly attends a religious service. The United States lost its protestant majority in 1993. Since then, the "nones"—atheists, agnostics, and the spiritually unaffiliated—have grown into a quarter of the population.[1]

Yet, the struggle over religion's role in public life hasn't faded. It's intensified. Three factions now battle for control.

The first consists of the remnants of the old evangelical religious right, pentecostal leaders from the New Apostolic Reformation, right-wing Catholics, and Latter-day Saints. They have forged a new coalition united by a single mission—to reassert Christian dominance in American governance. Though their share of the population has declined, their influence has surged. They've captured one of the nation's two major political parties and gained the favor of the US Supreme Court.

Opposing them is a second bloc: Christians in the liberationist tradition, many mainline protestant churchgoers, faith-based social justice advocates—and increasingly, the unaffiliated who claim to be "spiritual but not religious." They aim to build a more inclusive, pluralistic, and compassionate Christianity. They want to apply the ethics of Jesus to modern life.

A third group wants none of it. Regardless of their own personal convictions, they believe faith and politics should be kept entirely separate—and they're pushing to make that happen.

Each faction faces the same burning questions. Does the recent rise of a new form of Christian nationalism mark the dawn of a new theocracy—or Christian nationalism's last desperate gasp? Are we seeing the sunset of White Christian America—or its resurrection in a new, more potent form? Is the nation drifting steadily toward secularism—or witnessing the return of religious power, refashioned for the modern era?

And what lies beyond our borders? As Christianity's center of gravity shifts to Asia, Africa, and Latin America, how will believers from those regions reshape American worship, values, and identity? Are we the "heathens in the darkness" they will seek to transform? Are we on the brink of a global clash of civilizations—one driven not only by politics and economics but also by competing faiths and competing versions of Christianity?

Beneath these questions lie deeper issues that Americans have wrestled with since the nation's founding. What role should religion play in democracy? In politics? In culture? In foreign policy?

As we search for answers, one truth remains: the conviction that the United States is God's chosen land—and Americans his chosen people—has shaped our nation from the beginning. It continues to shape it now.

But will it shape our future?

The Constitution's disestablishment and free-exercise clauses do not dictate outcomes. They offer choices.

They entrust power not to presidents or preachers, not to judges or generals, but to the people. To each generation. To us.

We just have to use them.

ACKNOWLEDGMENTS

I am grateful to the many friends who endured my relentless musing about this book's core ideas—whether they cared to or not—and who helped sharpen my thinking with their questions and suggestions. My longtime mentors Jane Sherron De Hart, Grant Wacker, and David Hollinger all offered excellent advice and recommendations from the start. I had the benefit of superb suggestions and criticism on the entire manuscript from Grant and David, as well as from Paul Harvey, Brendan Pietsch, and David Sehat. Ryan Booth, Katherine Carté, Elesha Coffman, Emily Conroy-Krutz, Rebecca Davis, Timothy Gloege, Lawrence Hatter, Jeffrey Sanders, and Daniel K. Williams offered valuable feedback on various sections.

I had a top-tier team of professionals helping me along every step of the way. I am grateful to Sandra Dijkstra and Elise Capron at the Dijkstra Agency for their excellent support and advice. At Basic Books, Brian Distelberg showed me once again what a difference a great editor makes. Lara Heimert and Dan Gerstle helped me initially get this project off the ground. The rest of the team at Basic, including Roger Labrie, Alex Cullina, Michelle Welsh-Horst, Lillian Duggan, and Liz Miller made this a much better book. My son Jackson helped me double-check footnotes. I have told parts of this story in other publications and in other contexts, which helped me refine some of the arguments included here.

I also had support from numerous institutions. At Washington State University, Deans Courtney Meehan and Todd Butler provided critical support. I am also grateful to have had a Berry Family Distinguished Professorship in the Liberal Arts, which helped cover research expenses. A Lynn E. May Jr. Study Grant from the Southern Baptist Historical Library & Archives also provided assistance.

Most of all, I am grateful to my family for their everlasting championing of me and my work. Thanks always to John and Kathy Sutton and Dan and Roxey Coke. Once again, I am dedicating this book to my wife, Kristen, and our boys, Jackson and Nathan. They mean everything to me.

NOTES

ABBREVIATIONS USED IN THE NOTES

ABHS	American Baptist Historical Society, Atlanta, GA.
BGCA	Billy Graham Center Archives, Wheaton, IL.
BIOLA	Biola University Archives & Special Collections, La Mirada, CA.
BJU	Bob Jones University Library, Greenville, SC.
BURKE	Burke Library, Union Theological Seminary, New York, NY.
CWAL	Lincoln, Abraham. *The Collected Works of Abraham Lincoln*. Edited by Roy Basler. Rutgers University Press, 1953. https://quod.lib.umich.edu/l/lincoln/.
FDR	President's Personal File. Franklin D. Roosevelt Presidential Library, Hyde Park, NY.
FMD	Farmworker Movement Documentation Project. University of California, San Diego. https://libraries.ucsd.edu/farmworkermovement/.
FPHC	Flower Pentecostal Heritage Center, Springfield, MO.
FO	Founders Online. National Archives. https://founders.archives.gov/.
FTS	Fuller Theological Seminary Archives, Pasadena, CA.
GCTS	Gordon-Conwell Theological Seminary, South Hamilton, MA.
ICFG	Heritage Center. International Church of the Foursquare Gospel, Echo Park, CA.
JSP	Joseph Smith Papers. www.josephsmithpapers.org/.
LOC	Manuscript Division. Library of Congress, Washington, DC.
MLK	Martin Luther King, Jr. Papers Project. Martin Luther King, Jr. Research and Education Institute. Stanford University. https://kinginstitute.stanford.edu/king-papers/about-papers-project.

NAE	Papers of the National Association of Evangelicals (unprocessed). Wheaton College Archives & Special Collections, Wheaton, IL.
NARA	National Archives and Records Administration, College Park, MD.
PHS	Presbyterian Historical Society, Philadelphia, PA.
PU	Seeley G. Mudd Manuscript Library. Princeton University Library, Princeton, NJ.
SBHLA	Southern Baptist Historical Library & Archives, Nashville, TN.
SCH	Schomburg Center for Research in Black Culture, New York, NY.
UCSB	The American Presidency Project. Edited by Gerhard Peters and John T. Woolley. University of California, Santa Barbara. www.presidency.ucsb.edu/.
UW	Special Collections. University of Washington, Seattle, WA.
WCA	Wheaton College Archives and Special Collections, Wheaton, IL.
YALE	The Avalon Project. Lillian Goldman Law Library. Yale University. https://avalon.law.yale.edu/.

INTRODUCTION

1. Lincoln to Allen N. Ford, August 11, 1846, CWAL, vol. 1, 383.

2. Carl Sandburg, *Abraham Lincoln, The Prairie Years* (New York: Harcourt, Brace & Company, 1926), 337. Some historians doubt whether this encounter actually happened—there are many colorful stories about Lincoln's earlier years. Regardless, religion occupied the center of the campaign.

3. Handbill Replying to Charges of Infidelity, July 31, 1846, CWAL, vol. 1, 382.

4. "Religious Landscape Study" (2025), Pew Research Center, www.pewresearch.org/religious-landscape-study/.

5. On other approaches to US history, see especially Nikole Hannah-Jones, *The 1619 Project: A New Origin Story* (New York: Random House, 2021); Ned Blackhawk, *The Rediscovery of America: Native Peoples and the Unmaking of U.S. History* (New Haven: Yale University Press, 2023); and Jill Lepore, *These Truths: A History of the United States* (New York: Norton, 2019).

6. On the flaws in the "evangelical consensus" literature see my "Redefining the History and Historiography on American Evangelicalism in the Era of the Religious Right," *Journal of the American Academy of Religion* 92, no. 1 (2024): 37–60.

7. This is an argument Ann Braude made many years ago. See "Women's History *Is* American Religious History," in *Retelling U.S. Religious History*, Thomas A. Tweed, ed. (Berkeley: University of California Press, 1997).

CHAPTER 1: THE CHRISTIAN INVASION BEGINS

The following influenced my thinking about and understanding of the material in this chapter: Joseph R. Aguilar, "Asserting Sovereignty: An Indigenous Archaeology of the Pueblo Revolt Period at Tunyo, San Ildefonso Pueblo, New Mexico" (PhD diss., University of Pennsylvania, 2019); Ned Blackhawk, *The Rediscovery of America: Native Peoples and the Unmaking of U.S. History* (New Haven: Yale University Press, 2023); Henry Warner Bowden, "Spanish Missions, Cultural Conflict and the Pueblo Revolt of 1680," *Church History* 44, no. 2 (1975): 217–228; James F. Brooks, *Captives & Cousins: Slavery, Kinship, and Community in the Southwest Borderlands* (Chapel Hill: Omohundro Institute/University of North Carolina Press, 2002); Ramón A. Gutiérrez, *When Jesus Came, the Corn Mothers Went Away: Marriage, Sexuality, and Power in New Mexico, 1500–1846* (Palo Alto: Stanford University Press, 1991); Pekka Hämäläinen, *Indigenous Continent: The Epic Contest for North America* (New York: Liveright, 2022); and Sarah M. S. Pearsall, *Polygamy: An Early American History* (New Haven: Yale University Press, 2019).

1. *The Journal of Christopher Columbus, During His First Voyage, 1492–93*, translated by Clements R. Markham (London: Hakluyt Society, 1893), 16.
2. *Journal of Christopher Columbus*, 16.
3. Christopher Columbus, *The Book of Prophecies*, ed. Roberto Rusconi, translated by Blair Sullivan (Berkeley: University of California Press, 1997), 75.
4. *Journal of Christopher Columbus*, 38.
5. *Journal of Christopher Columbus*, 139.
6. Columbus, *Book of Prophecies*, 71, 77.
7. "Investigation of Conditions in New Mexico, 1601," in *Don Juan de Oñate: Colonizer of New Mexico, 1595–1628*, ed. George P. Hammond (Albuquerque: University of New Mexico Press, 1953), 667.
8. "Investigation of Conditions in New Mexico," 628.
9. Don Luis de Velasco, "Instructions to Don Juan de Oñate, October 21, 1595," in *Don Juan de Oñate*, 65.
10. "Breaking Camp at San Gabriel," in *Don Juan de Oñate*, 675.
11. "The Viceroy of New Spain Makes a Report," 3; and "Declaration of the Indian Juan, December 18, 1681," in *Revolt of the Pueblo Indians of New Mexico and Otermín's Attempted Reconquest, 1680–1682*, ed. George P. Hammond (Albuquerque: University of New Mexico Press, 1942), 234–235.
12. "Opinion of Fray Francisco de Ayeta, December 23, 1681," in *Revolt of the Pueblo Indians*, 309.

CHAPTER 2: THE CITY ON THE HILL

The following influenced my thinking about and understanding of the material in this chapter: Lisa Brooks, *Our Beloved Kin: A New History of King Philip's War* (New Haven: Yale University Press, 2019); Nicholas Guyatt, *Providence and the Invention of the United States, 1607–1876* (New York: Cambridge University Press, 2007); David D. Hall, *The Puritans: A Transatlantic History* (Princeton: Princeton University Press, 2019), and *Worlds of Wonder; Days of Judgment: Popular Religious Belief in Early New England* (Cambridge: Harvard University Press, 1989); Carol F. Karlsen, *The Devil in the Shape of a Woman: Witchcraft in Colonial New England* (New York: Norton, 1987); Mary Beth Norton, *In the Devil's Snare: The Salem Witchcraft Crisis of 1692* (New York: Knopf,

2003); John G. Turner, *They Knew They Were Pilgrims: Plymouth Colony and the Contest for American Liberty* (New Haven: Yale University Press, 2020); Abram C. Van Engen, *City on a Hill: A History of American Exceptionalism* (New Haven: Yale University Press, 2020); Wendy Warren, *New England Bound: Slavery and Colonization in Early America* (New York: Liveright, 2016); and Michael P. Winship, *Hot Protestants: A History of Puritanism in England and America* (New Haven: Yale University Press, 2019).

1. Samuel Danforth, "A Brief Recognition of New-Englands Errand into the Wilderness" (Cambridge, MA: 1671), 10, 14, 18, https://digitalcommons.unl.edu/cgi/viewcontent.cgi?article=1038&context=libraryscience.

2. Increase Mather, "The Day of Trouble Is Near" (Cambridge, MA: 1674), 22, https://quod.lib.umich.edu/e/evans/N00137.0001.001.

3. Samuel Danforth, "The Cry of Sodom Enquired Into" (Cambridge, MA: 1674), 8, 9, https://quod.lib.umich.edu/cgi/t/text/text-idx?c=evans;idno=N00131.0001.001.

4. Alexis de Tocqueville, *Democracy in America*, rev. ed., translated by Henry Reeve (New York: Colonial Press, 1900), 294.

5. William Bradford, *Of Plimoth Plantation* (Boston: Wright and Potter, 1898), 72.

6. "Mayflower Compact, 1620," YALE.

7. Bradford, *Of Plimoth Plantation*, 33–34.

8. John Winthrop, "A Modell of Christian Charity," 1630, https://history.hanover.edu/texts/winthmod.html.

9. Winthrop, "A Modell."

10. Winthrop, "A Modell."

11. Roger Williams, *The Bloudy Tenent of Persecution* (1644, reprinted London: Hanserd Knollys Society, 1848), 1, 2.

12. "Confirmatory Deed of Roger Williams and His Wife," and "Second Address from Rhode Island to King Charles the Second," in *Records of the Colony of Rhode Island and Providence Plantations, in New England*, ed. J. Russell Bartlett (Providence, RI: A. C. Greene and Brothers, 1856), 22, 491.

13. "The Examination of Mrs. Anne Hutchinson at the Court at Newtown," in *The Antinomian Controversy, 1636–1638: A Documentary History*, ed. David D. Hall (Middletown, CT: Wesleyan University Press, 1968), 312, 337.

14. "Examination of Mrs. Anne Hutchinson," 347.

15. Papers of the Winthrop Family, vol. 2, "General Observations," 120, www.masshist.org/publications/winthrop/index.php/view/PWF02d073#sn=0.

CHAPTER 3: VARIETIES OF CHRISTIAN LIBERTY

The following influenced my thinking about and understanding of the material in this chapter: Michael D. Breidenbach, *Our Dear-Bought Liberty: Catholics and Religious Toleration in Early America* (Cambridge, MA: Harvard University Press, 2021); Katharine Gerbner, *Christian Slavery: Conversion and Race in the Protestant Atlantic World* (Philadelphia: University of Pennsylvania Press, 2018); Michael A. Gomez, *Exchanging Our Country Marks: The Transformation of African Identities in the Colonial and Antebellum*

South (Chapel Hill: University of North Carolina Press, 1998), and *Black Crescent: The Experience and Legacy of African Muslims in the Americas* (New York: Cambridge University Press, 2005); Karen Ordahl Kupperman, *Pocahontas and the English Boys: Caught between Cultures in Early Virginia* (New York: New York University Press, 2019); Andrew Lipman, *The Saltwater Frontier: Indians and the Contest for the American Coast* (New Haven: Yale University Press, 2015); and Albert J. Raboteau, *Slave Religion: The "Invisible Institution" in the South* (New York: Oxford University Press, 1978), and *A Fire in the Bones: Reflections on African-American Religious History* (Boston: Beacon Press, 1995).

1. Richard Baxter, *The Quakers' Catechism* (London: Underhill and Tyton, 1655), n.p.
2. "The First Charter of Virginia, April 10, 1606," YALE.
3. John Rolfe, *A True Relation of the State of Virginia Lefte by Sir Thomas Dale in May Last 1616* (New Haven: Yale University Press, 1951), 41.
4. John Smith, *The Generall Historie of Virginia* (London: I. D. and I. H. for Michael Sparkes, 1624), 49, https://docsouth.unc.edu/southlit/smith/smith.html#p77.
5. "Letter from John Rolfe to Sir Thos. Dale," *Virginia Magazine of History and Biography* 22, no. 2 (April 1914): 154.
6. "Instructions to the Colonists by Lord Baltimore, 1633," in *Narratives of Early Maryland, 1633–1684*, ed. C. Colman Hall (New York: Scribner, 1925), 20.
7. "Instructions to the Colonists," 16.
8. "Maryland Toleration Act, September 21, 1649," YALE.
9. "Frame of Government of Pennsylvania, May 5, 1682," YALE.
10. "Frame of Government."

CHAPTER 4: THE BIRTH OF REVIVALIST CHRISTIANITY

The following influenced my thinking about and understanding of the material in this chapter: Richard J. Boles, *Dividing the Faith: The Rise of Segregated Churches in the Early American North* (New York: New York University Press, 2020); Catherine A. Brekus, *Strangers & Pilgrims: Female Preaching in America, 1740–1845* (Chapel Hill, NC: University of North Carolina Press, 1998), and *Sarah Osborn's World: The Rise of Evangelical Christianity in Early America* (New Haven: Yale University Press, 2013); Jon Butler, *Awash in a Sea of Faith: Christianizing the American People* (Cambridge, MA: Harvard University Press, 1990); Peter Y. Choi, *George Whitefield: Evangelist for God and Empire* (Grand Rapids, MI: Eerdmans, 2018); Linford D. Fisher, *The Indian Great Awakening: Religion and the Shaping of Native Cultures in Early America* (New York: Oxford University Press, 2012); Sylvia R. Frey and Betty Wood, *Come Shouting to Zion: African American Protestantism in the American South and British Caribbean to 1830* (Chapel Hill, NC: University of North Carolina Press, 1998); George M. Marsden, *Jonathan Edwards: A Life* (New Haven: Yale University Press, 2003); Mechal Sobel, *The World They Made Together: Black and White Values in Eighteenth-Century Virginia* (Princeton, NJ: Princeton University Press, 1987), and *Trabelin' On: The Slave Journey to an Afro-Baptist Faith* (Westport: Greenwood Press, 1979); Harry S. Stout, *The Divine Dramatist: George Whitefield and the Rise of Modern Evangelicalism* (Grand Rapids, MI: Eerdmans, 1991); Harry S. Stout and Peter Onuf, "James Davenport and the Great Awakening in New London," *Journal of American History* 70, no. 3 (1983): 556–578; and Douglas L. Winiarski, *Darkness Falls on the Land of Light: Experiencing Religious Awakenings in Eighteenth-Century New England* (Chapel Hill: University of North Carolina Press, 2019).

1. Alexander Hamilton, "Itinerarium," in *Colonial American Travel Narratives*, ed. Wendy Martin (New York: Penguin Books, 1994), 296.

2. Jonathan Edwards, *Sinners in the Hands of an Angry God: A Sermon Preached at Enfield, July 8th, 1741* (Boston: Kneeland and Green, 1741), 12–14.

3. Jonathan Edwards, "Some Thoughts Concerning the Revival," in *The Great Awakening: Works of Jonathan Edwards Online*, vol. 4 (Jonathan Edwards Center at Yale University).

4. Benjamin Franklin, *Autobiography*, part 12, https://franklinpapers.org/framedVolumes.jsp.

5. Franklin, *Autobiography*, part 11.

6. George Whitefield, *A Continuation of the Reverend Mr. Whitefield's Journal, From a Few Days After His Return to Georgia to His Arrival at Falmouth* (London: Strahan, 1744), 48–49.

7. Michael J. Crawford, "The Spiritual Travels of Nathan Cole," *William and Mary Quarterly* 33, no. 1 (1976): 92–93.

8. Gilbert Tennent, "The Danger of an Unconverted Ministry" (Philadelphia: printed by Benjamin Franklin, in Market-Street, 1740), 11, 12, 18.

9. Jonathan Edwards, "Advice to Mr. and Mrs. Kingsley, February 17, 1743," *Church and Pastoral Documents: Works of Jonathan Edwards Online*, vol. 39 (Jonathan Edwards Center at Yale University).

10. Edwards, "Advice to Mr. and Mrs. Kingsley."

11. Edwards, "Advice to Mr. and Mrs. Kingsley."

12. Samuel Hopkins and Sarah Osborn, *Memoirs of the Life of Mrs. Sarah Osborn* (Catskill, NY: Elliot, 1814), 43.

13. Samson Occom, *The Collected Writings of Samson Occom, Mohegan: Literature and Leadership in Eighteenth-Century Native America*, ed. Joanna Brooks (New York: Oxford University Press, 2006), 334.

14. George Whitefield, *The Two First Parts of His Life: With His Journals* (London: W. Strahan, 1756), 357.

15. Phillis Wheatley, "An Elegiac Poem, On the Death of That Celebrated Divine, and Eminent Servant of Jesus Christ, the Reverend and Learned George Whitefield" (Boston: Russell and Boyles, 1770), http://digital.library.upenn.edu/women/wheatley/whitefield/whitefield.html.

16. Charles Chauncy, *Seasonable Thoughts of the State of Religion in New England* (Boston: Rogers and Fowle, 1743), 226.

CHAPTER 5: REVOLUTION

The following influenced my thinking about and understanding of the material in this chapter: Chris Beneke, "The Critical Turn: Jonathan Mayhew, the British Empire, and the Idea of Resistance in Mid-Eighteenth-Century Boston," *Massachusetts Historical Review* 10 (2008): 23–56; Katherine Carté, *Religion and the American Revolution: An Imperial History* (Chapel Hill, NC: Omohundro Institute and University of North Carolina Press, 2021); Alan Heimert, *Religion and the American Mind: From the Great Awakening to the Revolution* (Cambridge, MA: Harvard University Press, 1966); J. Patrick Mullins, *Father of Liberty: Jonathan Mayhew and the Principles of the American Revolution* (Lawrence, KS: University Press of Kansas, 2017); John A. Ragosta, *Wellspring of Liberty: How Virginia's Religious Dissenters Helped Win the American Revolution and Secured Religious Liberty* (New York: Oxford University Press, 2010); and Charles Royster, *A Revolutionary People at War: The Continental Army & American Character, 1775–1783* (Chapel Hill, NC: University of North Carolina Press, 1979). For denominational statistics in this and the following chapters, see Roger Finke and Rodney Stark, *The Churching of America, 1776–2005: Winners and Losers in Our Religious Economy*, 2nd ed. (New Brunswick, NJ: Rutgers University Press, 2005), and Rodney Stark and Roger Finke, "American Religion in 1776: A Statistical Portrait," *Sociological Analysis* 49, no. 1 (1988), 39–51.

1. "To Benjamin Franklin from William Franklin, 30 April 1766," FO.

2. George Whitefield to Robert Keen, September 23, 1770, in *The Works of the Reverend George Whitefield* (London: Edward and Charles Dilly, 1771), 426.

3. "Proceedings of Farmington, Connecticut, on the Boston Port Act; May 19, 1774," YALE.

4. Samuel Sherwood, *A Sermon Containing Scriptural Instructions to Civil Rulers, and All Free-Born Subjects* (New Haven: T. and S. Green, 1774), n.p. 41.

5. Thomas Bradbury Chandler, *A Friendly Address to All Reasonable Americans, on the Subject of Our Political Confusions* (Boston: Mills and Hicks, 1774), 49, 53.

6. Nathaniel Bouton, ed., *Documents and Records Relating to the State of New-Hampshire from 1764–1776*, vol. 7 (Nashua, NH: Orren C. Moore, 1878), 545.

7. Jacob Bailey to Sir, March 1, 1775, Jacob Bailey Papers, LOC.

8. William Smith, *A Sermon on the Present Situation of American Affairs* (Philadelphia: James Humphreys, 1775), 20, 24.

9. John Wesley, *A Calm Address to Our American Colonies* (London: R. Hawes, 1775), 15.

10. Thomas Paine, *Common Sense* (Philadelphia: W. & T. Bradford, 1776), 39, 161.

11. John Witherspoon, *The Dominion of Providence over the Passions of Men* (Philadelphia: R. Aitken, 1776), 40–41.

12. Katherine Carté, *Religion and the American Revolution: An Imperial History* (Chapel Hill, NC: Omohundro Institute and University of North Carolina Press, 2021), 205.

13. Anthony Benezet, *Serious Considerations on Several Important Subjects* (Philadelphia: Joseph Crukshank, 1778), 11.

14. Quoted in Conor Cruise O'Brien, *God Land: Reflections on Religion and Nationalism* (Cambridge, MA: Harvard University Press, 1988), 29.

15. Samuel Sherwood, *The Church's Flight into the Wilderness: An Address on the Times* (New York: S. Loudon, 1776), n.p., 17.

CHAPTER 6: SANCTIFYING THE WEST

The following influenced my thinking about and understanding of the material in this chapter: William Deverell, *Whitewashed Adobe: The Rise of Los Angeles and the Remaking of Its Mexican Past* (Berkeley, CA: University of California Press, 2005); Lisbeth Haas, *Conquests and Historical Identities in California, 1769–1936* (Berkeley, CA: University of California Press, 1995); Steven W. Hackel, *Junípero Serra: California's Founding Father* (New York: Hill and Wang, 2013), and *Children of Coyote, Missionaries of Saint Francis: Indian-Spanish Relations in Colonial California, 1769–1850* (Chapel Hill, NC: University of North Carolina Press, 2005); Albert L. Hurtado, *Indian Survival on the California Frontier* (New Haven, CT: Yale University Press, 1988); Anna M. Nogar, *Quill and Cross in the Borderlands: Sor María de Ágreda and the Lady in Blue, 1628 to the Present* (Notre Dame, IN: University of Notre Dame Press, 2018), and "Junípero Serra's Mission Muse: Sor María de Jesús de Ágreda and Her Writings," in *Worlds of Junípero Serra: Historical Contexts and Cultural Representations*, ed. Steven W. Hackel (Berkeley, CA: University of California Press, 2018); and Gregory Orfalea, *Journey to the Sun: Junípero Serra's Dream and the Founding of California* (New York: Scribner, 2014). I drew many of the statistics in this chapter from James A. Sandos, *Converting California: Indians and Franciscans in the Missions* (New Haven: Yale University Press, 2004).

1. "Extracts Taken from a Letter," in Francisco Palou, *Francisco Palou's Life and Apostolic Labors of the Venerable Father Junípero Serra*, translated by C. Scott Williams (Pasadena, CA: George Wharton James, 1913), 329.
2. "Extracts Taken from a Letter," 330.
3. "Of the Declarations Which the Blessed Mother Mary of Jesus Writes to the Reverend Fathers of New Mexico," in Palou, *Francisco Palou's Life*, 331.
4. Palou, *Francisco Palou's Life*, 48.
5. Palou, *Francisco Palou's Life*, 257.
6. Palou, *Francisco Palou's Life*, 42–43.
7. "Diary of the Expedition from Loreto to San Diego, March 28 to July 1, 1769," in Junípero Serra, *Writings of Junípero Serra*, ed. Antonine Tibesar (Washington, DC: Academy of American Franciscan History, 1955), 65.
8. Palou, *Francisco Palou's Life*, 173.

CHAPTER 7: DISESTABLISHING CHRISTIANITY

The following influenced my thinking about and understanding of the material in this chapter: Steven K. Green, *Inventing a Christian America: The Myth of the Religious Founding* (New York: Oxford University Press, 2015); David L. Holmes, *The Faiths of the Founding Fathers* (New York: Oxford University Press, 2006); Isaac Kramnick and R. Laurence Moore, *The Godless Constitution: A Moral Defense of the Secular State*, rev. ed. (New York: Norton, 2005); Peter Manseau, *The Jefferson Bible: A Biography* (Princeton, NJ: Princeton

University Press, 2020); Alyssa Penick, "From Disestablishment to *Dartmouth College v. Woodward*: How Virginia's Fight over Religious Freedom Shaped the History of American Corporations," *Law and History Review* 39, no. 3 (2021): 479–512; Amanda Porterfield, *Conceived in Doubt: Religion and Politics in the New American Nation* (Chicago: University of Chicago Press, 2012); and David Sehat, *The Myth of American Religious Freedom* (New York: Oxford University Press, 2011).

1. The Barbary Treaties 1786–1816, Treaty of Peace and Friendship, Signed at Tripoli November 4, 1796, YALE.

2. James Madison, *The Records of the Federal Convention of 1787*, vol. 1, ed. Max Farrand (New Haven, CT: Yale University Press, 1911), 450–452.

3. "From George Washington to the Presbyterian Ministers of Massachusetts and New Hampshire, 2 November 1789," FO.

4. David Sehat, *The Myth of American Religious Freedom* (New York: Oxford University Press, 2011), 27.

5. Annals of Congress, House of Representatives, 1st Congress, 1st Session, June 8, 1789 (Washington, DC: Gales and Seaton, 1834), 451–452.

6. "82. A Bill for Establishing Religious Freedom, 18 June 1779," FO; Thomas Jefferson, July 27, 1821, Autobiography Draft Fragment, January 6 through July 27, LOC, www.loc.gov/resource/mtj1.052_0517_0609/?sp=22&st=text.

7. "82. A Bill for Establishing Religious Freedom."

8. Thomas Jefferson, *Notes on the State of Virginia* (Philadelphia: Prichard and Hall, 1788), 169.

9. Patrick Henry, "A Bill Establishing a Provision for Teachers of the Christian Religion," Virginia House of Delegates, December 24, 1784, Broadside, LOC.

10. *Memorial and Remonstrance Against Religious Assessments, [ca. 20 June] 1785*, FO.

11. Jefferson's Letter to the Danbury Baptists, The Final Letter, as Sent, January 1, 1802, www.loc.gov/loc/lcib/9806/danpre.html.

12. Amanda Porterfield, *Conceived in Doubt: Religion and Politics in the New American Nation* (Chicago: University of Chicago Press, 2012), 147.

13. From Alexander Hamilton to John Jay, 7 May 1800, FO; William Linn and John M. Mason, *Serious Considerations on the Election of a President* (New York: John Furman, 1800), 4, 18.

14. Linn and Mason, *Serious Considerations*, 17, 19, 24.

15. Joseph Story, *Commentaries on the Constitution of the United States*, vol. 3 (Boston: Hilliard, Gray, and Company, 1833), 726, 728.

16. Alexis de Tocqueville, *Democracy in America*, rev. ed., translated by Henry Reeve (New York: Colonial Press, 1900), 310.

CHAPTER 8: REVIVING THE NEW REPUBLIC

The following influenced my thinking about and understanding of the material in this chapter: Catherine L. Albanese, *The Spirituality of the American Transcendentalists:*

Selected Writings of Ralph Waldo Emerson, Amos Bronson Alcott, Theodore Parker, and Henry David Thoreau (Macon, GA: Mercer University Press, 1988); Catherine A. Brekus, *Strangers & Pilgrims: Female Preaching in America, 1740–1845* (Chapel Hill, NC: University of North Carolina Press, 1998); Jon Butler, *Awash in a Sea of Faith: Christianizing the American People* (Cambridge, MA: Harvard University Press, 1990); Paul Conkin, *Cane Ridge, America's Pentecost* (Madison, WI: University of Wisconsin Press, 1990); Ellen Eslinger, *Citizens of Zion: The Social Origins of Camp Meeting Revivalism* (Knoxville, TN: University of Tennessee Press, 1999); Nathan O. Hatch, *The Democratization of American Christianity* (New Haven, CT: Yale University Press, 1989); David Hempton, *Methodism: Empire of the Spirit* (New Haven, CT: Yale University Press, 2005); Christine Leigh Heyrman, *Southern Cross: The Beginnings of the Bible Belt* (New York: Knopf, 1997); E. Brooks Holifield, *Theology in America: Christian Thought from the Age of the Puritans to the Civil War* (New Haven, CT: Yale University Press, 2003); Paul E. Johnson, *A Shopkeeper's Millennium: Society and Revivals in Rochester, New York, 1815–1837* (New York: Hill and Wang, 1978); Eugene McCarraher, *The Enchantments of Mammon: How Capitalism Became the Religion of Modernity* (Cambridge, MA: Belknap Press of Harvard University Press, 2019); and John Wigger, *American Saint: Francis Asbury and the Methodists* (Oxford, UK: Oxford University Press, 2009).

1. Joshua Coit to Nancy Coit, March 18, 1794, and March 31, 1794, box 1, folder 2, Joshua Coit Papers, LOC.

2. Barton W. Stone and John Rogers, *The Biography of Eld. Barton Warren Stone: Written by Himself; With Additions and Reflections* (Cincinnati: J. A. & U. P. James, 1847), 39–41.

3. John Wesley, *The Journal of John Wesley* (London: C. H. Kelly, 1903), 54.

4. Matthew Simpson to Nephew, September 28, 1835, Family Correspondence, box 3, Papers of Matthew Simpson, LOC.

5. Joseph Anderson to Francis McFarland, December 7, 1840, folder 1, box 1, and J. Jones to Francis McFarland, September 2, 1833, folder 1, box 4, RG 459, Francis McFarland Papers, PHS.

6. Christine Leigh Heyrman, *Southern Cross: The Beginnings of the Bible Belt* (New York: Knopf, 1997), 147.

7. Elleanor Knight, *A Narrative of the Christian Experience* (Providence, RI: n.p., 1839), iii, 34; Harriet Livermore, *Scriptural Evidence in Favour of Female Testimony* (Portsmouth, NH: R. Foster, 1824).

8. Charles G. Finney, *Memoirs of Rev. Charles G. Finney* (New York: A. S. Barnes, 1876), 24; Charles G. Finney, *Lectures on Revivals of Religion* (Oberlin, OH: E. J. Goodrich, 1868), 10.

9. Finney, *Lectures on Revivals*, 11, 258.

10. Finney, *Lectures on Revivals*, 12, 14.

11. Lyman Beecher, *An Address to the Charitable Society for the Education of Indigent Pious Young Men for the Ministry of the Gospel* (New Haven, CT: n.p., 1814), 6.

12. Beecher, *Address to the Charitable Society*, 6.

13. Henry McNeal Turner, *Freedom's Witness: The Civil War Correspondence of Henry McNeal Turner*, ed. Jean Lee Cole (Morgantown, WV: West Virginia University Press, 2013), 210–211.

14. From Thomas Jefferson to James Smith, 8 December 1822, FO.

15. William Ellery Channing, "The Evidences of Christianity," in *The Works of William E. Channing, D. D.*, vol. 3 (Boston: James Munroe, 1846), 328.

16. William Ellery Channing, *A Sermon Delivered at the Ordination of the Rev. Jared Sparks* (Boston: Cummings and Hilliard, 1819), 30, 34.

17. Channing, *Sermon Delivered*, 39.

18. Ralph Waldo Emerson, *An Address Delivered Before the Senior Class in Divinity College* (Boston: Munroe and Company, 1838), 3, 4.

19. Emerson, *Address*, 13, 30.

20. Robert Baird, *Religion in America* (New York: Harper, 1844); on the use of "evangelical" see Linford D. Fisher, "Evangelicals and Unevangelicals: The Contested History of a Word, 1500–1950," *Religion and American Culture* 26, no. 2 (2016): 184–226.

CHAPTER 9: LIBERATED CHRISTIANITY

The following influenced my thinking about and understanding of the material in this chapter: Patrick H. Breen, *The Land Shall Be Deluged in Blood: A New History of the Nat Turner Revolt* (New York: Oxford University Press, 2016); Dennis C. Dickerson, *The African Methodist Episcopal Church: A History* (New York: Cambridge University Press, 2020); Douglas R. Egerton and Robert L. Paquette, *The Denmark Vesey Affair: A Documentary History* (Gainesville, FL: University Press of Florida, 2017); Sylvia R. Frey and Betty Wood, *Come Shouting to Zion: African American Protestantism in the American South and British Caribbean to 1830* (Chapel Hill, NC: University of North Carolina Press, 1998); Paul Harvey, *Through the Storm, Through the Night: A History of African American Christianity* (Lanham, MD: Rowman & Littlefield, 2011), and *Christianity and Race in the American South: A History* (Chicago: University of Chicago Press, 2016); Vanessa Holden, *Surviving Southampton: African American Women and Resistance in Nat Turner's Community* (Urbana, IL: University of Illinois Press, 2021); Richard S. Newman, *Freedom's Prophet* (New York: New York University Press, 2008); Albert J. Raboteau, *Slave Religion: The "Invisible Institution" in the South* (New York: Oxford University Press, 1978); and Alexis Wells-Oghoghomeh, *The Souls of Womenfolk: The Religious Cultures of Enslaved Women in the Lower South* (Chapel Hill, NC: University of North Carolina Press, 2021).

1. Richard Allen, *The Life, Experience, and Gospel Labours of the Rt. Rev. Richard Allen* (Philadelphia: Martin and Boden, 1833), 5.

2. Allen, *Life, Experience, and Gospel Labours*, 45, 46.

3. Allen, *Life, Experience, and Gospel Labours*, 12.

4. Allen, *Life, Experience, and Gospel Labours*, 13.

5. Allen, *Life, Experience, and Gospel Labours*, 17.

6. Jarena Lee, *Religious Experience and Journal of Mrs. Jarena Lee* (Philadelphia: published for the author, 1849), 5, 10.

7. Lee, *Religious Experience and Journal*, 11.

8. Lee, *Religious Experience and Journal*, 11.

9. Lee, *Religious Experience and Journal*, 18.

10. Lee, *Religious Experience and Journal*, 63.

11. Denmark Vesey, Lionel Henry Kennedy, and Thomas Parker, *An Official Report of the Trials of Sundry Negroes, Charged with an Attempt to Raise an Insurrection in the State of South-Carolina* (Charleston, SC: James R. Schenck, 1822), 23.

12. Nat Turner, *The Confessions of Nat Turner* (Baltimore: Thomas R. Gray, 1831), 10–11.

13. Turner, *Confessions*, 11.

14. Harriet Jacobs, *Incidents in the Life of a Slave Girl* (Boston: published for the author, 1861), 103, 105.

CHAPTER 10: CREATING AMERICAN ORIGINALS

The following influenced my thinking about and understanding of the material in this chapter: Benjamin Baker, "'The Year of Jubilee Is Come': Black Millerites and the Politics of Christian Apocalypticism," *Church History* 92, no. 1 (2023): 68–98; Christopher James Blythe, *Terrible Revolution: Latter-day Saints & the American Apocalypse* (New York: Oxford University Press, 2020); Richard Lyman Bushman, *Joseph Smith: Rough Stone Rolling* (New York: Knopf, 2005); Stewart Davenport, *Sex and Sects: The Story of Mormon Polygamy, Shaker Celibacy, and Oneida Complex Marriage* (Charlottesville, VA: University of Virginia Press, 2022); Kara M. French, *Against Sex: Identities of Sexual Restraint in Early America* (Chapel Hill, NC: University of North Carolina Press, 2021); Rodney Hessinger, *Smitten: Sex, Gender, and the Contest for Souls in the Second Great Awakening* (Ithaca, NY: Cornell University Press, 2022); Scott Larson, "'Indescribable Being': Theological Performances of Genderlessness in the Society of the Publick Universal Friend, 1776–1819," *Early American Studies* 12, no. 3 (2014): 576–600; Spencer W. McBride, *Joseph Smith for President: The Prophet, the Assassins, and the Fight for American Religious Freedom* (New York: Oxford University Press, 2021); Paul B. Moyer, *The Public Universal Friend: Jemima Wilkinson and Religious Enthusiasm in Revolutionary America* (Ithaca, NY: Cornell University Press, 2015); Ronald L. Numbers, Jonathan M. Butler, and James R. Nix, eds., *The Disappointed: Millerism and Millenarianism in the Nineteenth Century* (Knoxville, TN: University of Tennessee Press, 1993); Benjamin E. Park, *American Zion: A New History of Mormonism* (New York: Liveright, 2024); Sarah M. S. Pearsall, *Polygamy: An Early American History* (New Haven: Yale University Press, 2019); David L. Rowe, *God's Strange Work: William Miller and the End of the World* (Grand Rapids, MI: Eerdmans, 2008); John Howard Smith, *A Dream of the Judgment Day: American Millennialism and Apocalypticism, 1620–1890* (Oxford, UK: Oxford University Press, 2021); Stephen J. Stein, *The Shaker Experience in America: A History of the United Society of Believers* (New Haven, CT: Yale University Press, 1992); and Anthony Wonderley, *Oneida Utopia: A Community Searching for Human Happiness & Prosperity* (Ithaca, NY: Cornell University Press, 2017).

1. François Jean de Beauvoir, Marquis de Chastellux, *Travels in North-America, in the Years 1780–81–82* (New York: White, Gallaher, & White, 1827), 135.

2. William Miller, *Evidence from Scripture and History of the Second Coming of Christ, About the Year 1843* (Troy, NY: Tuttle, Belcher, and Burton, 1838), 277; William Miller and Joshua V. Himes, *Views of the Prophecies and Prophetic Chronology* (Boston: J. V. Himes, 1842), 12.

3. Miller to Himes, August 12, 1840, in Miller and Himes, *Views of the Prophecies*, 236.

4. William Ramsey to Robert W. Landis, February 6, 1844, folder 5, box 1, RG 260, Robert W. Landis Papers, PHS.

5. John Humphrey Noyes, *Confessions of John H. Noyes: Part I. Confession of Religious Experience: Including a History of Modern Perfectionism* (Oneida, NY: Leonard & Co., 1849), 2.

6. Noyes, *Confessions*, 15.

7. Oneida Association, *First Annual Report of the Oneida Association* (Oneida, NY: Leonard and Co., 1849), 21.

8. John Humphrey Noyes, *Male Continence* (Oneida, NY: published by the Oneida Community, 1872), 18.

9. "Revelation, 12 July 1843 [D&C 132]," 1, 3, JSP.

CHAPTER 11: BUILDING THE MORAL ESTABLISHMENT

The following influenced my thinking about and understanding of the material in this chapter: Kathleen Sprows Cummings, "Elizabeth Ann Seton: A Wholly American Saint," *American Catholic Studies* 132, no. 3 (2021): 107–115; John Fea, *The Bible Cause: A History of the American Bible Society* (New York: Oxford University Press, 2016); and Michael Pasquier, *Fathers on the Frontier: French Missionaries and the Roman Catholic Priesthood in the United States, 1789–1870* (New York: Oxford University Press, 2010).

1. Lyman Beecher, *Autobiography, Correspondence, Etc. of Lyman Beecher*, ed. Charles Beecher (New York: Harper & Brothers, 1865), 344.

2. L. Beecher, *Autobiography*, 344.

3. Lyman Beecher, *The Memory of Our Fathers: A Sermon Delivered at Plymouth, on the Twenty-Second of December, 1827* (Boston: T. R. Marvin, 1828), 7.

4. L. Beecher, *Memory of Our Fathers*, 17.

5. George Washington, "Farewell Address" (September 19, 1796), FO.

6. L. Beecher, *Memory of Our Fathers*, 18; Lyman Beecher, *A Reformation of Morals Practicable and Indispensable* (Andover, CT: Flagg and Gould, 1814), 18.

7. L. Beecher, *Memory of Our Fathers*, 26.

8. Horace Mann, *Twelfth Annual Report of the Board of Education* (Boston: Dutton and Wentworth, 1849), 116–117.

9. William Holmes McGuffey, *McGuffey's New First Eclectic Reader for Little Children* (Cincinnati: Sargent, Wilson & Hinkle, 1857), 25, 56.

10. William Holmes McGuffey, *The Eclectic Second Reader: Consisting of Progressive Lessons in Reading and Spelling: For the Younger Classes in Schools, with Engravings* (Cincinnati: Truman and Smith, 1836), 118, 163.

11. Catharine E. Beecher, *A Treatise on Domestic Economy, for the Use of Young Ladies at Home, and at School*, rev. ed. (Boston: T. H. Webb, 1842), 37.

12. C. E. Beecher, *Treatise*, 33.

13. Lyman Beecher, *Six Sermons on the Nature, Occasions, Signs, Evils, and Remedy of Intemperance*, 10th ed. (New York: American Tract Society, 1833), 7.

14. L. Beecher, *Autobiography*, 343; L. Beecher, *Memory of Our Fathers*, 37.

15. Phoebe Palmer, *The Way of Holiness* (New York: Piercy and Reed, 1843), 120.

16. Palmer, *Way of Holiness*, 230.

17. Samuel F. B. Morse, *Foreign Conspiracy Against the Liberties of the United States*, rev. ed. (New York: Van Nostrand & Dwight, 1835), 55, 99–100.

18. Rebecca Theresa Reed, *Six Months in a Convent, or, The Narrative of Rebecca Theresa Reed* (Boston: Russell, Odiorne & Metcalf, 1835), 163.

19. Committee to Investigate the Destruction of the Ursuline Convent, *Report of the Committee, Relating to the Destruction of the Ursuline Convent, August 11, 1834* (Boston: J. H. Eastburn, 1834), 2.

20. Maria Monk, *Awful Disclosures of Maria Monk, or, The Hidden Secrets of a Nun's Life in a Convent Exposed!* (Philadelphia: T. B. Peterson, 1836), 38, 39.

21. Monk, *Awful Disclosures*, vi, 118.

22. Alexis de Tocqueville, *Democracy in America*, rev. ed., translated by Henry Reeve (New York: Colonial Press, 1900), 308.

23. L. Beecher, *Memory of Our Fathers*, 20.

CHAPTER 12: GOING INTO ALL THE WORLD

The following influenced my thinking about and understanding of the material in this chapter: David A. Chang, *The World and All the Things upon It: Native Hawaiian Geographies of Exploration* (Minneapolis: University of Minnesota Press, 2016); Emily Conroy-Krutz, *Missionary Diplomacy: Religion and Nineteenth-Century American Foreign Relations* (Ithaca, NY: Cornell University Press, 2024), and *Christian Imperialism: Converting the World in the Early American Republic* (Ithaca, NY: Cornell University Press, 2015); Peter Cozzens, *Tecumseh and the Prophet: The Shawnee Brothers Who Defied a Nation* (New York: Knopf, 2020); Gregory Evans Dowd, *A Spirited Resistance: The North American Indian Struggle for Unity, 1745–1815* (Baltimore, MD: Johns Hopkins University Press, 1992); Blaine Harden, *Murder at the Mission: A Frontier Killing, Its Legacy of Lies, and the Taking of the American West* (New York: Viking, 2021); Christine Leigh Heyrman, *American Apostles: When Evangelicals Entered the World of Islam* (New York: Hill and Wang, 2016); Sarah Koenig, *Providence and the Invention of American History* (New Haven: Yale University Press, 2021); Drew Lopenzina, *Through an Indian's Looking-Glass: A Cultural Biography of William Apess, Pequot* (Amherst, MA: University of Massachusetts Press, 2017); Kathryn Gin Lum, *Heathen: Religion and Race in American*

History (Cambridge, MA: Harvard University Press, 2022); Joel W. Martin, "Crisscrossing Projects of Sovereignty and Conversion: Cherokee Christians and New England Missionaries During the 1820s," in *Native Americans, Christianity, and the Reshaping of the American Religious Landscape*, Joel W. Martin and Mark A. Nicholas, eds. (Chapel Hill, NC: University of North Carolina Press, 2010), 67–89; Andrew Preston, *Sword of the Spirit, Shield of Faith: Religion in American War and Diplomacy* (New York: Knopf, 2012); and Jennifer Thigpen, *Island Queens and Mission Wives: How Gender and Empire Remade Hawai'i's Pacific World* (Chapel Hill, NC: University of North Carlina Press, 2014).

1. American Board of Commissioners for Foreign Missions, *First Ten Annual Reports of the American Board of Commissioners for Foreign Missions* (Boston: Crocker and Brewster, 1834), 9.

2. Emily Conroy-Krutz, *Missionary Diplomacy: Religion and Nineteenth-Century American Foreign Relations* (Ithaca, NY: Cornell University Press, 2024), 12.

3. American Board of Commissioners for Foreign Missions, *First Ten Annual Reports*, 13.

4. Gordon Hall and Samuel Newell, *The Conversion of the World* (Andover, CT: Flagg & Gould, 1818), 80.

5. David Abeel, *The Missionary Fortified Against Trials* (Boston: Perkins, Marvin & Co, 1835), 6, 7, 8.

6. Alvan Bond and Pliny Fisk, *Memoir of the Rev. Pliny Fisk, A.M., Late Missionary to Palestine* (Boston: Crocker and Brewster, 1828), v.

7. E. W. Dwight, *Memoirs of Henry Obookiah: A Native of Owhyhee*, rev. ed. (Philadelphia: American Sunday School Union, 1830).

8. Jennifer Thigpen, *Island Queens and Mission Wives: How Gender and Empire Remade Hawai'i's Pacific World* (Chapel Hill, NC: University of North Carlina Press, 2014), 2.

9. "Speech of Indian Chief to Various Tribes, May 4, 1807," in *Michigan Historical Collections*, v. 40 (Lansing, MI: 1929), 129.

10. American Board of Commissioners for Foreign Missions, *First Ten Annual Reports*, 153.

11. American Board of Commissioners for Foreign Missions, *First Ten Annual Reports*, 124.

12. William Penn [Jeremiah Evarts], "Present Crisis in the Condition of the American Indians. No. 1," *Cherokee Phoenix*, September 16, 1829; Theodore Frelinghuysen, *Speech of Mr. Frelinghuysen, of New Jersey*, delivered in US Senate, April 6, 1830 (Washington, DC: Office of the National Journal, 1830), 7.

13. William Apess [the author's name is spelled as Apes in the published book], *The Experiences of Five Christian Indians of the Pequod Tribe* (Boston: published for the author, 1833), 16, 17.

14. William Apess, "An Indian's Looking-Glass for the White Man," in *Experiences of Five Christian Indians*, 56.

15. John L. O'Sullivan, "The Great Nation of Futurity," *United States Democratic Review* (November 1839), 427.

16. Hall and Newell, *Conversion of the World*, 81.

CHAPTER 13: SETTING CAPTIVES FREE

The following influenced my thinking about and understanding of the material in this chapter: David W. Blight, *Frederick Douglass: Prophet of Freedom* (New York: Simon & Schuster, 2018); Kerri K. Greenidge, *The Grimkes: The Legacy of Slavery in an American Family* (New York: Liveright, 2023); Charles F. Irons, *The Origins of Proslavery Christianity: White and Black Evangelicals in Colonial and Antebellum Virginia* (Chapel Hill, NC: University of North Carolina Press, 2008); Manisha Sinha, *The Slave's Cause: A History of Abolition* (New Haven, CT: Yale University Press, 2016); Margaret Washington, *Sojourner Truth's America* (Champaign, IL: University of Illinois Press, 2009); and Ben Wright, *Bonds of Salvation: How Christianity Inspired and Limited American Abolitionism* (Baton Rouge, LA: Louisiana State University Press, 2020).

1. Sojourner Truth and Olive Gilbert, *The Narrative of Sojourner Truth: A Northern Slave* (Boston: printed for the author, 1850), 100–101.

2. *The Anti-Slavery Bugle* (New-Lisbon, Ohio), June 21, 1851, Chronicling America: Historic American Newspapers, Library of Congress, https://chroniclingamerica.loc.gov/lccn/sn83035487/1851-06-21/ed-1/seq-4/.

3. Angelina Grimké, *Appeal to the Christian Women of the South* (New York: American Anti-Slavery Society, 1836), 16, 25.

4. Sarah Grimké, *Letters on the Equality of the Sexes and the Condition of Woman* (Boston: Isaac Knapp, 1838), 51–52.

5. S. Grimké, *Letters*, 15, 20.

6. S. Grimké, *Letters*, 4, 10.

7. Catharine Beecher, *An Essay on Slavery and Abolitionism, with Reference to the Duty of American Females*, 2nd ed. (Philadelphia: H. Perkins, 1837), 104.

8. Robert Finley, *Thoughts on the Colonization of Free Blacks* (Washington, DC: n.p., 1816), 7–8.

9. Allen's letter, which originally appeared in *Freedom's Journal* on November 2, 1827, was reprinted by David Walker in *Walker's Appeal, in Four Articles*, 3rd ed. (Boston: D. Walker, 1830), 64–65.

10. Walker, *Walker's Appeal*, 2, 14.

11. Walker, *Walker's Appeal*, 15, 21.

12. William Lloyd Garrison, "To the Public," *The Liberator*, January 1, 1831; William Lloyd Garrison, *Thoughts on African Colonization* (Boston: Garrison and Knapp, 1832), 146.

13. Maria W. Stewart, *Meditations from the Pen of Mrs. Maria W. Stewart* (Washington, DC: W. Lloyd Garrision & Knap[p], 1879), 33.

14. William Lloyd Garrison, "An Address," *The Liberator* (July 13, 1838), and "The Meeting at Framingham," *The Liberator* (July 7, 1854).

15. Frederick Douglass, *Narrative of the Life of Frederick Douglass* (Boston: Anti-Slavery Office, 1845), 118; *Oration Delivered in Corinthian Hall* (Rochester, NY: Lee, Mann and Co., 1852), 29; and "Dialogue Between a Slaveholder and the Bible," *Frederick Douglass' Paper*, July 9, 1852, 1.

16. Henry Highland Garnet, "Garnet's Address," in David Walker, *Walker's Appeal, with a Brief Sketch of His Life and Also Garnet's Address* (New York: J. H. Tobitt, 1848), 93, 94.

17. Douglass, *Oration*, 15, 20, 34.

18. William Ellery Channing, *Slavery* (Boston: J. Munroe and Co., 1835), 109, 113.

19. Charles Hodge, "Slavery," *Biblical Repertory and Theological Review* 8, no. 2 (1836): 276–277, 280.

20. James Henley Thornwell, *The Rights and the Duties of Masters* (Charleston, SC: Walker & James, 1850), 11, 14, 44.

21. George Fitzhugh, *Cannibals All! or, Slaves Without Masters* (Richmond, VA: A. Morris, 1857), 143–144.

22. Charles Colcock Jones, *The Religious Instruction of the Negroes in the United States* (Savannah, GA: Thomas Purse, 1842), 167.

23. Thornton Stringfellow, *A Brief Examination of Scripture Testimony on the Institution of Slavery* (Richmond, VA: Religious Herald, 1841), 27.

24. Peter Cartwright, *Autobiography of Peter Cartwright: The Backwoods Preacher*, edited by W. P. Strickland (New York: Carlton & Porter, 1856), 157.

25. Herman Melville, *White-Jacket, or, The World in a Man-of-War* (New York: Harper & Brothers, 1855), 180, 181.

CHAPTER 14: AN ALMOST CHOSEN PEOPLE

The following influenced my thinking about and understanding of the material in this chapter: James P. Byrd, *A Holy Baptism of Fire and Blood: The Bible and the American Civil War* (New York: Oxford University Press, 2021); Drew Gilpin Faust, *This Republic of Suffering: Death and the American Civil War* (New York: Knopf, 2008); Luke E. Harlow, *Religion, Race, and the Making of Confederate Kentucky, 1830–1880* (New York: Cambridge University Press, 2014); John H. Matsui, *Millenarian Dreams and Racial Nightmares: The American Civil War as an Apocalyptic Conflict* (Baton Rouge, LA: Louisiana State University Press, 2021); Mark A. Noll, *The Civil War as a Theological Crisis* (Chapel Hill, NC: University of North Carolina Press, 2006); Andrew Preston, *Sword of the Spirit, Shield of Faith: Religion in American War and Diplomacy* (New York: Knopf, 2012); George C. Rable, *God's Almost Chosen Peoples: A Religious History of the American Civil War* (Chapel Hill, NC: University of North Carolina Press, 2010); and Harry S. Stout, *Upon the Altar of the Nation: A Moral History of the American Civil War* (New York: Viking, 2006).

1. Abraham Lincoln, "Address to the New Jersey Senate at Trenton, New Jersey, February 21, 1861," CWAL, vol. 4, 236.

2. Gilbert Haven, *Te Deum Laudamus: The Cause and the Consequence of the Election of Abraham Lincoln* (Boston: J. M. Hewes, 1860), 6.

3. Abraham Lincoln, "'A House Divided': Speech at Springfield, Illinois, June 16, 1858," CWAL, vol. 2, 461.

4. B. F. Brooke, *The Olive Branch: or, The Conservatism of Christianity* (Winchester, VA: The Republican Office, 1861), 13–14.

5. Abraham Lincoln, "First Inaugural Address, March 4, 1861," CWAL, vol. 4, 271.

6. Henry Ward Beecher, *Freedom and War* (Boston: Ticknor and Fields, 1863), 103.

7. Abraham Lincoln, "Proclamation of a National Fast Day, August 12, 1861," CWAL, vol. 4, 482.

8. Jefferson Davis, "Proclamation by the President of the Confederate States of America," Alfred Whital Stern Collection of Lincolniana [Montgomery, 1861], www.loc.gov/item/2021773881/.

9. John T. Wightman, *The Glory of God, the Defense of the South* (Portland, ME: B. Thurston & Company, 1871), 8.

10. Benjamin Morgan Palmer, *National Responsibility Before God* (New Orleans, LA: Price-Current, 1861), 12, 13.

11. R. L. Dabney, *Life and Campaigns of Lieut.-Gen. Thomas J. Jackson* (New York: Blelock & Co., 1866), 644.

12. Horace Bushnell, *Reverses Needed* (Hartford, CT: L. E. Hunt, 1861), 26.

13. National Convention to Secure the Religious Amendment of the Constitution of the United States, *Proceedings of the National Convention to Secure the Religious Amendment of the Constitution of the United States* (Philadelphia: Rodgers Co., 1872), iv–v, x.

14. Palmer, *National Responsibility*, 5; J. W. Tucker, *God's Providence in War* (Fayetteville, NC: Presbyterian Office, 1862), 11.

15. W. H. Seat, *The Confederate States of America in Prophecy* (Nashville, TN: Southern Methodist Publishing House, 1861), 93.

16. Wightman, *Glory of God*, 14.

17. Tucker, *God's Providence*, 8, 10.

18. Bushnell, *Reverses Needed*, 23, 25.

19. F. B. Carpenter, *Six Months at the White House with Abraham Lincoln* (New York: Hurd and Houghton, 1866), 282.

20. J. William Jones, *Christ in the Camp: or, Religion in Lee's Army* (Richmond, VA: B. F. Johnson & Co, 1887), 372.

21. Jones, *Christ in the Camp*, 289, 297.

22. Jones, *Christ in the Camp*, 301.

23. William W. Bennett, *A Narrative of the Great Revival Which Prevailed in the Southern Armies* (Philadelphia: Claxton, Remsen & Haffelfinger, 1877), 227.

24. Henry McNeal Turner, *Freedom's Witness: The Civil War Correspondence of Henry McNeal Turner*, ed. Jean Lee Cole (Morgantown, WV: West Virginia University Press, 2013), 155.

25. "The War Letters of Father Peter Paul Cooney of the Congregation of the Holy Cross," *Records of the American Catholic Historical Society of Philadelphia* 44, no. 1 (1933), 69.

26. Joseph Fransioli, *Patriotism, A Christian Virtue* (New York: Loyal Publication Society, 1863), 3, 7.

27. John Hampden Chamberlayne, *Ham Chamberlayne—Virginian* (Richmond, VA: Dietz Printing Co., 1932), 123.

28. "Battle Hymn," box 1, Papers of Julia Ward Howe, LOC.

29. William Barrows, *Our War and Our Religion, and Their Harmony* (Boston: J. M. Whittemore & Co., 1862), 7.

30. Daniel Alexander Payne, *Welcome to the Ransomed* (Baltimore: Bull & Tuttle, 1862), 15–16.

31. Gideon Welles, *Diary of Gideon Welles, Secretary of the Navy Under Lincoln and Johnson* (Boston: Houghton Mifflin, 1911), 143.

32. James Lynch, *The Mission of the United States Republic* (Augusta, GA: Chronicle & Sentinel Office, 1865), 8–9.

33. Abraham Lincoln, "Proclamation Appointing a National Fast Day, March 30, 1863," CWAL, vol. 6, 156.

34. Thomas Brainerd, *Patriotism Aiding Piety* (Philadelphia: W. F. Geddes, printer, 1863), 19–20.

35. Stephen Elliott, *Ezra's Dilemna [sic]* (Savannah, GA: George N. Nichols, 1863), 15, 17.

36. Abraham Lincoln, "Proclamation of Thanksgiving, October 3, 1863," CWAL, vol. 6, 497.

37. *The Lincoln Catechism Wherein the Eccentricities & Beauties of Despotism Are Fully Set Forth: A Guide to the Presidential Election of 1864* (New York: J. F. Feeks, 1864), 39.

38. Abraham Lincoln, "Second Inaugural Address, March 4, 1865," CWAL, vol. 8, 332–333.

39. Henry Ward Beecher, *Patriotic Addresses in America and England*, ed. John R. Howard (New York: Fords, Howard & Hulbert, 1887), 702, 711.

CHAPTER 15: RECONSTRUCTING THE NATION

The following influenced my thinking about and understanding of the material in this chapter: Matthew Bowman, *The Mormon People: The Making of an American Faith* (New York: Random House, 2012); Dennis C. Dickerson, *The African Methodist Episcopal Church: A History* (New York: Cambridge University Press, 2020); C. Joseph Genetin-Pilawa, "Ely Parker and the Contentious Peace Policy," *Western Historical Quarterly* 41, no. 2 (2010): 196–217; Sarah Barringer Gordon, *The Mormon Question: Polygamy and Constitutional Conflict in Nineteenth-Century America* (Chapel Hill, NC: University of North Carolina Press, 2002); Jennifer Graber, "'If a War It May Be Called': The Peace Policy with American Indians," *Religion and American Culture* 24, no. 1 (2014): 36–69, and *The Gods of Indian Country: Religion and the Struggle for the American West* (New York: Oxford University Press, 2018); Paul Harvey, *Christianity and Race in the American South: A History* (Chicago: University of Chicago Press, 2016), and *Freedom's Coming:*

Religious Culture and the Shaping of the South from the Civil War Through the Civil Rights Era (Chapel Hill, NC: University of North Carolina Press, 2007); Elizabeth L. Jemison, *Christian Citizens: Reading the Bible in Black and White in the Postemancipation South* (Chapel Hill, NC: University of North Carolina Press, 2020); Joshua Paddison, *American Heathens: Religion, Race, and Reconstruction in California* (Berkeley, CA: University of California Press, 2012); Benjamin E. Park, *American Zion: A New History of Mormonism* (New York: Liveright, 2024); and Louis Warren, *God's Red Son: The Ghost Dance Religion and the Making of Modern America* (New York: Basic Books, 2017).

1. Charles Shelton, "The Indians from a Christian Stand-point," *American Missionary* 39, no. 12 (1885), 371, 372.

2. Theophilus Gould Steward, *Fifty Years in the Gospel Ministry* (Philadelphia: A. M. E. Book Concern, 1921), 33.

3. James M. Simms, *The First Colored Baptist Church in North America* (Philadelphia: J. B. Lippincott, 1888), 151–152.

4. *Report On the Alleged Outrages in the Southern States by the Select Committee of the Senate: March 10, 1871* (Washington, DC: Government Printing Office, 1871), 103.

5. Henry McNeal Turner, *The Barbarous Decision of the United States Supreme Court* (Atlanta: published by the author, 1893), 3.

6. Henry McNeal Turner, *Respect Black: The Writings and Speeches of Henry McNeal Turner*, ed. Edwin S. Redkey (New York: Arno Press, 1971), 176–177.

7. W. E. B. Du Bois, *The Souls of Black Folk* (Chicago: A. C. McClurg, 1903), 193.

8. Grover Cleveland, "Inaugural Address," March 4, 1885, UCSB.

9. *Memorial of the Yearly Meetings of the Society of Friends, Relative to the Treatment of Indians* (January 25, 1869), 40th Cong., 3rd Sess., House Miscellaneous Doc. No. 29 (Washington, DC: Government Printing Office, 1869).

10. *Fifth Annual Report of the Board of Indian Commissioners to the Secretary of the Interior* (Washington, DC: Government Printing Office, 1874), 54.

11. *First Annual Report of the Board of Indian Commissioners to the Secretary of the Interior* (Washington, DC: Government Printing Office, 1870), 10.

12. *Fifth Annual Report*, 178.

13. Isabel C. Barrows, ed., *Proceedings of the National Conference of Charities and Correction* (Boston: Geo. H. Ellis, 1892), 46.

14. *Report of the Commissioner of Indian Affairs*, November 1, 1872, H.R. Exec. Doc. No. 1, 42nd Cong., 3rd Sess. (Washington, DC: Government Printing Office, 1872), 462.

15. US Sec. of the Interior, *Regulations of the Indian Department: With an Appendix Containing the Forms Used* (Washington, DC: Government Printing Office, 1884), 86.

16. US Sec. of the Interior, *Regulations of the Indian Department*, 89.

17. Brigham Young, *Journal of Discourses*, vol. 5 (London: Asa Calkin, 1858), 78.

18. Belinda Marden Pratt, *Defence of Polygamy, by a Lady in Utah* (n.p., 1854), 3.

19. Reynolds v. United States, 98 US 145 (1879).

20. James Cardinal Gibbons, "Some Defects in Our Political and Social Institutions," *North American Review* (October 1887), 346.

21. Journal of Wilford Woodruff (1886–1892), January 1, 1886, and January 1, 1887, Wilford Woodruff Papers, wilfordwoodruffpapers.org.

22. Journal of Wilford Woodruff, September 25, 1890.

23. Frederick Jackson Turner, "The Significance of the Frontier in American History," in *Annual Report of the American Historical Association for the Year 1894* (Washington, DC: Government Printing Office, 1895), 225–226.

24. Turner, "Significance of the Frontier," 227.

CHAPTER 16: IMMIGRATING FAITH

The following influenced my thinking about and understanding of the material in this chapter: William S. Cossen, *Making Catholic America: Religious Nationalism in the Gilded Age and Progressive Era* (Ithaca, NY: Cornell University Press, 2023); Linda Gordon, *The Great Arizona Orphan Abduction* (Cambridge, MA: Harvard University Press, 1999); Ruth Harris, *Guru to the World: The Life and Legacy of Vivekananda* (Cambridge, MA: Belknap Press of Harvard University Press, 2022); Kathryn Gin Lum, *Heathen: Religion and Race in American History* (Cambridge, MA: Harvard University Press, 2022); Andrew Preston, *Sword of the Spirit, Shield of Faith: Religion in American War and Diplomacy* (New York: Knopf, 2012); Jeffrey Rosario, "Seventh-day Adventism and Apocalyptic Political Dissent, 1898–1919" (PhD diss., Cambridge University, 2022); and Tisa Wenger, *Religious Freedom: The Contested History of an American Ideal* (Chapel Hill, NC: University of North Carolina Press, 2017).

1. Robert Anderton Naylor, *Across the Atlantic* (London: Roxburghe Press, 1893), 121.

2. "Speech of Bishop Arnett," in John Henry Barrows, *The World's Parliament of Religions: An Illustrated and Popular Story*, vol. 1 (Chicago: Parliament Publishing Company, 1893), 107.

3. Barrows, *World's Parliament of Religions*, vol. 1, ix, and vol. 2, 1578.

4. Swami Vivekananda, *Chicago Addresses*, 5th ed. (Calcutta: Advaita Ashrama, 1915), 32, 33.

5. Isaac Thomas Hecker, *The Church and the Age: An Exposition of the Catholic Church* (New York: Catholic World, 1887), 67, 79.

6. Hecker, *Church and the Age*, 89.

7. John A. Russell, "The Catholic Church in the United States," in *The Memorial Volume: A History of the Third Plenary Council of Baltimore* (Baltimore: Baltimore Publishing Co., 1885), 26–27.

8. Pope Leo XIII, *Longinqua*, January 6, 1895, www.vatican.va/content/leo-xiii/en/encyclicals/documents/hf_l-xiii_enc_06011895_longinqua.html.

9. Pope Leo XIII, *Testem Benevolentiae Nostrae*, January 22, 1899, www.papalencyclicals.net/leo13/l13teste.htm.

10. Isaac Mayer Wise, David Philipson, and Louis Grossmann, *Selected Writings of Isaac M. Wise* (Cincinnati, OH: Robert Clarke, 1900), 261.

11. "Address of Rev. S. V. Blakeslee," in *Chinese Immigration: Its Social, Moral, and Political Effect*, Report to the California State Senate of Its Special Committee on Chinese Immigration (Sacramento: State Printing, 1878), 241, 245.

12. Wong Chin Foo, "Why Am I a Heathen?" *North American Review* (August 1887), 175, 179.

13. Yan Phou Lee, "Why I Am Not a Heathen," *North American Review* (September 1887), 309, 312.

14. Robert E. Speer, *Missionary Principles and Practice* (New York: Revell, 1902), 501–502.

15. Josiah Strong, *Our Country: Its Possible Future and Its Present Crisis* (New York: Baker & Taylor, 1885), 161.

16. John R. Mott, *The Evangelization of the World in This Generation* (New York: Student Volunteer Movement, 1900).

17. Judson Smith and James L. Barton, "Annual Survey of the Work of the American Board, 1897–1898," *Missionary Herald*, November 1898, 445; Washington Gladden, "The Issues of the War," *Outlook*, July 16, 1898, 673, 675.

18. General James Rusling, "Interview with President William McKinley," *Christian Advocate*, January 22, 1903, 17.

19. William Newton Clarke, *A Study of Christian Missions* (New York: Scribner, 1900), 107–108.

20. "Mr. Bryan's Notification Speech, August 8, 1900," in William Jennings Bryan, *Life and Speeches of Hon. Wm. Jennings Bryan* (Baltimore: R. H. Woodward, 1900), 408.

21. Pan-African Association, "To the Nations of the World," Manuscript [1900]. Digital Commonwealth, http://credo.library.umass.edu/view/full/mums312-b004-i321.

22. John Ireland, "The Religious Conditions in Our New Island Territory," *Outlook*, August 26, 1899, 933.

23. Congressional Record—56th Congress (Senate) 33, part 1 (January 9, 1900), 704.

CHAPTER 17: SAVING AND PURIFYING BODIES

The following influenced my thinking about and understanding of the material in this chapter: Catherine L. Albanese, *A Republic of Mind and Spirit: A Cultural History of American Metaphysical Religion* (New Haven, CT: Yale University Press, 2007); Heather D. Curtis, *Faith in the Great Physician: Suffering and Divine Healing in American Culture, 1860–1900* (Baltimore: Johns Hopkins University Press, 2007); Richard Wightman Fox, *Trials of Intimacy: Love and Loss in the Beecher-Tilton Scandal* (Chicago: University of Chicago Press, 1999); Timothy E. W. Gloege, "Faith Healing, Medical Regulation, and Public Religion in Progressive Era Chicago," *Religion and American Culture* 23, no. 2 (2013): 185–231, and *Guaranteed Pure: The Moody Bible Institute, Business, and the Making of Modern Evangelicalism* (Chapel Hill, NC: University of North Carolina Press, 2015); Fran Grace, *Carry A. Nation: Retelling the Life* (Bloomington, IN: Indiana University Press, 2001); Ronald L. Numbers, *Prophetess of Health: A Study of Ellen G. White* (New York: Harper & Row, 1976); Leigh Eric Schmidt, *Village Atheists: How America's

Unbelievers Made Their Way in a Godly Nation (Princeton, NJ: Princeton University Press, 2016); Amy B. Voorhees, *A New Christian Identity: Christian Science Origins and Experience in American Culture* (Chapel Hill, NC: University of North Carolina Press, 2021); and Grant Wacker, "Marching to Zion: Religion in a Modern Utopian Community," *Church History* 54, no. 4 (1985): 496–511.

1. Carry A. Nation, *The Use and Need of the Life of Carry A. Nation* (Topeka, KS: F. M. Steves & Sons, 1904), 61.

2. Nation, *Use and Need*, 60, 64.

3. Ellen G. White, *An Appeal to Mothers* (Battle Creek, MI: Steam Press, 1864), 11, 17.

4. John Harvey Kellogg, *Plain Facts for Old and Young* (Burlington, IA: Segner & Condit, 1881), 320, 383–384.

5. Sarah Mix, *Faith Cures and Answers to Prayer* (Springfield, MA: Springfield Printing, 1882), 8.

6. Carrie Judd Montgomery, *The Prayer of Faith* (San Francisco: Hicks-Judd, 1894).

7. "Torrey Holds His Faith," *Chicago Tribune*, October 8, 1899.

8. Mary Baker Eddy, *Retrospection and Introspection* (Boston: Joseph Armstrong, 1900), 39.

9. Eddy, *Retrospection and Introspection*, 39, 40.

10. Frances E. Willard, *Woman and Temperance*, 4th ed. (Hartford, CT: Park Pub. Co., 1884), 42, 43.

11. Victoria C. Woodhull, *A Speech on the Principles of Social Freedom Delivered in Steinway Hall* (New York: Woodhull, Claflin, and Co., 1872), 23.

12. Anthony Comstock, *Traps for the Young*, 2nd ed. (New York: Funk & Wagnalls, 1884), 239, 240.

13. Robert Ingersoll, *Lectures of Col. R. G. Ingersoll, Including His Letters on the Chinese God* (Chicago: Rhodes & McClure, 1898), 746; Ingersoll to Scotch Presbyterians, January 22, 1887, and Catie Hansen to Robert Ingersoll, November 9, 1891, microfilm reel 18, Robert Ingersoll Papers, LOC.

14. Comstock, *Traps for the Young*, 184.

15. Comstock, *Traps for the Young*, 199.

16. On the Beecher-Tilton scandal, see *Theodore Tilton vs. Henry Ward Beecher, Action for Crim. Con. Tried in the City Court of Brooklyn* (New York: McDivitt, Campbell & Co., 1875).

17. Victoria Woodhull, "The Beecher-Tilton Scandal Case," *Woodhull & Claflin's Weekly*, November 2, 1872.

CHAPTER 18: CHRISTIANITY, CAPITALISM, AND THE SIGNS OF THE TIMES

The following influenced my thinking about and understanding of the material in this chapter: Donald Harman Akenson, *The Americanization of the Apocalypse: Creating America's Own Bible* (New York: Oxford University Press, 2023); Edward J. Blum,

Reforging the White Republic: Race, Religion, and American Nationalism, 1865–1898, 2nd ed. (Baton Rouge, LA: Louisiana State University Press, 2015); Heath W. Carter, *Union Made: Working People and the Rise of Social Christianity in Chicago* (New York: Oxford University Press, 2015); Seth Dowland, *Purity and Power: A History of White Christian Masculinity in America* (New York: Oxford University Press, forthcoming); Timothy E. W. Gloege, *Guaranteed Pure: The Moody Bible Institute, Business, and the Making of Modern Evangelicalism* (Chapel Hill, NC: University of North Carolina Press, 2015); Crawford Gribben, *J. N. Darby and the Roots of Dispensationalism* (New York: Oxford University Press, 2024); Evelyn Brooks Higginbotham, *Righteous Discontent: The Women's Movement in the Black Baptist Church, 1880–1920* (Cambridge, MA: Harvard University Press, 1993); Daniel G. Hummel, *The Rise and Fall of Dispensationalism: How the Evangelical Battle over the End Times Shaped a Nation* (Grand Rapids, MI: Eerdmans, 2023); Abigail Modaff, "'The Hidden Life': Ellen Gates Starr, Vida Dutton Scudder, and Catholic Socialist Progressivism," *Modern Intellectual History* 20, no. 4 (2023); B. M. Pietsch, *Dispensational Modernism* (New York: Oxford University Press, 2015); and Diane Winston, *Red-Hot and Righteous: The Urban Religion of the Salvation Army* (Cambridge, MA: Harvard University Press, 1999).

1. August Spies, *August Spies' Auto-Biography* (Chicago: Nina van Zandt, 1887), 77.

2. Russell H. Conwell, *Acres of Diamonds* (New York: Harper & Brothers, 1915), 18, 20.

3. Washington Gladden, *The New Idolatry* (New York: McClure, Phillips & Co., 1905), 47–48.

4. Washington Gladden, *Social Salvation* (Boston: Houghton Mifflin, 1902), 26, 30.

5. Walter Rauschenbusch, *Christianity and the Social Crisis* (New York: Macmillan, 1907), xiii.

6. Jane Addams, "A New Impulse to an Old Gospel," *The Forum*, November 1892, 353.

7. Vida Scudder, *On Journey* (New York: E. P. Dutton, 1937), 368; Vida Scudder, *The Church and the Hour, Reflections of a Socialist Churchwoman* (New York: E. P. Dutton, 1917), 100.

8. Scudder, *On Journey*, 163.

9. *Official Program of the Twentieth Annual Session of the National Baptist Convention* (Nashville, TN: National Baptist Publishing Board, 1900), 196. See also, for example, Nannie Helen Burroughs to Mrs. Alvin T. Hert, August 19, 1929, folder 16, box 37, Nannie Helen Burroughs Papers, LOC.

10. Salvation Army, *What Is the Salvation Army?* (New York: Eastern Territorial Headquarters, 1924), 7.

11. Fred B. Smith, *A Man's Religion* (New York: Association Press, 1913), 33.

12. John Richard Brown, *Jesus the Joyous Comrade* (New York: Association Press, 1911), 5–6.

13. Mary E. Lease, "Women in the Farmers' Alliance," in *Transactions of the National Council of Women of the United States*, ed. Rachel Foster Avery (Philadelphia: J. B. Lippincott, 1891), 215, 216.

14. Isom P. Langley, "Religion in the Alliance," in Nelson A. Dunning, *The Farmers' Alliance History and Agricultural Digest* (Washington, DC: Alliance, 1891), 314, 316.

15. *Official Proceedings of the Democratic National Convention Held in Chicago* (Logansport, IN: Wilson, Humphreys & Co., 1896), 234.

16. Elias B. Sanford, ed., *Church Federation, Inter-Church Conference on Federation* (New York: Revell, 1906), 30.

17. Scudder, *Church and the Hour*, 10.

18. J. N. Darby to brother, October 1866, in *Letters of J. N. D., vol. I, 1832–1868* (Kingston-on-Thames, UK: Stow Hill Bible and Tract Depot, n.d.), 460–461.

19. T. G. Steward, *The End of the World* (Philadelphia: A. M. E. Book Concern, 1888), 67–68, 121.

20. Steward, *End of the World*, 71, 125.

21. James Theodore Holly, "The Divine Plan of Human Redemption in Its Ethnological Development," *A. M. E. Church Review* (October 1884), 83, 85.

22. Charles Taze Russell, *Millennial Dawn*, vol. 1 (Allegheny, PA: Tower Publishing, 1886), 13.

23. Although the Scofield Bible is certainly one of the best-selling books in Oxford history, the press does not have reliable statistics from the pre–World War II era, so it is impossible to determine conclusively if this is in fact their best-selling book.

24. Dwight L. Moody, "The Second Coming of Christ," in Moody et al., *The Second Coming of Christ* (Chicago: Moody Press, 1896), 28. See also, "The Revival: Mr. Moody's Sermon on the Coming of the Lord," *Chicago Tribune*, January 6, 1877.

25. "Moody and Sankey," *The Nation*, March 9, 1876, 157.

26. "Moody and Sankey," *The Nation*, 156, 157.

27. "Could Not Preach in a Barn," *Brooklyn Eagle*, June 11, 1887; "Oration of Frederick Douglass," *American Missionary* 39, no. 6 (June 1885), 164.

CHAPTER 19: NEW CHRISTIANITIES FOR THE NEW CENTURY

The following influenced my thinking about and understanding of the material in this chapter: Lloyd Daniel Barba, *Sowing the Sacred: Mexican Pentecostal Farmworkers in California* (New York: Oxford University Press, 2024); Gastón Espinosa, "'El Azteca': Francisco Olazábal and Latino Pentecostal Charisma, Power, and Faith Healing in the Borderlands," *Journal of the American Academy of Religion* 67, no. 3 (1999), 597–616; Daniel Ramírez, *Migrating Faith: Pentecostalism in the United States and Mexico in the Twentieth Century* (Chapel Hill, NC: University of North Carolina Press, 2015); and Grant Wacker, *Heaven Below: Early Pentecostals and American Culture* (Cambridge, MA: Harvard University Press, 2001), and *Augustus H. Strong and the Dilemma of Historical Consciousness* (Macon, GA: Mercer University Press, 1985).

1. "Weird Babel of Tongues," *Los Angeles Times*, April 18, 1906; Frank Bartleman, "How Pentecost Came to Los Angeles," in Frank Bartleman, *Witness to Pentecost: The Life of Frank Bartleman* (New York: Garland, 1985), 54.

2. Bartleman, "How Pentecost Came," 44, 49, 58.

3. William J. Seymour, "Behold the Bridegroom Cometh!" *Apostolic Faith*, January 1907, 2.

4. Grant Wacker, *Heaven Below: Early Pentecostals and American Culture* (Cambridge, MA: Harvard University Press, 2001), 266.

5. Andrew Dickson White, *A History of the Warfare of Science with Theology in Christendom* (London: Macmillan, 1896), v–vi.

6. Sydney E. Ahlstrom, *A Religious History of the American People* (New Haven: Yale University Press, 1972), 767.

7. Kathryn Lofton, "The Methodology of the Modernists: Process in American Protestantism," *Church History* 75, no. 2 (2006): 378.

8. Shailer Mathews, "The Awakening of American Protestantism," *Constructive Quarterly* (March–December 1913), 102, 105, 109.

9. Mathews, "Awakening of American Protestantism," 103, 108.

10. Lyman Stewart to Arthur Hicks, July 9, 1908, Lyman Stewart Papers, BIOLA.

11. James Orr, "Science and Christian Faith," in *The Fundamentals: A Testimony to the Truth*, vol. 4 (Chicago: Testimony Publishing Company, 1910–1915), 91–104; Charles R. Erdman, "The Church and Socialism," in *The Fundamentals: A Testimony to the Truth*, vol. 12 (Chicago: Testimony Publishing Company, 1910–1915), 116, 119.

12. Lyman Stewart to Will, May, and Fred, September 4, 1914, Lyman Stewart Papers, BIOLA.

CHAPTER 20: MAKING THE WORLD SAFE FOR DEMOCRACY

The following influenced my thinking about and understanding of the material in this chapter: Cara Lea Burnidge, *A Peaceful Conquest: Woodrow Wilson, Religion, and the New World Order* (Chicago: University of Chicago Press, 2016); Jonathan H. Ebel, *Faith in the Fight: Religion and the American Solider in the Great War* (Princeton, NJ: Princeton University Press, 2010); Michael Kazin, *A Godly Hero: The Life of William Jennings Bryan* (New York: Knopf, 2006); and Andrew Preston, *Sword of the Spirit, Shield of Faith: Religion in American War and Diplomacy* (New York: Knopf, 2012).

1. Billy Sunday, *Address by Billy Sunday: Americanism* (Philadelphia: Law Enforcement League of Philadelphia, April 10, 1922), 36–37; "The Rev. Billy Sunday," *Atlanta Constitution*, September 22, 1907.

2. "$25,000 Subscribed to Liberty Loan by Billy Sunday," *New York Tribune*, June 6, 1917; "Billy Sunday Says America Will Win," *Boston Globe*, April 8, 1917; "40,000 Cheer for War and Religion Mixed by Sunday," *New York Times*, April 9, 1917; "45,000 Cheer Sunday in Attacks on Kaiser," *Washington Post*, January 7, 1918; "Billy Sunday's Prayer," *The Mercury* (Australia), April 5, 1918; and "When Billy Prays, Congressmen Cheer and Applaud," *Spokesman-Review*, January 27, 1918.

3. Henry S. Coffin, "The Preparedness of a Christian Nation," *King's Business*, August 1916, 694; "The World War Mad," *King's Business*, June 1916, 487.

4. Martin D. Hardin, "Civilization at the Crossroads," Congressional Record 53:14, Sixty-Fourth Congress, Appendix (Washington, DC: Government Printing Office, 1916), 409, 410, 412.

5. A. C. Dixon to Mary Dixon, November 26, 1915, folder 4, box 7, Amzi Clarence Dixon Papers, SBHLA.

6. William Jennings Bryan to Woodrow Wilson, May 12, 1915, and W. B. Fleming to William Jennings Bryan, June 2, 1915, box 30, William Jennings Bryan Papers, LOC.

7. William Jennings Bryan to M. A. Matthews, February 2, 1916, folder 10, box 1, accession 97-2, Mark A. Matthews Papers, UW; H. O. Rowlands to William Jennings Bryan, June 10, 1915, box 30, William Jennings Bryan Papers, LOC.

8. P. A. Klein, "Compulsory Military Service," *Christian Workers Magazine*, July 1916, 836; Frank Bartleman, "Christian Preparedness," *Word and Work*, Papers of Frank Bartleman, FPHC.

9. C. H. Mason, "The Kaiser in the Light of the Scriptures," in *The History and Life Work of Elder C. H. Mason* (Memphis: Howe Print. Dept., 1920), 49.

10. Shailer Mathews, *Patriotism and Religion* (New York: Macmillan, 1918), 78.

11. Woodrow Wilson, "Necessity of War Against Germany (April 2, 1917)," in *Selected Addresses and Public Papers of Woodrow Wilson*, ed. Albert Bushnell Hart (New York: Boni and Liveright, 1918), 195; William E. Blackstone to Woodrow Wilson, April 24, 1917, folder 5, box 7, collection 540, William E. Blackstone Papers, BGCA.

12. James Morris Webb, *A Black Man Will Be the Coming Universal King* (Chicago: published by the author [1918?]), 3, 4.

13. *Handbook of the National Catholic War Council* (Washington, DC: Administrative Committee of Bishops, 1918), 7, 8.

14. *Handbook of the National Catholic War Council*, 9.

15. *Handbook of the National Catholic War Council*, 24.

16. Harry Emerson Fosdick, *The Challenge of the Present Crisis* (New York: George H. Doran, 1917), 24.

17. Henry Sloane Coffin, *In a Day of Social Rebuilding* (New Haven, CT: Yale University Press, 1918), 27; Walter Rauschenbusch, *A Theology for the Social Gospel* (New York: Macmillan, 1917), 4.

18. "Safe for Democracy," *Christian Workers*, July 1917, 852; "Will This Be the Last War?" *King's Business*, June 1917, 483.

19. Frank Bartleman, "War and the Christian," *Word and Work*, Papers of Frank Bartleman, FPHC; Philip Mauro, *The Number of Man*, 2nd ed. (Boston: Scripture Truth Depot, 1919), 372, 373.

20. The Blackstone Memorials, 1891 and 1916, folder 6, box 6, collection 540, William E. Blackstone Papers, BGCA.

21. Nathan Straus to William E. Blackstone, May 8, 1916, folder 6, box 7, collection 540, William E. Blackstone Papers, BGCA.

22. William E. Blackstone to Justice Brandeis, March 19, 1917, and William E. Blackstone to Justice Brandeis, April 18, 1917, folder 6, box 7, collection 540, William E. Blackstone Papers, BGCA.

23. Louis Brandeis to Jacob deHaas, May 8, 1917, and Louis Brandeis to Jacob deHaas, December 6, 1917, in *Letters of Louis D. Brandeis,* vol. iv ed. Melvin I. Urofsky and David W. Levine (Albany, NY: State University of New York Press, 1975), 289, 327.

24. Leonard Newby, "Light on the Present Crisis," *Christian Workers Magazine*, December 1916, 277; "Has Christianity Failed, or Has Civilization Failed, or Has Man Failed?" *King's Business*, November 1914, 595; Stanley H. Frodsham, "Our Heavenly Citizenship," *Weekly Evangel*, September 11, 1915, 3.

25. Shirley Jackson Case, "The Premillennial Menace," *Biblical World* 52, no. 1 (July 1918), 17; Herbert L. Willett, "Activities and Menace of Millennialism," *Christian Century*, August 29, 1918, 8.

26. Shailer Mathews, *Will Christ Come Again?* (Hyde Park, IL: American Institute of Sacred Literature, 1917), 3, 15–16.

27. James Allen Geissinger, "Premillennialism Tested by Its Fruits," *Sunday School Journal*, March 1916, 179, 180; George Preston Mains, *Premillennialism: Non-Scriptural, Non-Historic, Non-Scientific, Non-Philosophical* (New York: Abingdon, 1920), 50, 51–52.

28. T. C. Horton, "Persecuting the Premillennialists," *King's Business*, October 1920, 917, 918.

29. "Postmillennialism and Pacifism," *Christian Workers*, October 1918, 83.

CHAPTER 21: THE RISE OF FUNDAMENTALISM

The following influenced my thinking about and understanding of the material in this chapter: Tona J. Hangen, *Redeeming the Dial: Radio, Religion, and Popular Culture in America* (Chapel Hill, NC: University of North Carolina Press, 2002); Mary Beth Swetnam Mathews, *Doctrine and Race: African American Evangelicals and Fundamentalism Between the Wars* (Tuscaloosa, AL: University of Alabama Press, 2018); and Grant Wacker, *Heaven Below: Early Pentecostals and American Culture* (Cambridge, MA: Harvard University Press, 2001).

1. William Bell Riley, *The Menace of Modernism* (New York: Christian Alliance Publishing Company, 1917), 155, and "The Great Divide, or Christ and the Present Crisis," in World Conference on Christian Fundamentals, *God Hath Spoken* (Philadelphia: Bible Conference Committee, 1919), 27.

2. Curtis Lee Laws, "Convention Side Lights," *Watchman-Examiner*, July 1, 1920, 834. See also Curtis Lee Laws, "Fundamentalism from the Baptist Viewpoint," *Moody Monthly*, September 1922, 14–17.

3. Harry Emerson Fosdick, *Shall the Fundamentalists Win?* (n.p., 1922), 4, 9, 10.

4. Walt Holcomb to Harry Emerson Fosdick, January 21, 1924, folder 7, box 5, series 2A, Harry Emerson Fosdick Papers, BURKE.

5. Harry Emerson Fosdick to Walt Holcomb, February 4, 1924, folder 7, box 5, series 2A, Harry Emerson Fosdick Papers, BURKE.

6. H. L. Mencken, "Doctor Fundamentalist," *Baltimore Evening Sun*, January 18, 1937.

7. William Bell Riley, "The Faith of the Fundamentalists," *Current History* 26, no. 3 (1927), 436.

8. Riley, "Faith of the Fundamentalists."

9. Aimee Semple McPherson, "Converting the World by Radio," *Bridal Call*, July 1923, 15.

10. Herbert Hoover, "The Reminiscences of Herbert Clark Hoover," Columbia University Oral History Project, 1951 (New York: Columbia University, 1975), 11.

11. "Fundamentalism and Modernism: Two Religions," *Christian Century*, January 3, 1924, 5, 6.

12. "White Baptists," *National Baptist Union-Review*, April 17, 1926, 4; "He Wants to Know," *National Baptist Union-Review*, April 30, 1927, 2; "Among White Baptists," *National Baptist Union-Review*, May 7, 1927, 4; "No Time to Study Isms," *National Baptist Union-Review*, July 1, 1916, 9.

13. E. C. Morris, "Twenty-seventh Annual Address of E. C. Morris, President, National Baptist Convention," *National Baptist Voice*, September 17–24, 1921.

14. T. G. Steward to Frank [Steward], March 3, 1923, Theophilus G. Steward Papers, SCH.

15. A. B. Adams, "The Light House," *Pittsburgh Courier*, June 18, 1932, and September 16, 1933.

16. Ernest Rice McKinney, "This Week," *Amsterdam News*, April 15, 1925, and "Views and Reviews," *Pittsburgh Courier*, March 19, 1932.

17. Lester A. Walton, "Negro, Freed from Religious Bugaboos of 'Slave' Days, Gradually Drifting from Church," *Pittsburgh Courier*, September 25, 1926.

18. Roscoe Simmons, "The Week," *Chicago Defender*, February 7, 1925, December 15, 1923, December 29, 1923, January 5, 1924, and September 20, 1924.

19. "The Church Caucasian," *Pittsburgh Courier*, May 31, 1924.

20. Charles H. Corbett to Henry Sloane Coffin, November 1, 1925, folder 3, box 2, series 1A, Henry Sloane Coffin Papers, BURKE.

21. William Ernest Hocking, *Re-Thinking Missions: A Laymen's Inquiry After One Hundred Years* (New York: Harper, 1932), 326; "The Betrayal Commission," *Sunday School Times*, January 7, 1933, 7.

22. Sarah Comstock, "Aimee Semple McPherson: Prima Donna of Revivalism," *Harper's Monthly*, December 1927, 13.

23. Aimee Semple McPherson, *In the Service of the King: The Story of My Life* (New York: Boni and Liveright, 1927), 152, 211; Roberta Semple Salter, interview by author, New York City, March 16, 2004.

24. Aimee Semple McPherson, "Trial of the Modern Liberalist College Professor Versus the Lord Jesus Christ," sermon transcript (October 14, 1923), ICFG.

25. Aimee Semple McPherson, "To the Servants and the Handmaidens: Baccalaureate Sermon," *Bridal Call Foursquare*, February 1930, 5.

CHAPTER 22: RELAUNCHING CULTURE WARS

The following influenced my thinking about and understanding of the material in this chapter: Linda Gordon, *The Second Coming of the KKK: The Ku Klux Klan of the 1920s and the American Political Tradition* (New York: Liveright, 2017); Raymond J. Haberski Jr., *It's Only a Movie!: Films and Critics in American Culture* (Lexington, KY: University Press of Kentucky, 2015); Edward J. Larson, *Summer for the Gods: The Scopes Trial and America's Continuing Debate over Science and Religion*, 2nd ed. (New York: Basic Books, 2020); and Mary Beth Swetnam Mathews, *Doctrine and Race: African American Evangelicals and Fundamentalism Between the Wars* (Tuscaloosa, AL: University of Alabama Press, 2017).

1. Herbert Blumer and Philip M. Hauser, *Movies, Delinquency, and Crime* (New York: Macmillan, 1933), 85.

2. W. S. Lockhart to Chas. S. Macfarland, fall 1922, folder 24, box 14, RG NCC 18, Federal Council of the Churches of Christ in America Records, PHS; T. C. Horton, "Clean Up the Movies," *King's Business*, October 1922, 990; "Will the Movies Clean Up?" *Christian Century*, April 2, 1925, 432.

3. Frederick Lewis Allen, *Only Yesterday: An Informal History of the 1920s* (New York: Perennial Classics, 1931), 88.

4. New York (State) Legislature Joint Committee Investigating Seditious Activities, *Revolutionary Radicalism: Its History, Purpose and Tactics* (Albany, NY: J. B. Lyon, 1920), 2708.

5. Archibald Stevenson to James F. Forbes, November 30, 1920, in "Correspondence Relative to the Conduct of the Labor Temple," folder 2, box 1, RG 14, Labor Temple Records, PHS.

6. New York (State) Legislature, *Revolutionary Radicalism*, 2701, 2705; Edmund Chaffee to Kenneth Miller, March 28, 1921, folder 7, box 1, RG 14, Labor Temple Records, PHS.

7. John D. Rockefeller Jr. to Harry Emerson Fosdick, December 19, 1927, folder 20, box 8, series 2A, Harry Emerson Fosdick Papers, BURKE.

8. Harry Emerson Fosdick to John D. Rockefeller Jr., December 22, 1927, and January 4, 1928, folder 20, box 8, series 2A, Harry Emerson Fosdick Papers, BURKE.

9. Bruce Barton, *The Man Nobody Knows: A Discovery of the Real Jesus* (Indianapolis: Bobbs-Merrill, 1925), n.p.

10. Elizabeth Cady Stanton, *The Woman's Bible*, vol. 1, 8–9, and vol. 2, 213 (New York: European Publishing, 1898).

11. Stanton, *Woman's Bible*, vol. 1, 14.

12. Annie Armstrong to T. P. Bell, December 13, 1893, folder 26, box 1, AR 795-109, James Marion Frost Papers, SBHLA.

13. Billy Sunday, *Address by Billy Sunday: Americanism* (Philadelphia: Law Enforcement League of Philadelphia, April 10, 1922), 42.

14. Peter Z. Easton, "Does Woman Represent God?" *Christian Workers*, August 1912, 785–787.

15. Frank Bartleman, *Flapper Evangelism: Fashion's Fools, Headed for Hell* (Los Angeles: printed by the author [1920?]); John R. Rice, *Bobbed Hair, Bossy Wives, and Women Preachers* (Wheaton, IL: Sword of the Lord Publishers, 1941).

16. Harold L. Lundquist, "The Decline of the American Home," *Moody Monthly*, November 1937, 115; "The Education of Women," *King's Business*, April 1916, 294; M. A. Matthews, "Woman's Throne," Punchettes, folder 7, box 7, accession 97-2, Mark A. Matthews Papers, UW; M. A. Matthews, "Cowardly Husbands," Sermonettes 1923, box 17, accession 97-2, Mark A. Matthews Papers, UW.

17. "Religion and Sex," *Christian Century*, January 25, 1923, 104.

18. "Evangelist Shows Atlanta Girls How to Catch Husbands," *Boston Globe*, December 15, 1917; Heartbroken Mother to John Roach Straton, January 13 [n.y.], and Edwin B. Van Aken to John Roach Straton, April 12, 1920, John Roach Straton Papers, ABHS; John R. Rice, "The President's Birthday Balls," *Sword of the Lord*, January 28, 1938, 2; John R. Rice, *The Home: Courtship, Marriage, and Children* (Wheaton, IL: Sword of the Lord Publishers, 1946), 156; "Birth Control," *Moody Monthly*, March 1931, 336.

19. Donald Grey Barnhouse, "Tomorrow: Current Events in the Light of Bible Prophecy," *Revelation*, September 1937, 398; Dan Gilbert, *One Minute Before Midnight* (Los Angeles: Jewish Hope, 1945), 28–29; Wilbur Smith, "Paul's Final Description of the End of This Age," *Our Hope*, February 1941, 528.

20. *The World's Most Famous Court Trial, Tennessee Evolution Case* (complete stenographic report) (Cincinnati: National Book Company, 1925), 4–5.

21. William Jennings Bryan, "Misrepresentations of Darwinism and Its Disciples," *Moody Monthly*, April 1923, 331.

22. Clarence Darrow, *The Story of My Life* (New York: Scribner's, 1932), 249.

23. *World's Most Famous Court Trial*, 74, 79, 87.

24. Albert Henry Newman to Mrs. Newman [n.d., 1925], folder 16, box 1, AR 11, Albert Henry Newman Collection, SBHLA.

25. H. L. Mencken, "Mencken Declares Strictly Fair Trial Is Beyond Ken of Tennessee Fundamentalists," *Baltimore Evening Sun*, July 16, 1925.

26. *World's Most Famous Court Trial*, 317.

27. Hiram Wesley Evans, "The Klan's Fight for Americanism," *North American Review* 223 (March 1926), 38–39, 52, 54.

28. M. A. Matthews to Woodrow Wilson, August 20, 1919, folder 3, box 5, accession 97-2, Mark A. Matthews Papers, UW.

29. Charles C. Marshall, "An Open Letter to the Honorable Alfred E. Smith," *Atlantic*, April 1927, 540.

30. An Ardent Roman Catholic to Charles C. Marshall, April 21, 1927, and An Admirer of the Governor to Charles C. Marshall, April 19, 1927, box 2, Charles C. Marshall Papers, LOC.

31. Alfred E. Smith, "Catholic and Patriot," *Atlantic*, May 1927, 728.

32. "Browbeating the Protestants," *Christian Century*, October 11, 1928, 1219.

33. Anonymous to John Roach Straton, n.d., and A 200% AMERICAN to John Roach Straton, n.d., John Roach Straton Papers, ABHS.

34. Walter Lippman, *A Preface to Morals* (New York: Macmillan, 1929), 8, 12.

CHAPTER 23: THE POPULIST REVOLT

The following influenced my thinking about and understanding of the material in this chapter: Joel A. Carpenter, "Fundamentalist Institutions and the Rise of Evangelical Protestantism, 1929–1942," *Church History* 49, no. 1 (1980), 62–75; Jay P. Dolan, *The American Catholic Experience: A History from Colonial Times to the Present* (New York: Doubleday, 1985); Jonathan H. Ebel, *From Dust They Came: Government Camps and the Religion of Reform in New Deal California* (New York: New York University Press, 2023); Alison Collis Greene, "The End of 'The Protestant Era'?" *Church History* 80, no. 3 (2011): 600–610, and *No Depression in Heaven: The Great Depression, the New Deal, and the Transformation of Religion in the Delta* (New York: Oxford University Press, 2016); Robert T. Handy, "The American Religious Depression, 1925–1935," *Church History* 29, no. 1 (1960), 3–16; Lerone A. Martin, *Preaching on Wax: The Phonograph and the Shaping of Modern African American Religion* (New York: NYU Press, 2014); Kim Phillips-Fein, "'A Fight Between Two Systems of Thought': Gerald B. Winrod and the Kansas Senate Race of 1938," *Journal of American History* 108, no. 3 (2021), 521–544; and Randal Powell, "Social Welfare at the End of the World: How the Mormons Created an Alternative to the New Deal and Helped Build Modern Conservatism," *Journal of Policy History* 31, no. 4 (2019): 488–511.

1. "Full Text of Hoover's Speech," *New York Times*, August 12, 1928.

2. "Babson's View of Slumps," *New York Times*, September 13, 1930.

3. Samuel C. Kincheloe, *Research Memorandum on Religion in the Depression* (New York: Social Science Research Council, 1937), 95; "Why No Revival?" *Christian Century*, September 18, 1935, 1168.

4. Franklin Delano Roosevelt, "Inaugural Address," March 4, 1933, UCSB.

5. *Speaking Freely*, WNBC Television, Edwin Newman interviewing Anthony Quinn, taped November 12, 1968, aired November 30, 1968.

6. Alison Collis Greene, "The End of 'The Protestant Era'?" *Church History* 80, no. 3 (2011): 609.

7. Dorothy Day, *From Union Square to Rome* (Silver Spring, MD: Preservation of the Faith Press, 1938), 10.

8. "To Our Readers," *Catholic Worker*, May 1933, 4.

9. Rev. Chas. E. Coughlin, *A Series of Lectures on Social Justice* (Royal Oak, MI: Radio League of the Little Flower, 1935), 16, 17–18; Marquis W. Childs, "Father Coughlin, A Success Story of the Depression," *New Republic*, May 2, 1934, 326.

10. Coughlin, *Series of Lectures*, 123, 134.

11. "Washington Notes," *New Republic*, August 21, 1935, 46.

12. John D. Ryan, *Roosevelt Safeguards America* (New York: Democratic National Committee, 1936), 12.

13. St. Clair McKelway and A. J. Liebling, "Who Is This King of Glory?—II," *New Yorker*, June 20, 1936, 28.

14. J. Edgar Hoover to L. E. Kennedy, October 5, 1936, Peter Pelosi to J. Edgar Hoover, December 17, 1938, and Brother William Ross to J. Edgar Hoover, May 28, 1936, Father Divine FBI File 62-32932.

15. "Articles of Faith," Church Discipline, Constitution, and By-Laws, folder 1, box 1, Father Divine Collection, SCH; NY File No. 9-524 (August 30, 1939), Father Divine FBI File 9-2512-8.

16. St. Clair McKelway and A. J. Liebling, "Who Is This King of Glory?—III," *New Yorker*, June 27, 1936, 25.

17. "Military Service," Church Discipline, Constitution, and By-Laws, folder 1, box 1, and "Father Divine's Righteous Government Platform," folder 4, box 3, Father Divine Collection, SCH.

18. Gerald B. Winrod, *Communism and the Roosevelt Brain Trust* (Wichita, KS: Defender Publishers, 1933), 5.

19. Gerald Winrod, "Viewing the Facts," July 14, 1938, folder 25, box 22, RG NCC 18, Federal Council of the Churches of Christ in America Records, PHS.

20. Samuel McCrea Cavert to John W. Meloy, June 22, 1938, folder 25, box 22, RG NCC 18, Federal Council of the Churches of Christ in America Records, PHS.

21. Mark Matthews to J. Frank Norris, July 27, 1932, and J. Frank Norris to Mark Matthews, July 30, 1932, folder 1182, box 26, collection 124, J. Frank Norris Papers, SBHLA; A. V. Bradley to FDR, October 16, 1935, Texas File, collection 21-A, FDR.

22. Lightfoot Solomon Michaux to FDR, October 26, 1935, Washington, DC, File, collection 21-A, FDR.

23. John Collier, "Do Indians Have Rights of Conscience?" *Christian Century*, March 12, 1925, 349.

24. John Collier and Harold Ickes, "Circular No. 2970," in *Indian Conditions and Affairs: Hearings Before the Subcommittee, HR 7781*, February 11, 1935 (Washington, DC: US Government Printing Office, 1935), 372.

25. John Collier, "A Reply to Mrs. Eastman," *Christian Century*, August 8, 1934, 1020.

26. Franklin Delano Roosevelt to Reverend and Dear Sir, September 24, 1935 (version #3), box 35, collection 21-A, FDR.

27. J. Oliver Buswell to Franklin D. Roosevelt, September 26, 1935, box 15, J. Oliver Buswell Papers, WCA; Percy Crawford to FDR, November 4, 1935, Pennsylvania File, and Audie Ellis to FDR, November 25, 1935, Florida File, collection 21-A, FDR.

28. J. Gresham Machen to FDR, September 28, 1935, Pennsylvania File, and H. McAllister Griffiths to FDR, October 19, 1935, Authors and Editors File, collection 21-A, FDR.

29. "Weighs Roosevelt Issue," *New York Times*, June 1, 1936.

30. "A Year of Roosevelt," *Christian Century*, March 7, 1934, 311.

31. Franklin D. Roosevelt, "Radio Address on Brotherhood Day," February 23, 1936, UCSB.

32. "The Meaning of Liberalism," *National Baptist Union-Review*, September 22 and 29, 1934, 6; J. G. Robinson to FDR, September 28, 1935, Authors and Editors File, collection 21-A, FDR.

33. Nannie Helen Burroughs to Fannie Cobb Carter, September 19, 1932, folder 21, box 34, Nannie Helen Burroughs to Fannie Cobb Carter, May 30, [illegible], folder 21, box 34, and Nannie Helen Burroughs to Franklin Roosevelt, October 18, 1940, folder 8, box 42, Nannie Helen Burroughs Papers, LOC.

34. Smallwood Edmond Williams, *This Is My Story: A Significant Life Struggle* (Washington, DC: Wm. Willoughby Publishers, 1981), 90–91; Lightfoot Solomon Michaux to FDR, October 26, 1935, Washington, DC File, collection 21-A, FDR; Adam Clayton Powell Jr., "Soap Box," *Amsterdam News*, October 24, 1936.

35. R. C. Lawson, "I Was Glad for Your Sake," *Contender for the Faith*, May 1935, 2.

36. US Bureau of the Census, *Census of Religious Bodies*, 1936, vol. i (Washington, DC: Government Printing Office, 1941), 49; John C. Bennett, "After Liberalism—What?" *Christian Century*, November 8, 1933, 1403; Harry Emerson Fosdick, "Beyond Modernism," *Christian Century*, December 4, 1935, 1552.

37. Kincheloe, *Research Memorandum*, 92.

38. Kincheloe, *Research Memorandum*, 92.

CHAPTER 24: WARS OF FAITH

The following influenced my thinking about and understanding of the material in this chapter: Elesha J. Coffman, *The Christian Century and the Rise of the Protestant Mainline* (New York: Oxford University Press, 2013); David A. Hollinger, *Protestants Abroad: How Missionaries Tried to Change the World but Changed America* (Princeton, NJ: Princeton University Press, 2017); G. Kurt Piehler, *A Religious History of the American GI in World War II* (Lincoln, NE: University of Nebraska Press, 2021); Andrew Preston, "The Limits of Brotherhood: Race, Religion, and World Order in American Ecumenical Protestantism," *American Historical Review* 127, no. 3 (2022): 1222–1251, and *Sword of the Spirit, Shield of Faith: Religion in American War and Diplomacy* (New York: Knopf, 2012); Ronit Y. Stahl, *Enlisting Faith: How the Military Chaplaincy Shaped Religion and State in Modern America* (Cambridge, MA: Harvard University Press, 2017); and Gene Zubovich, *Before the Religious Right: Liberal Protestants, Human Rights, and the Polarization of the United States* (Philadelphia: University of Pennsylvania Press, 2022).

1. Franklin D. Roosevelt, "Annual Message to Congress," January 4, 1939, UCSB.

2. Walter W. Van Kirk, *Religion Renounces War* (Chicago: Willet, Clark and Co., 1934), vi.

3. Reinhold Niebuhr, *Moral Man and Immoral Society: A Study in Ethics and Politics* (New York: Scribner, 1932), xii.

4. Reinhold Niebuhr, *Christianity and Power Politics* (New York: Scribner, 1940), ix.

5. Charles S. Aldrich to Reinhold Niebuhr, December 17, 1940, folder 7, box 2, and John B. Cottrell to Reinhold Niebuhr, May 12, 1941, folder 3, box 4, Reinhold Niebuhr

Papers, LOC; Harold Bosley, "Illusions of the Disillusioned," *Christian Century*, January 1, 1941, 14.

6. Reinhold Niebuhr, "Pacifism and America First," *Christianity and Crisis*, June 16, 1941, 6.

7. Charles P. Proudfit to Reinhold Niebuhr, December 21, 1941, folder 3, box 10, Reinhold Niebuhr Papers, LOC.

8. John Ryan and the Ethics Committee, *The Obligation of Catholics to Promote Peace* (New York: Paulist Press, 1940), 10–11.

9. Alva J. McClain, "The Four Great Powers of the End-Time," *King's Business*, February 1938, 49; Charles Fuller, KHJ sermon (no title), December 31, 1939, box 33, collection 11, Charles E. Fuller Papers, FTS.

10. Franklin D. Roosevelt, "Annual Message to Congress on the State of the Union," January 6, 1941, UCSB.

11. Franklin D. Roosevelt, "Radio Address Announcing an Unlimited National Emergency," May 27, 1941, and Franklin D. Roosevelt, "Address for Navy and Total Defense Day," October 27, 1941, UCSB.

12. Franklin D. Roosevelt, "Address to Congress Requesting a Declaration of War with Japan," December 8, 1941, UCSB.

13. Harold L. Ickes to FDR, January 6, 1942, box 128, President's Secretary's File, FDR, http://www.fdrlibrary.marist.edu/_resources/images/psf/psf000511.pdf.

14. John Foster Dulles, "The American People Need Now to Be Imbued with a Righteous Faith," 5; Everett R. Clinchy, "Christians Must Seek the Cooperation of Other Faiths," 35; and Harry Emerson Fosdick, "Christians, as Citizens, Have an Imperative Duty," 100, in *A Righteous Faith for a Just and Durable Peace*, John Foster Dulles, ed. (New York: n.p., 1942).

15. Committee to Study the Bases of a Just and Durable Peace, *Six Pillars of Peace: A Study Guide Based on "A Statement of Political Propositions"* (New York: Federal Council of Churches, 1943).

16. Fulton J. Sheen, *Seven Pillars of Peace* (New York: Scribner, 1944), 9.

17. Stanley High, "The Church Unmilitant," *New Republic*, June 22, 1942, 850.

18. Aimee Semple McPherson, "Foursquaredom and Uncle Sam," *Foursquare Crusader* 14, February 1942, 24; Aimee Semple McPherson, "Happy New Year," *Foursquare Crusader* 15, January 1943, 3.

19. "The Christian in Time of War," *Prophecy Monthly*, June 1940, 23; "Non-Resisters Who Resist Government," *Prophecy Monthly*, July 1940, 12; "Objectors to War," *Our Hope*, February 1942, 517.

20. West Virginia State Board of Education v. Barnette, 319 US 624 (1943).

21. "Statement of the Executive Committee, January 26, 1940," and Franklin D. Roosevelt to George A. Buttrick, March 14, 1940, folder 5, box 22, RG NCC 18, Federal Council of the Churches of Christ in America Records, PHS.

22. William Alfred Eddy, "Arms and the Man," *Outlook*, November 5, 1924, 374.

23. Ralph T. Davis to Will H. Houghton, J. Davis Adams, Howard W. Ferrin, Louis T. Talbot, December 11, 1940, box 67, collection 113, NAE.

24. Harold John Ockenga, "The Unvoiced Multitudes" (April 1942), box 1, collection 113, NAE.

25. Harry S. Truman, "Radio Report to the American People on the Potsdam Conference," August 9, 1945, UCSB.

26. "Obliteration Raids on German Cities Protested in US," *New York Times*, March 6, 1944; Harold J. Ockenga, "Letters to the Times," *New York Times*, March 9, 1944.

27. William Axling to Dr. Van Kirk, August 7, 1945, folder 12, box 24, RG NCC 18, Federal Council of the Churches of Christ in America Records, PHS; "America's Atomic Atrocity," *Christian Century*, August 29, 1945, 975; Samuel McCrea Cavert to Harry S. Truman, August 9, 1945, folder 12, box 24, RG NCC 18, Federal Council of the Churches of Christ in America Records, PHS.

28. Clarence E. Benson, "The Sunday School's Place in the Atomic Age," *Sunday School Times*, October 6, 1945, 767; "That Atomic Bomb: Editor's Note," *United Evangelical Action*, September 15, 1945, 2.

29. Fosdick, "Christians, as Citizens," 48.

30. "World Needs," *Moody Monthly*, October 1944, 62; R. C. Lawson, "Bird's Eye View of Things to Come, December 1958–January 1959," in *For the Defense of the Gospel*, ed. Arthur M. Anderson (New York: Church of the Lord Jesus Christ of the Apostolic Faith, 1971), 246; Dan Gilbert, *The United Nations and the Coming Antichrist* (Washington, DC: Christian Press Bureau, n.d.), 13, 28.

CHAPTER 25: ONE NATION UNDER GOD

The following influenced my thinking about and understanding of the material in this chapter: K. Healan Gaston, *Imagining Judeo-Christian America: Religion, Secularism, and the Redefinition of Democracy* (Chicago: University of Chicago Press, 2019); Steven K. Green, *The Third Disestablishment: Church, State, and American Culture, 1940–1975* (New York: Oxford University Press, 2019); Raymond Haberski Jr., *God and War: American Civil Religion Since 1945* (New Brunswick, NJ: Rutgers University Press, 2012); Laura Harrington, "The Greatest Movie Never Made: The Life of the Buddha as Cold War Politics," *Religion and American Culture* 30, no. 3 (2020): 397–425; Paul Harvey, *Martin Luther King: A Religious Life* (Lanham, MD: Rowman & Littlefield, 2021); William Inboden, *Religion and American Foreign Policy, 1945–1960: The Soul of Containment* (Cambridge, UK: Cambridge University Press, 2008); Kevin M. Kruse, *One Nation Under God: How Corporate America Invented Christian America* (New York: Basic Books, 2015); Lerone A. Martin, *The Gospel of J. Edgar Hoover: How the FBI Aided and Abetted the Rise of White Christian Nationalism* (Princeton, NJ: Princeton University Press, 2023); Walter Russell Mead, *The Arc of a Covenant: The United States, Israel, and the Fate of the Jewish People* (New York: Knopf, 2022); Kevin M. Schultz, *Tri-Faith America: How Catholics and Jews Held Postwar America to Its Protestant Promise* (New York: Oxford University Press, 2011); Daniel Silliman, *One Lost Soul: Richard Nixon's Search for Salvation* (Grand

Rapids, MI: Eerdmans, 2024); and Grant Wacker, *America's Pastor: Billy Graham and the Shaping of a Nation* (Cambridge, MA: Harvard University Press, 2014).

1. J. B. Matthews, "Reds and Our Churches," *American Mercury*, July 1953, 3, 13.

2. Reinhold Niebuhr, "Communism and the Clergy," *Christian Century*, August 19, 1953, 936; Dwight D. Eisenhower, "Message to the National Co-Chairmen, Commission on Religious Organizations, National Conference of Christians and Jews," July 9, 1953, UCSB.

3. Fred Schwarz, *You Can Trust the Communists* (Englewood Cliffs, NJ: Prentice Hall, 1960), 174.

4. Lowell Blanchard with the Valley Trio, "Jesus Hits Like an Atom Bomb," on *Atomic Platters: Cold War Music from the Golden Age of Homeland Security*, Bear Family Records, 2005.

5. "Harry S. Truman, Exchange of Messages with Pope Pius XII," August 28, 1947, UCSB.

6. Harry Emerson Fosdick to Harry S. Truman, October 22, 1951, folder 11, box 10, series 2A, Harry Emerson Fosdick Papers, BURKE; "Spellman Sees Call to Disunion in Protest on Envoy to Vatican," *New York Times*, June 13, 1946.

7. Louis T. Talbot and William W. Orr, *The New Nation of Israel and the Word of God!* (Los Angeles: Bible Institute of Los Angeles, 1948), 4; "What Next?" *Pentecostal Evangel*, June 12, 1948, 10; "Israel Is a Nation!" *King's Business*, August 1948, 4.

8. "Text of Eisenhower Speech," *New York Times*, December 23, 1952.

9. Reinhold Niebuhr, "Varieties of Religious Revival," *New Republic*, June 6, 1955, 14.

10. Charles Oakman, "Lincoln Day: Extension of Remarks," Congressional Record, 83rd Congress, 2nd sess., vol. 100, part 2 (February 12, 1954), 1697.

11. Clayton Knowles, "Big Issue in DC: The Oath of Allegiance," *New York Times*, May 23, 1954.

12. Dwight D. Eisenhower, "Statement by the President Upon Signing Bill to Include the Words 'Under God' in the Pledge to the Flag," June 14, 1954, UCSB.

13. "Roosevelt Dropped 'In God We Trust,'" *New York Times*, November 14, 1907.

14. "Christian Amendment," Hearings Before the United States Senate Committee on the Judiciary, Subcommittee on Constitutional Amendments, 83rd Congress, 2nd Session, May 13, 17, 1954 (Washington: US Government Printing Office, 1954), 1.

15. Everson v. Board of Education, 330 US 1 (1947).

16. McCollum v. Board of Education, 333 US 203 (1948).

17. "Statement on Church and State," *Christianity and Crisis*, July 5, 1948, 90.

18. Norman Vincent Peale, *The Power of Positive Thinking* (New York: Prentice Hall, 1952), vii, viii, 55.

19. Fulton J. Sheen, *Peace of Soul* (New York: Whittlesey House, 1949), 6.

20. "Microphone Missionary," *Time*, April 14, 1952, 72.

21. Billy Graham, *Revival in Our Time: The Story of the Billy Graham Evangelistic Campaigns* (Wheaton, IL: Van Kampen Press, 1950), 70.

22. Billy Graham, *Christianism vs. Communism* (Minneapolis: Billy Graham Evangelistic Association, 1951), n.p.

23. "The Evangelical Witness in a Modern Medium," *Christianity Today*, October 15, 1956, 21; Carl Henry to Members of Christianity Today Board, June 7, 1960, Harold John Ockenga Papers, GCTS.

24. Martin Luther King Jr., "Address," Montgomery Improvement Association Mass Meeting at Holt Street Baptist Church, December 5, 1955, MLK.

25. Martin Luther King Jr., "Communism's Challenge to Christianity," August 9, 1953, Ebenezer Baptist Church, Atlanta, GA, MLK.

26. "Separation of Church and State," *Christian Century*, January 21, 1948, 79.

27. "Protestant Groups' Statements," *New York Times*, September 8, 1960.

28. John F. Kennedy, "Address to the Houston Ministers Conference, 12 September 1960," John F. Kennedy Presidential Library, video recording, www.jfklibrary.org/learn/about-jfk/historic-speeches/address-to-the-greater-houston-ministerial-association.

29. Engel v. Vitale, 370 US 421 (1962).

30. Kennedy News Conference 37 (June 27, 1962), Kennedy Presidential Library and Museum, audio and transcript, www.jfklibrary.org/archives/other-resources/john-f-kennedy-press-conferences/news-conference-37.

31. Abington School District v. Schempp, 374 US 203 (1963).

32. Niebuhr, "Varieties of Religious Revival," 13.

33. Will Herberg, *Protestant-Catholic-Jew: An Essay in American Religious Sociology* (New York: Doubleday, 1955), 276.

CHAPTER 26: STILL SEEKING LIBERATION

The following influenced my thinking about and understanding of the material in this chapter: Edward J. Blum and Paul Harvey, *The Color of Christ: The Son of God and the Saga of Race in America* (Chapel Hill, NC: University of North Carolina Press, 2012); David L. Chappell, *A Stone of Hope: Prophetic Religion and the Death of Jim Crow* (Chapel Hill, NC: University of North Carolina Press, 2004); Jesse Curtis, *The Myth of Colorblind Christians: Evangelicals and White Supremacy in the Civil Rights Era* (New York: New York University Press, 2021); Jane Dailey, "Sex, Segregation, and the Sacred After Brown," *Journal of American History* 91, no. 1 (2004): 119–144; Angela D. Dillard, *Faith in the City: Preaching Radical Social Change in Detroit* (Ann Arbor, MI: University of Michigan Press, 2009); Paul Harvey, *Howard Thurman & the Disinherited: A Religious Biography* (Grand Rapids, MI: Eerdmans, 2020), and *Martin Luther King: A Religious Life* (Lanham, MD: Rowman & Littlefield, 2021); and L. Heidenreich, "Saintly Protest: Women Religious, Religious Women, and the Early United Farm Worker Movement," *U.S. Catholic Historian* 42, no. 2 (2024): 39–60.

1. Albert B. Cleage Jr., *The Black Messiah* (New York: Sheed and Ward, 1968), 85.

2. Albert B. Cleage Jr., *Black Christian Nationalism: New Directions for the Black Church* (New York: Morrow, 1972), 16.

3. Howard Thurman, *Jesus and the Disinherited* (New York: Abingdon-Cokesbury Press, 1949), 7.

4. Martin Luther King Jr., "Draft of Chapter 13; Our God Is Able" (late 1962–early 1963), MLK.

5. Martin Luther King Jr. to Bishop C. C. Carpenter et al., April 16, 1963, MLK.

6. Anne Moody, *Coming of Age in Mississippi* (New York: Dell, 1968), 318.

7. Student Nonviolent Coordinating Committee, Statement of Purpose, 1960, James Forman Papers, LOC, loc.gov/exhibits/civil-rights-act/images/cr0108_enlarge.jpg.

8. Mary King, *Freedom Song: A Personal Story of the 1960s Civil Rights Movement* (New York: Morrow, 1987), 273.

9. Fannie Lou Hamer, Oral History Interview, KZSU Project South Interviews, Department of Special Collections and University Archives, Stanford University Libraries, Stanford, CA; Fannie Lou Hamer, *Speeches of Fannie Lou Hamer: To Tell It Like It Is*, ed. Maegan Parker Brooks (Jackson, MS: University Press of Mississippi, 2010), 71.

10. Tom Skinner, "The US Racial Crisis and World Evangelism," Urbana Address (1970), Collection 430, Papers of Tom Skinner, WCA.

11. Billy Graham, *Four Great Crises* (Minneapolis: Billy Graham Evangelistic Association, 1957), n.p.; "Billy Graham Urges Restraint in Sit-Ins," *New York Times*, April 18, 1963.

12. Jerry Falwell, *Falwell: An Autobiography* (Lynchburg, VA: Liberty House Publishers, 1997), 308, 312; Jerry Falwell, *Ministers and Marches* (Lynchburg, VA: Thomas Road Baptist Church, 1965), 7–8; Carl McIntire to Lyndon Baines Johnson, March 26, 1964, Carl McIntire Papers, Princeton Theological Seminary.

13. Malcolm X as told to Alex Haley, *The Autobiography of Malcolm X* (New York: Ballantine Books, 1964), 224.

14. James H. Cone, *Black Theology & Black Power* (New York: Seabury Press, 1969), 1, 31.

15. Cone, *Black Theology*, 108.

16. Cone, *Black Theology*, 68, 69.

17. "The Little Strike That Grew to La Causa," *Time*, July 4, 1969, 19.

18. César Chávez, "Peregrinacion, Penitencia, Revolucion," March 14, 1966, FMD.

19. César Chávez, "The Mexican-American and the Church," FMD.

20. Interview with Obdulia "Abby" Flores Rivera, FMD.

21. Gustavo Gutiérrez, *A Theology of Liberation: History, Politics, and Salvation* (Maryknoll, NY: Orbis Books, 1973), xiii, xiv.

22. Vine Deloria Jr., *God Is Red* (New York: Dell, 1973), 301.

23. Clarence Hilliard, "Down with the Honky Christ—Up with the Funky Jesus," *Christianity Today*, January 30, 1976, 430.

CHAPTER 27: APOCALYPSE NOW

The following influenced my thinking about and understanding of the material in this chapter: Larry Eskridge, *God's Forever Family: The Jesus People Movement in America* (New

York: Oxford University Press, 2013); Jill K. Gill, *Embattled Ecumenism: The National Council of Churches, the Vietnam War, and the Trials of the Protestant Left* (DeKalb, IL: Northern Illinois University Press, 2011); Jeff Guinn, *The Road to Jonestown: Jim Jones and Peoples Temple* (New York: Simon & Schuster, 2017); Mitchell K. Hall, *Because of Their Faith: CALCAV and Religious Opposition to the Vietnam War* (New York: Columbia University Press, 1990); Adam Morris, *American Messiahs: False Prophets of a Damned Nation* (New York: Liveright, 2019); Leah Payne, *God Gave Rock & Roll to You: A History of Contemporary Christian Music* (New York: Oxford University Press, 2024); Randall J. Stephens, *The Devil's Music: How Christians Inspired, Condemned, and Embraced Rock 'n' Roll* (Cambridge, MA: Harvard University Press, 2018); and Lawrence Wright, "The Orphans of Jonestown," *New Yorker*, November 22, 1993, 66–89.

1. Hal Lindsey with C. C. Carlson, *The Late Great Planet Earth* (Grand Rapids, MI: Zondervan, 1970), 50–51.

2. Lindsey, *Late Great Planet Earth*, 54.

3. Harold J. Ockenga to the President, May 28, 1966, Harold John Ockenga Papers, GCTS; Grant Wacker, *America's Pastor: Billy Graham and the Shaping of a Nation* (Cambridge, MA: Harvard University Press, 2014), 235–236.

4. "We, Too, Protest," *New York Times*, September 15, 1963.

5. "18 Clerics Back Draft Resisters," *New York Times*, October 26, 1967.

6. Martin Luther King Jr., "Beyond Vietnam," April 4, 1967, MLK.

7. Edward B. Fiske, "Religion; The Clergy on Vietnam," *New York Times*, January 7, 1968, and "Religion; Some Clergy Say 'No' on War," *New York Times*, February 11, 1968.

8. Philip O. Evaul to George A. Chauncey, June 9, 1971, Robert Strong to George A. Chauncey, May 12, 1971, and Jesse Cooke Jr. and T. H. Stevens to George A. Chauncey, May 23, 1971, folder 3, box 2, RG 503, Presbyterian Church in the US Board of Christian Education Office of Church and Society Records, PHS.

9. John Reels to Office of Church and Society, May 15, 1971, Dorsey D. Ellis to Senator Robert Byrd, June 2, 1971, and J. Q. and Mary C. Wray to Richard Nixon, May 27, 1971, folder 3, box 2, RG 503, Presbyterian Church in the US Board of Christian Education Office of Church and Society Records, PHS.

10. C. H. Sider to Office of Church and Society, and Paul W. Gess to Office of Church and Society, May 14, 1971, folder 3, box 2, RG 503, Presbyterian Church in the US Board of Christian Education Office of Church and Society Records, PHS.

11. "Methodists Score U.S. Vietnam Role," *New York Times*, April 26, 1972.

12. "The Alternative Jesus: Psychedelic Christ," *Time*, June 21, 1971.

13. "1000 'Jesus People' Baptized in Ocean Off California," *Pentecostal Evangel*, June 13, 1971.

14. Robert S. Ellwood, *One Way: The Jesus Movement and Its Meaning* (Englewood Cliffs, NJ: Prentice-Hall, 1973), 89.

15. Larry Norman, "Why Should the Devil Have All the Good Music?" *Only Visiting This Planet*, Verve Records, 1972.

16. Dean A. Anderson, "The Original 'Left Behind,'" *Christianity Today*, March 7, 2012; *Finding God in the Final Days* (Des Moines, IA: Mark IV Pictures, 1981).

17. Marshall Kilduff and Phil Tracy, "Inside Peoples Temple," *New West*, August 1, 1977.

18. Lawrence Wright, "Orphans of Jonestown," *New Yorker*, November 14, 1993, 72.

19. "Excerpts from Transcript of Tape Describing the Final Moments at Jonestown," *New York Times*, March 15, 1979.

CHAPTER 28: THE TERMINUS OF THE MAINLINE

The following influenced my thinking about and understanding of the material in this chapter: David A. Hollinger, *Christianity's American Fate: How Religion Became More Conservative and Society More Secular* (Princeton, NJ: Princeton University Press, 2022), and *After Cloven Tongues of Fire: Protestant Liberalism in Modern American History* (Princeton, NJ: Princeton University Press, 2013); Rosalind Rosenberg, *Jane Crow: The Life of Pauli Murray* (New York, NY: Oxford University Press, 2020); David Sehat, *This Earthly Frame: The Making of American Secularism* (New Haven, CT: Yale University Press, 2022); and William Stell, *Born Again Queer: A History of Evangelical Gay Activism and the Making of Antigay Christianity* (Princeton, NJ: Princeton University Press, forthcoming).

1. John T. Elson, "Toward a Hidden God," *Time*, April 8, 1966, 84, 85.

2. Bernhard M. Auer, "A Letter from the Publisher," *Time*, April 8, 1966, 21.

3. David A. Hollinger, *Christianity's American Fate: How Religion Became More Conservative and Society More Secular* (Princeton, NJ: Princeton University Press, 2022), 93.

4. Harvey Cox, *The Secular City* (New York: Macmillan, 1965), 2, 3.

5. "Rector and a Rumpus," *Newsweek*, July 4, 1960, 77.

6. *Annual of the Southern Baptist Convention* (Nashville, TN: Executive Committee, Southern Baptist Convention, 1984), 65.

7. Andrew Manis to Charles Stanley, July 12, 1984, and Mary B. Parker to Charles Stanley, n.d., folder 79, box 1, AR 666, Charles Stanley Papers, SBHLA.

8. J. J. Melvin to Chairman, Christian Life Commission, October 29, 1957, folder 1, box 21, R. J. Burrow to Rev. Roy Magill, November 11, 1956, folder 1, box 21, and Carey Daniel to A. C. Miller, September 23, 1956, folder 13, box 20, AR 138, Christian Life Commission, SBHLA.

9. Mrs. Ralph (Lois) Stair, "A Special Communication to Presbyterian Pastors," May 26, 1971, "background," box 1, RG 532, Angela Davis Legal Defense Records, PHS.

10. Edwin F. Dalstrom to William Thompson, July 16, 1971, folder 4, box 1, RG 532, Angela Davis Legal Defense Records, PHS.

11. W. G. Rowe to the General Council of the General Assembly, June 8, 1971, folder 3, box 1, W. S. Magers to Sirs, June 11, 1971, folder 10, box 1, and Grace G. Sweetland to Theophilus M. Taylor, June 15, 1971, folder 10, box 1, RG 532, Angela Davis Legal Defense Records, PHS.

12. Mrs. Donald E. Lockwood to the General Council of the General Assembly, June 15, 1971, folder 10, box 1, and Mrs. John Freeman to General Council of Church Presbytery of New Castle, November 4, 1971, folder 4, box 1, RG 532, Angela Davis Legal Defense Records, PHS.

13. Carol Van Norman to Theophilus M. Taylor, n.d., folder 3, box 1, RG 532, Angela Davis Legal Defense Records, PHS.

14. "The Southern Churches and the Race Question," *Christianity and Crisis*, March 3, 1958, 17–18.

15. Edward B. Fiske, "Homosexuals in Los Angeles, Like Many Elsewhere, Want Religion and Establish Their Own Church," *New York Times*, February 15, 1970.

16. Troy Perry, *The Lord Is My Shepherd and He Knows I'm Gay* (Los Angeles: Nash, 1972), 3, 4.

17. Elliott Wright, "The Church and Gay Liberation," *Christian Century*, March 3, 1971, 284.

18. Anne Amacher to James E. Andrews, March 8, 1991, folder 9, box 2, Eleanor J. Haley to James E. Andrews, April 22, 1991, folder 15, box 4, and Robert E. Harvey to James E. Andrews, May 9, 1991, folder 11, box 3, RG 517, Presbyterian Church (USA) Special Committee to Study Human Sexuality, PHS.

19. Jeffrey K. Hadden, *The Gathering Storm in the Churches* (Garden City, NY: Doubleday, 1969), 6, 15, 222.

CHAPTER 29: THE RELIGIOUS RIGHT

The following influenced my thinking about and understanding of the material in this chapter: Darren Dochuk, *From Bible Belt to Sunbelt: Plain-Folk Religion, Grassroots Politics, and the Rise of Evangelical Conservatism* (New York: Norton, 2011); Seth Dowland, *Family Values and the Rise of the Christian Right* (Philadelphia: University of Pennsylvania Press, 2015); Kristin Kobes Du Mez, *Jesus and John Wayne: How White Evangelicals Corrupted a Faith and Fractured a Nation* (New York: Liveright, 2020); Brantley W. Gasaway, *Progressive Evangelicals and the Pursuit of Social Justice* (Chapel Hill, NC: University of North Carolina Press, 2014); R. Marie Griffith, *Moral Combat: How Sex Divided American Christians & Fractured American Politics* (New York: Basic Books, 2017); Hilde Løvdal Stephens, *Family Matters: James Dobson and Focus on the Family's Crusade for the Christian Home* (Tuscaloosa, AL: University of Alabama Press, 2019); David R. Swartz, *Moral Minority: The Evangelical Left in an Age of Conservatism* (Philadelphia: University of Pennsylvania Press, 2012); Daniel K. Williams, *God's Own Party: The Making of the Christian Right* (New York: Oxford University Press, 2010), and *Defenders of the Unborn: The Pro-Life Movement Before Roe v. Wade* (New York: Oxford University Press, 2016); and Neil J. Young, *We Gather Together: The Religious Right and the Problem of Interfaith Politics* (New York: Oxford University Press, 2015).

1. Peter Marshall and David Manuel, *The Light and the Glory* (Old Tappan, NJ: Revell, 1977), 16.

2. Marshall and Manuel, *Light and the Glory*, 26, 359.

3. Carol Beth Cade to Reinhold Niebuhr, November 20, 1955, and Reinhold Niebuhr to Carol Beth Cade, November 22, 1955, folder 27, box 3, Reinhold Niebuhr Papers, LOC.

4. Gordon V. Drake, *Is the School House the Proper Place to Teach Raw Sex?* (Tulsa, OK: Christian Crusade Publications, 1968), 18.

5. Tim F. LaHaye, *A Christian View of Radical Sex Education* (San Diego: Family Life Seminars, c. 1969), 2, 7, 28, 31.

6. Amicus Curiae Brief from the National Association of Evangelicals re: Bob Jones University vs. the United States (1981).

7. "Dialogue with Phyllis Schlafly," *Moody Monthly*, November 1978, 44–49.

8. Marabel Morgan, *The Total Woman* (Old Tappan, NJ: F. H. Revell, 1973), 80.

9. Morgan, *Total Woman*, 117.

10. Tim and Beverly LaHaye, *The Act of Marriage: The Beauty of Sexual Love* (Grand Rapids, MI: Zondervan, 1976), 212.

11. Pope Paul VI, *Humanae Vitae*, July 25, 1968, www.vatican.va/content/paul-vi/en/encyclicals/documents/hf_p-vi_enc_25071968_humanae-vitae.html.

12. "Playboy Interview: Anita Bryant," *Playboy*, May 1978, 78, 79.

13. "Playboy Interview: Anita Bryant," 74, 78.

14. James Robison, *Homosexuality: God's Pattern or Man's Perversion?* (Hurst, TX: Life's Answer, 1977), 1, 2.

15. *Chicago Declaration of Evangelical Social Concern*, November 25, 1973, https://fromthevault.wheaton.edu/2023/11/01/a-prophetic-document/.

16. *Chicago Declaration.*

17. Kenneth L. Woodward, John Barnes, and Laurie Lisle, "Born Again," *Newsweek*, October 25, 1976, 68–78; Kenneth A. Briggs, "An Evangelical's Rise," *New York Times*, July 30, 1977.

18. Jerry Falwell, *Falwell: An Autobiography* (Lynchburg, VA: Liberty House Publishers, 1997), 384.

19. Falwell, *Falwell*, 389.

20. Falwell, *Falwell*, 390.

21. Ronald Reagan, "Remarks at the Annual Convention of the National Association of Evangelicals," March 8, 1983, UCSB; "On Separation of Church and State," *New York Times*, September 6, 1984.

22. "Pat Buchanan's Greatest Hits," *Washington Post*, February 3, 1987; "AIDS Called Punishment," *Washington Post*, January 17, 1986; Jonathan R. Crosby to Charles Stanley, February 27, 1986, folder 4, box 1, AR 666, Charles Stanley Papers, SBHLA.

23. Oral Roberts, *If You Need Healing Do These Things* (Tulsa, OK: Healing Waters, Inc., 1947), 15.

24. "Oral Roberts Tells of Talking to 900-foot Jesus," *Tulsa World*, October 16, 1980.

25. James Davison Hunter, *Culture Wars: The Struggle to Define America* (New York: Basic Books, 1991), 34, 42.

26. Robert Wuthnow, *The Restructuring of American Religion: Society and Faith Since World War II* (Princeton, NJ: Princeton University Press, 1988).

CHAPTER 30: LIVING AT THE CLOSE OF THE MILLENNIUM

The following influenced my thinking about and understanding of the material in this chapter: Damon T. Berry, *The New Apostolic Reformation, Trump, and Evangelical Politics: The Prophecy Voter* (London: Bloomsbury, 2023); Kate Bowler, *Blessed: A History of the American Prosperity Gospel* (New York: Oxford University Press, 2013); Amy Johnson Frykholm, *Rapture Culture: Left Behind in Evangelical America* (New York: Oxford University Press, 2004); Crawford Gribben, *Survival and Resistance in Evangelical America: Christian Reconstruction in the Pacific Northwest* (New York: Oxford University Press, 2021); Michael J. McVicar, *Christian Reconstruction: R. J. Rushdoony and American Religious Conservatism* (Chapel Hill, NC: University of North Carolina Press, 2015); Jonathan Root, *Oral Roberts and the Rise of the Prosperity Gospel* (Grand Rapids, MI: Eerdmans, 2023); Daniel Silliman, *Reading Evangelicals: How Christian Fiction Shaped a Culture and a Faith* (Grand Rapids, MI: Eerdmans, 2021); and John Wigger, *PTL: The Rise and Fall of Jim and Tammy Faye Bakker's Evangelical Empire* (New York: Oxford University Press, 2017).

1. Pew Research Center, "The Religious Affiliation of U.S. Immigrants: Majority Christian, Rising Share of Other Faiths," May 17, 2013, www.pewresearch.org/religion/2013/05/17/the-religious-affiliation-of-us-immigrants/#overview.

2. Matt Carroll, Sacha Pfeiffer, and Michael Rezendes, "Church Allowed Abuse by Priest for Years," *Boston Globe*, January 6, 2002. This and the following articles from the *Globe* series are available at The Pulitzer Prizes, www.pulitzer.org/winners/boston-globe-1.

3. Matt Carroll, Sacha Pfeiffer, and Michael Rezendes, "Scores of Priests Involved in Sex Abuse Cases," *Boston Globe*, January 31, 2002; Thomas Farragher, "Church Cloaked in Culture of Silence," *Boston Globe*, February 24, 2002.

4. Pew Research Center, "Americans See Catholic Clergy Sex Abuse as an Ongoing Problem," June 11, 2019, www.pewresearch.org/religion/2019/06/11/americans-see-catholic-clergy-sex-abuse-as-an-ongoing-problem/.

5. On the Waco siege see United States House of Representatives, Committee on Government Reform and Oversight, *Investigation into the Activities of Federal Law Enforcement Agencies Toward the Branch Davidians: Thirteenth Report* (Washington, DC: US GPO, 1996); and John C. Danforth, *Final Report to the Deputy Attorney General: Concerning the 1993 Confrontation at the Mt. Carmel Complex, Waco, Texas* (Washington, DC: Dept. of Justice, 2000).

6. US Department of the Treasury, Bureau of Alcohol, Tobacco, and Firearms, *911 Tape #1AA* (2/28/93), 6-7, 911 Calls, folder 1, box 18, Dick J. Reavis Papers, SWWC-086, The Wittliff Collections, Texas State University Libraries.

7. "Waco FBI Transcripts Tapes 10B" (March 1, 1993), 23, https://vault.fbi.gov/waco-branch-davidian-compound.

8. "Waco FBI Transcripts Tapes 01-003" (February 28, 1993), 50, https://vault.fbi.gov/waco-branch-davidian-compound/Waco%20FBI%20Transcripts%20Tapes%20001%20-%20003%20Part%2001/view.

9. United States House of Representatives, Committee on Government Reform and Oversight, *Investigation into the Activities*, 61.

10. John Cloud, "Meet the Prophet," *Time*, July 1, 2002; Madeleine Albright, *The Mighty & the Almighty: Reflections on America, God, and World Affairs* (New York: Harper, 2006), 134–136.

11. "Falwell Apologizes to Gays, Feminists, Lesbians," *CNN*, September 14, 2001.

12. Hanna Rosin, "Bush's 'Christ Moment' Is Put to Political Test by Christians," *Washington Post*, December 16, 1999.

13. Ron Suskind, "Faith, Certainty and the Presidency of George W. Bush," *New York Times Magazine*, October 17, 2004.

14. George W. Bush, "Remarks on Arrival at the White House and an Exchange with Reporters," September 16, 2001, UCSB.

15. Richard Land to George W. Bush, October 3, 2002 and Richard Land et al. to Editor, *Wall Street Journal*, February 20, 2003, folder 4, box 7, AR 138-8, Ethics and Religious Liberty Commission, SBHLA.

16. Bush quoted in Kurt Eichenwald, *500 Days: Secrets and Lies in the Terror Wars* (New York: Simon and Schuster, 2012), 459. See also Stephen Spector, "Gog and Magog in the White House: Did Biblical Prophecy Inspire the Invasion of Iraq?" *Journal of Church & State* 56, no. 3 (2014), 534–552.

CHAPTER 31: THE END OF CHRISTIAN AMERICA OR A NEW BEGINNING?

The following influenced my thinking about and understanding of the material in this chapter: Damon T. Berry, *The New Apostolic Reformation, Trump, and Evangelical Politics: The Prophecy Voter* (London: Bloomsbury, 2023); Kristin Kobes Du Mez, *Jesus and John Wayne: How White Evangelicals Corrupted a Faith and Fractured a Nation* (New York: Liveright, 2020); David W. Congdon, *Who Is a True Christian?: Contesting Religious Identity in American Culture* (Cambridge, UK: Cambridge University Press, 2024); Katherine Stewart, *Money, Lies, and God: Inside the Movement to Destroy American Democracy* (New York: Bloomsbury, 2025); and Andrew L. Whitehead and Samuel L. Perry, *Taking America Back for God: Christian Nationalism in the United States* (New York: Oxford University Press, 2020).

1. Barack Obama, *The Audacity of Hope: Thoughts on Reclaiming the American Dream* (New York: Crown, 2006), 203–204, and "Address at the National Constitution Center in Philadelphia: 'A More Perfect Union,'" March 18, 2008, UCSB.

2. Wright's sermons including "The Day of Jerusalem's Fall" and "Confusing God and Government" are available in various places on YouTube.

3. Obama, "Address at the National Constitution Center."

4. Barack Obama, "Keynote Address at the 2004 Democratic National Convention," July 27, 2004, UCSB.

5. Barack Obama, "Obama's 2006 Speech on Faith and Politics," *New York Times*, June 28, 2006.

6. Obama, "Obama's 2006 Speech."

7. Katharine Q. Seelye and Jeff Zeleny, "On the Defensive, Obama Calls His Words Ill-Chosen," *New York Times*, April 13, 2008.

8. Barack Obama, "Remarks to the Hampton University Annual Ministers' Conference in Hampton, Virginia," June 5, 2007, UCSB.

9. Barack Obama, "Inaugural Address," January 20, 2009, "The President's News Conference with President Abdullah Gul of Turkey in Ankara, Turkey," April 6, 2009, and "Remarks in Cairo," June 4, 2009, UCSB.

10. Josh Earnest, "President Obama Supports Same-Sex Marriage," White House blog, May 10, 2012, https://obamawhitehouse.archives.gov/blog/2012/05/10/obama-supports-same-sex-marriage.

11. This story is told in, and I consulted on and appear in, *God Forbid: The Sex Scandal That Brought Down a Dynasty*, produced by Rakontur for Hulu, aired November 11, 2022.

12. See "The Lord's Favor on Trump with Frank Amedia," Charisma Podcast Network, June 1, 2016, www.charismapodcastnetwork.com/show/strangreport/the-lords-favor-on-trump-with-frank-amedia/.

13. C. Peter Wagner, *Churchquake!: How the New Apostolic Reformation Is Shaking Up the Church as We Know It* (Ventura, CA: Regal, 1999), 5, 6, 12.

14. Lance Wallnau, "The Seven Mountain Mandate," in *The Reformer's Pledge*, Ché Ahn, ed. (Shippensburg, PA: Destiny Image, 2010), 193.

15. Jessica Martínez and Gregory A. Smith, "How the Faithful Voted: A Preliminary 2016 Analysis," Pew Research Center, November 9, 2016, www.pewresearch.org/fact-tank/2016/11/09/how-the-faithful-voted-a-preliminary-2016-analysis/.

16. Justin Nortey, "Most White Americans Who Regularly Attend Worship Services Voted for Trump in 2020," Pew Research Center, August 30, 2021, www.pewresearch.org/fact-tank/2021/08/30/most-white-americans-who-regularly-attend-worship-services-voted-for-trump-in-2020/.

17. Elizabeth Dias and Ruth Graham, "How White Evangelical Christians Fused with Trump Extremism," *New York Times*, January 11, 2021.

18. See Matthew Avery Sutton, "The Capitol Riot Revealed the Darkest Nightmares of Evangelical America," *New Republic*, January 14, 2021.

19. Burwell v. Hobby Lobby Stores, Inc., 573 US 682 (2014).

20. Kennedy v. Bremerton School District, 597 US ___ (2022).

21. Masterpiece Cakeshop, Ltd. v. Colorado Civil Rights Commission, 584 US ___ (2018).

22. 303 Creative LLC v. Elenis, 600 US ___ (2023).

23. Dobbs v. Jackson Women's Health Organization, 597 US ___ (2022).

24. Alabama Supreme Court, SC-2022-0515 and SC-2022-0579 (February 16, 2024), 33, 37–38.

25. Chris Lehmann, "The Trump Revival," *The Nation*, April 15, 2024.

26. Food and Drug Administration v. Alliance for Hippocratic Medicine, 602 US ___ (2024).

27. Robert P. Jones, *White Too Long: The Legacy of White Supremacy in American Christianity* (New York: Simon & Schuster, 2020); Pew Research Center, "Modeling the Future of Religion in America," September 13, 2022, www.pewresearch.org/religion/2022/09/13/modeling-the-future-of-religion-in-america.

28. "Republican Party Platform, 2024," UCSB.

29. "Republican Party Platform."

30. Public Religion Research Institute, "Analyzing the 2024 Presidential Vote: PRRI's Post-Election Survey, December 13, 2024," www.prri.org/research/analyzing-the-2024-presidential-vote-prris-post-election-survey/.

CONCLUSION

1. On the "nones" see Pew Research Center, "Religious 'Nones' in America: Who They Are and What They Believe," January 24, 2024, www.pewresearch.org/religion/2024/01/24/religious-nones-in-america-who-they-are-and-what-they-believe/; Public Religion Research Institute, "Religious Change in America," March 27, 2024, www.prri.org/research/religious-change-in-america/.

INDEX

Abeel, David, 194
Abington School District v. Schempp, 452
abolitionism
  Black Christians and, 211–212, 213, 214–217
  divided nation and, 207, 220–222
  Grimké sisters and, 207–208
  John Brown and, 225
  multi-faith leadership and, 214
  opposition's condemnation of, 218, 219
  reform vs. evangelism split and, 217
  Sojourner Truth and, 206–207
  Uncle Tom's Cabin and, 209
  White American reformers and, 212–214, 224
  women's equality and, 207–208, 213
abortion
  culture wars and, 380, 515–517
  national abortion ban, 561–562
  Supreme Court and, 516, 553, 558–560
Act of Marriage: The Beauty of Sexual Love (LaHaye), 515
Adams, A. B., 363
Adams, John, 84, 109, 119–120
Adams, Samuel, 84
Addams, Jane, 300, 301, 339
Affordable Care Act, 557
Africa
  Black Americans emigrating to, 245
  sending free Black Americans to, 209, 210–211
African Episcopal Church of St. Thomas, 145
African Methodist Episcopal (AME) Church, 146, 151–152, 214, 244
African Methodist Episcopal Zion (AMEZ) Church, 147
African nationalism, 340
Ágreda, María de Jesús de, 93–95, 98, 99
Agricultural Workers Organizing Committee, 468
Ahlstrom, Sydney, 325
Albright, Madeleine, 537
alcohol consumption
  Prohibition and, 346, 402
  social activism and, 178–179, 279–280, 288–289
Algonquins, 52–53
Alito, Samuel, 559, 560
Allen, Frederick Lewis, 371–372
Allen, Richard, 142–148, 211
Allenby, Edmund, 348
al-Qaeda terrorists, 539–540, 541
Amedia, Frank, 550
America First Committee, 414
American Bible Society (ABS), 175
American Board of Commissioners for Foreign Missions (ABCFM), 192–193, 211, 298. *See also* missionary movement
American Christianity
  celebrity ministries and, 366–368, 443–447

Church of England and, 56, 78, 81
crisis and great re-sorting of (1960s), 504–506
current state of, 551–552, 565–567
different views of religious liberty in 1780s, 113–114
diversity of colonial, 49–50, 59–60, 78–79, 89, 156
fascism and, 400–401
four distinctive streams of, 11–15, 75–76, 140–141
free-market religious landscape and, 7, 125
gay rights and, 501–504
God's chosen land and, 3, 79, 143, 155–156, 222, 223–224, 226–227, 349, 399, 430, 509
impact of modernism on, 324–330
impact of revivalism on, 75, 173
leaders' support of patriot cause, 80–81, 84–86, 87, 90
majority of new immigrants now identified as, 530
membership decline (early-1800s), 122–123, 124–125
membership decline (1930s), 408–409
membership decline (1960s), 504–506
opposition to Vietnam War, 476–480
ordination of women, 496–498, 512–513
overview of mid-1800s, 140–141
post-world war shallowness of, 454–455
pre-revolution discord among groups, 83–84
racism and, 14, 222, 244, 313–314, 319, 322, 323, 362, 427, 460, 463–465, 471, 498–501, 516–520
remaining central in modern America, 3–8, 545–546
response to Depression era, 390–394, 409–410
rise of political parties and, 119–120
secularization of, 491–494
socialism and, 300–301
support of capitalism, 134, 156, 174, 296, 305, 314–315, 374–376, 391
Trump presidency and, 550–555
viewed as political entity (1830s), 122
views of New Deal policies, 402–408
women's rights and, 14, 72–73, 131–132, 147–149, 185, 205–207, 289, 302, 496–498, 512–513, 520
WWII policy tied to, 411, 416–418
See also protestants, mainstream; *specific denominations*
American Church in Berlin, 424–425
American Civil Liberties Union (ACLU), 388
Scopes trial and, 382–384
American Colonization Society (ACS), 211
American Communist Party, 400
American exceptionalism, 7, 47, 410, 441, 480, 509
American Friends Service Committee, 339
American Home Missionary Society (AHMS), 202–203
American Indian Movement, 470–471
American Medical Association, 515
American Party (Know-Nothings), 184–185, 233
American Protective Association (APA), 270
American Revolution. *See* Revolutionary War
American Temperance Society, 179
American Tract Society, 176
American Unitarian Association, 137
Andover Theological Seminary, 192, 218
Anglicans
in colonial America, 50, 59, 78, 83–84
conservatism of, 63, 71
loyalty to England, 90, 115
anti-evolution movement, 382–384
anti-federalists, 111
anti-Semitism, 271, 385–386
Catholics and, 397
fundamentalists and, 400, 401
Apess, William, 201–202
apocalyptic revivalists
contemporary music and film of, 483–484
Dwight Moody and, 312–314
economic crisis (1930s) and, 409–410
establishment of modern Israel and, 346–349
Iraq war and, 541–542
Jesus-people movement, 481–484

apocalyptic revivalists (*Continued*)
responses to New Deal policies, 402, 404–405
responses to WWI, 344–345, 349–350
responses to WWII, 415–416
schism with modernism, 349–352, 355–356
Steward brothers' financing of, 328–330
See also end-times beliefs; premillennialists
Apostolic Faith Mission, 320
Appeal to the Christian Women of the South (Grimké), 207
Appeal to the Colored Citizens of the World, An (Walker), 212
Armageddon, 344, 416, 484, 490
Branch Davidians and, 532, 534 (fig)
Middle East and, 312, 346–347, 474, 536
Arminianism, 39, 129
Armour, George, 314
Armstrong, Annie, 377
Arnold, Benedict, 77
Articles of Confederation, 89, 110, 111, 112
Art of the Deal, The (Trump), 524
Asbury, Francis, 129–130, 131, 141, 143–144, 146, 180
Assemblies of God, 322, 323, 349, 357, 366, 506
atomic weapons, church response to use of, 427–428
Auer, Bernhard M., 492
"Awakening of American Protestantism, The" (Mathews), 327
Awful Disclosures of Maria Monk, or, The Hidden Secrets of a Nun's Life in a Convent Exposed! (Monk), 184–185
Ayer, William Ward, 426–427
Aztec empire, 25
Azusa street revival, 316–317, 319–322

Babson, Roger, 390
Backus, Isaac, 116
Baird, Robert, 140
Baker, Ella, 462
Bakker, Jim and Tammy Faye, 525, 526–527
Baldwin, Ebenezer, 91
Balfour, Arthur, 348
Baptists, 141
in colonial America, 50, 59, 78
first American church of, 57
Indigenous peoples and, 249
ordination of women, 497–498
racism and, 147, 498–499
religious liberty and, 116
slavery and, 214, 222
Barnhouse, Donald Grey, 358, 359
Barrows, John Henry, 264
Barrows, William, 235
Barth, Karl, 413
Bartleman, Frank, 319, 338–339, 344–345, 378–379
Barton, Bruce, 375–376
Battle Creek Sanitarium, 282–284
"Battle Hymn of the Republic" (Howe), 235
Baumfree, Isabella. *See* Truth, Sojourner
Beecher, Catharine, 178, 199, 208–209
Beecher, Henry Ward, 227, 239–240, 292–294
Beecher, Lyman, 135, 172–173, 175, 179, 187
Benezet, Anthony, 90–91
Ben-Gurion, David, 437
Bennett, Dennis, 494–495
Bennett, John C., 408
Benson, Clarence, 428
Berrigan, Daniel, 476, 477
Berrigan, Philip, 476
Bethel African Methodist Episcopal Church of Philadelphia, 146
Beveridge, Albert, 277–278
Bible
Civil War soldiers and, 234
Elizabeth Cady Stanton's revision of, 376–377
higher criticism and, 325–326
Jefferson and, 119
John Eliot's indigenous language, 45
protestant social reformers view of, 175
reading in public schools, 177, 185, 452, 494
Bible Institute of Los Angeles (Biola University), 357, 359, 360, 421, 437
Bible institutes and colleges, fundamentalist, 357–358
biblical prophecy
American Revolution and, 91–92
Civil War and, 230
Iraq war and, 541–542
Late Great books and, 473–474

William Miller and, 160–163.
World Wars and, 346–349, 415–416
See also end-times beliefs
Biden, Joe, 549, 554, 556, 561
Bill of Rights, 112–113. *See also* First Amendment
Birch, John, 424
Birmingham, Alabama, protests, 459–460, 461
birth control
Comstock laws and, 290, 291, 560
culture wars and, 379–380, 515–517
Supreme Court ruling on, 557
Black, Hugo, 441–443, 451–452
Black Christianity
as authentic version of Christianity, 462–463
central role of Black churches, 245
depictions of Black Madonna and Black Jesus and, 456–457, 458 (fig)
Malcolm X's critique of, 465–466
Martin Luther King Jr.'s ministry, 447–448, 458–460
ministry of women, 147–149, 205–207, 302, 496
need for Black theology, 457, 466–467
premillennialism and, 309–310
Reconstruction era growth of, 242–244
reframing of White Methodist ideas, 142–147
renouncement of Christian nationalism, 463–464
as threat to White Southerners, 152–154, 245
Turner's claim that "God is a Negro," 245, 466
Vietnam War and, 477–478
Black Christian nationalism, 457, 466
Black Christians
condemnation of slavery, 144, 147, 149, 211–212, 213, 214–217
evangelical segregation and, 427
fundamentalist-modernist controversy and, 361–365
Millerites and, 161
in pre-civil war South, 147
response to WWI, 340–341
revivalism and, 73, 74, 75, 126, 135–136, 142
social gospel and, 302, 363, 364
views of New Deal policies, 406–408
See also enslaved Christians
Black civil rights
clergy's advocating for, 243–244
desegregation and, 459, 464–465, 498–499
lack of White support for, 313–314, 460, 463–465, 498–501
liberationist themes and, 457, 458, 463
nation's indifference to, 463
New Deal era and, 406–407
1960s-era, 456–467
post-Reconstruction era collapse of, 313–314
theology of nonviolence and, 458–459, 462
See also race and racism; racial violence
Black liberation movements, 457, 498
Black Lives Matter movement, 553
Blackstone, William, 340, 347–349
Black Theology & Black Power (Cone), 466
Blakeslee, S. V., 272
Blanchard, Lowell, 436
Board of Indian Commissioners (BIC), 247–248
Bobbed Hair, Bossy Wives, and Women Preachers (Rice), 379
Bob Jones University (BJU), 512
body, Christian ministry to, 280–281, 284–285. *See also* health and wellness
Bolshevik Revolution, 373
Book of Mormon, 167–168, 170
Book of Prophecies (Columbus), 23
Boone, Pat, 482
Booth, Catherine, 302, 368
Booth, John Wilkes, 239
Booth, William, 302
Boston Globe, The, 531
Boston Massacre, 82
Boxer Uprising, 277
Bradford, William, 36–37
Brainerd, Thomas, 237
Branch Davidians, 532–535
Brandeis, Louis, 348–349
Breen, Joseph, 371
Brennan, William, 452–453
Briggs, Kenneth, 520
Brooke, B. F., 226–227

Brooks, Keith, 421
Brown, Jerry, 486, 487
Brown, John, 225, 226 (fig)
Brown, Willie, 486
Brown v. Board of Education, 459, 498
Bryan, William Jennings, 276, 305–306, 307 (fig), 337–338, 382–384
Bryant, Anita, 518
Buchanan, James, 254
Buchanan, Pat, 523
Buddhism, 476
Bureau of Alcohol, Tobacco, Firearms and Explosives (ATF), 533, 535
Bureau of Catholic Indian Missions, 250
Burroughs, Nannie Helen, 302, 406–407
Bush, George W., 530, 540–541, 546
Bushnell, Horace, 229, 231
Buswell, J. Oliver, 404–405
Byrd, Robert, 479

California
- American seizure of, 203
- Jesus-people movement and, 482, 484
- Spanish mission system in, 95, 96, 99–105

Calm Address to Our American Colonies, A (Wesley), 86
Calvary Chapel, 482
Calvert, Cecil, 55, 56
Calvin, John, 38–39
Calvinism, 64, 129, 131, 537
Campbell, Alexander, 128
Campus Crusade for Christ, 483
capitalism
- early republic growth, 174
- imperialism and, 337, 339
- late-1800s growth and shortcomings, 296–298, 300, 304–306, 314
- mainstream Christianity's support of, 134, 156, 174, 296, 305, 314–315, 374–376, 391
- Puritan foundations for, 40
- social gospel and, 296
- views of incompatibility with religion, 394–395

Carnegie, Andrew, 342
Carpenter, Francis Bicknell, 231
Carroll, Charles, 89, 182
Carroll, John, 182
Carté, Katherine, 89
Carter, Jimmy, 520–521, 522
Carter, Rosalynn, 486
Cartwright, Peter, 1–3, 12, 221, 223
Case, Shirley Jackson, 349–350
Catholic Association for International Peace, 415
Catholic Church
- abortion and, 515–516
- California mission system and, 95, 99–104
- Cold War and, 437, 449
- Latin American radical forms of, 470
- Martin Luther and, 24–25
- new ideas and practices of (1960s), 495–496
- sexual abuse scandal and, 531–532
- Spanish colonization in Americas, 20–23, 25–31
- women leadership and, 496
- WWII and, 423

Catholic parochial schools, 182, 185, 268–269, 441
Catholics, American, 8
- adapting to American political context (late 1800s), 267–270
- Al Smith's presidential campaign, 386–388
- anti-communist hysteria and, 435–436
- charismatic renewal and, 495
- church-state separation controversy and, 268–270, 423, 437, 448–451
- in colonial America, 55–56, 59, 78
- conservatism of, 12, 141
- criticism of Latter-day Saints, 256–257
- early republic expansion of, 181–183
- Father Coughlin and, 395–397
- Fulton Sheen and, 444–445
- great Arizona orphan abduction and, 267
- immigration surge in late 1800s, 266–267
- Indigenous peoples and, 249–250
- Irish leadership of, 266
- Kennedy's presidency, 449–451
- New Deal and, 396–398
- occupation of Philippines and, 276–277
- patriotism during Civil War, 233–234
- protestant attacks on, 183–186, 270, 448–451
- Quebec Act and, 82–83
- responses to Depression era, 394–398

responses to WWI, 341–342, 345 (fig)
responses to WWII, 415, 420, 428
social reform and, 467–469
as threat to evangelicalism, 426
Vietnam War and, 475–476
Catholic Worker, The, 395
Católicos por La Raza, 469
Cavert, Samuel McCrea, 401
Cayuse, 200–201
celebrity ministries, 366–368, 443–447
Central Intelligence Agency (CIA), 436
Chafer, Lewis Sperry, 357
Chalcedon Foundation, 537–538
Chandler, Thomas Bradbury, 83–84
Channing, William Ellery, 137–138, 217–218
Charles I, King of England, 37, 55
Chastellux, Marquis de, 158
Chauncy, Charles, 75, 135
Chauncy, George, 479
Chávez, César, 467–469, 486
Cherokee Nation, 198–200
"Chicago Declaration of Evangelical Social Concern," 519, 520
children
clergy molestation of, 531
communal rearing of, 164
revivalism and, 75, 126
China, missionary movement in, 277, 424
Chinese Exclusion Act (1882), 272
Chinese immigrants, 271–273
Christian Anti-Communism Crusade, 436
Christian Broadcasting Network (CBN), 525
Christian Century, The, 350, 361, 371, 387, 403, 404, 405–406, 414, 421, 428, 502
Christian Crusade, 436, 511
Christianity and Crisis, 414
Christianity Today, 446–447
Christian-Jewish interfaith dialogues, 438
Christian nationalism
apocalyptic revivalists' view of, 349
Black Christian rejection of, 463–464
evangelicals and, 10, 426–427, 429–430, 481, 493
Federal Council of Churches and, 306–308
historical scope of, 9
modern day coalition supporting, 11, 566
New Apostolic Reformation and, 552
Republican Party and, 10
revivalism and, 422
"seven mountain mandate" and, 552, 560
Supreme Court rulings and, 545–546, 556–560
Vietnam War and, 480, 481
Christian realism, 413–415
Christian Reformed Church (CRC), 271
"Christians" (revivalist group), 128
Christian Scientists, 287–288
Christians for Social Action, 519
Christian Workers, 344
Christian Zionists, 439
Church of England, 34
Anglican bishop controversy, 81
colonial churches' affiliation with, 50, 51, 56, 78, 81
Puritans and, 32, 35, 37, 41–42
Virginia and, 51, 115
Church of God in Christ (COGIC), 322, 339, 506
Church of Jesus Christ of Latter-day Saints, 186 (fig), 187, 242, 318, 393
establishment in Salt Lake region, 170, 252–254
Joseph Smith Jr. and, 166–170
Mountain Meadows Massacre and, 254–255
plural marriage and, 169, 254–258
Church of the Nazarene, 181
Church Peace Union (Carnegie Endowment for International Peace), 342
Churchquake! (Wagner), 551
church-state separation
adding God to pledge of allegiance and, 439–440, 453
American Catholics and, 268–270, 423, 437, 448–451
Constitution and, 3, 4, 5
George Washington on, 112
Kennedy's speech on, 451
modern day battle over, 11
myth of, 9, 118
Puritans and, 39–40, 42
Supreme Court rulings on, 441–443, 451–453, 556–557
Treaty of Tripoli and, 109–110
See also First Amendment

city on the hill, 38, 39, 47, 48, 475
civil rights, 10, 430
  impact on American Christianity, 505
  for Indigenous peoples, 470–471
  Latine Christian, 467–470
  See also Black civil rights
Civil Rights Act of 1964, 464–465
Civil War
  attack on Fort Sumter, 227
  biblical prophecy and, 230
  efforts to amend the Constitution during, 229–230
  ending of, 239
  importance of Bibles and hymns, 234–235
  justifying violence of, 224, 235
  opposing religious convictions and, 224, 227–229, 230–231
  as punishment for sinfulness, 237
  secession of South and, 226–227
  soldier religiosity and, 232–233
  Southern revisionist accounts of, 242, 245–246
Clark, Tom, 452
Clarke, William Newton, 276
class distinctions
  late-1800s economy and, 296–298, 304–306
  Puritan view of, 40
  revivalism and, 67, 74, 135
  See also economic inequalities
Cleage, Albert, Jr., 456, 457, 458 (fig), 466, 467
Clergy and Laymen Concerned About Vietnam (CALCAV), 477
Cleveland, Grover, 246
Clinton, Bill, 549
Clinton, Hillary, 543, 547–548, 549
Coffin, Henry Sloane, 336–337, 343, 365
Cohen, Michael, 550
Cold War
  anti-communist hysteria and, 433–436
  revival of religion and, 434, 439–441, 453–454
  Truman and, 436–437
Cole, Nathan, 69–70
Collier, John, 402–404
Columbus, Christopher, 10, 20–23, 177
Commission on a Just and Durable Peace, 419–420, 429
Common Sense (Paine), 87
"Communion of Reformed Evangelical Churches," 538–539
communism
  anti-communist gospel and, 443–446
  anti-communist hysteria, 433–436
  Depression-era, 394–395
  Martin Luther King Jr. and, 448
  as threat to religion, 433–434
Compromise of 1850, 253
Comstock, Anthony, 290–292, 293, 294, 380
Comstock, Sarah, 367
Comstock laws, 291, 560
Concerned Women for America, 519
Cone, James, 466–467
Confederate States of America
  attack on US Constitution, 228–229
  biblical prophecy and, 230
  religious convictions of, 228–229, 230–231, 237–238
  revisionist views of righteousness of, 242, 246
  secession and, 226–227
Congregationalists, 13, 41, 64
  conservatism of, 63, 141
  disestablishment and, 172
  early dominance of, 61, 78
  Indigenous peoples and, 249
  as missionaries, 203
  pre-revolution views of, 83
Congress of Racial Equality (CORE), 462
Conroy-Krutz, Emily, 193
conscientious objectors, 339, 422
conservative Christianity
  economic crisis (1930s) and, 409
  religious liberty and, 113–114
  as stream of American Christianity, 12, 75–76, 141
  views of New Deal policies, 405
  See also apocalyptic revivalists; evangelicals; fundamentalists; revivalist Christianity
Constitution
  Civil War efforts to amend, 229–230
  Confederate attack of, 228–229
  creation and ratification of, 111–113, 125
  rejection of "Christian" amendment to, 441

secular nature of, 112, 173
Constitutional Convention, 111
Contemporary Christian music (CCM), 483–484
Continental Congress, 84–85, 87, 91, 111
conversion experiences
enslaved Christians and, 150
Methodism and, 129
revivalism and, 62, 64–65, 67, 74, 134–135
Conwell, Russell, 297–298
Cooney, Peter Paul, 233
Cornell, Ezra, 324–325
Cornell University, 324–325
Coronado, Francisco Vázquez de, 26
corporations
late-1800s growth of, 297
religious rights of, 557
See also capitalism
Cortés, Hernán, 25
Coughlin, Charles, 395–397
Council on Church and Race, 499, 500
counterculture, Vietnam-era, 481–484
Court of Indian Offenses, 251
Covey, Stephen, 524
Cox, Harvey, 477, 494
Crawford, Percy, 405
Crowell, Henry Parsons, 314
Cruz, Ricardo, 469
culture wars
abortion, 515–517, 558–560
anti-evolution movement, 382–384
Bush presidency and, 540–541
gay rights, 380–381, 517–519, 523, 549
Hollywood moral code and, 370–372
Hunter on new American, 527–528
immigration restrictions, 384–386
sexual revolution and, 510–512
women's roles and rights, 376–380, 513–517
working class conditions and, 372–374
currency, adding "In God We Trust" to, 439–440

Danforth, Samuel, 32
"Danger of an Unconverted Ministry, The" (Tennent), 70–71
Darby, John Nelson, 308–309, 312
Darrow, Clarence, 382–384
Darwin, Charles, 325
Davenport, James, 61–63, 71
Davis, Angela, 486, 499–500
Davis, Jefferson, 228
Davis, Ralph T., 425–426
Day, Dorothy, 394–395, 467
Declaration of Independence, 87–89, 112, 182
slavery and, 210, 214
Defenders of the Christian Faith, 400
Deists, 13, 88, 111, 120
Delawares, 79, 80
Deloria, Vine, 470–471
Democratic Party
Black leaders and, 406, 407
evangelical growing distrust of, 465
secularism and, 10
Dewey, George, 275
Dickinson, John, 89
Disciples of Christ, 128, 141
disestablishment
Christian social activism and, 172–174
state-level, 172, 186
disestablishment clause, 5–6, 117–118, 125, 156
Divine, Father, 398–400
Dixon, A. C., 337
Dobbs v. Jackson Women's Health Organization, 559
Dobson, James, 514, 551
Docherty, George M., 439
domestic violence, 514
Douglass, Frederick, 9, 150, 214–216, 217, 313–314
Dow, Lorenzo, 131
Dowie, John Alexander, 286–287, 318
Du Bois, W. E. B., 150, 245, 276
Duché, Jacob, 84, 85 (fig)
Duffield, George, Jr., 234–235
Dulles, John Foster, 419–420
Dutch Reformed Church, 57, 271
Dwight, Timothy, 195

Easton, Peter Z., 378
economic depression
Catholic responses to, 394–398
impact on American Christianity, 390–392
welfare ministries and, 392–394

economic inequalities
early republic increase in, 174
in late-1800s, 296, 297, 298
See also class distinctions; workers' rights
ecumenism
Eisenhower and, 438–439
Federal Council of Churches and, 306–308
opposition to Vietnam War and, 476–477
Unitarians and, 138
Eddy, Mary Baker, 287–288
Eddy, William, 425
education
Bible institutes and colleges, 357–358
Catholic parochial schools, 182, 185, 268–269, 441
Christian social reform and, 175–178
higher, growth of secular, 324–325
of Indigenous peoples, 249
private vouchers, 540
protestant view of Bible as foundation of, 175
Puritan commitment to, 41
See also public school system
educational hierarchies, revivalism and, 71, 75, 135, 146
Edwards, Jonathan, 12, 64–66, 69, 72, 313
Edwards, Sarah, 65, 69
Eisenhower, Dwight, 425, 435, 438–440, 449
Eliot, John, 45
Elliott, Stephen, 237–238
Ellwood, Robert, 482
Elson, John, 491–492
Emancipation Proclamation 236, 238
Emerson, Ralph Waldo, 138–139
End of the World, The (Steward), 309
end-times beliefs
Columbus and, 20, 23
Ellen G. White and, 281–282
establishment of modern Israel and, 346–349, 415–416, 437–438
false prophets and, 330
Latter-day Saints and, 166 168, 170
Left Behind books and, 536
pentecostals, 320
premillennial, 308–314
reconstructionists, 537–538
Southern Confederacy and, 230
William Miller and, 160–163, 282
See also apocalyptic revivalists; premillennialists
Engel v. Vitale, 451–452
England
abolitionism in, 210–211
growing colonial dissent with, 80–84
persecution of Catholics in, 55
Enlightenment, 64, 87–89, 116, 491
enslaved Africans
early attitude toward Christian faith, 54, 143
native religions of, 50, 143
in Virginia colony, 53–54
enslaved Christians
enslavers' use of religion to control, 150–151
insurrections of, 151–154
Old Testament God and, 143
ordination of, 151
religious practices of, 149–151
enslavement
biblical defenses of, 217–219
Black Christian condemnation of, 144, 147, 149, 211–212, 213, 214–217
Christianization defense of, 220, 224
defenders' romantic depictions of, 219–220
early Christian attitudes toward, 40, 54
early republic growth of, 174
ending of, 235–236
incongruity with Christian ideals, 207–208, 210, 215, 217–218
of Indigenous peoples, 22, 40, 102
recognition of sin of, 217
revivalism and, 67, 74, 75
social reformers avoidance of, 175–176, 181
treatment of Black women, 207–208
westward expansion and, 225
White Southern political power and, 212
See also abolitionism
Episcopalians, 141, 401
charismatic renewal and, 494–495
gay rights, 503–504
Indigenous peoples and, 249
membership loss of, 505
Vietnam War and, 480
equal rights amendment (ERA), 513–514

Erdman, Charles, 329
Eskridge, Larry, 482–483
establishment clause. *See* disestablishment; First Amendment
eugenics, 164
European Christianity, 11, 22, 49–50, 75
evangelicals
 Billy Graham, 445–447
 Black civil rights and, 427, 463–465
 Carter presidency and, 520–521
 Christian nationalism and, 10, 426–427, 429–430, 481, 493
 Cold War-era growth of, 446–447, 453
 dislike of internationalism, 429
 in mid-1800s, 140
 Ockenga on major threats to, 426
 post-WWII creation of, 9–10, 140, 425–426
 proper roles for women and, 512–513, 520
 religious right and, 521–523
 Republican Party and, 528
 response to 2020 election result, 555–556
 support of Trump, 553, 554–555, 562
 support of Vietnam War, 475, 481
 unapologetic WWII-era patriotism of, 427–428
 See also fundamentalists; revivalist Christianity
Evangelical Women's Caucus, 520
Evangelization of the World in This Generation, The (Mott), 274
Evans, Hiram Wesley, 385
Evarts, Jeremiah, 199
Evers, Medgar, 467
Everson v. Board of Education, 441–442
evolutionary theory
 Darwin's, 325, 381–382
 Scopes trial and, 381–384
 theistic version of, 329
Explo '72, 483

faith healing, 285–287, 288, 321 (fig)
Falwell, Becki, 550
Falwell, Jerry, 9, 465, 521–522, 539–540
Falwell, Jerry, Jr., 550
family hierarchy
 early-1900s culture wars and, 378–380
 Puritans and, 40–41
family values, new culture wars and, 513–517, 519
farmworkers' movement, 467–469
fascism, blending of Christianity with, 400–401
Federal Council of Churches (FCC), 425, 428, 449
 creation of, 306–308
 far-right attack on, 400–401
 WWI and, 340, 342
Federalist Party, 111, 119–120
Federation of American Zionists, 347
Fellowship of Reconciliation, 339
feminism. *See* women's equality
Ferdinand, Archduke Franz, 336
Ferdinand, King of Spain, 20–21
Fifield, James W., Jr., 405
Fillmore, Millard, 253
Finding God in the Final Days, 484
Finley, Robert, 211
Finney, Charles, 132–134, 141
First Amendment, 8, 11
 ambiguous nature of, 117–118
 Christian activism and, 4
 Indian policy and, 248
 plural marriage and, 255–256
 Reagan's view of, 522–523
 religious clauses of, 5–8, 113–114, 117–118, 156, 170
 religious dissenters and, 292
 Supreme Court rulings on, 441–443, 451–453
First Baptist Church of Williamsburg, 147
Fisk, Pliny, 194
Fiske, Edward B., 479
Fitzgerald, F. Scott, 389
Fitzhugh, George, 219
flag, pledging allegiance to, 422–423
 adding God to, 439–440, 453
Flapper Evangelism: Fashion's Fools Headed for Hell (Bartleman), 378–379
Focus on the Family, 514, 551
Ford, Gerald, 520
Ford, Henry, 386
foreign missionary movement. *See* missionary movement
foreign policy, American interfaith postwar plans for, 419–420
For God and Country, 417

Forman, James, 471
Fosdick, Harry Emerson, 362, 363, 368, 427, 437, 443
  business interests and, 374–375
  on fundamentalism, 356
  international peace and, 343, 419
  on liberal crisis, 408–409
  on United Nations, 429
  Vietnam War and, 476
Fourteenth Amendment, 549
Franciscan missionaries
  bilocated evangelism and, 93–95
  in California, 95, 96, 99–104
  colonization of Pueblo peoples, 26–31
Franco, Francisco, 400
Frankfurter, Felix, 441–442
Franklin, Benjamin, 68–69, 70, 76, 80, 111
Fransioli, Joseph, 233–234
Free African Society, 144
Freedman's Bureau, 244
free exercise clause, 5, 6–7, 113, 156, 169, 170, 242
Frelinghuysen, Theodore, 199
French and Indian War (Seven Years' War), 79–80, 82, 92, 96
Frisbee, Lonnie, 482
Frodsham, Stanley, 349
Fugitive Slave Act, 214
Fuller, Charles, 360, 416
Fuller, Margaret, 139
fundamentalist-modernist controversy
  Black Christians and, 361–365
  Christian Century on, 361
  evolution of, 355–356
  institutional battles, 358–359
  missionary movement and, 365–366
  negative impact of, 384, 391
  publication of *The Fundamentals* and, 328–330
  Scopes trial and, 381–384
  WWI influences, 349–352, 355
fundamentalists, 9, 286
  Aimee Semple McPherson and, 366–369
  Bible institutes and colleges of, 357–358
  Black Christians and, 362, 363–364
  early rapid growth of, 361
  early use of radio broadcasts, 359–361
  economic crisis (1930s) and, 409–410
  evangelizing efforts of, 357
  far-right-leaning aspects of, 400–401
  formation of, 354–355
  marriage of faith and patriotism and, 368
  reorganization and renaming of, 425–426
  responses to New Deal policies, 401–402, 403 (fig)
  responses to WWII, 415–416, 421–423, 427–428, 430
  Scopes trial and, 384
  See also evangelicals
Fundamentals, The, 329, 337, 348, 354

Gaebelein, Arno, 421–422
Gandhi, Mohandas, 458
Garnet, Henry Highland, 215–216
Garrison, William Lloyd, 212–214, 216, 217
Gathering Storm in the Churches, The (Hadden), 505
Gay Liberation Front (GLF), 517
gay rights
  AIDS crisis and, 523
  Christian ministries and, 501–504
  culture wars and, 380–381, 517–519
  overturning of "don't ask, don't tell," 549
  same-sex marriage, 502, 549
  Supreme Court rulings on, 558
Geissinger, James Allen, 350–351
gender norms
  Catharine Beecher on, 208–209
  Christian leaders' affirmation of, 156, 185, 377–380
  Elizabeth Cady Stanton and, 376–377
  Francis Willard and, 289
  Grimké sisters and, 208–209
  Phoebe Palmer and, 181
  revivalism and, 75, 131–132
  See also marriage, sexuality, and gender; women; women's equality
General War-Time Commission, 342
Geoghan, John J., 531
George, David, 210–211
German immigrants, 174, 181, 266, 271
Ghost Dance movement, 251–252
Gibbons, James Cardinal, 256–257, 269, 341
Gilbert, Dan, 429
"gilded age," 297
Gladden, Washington, 275, 298–299, 301

Goad, Benjamin, 33
God
 as a Black man, 245, 466
 Times story on death of, 491–492
Godspell, 484
"Godstock" festival, 483
Gorsuch, Neil, 557
Government and Liberty Described, and Ecclesiastical Tyranny Exposed (Backus), 116
Graham, Billy, 12, 445–447, 450, 464–465, 475, 483
Granda, Giancarlo, 550
Grant, Ulysses S., 239
Gray, James, 352
Gray, William Henry, 200
Greene, Alison Collis, 393
Grimké, Sarah and Angelina, 207–209, 210
Guideposts, 444
Gutiérrez, Gustavo, 470

Hadden, Jeffrey, 505
Hagin, Kenneth, 524–525
Hahn, Jessica, 526
Hale, Sarah Josepha, 238
Hamer, Fannie Lou, 462–463
Hamilton, Alexander, 62–63, 111, 120
Hardin, Martin D., 337
Hargis, Billy James, 436, 511
Harpers Ferry raid, 225
Harris, Kamala, 561
Harrison, Benjamin, 252, 347
Harrison, William Henry, 197
Harry Potter, 536
Harvard
 intellectual renaissance (late 1800s) and, 324
 liberal Christianity and, 137, 138–139, 141, 192
 Puritans and, 41
Hawai'i, missionary work in, 194–196
Hayes, Rutherford B., 163
Haymarket Square rally, 295–296
Hays, Will, 371–372
Head of Christ (Sallman), 457
health and wellness
 Adventist medical clinics and, 282–284
 antiliquor crusade, 279–280, 288–289
 Christian ministry for, 280–281, 284–285
 faith and metaphysical healing, 285–288
Hearst, William Randolph, 369
Hecker, Isaac, 267–268, 269
Hegseth, Pete, 539
Henry, Carl, 447, 450
Henry, Patrick, 80, 84, 89, 90, 121
 religious liberty and, 114, 116, 117
Henry VIII, King of England, 34
Herberg, Will, 454
Herman, Stewart, 424–425
Herzl, Theodor, 348
Heyrman, Christine, 130
High, Stanley, 420–421
higher criticism, 325–326
Himes, Joshua, 161, 162
Hitler, Adolph, 400, 416, 421
Hobby Lobby, 557
Hocking, William E., 365–366
Hodge, Charles, 217, 218, 219, 358
holiness movement, 180–181, 318, 319
Hollinger, David, 493
Holly, James T., 310
Hollywood studios
 anti-communism and, 436
 moral impositions on, 370–372
Holocaust, 438
Holy Spirit, pentecostals and, 317, 318, 319, 320, 324, 495
homeschooling, 538
Honest to God (Robinson), 493
Hoover, Herbert, 360, 388, 390, 406
Hoover, J. Edgar, 398–399, 435
Horton, T. C., 351, 371
House Un-American Activities Committee, 434–435
Houston Chronicle, 532
Howe, Julia Ward, 235
How Should We Then Live? (Schaeffer), 516–517
Huerta, Dolores, 468
Huguenots, 50, 78
Hull House, 300
Hunter, James Davison, 527–528
Hussein, Saddam, 541, 544
Hutchinson, Anne, 43–44, 72
hymns, Civil War inspired, 225, 234–235

Ickes, Harold, 417
immigrants/immigration
  conservative Christianity and, 12
  early-1900s laws restricting, 384–386
  in early colonies, 50
  early republic increase of, 174, 181
  Johnson-era growth in, 529
  settlement houses and, 300
  surge in late 1800s, 265–267, 270, 271
  Trump and, 561
Immigration Act of 1924 (Johnson-Reed Act), 386, 394, 529
imperialism, American
  debate over WWI intervention and, 337, 339
  Philippines and, 275–277
India, missionary work in, 194
Indian Reorganization Act (1934), 403–404
"Indian's Looking-Glass for the White Man, An" (Apess), 201–202
Indigenous peoples
  account of White racism, 201–202
  boarding schools and, 249
  brief description of pre-invasion, 19–20
  California mission system and, 99–104
  Cherokee Nation's forced migration, 198–200
  civil rights and, 470–471
  colonization of Pueblo peoples, 26–31, 95, 403
  Columbus and, 20–23
  educational material denigrating, 177
  enslavement of, 22, 40, 102
  Ghost Dance movement and, 251–252
  Latter-day Saints and, 253
  missionary interventions with, 198–201, 241, 248–250
  New Deal policies supporting, 402–404
  post-French and Indian War violence and, 79–80
  Puritans and, 36–37, 44–45
  Quakers and, 59, 247, 249
  Removal Act of 1830 and, 198–199
  restriction of religious freedom of, 250–252
  revivalism and, 73–74, 201–202
  Shawnee warfare with White settlers, 196–197
  Virginia colony and, 52–53
  Western reservation system for, 242, 247–251
Ingersoll, Robert, 291–292, 313–314, 362, 492
In His Steps (Sheldon), 301
Institutes of Biblical Law (Rushdoony), 538
intellectual renaissance
  American universities and, 324–326
  evolutionary theory, 325
  higher criticism, 325–326
  impact on American Christianity, 324–330
Interdenominational Mexican Council of Christian Churches, 323
Internal Revenue Service (IRS), 512
International Church of the Foursquare Gospel, 367, 421
international peace movements, 342, 343, 419–420, 429, 430
Iraq war, 541–542
Ireland, John, 276–277
Irish immigrants, 174, 181
Ironside, Edmund, 357
Isabella, Queen of Spain, 20–21
"Is God Dead?" (*Time* magazine, 1966), 491–492
isolationism
  Catholics and, 396, 397
  liberalism and, 414
  WWI debate over, 334, 336, 337, 339
  WWII and, 411
Israel (Palestine)
  creation of State of, 437–439, 474
  importance of, 194
  prophecy of restoration of, 346–349, 415–416
Is the School House the Proper Place to Teach Raw Sex? (Hargis), 511
Italian immigrants, 266

Jackson, Andrew, 198
Jackson, Robert H., 422
Jackson, Stonewall, 229, 246
Jacobs, Harriet, 153–154
Jamestown, 36, 50–51
James VI of Scotland (James I of England), 35
January 6 insurrection, 555–556
Jay, John, 84, 89, 120

Jefferson, Thomas, 5, 111, 137, 174, 197, 442
Declaration of Independence and, 87–89
presidential campaign of, 119–120
religious liberty and, 114–116, 117, 118
religious views of, 88–89, 119, 137, 141
Jehovah's Witnesses, 311, 422–423
Jenkins, Jerry, 536
Jesus Christ
as a Black man, 340–341, 456–457, 466–467
liberal modernist portrayal of, 326
modern business parable and, 376
revolutionary teachings of, 296, 300, 301, 305
Unitarianism and, 136–138
Jesus Christ Superstar, 484
"Jesus Hits Like an Atom Bomb" (Blanchard), 436
Jesus-people movement, Vietnam-era, 481–484
Jews
American practices of, 270–271
anti-Semitism and (*see* anti-Semitism)
establishment of modern Israel and, 346–349, 437–439
in colonial America, 50, 57, 78
immigration surge in late 1800s, 270, 271
"John Brown's Body," 225, 235
Johnson, Lyndon, 464, 475, 529
Johnson-Reed Act (*see* Immigration Act of 1924)
Jones, Absalom, 144–146
Jones, Bob, 357
Jones, Charles Colcock, 220
Jones, Charles Price, 318, 322
Jones, Jim, 484–490
Jones, Robert P., 561
Judeo-Christian tradition, United States as, 438, 441, 462, 547

Ka'ahumanu, 196
Kansas-Nebraska Act (1854), 225
Kellogg, John Harvey, 282–284
Kennedy, John F., 449–451, 476
Kennedy, Joseph, 557
Kennedy, Robert, 468
Kentucky revival (Cane Ridge), 126–127, 317
Kerry, John, 546
King, Martin Luther, Jr., 467
ministry of, 447–448, 458–460, 462
Vietnam War and, 477–478
White revivalists and, 464–465
King, Mary, 462
Kingdom of Matthias, 205
King's Business, 344, 349, 379, 438
Kingsley, Bathsheba, 72, 75
Klein, P. A., 338
Knight, Elleanor, 132
Know-Nothings, 184–185, 233, 270
Koop, C. Everett, 517
Koresh, David (Vernon Howell), 532–535
Ku Klux Klan, 244, 385, 460
Kumeyaay attack, 103–104

labor movements
Latine Christians and, 467–469
social gospel and, 299
See also workers' rights
Labor Temple, 373–374
LaHaye, Beverly, 515, 519
LaHaye, Tim, 511–512, 515, 521, 536–537
Lakota, 252
Lamanites, 167–168, 253
Land, Richard, 541
Langley, Isom P., 305
Las Casas, Bartolomé de, 22
Late Great Planet Earth, The (Lindsey), 473–474, 482–483
Latine Christians
civil rights organizers, 467–470
pentecostal, 322–323
See also Mexican Americans
Latter-day Saints. *See* Church of Jesus Christ of Latter-day Saints
Laws, Curtis Lee, 355
Lawson, R. C., 408, 429
League of Nations, 352–353, 412, 429
Lear, Norman, 523
Lease, Mary Elizabeth, 305
Lee, Ann, 158–160, 163
Lee, Jarena, 147–149
Lee, John D., 254
Lee, Robert E., 225, 239, 246
Left Behind books (LaHaye, Jenkins), 536–537
Lennon, John, 484

"Letter from a Birmingham Jail" (King), 464
LGBTQ+ activism, 10. *See also* gay rights
liberal Christianity
  anti-communist attack on, 435
  capitalism and, 296
  Christian realism and, 413–415
  crisis of (1930s), 408–409
  declining membership and, 504–506, 545
  ecumenism and, 138, 306–308, 476–477
  intellectual renaissance and, 324–326
  international peace movements and, 342, 343, 419–420, 429, 430
  Jefferson and, 137, 141
  missionary movement and, 365–366
  modernism and, 317, 324–330
  responses to WWI, 336–337, 339–340, 342–343
  responses to WWII, 412, 414, 419–421, 427, 428, 430
  secularization and, 491–494, 545
  social gospel and, 296, 298–304
  as stream of American Christianity, 13, 76, 141
  Unitarianism, 125, 136–138
  United Nations and, 428–429
  Vietnam War and, 476–477, 480
  view of religious liberty, 114
  views of New Deal policies, 405–406
  World's Parliament of Religions and, 263–264
  WWII challenges for, 420–421
  See also modernists, protestant
liberationist Christianity, 141, 166, 471
  Black Christians and, 142–149, 222, 244–245
  Black civil rights movement and, 457–467
  enslaved Christians and, 149–154
  Martin Luther King Jr. and, 448, 478
  Obama and, 544, 545
  pentecostals and, 317, 321, 322
  social gospel and, 302
  as stream of American Christianity, 13–14, 76
  views of New Deal, 408
Liberator, The, 213, 217
Liberia, 211
Life Is Worth Living (Sheen), 445
Lincoln, Abraham
  assassination of, 239
  Northern critics of, 238
  as president, 227, 238–239
  religious views of, 1–3, 223–224, 231–232, 237
  slavery and, 226, 235–236
  on soldier religiosity, 232–233
Lindsey, Hal, 473–474, 482
Linn, William, 120
Lippman, Walter, 389
Livermore, Harriet, 132
Locke, John, 64, 88
Lofton, Kathryn, 327
Louisiana Territory, 174, 182
Louverture, Toussaint, 152
Luce, Henry, 475
Lundquist, Harold, 379
Luther, Martin, 24–25
Lutheran Hour, The, 360
Lutherans, 12, 78, 249, 271, 360, 409
Lynch, James, 236

Machen, J. Gresham, 358, 405
Madison, James, 111, 442
  Bill of Rights and, 112–113, 114, 117–118
  religious liberty and, 114, 116–117
Maier, Walter, 360, 395
Mains, George Preston, 351
Malcolm X, 463, 465–466
manifest destiny, 203, 247
Mann, Horace, 176–177
Man Nobody Knows, The (Barton), 376
Manuel, David, 509–510
March on Washington for Jobs and Freedom, 460
market economy. *See* capitalism
marriage, sexuality, and gender
  Adventist view of, 283–284
  fear of evolutionary theory's impact on, 381–382
  Latter-day Saints and, 169, 254–258
  masturbation and, 283–284, 290
  moral crusaders and, 289–294
  new culture wars and, 510–519
  Oneida community and, 164–166
  Public Universal Friend's view of, 158
  questioning of traditional, 156

sexual abstinence, 158, 159, 163
Shakers and, 159
Woodhull's free love views, 290, 293
See also gender norms
Marshall, Charles, 386–387
Marshall, Peter, 509–510
Marty, Martin, 477
Marxism
blended with Catholicism, 470
view of religion, 301
Maryland, religious tensions in colonial, 55–56
Mason, Charles H., 318, 322, 339
Massachusetts Bay Puritans, 37–47. *See also* Puritans
Massasoit, 37
Mather, Increase, 32–33
Mathews, Shailer, 327–328, 339–340, 350, 368
Matoaka (Pocahontas), 52–53
Matthews, J. B., 434–435
Matthews, Mark, 338, 379, 385–386, 402
Matthews, Robert, 205
Maurin, Peter, 395
Mauro, Philip, 345
McCain, John, 548
McCarthy, Joseph, 434, 435
McClain, Alva, 416
McCollum, Vashti, 442
McCollum v. Board of Education, 442–443
McCormick, Cyrus, 314
McGuffey, William Holmes, 177
McIntire, Carl, 358, 465, 475
McKinley, William, 275, 306, 347
McKinney, Ernest Rice, 363–364
McPherson, Aimee Semple, 357, 359–360
response to WWII, 421
successful ministry of, 366–369
welfare ministry of, 392–393
McQuilkin, Robert C., 357
McVeigh, Timothy, 535
Melville, Herman, 222
Memorial and Remonstrance Against Religious Assessments (Madison), 116–117, 442
Mencken, H. L., 358, 383, 384
Mennonites, 78, 90
Metacom (Philip), 45
Metaxas, Eric, 556
Methodist Episcopal Church, South, 221–222, 244
Methodists, 78, 181
Black Christian refashioning and, 142–147
Indigenous peoples and, 201–202, 249, 250
membership loss of, 505
revivalism and, 129–131, 141
slavery and, 221
Vietnam War and, 480
Metropolitan Community Church (MCC), 502–503
Mexican Americans
civil rights and, 467–469
as immigrants, 266–267
pentecostalism and, 322–323
Mexico
Spanish colonization of, 25–26
US seizure of lands, 203, 253
Michaux, Lightfoot Solomon, 359, 402, 407
middle class
late-1800s growth of, 297, 298
self-help ministries for, 443–445, 447
Middle East
missionary work in, 194
WWI and, 346–349
Midnight Cry, The, 161
military, WWI debate over enlarging, 336–337
military service, compulsory
Vietnam War and, 477, 481
WWI and, 338, 339, 349
Miller, Kenneth, 373–374
Miller, William, 160–163, 166, 281
Mills, Samuel, 191–192
Minersville School District v. Gobitis, 422
missionary movement
American imperialism and, 275–277
Chinese immigrants and, 271
combining religion and American values, 274
creation of ABCFM, 192–193
Du Bois's criticism of, 276
early 1900s growth of, 273–274
fundamentalist-modernist controversy and, 365–366
Hawai'i mission, 194–196
Haystack Prayer Meeting and, 191–192

missionary movement (*Continued*)
Hocking's study on, 365–366
home missions, 202–203, 374
Indigenous peoples and, 196–201, 241, 242, 248–250
millennium and, 193
New Deal Indian policies and, 402, 404
scope and success of, 203–204
women missionaries, 195–196
WWII spycraft and, 423–425
Missionary Society of St. Paul, 267
Mix, Sarah, 285
Moctezuma II, 25
modern consumer culture, Jesus and, 376
modernists, protestant
awakening of liberal protestantism and, 317, 327–328
Black leaders' criticism of, 362–363
crisis of (1930s), 408–409
impact on American Christianity, 324–330
lack of evangelistic method, 356–357
portrayal of Jesus, 326
revivalist attacks on, 328–330, 367–368
schism with apocalyptical revivalists, 349–352, 355–356
as threat to evangelicalism, 426
See also fundamentalist-modernist controversy; liberal Christianity
Mohegans, 45, 73
Mondale, Walter, 486
Monk, Maria, 184–185, 233
Montgomery, Carrie Judd, 285
Montgomery bus boycott, 459
Moody, Anne, 461
Moody, Dwight, 273, 312–314, 333
Moody Bible Institute, 314, 323, 359
moral establishment
anti-Catholic fervor and, 183–186
challenges to creation of, 174–175
curbing of alternative religions and, 171
early republic need for, 172–175
influencing voting behavior and, 179
See also social activism, Christian
morality, Christian
challenge of freethinkers to, 291–292
Christian realism and, 413
colonial, 43, 51, 58
early debate over government role in, 117, 121
modernism and, 326
Unitarians and, 136, 138
women's vote for establishing, 289
Moral Majority, 521–523. *See also* religious right
Moral Man and Immoral Society (Niebuhr), 413
Moravians, 78, 90
Morgan, J. P., 347
Morgan, Marabel, 514–515
Mormons. *See* Church of Jesus Christ of Latter-day Saints
Moroni, 166–167, 168
Morrill Anti-Bigamy Act, 255
Morris, E. C., 362
Morrison, Charles Clayton, 387–388, 391, 414, 448
Morse, Samuel F. B., 183
Mott, John R., 274
Mott, Lucretia, 209–210
Moyamensing Temperance Society, 179
Murray, Pauli, 496–497
Mussolini, Benito, 400
Mutual Broadcasting, 360

Narragansett tribe, 37, 43, 45
Nation, Carry A., 279–280, 281(fig), 346, 368
National Association for the Advancement of Colored People (NAACP), 447, 459
National Association of Evangelicals (NAE), 426, 449, 450, 512, 522
National Baptist Convention, 302, 362
National Baptist Union-Review, 362, 406
National Catholic War Council, 341–342
National Conference of Christians and Jews, 406, 419
National Convention of Colored Citizens (1843), 215
national identity and culture
Christian dominance of, 3–8, 545–546
protestant moral establishment and, 173–174
See also Christian nationalism; culture wars
National Organization for Women (NOW), 519

National Union for Social Justice, 396
Nation of Islam (NOI), 465–466
Neolin, 79
neoorthodoxy, 413–414
neutrality acts, 412
New Amsterdam, religious diversity in, 56–57
New Apostolic Reformation (NAR), 551–552, 560
Newby, Leonard, 349
New Deal policies, 401–408, 426
New Mexico, Spanish colonization of, 26–31, 93–95
New Republic, The, 396, 421
Newton, Huey, 486
Newton, Isaac, 64, 87–88, 325
New Yorker, The, 398, 487
New York Society for the Suppression of Vice, 290
New York Times, The, 334, 427, 440, 476, 478–479, 502, 520, 555
Ngô Đình Diệm, 476
Niebuhr, Reinhold, 435, 439, 443, 460
  on sexual prohibitions, 510–511
  Vietnam War and, 476
  WWII and, 412–415
Nightingale, Florence, 368
Nimiipuu (Nez Perce), 200
9/11 attacks, 537, 539–540, 541
Nixon, Richard, 450, 475, 479, 480
Norman, Larry, 483–484
Norris, J. Frank, 359, 402
North American Review, 272, 385
Northampton, Massachusetts, revivalism, 64–66
Notes on the State of Virginia (Jefferson), 115
Noyes, John Humphrey, 163–166

Obama, Barack, 10, 555
  Jeremiah Wright and, 543–545
  policies of, 548–549
  vision of faith and politics, 546–549
Obergefell v. Hodges, 549
Occom, Samson, 73–74, 75
Ockenga, Harold, 358, 359, 426, 427–428, 450, 475
Office of Faith-Based and Community Initiatives, 540
Office of Strategic Services (OSS), 424–425
Oklahoma City bombing, 535
Olazábal, Francisco, 322–323
Old Fashioned Revival Hour, 360
Oñate, Juan de, 27–28
Oneida community, 164–166
On the Origin of Species (Darwin), 325
ʻŌpūkahaʻia ("Henry Obookiah"), 195, 200
Oregon Territory, 200–201, 203
Orr, James, 329
Osborn, Sarah, 72–73
O'Sullivan, John L., 203
Osuna, Luciano, 250
Ottoman Empire, missionary work in, 194
Our Lady of Guadalupe, 266, 468, 469
Oxford University Press, 311, 312
Oxnam, G. Bromley, 448
Ozman, Agnes, 318–319

pacifism
  international peace movements, 342, 343, 419–420, 429, 430
  peace churches, 90–91
  WWI-era revivalists and, 338–339
  WWII-era liberal promotion of, 412, 414, 420–421
Padres Asociados para Derechos Religiosos, Educativos, y Sociales (PADRES), 469–470
Paine, Thomas, 87
Palmer, Benjamin Morgan, 228–229, 230
Palmer, Phoebe, 180–181, 318
Palóu, Francisco, 98–99
Parham, Charles Fox, 318–319, 320
Parker, Tom, 559–560
Parks, Rosa, 447
Patton, George, 425
Paul, Rand, 538
Payne, Daniel, 236
peace churches, 90–91, 339
Peace Mission movement, 399–400
Peace of Soul (Sheen), 445
Peale, Norman Vincent, 405, 443–444, 450–451, 550
Pearl Harbor, attack on, 417, 421, 422
Pearl of Great Price, Doctrine and Covenants, 168

Penn, William, 57–59
Pennsylvania colony, 57–59
pentecostals, 316–324
  Aimee Semple McPherson and, 366–369
  Azusa street revival, 316–317, 319–322
  creation of, 318–319
  distinguishing characteristics of, 320–321
  independent pentecostalism, 551–552
  interracial fellowship and, 322
  mainstream protestants experiences of, 494–495
  membership growth of, 506
  "oneness" pentecostalism, 323
People's Party, 304–306
Peoples Temple, 485–490
Perry, Troy, 501–503
Philadelphia
  Black Christianity in, 144–146
  founding of, 58, 59
Philippines, US seizure of, 275–277
Pierson, A. T., 274
Pietism, 63–64, 66
Pilgrims, 36–37, 38, 45
Pittsburgh Courier, 363, 364
plural marriage
  crusade against, 254–258
  Latter-day Saints' defense of, 169, 255
Polish immigrants, 266
Pontiac, 80
Popé, 30–31
Pope Benedict XV, 341
Pope John XXIII, 495
Pope Leo XIII, 269–270
Pope Paul VI, 183
Pope Pius XI, 394
Pope Pius XII, 437
populist nativism, Catholic immigration and, 270
Populists, 304–306
Porterfield, Amanda, 120
Powell, Adam Clayton, Jr., 407–408
Power of Positive Thinking, The (Peale), 444
Pratt, Richard H., 249
"praying towns," 45
premillennialists
  Black Christian view of, 309–310
  Branch Davidians as, 532–535
  Dwight Moody and, 312–314
  establishment of modern Israel and, 346–349
  Jehovah's Witnesses and, 311
  post-Civil War reshaping of, 308–314
  responses to WWI, 344–345, 349–351
  Scofield Reference Bible and, 311–312
  See also apocalyptic revivalists; end-times beliefs
Presbyterians
  Black civil rights and, 499–501
  in colonial America, 50, 59, 78
  gay rights and, 504
  Indigenous peoples and, 249
  membership loss of, 505
  as missionaries, 203
  slavery and, 214, 220–221
  Vietnam War and, 479–480
Price, Hiram, 251
Princeton Theological Seminary, 358
Princeton University, 70
prison reform, 180, 289
Prohibition, 346, 402
pro-life movement, 516–517, 519, 559–560, 561–562
prophecy conferences, 309, 312, 361
Prophetstown, 197
prosperity gospel, 523–527
Protestant-Catholic-Jew (Herberg), 454
protestant establishment, unofficial
  First Amendment and, 6–7, 121–122
  social and cultural reform and, 173–174, 187
protestantism, Martin Luther and, 25
Protestant Reformation, 9, 34
protestants
  affiliation with Church of England, 50, 51, 56, 78, 81
  early tension with Catholics, 55–56
  immigration surge in late 1800s, 271
protestants, mainstream
  anti-Catholic sentiment of, 183–186, 270, 448–451
  anti-Chinese sentiment of, 272–273
  creation of Federal Council of Churches, 306–308
  declining membership and, 504–506, 545, 551
  early-1900s anxiety of, 388–389

early republic dissatisfaction with, 156–157
foreign missionary work and, 192–193
fracture over involvement in WWI, 334–335, 336–340
fundamentalist-modernist controversy, 355–356
government favoring of, 6–7, 118–119, 121–122
moral pressures on Hollywood (1920s), 370–372
moral standards and (*see* moral establishment)
multicentury activism of, 11
Native reservation system and, 247, 249–250
new charismatic revival's impact on, 494–495
opposition to utopian visionaries, 156, 169, 170, 171
overview of pre-revolution, 78–79
as predominantly White activists, 8–9
racism and, 14, 222, 244, 313–314, 498–501
Reconstruction and, 242
religious liberty and, 8–9, 156, 169, 170, 171
sex abuse and, 532
slavery-related religious schism and, 220–222
state government support of, 113–114
support of capitalism, 134, 156, 174, 296, 305, 314–315, 374–376, 391
threat of colonial revivalism to, 70–71
united around early republic social reform, 175
upholding of gender norms (1920s), 377–380
Vietnam War and, 477
views of New Deal policies, 402–408
See also American Christianity; *specific denominations*

"Protestants and Other Americans United for Separation of Church and State" (POAU), 448–449, 450
Protocols of the Elders of Zion, 385
PTL (Praise the Lord) Network, 525
public school system
Bible reading in, 177, 185, 452, 494
Catholic view of, 268
Christian social reform and, 176–178, 289
desegregation and, 464, 498–499
prayers in, 177, 451–452, 494, 557
rulings on church-state separation in, 441–443, 451–453, 557
sex education and, 511–512
Public Universal Friend, 155, 157–158, 159
Pueblo peoples
New Deal Indian policies and, 403
Spanish colonization of, 26–31
Pueblo revolt, 31, 96
Puritans, 41, 59
crises and failure of, 32–34, 41–46
Indigenous peoples and, 36–37, 44–45
Massachusetts Bay, 37–47
Quakers and, 48, 49
religious views of, 34–36, 38–39
separatist Pilgrims, 36–37, 38

QAnon, 555–556
Quakers. *See* Society of Friends
Quebec Act, 82–83
Quimby, Phineas P., 287
Quinn, Anthony, 393

race and racism
Black civil rights and, 456–467, 498–501
in North, 216
Indigenous account of White, 201–202
Latine Christians and, 467–470
mainstream Christianity and, 14, 222, 244, 313–314, 471, 498–501
in pentecostal movement, 319, 322, 323
revivalism and, 73–75, 126, 313–314, 362, 427, 463–465, 519–520
social gospel and, 302
social reformers avoidance of, 175–176, 181, 289
racial violence
in Birmingham, 459–460, 461
Detroit riots, 456–457
Martin Luther King Jr. and, 448, 459–460
in post-war South, 244
Rader, Paul, 359
radio broadcasts
Father Coughlin and, 395
fundamentalist early use of, 359–361

rapture, 308–309, 340, 348, 474, 536
Rauschenbusch, Walter, 299, 301, 343, 368
Reagan, Ronald, 515, 522–523
Reconstruction
  Black Christianity and, 242–244
  Christian activism and, 242
  Southern White revisionist accounts and, 242, 245–246
reconstructionist movement, 537–538
"Reds and Our Churches" (Matthews), 435
Red Scare, 372, 374, 384, 434–436
Reed, Rebecca, 183–184
religion
  Cold War-era revival of, 434, 439–441, 453–454
  communism as threat to, 433–434
  Constitution's omission of, 112
  Declaration of Independence and, 87–89
  as incompatible with capitalism, 394–395
  as incongruous with enslavement, 207–208, 210, 215, 217–218
  official disestablishment of, 117–119, 121, 125
  pressing issue of role in new US government, 110
  science eclipsing in universities (late 1800s), 324–325
  WWII policy tied to, 411, 416–418
religious diversity, in modern US, 529–530
Religious Instruction of the Negroes in the United States, The (Jones), 220
religious liberty
  amendment debates over, 113–114, 117–118
  Articles of Confederation and, 89
  Jefferson and, 114–116
  linking political liberty with, 84–86, 87, 129
  Madison and, 114, 116–117
  protestant dominance and, 8–9, 156, 169, 170, 171
  Supreme Court rulings and, 556–560
  World's Parliament of Religions and, 263–265
religious right
  Iraq war and, 541
  Moral Majority and, 521–523
  Republican Party and, 528, 547, 562
  "seven mountain mandate" and, 552, 560
  support of Trump, 552–553, 562
  2020 election and, 555–556
Removal Act of 1830, 198–199
Republican Party
  Black leaders' criticisms of, 407
  Christian nationalism and, 10
  family values and, 513–514
  religious right and, 521–523, 528, 547, 562
  rise of, 119–120
  slavery and, 226
revivalist Christianity
  alternatives to sexual revolution, 514–515
  apocalyptic (*see* apocalyptic revivalists)
  Black Christians and, 73, 74, 135–136, 142–147
  camp-meeting revivals, 126–129, 133
  Charles Finney and, 132–134
  Civil War soldiers and, 232, 233
  Cold War-era growth of, 446–447, 453
  conversion experiences and, 62, 64–65, 67, 134–135
  early criticisms and concerns about, 75, 135–136
  early republic surge of, 125–136
  economic crisis (1930s) and, 409–410
  enslavement and, 67, 74
  faith healing and, 285, 286
  family values and, 514–517
  George Whitefield and, 66–70
  growing membership of (1960s), 504
  impact on American Christianity, 75, 173
  inclusiveness of early, 71–75
  Indigenous peoples and, 73–74, 201–202
  itinerant and outdoor ministries of, 67, 129–131, 133–134
  James Davenport and, 61–63
  Jesus-people movement and, 481–484
  Jonathan Edwards and, 64–66
  market economy and, 134, 296
  Methodists and, 129–131
  new charismatic revival and, 494–495
  pentecostals, 317–324
  physical manifestations of revival, 127, 131
  Pietism and, 63–64
  pop-up cities and spaces, 126
  race issues and, 126, 313–314, 362, 427, 463–465, 519–520
  responses to WWI, 344–345

responses to WWII, 421–423
rural settings and, 125–126, 127
slavery and, 221
as stream of American Christianity, 12–13, 75, 141
success of, 63, 70
support of Vietnam War, 475
threat to mainstream protestants, 70–71
use of music, 313
view of religious liberty, 113–114
view of salvation, 61–62, 66–67, 71
women leadership and, 72–73, 131–132
WWI-era pacifism and, 338–339
revolutionary suicide, 488–489
Revolutionary War, 11
biblical prophecy and, 91–92
church leaders support of, 87, 90
conclusion of war, 91
Declaration of Independence and, 87–89
God's chosen land and, 79
growing dissent with English rule and, 80–84
linking religion and politics and, 84–86, 87
overview of religious life before, 78–79
peace churches and, 90–91
Reynolds v. United States, 255–256
Rhode Island, religious diversity in colonial, 42–43, 57
Rice, John R., 379, 380
Rice, Tim, 484
Riley, William Bell, 354–355, 357, 359, 369
Ritchings, Edna Rose, 400
Rivera, Abby Flores, 469
Roberts, Oral, 524, 525–526
Robertson, Pat, 521, 525, 539–540
Robinson, Gene, 503–504
Robinson, J. G., 406
Robinson, John A. T., 493
Robison, James, 518
Rochester Theological Seminary, 299
Rockefeller, John D., 298, 299 (fig), 327, 347
Rockefeller, John D., Jr., 365, 374–375
Roe v. Wade, 516, 558–560
Rolfe, John, 51, 53
Roman Empire, prediction of restored, 309
Roosevelt, Franklin Delano, 401, 427
Black leaders' response to, 406–408
Catholics and, 396–398, 423
election of, 392, 396
on four essential human freedoms, 416
New Deal policies and, 401–408
religion and WWII policy of, 411, 416–418, 423
religious leaders' views of policies of, 402–408
"Roosevelt Safeguards America" (Ryan), 397
Rothschild, Lord, 348
rural economy, late-1800s exploitation and, 296–297, 304–306
Rushdoony, Rousas John, 537–538
Russell, Charles Taze, 310–311
Rutledge, Wiley, 441–442
Ryan, John, 397, 415
Ryan, Leo, 489

Saint Francis, 93, 94, 95, 97
Salem witch trials, 46
Sallman, Walter, 457
salvation
grace vs. moral code in, 43
Martin Luther and, 24
Puritan view of, 38–39
real-world reform vs., 308
revivalist view of, 61–62, 66–67, 71, 129
Salvation Army, 302–303, 342, 367
same-sex marriage, 502, 549. *See also* gay rights
Sandford, Frank, 318
San Diego mission attack, 103–104
San Francisco earthquake, 320
Sanger, Margaret, 380
Sankey, Ira, 312–313
Save Our Children, 518
Scandinavian immigrants, 174, 271
Schaeffer, Francis, 516–517
Schlafly, Phyllis, 513–514
schools. *See* education; public school system
Schwarz, Fred C., 436
scientific thought
challenge to Christian theology, 325
death of God and, 491–492
higher education's focus on, 324–325
Scofield, Cyrus Ingerson, 311–312, 357
Scofield Reference Bible, 311–312
Scopes, Thomas, 382–384

Scopes trial, 381–384, 391
Scriptural Evidence in Favour of Female Testimony in Meetings for Christian Worship (Livermore), 132
Scudder, Vida, 300–301, 307
Second Coming of Jesus
  Branch Davidians and, 535
  signs of, 320
  William Miller and, 160–163
  See also end-times beliefs
Secular City, The (Cox), 494
secularism
  Democratic Party and, 10
  religious liberals and, 491–494, 545
  Time's 1966 cover story and, 491–492
Sehat, David, 113
Selective Service Act, 338
self-help ministries, 443–445, 447, 454
Serra, Father Junípero, 95–104, 131, 182
Seton, Elizabeth Ann, 182–183
settlement houses, 300
7 Habits of Highly Effective People, The (Covey), 524
"seven mountain mandate," 552, 560
Seven Pillars of Peace (Sheen), 420
Seventh-day Adventists, 161, 163, 532
  medical clinics of, 282–284
sex education, 511–512
sex reform, moral crusaders and, 289–294
sexual abuse, by clergy, 530–532
sexuality. *See* marriage, sexuality, and gender
sexual revolution, 510–512
  revivalist alternative to, 514–515
Seymour, William J., 316–317, 319, 320
Shakers (United Society of Believers in Christ's Second Appearing), 159–160, 170, 187, 219, 318
Shawnees, 80, 196–197
Sheen, Fulton J., 420, 444–445
Sheldon, Charles, 301
Shelton, Charles, 241, 250
Sherwood, Samuel, 83, 91–92
Shrine of the Black Madonna, 456
Signs of the Times, 161
Simmons, Roscoe, 364
Simms, James, 243
"Sinners in the Hands of an Angry God" (Edwards), 64–65
Sisters of Charity of St. Joseph, 182
Sitting Bull, 252
Six Pillars of Peace (Dulles), 419–420
Skinner, Tom, 463–464
slavery. *See* enslaved Africans; enslaved Christians; enslavement
Smith, Al, 386–388
Smith, Chuck, 482
Smith, Fred B., 303
Smith, Hyram, 170
Smith, John, 52–53
Smith, Joseph, Jr., 166–170
Smith, William, 86
Social Action Department of the National Catholic Welfare Conference, 420
social activism, Christian
  antiliquor crusade, 178–179, 279–280, 288–289
  avoidance of race and racism, 175–176, 181, 289
  early republic need for, 173–175
  educational reform, 175–178
  holiness movement and, 180–181
  for improving American society, 179–180
  Jim Jones and, 485
  Latine organizers, 467–469
  liberal Christians and, 13, 492
  mainstream protestant unity for, 175
  settlement houses, 300
  sex reform, 289–294
  Sojourner Truth and, 206–207
  women's roles in, 178
social gospel
  anti-communist attack on, 435
  Black Christians and, 302, 363, 364
  conservative criticism of, 308, 329
  focus on transforming communities, 301–302
  labor movements and, 299
  urban poverty and, 296, 298–304
  WWI-era and, 343
socialism
  attack on, 329, 345
  Christian faith and, 300–301
social radicalism
  Dorothy Day and, 394–395
  Labor Temple and, 373–374
Social Security Act, 405

Society for the Propagation of the Faith, 444
Society of Friends (Quakers), 78, 179
  evangelizing Puritans, 48, 49
  Indigenous peoples and, 59, 247, 249
  pacifism of, 90–91, 339
  religious views of, 48–49, 57–59, 157
  slavery and, 214
  utopian visionaries and, 157, 158–159
Society of Universal Friends, 158
Soledad brothers, 499
Soros, George, 556
Sotomayor, Sonia, 557, 558
Southern Baptist Convention, 222, 498, 532, 541
Southern Baptists, membership growth of, 506
Southern Christian Leadership Conference (SCLC), 459, 462
Spain
  California mission system and, 95, 96, 99–104
  colonization of Pueblo peoples, 26–31
  Columbus's exploration of Americas, 20–23
  expansion into Mexico, 25–26
Spalding, Henry and Eliza, 200
Spanish-Cuban-American War, 275, 278
Speer, Robert, 273
Spellman, Francis, 437
Spies, August, 296
Spiritual Mobilization, 405
Stair, Lois, 499
Stamp Act (1765), 80
Stanley, Charles, 523
Stanton, Elizabeth Cady, 209–210, 376–377
state government
  abortion issue and, 559–560
  disestablishment and, 172, 186
  support of mainstream protestants, 113–114
Steward, Theophilus Gould (T. G.), 243, 309–310, 362–363
Stewart, Lyman, 328–329, 357
Stewart, Maria, 213
Stewart, Milton, 328, 329, 348
St. Mary's Seminary, 182
Stoddard, Solomon, 64, 69
Stone, Barton, 126–128
Story, Joseph, 121–122
Stowe, Harriet Beecher, 209
Straton, John Roach, 359, 380, 388
Stringfellow, Thornton, 220
Strong, Josiah, 274
Student Nonviolent Coordinating Committee (SNCC), 462
suffrage movement, 378, 394
Sunday, Billy, 333–334, 335 (fig), 378, 380
Suskind, Ron, 540
Swami Vivekananda, 264–265
Synagogue Council of America, 420

Talbot, Louis, 359, 437–438
Tammany Hall, 386
Tanner, B. T., 313
Taylor, Myron, 423
Tecumseh, 196, 197
television
  prosperity gospel and, 525
  Sheen's use of, 445
Teller, Henry M., 251
temperance movement, 179, 181, 279–280, 288–289
  Prohibition and, 346, 402
Ten Commandments, in school curriculum, 177
Tennent, Gilbert, 70–71, 72
Tenskwatawa, 196–197, 201
Terry, Randall, 517
Thanksgiving, 37, 238
Theology of Liberation, A (Gutiérrez), 470
Thief in the Night, A, 484
Thigpen, Jennifer, 196
Thomas, Clarence, 559, 560
Thomas, Norman, 339
Thoreau, Henry David, 139
Thornwell, James Henley, 218–219
Thurman, Howard, 458–459
Tilton, Elizabeth, 292–293
Tilton, Theodore, 293
Tippecanoe, Battle of, 197
Tocqueville, Alexis de, 33, 122, 187
Todd, Mary, 238
Tomlinson, A. J., 318
tongues, speaking in, 158, 316–324, 421, 494–495, 553, 565
Torrey, R. A., 286–287
Total Woman, The (Morgan), 514

Tracy, Joseph, 75
Trail of Tears, 199
transcendentalism, 139–140
Treatise Concerning Religious Affections, A (Edwards), 65
Treaty of Paris, 91
Treviño, Juan Francisco, 29–30
"Trial of the Modern Liberalist College Professor Versus the Lord Jesus Christ" (McPherson), 367–368
Trinity Broadcasting Network, 525
Tripoli, US treaty with, 109–110, 122
Truman, Harry S., 427, 436–437, 449
Trump, Donald, 524
  Christian supporters of, 550–555
  and 2020 election, 554–556
  reelection of, 561–563
Truth, Sojourner, 205–207, 210, 213, 279
Tucker, J. W., 231
Turner, Frederick Jackson, 258–259
Turner, Henry McNeal, 135–136, 233, 244, 246, 466
Turner, Nat, 152–153, 215, 217
Twain, Mark, 297

Uncle Tom's Cabin (Stowe), 209
Union Oil, 328
Unitarians, 125, 136–138, 139, 141, 192
United Church of Christ, 477, 480, 505
United Farm Workers (UFW), 468
United Nations, 428–429
United Society of Believers in Christ's Second Appearing. *See* Shakers
United States
  early republic growth of, 174
  formation of, 110–113
  as God's chosen land, 3, 79, 143, 155–156, 222, 223–224, 226–227, 349, 399, 430, 509
  impact of war in Vietnam, 480–481
  modern religious diversity and, 529–530
  race for empire (1890s) and, 265
  as world superpower, 433
Universalists, 138, 141
University of Chicago, 324, 349
University of Chicago Divinity School, 327, 339
urban poverty, social gospel and, 296, 298–304
Ursuline Convent, 183–184
US Supreme Court
  abortion and, 516, 558–560
  Christian nationalism and, 11, 545–546, 556–559
  on church-state separation, 121–122, 441–443, 451–453, 556–557
  corporate religious rights and, 557
  on pledging allegiance to the flag, 422, 453
  on plural marriage, 255–256
  same-sex marriage and, 549
  Trump's appointments to, 553
utopian Christian visionaries
  dissatisfaction with mainstream religion, 156–157
  Latter-day Saints, 166–171
  Millerites, 160–163
  Oneida community, 163–166
  persecution of, 156, 159–160, 169, 171
  Public Universal Friend, 157–158
  Shakers, 158–160

Van Kirk, Walter W., 412
Varick, James, 147
Vesey, Denmark, 151–152, 215
vice crusaders, 290–294, 560
Vietnam War
  American opposition to, 476–480
  Catholics and, 475–476
  counterculture and, 481–484
  end of, 480
  evangelical support of, 475, 481
Viguerie, Richard, 521
Virginia
  colonial, 36, 50–54
  religious liberty in, 114–117
voting behavior
  Christian social activism and, 179
  religious affiliation and, 10, 546–547
voting rights, 464

Wacker, Grant, 323
Wagner, C. Peter, 551
Wahunsonacock (Powhatan), 52–53
Walker, David, 212
Wallnau, Lance, 552
Wall Street Journal, The, 541
Wampanoag tribe, 36, 37, 45

Wanamaker, John, 314
Warfield, B. B., 358
War of 1812, 160, 197
Washington, George, 84, 89, 90, 111, 114, 197
  on national morality, 174
  on separation of church and state, 112
Way of Holiness, The (Palmer), 181
wealth
  church affiliation and, 134, 135
  higher education and, 324
  in late-1800s economy, 297–298
  prosperity gospel and, 523–527
  Puritan positive view of, 40
Webb, James Morris, 340–341
Webber, Andrew Lloyd, 484
welfare ministries, 392–394
welfare state, criticism of, 447
Welles, Orson, 474
Wesley, John, 80, 86–87, 129, 180
Wesleyan Church, 181
Western Health Reform Institute, 282
Western states and territories
  Asian immigrants and, 271–272
  California mission system in, 95, 96, 99–105
  conversion of Indigenous peoples in, 241
  discovery of gold and silver in, 247
  enslavement and, 225
  Latter-day Saints and, 252–258
  missionary work in, 200–201
  Native reservation system in, 247–251
  post-Civil War "peace policy" for, 247
  revivalism in, 125–126
Westminster Theological Seminary, 358
West Virginia State Board of Education v. Barnette, 422
Weyrich, Paul, 521
Wheatley, Phillis, 74
Wheaton College, 357–358
Whipple, George, 249
White, Alma, 318
White, Andrew, 55
White, Andrew Dickson, 324–325
White, Ellen G., 281–282, 532
White-Cain, Paula, 551–553
White Christian America, forecasts of decline of, 561
White Citizens' Council, 460
Whitefield, George, 61–62, 98, 131, 157, 367
  Bethesda orphanage and, 67
  inspiration to ministers, 74
  revolution and, 77–78, 80, 82
  slavery and, 67, 74
  successful ministry of, 66–70
White nationalism, 535–536, 539. *See also* Christian nationalism
White protestant dominance, 8–9. *See also* protestants, mainstream
White Southerners
  political power of, 212
  revisionist accounts of Civil War, 242, 245–246
  threat of Black Christianity to, 152–154, 245
  See also Confederate States of America; enslavement
Whitman, Marcus and Narcissa, 200–201
Whitney, Thomas R., 185
Wightman, John T., 230
Wilkinson, Jemima, 155, 157–158
Willard, Francis, 289, 346, 368
Williams, Roger, 41–43, 57, 116
Williams, Smallwood, 407
Wilson, Doug, 538–539
Wilson, Woodrow
  apocalyptic revivalist critique of, 344–345
  debate over WWI intervention and, 334–335, 337–338
  entry into war, 340
  postwar world and, 352–353
  prewar views of, 335–336
  suffrage and, 378
Winrod, Gerald, 400–401
Winthrop, John, 37–38, 40, 43, 44, 203, 510
Wise, Isaac Mayer, 270
Witherspoon, John, 87, 89
Woman's Bible, The (Stanton), 377
Woman's Christian Temperance Union (WCTU), 279
women
  antiliquor crusade and, 181, 279–280, 289
  Black women's ministries, 147–149, 302, 496
  Catholic Church and, 496
  early-1900s culture wars and, 376–380

women (*Continued*)
"flappers," response to, 378–379
as foreign missionaries, 195–196
mainstream Christianity and, 14, 72–73, 131–132, 147–149, 185, 205–207, 289, 302, 496–498, 512–513, 520
pentecostal leadership and, 320–321
Puritan ministry and, 43–44
Quaker leadership and, 157
religious communities for, 182
revivalist ministries of, 72–73, 75, 131–132
social activism and, 178, 300, 302
utopian visionaries embrace of, 158–159, 160
See also gender norms; marriage, sexuality, and gender; women's equality
Women's Christian Temperance Union (WCTU), 289, 346
women's equality
abolitionism and, 213
Aimee Semple McPherson and, 368
birth control and, 379–380
Elizabeth Cady Stanton and, 376–377
Francis Willard and, 289
Grimké sisters and, 207–209
Mott and Stanton and, 209–210
new culture wars and, 513–517, 519
Pauli Murray and, 496–497
social gospel and, 302
Sojourner Truth and, 205–207
suffrage and, 378, 394
women's ordination and, 496–498, 512–513
Wong Chin Foo, 272
Woodhull, Victoria, 290, 292–293, 376
Woodruff, Wilford, 257–258
Worcester v. Georgia, 199
workers' rights, 289
business efforts to quash, 373–374
early-1900s labor strikes, 372–373, 386
Haymarket Square rally and, 295–296
working class
Labor Temple and, 373–374
late-1800s impoverishment of, 296, 297, 298
men, social activism focused on, 304
social gospel ministries for, 298–304
World Anti-Slavery Convention, 209
World Conference on Christian Fundamentals, 354
World Court, 396
World's Fair, 263–265, 286
World's Parliament of Religions, 263–265
World War I
beginning of, 336
debate over intervention in, 334–335, 336–340
ending of, 352
international Christian unity and, 342, 343
modernist-apocalyptical revivalist schism and, 349–352, 355–356
US entry into, 340
wartime sermons and, 334
World War II
American interfaith postwar plans and, 419–420
atomic weapons and, 427–428
FDR and religious nature of, 411, 416–418
fundamentalist responses to, 421–423
liberal responses to, 419–421
Wounded Knee, 252
Wovoka, 251
Wright, Jeremiah, 543–545, 548
Wright, Lawrence, 487
Wuthnow, Robert, 528

Yan Phou Lee, 272–273
Young, Brigham, 170, 219, 253
Young Men's Christian Association (YMCA), 290, 303–304, 342
Young People's Church of the Air, 405
yuppie culture, 523–524

Zionism, 347–348, 349
Zion's Watch Tower Tract Society, 311. *See also* Jehovah's Witnesses

Credit: Kristen Coke-Sutton

Matthew Avery Sutton is the Claudius O. and Mary Johnson Distinguished Professor and department chair in history at Washington State University. He is the author of five other books on the history of American Christianity, including *Double Crossed* and *American Apocalypse*, and the recipient of a Guggenheim Fellowship. He lives in Pullman, Washington.

RAISING READERS

Books Build Bright Futures

Thank you for reading this book and for being a reader of books in general. We are so grateful to share being part of a community of readers with you, and we hope you will join us in passing our love of books on to the next generation of readers.

Did you know that reading for enjoyment is the single biggest predictor of a child's future happiness and success?

More than family circumstances, parents' educational background, or income, reading impacts a child's future academic performance, emotional well-being, communication skills, economic security, ambition, and happiness.

Studies show that kids reading for enjoyment in the US is in rapid decline:

- In 2012, 53% of 9-year-olds read almost every day. Just 10 years later, in 2022, the number had fallen to 39%.
- In 2012, 27% of 13-year-olds read for fun daily. By 2023, that number was just 14%.

TOGETHER, WE CAN COMMIT TO RAISING READERS AND CHANGE THIS TREND.

HOW?

- Read to children in your life daily.
- Model reading as a fun activity.
- Reduce screen time.
- Start a family, school, or community book club.
- Visit bookstores and libraries regularly.
- Listen to audiobooks.
- Read the book before you see the movie.
- Encourage your child to read aloud to a pet or stuffed animal.
- Give books as gifts.
- Donate books to families and communities in need.

Books build bright futures, and **Raising Readers** is our shared responsibility.

For more information, visit JoinRaisingReaders.com

Sources: National Endowment for the Arts, National Assessment of Educational Progress, WorldBookDay.com, Nielsen BookData's 2023 "Understanding the Children's Book Consumer"